Supply Chain Management

10e

Supply Chain Management

A LOGISTICS PERSPECTIVE

10e

JOHN J. COYLE
The Pennsylvania State University

•

C. JOHN LANGLEY, JR.
The Pennsylvania State University

•

ROBERT A. NOVACK
The Pennsylvania State University

•

BRIAN J. GIBSON
Auburn University

CENGAGE
Learning®

Australia • Brazil • Mexico • Singapore • United Kingdom • United States

Supply Chain Management: A Logistics Perspective, Tenth Edition
John J. Coyle, C. John Langley, Jr., Robert A. Novack and Brian J. Gibson

Vice President, General Manager, Science, Math & Quantitative Business: Balraj Kalsi

Product Director: Mike Schenk

Sr. Product Team Manager: Joe Sabatino

Product Manager: Aaron Arnsparger

Sr. Product Assistant: Adele Scholtz

Content Developer: Theodore Knight

Marketing Director: Kristen Hurd

Sr. Marketing Manager: Nate Anderson

Sr. Marketing Coordinator: Eileen Corcoran

Art and Cover Direction, Production Management, and Composition: Cenveo Publisher Services

Intellectual Property

   Analyst: Brittani Morgan

   Project Manager: Nick Barrows

Manufacturing Planner: Ron Montgomery

Cover Image(s): Shutterstock/Cienpies Design

For product information and technology assistance, contact us at **Cengage Learning Customer & Sales Support, 1-800-354-9706**

For permission to use material from this text or product, submit all requests online at **www.cengage.com/permissions**
Further permissions questions can be emailed to **permissionrequest@cengage.com**

Library of Congress Control Number: 2016930710

ISBN: 978-1-305-85997-5

Cengage Learning
20 Channel Center Street
Boston, MA 02210
USA

Cengage Learning is a leading provider of customized learning solutions with employees residing in nearly 40 different countries and sales in more than 125 countries around the world. Find your local representative at **www.cengage.com.**

Cengage Learning products are represented in Canada by Nelson Education, Ltd.

To learn more about Cengage Learning Solutions, visit **www.cengage.com**

Purchase any of our products at your local college store or at our preferred online store **www.cengagebrain.com**

Printed in the United States of America
Print Number: 01   Print Year: 2016

Dedication

A very special note of thanks and appreciation is due to our families. John Coyle would like to thank his wife Barbara, their children John and Susan, and their grandchildren Lauren, Matthew, Elizabeth Kate, Emily, Ben, Cathryn, and Zachary. John Langley would like to thank his wife Anne, their children Sarah and Mercer, and their grandchildren Bryson, Molly, and Anna. Bob Novack would like to thank his wife Judith and their children Tom, Elizabeth, and Alex. Brian Gibson would like to thank his wife Marcia, son Andy, and his longtime mentor Dr. Bob Cook (1947–2014).

Another note of gratitude is due to Ms. Kusumal Ruamsook, Research Associate and Instructor, The Center for Supply Chain Research and Department of Supply Chain and Information Systems, Penn State University. We thank Kusumal for her many contributions to the preparation of this 10th edition, including not only certain areas of subject matter but also for her preparation of PowerPoint slide decks that will be of great value to those who use the text in a classroom environment. Appreciation is extended also to the staff and students who work with the Center for Supply Chain Research who contributed significantly to the overall effort related to the preparation of this edition.

The authors of Supply Chain Management: A Logistics Perspective would like to express their sincere appreciation and respect for the many contributions made to this text by Dr. John Coyle, Professor Emeritus of Logistics and Supply Chain Management at The Pennsylvania State University. The first edition was published in 1976 by Dr. Coyle and co-author Dr. Edward J. Bardi. Looking back at the preface to that first edition, the first sentence reads: "Business logistics is a relatively new field of study in business administration." While this discipline has grown in many ways over many years, we find that excellence today in areas such as supply chain and value chain are heavily dependent on sound planning and execution in the area of logistics. In fact, the subtitle of this text was carefully crafted to underscore the importance of logistics as a key element of supply chain management. It has been a great privilege for the authors of this text to have had the opportunity to work in close quarters with Dr. Coyle to provide a textbook that hopefully has been and will continue to be valuable to students, professors, and industry practitioners who have relied on our book as a useful resource. Also, the authors wish to express special recognition to John's wife, Barbara, who has had "up close and personal" involvement with these first 10 editions of Supply Chain Management: A Logistics Perspective. In appreciation for her support of our collective writing effort, we would like to bestow on Mrs. Barbara Coyle the title of "Honorary Author" of this 10th edition.

Brief Contents

Contents

Part II

Part III

Part IV

Preface

The publication of the 10th edition of this text, Supply Chain Management: A Global Logistics Perspective, in the spring of 2016 will mark the 40th anniversary of the first edition. While the original edition was titled THE MANAGEMENT OF BUSINESS LOGISTICS, the title and content changes made to the original text over the course of that 40 years period reflect the dynamic happenings in the United States and other countries throughout the world. If we had predicted drones making deliveries, 3-D printing replacing inventory, robots filling orders in warehouses and modern mobile phones for shopping in 1976, we may have been committed to an appropriate institution or accused of writing science fiction. Albeit, in this edition these developments plus numerous others are given coverage and acceptance with an explanation of their impact on global economies and specifically the logistics and supply chain systems of many businesses in the twenty-first century. The World has changed dramatically, especially the business environment, which has been described by some pundits as a "white water" world. You had to "fasten your seat belt" and put on your protective "helmet" to survive the tumultuous changes and fast pace of the last 40 years. Through it all, logistics and supply chain management played an increasingly important role to improve organizational efficiency, effectiveness, and competitiveness.

In 1976, some individuals suggested that the United States was destined to become a second class economic power and would be surpassed by Japan, West Germany and others in the highly competitive, global marketplace for producing products and services. The U.S. economy was in the "doldrums," but the seeds of change were being sowed. The first important change was the deregulation of major elements of the transportation system in the United States that occurred over a several year period in the late 1970s and early 1980s. The net result of deregulation was that the purchase and sale of transportation services became similar to the selling and buying of other goods and services with limited government oversight. The more competitive prices spurred economic activity by lowering the cost of goods sold and helped to make U.S. products more competitive in domestic and global markets. The subsequent deregulation of the financial and communication industries contributed to additional economic vitality in the 1980s as pointed out in Chapter 1.

Globalization, technology, and more informed consumers also influenced and changed the dynamics of the U.S. economy in the 1990s (discussed in more detail in Chapter 1). A critical ingredient for all the changes and the resurgence of the U.S. economy was the development of efficient and effective supply chains by many organizations as well as logistics and supply chain service providers (3PLs) that contributed to the growth of the U.S. economy and its global presence throughout the world. It was an amazing set of changes that we hope have been adequately reflected in the various editions of this text over the previous 40 years (hence the content and title changes noted above). Global organizations learned that lean, fast, agile, and flexible supply chains were a requirement of the twenty-first century where economic swings would likely be quicker and of shorter duration than in the past. Adaptability and readiness were also ingredients for continuing growth and profitability.

Another important lesson for success was a recognition that "finance" had to be a common language for supply chain executives because that was the basic language of the boardroom. EPS, ROA, ROI, cash flow, and shareholder value had to be embraced by supply chain executives in reporting their contributions to the success of the organization. These were the metrics the executive board would use to evaluate performance. While order cycle time, inventory turns and order fill rates could be used as internal metrics for judging supply chain and logistics performance, they had to be translated into terms that resonated well with executive management.

Recognizing the fast paced change that has continued into the twenty-first century and the criticality of efficient and effective supply chain management, the authors have attempted to reflect these dimensions in the 10th edition of this text with new content and some reordering of the topics to improve the flow of material.

Part I-Supply Chain Foundations

This section of the text provides a framework for an appreciation and understanding of supply chain management as it developed and expanded to meet the challenges of the last 30 years. Chapter 1 provides an overview of the role and importance of supply chain management in the twenty-first century. This is followed by Chapter 2 that has been added to explore the global issues of the twenty-first century among the various countries of the world with an in-depth look at demographics. Chapter 3 explores the important dimensions of logistics management in support of global supply chain challenges. This provides due recognition to the critical role played by logistics as the backbone of supply chains. The final chapter in Part 1, Chapter 4 explores the challenges of supply chain design in a traditional sense, as well as in the rapidly-emerging context of omni-channel distribution.

Part II-Supply Chain Fundamentals

The underlying fundamentals of supply chains can be visualized in the so-called SCOR® Model that provides a solid conceptual view of the key ingredients of a supply chain. The content of this section continues in the spirit of the SCOR® model, with each chapter exploring one of the critical components of the model. Strategic sourcing is the topic for Chapter 5 with consideration being given to sourcing materials and services. In this era of outsourcing, the strategic global procurement of goods and services has taken on increased importance and relevance. The focus of Chapter 6 is on operations. Efficient and effective operations in manufacturing and related areas such as maintenance are of great significance in the supply chain. Chapter 7 in this section examines the outbound-to-customer needs and requirements to add value for customers. The fourth and final Chapter 8 in this section considers customer service and order management with emphasis on measurement and financial impact.

Part III-Cross-Chain Logistics Processes

This section takes an in-depth look at the major supply chain process areas that are essential to achieving the objectives of customer order fulfillment. Referred to as "cross-chain logistics processes," these areas of competency are major contributors to the successfully executing the delivery of raw materials, components, and finished processes, consistent with requirements. To provide useful insight and perspectives on this topic, Chapter 9 focuses on contemporary and futuristic approaches to managing inventory in the supply chain. Chapter 10 highlights the role of distribution as a key supply chain responsibility and Chapter 11 provides broad coverage of the importance of transportation as a key element of overall supply chain success.

Collectively, the successful execution of these processes contribute significantly to achieving the promise of the efficient and effective supply chain by ensuring that customers receive the right product in the right quantities at the right place, right time, and at the right cost. Customers will therefore be satisfied and the order-to-cash flow should be maximized. While seemingly not as "glamorous" to some as other aspects of supply chain management, they are nevertheless an essential components of successful supply chains.

Part IV-Supply Chain Challenges and Future Directions

Part IV examines the strategic issues that face supply chain managers as organizations strive to remain competitive in the global economy. One of the issues is that of supply chain alignment which has been receiving increasing attention by supply chain professionals and academics. Covered in Chapter 12 is the need for alignment on both internal and external perspectives because of the need for collaboration among supply chain participants. Chapter 12 also provides useful information regarding the role of third party providers of logistics services, and how they may contribute to desired degrees of alignment among members of the supply chain. Chapter 13 provides insight into the important areas of performance measurement and financial analysis that are so critical to successfully executing today's supply chain responsibilities. The topic of technology is examined in Chapter 14 because of its increasingly critical role in achieving supply chain success. Not only are supply chain technologies important to the functioning of supply chains and the organizations that are involved, but they have become key contributors to creating customer value and making significant contributions to the success of overall organizations. In short, it has become apparent that the use of capable technologies has become a very important change agent to help deal with the increasing pressures faced by supply chains. Last, Chapter 15 provides an insightful look at some of the governing principles of supply chain management, and how they continue to evolve and remain current in the fast-changing world of supply chain management. This concluding chapter also provides in-depth commentaries on several topics that are of great contemporary and future interest to achieving the goals of supply chain management and overall business success.

Features

- Learning Objectives at the beginning of each chapter provide students with an overall perspective of chapter material and also serve to establish a baseline for a working knowledge of the topics that follow.
- Supply Chain Profiles are the opening vignettes at the beginning of each chapter that introduce students to the chapter's topics through familiar, real-world companies, people, and events.
- On the Line features are applied, concrete examples that provide students with hands-on managerial experience of the chapter topics.
- End-of-chapter summaries and study questions reinforce material presented in each chapter.
- Short cases at the end of each chapter build upon what students have learned. Questions that follow the cases sharpen critical thinking skills.

Ancillaries

The website contains three essential resources:
- The Instructor's Manual includes chapter outlines, answers to end-of-chapter study questions, commentary on end-of-chapter short cases and end-of-text comprehensive cases, and teaching tips.
- A convenient Test Bank offers a variety of true/false, multiple choice, and essay questions for each chapter.
- PowerPoint slides cover the main chapter topics and contain graphics from the main text.

About the Authors

John J. Coyle is currently director of corporate relations for the Center for Supply Chain Research and professor emeritus of logistics and supply chain management in the Smeal College of Business at Penn State University. He holds a BS and MS from Penn State and earned his doctorate from Indiana University in Bloomington, Indiana, where he was a U.S. Steel Fellow. He joined the Penn State faculty in 1961 and attained the rank of full professor in 1967. In addition to his teaching responsibilities, he has served in a number of administrative positions, including department head, assistant dean, senior associate dean, special assistant for strategic planning to the university president, and executive director of the Center for Supply Chain Research. He also served as Penn State's faculty representative to the NCAA for 30 years and to the Big Ten for 10 years. Dr. Coyle was the editor of the *Journal of Business Logistics* from 1990 to 1996. He has authored or coauthored 20 books or monographs and numerous articles in professional journals. He has received 14 awards at Penn State for teaching excellence and advising. In addition, he received the Council of Logistics Management's Distinguished Service Award in 1991; the Philadelphia Traffic Club's Person of the Year Award in 2003; and the Eccles Medal from the International Society of Logistics for his contributions to the Department of Defense and the Lion's Paw Medal from Penn State for Distinguished Service, both in 2004. Dr. Coyle currently serves on the boards of two logistics and supply chain service companies.

C. John Langley Jr. is clinical professor of supply chain management in the Smeal College of Business at Penn State University and also serves as director of development in the Center for Supply Chain Research. Previously, he served as the John H. Dove professor of supply chain management at the University of Tennessee and the SCL professor of supply chain management at the Georgia Institute of Technology. Dr. Langley is a former president of the Council of Supply Chain Management Professionals and a recipient of the Council's Distinguished Service Award. He has been recognized by the American Society of Transportation and Logistics as an honorary distinguished logistics professional for his long-term contributions and continuing commitment to the transportation logistics community, and he is a recipient of the Outstanding Alumnus Award from Penn State's Business Logistics Program. Dr. Langley received his BS degree in mathematics, MBA in finance, and Ph.D. in business logistics, all from Penn State University. Dr. Langley has coauthored several books, including *Supply Chain Management: A Logistics Perspective*. Also, he is lead author of the annual *Third Party Logistics Study and recently completed the 2016 20th Annual 3PL Study*. His research publications have appeared in journals such as the *Journal of Business Logistics, International Journal of Physical Distribution and Logistics Management, International Journal of Logistics Management, Supply Chain Management Review, and Land Economics*. Dr. Langley serves on the Boards of Directors of UTi Worldwide, Inc., Forward Air Corporation, and Averitt Express, Inc., in addition to several involvements on academic advisory boards to logistics organizations. He also participated as a member of the Program Faculty for the Kühne Logistics University in Hamburg, Germany, currently serves as education advisor for NASSTRAC.

Robert Novack is an associate professor of supply chain management in the Department of Supply Chain and Information Systems at Penn State University. From 1981 to 1984 he worked in operations management and planning for the Yellow Freight Corporation in Overland Park, Kansas, and from 1984 to 1986 he worked in planning and transportation at Drackett Company in Cincinnati, Ohio. Dr. Novack's numerous articles have been published in such publications as the *Journal of Business Logistics, Transportation Journal, and International Journal of Physical Distribution and Logistics Management.* He also is a coauthor of *Creating Logistics Value: Themes for the Future.* Active in the Council of Supply Chain Management Professionals, he has served as overall program chair for the annual conference, as a track chair, and as a session speaker as well as a member of numerous committees. Dr. Novack holds the CTL designation from AST&L and is a member of WERC. He earned a BS degree and an MBA in logistics from Penn State University and a Ph.D. in logistics from the University of Tennessee.

Brian J. Gibson is executive director of the Center for Supply Chain Innovation and the Wilson Family Professor of supply chain management at Auburn University. Previously, he served on the faculty of Georgia Southern University and as a logistics manager for two major retailers. He has received multiple awards for outstanding teaching, research, and outreach. Gibson's research has been published in the *Journal of Business Logistics, International Journal of Logistics Management, International Journal of Physical Distribution and Logistics Management, Supply Chain Management Review, Supply Chain Quarterly,* and other leading publications. He is coauthor of *Transportation: A Supply Chain Perspective,* author of the electronic textbook *Supply Chain Essentials,* and lead author of the annual State of the *Retail Supply Chain Report.* Dr. Gibson serves as SCPro certification chair and board member for the Council of Supply Chain Management Professionals, education advisor for NASSTRAC, and supply chain steering committee member for the Retail Industry Leaders Association. Dr. Gibson earned a BS from Central Michigan University, an MBA from Wayne State University, and a Ph.D. in logistics and transportation from the University of Tennessee.

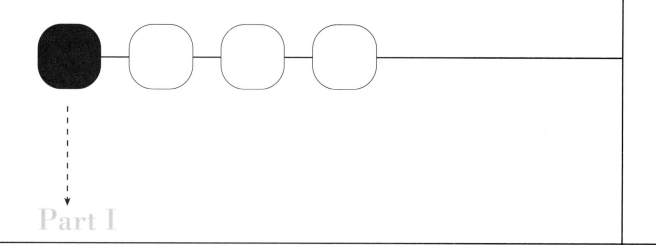

This section of the text provides a framework and overview to provide an appreciation, some insights and an understanding of supply chain management as it expanded and developed over the course of the last 30 years. This part of the text has been updated and revised again to better reflect the authors' view of the dynamic happenings of the 21st century for global supply chains. Companies and other organizations will need to navigate the associated challenges to achieve efficiency and effectiveness while executing to meet the expectations of their "customers."

The first chapter provides an overview of the role and increasing importance of supply chain management in today's tumultuous environment. This chapters explores the external forces impacting global supply chains and the major challenges and issues in the 21st century. The chapter also provides an overview the basis tenets of supply chain management and its development.

The second chapter covering the global dimensions of supply chains has been repositioned in the text and expanded to explicate more fully the complexity of the global demographic and economic issues that will continue to impact global supply chains. Effective response to these global dynamics will be critical for survival.

Chapter 3 discusses and explores the dimensions of logistics management and its importance to the proficiency of global supply chains. The role of logistics as the "backbone" for world class supply chains is examined and explained.

Chapter 4 has been repositioned in Part I and expanded to include an analysis and discussion of omni-channel distribution and the related network design. This is an important issue and growing challenge for many supply chains as they respond to the needs of today's demanding and technology savvy consumers.

Chapter 1

SUPPLY CHAIN MANAGEMENT: AN OVERVIEW

Learning Objectives

After reading this chapter, you should be able to do the following:

- Explain how efficient and effective supply chains can improve customer fulfillment and cash flow.

- Discuss the development and shaping of supply chains in leading organizations and understand their contributions to their financial viability.

- Appreciate the important role of supply chain management among private as well as public or nonprofit organizations.

- Understand the contributions of supply chain management to organizational efficiency and effectiveness for competing successfully in the global marketplace.

- Explain the benefits that can be achieved form implementing supply chain best practices.

- Understand the major supply chain challenges and issues faced by organizations currently and in the future.

Supply Chain Profile   *SAB Distribution: The Final Chapter*

SAB was established as a classic, middle-of-the-supply chain organization since it purchased consumer products from major manufacturers such as Kraft, Kimberly-Clark, Procter & Gamble (P&G), Unilever, and others and sold them to smaller distributors, wholesalers, and retailers. When Susan Weber assumed the role CEO of SAB in 2010, she knew that in spite of several major changes, its continued survival depended upon the company reexamining its role in various supply chains and making appropriate strategic and tactical changes.

COMPANY BACKGROUND

SAB Distribution was established in 1949 in Harrisburg, Pennsylvania, by three World War II veterans (Skip, Al, and Bob) who had served as navy supply officers. Harrisburg was selected because of its central location in the mid-Atlantic region and because of its access to rail and highways for suppliers and potential customers. The founders of SAB recognized the need for a consumer products wholesaling company to serve medium- and small-size retailers within a 200-mile radius of Harrisburg. The company grew and prospered in subsequent years. The company was incorporated in 1978, and a CEO, Pete Swan, was appointed in 1980 when the founders retired. SAB's market area expanded into nearby states, such as New York, New Jersey, and Delaware, and its product line expanded from nonperishable food products to include perishables and nonfood consumer products. Sue Purdum took over from Pete Swan in 1995 when the company was facing major competitive challenges that could have led to the sale of the company, but she "navigated" the company successfully. Susan Weber assumed the CEO role with the full knowledge that significant change was necessary if SAB was to continue to survive as a profitable organization. Essentially, SAB needed a transformation in the scope of its activities.

CURRENT SITUATION

SAB is faced with a number of challenges to its future existence. First and foremost, many of its customers compete against large retailers like Walmart that can buy directly from the same consumer product manufacturers as SAB, with no "middleman." Walmart's buying advantage had to be offset in some way to keep SAB's customers competitive. In addition, globalization was affecting SAB's business because of an increase in imported products for the more diverse population of the United States and the ongoing search for lower-priced alternatives. The net effect was a much more complex and competitive business environment with more potential volatility.

When Sue Purdum assumed the role of CEO in 1995, she analyzed the competitive environment and understood the need to change to SAB's business practices. She focused upon efficiency in warehouse operations, improved fulfillment, and developed partnerships with a core group of motor carriers. Finally, she invested in information technology. The net effect of these changes lowered the cost of doing business for SAB's customers and enabled them to be more competitive. It was a win-win since SAB also became more efficient and effective as well as more profitable.

Initially, Susan Weber followed the lead of Sue Purdum, but she knew that she had to transform the company to attract large retailers as customers. Their current customers were losing market share to the larger retailers which negatively impacted SAB's profitability.

Susan Weber realized that the large retailers outsourced part of their logistics operations to third-party logistics companies to lower their cost of doing business. Given SAB's proficiency in logistics, she believed that there were opportunities for SAB to eliminate duplicative echelons in those supply chains. For example, between a producer's plant and a retail store, there were often three or more distribution locations where products were stored and handled.

The SAB managers recognized the challenge of Susan Weber's assessment of their competitive market but also the opportunities associated with the changes that she outlined. After five years of Susan Weber's leadership, SAB attracted five large regional retail chains in the Northeast and developed a distribution park for warehousing, a transportation hub, and a call center near Scranton, Pennsylvania.

The new distribution park allowed SAB to expand their value-added services to customers by providing third-party logistics services (warehousing and inventory management, order fulfillment, delivery and special packaging).

SAB hopes to attract additional regional chains such as Wegman's. A focus for their new distribution park is fresh fruits, vegetables, and other perishable food items, commonly referred to as the cold supply chain. SAB's success with their distribution park has caught the attention of several other companies who are planning similar operations along the eastern seaboard.

Recently, Susan was informed by a daughter of one of the founders of SAB that the family had been contacted by a representative of a major investment group that wanted to buy the family's share of the stock (65%) and take the company private. The potential buyout had major implications for Ms. Weber and her valued employees. She felt that SAB could survive in the current environment, but she would have to present a plan to the family owners that would convince them to maintain their current ownership position. As you read this text, consider how SAB could address the challenges of their current environment including: (1) cost pressure; (2) having a responsive/demand driven supply chain; (3) supply chain visibility; (4) more collaborative supply chain relationships; and (5) improved information flow and data analytics.

1-1 Introduction

The first decade of the twenty-first century was a period of rapid change for most organizations, especially businesses. That rate of change has not slowed down, and the second decade has been more volatile than previous years. The external forces of change require organizations to be much more nimble and responsive; that is, organizations need to be able to change and/or transform themselves to survive in the intensely competitive, global environment. The SAB case is a good example of this survivor mode which forces companies to transform. SAB would have been driven out of business in the 1990s if it had not changed, and it now faces an even more daunting challenge, which will necessitate still bigger changes.

Several quotes cited in a previous edition of this book are still apropos. They are as follows:

"Change is inevitable, but growth and improvement are optional."[1]

"When the rate of change outside the organization is faster than inside, the end is near."[2]

Susan Weber, CEO of SAB, understands the wisdom of these comments and the need to collaborate with their customers. The rationale for SAB to change can be made by comparing the top retail establishments in 2000, 2010, and 2014 (see Table 1.1). One could argue that most retailers are essentially supply chain companies since they buy products produced by others and sell these same products to their customers. While other factors such as merchandising, pricing, store location, and layout are very important, supply chain management and logistics are key ingredients for success in today's highly competitive global environment.

Table 1.1	Leading Retailers (Sales/Year)	
2000	**2010**	**2014**
1. Wal-Mart	1. Wal-Mart	1. Wal-Mart
2. Kroger	2. Kroger	2. Kroger
3. The Home Depot	3. Target	3. Costco
4. Sears, Roebuck & Company	4. Walgreen	4. The Home Depot
5. Kmart	5. The Home Depot	5. Walgreen
6. Albertson's	6. Costco	6. Target
7. Target	7. CVS Caremark	7. CVS Caremark
8. JC Penny	8. Lowe's	8. Lowe's
9. Costco	9. Best Buy	9. Amazon.com
10. Safeway	10. Sears Holdings	10. Safeway

Source: National Retail Federation (NRF) https://nrf.com/resources/annual-retailer-lists/top-100-retailers

Susan Weber (CEO, SAB) appears to comprehend the potential role that supply chains can play in making retail organizations successful. She also seems to understand that the dynamics of today's global environment requires thinking "out of the box." Table 1.1 demonstrates the forces of change and the need to adapt with the shifts which have occurred. In 2010, five of the top 10 retailers of 2000 are not on the list anymore with the caveat that Sears and Kmart were merged. Note that Sears and Kmart were #4 and #5 in 2000, but after the merger, the combined company was #10. Four new companies were on the 2010 list. In 2014, two new companies (Amazon and Safeway) joined the top 10 while Sears and Best Buy were eliminated. Amazon's appearance on the list is most notable because of their business model with no stores. Amazon's impact will be the basis of discussion in following chapters.

At this juncture, an examination of the major external forces or change drivers shaping supply chains is appropriate to examine their impact on various organizations and their supply chains.

1-2 Shaping the Supply Chains of the Twenty-First Century: Evolution and Change

The dynamics of the global environment changed dramatically during the 1990s, and organizations had to adapt to these changes or perish. Unfortunately, there were a number of casualties along the way. Some previously successful companies did not survive in the more competitive global marketplace because they did not adapt and change. Leading companies such as Westinghouse, Bethlehem Steel, and RCA are no longer in business. Currently successful leaders such as IBM, General Electric, and McDonald's are struggling to survive as they try to make appropriate changes in their business models. Some individuals argue that an appropriate business mantra should be "disrupt or be disrupted" which may be a way of stating an older axiom, "think outside the box".

Five major external forces are driving the rate of change: globalization, technology, organizational consolidation, the empowered consumer, and government policy and

Figure 1.1	External Change Drivers

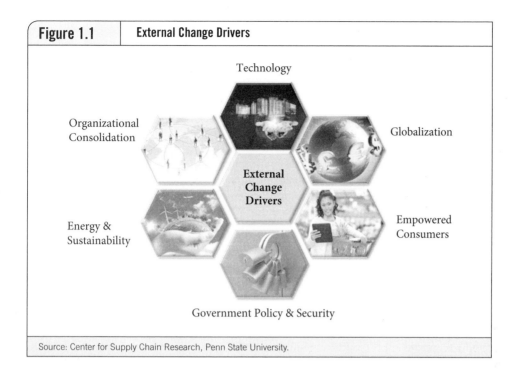

Source: Center for Supply Chain Research, Penn State University.

regulation. (See Figure 1.1) The confluence of these factors in the twenty-first century has dramatically changed the economic landscape and provided an opportune business climate for the development of global supply chains and supply chain management.

1-2-1 Globalization

Globalization was the most frequently cited change factor by business leaders, and it replaced the post–World War II Cold War as the dominant driving force in world economics. The concept of the global marketplace or the global economy took on a special meaning for all enterprises (profit and nonprofit; small, medium, and large; products or services) and for individual consumers in the 1990s and the first decade of the twenty-first century. Globalization led to a more competitive economic and geopolitical environment which resulted in opportunities and threats both economic and political. Some individuals have argued that there is no "geography" in the current global environment (figuratively speaking) or, perhaps more aptly, that **time** and **distance** have been compressed. For example, companies seeking to rationalize their global networks ask such questions as: (1) Where in the world should we source our materials and/or services? (2) Where in the world should we manufacture or produce our products or services? (3) Where in the world should we market and sell our products or services? (4) Where in the world should we warehouse and distribute our products? (5) What global transportation and related service alternatives should we consider?

Some important issues or challenges for supply chains in the global economy are more economic and political risk; shorter product life cycles; and the blurring of traditional organizational boundaries. All three deserve some discussion.

Supply and demand have become more volatile for a number of reasons. Acts of terrorism, for example, the ISIS attacks in the Middle East and pirates attacking cargo ships, have serious implications for the flow of commerce. Companies have put security measures in place to protect their global supply chains and to act quickly to offset challenges to their supply chains which has increased their cost, but the risk is ever present. Natural catastrophes such as hurricanes, floods, typhoons, and earthquakes have become more problematic because of climate changes and because they pose a very significant challenge for global supply chains. Challenges to supply and demand are usually exacerbated in number and severity by the distances involved, which necessitates risk mitigation strategies.

It has been argued that an interruption or disruption to a supply chain that cuts off the flow of information and products is analogous to a "heart attack" that cuts off the flow of blood to the heart. Like a heart attack, supply chain disruption can have lasting effects. The global supply chains of the best companies must be adaptive, resilient, and responsive to meet the challenges of the global economy and develop mitigating strategies for disruptive forces.

Shorter product life cycles are a manifestation of the ability of products and services to be duplicated quickly. Technology companies are particularly vulnerable to the threat of their new products being reengineered. However, almost all products in the highly competitive global environment are faced with this issue. From a supply chain perspective, shorter product life cycles present a challenge for inventory management. Products that are duplicated will most likely face a faster reduction in demand and require new pricing policies, both of which present challenges to effective inventory management. The risk of obsolescence as new products are developed is another challenge for inventory management. It also means continually developing new products or reconfiguring old products to maintain market share. The rate of development and change in technology is particularly disruptive to existing enterprises and has led to the demise of some.

The blurring of traditional organizational boundaries is the result of companies having to adjust or transform their business model or the way that they do business in the more competitive global economy. For example, to maintain financial viability (read profitability), companies may outsource activities and processes to another company that can provide what they need more efficiently and hopefully more effectively. They may also add to their current operations or services to provide additional value for customers. SAB followed this strategy to retain and add customers.

Outsourcing is not new. No organization is completely independent. The competitiveness of the global environment, however, has increased the scope of outsourcing both domestically and globally. As previously mentioned, companies need to analyze how they do business in order to stay competitive and financially viable. Nike, for example, outsources all of its manufacturing and has done so for many years. Many automobile and computer manufacturers outsource components or parts that they need for finished products as well as logistics related services. From a supply chain and logistics perspective, the growth in outsourcing is noteworthy because it increases the importance of effective and efficient supply chain management because supply chains are longer and more complex.

A strong compliment to the growth in the global economy has been the growth and development in the technology related to supply chains. Mention has been made of time and distance being compressed, and technology has certainly played a major role in making this happen. Technology will be discussed as the next external change factor. It should be noted that some organizations think that technology has become a more important driver of change than globalization.

1-2-2 Technology

Technology has had a major impact on supply chains as a facilitator of change as companies have transformed their processes. However, it is also a major force in changing the dynamics of the marketplace. Individuals and organizations are "connected" 24/7 and have access to information on the same basis via the Internet. Search engines, such as Google and others, have made it possible to gather timely information quickly. We no longer have to wait for information to be "pushed out" to us; we can "pull" information as we need it. Vast stores of data and information are virtually at our fingertips. Social networks such as Facebook or Twitter are playing an ever increasing role in business organizations and influence supply chains because of their impact on customer demand and the speed of information transfers. Some individuals have argued that another relevant mantra for businesses in the twenty-first century is "twitter and tweet or retreat." Many companies see opportunities to "data mine" the social media to uncover demand related information for improved forecasting and marketing. As will be discussed in more detail, "cloud computing", is more than a "buzz word" and is revolutionizing information systems.

Technology has allowed individuals and smaller organizations to connect to the world's "knowledge pools" to create and establish opportunities for collaboration in supply chains. Outsourcing to the less-developed countries was enhanced by technology. Collaboration opportunities with individuals and companies throughout the globe have increased which has created market opportunities as employment opportunities increased. Technology has spawned the development of Uber, Airbnb, and other such organizations which have disrupted their respective marketplaces.

Susan Weber, as SAB's new CEO, will have to more fully exploit the opportunities presented by technology both on the procurement side of business and in marketing products to customers. Her predecessor used technology to improve internal processes, for example, warehouse operations and order fulfillment as well as transportation carrier collaboration. SAB will need to focus more externally with information technology to improve overall supply chain efficiency and effectiveness.

1-2-3 Organizational Consolidation and Power Shifts

After World War II, product manufacturers became the driving force in supply chains. They developed, designed, produced, promoted, and distributed their products. Frequently, they were the largest organizations in the supply chain in terms of sales volume, employees, buying power, locations, and other factors. They typically exerted their influence throughout the supply chain often to their specific economic advantage, especially in the distribution of their products.

During the 1980s and especially the 1990s, a significant change occurred as retail giants such as Walmart, Sears, Kmart, Home Depot, Target, Kroger, McDonald's, etc., became powerful market leaders and engines for change. While other retailers are not as large as Walmart, their size and economic buying power have also increased significantly. An important aspect of the economic power shift toward the retail end of the supply chain is that many consumer product companies find that 15 to 20 percent of their customers account for 70 to 80 percent of their total sales.

The large retailers were accorded services such as scheduled deliveries, "rainbow" pallets (mixed arrays of products or stock-keeping units [SKUs]), advance shipments notices (ASNs) shrink-wrapped pallets, etc. These services allowed retailers to operate more efficiently and often more effectively and provide scale economies to the producers which was a win-win arrangement with savings passed on to the consumer. Subsequent chapters will more fully explicate the benefits.

As more collaboration is practiced among organizations in the supply chains, they can gain shared cost savings and improved customer service. For example, sharing point-of-sale data is a powerful collaborative tool for mitigating the so-called "bullwhip effect" of inventory in the supply chain which has multiple benefits for supply chain collaborators. Companies that report innovative best practices usually obtain about half of their innovative insights outside their company through collaboration with suppliers and customers. The power of information sharing and collaboration cannot be overstated. This is a key area for SAB to exploit as it tries to adapt to its competitive environment and increase sales with existing and new customers. Data sharing will help SAB to lower product stock-outs and related lost sales to improve on-shelf availability of their products for increased sales.

1-2-4 The Empowered Consumer

The impact of the consumer is more direct for supply chains today because the consumer has placed increased demands at the retail level for an expanded variety of products and services. The implementation of an omni-channel distribution strategy by large retailers, which will be discussed in Chapter 4, is an excellent example of a current strategy made feasible with technology that is having a major impact on marketing sales at the retail level.

Consumers are empowered by the information that they have at their disposal from the Internet and other sources. Their access to product sources and related information has expanded exponentially. Consumers have the opportunity to compare prices, quality, and service. Consequently, they demand competitive prices, high quality, tailored or customized products, convenience, flexibility, and responsiveness. They tend to have a low tolerance level for poor quality in products and services. They report their likes and dislikes on the Internet to third party organizations such as Yelp. Some consumers have increased buying power due to high income levels. They demand the best quality, at the best price, with the best service. These demands place increased challenges and pressure on the various supply chains for consumer products.

The demographics of our society with the increase in two-career families and single-parent households have made time and convenience critical factors for many households. The expectation for service is frequently 24/7 availability with a minimum of wait time. The age old axiom of "let the buyer beware" should probably be changed to "let the seller beware." The Internet enables buyers to expand their buying alternatives and quickly make comparisons before they purchase. The omni-channel distribution option provides additional flexibility for consumers. The power of the consumer has caused much change in how supply chains function. Supply chains have felt the pressure to keep prices stable even during inflationary periods. Collaboration has frequently been the basis for efficiencies to mitigate increased costs.

1-2-5 Government Policy and Regulation

The fifth external change factor is the various levels of government (federal, state, and local) that establish and administer policies, regulations, taxes, etc., which impact businesses and their supply chains. The deregulation of several important sectors of our economy that occurred in the 1980s and 1990s is a good example. The deregulated sectors include transportation, communications, and financial institutions, which are cornerstones of the infrastructure for most organizations.

Beginning in the late 1970s and into the 1980s, the U.S. transportation industry was deregulated at the federal level in terms of economic controls such as rates and areas of service. The net effect was that it became possible for transportation services to be purchased and sold in a more competitive environment. Transportation companies were also allowed to offer more than just transportation services. Many motor carriers, for example, became logistics services companies and offered services that include order fulfillment, inventory management, and warehousing. They have moved aggressively ahead in the deregulated environment to view themselves as outsourcing partners for potential strategic advantages (see Case 1.1).

The financial sector was also deregulated at the federal level. Financial markets became more competitive, flexible, and responsive to customer needs. The deregulation of financial institutions fostered changes in how businesses can operate with respect to cash flow, purchase cards, and short-term investment. These changes made organizations more

---

On the Line   *Changing Times for Drugs*

One of the U.S. industries being buffeted by the "winds of change" in the twenty-first century is the pharmaceutical industry which has been a major force in the U.S. economy for many years. The industry has provided consistent and excellent employment opportunities and inceased returns to shareholders for years. However, the industry has been challenged in recent years by more intense global competition; a related growth in the prescription and use of generic drugs; the end of patent protection for a growing number of their major drugs; a slower development of new "blockbuster" drugs to treat major illnesses; more regulation; and an unresponsive supply chain.

One of several "cures" may come to mind for the challenges enumerated in earlier paragraph, but there is no question that there is a glaring need for managing their supply chains more efficiently and effectively along with better execution. Discussion with key executives noted a need to change their strategy from a push approach to a pull strategy. The push approach has led to overstocks of some SKU's and stock-outs of others with consequent higher inventory costs and perhaps lost sales. There is also a need for their supply chains to be more responsive to demand "signals" in a timely manner.

Another needed change is a more collaboration with suppliers, customers, and logistics service providers. In the past, pharmaceutical companies could essentially dictate and control what happened in their supply chains. Participants in the supply chain were usually not considered to be "partners" or needed collaborators. Valuable information and potential innovations were probably squandered along the way. As has been pointed out in recent years, supply chain collaborators and partners often provide half or more of the innovative changes that lowered cost and/or improved service.

Another need is for improved information flow and management as well as more visibility along the supply chain. This is a necessary ingredient for improved decisions in logistics and transportation. Too frequently, data has been incomplete or incorrect resulting in higher cost and/or ineffective customer service. Timely and accurate Information flow is important and is a necessary part of improving pharmaceutical supply chains and the financial viability of the industry.

The pharmaceutical industry is still an important part of the economy but like some other sectors and individual companies, they need to make innovative changes in their supply chains and related activities to be more competitive and financially viable in the twenty-first century.

Source: John J. Coyle and Kusumal Ruamsook, Center for Supply Chain Research, Penn State University.

cognizant of the role that supply chain management could play with asset efficiency and cash flow. All of the above have contributed to the focus on cash flow as previously discussed. It should be noted that there have been some negative aspects associated with the financial deregulation which contributed, for example, to the great recession of 2008–2010.

The communications industry also became more competitive. This scenario was different since the major cause of change was a Supreme Court decision that split up the AT&T/Bell telephone system into regional companies; separated the "long-lines" system of AT&T, and made it accessible to other companies such as Sprint that wanted to sell telephone services. Like the other two industries discussed earlier, the communications industry has undergone dramatic change and has become part of the information revolution with a number of other "players" including cable companies, Internet companies, etc.

Businesses and the general consumer population have been impacted by the many changes in the communications industry from cell phones and pagers to e-mail, text messaging, twitter-tweets, and the Internet. Communications efficiency and effectiveness have led to dramatic improvements and opportunities in logistics and supply chains. Examples include asset visibility, quick response replenishment, improved transportation scheduling, rapid order entry, and same day delivery. The omni-channel option discussed in Chapter 4 is a major change in meeting customer needs at the retail level. Supply chain practices have been improved leading to lower cost and better customer service. The supply chain technology continues to improve and more examples will be delineated in subsequent chapters.

SAB Distribution is being buffeted by all of these change drivers. The marketplace is much more competitive; consumers are much more demanding and knowledgeable. Globalization and deregulation have made SAB much more vulnerable in its regional marketplace and much less insulated against larger competitors. These change drivers represent both opportunities and threats for SAB, as well as for other businesses both large and small. SAB needs to use technology to improve their supply chain operations and changes in their business model and practices to survive.

1-3 Supply Chains: Development and Shaping for the Twenty-First Century

1-3-1 Development of the Concept

It can be argued that supply chain management represents the third phase of an evolution that started in the 1960s with the development of the **physical distribution** concept that focuses on the outbound side of a firm's logistics system (see Figure 1.2). The system relationships among transportation, inventory requirements, warehousing, exterior packaging, materials handling, and other activities or cost centers were recognized. For example, the selection and use of a mode of transportation, such as rail, affects inventory, warehousing, packaging, customer service, and materials-handling costs, whereas motor carrier service would probably have a different impact on the same cost centers. The transportation decision should be based upon lowest total system cost. The systems perspective is also an important concept underlying supply chain management and will be explored in more detail in Chapter 3.

The 1980s, as noted, was a decade of change in the United States with the deregulation of transportation and financial institutions, and the **integrated logistics management**

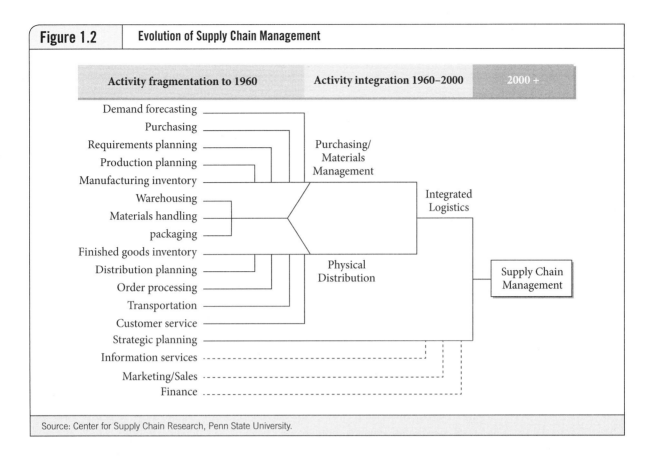

Figure 1.2 | **Evolution of Supply Chain Management**

Source: Center for Supply Chain Research, Penn State University.

concept that added inbound logistics to the outbound logistics of physical distributions developed in a growing number of organizations. This was logical since deregulation of transportation provided an opportunity to coordinate inbound and outbound transportation movements of large shippers that could positively impact a carrier's operating cost by minimizing empty backhauls, leading to lower rates for the shipper. Also, international or global sourcing of materials and supplies for inbound systems was growing in importance. Therefore, it became increasingly apparent that coordination between the outbound and inbound logistics system provided opportunities for increased efficiency and improved customer service.

The underlying logic of the **systems** or **total cost concept** was the rationale for logistics management. In addition, Porter's **value chain concept** developed as a tool for competitive analysis and strategy was a complement to integrated logistics. The value chain illustration where (see Figure 1.3), inbound and outbound logistics are identified as primary components of the value chain; that is, they can contribute value for customers and make the company financially viable to increase sales and improve cash flow. The more integrated nature of marketing, sales, and manufacturing with logistics is also an important dimension of the value chain and has become more important with the supply chain management focus.

Supply chain management gained traction in the 1990s because of two major studies. The Grocery Manufacturers Association (GMA) commissioned a study by the Cleveland Consulting Company to analyze the supply chains or grocery manufacturers. The impactful conclusions indicated a potential savings of $30 billion a year by reducing inventory levels from 104 days of inventory to 61 days of inventory in their outbound supply chains.

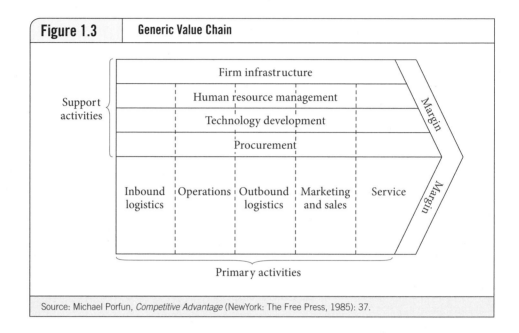

Figure 1.3	Generic Value Chain

Source: Michael Porfun, *Competitive Advantage* (NewYork: The Free Press, 1985): 37.

The other example of the importance of focusing upon the supply chain came from the Supply Chain Council, which published a comparison for 1996 and 1997 of "best-in-class" companies (top 10 percent) and the median companies that were reporting their metrics to the Council. The related costs of the best-in-class (BIC) companies were 7.0 percent of total sales, while the median company experienced 13.1 percent. In other words, the best-in-class companies spent 7.0 cents of every sales/revenue dollar for supply chain-related costs, while the median company spent 13.1 cents of every sales dollar on supply chain-related costs. In 1997, the respective numbers were 6.3 percent and 11.6 percent for best-in-class companies versus the median company. A simple application of these numbers for a hypothetical company with $100 million sales in 1997, being best in class would mean an additional $5.3 million of gross profit to an organization, which frequently would be the equivalent profit from an additional $80 to $100 million of sales.

At this point, a more detailed analysis and discussion of the supply chain is appropriate. Figure 1.4 presents a linear or basic example of a hypothetical supply chain. Real-world supply chains are usually more complex than this example because they may be nonlinear or have more supply chain participants (see Figure 1.5). Also, this supply chain does not adequately portray the importance of transportation and other service suppliers in the supply chain. In addition, some companies may be part of several supply chains. For example, chemical companies provide the ingredients for many different products manufactured by different companies.

Figure 1. 4 provides perspective of the basic supply chain. The illustration indicates that a **supply chain** is an **extended enterprise** that usually crosses the boundaries of several individual firms to coordinate the related flows of all the companies. This extended enterprise should attempt to execute a coordinated, two-way flow of goods and services, information, cash, and demand. The four supply flows described in Figure 1.7 are very important to the success of supply chains (see Figure 1.7). Integration across the boundaries of several organizations in essence means that the supply chain needs to function similar to a single organization in satisfying the ultimate consumer. The management of a supply chain(s) is both an art and a science. There are many scientific applications and models utilized today

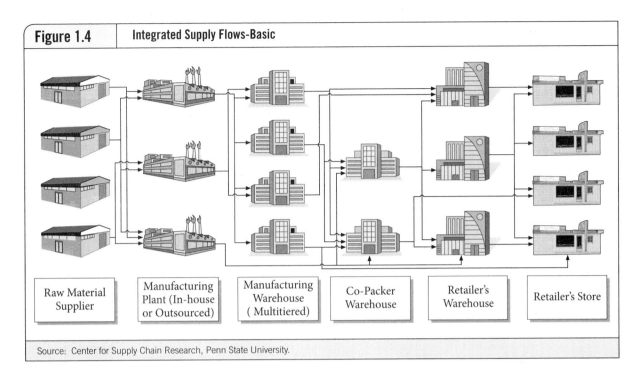

| Figure 1.4 | Integrated Supply Flows-Basic |

| Raw Material Supplier | Manufacturing Plant (In-house or Outsourced) | Manufacturing Warehouse (Multitiered) | Co-Packer Warehouse | Retailer's Warehouse | Retailer's Store |

Source: Center for Supply Chain Research, Penn State University.

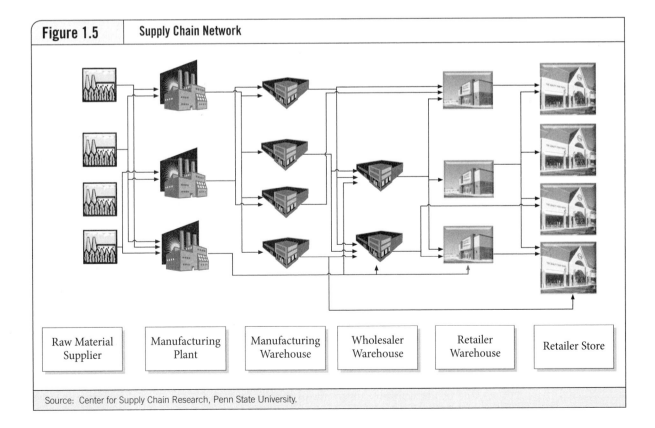

| Figure 1.5 | Supply Chain Network |

| Raw Material Supplier | Manufacturing Plant | Manufacturing Warehouse | Wholesaler Warehouse | Retailer Warehouse | Retailer Store |

Source: Center for Supply Chain Research, Penn State University.

Figure 1.6 | **Integrated Supply Chain - Basics**

SCM is the art and science of integrating the flows of products, information and financials through the entire supply pipeline from the vendor's vendor to the customer's customer.

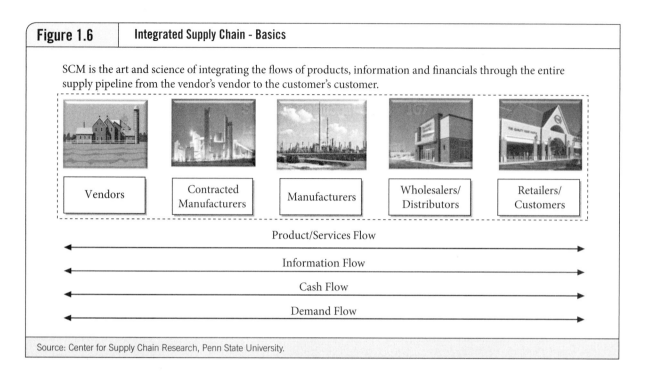

| Vendors | Contracted Manufacturers | Manufacturers | Wholesalers/ Distributors | Retailers/ Customers |

Product/Services Flow

Information Flow

Cash Flow

Demand Flow

Source: Center for Supply Chain Research, Penn State University.

---

in the management of supply chains from forecasting to distribution which will be explicated in following chapters. However, supply chain management is also an "art" because of its dynamic and complex environment which requires collaboration along the supply chain and continuing analysis and planning. This direct management involved in short- and long-run decisions is the key to innovation and successful management. The modeling applications are usually less challenging.

The top flow—*products and related services*—has traditionally been an important focus of logisticians and can be considered the "life blood" of the supply chain. Customers expect their orders to be delivered in a timely, reliable, and damage-free manner. Figure 1.7 also indicates that product flow is a two-way flow in today's environment because of the growing importance of reverse logistics systems for returning products that are unacceptable to the buyer, because they are damaged, obsolete, or worn out. Reverse supply chains are very important for many consumer product companies and retailers, and will be discussed in more detail in a later chapter. Third-party logistics companies that specialize in offering reverse flow systems can provide a valuable service for many companies.

The second flow indicated is the *information flow*, which has become an extremely important factor for success in supply chain management and can be considered the fuel for the supply chain. Traditionally, information was viewed as flowing in the opposite direction of products, that is, from the market or customer back into the supply chain. The information was primarily customer orders, which were the trigger for replenishment and the basis for forecasting. If there were long intervals between orders, the members of the supply chain were faced with more uncertainty about the level and pattern of the demand, which usually resulted in higher inventory or stock-out costs **(bullwhip effect)**.

One of the realizable outcomes of supply chain management is the sharing of sales information on a more real-time basis, which leads to less uncertainty and, therefore,

Figure 1.7	Supply Chain Flows

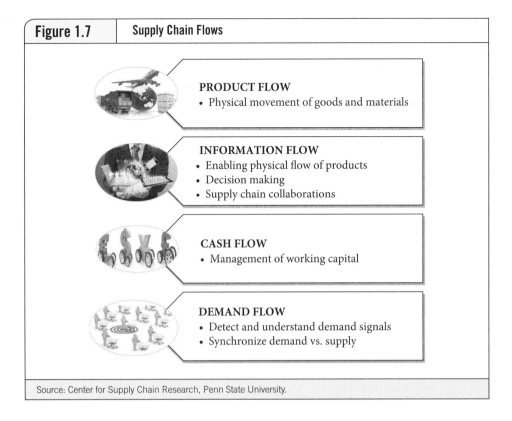

PRODUCT FLOW
- Physical movement of goods and materials

INFORMATION FLOW
- Enabling physical flow of products
- Decision making
- Supply chain collaborations

CASH FLOW
- Management of working capital

DEMAND FLOW
- Detect and understand demand signals
- Synchronize demand vs. supply

Source: Center for Supply Chain Research, Penn State University.

less safety stock. In a sense, the supply chain is being compressed or shortened through timely information flows back from the marketplace, which leads to a type of supply chain compression or inventory compression. In other words, inventory can be eliminated from the supply chain by timely, accurate information about demand. Simply stated, "Information can be a substitute for inventory." If point-of-sale (POS) data is available from the retail level on a real-time basis, it helps to mitigate the bullwhip effect associated with supply chain inventories and could significantly reduce cost.

Note that the illustration also indicates a two-way flow for information. In a supply chain environment, information flowing forward in the supply chain has taken on increased significance and importance. Forward information flow can take many forms such as advance shipment notices, order status information, inventory availability information, etc. The forward information flow can also help to reduce uncertainty. A related aspect of forward information flow has been the increased utilization of barcodes and radio-frequency tags, which can increase inventory visibility and help to reduce uncertainty and safety stock. The improved visibility of pipeline inventory also makes possible many opportunities for improved efficiency such as transportation consolidation and merge-in-transit strategies. The combined two-way flow of timely, accurate information lowers supply chain-related costs while also improving customer service.

The third flow is *financials* or, more specifically, cash. Traditionally, financial flow has been viewed as one-directional (backward) in the supply chain, as payment for goods, services, and orders received. A major impact of supply chain compression and faster order cycle times has been faster cash flow. Customers receive orders faster, they are billed sooner, and companies can collect sooner. The faster cash-to-cash cycle or order-to-cash cycle has been a bonanza for companies because of the impact on reducing working capital. In fact, some companies have what financial organizations refer to as "free" cash flow. They collect from their customers before they have to pay their vendors or suppliers. The cash can be used for a source of funding when it occurs on a regular basis. Cash flow has become an important metric for the financial markets to gauge the economic viability or vulnerability of companies. Most companies recognize the importance of accelerated cash flow or free cash flow and that supply chain management plays an important role in improved cash flow.

The fourth and final flow is **demand flow** which has received increased attention from supply chain managers with demand-driven systems. This is not a new concept for supply chain management but rather reflects the growth in technology which provides organizations the ability to better synchronize supply and demand by detecting and understanding demand "signals" and making appropriate adjustments to inventory replenishment and order fulfillment. For example, consumer product companies frequently had a 30-day production schedule "locked in" based upon a demand forecast by SKU. Consequently, these products rolled out to distribution centers regardless of what was actually being sold at the retail level. Production runs were rigid until the next period.

Best-in-class companies have developed a more flexible production schedule with the opportunity to make adjustments in 24 hours. Production costs can be higher, but the trade-off is the ability to meet spikes in demand or to slow down production of some SKUs that may not be selling at the level anticipated (higher cost but with more profit). It should be noted that some companies cannot make adjustments on such a short-term basis. Global supply chains present a special challenge because of the longer lead times, but technology has enabled companies to detect demand signals or market changes and make quicker adjustments, as will be discussed in subsequent chapters.

SAB Distribution is obviously part of a supply chain with an intermediate position between manufacturers and retailers. Wholesalers had a traditional role, which was buying products in volume quantities at lower prices and selling a mix of products in smaller quantities at higher prices to retailers. They frequently played a role in promoting and financing product sales in addition to distributing the item. Manufacturers and retailers depended upon them for efficiency in their operations. Large-scale retailers and manufacturers willing and able to provide more tailored, customized services have put wholesalers in jeopardy. SAB has felt this changing environment. It needs to reevaluate its role in relation to retailers, and to add "value" services to help reduce costs for their customers or help improve their sales revenue, and make other strategic moves.

Supply chain management provides organizations an opportunity to reduce cost (improve efficiency) and improve customer service (effectiveness) to increase revenue.

1-4 Major Supply Chain Issues

The challenge to develop and sustain an efficient and effective supply chain(s) requires organizations to address a number of issues. The issues are discussed here, but will be explored in much more depth in later chapters.

1-4-1 Supply Chain Networks

Network facilities (plants, distribution centers, terminals, etc.) and the supporting transportation services are considered to be very important. However, the network system in a dynamic, global environment is critical. One of the challenges is the rapid changes that can take place. Companies and other organizations need a network system that is capable and flexible to respond and change with the dynamics of the marketplace whether in the short run or the long run.

Technology companies, for example, may have to move manufacturing operations to a different country in six to nine months because of changes that can occur which affect their cost or customer service. The need for flexibility frequently means leasing facilities, equipment, and maybe supporting services. At times, the flexibility may be required for a shorter duration—for example, to respond to port strikes, floods, hurricanes, political uprisings, terroristic attacks and other disruptions. Mitigating the risk from such disruptions is a critical strategy in today's global networks. Private sector companies are placing increased emphasis on strategies to deal with the risk of disruptions whether they be natural dictators or other disruptive forces. Such a level of responsiveness requires information systems to provide as much warning as possible and plans in place on how to respond.

1-4-2 Complexity

The globalization and consolidation in supply chains that were previously discussed have caused an increased complexity for organizations in terms of SKUs, customer and supplier locations, transportation requirements, trade regulations, taxes, and so forth. Companies need to take steps to simplify, as much as possible, the various aspects of their supply chains. For example, the number of SKUs has expanded for many companies, which exacerbates problems for inventory management and order fulfillment. Consequently, companies have been rationalizing SKUs to eliminate the slow movers and items that do not contribute to profitability. Locations also need to be analyzed to eliminate high-cost or duplicative operations. Customer service levels need to be rationalized as do vendors or supplier alternatives. Layers of complexity develop and may seem necessary, but organizations need to continually evaluate those areas of complexity by evaluating processes, training people and exploiting technology.

1-4-3 Inventory Deployment

Two interesting characteristics of supply chains are that inventory is often being duplicated along the chain and the bullwhip effect. Effective SCM usually provides an opportunity to reduce inventory levels. Coordination or integration can help reduce inventory levels on horizontal single-firm) and vertical (multiple-firms) levels in the supply chain. Strategies such as compression and postponement can also have a positive impact. Inventory deployment is an important issue for supply chains because of the associated cost and related opportunities for increased efficiency. However, it is important to remember that inventory is a necessary ingredient for successful supply chains, but inventory levels must be managed carefully to reduce working capital. As discussed in the next section and subsequent chapters, information technology is a key ingredient for efficiency of inventory management.

1-4-4 Information

The technology and communication systems that are available to organizations today lead to the collection and storage of vast amounts of data, but interestingly enough, organizations may not be taking advantage of the abundant data to develop information systems to improve decision making. The accumulation and storage of data unless it is shared horizontally and vertically in the supply chain and is used to make better decisions about inventory, customer service, transportation, etc, is almost useless. Information can be a powerful tool if it is timely, accurate, managed, and shared. It can be a substitute for inventory because it can reduce uncertainty. The latter is one of the major causes of higher inventory levels because it leads to the accumulation of safety stock. The challenge, frequently, is the sharing of information along the supply chain and the discipline to ensure the integrity of the data collected—a big challenge but one with much potential.

1-4-5 Cost and Value

Frequent reference has been made in this chapter to efficiency (cost) and effectiveness (value). A challenge for supply chains is the prevention of sub-optimization. In today's environment, global supply chains compete against global supply chains, which means that the cost and value at the end of the supply chain are critical. This is another reason why supply chain collaboration is so important. All the members of a supply chain need to appreciate and understand the challenges and issues along the supply chain.

Consider SAB's situation. It has to be cognizant of the cost and value being offered by the large retailers who compete against its customers. It must think in terms of making its customers more competitive or attracting different customers where the synergies will lead to better outcomes. SAB's expertise in warehousing, distribution, and inventory management can be exploited to ensure that their customers are efficient and effective. The supply chain perspective with vertical and horizontal views provides an opportunity to "think outside the box." (See Case 1.2)

1-4-6 Organizational Relationships

Supply chain management emphasizes a horizontal process orientation that cuts across traditional functional silos within organizations and necessitates collaboration with external vendors, customers, transportation companies, 3PLs, and other service providers in the supply chain. In other words, internal collaboration or cooperation with marketing, sales, operations or manufacturing, and accounting or finance are very important as well as collaboration or cooperation with external organizations.

Communication is critical to explain the opportunities for system tradeoffs that will make the supply chain more competitive. For example, the vice president of manufacturing may present a rationale for operating plants on a 24/7 basis to lower production costs, but what about the cost of warehousing and inventory of goods that have to be stored until sales are finalized? Looking at manufacturing cost in isolation could lead to higher overall system costs. In Chapter 3, we will explore the concept of systems analysis in more detail and the importance of Sales and Operations Planning (S&OP) will be explored in a later chapter. The internal and external collaborative effort in supply chains is a critical ingredient for success, but it is an ongoing challenge for most organizations.

1-4-7 Performance Measurement

Most organizations have measures of performance or metrics in place to analyze and evaluate their efficiency and progress over different time periods. Sometimes, such measures are used for setting baseline performance objectives or expected outcomes, for example, orders filled and shipped per day. Measurement is important, and more attention will be devoted to this topic in Chapter 5. At this juncture, it is important to recognize that lower-level metrics in an organization must connect directly to the high-level performance measures of the organization and the supply chain, which are usually net profit, return on investment, or assets and cash flow. In some instances, metrics are set that appear logical for the subunit of the organization, but are suboptimal for the overall organization or supply chain. The previous example of the vice president running the plants 24/7 to achieve the lowest possible unit cost of products could have been saving 3 cents per unit on manufacturing, but the extra expense of holding excess inventory could have cost 4 to 5 cents per unit, thus lowering the company's net profit margin. The warehouse manager who is measured by the cost per cubic foot of units stored will be motivated to fill the warehouse to the ceiling (what is the tradeoff cost?). Consequently, the overall financial metrics of an organization should be the "drivers" of the lower level metrics.

1-4-8 Technology

Technology, as indicated previously, can be viewed as a change driver, but it is also important as a facilitator of change that can provide improved efficiency and effectiveness. The challenge is to evaluate and successfully implement the technology to make the improvements desired. Sometimes technology is, figuratively speaking, thrown at a problem, which usually leads to frustration and then failure. The approach necessary is to analyze and then adjust or change processes, educate the people involved, and then select and implement the technology to facilitate the changes in the processes. Skipping the first two steps is analogous to the frequently cited bad approach to strategic planning—ready, fire, aim. The technology available today is almost overwhelming, but analysis and planning are necessary to achieve the expected outcomes. Technology cannot solve or mitigate problems without appropriate up-front analysis and planning.

1-4-9 Transportation Management

Transportation can be viewed as the glue that helps the supply chain system function. The critical outcomes of the supply chain are "to deliver the right product at the right time, in the right quantity and quality, at the right cost, and to the right destination." Transportation plays an important role in making these "rights" happen. Another aspect of the importance of transportation is related to some of the strategies that are being used by companies to remain competitive in today's economy—for example, just-in-time inventory, lean logistics and manufacturing, and scheduled and one-day deliveries, etc. The challenge has been exacerbated by challenges and changes among transportation providers; shortages of drivers, fuel costs, and changes in driver hour regulations, which have led to what some individuals have called a transportation crisis or the "perfect storm." Transportation has gone from being a readily available commodity to potential users, especially in the 1990s, to today where transportation service can be scarce in some market areas. A major challenge is the maintenance of the existing transportation infrastructure (roads, bridges, ports, waterways, tracks, and airports) and the need to increase capacity to meet the growth in demand. The transportation infrastructure is a major cause of concern for global supply chains especially for water transportation in the port areas.

1-4-10 Supply Chain Security

As indicated, safe and reliable delivery of products to customers is expected of the supply chain. In the past, this was often accepted as a given, but today it is a concern and potential challenge. Globalization has obviously increased the risk of supply chain disruptions. Consequently, organizations must be prepared for potential disruption. Terroristic threats have changed some of the planning and preparation for supply chains that now often include some type of scenario analysis that can consider possible threats, assess probabilities, and plan for alternatives. This situation is not likely to improve in the near future, and companies need to be prepared. With global supply chains, vulnerability is exacerbated by distance and complexity.

1-4-11 Talent Management

As supply chains have become more complex and comprehensive for reasons explicated in this chapter and subsequent chapters, the criticality of having educated and talented managers involved in supply chains has attracted much more attention in many organizations. The effort to attract, develop, and maintain the appropriate pool of talent from entry level to executive level is attracting much more attention. At one time, it was assumed that anyone with experience in another functional area of the organization (marketing, manufacturing, accounting, etc.) could easily transition to a position in logistics and/or supply chain management. While that still does occur, most organizations recognize that the complex and special challenge of twenty-first century supply chains require experience and expertise in this area. Consequently active recruiting at universities with supply chain and logistic programs is taking place. In addition, educational programs offered for logistics and supply chain managers are increasing in number and popularity. These are offered by universities and professional organizations. There are other examples, but all are indicative of the growing importance and need for talented and experienced managers.

SUMMARY

- Cash flow has become one of the most important measures of financial viability for business organizations in today's global markets. Supply chains are very important determinant of improved cash flow since they directly impact cost, revenues, and asset requirements.

- Supply chains are an important determinant of working capital consumption since they impact inventory, accounts receivable, and cash.

- Efficient and effective supply chains can free up valuable resources and improve customer fulfillment so as to increase return on investment or assets and improve shareholder value.

- The accelerated rate of change in the global economy has increased the necessity of continual changes in supply chains or even transformation of the organization to remain competitive.

- The rate of change has been driven by a set of external forces including but not limited to globalization, technology, organizational consolidation and shifts in power in supply chains, an empowered consumer, and government policy and regulations.

- The conceptual basis of the supply chain is not new. In fact, organizations have evolved from physical distribution management to logistics management to supply chain management which are all based upon effective systems analysis.

- Supply chains are extended enterprises which require managing four flows—products, information, financials (cash), and demand on a collaborative basis.

- Information systems and technology are an important part of successful supply chains.

- Supply chain performances should be measured in terms of overall corporate goals for success and supply chain strategies must be consistent with organizational strategies.

- Supply chains need to focus on the customers at the end of the supply chain and be flexible and responsive.

- Technology is important to facilitate change, but it should follow process change and employee education to address problems and issues appropriately.

- Transportation management, security and sustainability have become increasingly important in the twenty-first century because of the political and economic changes that have occurred.

- Change with the changes, or you will be changed by the changes!

STUDY QUESTIONS

1. Globalization and technology developments have led to some significant changes in the global economy. Discuss the importance of such changes to the United States. What is the impact upon supply chains?

2. The consolidation that has developed at the retail end of many supply chains has had an important impact. What changes have occurred in supply chain management because of retail consolidation and the related power shift?

3. Consumers have much more influence in the marketplace today. What factors have led to this "empowered consumer" situation? How has this factor changed supply chains in the last 10 years? Will consumer influence continue, and what will be the impact on supply chains?

4. Describe the three phases of the evolution of the supply chain concept.

5. Why should senior executives be concerned about supply chain management in their organizations? How can effective supply chain management improve the financial viability of their companies?

6. Supply chains encompass four flows. Describe the four flows, and why are they important? How are they related to each other?

7. During the 1980s and 1990s, managing the transportation function in supply chains was recognized as being important but not critical. Has this perspective changed, and, if so, how and why? What special challenges does transportation face in the future?

8. Collaboration is a very critical ingredient for successful supply chains. Why? What types of collaboration are important? What are some of the challenges and issues that need to be addressed?

9. Why is information so important in supply chains? What are the challenges to the successful development and implementation of effective information? What is the role of technology and information management?

10. Describe the major challenges and issues facing supply chains in the future.

NOTES

1. James Tompkins, speech presented at the Warehouse of the Future Conference (Atlanta, GA: May 2000).

2. Anonymous, *Logistics* (July/August 2000): 43.

CASE 1.1

Lehigh Valley Transport and Logistics Service (LVTLS)

LVTLS was established in 1960 by Mason Delp as a local cartage company to provide pickup and delivery service for several interstate trucking companies in the Greater Lehigh Valley area of Pennsylvania. Mason saw signs of change in the area between Allentown and Philadelphia with the improvement of the interstate highway system and the improvements in the Pennsylvania Turnpike System providing North-South and East-West corridors along with other roadway additions and improvements. In addition there was a definite population sprawl around Philadelphia. The roadway additions and improvements provided transportation access to many communities. Mason's observations were correct and the area changed from predominantly agriculture to companies producing and manufacturing products and services.

One very significant development was the establishment of a number of facilities for producing pharmaceutical products and an agglomeration of companies and services to support that industry. The growth and success of these companies provided the opportunity for Mason Delp to expand his motor carrier services to provide both less-than-truckload and truckload service throughout the mid-Atlantic states. When the motor carriers were deregulated in 1980, Mason established warehousing services in Lansdale, Pennsylvania as a complement to his trucking services. At that point "Logistics" was added to the name of the company. He promoted his son, Paul, to vice president of the warehousing division because of his experience and education.

In 2000, Mason retired and Paul became the CEO. The company experienced growth in the warehousing business as the economy was expanding in the early years of the twenty-first century and Paul invested heavily in information systems and technology. However, the great recession of 2008 caused challenges and financial pain for LVTLS because of a downturn in business activity. The investments in information systems and technology mitigated the impact of the downturn.

The organization has fully recovered by 2012 but Paul now recognizes the need for cost control and strategic relationships to buffer future economic volatility. He is particularly concerned about the business activity he has with pharmaceutical companies because of the challenges that they are facing. However, Paul recognizes that their challenges may be opportunities for LVTLS to develop collaborative relationships with a number of these companies to help them improve their supply chains management.

CASE QUESTIONS

1. Discuss the challenges faced by the pharmaceutical industry.
2. Which of these challenges provide the best opportunity for LVTLS? Why?

CASE 1.2

Central Transport, Inc.

Jamie Corman, the new president and CEO of Central Transport, recently met with Susan Weber, the current president and CEO of SAB Distribution. Jaime was promoted from CMO at Central Transport to CEO. Her predecessor had worked closely with the former CEO of SAB Distribution when SAB had transformed its operations about 10 years earlier to respond to changes in its competitive marketplace. Now, Ms. Weber was faced with new challenges and again needed the collaboration of Jaime and Central Transport to meet some new challenges.

Susan has met extensively with the members of her executive team to develop a tentative plan for modifying the strategic direction of SAB and thwart the buyout of the company by a private investment firm.

Susan was convinced that SAB could attract additional retailers in the mid-Atlantic states if it added to and improved its logistics services, namely, warehousing, transportation delivery, and inventory management. However, Susan felt that she needed a major collabo-rator with experience in these areas. She also felt that it would be better if the collaborator was a company SAB had worked with previously on a successful basis and was willing to take on some new challenges.

Susan had decided to approach Wegman's Food Markets, Inc. as a customer for these new services. Wegman's was a very successful company in the Northeast that was privately owned and had expanded carefully into new market areas over the last 15 years. It offered more value services to its customers, including an in-store bakery, a restaurant and deli, more take-out options, and in-store cooking demonstrations.

Wegman's primary distribution point for their stores was located in a distribution park in Rochester, New York near their corporate headquarters. With their store expansion into the Washington, D.C. area and points further south into Virginia, they are developing a new distribution park in northwestern Pennsylvania to lower their cost and improve their service. Wegman's was feeling the pressure to be more price competitive with Walmart and other food chains but also wanted to maintain their unique value added in store services for customers.

Susan was also convinced that Wegman's could be price competitive and to continue to increase their in-store services and expand their market opportunities. She felt that they would listen to her proposal to offer expanded services to help their company be more competitive. Now, she wanted Central to join with SAB in making Wegman's a proposal.

Jaime needs your help in developing a response to Susan.

CASE QUESTIONS

1. Why and how has the competitive market place for SAB changed in the last five to seven years?
2. What advantages might Central experience in the proposed new venture?
3. What issues would SAB and Central face in the proposed new approach?

Source: John J. Coyle, DBA, Used with permission.

Chapter 2

GLOBAL DIMENSIONS OF SUPPLY CHAINS

Learning Objectives

After reading this chapter you should be able to do the following:

- Appreciate the complex issues facing managers of global supply chains and the challenges of the more volatile global economy.

- Understand the rationale for global trade flows (imports and exports) and especially the concepts of absolute and comparative advantage in explaining international trade.

- Discuss the role and importance of the factors of production in providing a trade advantage to countries and/or regions for participating in global trade.

- Appreciate how population size and age distribution differ among various countries and the impact that they have on their economic growth and vitality.

- Recognize and understand how the growth in urban areas around the world provides challenges and opportunities for their countries especially, the development of the so-called mega-cities.

- Discuss the challenges and importance of migration for the economies of the world, especially the developed countries.

- Understand the internal and external roles of technology and information systems for economic growth and development.

- Appreciate and discuss the trade flow volumes (imports and exports) among and between countries of the world.

- Recognize and appreciate the importance of the various trading partners of the United States.

- Discuss the importance and nature of the major trade agreements that impact the United States and its trading partners.

Supply Chain Profile   *"The Impact of Changing Weather Patterns"*

As supply chains have become more global in scope, executives became increasingly aware of the inherent risks associated with managing global supply chains. Initially, the focus was usually upon the risks associated with the complexity of managing suppliers, customers and service partners who were separated by distance, culture, customs, language, business practices, etc. Also the threat or risk associated with intense competition from rivals in other countries as they also became more efficient and effective in the global marketplace. Managing risk has become a major focus for supply chain executives in the twenty-first century and the scope of the risks has increased, especially in the area of weather-related risks. The latter concerns are usually associated with catastrophic events which can result in supply chain disruptions, stock-outs of needed materials and finished products and of course the costs associated with emergency responses as well as costs associated with preparing to mitigate the impact of the potential catastrophe.

There are also more subtle risks associated with changing global weather patterns, especially so-called global warming which can transform global shipping patterns and influence geopolitics. The improvements being made to the Suez Canal and especially, the Panama Canal have been discussed widely in various publications. The impact of being able to accommodate the new larger container ships has resulted in much discussion about maritime trade patterns with respect to port deliveries. Ports on the West Coast of the United States have benefited from the great growth in shipments from Asia even though some of the containers move relatively long distances to Midwest and East Coast destinations. When the Panama Canal can accommodate these larger size vessels, it will open up the possibility of more direct shipments to East Coast ports and possibly Europe.

There is, however, another "mystical" northern maritime route that is likely to open up because of the so-called Artic ice melt being caused by global warming. This "Northeast Passage," as opposed to the Northwest Passage across the Canadian Artic, would provide a maritime route from Europe to Asia through Russia's remote Artic region. This maritime route could have a dramatic impact on supply chains by shortening shipping times between Europe and Asia by 35 to 40 percent and also shortening shipping times from Europe to West Coast U.S. ports. This alternate route would likely have a significant negative impact on Suez Canal traffic. The geopolitical ramifications of the Northeast Passage are perhaps even more important than the economic impact. For countries boarding the Artic, there is much at stake in terms of the economic potential of unexploited natural resources, especially gas and oil. These developments are not going to happen in the near future, but a long-term vision for countries and businesses is critical. The debate over who has sovereignty over the North Pole will really heat up!

Source: John J. Coyle and Kusumal Ruamsook, Center for Supply Chain Research, Penn State University.

2-1 Introduction

Global supply chains are dependent on the efficient and effective flow of commerce between and among the countries and regions of the world. There are numerous factors that can impact and influence the flow of global goods and services, especially economic and political factors. Additional important factors range from weather (see the Chapter Profile) to the threat of terrorism to demographics. The number of such factors that can possibly impact global trade flows are too numerous to discuss each one in detail in this chapter or the text. The authors used their judgment to select those important factors that will most likely impact and shape global trade flows in the twenty-first century. In other words, what factors are the "drivers" of global commerce and need to be discussed to gain an appreciation and understanding of global supply chain flows. Before discussing the Global Drivers, the rationale for global and regional trade will be summarized.

2-2 Rationale for Global Trade and Commerce

Anyone familiar with economic and political history realizes that international trade is not a phenomenon of the twenty-first or even the twentieth century. Such activity can actually be traced to the so-called Middle-Ages when trade merchants from various countries traversed by land and sea to barter or trade for selected commodities not available in their own country. The exploits of European explorers and others have long been noted, especially their quest for new territory to annex, but trade was a very important aspect of their travels, viz., the opportunity to find and trade for valuable commodities.

As European countries advanced economically, particularly during the eighteenth century, there was a growing awareness of the potential value of international trade. Adam Smith in his renowned treatise, THE WEALTH OF NATIONS, provided not only a rationale for a market economy based upon competition, but also advanced a rationale for trade among nations called the Theory of Absolute Advantage. Smith argued that countries would be better off if they would trade commodities where each country had an economic or cost advantage for one or more of the products that they produced. In other words, sell or trade products where they had a cost advantage and buy or trade for products where they did not have an advantage. Smith concluded that all participants in such transactions would be better off than trying to be self-sufficient. While the analysis was relatively simplistic, it was valuable advice, especially for that time period.

The underlying logic of absolute advantage was also used by Adam Smith to advance the rationalization what he called "division of labor" or specialization of labor. The latter concept led to mass production or assembly lines in manufacturing plants. The underlying logic was that the specialization led to increased aggregate output and lower unit cost, and provided an opportunity for regional specialization and inter-region commerce for an overall economic benefit.

The theory of comparative advantage was advanced about 40 years later by several economists. They maintained that even if one country had a comparative advantage (lower cost) in the production of two products, they should focus on the production of the one that they had the greatest advantage and trade for the other. The analyses were also somewhat simplistic because not all of the relevant costs were considered. However, the logic was sound as long as total landed costs were considered. The importance of both absolute and comparative advantage is they demonstrate that global trade and related global supply chain flows can be based not only upon scarcity of items among countries but also differences in the cost of production with implicit benefit to all parties involved.

As one would expect, later economists explored more fully the rational of global trade and specialization. For example, the Factor Endowment Theory postulates that when a country has more of one of the four so-called Factors of Production (land, labor, capital and entrepreneurship), they may have a comparative advantage in producing one or more products. For example, a country with an abundance of capital and an educated workforce may produce high tech products and import labor intensive products and agriculture products.

The current more complex global economy means that there are more variables than the traditional factors of production that can provide advantages to countries and be a basis for global trade flows. Some of these factors help to explain the development of the so-called BRIC (Brazil, Russia, India and China) and VISTA (Viet Nam, Indonesia, South Africa, Turkey and Argentina) countries. India and China have developed and prospered in recent years because of improved global transportation, faster communication systems, population growth, education, and technology advancement. The discussion of contributing factors for global development which follows is very important for appreciating and understanding current global supply chain flows, and it also provides insights into future challenges and potential development.

2-3 Contributing Factors for Global Commerce and Supply Chain Flows

Essential factors for economic growth and increased development of global trade flows include population growth and age distribution, urbanization, land and resources, economic integration, knowledge dissemination, labor mobility, financial flows and investment in infrastructure by public and/or private sources, faster communication systems, improved financial services for the effective flow of goods and services. These factors are the driving forces for globalization around the world and need to be discussed in order to understand the future course of global trade and development.

2-3-1 Population Size and Distribution

Table 2.1 displays the total population for the ten largest countries for 2000, 2010, and 2015 as well as the projected population for 2050 which can be used to gain some perspective and understanding of current and future economic growth and development. The top ten countries account for almost 60% of the total world population. Interestingly, two countries account for about 36% of the total, China and India. The United States is a distant third and China and India have over four times as many people as the United States. Another interesting statistic is that India is projected to have a larger population than China by 2050 and that Russia (#9) and Japan (#10) are projected to have fewer people in 2050 than they had in 2015.

The sheer size of the populations in China and India will provide these two countries with a potential economic advantage in terms of labor for growth as long as the economies can support that population size. The decrease in size for Russia and Japan reflects an aging population and has the potential of being an economic disadvantage in terms of labor availability and the social cost to support an aging population. Immigration into these two countries could be an economic benefit especially for Russia, but also Japan, not only for labor availability in general but also to provide services for assisting seniors.

As suggested earlier, not only is the total population of countries important, but also the age distribution deserves consideration. Figure 2.1 provides some insight into this area with median age data for four years. Each of the four years shows the median age for the world for that year (note that the last two years are projections), and then for more developed countries, less developed countries and least developed countries. As one would probably expect, the median age is increasing, with one exception, over the course of the four years for all categories. Developed countries have the highest median age in each year, and the least developed counties have the lowest median age. The differences are generally explained

Table 2.1	Top Ten Countries with the Highest Population			
RANK	COUNTRY	2000 POPULATION	2010 POPULATION	2015 POPULATION	2050 EXPECTED POPULATION
1	China	1,268,853,362	1,330,141,295	1,361,512,535	1,303,723,332
2	India	1,004,124,224	1,173,108,018	1,251,695,584	1,656,553,632
3	United States	282,338,631	310,232,863	321,362,789	439,010,253
4	Indonesia	213,829,469	242,968,342	255,993,674	313,020,847
5	Brazil	176,319,621	201,103,330	204,259,812	260,692,493
6	Pakistan	146,404,914	184,404,791	199,085,847	276,428,758
7	Nigeria	123,178,818	152,217,341	181,562,056	264,262,405
8	Bangladesh	130,406,594	156,118,464	168,957,745	233,587,279
9	Russia	146,709,971	139,390,205	142,423,773	109,187,353
10	Japan	126,729,223	126,804,433	126,919,659	93,673,826
TOP TEN Countries		3,618,894,827	4,016,489,082	4,213,773,474	4,950,140,178
Rest of the World		2,466,012,769	2,829,120,878	3,050,850,319	4,306,202,522
TOTAL World Population		6,084,907,596	6,845,609,960	7,264,623,793	9,256,342,700

Figure 2.1	Median Age of Population

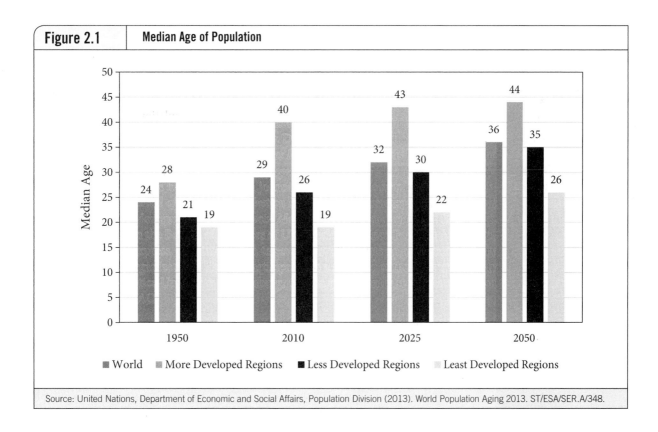

Source: United Nations, Department of Economic and Social Affairs, Population Division (2013). World Population Aging 2013. ST/ESA/SER.A/348.

by the level of education, quality of health care and economic well-being. The difference in median age between the most developed and least developed is interesting to note. It is 21 years in 2010 and 2025 but drops to a projected 18 years by 2050. Overall, however, the challenge is evident that the more developed countries have a lower birth rate and an aging citizenry which has implications for future economic development and prosperity.

The challenge is even greater if you examine the data for individual countries. For example, Japan and three European countries are projected to have populations with median ages over 50 (see Table 2.2). As suggested, the aging populations in these countries will result in increased health care costs and a reduction in the size of the working population or labor pool. This could result in a lowering of labor productivity and increased taxes. In comparison, many of the least developed countries currently have and are projected to have median age populations under 20 years old (see Table 2.3). The consequences of this phenomenon could mean high unemployment, scarcity of some resources, and a need for more housing, infrastructure (water, sewers, roads, etc.), education and other services thus straining their economic viability even more. However, the size of the potential workforce can attract industries that are labor intensive. Migration to countries with aging populations is another possibility if not constrained.

From the perspective of world business and global supply chains, this data has some important implications relative to economic growth, market size and development, capital flows, labor availability consumer needs and utilization of natural and strategic resources. There will be challenges and opportunities for not only the private sector but also for the public sector.

A related issue is urbanization with the increase in migration in many countries from rural areas to cities or urban areas. As one would expect this shift will be most profound in the less and least developed countries of the world. The United Nations projects by 2025 that 50% or more of the total Asian population will be in cities with China having the

Table 2.2	Ten Countries With the Oldest Populations 2015, 2030				
2015			**2030**		
RANK	COUNTRY/AREA	MEDIAN AGE	RANK	COUNTRY/AREA	MEDIAN AGE
1	Japan	46.5	1	Japan	51.5
2	Germany	46.2	2	Italy	50.8
3	Martinique	46.1	3	Portugal	50.2
4	Italy	45.9	4	Spain	50.1
5	Portugal	44.0	5	Greece	48.9
6	Greece	43.6	6	China, Honk Kong SAR	48.6
7	Bulgaria	43.5	7	Germany	48.6
8	Austria	43.2	8	Other non-specified areas	48.1
9	China, Honk Kong SAR	43.2	9	Slovenia	48.1
10	Spain	43.2	10	Republic of Korea	47.5
	WORLD	29.6		WORLD	33.1

Table 2.3	Ten Countries With the Youngest Populations 2015, 2030				
2015			**2030**		
RANK	COUNTRY/AREA	MEDIAN AGE	RANK	COUNTRY/AREA	MEDIAN AGE
1	Niger	14.8	1	Niger	15.2
2	Uganda	15.9	2	Somalia	17.7
3	Chad	16.0	3	Angola	17.7
4	Angola	16.1	4	Chad	17.9
5	Mali	16.2	5	Mali	17.9
6	Somalia	16.5	6	Uganda	18.1
7	Gambia	16.8	7	Gambia	18.3
8	Zambia	16.9	8	Burundi	18.5
9	Dem. Republic of the Congo	16.9	9	Zambia	18.5
10	Burkina Faso	17.0	10	Dem. Republic of the Congo	18.6
	WORLD	29.6		WORLD	33.1

largest urban population. A new category of city has been identified, namely, Megacities (10 million or more inhabitants) which is a manifestation of the migration to urban areas. One of the interesting and important dimensions of the new Megacities is "where" they will develop. The prediction is that Asia will have 18 Megacities, Latin America will have four and North America will have two. Europe will not have any cities of this size. Mumbai and Lagos will challenge Tokyo for being the World's largest city.[1]

The rise of the Megacities will present opportunities and many challenges. The private sector can play an important role in the development of these large urban communities. The sheer size and density of the cities will require much effort and innovation. To address the infrastructure shortages of transportation, fresh water, sewage disposal, health services, educational facilities, etc. Meeting these needs will require public and private funding. Global trade flows and global supply chains will be impacted and businesses must be prepared to take advantage and participate for the welfare of the citizenry.[2]

Migration was mentioned earlier as a means to balance the population distribution especially with respect to age distribution. However, migration can be disruptive and dysfunctional when it occurs with large numbers under conditions of political upheaval as was the case in the middle of this decade with individuals and families fleeing their native lands to go to areas which were viewed as safe havens to escape the threat of terroristic acts including death. Absorbing that crush of humanity strains the existing economic and social systems and causes unstable conditions. However, humanitarian concerns dictate that every effort possible be made to accommodate this mass migration from Syria and other nearby countries. The European Union countries have felt the major impact of migration pattern because of their proximity and economic status.

Before leaving this discussion of population and age distribution, the United States should be given some attention. Table 2.4 addresses the U.S. population (third largest) by age and gender for five years from 2010 to 2014. While the population has increased during

On the Line

Economic Growth and the Birth Rate

In spite of the hue and cry of some political pundits and politicians, the population of the world is not overflowing and the doomsday forecasts of some are completely out of line with reality. There was a time after World War II that the population growth rate was about 2.2% per year, and there were fears of a population explosion with consequent dire outcomes. While the total world population has been increasing on an absolute basis the rate of increase has declined to about 1% per year with a projected rate of about 0.75% by 2025.[3] The challenge is that the population has been rapidly increasing in the countries that can least afford the increases. However, in the more economically advanced countries that have been a dynamic engine for economic advancement, the working age population is shrinking causing an imbalance between workers and retirees, for example, Japan.

The importance of the 20- to 60-year-old segment of the population is critical not only for labor input but also for the economic vitality associated with innovation and change. Thus, the conundrum of immigration is the possible stagnation versus economic growth with immigrants. The United States is probably a classic case study of the value of immigration not only for mitigating an aging population but also for innovation and economic growth. Many U.S. Citizens would be surprised to learn that in the relatively near future, Caucasians will be the third largest segment of our population. The largest will be of Asian descent followed by Latinos. Consider Germany, which has the lowest birthrate in the world at just over 8 births per year per 1000 citizens. To maintain its current distribution of working age citizens versus retirees, it would have to accept 1.5 million immigrants per year for the next 15 years. Maybe the controversy over immigrants will fade as countries come to realize their desperate need for attracting and developing talented workers.[4]

Source: John J. Coyle and Kusumal Ruamsook, Center for Supply Chain Research, Penn State University.

this period, the increase has been modest, an increase of about 9.5 million people over the five year period. Interestingly, there are more females than males which is primarily due to their longer life expectancy. The median age has remained stable during this period unlike some other developed countries because of migration from various countries of the world.

2-3-2 Land and Resources

In addition to labor availability as related to the above population discussion, two other "Factors of Production" land and resources are also important for economic advancement and development.

These are general terms and would include such items as energy, food, and water which are critical for economic viability and future development. Technology can play an important role in mitigating scarcity of key resources, from desalinization of ocean water and fracking for gas and oil production to biotechnology for improving crop yield and agricultural production. Fracking, for example, has already changed the global dynamics of the oil and gas industry with North America becoming a major producer and a potential exporter of gas and oil. With the required changes forthcoming in the transportation infrastructure, these developments will be key factors for future economic growth. Public and private sector collaboration and partnerships could be very instrumental in alleviating global economic disparities that currently exist around the world. Investment in infrastructure will be required but most important will be the elimination of terroristic acts along with economic and political stability!

2-3-3 Technology and Information

Technology has two important dimensions. It can be viewed as an internal change agent that can enhance organizational efficiency and effectiveness and enhance the ability to compete in the global marketplace. Technology, however, can also be viewed as an external driver of change similar to globalization. In fact, one could argue that its external role in recent years has moved technology ahead of globalization as an agent or driver of change. The rapid development of new technology whether it be hardware or software has changed the "rules of engagement" and enabled new sources and forms of competition and especially new "business models." The new companies along with their new technologies have changed the nature of competition which often has meant that established companies have had to change or "perish." There are numerous examples of organizations that have been "blindsided" and have perished. Information technology, particularly, the internet has been the biggest "culprit" because it made relevant information available to the general public efficiently on a real time basis via personal computers, telephones, and other devices.

The availability and sharing of such information has become a major force for driving competition and the development of new business models. For example, Amazon or Zappos without stores can compete effectively with established retailers. In fact, this competition has caused the "bricks and mortar stores" to establish an omni-channel distribution approach which will be discussed in Chapter 4. Technology and transportation services have played a major role in these changes. A very important outcome of these developments has been the opportunities for expanding global participation with efficient and effective supply chains via outsourcing to other countries of the world. It has made it possible for relatively small companies to participate in some of the processes and expand their footprint. India for example, has capitalized on their large and educated workforce, noted previously, to participate in global supply chains via call centers for tech companies, financial services for businesses and accounting firms, research and development, manufacturing components, etc. The internet and information system technology have allowed processes to be separated or split off from a company for outsourcing on a competitive and efficient basis. This is a major change from the large, hierarchal and vertically integrated organizations of the twentieth century, and provided a major opportunity for global participants and partnerships.

2-4 Global Supply Chain Flows

As indicated previously, early in the twenty-first century there was frequent reference made to the acronyms, the BRIC countries and the VISTA countries. The former were identified as the top emerging economies and the latter as developing at a fast pace. The development of global supply chains provided an opportunity for these economies to participate in the global landscape because of material resources, the size of their workforce, their technical skills or some other economic advantage that made them attractive to companies from more developed economies. Their population size also made them attractive as potential markets to businesses in the United States, the European Union (EU), and Japan. They were hailed as a sign of more global economic balance, and one author declared that the "world was becoming flat" on an economic development basis.[5] Their status at the time was largely based on inherent factors of production and related development. At this point there have already been some shifts and the future importance of some of the VISTA countries is not clear. The political upheaval occurring during the second decade of the twenty-first century along with terrorism have disrupted some economic development. Never-the-less, global supply chain flows are significant and an examination of some of the related trade data provides some important insights into the significance of various countries on the world stage.

Figure 2.2 and the related table provides data on the volume of export trade moving from the top 12 countries of the world and the associated world map depicts numerous circles which indicate, by their size, the volume of exports. Looking at the map with its numerous circles indicating exports or out flow of merchandise, it reflects good news and bad news. The good news is the number of countries participating in exporting or global commerce. The bad news is the disparity among the countries in terms of volume of exports. Certainly, some of this is attributable to the size of the country, its stage of economic development, and the value of the merchandise being exported, but the concentration of economic power is obvious.

The table indicates that the European Union as a whole with its 28 countries is the leader in terms of exports. This listing may seem unfair to some readers. But, the total geographic size of the EU is smaller than of Russia and China, for example, and it is considered an economic entity. Also, it is interesting to note, that in spite of their relatively small geographic size, four European countries are among the top nine countries on the list. Overall, the EU is an important component of the global economy and a major economic force.

As one might expect, China is the leading individual, exporting country followed the United States which exports about 30% less than China. The U.S. is followed closely by Germany, and Japan is a somewhat distant fourth on the list. It is also, interesting to note that the Republic of Korea and Hong Kong and both compare favorably with Italy and France in terms of their exports. If the table were expanded to include the top 12, the United Kingdom and the Russian Federation would make the list at eleventh and twelfth respectively.

Figure 2.2	Table Export-Trade Flows of Merchandise 2014

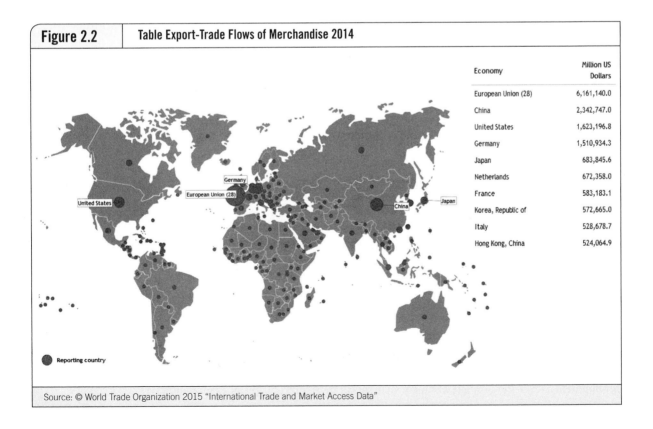

Economy	Million US Dollars
European Union (28)	6,161,140.0
China	2,342,747.0
United States	1,623,196.8
Germany	1,510,934.3
Japan	683,845.6
Netherlands	672,358.0
France	583,183.1
Korea, Republic of	572,665.0
Italy	528,678.7
Hong Kong, China	524,064.9

Source: © World Trade Organization 2015 "International Trade and Market Access Data"

Figure 2.3 and the related table provide data on the volume of imports moving into various countries. Again, the EU is at the top of the list, but the United States and China have changed positions with the United States being number two. The two tables indicate China's position as a net exporter and the United States as a net importer. Keep in mind, however, that these tables are showing merchandise flows, and are not the equivalent of the balance of payments which also reflects financial flows. The trade data in terms of value is the most relevant to the instant discussion for global supply chains but one could argue that the actual physical volume of the flows could also be important from a supply chain perspective. An overall comparison of imports and exports is interesting. Note the data for China and Germany in terms of exports versus imports.

Another set of data that is of interest for this discussion is the trading partners of the United States with respect to exports and imports. Table 2.4 shows the total exports of the United States and their top 25 export partners for 2014. Canada, Mexico and China are the top three recipients of exports from the United States, in that order. Japan is a distant fourth with about half of what is exported to China, and China only receives about half of what is exported to Mexico. Canada is by far the most important trading partner of the United States, in terms of exports. Note that six European countries are in the top 25 and an array of Asian and South American countries, for the most part, complete the list. As indicated earlier, United States is a major global exporting country with some concentration of trade with its two closest "neighbors," but also with a broad reach throughout the world.

The U.S. imports presented in Table 2.5 indicate a counterbalancing global flow as one might expect. However, in this case China is the top partner followed by Canada and Mexico. Most of the same countries listed in Table 2.4 appear on Table 2.5, but there are some differences. For example, Belgium is number 11 in terms of export partners but is 22 on the

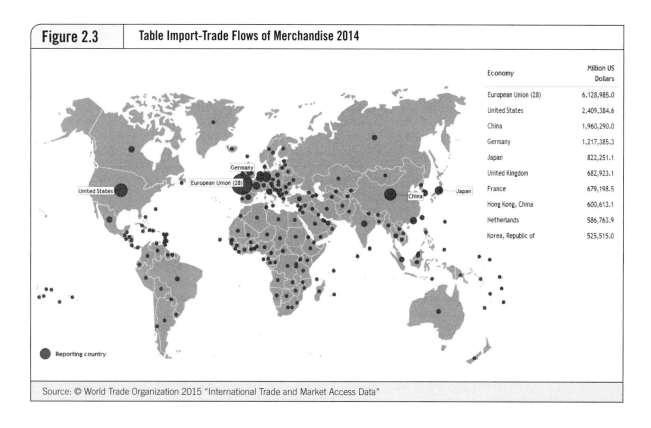

Figure 2.3	Table Import-Trade Flows of Merchandise 2014

Economy	Million US Dollars
European Union (28)	6,128,985.0
United States	2,409,384.6
China	1,960,290.0
Germany	1,217,385.3
Japan	822,251.1
United Kingdom	682,923.1
France	679,198.5
Hong Kong, China	600,613.1
Netherlands	586,763.9
Korea, Republic of	525,515.0

Reporting country

Source: © World Trade Organization 2015 "International Trade and Market Access Data"

Table 2.4	U.S. Population by Age and Gender, 2010–2014				
	POPULATION ESTIMATES (AS OF JULY 1)				
	2010	2011	2012	2013	2014
Total Population	309,347,057	311,721,632	314,112,078	316,497,531	318,857,056
By Gender					
Male	152,089,484	153,294,635	154,528,573	155,741,368	156,936,487
Female	157,257,573	158,426,997	159,583,505	160,756,163	161,920,569
By Age Groups					
<18 years	74,123,041	73,917,259	73,711,826	73,610,207	73,583,618
18–24 years	30,766,571	31,094,473	31,397,205	31,534,166	31,464,158
25–44 years	82,201,194	82,491,713	82,905,066	83,441,231	84,029,637
45–64 years	81,776,898	82,851,559	82,933,072	83,188,886	83,536,432
65 and over	40,479,353	41,366,628	43,164,909	44,723,041	46,243,211
Median Age (years)	37.2	37.3	37.5	37.6	37.7

https://www.census.gov/popest/data/national/asrh/2014/index.html

import list. Saudi Arabia is number 8 with respect to imports but number 20 on the export list (the reason should be obvious). Surprisingly, the Russian Federation is number 20 on the import list but is not included in the top 25 for U.S. exports. Likewise, Israel is number 21 for imports into the United States but does not appear on the top 25 list of export partners. Overall, both tables reflect the importance of the United States as a global economy.

Global supply chain flows reflect the world economy and the trade patterns between and among the countries of the world. As stated previously in this chapter, there is an underlying economic rationale for global trade which can bring benefits to the various trading partners. That said, the "economic pie" is not evenly divided. The economic strength of the various countries is based upon their inherent "factors of production" and some related economic, social, and political factors. Overall global economic progress is dependent upon a united effort from the more developed economies to aid in the development of the lesser developed countries.

Global interdependence can be good news or bad news on a macro basis. On the positive side, it can result in lower prices, wider availability of goods and services, land and resource development, and new employment opportunities for countries and regions of the world, both developed and developing regions. On the negative side, the interdependence can lead to global economic downturns or recessions, as was the case in 2008–2009, requiring government intervention to mitigate the problems. The recovery process was slow in some countries causing some economic turbulence.

Our focus in this text is on the micro level and how individual firms respond to the increased complexity and competiveness of a global economy. These changes have resulted in shorter product life cycles, new forms of competition, and new business models. Out sourcing, off-shoring, and insourcing have become part of the lexicon of twenty-first century businesses. Information technology has allowed supply chains to be redesigned

Table 2.5	Top U.S. Trading Partners ($ Billions)		
COUNTRY	2008	2010	2014
Canada	$601	$525	$660
China	$408	$457	$589
Mexico	$367	$393	$534
Japan	$204	$181	$201
United Kingdom	$112	$98	$107
Germany	$152	$131	$172
Korea	$83	$88	$114
Netherlands	$61	$54	$64
Brazil	$63	$59	$72
Hong Kong	$28	$31	$46
Total	$2,079	$2,017	$2,559

Sources: US Department of Commerce, Census Bureau, 2014 - US Census Bureau, Foreign Trade.

for more efficiency and effectiveness as well as better execution. Supply chain management has become an important and for some organizations, even critical ingredient for their competitive strategy and success in this global environment. These companies have transformed themselves by changing their supply chains to take advantage of global opportunities.

Chapter 1 argued that the rate of change has accelerated and is being fueled by a number of major external forces or change drivers. The synergism between globalization and technology, especially, has permanently changed the dynamics of the world's marketplace. The outcry in some quarters about outsourcing is 40 years too late and may be misguided. This new era has and will continue to spotlight supply chains as a critical part of the ability of organizations to compete economically, and it deserves special discussion.

2-5 Supply Chains in a Global Economy

In Chapter 1, a supply chain was depicted as being boundary spanning; that is, encompassing a group of interrelated firms focused on delivering the best price or value products and services to the ultimate customer at the end of the supply chain. It was also noted a supply chain also should manage four important flows, namely, materials/products, information, financials, and demand.

An important characteristic of today's world economy is the increasing regional economic integration. The globalized economy, the establishment of the General Agreement on Tariffs and Trade (GATT) and its 1995 successor, the World Trade Organization (WTO) have together led to multilateral trade promotion and lowered barriers to international business transactions. Nevertheless, a growing number of countries have grouped together to form Regional Trade Agreements (RTAs). The biggest and best known example of an RTA is the EU, with number of memberships growing from six members in the 1950s to 28 members by 2015. The number of RTAs grew significantly during the 1990s. As of July 2005, 330 RTAs had been ratified by the GATT or the WTO, over 200 of which were ratified after the establishment of WTO in 1995. Today, 180 are still in force. Members of an RTA are usually subjected to membership requirements and rules, while receiving special trade preferences among members of the RTA that are not available to nonmembers. The specific details of these preferences vary across RTA's.[6] Comparative advantages of different regions and member countries change as a result of regional position shift with new RTAs being proposed, new members joining the existing RTAs, and new activities of integration (such as customs unions, currency unions, and visa-free transit) being enforced or proposed among member states. The best supply chains compete very successfully on a national, regional, and global basis.

On the Line   *More Deliveries, Same Cost*

Kimberly-Clark, a 140-year-old company headquartered in Irving, Texas, USA, makes an assortment of personal care products, including such well-known items as Kleenex facial tissues, Huggies diapers, and Scott's paper towels. In 2010 it reported worldwide revenue of US $19.7 billion from sales in more than 150 countries.

In Europe, Kimberly-Clark sold its products in 45 countries and operated 15 factories. Finished goods were stored in 32 distribution centers, all of which were operated by third-party logistics (3PL) companies.

In 2003, some retailers in the Netherlands were trying to restock store inventory based on point-of-sale data, which would allow them to make replenishment decisions based on actual customer transactions. As part of the initiative, retailers wanted to increase the frequency of deliveries and resupply stores by replenishing only what had been sold. "They really wanted delivery more frequently to align to point-of-sale data, on a real time basis."

The question facing Kimberly-Clark was this: How could they shorten the replenishment cycle and deliver smaller quantities without incurring additional transportation costs?

The solution was to collaborate with another company also making shipments to those same retail stores. If Kimberly-Clark and its partner split a truckload, with each filling half a trailer, both companies could increase delivery frequency without increasing transportation costs.

Kimberly-Clark contracted with a cosmetics manufacturer, Lever Faberge, about the proposal. The two companies conducted a successful trial with Makro, which operates a chain of warehouse club stores in the Netherlands. The experiment produced other benefits besides transportation savings: it also demonstrated by shortening cycle time for deliveries, collaborative distribution could reduce store inventories while increasing on-shelf availability of products. When they did the trial with Makro, there was a 30 percent reduction in the value of the products they were storing. They also got an out-of-stock reduction of 30 percent.

Collaboration is more prevalent in Europe, especially for CPGs (consumer packaged goods companies). The concept of shared supply chains has proved attractive and a nonprofit organization has been formed to foster such collaboration among other CPG companies, retailers, and third-party logistics companies.

For Kimberly-Clark, its positive experience with collaborative distribution in the Netherlands prompted the consumer goods giant to extend that program to additional countries and business partners.

Source: "Sharing Supply Chains for Mutual Gain", James A. Cooke, CSCMP's Supply Chain Quarterly, Quarter 2/2011, p. 39.

Kimberly-Clark and others have transformed themselves by changing their supply chains and their business models, which, in turn, has significantly changed the business landscape in the twenty-first century. Consider, for example, some U.S. companies derive over 25 percent of their profit from global sales, which helps to mitigate declines or instability in domestic markets. We argued in 1976, in the first edition of this text, that an important role of logistics was to help extend the market area of countries or companies through improved efficiency to lower the landed cost in new market areas.

It is even more apropos for supply chains. It can be argued supply chains help to establish the limits of what is competitively possible in the market. In other words, the cost and value at the end of the supply chain help determine a firm's ability to compete in a global marketplace. Good supply chains are business power and good supply chain managers are continually pushing the limits of their supply chains to be viable in both domestic and global markets.

Operating globally has become easier to accomplish for even individuals and small companies, because of the advances in information/communications technology, as noted above, and the continuing improvement of specialists such as UPS, FedEx, DHL, etc., which can provide global supply chain services at a very reasonable cost. A growing number of specialists and continuing improvements in information technology/communications are contributing to the flattening of the world. Obviously, large global companies are also contributing to this phenomenon.

It is safe to conclude supply chains and supply chain management play an important role in the global economy and have helped to push the growth and success of companies that do "supply chaining" very well. Global supply chains impact all with lower prices, increased array of products, and convenience (read 24/7, one-stop shopping, etc.), but some are critical of the outcomes when individuals lose their jobs; businesses are closed, and so forth. Many would argue the advantages outweigh the disadvantages, for instance, lower prices have saved consumers billions of dollars in purchase prices. There are tradeoffs (advantages and disadvantages), but there is no turning back. Successful organizations will continue to need effective and efficient supply chain management as they move ahead aggressively in the twenty-first century.

2-6 Global Markets and Strategy

The global business environment has changed significantly and companies are not just importing and exporting products but are also locating plants and other facilities in other parts of the world. Honda and Toyota used to produce cars in Japan and ship them to the United States. Now their cars are also produced in the United States for sale in North America. Toyota, for example, has been producing automobiles for 25 years in the state of Indiana. U.S. companies have also located plants in other countries, for example, Mexico and Canada as well as some South American countries.

Tariffs and other trade barriers have been significantly reduced among many countries, allowing a much more competitive global economy. Some companies have not responded well and have lost market share or gone out of business. Other companies have taken advantage of the opportunity and expanded aggressively into global markets, for example, General Electric, IBM, Wal-Mart, McDonald's, P&G, Kimberly-Clark, etc. Many *Fortune* 500 companies experience 50 percent or more of their sales in global markets. Small and medium-sized companies have also been able to be players in global markets, with the opportunity to source and sell on a global basis by developing appropriate relationships.

Success in the global marketplace requires development of a cohesive set of strategies including product development, technology, marketing, manufacturing, and supply chains. Global companies tend to be more successful when their strategies help them to simultaneously achieve their business objectives at their various global locations. From a supply chain perspective, this means strategically sourcing materials and components worldwide, selecting global locations for key supply depots and distribution centers, evaluating transportation alternatives and channel intermediaries, providing customer service, understanding governmental influences on global supply chain flows, examining opportunities for collaboration with third-or fourth-party logistics companies, and other supply chain issues.

From a customer service perspective, global markets and strategy have four important characteristics. First, companies attempt to standardize to reduce complexity, but they have to recognize that global markets need some customization. For example, in contrast to the U.S. market where large retail stores buy in volume quantities for delivery to their large warehouses, less developed countries may have tiny retail stores that are only 80 to 100 square feet. This means deliveries of small quantities, more frequent deliveries, different packaging, etc. Customer service levels have to be adjusted for these markets in terms of delivery schedules, volumes, order fulfillment, and other areas.

Second, global competition often reduces the product life cycle, as previously mentioned, since products can be copied or reengineered quickly by competitors. Technology companies are faced with this phenomenon even in the U.S. market, but globally other products are faced with similar experiences. Technology companies counteract with continual upgrades and new products. Apple, for example, had great success with its iPod, but it quickly followed this with the iPhone, and now the iPad, to maintain financial momentum. Shorter product life cycles present challenges for inventory management with respect to obsolete items. Customer service levels are also impacted because changes have to be made as the product matures in terms of sales volume and then declines, which reduces product profitability. Usually, companies cannot afford to provide the same level of customer service when the product volume declines.

Third, traditional organizational structures and related business models frequently change since companies get more involved in outsourced manufacturing and some logistical activities such as transportation, warehousing, and order fulfillment. All of this impacts the supply chain and its related customer service activities. The collaboration indicated requires effective coordination among the various parties to ensure that customer service levels (on-time delivery, complete orders, reliability, etc.) are maintained.

There are many challenges for supply chain managers. The soft side of global supply chain management presents significant challenges. The social and cultural elements come into play when dealing with foreign business partners and require daily effort to ensure smooth supply chain execution. This is because "soft" issues and physical problems are, in many cases, not mutually exclusive. Misunderstanding the culture and miscommunicating can cause havoc on the physical side of global supply chain planning and execution. Cross-cultural communication is made complicated by not only different languages and time zones, but also other culturally-rooted practices such as communication styles, different approaches to completing tasks, different attitudes toward conflict, and different decision-making styles, among other factors.

Fourth, globalization introduces more volatility and complexity, as noted in Chapter 1. It is much more likely that global supply chains will experience challenges with weather, terrorism, strikes, and other disruptions. The need for flexibility and responsiveness is a requisite for customer service throughout the supply chain. The expanded networks cover long distances and many are complex. Trade policy, regulations, tariffs and currency exchange rates exacerbate the level of complexity for global supply chains. Furthermore, the number of intermediaries that can be involved adds another additional layer of complexity.

In addition to the four areas indicated earlier, some of the customary strategies used in the domestic market are also challenged. Reduced order cycle time, for example, has become an important part of supply chain management since it can lead to lower inventory levels for customers, improved cash flow, lower current assets and accounts receivable. The increased length and complexity of the supply chain make it more difficult to achieve shorter lead times.

Also, demand-driven supply or pull systems can lower inventory levels significantly, but they are challenged by the longer distance and complexity of multi-layered supply chains. Other strategies such as compression and lean supply chains are also more difficult to achieve in the global environment. None of this discussion is meant to imply that companies should not be involved in globalization. Rather it is meant to provide understanding of the challenges necessary to improve the likelihood of success. Without a doubt, globalization has helped many U.S. companies as previously noted. Much higher sales and profits and more revenue stability are some of the advantages that have been pointed out thus far, but globalization is a two-edged sword that requires a company to be nimble and continually proactive in managing and responding to change. The topic of the next section, global supply chain security, ties in directly with this discussion of global supply chain strategy.

2-7 Supply Chain Security: A Balancing Act

Before the events of September 11, 2001, ships would frequently clear U.S. ports in a matter of hours. The scenario has changed because of security measures that were put in place. More cargo inspections, much more paperwork, and a longer time to clear U.S. borders are now a reality. Ships may be stopped and inspected and cargo inspected and checked. Some ships and items are given very close scrutiny because of their country of origin.

Given the importance of global trade to the United States, a delicate balance exists between security and the efficient flow of global commerce. If security is too tight it could impede the flow of needed goods or materials, causing delays and decreased efficiency. Ports and border gateways can become congested because of security measures. Consequently, clearance time has increased from hours to days in some instances. Steps have been taken to improve the flow through border crossing. This is necessary for our global economy.

Electronic filing of cargo information has helped to improve the border clearance times. The Trade Act of 2002 requires exporters to electronically submit shipping documents to U.S. Customs 24 hours after delivery to a port or 24 hours before vessel departure. For imports, the manifest must be filed by the ocean carrier or the consolidator 24 hours before the U.S.-bound cargo is loaded on the vessel in the foreign port. Because of Canada's importance as a trading partner, an expedited procedure (FAST) has been developed to speed up clearance through the U.S.-Canadian border.

The U.S. Coast Guard was authorized by the U.S. Maritime Transportation Security Act of 2002 to assess the vulnerability of U.S. ports and to deny entry to ships from countries that do not meet U.S. security standards. This act requires the development of standards for container seals and locks, cargo tracking, identification, and screening systems for ocean containers.

In addition, the Customs Trade Partnership Against Terrorism (C-TPAT) was established under the direction of the U.S. Department of Homeland Security in November 2001. This voluntary initiative to secure the global supply chain was started with seven companies; by 2007, some 7,400 corporations were involved in this cooperative effort to secure the global supply chain and to facilitate legitimate cargo and conveyance. C-TPAT functions under the U.S. Customs and Border Protection (CBP) Agency, which previously was known as the U.S. Customs Service.[7]

CBP has responsibility for the traditional role of the U.S. Customs Service, namely, preventing illegal entry of people and drugs, protecting agriculture from harmful pests and diseases, protecting the intellectual property of businesses, collecting import duties, and regulating and facilitating global trade. Partner companies in C-TPAT agree to be responsible for keeping their supply chains secure to agreed standards and to implement needed changes. One of the key features of this program is information sharing of best practices for security among members. The goal is to develop a "green lane" to speed goods across the border but also to protect the United States and the global supply chains of the participants.

2-8 Ports

Ports are a critical part of global supply chains and also a major focus for global security. Every day, thousands of containers from countries all around the world arrive at U.S. seaports. Each shipment is usually for a specific supply chain—for example, porch furniture from Thailand bound for a St. Louis retailer or shoes from China destined for a Chicago distributor.

Over $2 trillion in trade value per year passes through U.S. ports, and over $20 billion is collected in industry fees and taxes. The 50 states utilize about 15 ports to handle their imports and exports; over $6 billion worth of goods moves in and out every day. About 99 percent of the international cargo of the United States moves through its ports, or about 3 billion tons annually. In 1960, international trade accounted for about 9 percent of U.S. gross domestic product (GDP). Today, it is over 30 percent.[8]

U.S. ports also play a vital role for the cruise industry. In 2015, about 80 million passenger nights were booked on North American cruises. The top five departure ports account for about 60 percent of the North American cruise passenger departures. The top three are Florida ports: Miami, Fort Lauderdale and Port Canaveral. This flow of passenger traffic has a very positive economic impact on the U.S. economy because of the expenditures to support the cruise industry.[9]

The ports also play a vital role in national defense and security. The ports are bases of operation to deploy troops and equipment. Port security is very important for military and civilian purposes, and it is a shared responsibility between the public and private sectors. C-TPAT is an excellent example of this shared responsibility.

As indicated previously in this chapter, Canada and Mexico are very important trade partners for the United States; they ranked number 1 and 2, respectively, in 2014 for exports and 2 and 3 for imports. Given their importance, the next section of this chapter will discuss the **North American Free Trade Agreement (NAFTA)**.

2-9 North American Free Trade Agreement

The North American Free Trade Agreement was signed by leaders of Canada, the United States, and Mexico in 1993 and was ratified by Congress in early 1994. NAFTA establishes free trade between these three countries and provides the way the agreement is to be interpreted. NAFTA states that the objectives of these three countries is based on the principles of an unimpeded flow of goods, most favored nation (MFN) status, and a commitment to enhance the cross-border movement of goods and services. MFN status provides the lowest duties or customs fees, if any, and simplifies the paperwork required to move goods between the partner countries.

In the long run, the goal of NAFTA is to create a better trading environment. NAFTA's goals involve making structural changes to operate a borderless logistics network in North America. Information systems, procedures, language, labels, and documentation are being redesigned to expedite the border crossings and the flow of commerce. There are continuing challenges to achieving the established goals among all three countries. Migration from Mexico into the United States continues to be a political "hot button" because of the relative ease of entry into the United States.

As new markets and supply sources develop, new transportation and storage facilities as well as intermediaries need to be developed. Storage facilities are particularly important to facilitate efficient and effective global trade flows. An overview of these topics is included in Chapter 10.

SUMMARY

- Global companies usually are faced with more complex and longer supply chains which challenge them in terms of efficiency, effectiveness, and execution.

- Successful global companies have transformed their supply chains on a continuing basis as economic and political circumstances have changed to enable them to deliver best cost and best value to the ultimate customer.

- The scope and magnitude of trade flows between the United States and other countries have grown considerably in the last several decades. One very important development has been the growth in the volume of trade with China and several other Asian countries.

- Global trade is based upon economic factors of production including land, labor, capital, and entrepreneurship. Population and the age distribution of a country total population are important factors for labor availability.

- Migration and urbanization are important issues for economic development and vitality of the economy.

- Success in the global marketplace requires ongoing development of a cohesive set of strategies including customer service, product development, business model, and supply chains management. Supply chains have become increasingly more important during the twenty-first century.

- Supply chain security has taken on increased significance since September 11, 2001. Companies individually, jointly, and in cooperation with the various levels of government are actively involved. The federal government, in particular, has expanded the scope of its regulations and policies for global security.

- U.S. ports play a critical role in global supply chains since over 90 percent of global trade United States. passes through them. Ports are also an important focus for security. The United States needs to focus more attention upon port infrastructure.

- Canada and Mexico are ranked number 1 and 3, respectively, on the list of most important trading partners with the United States. That relationship is enhanced by the North American Free Trade Agreement ratified by Congress in 1994. While the treaty had lofty goals, it still is experiencing problems with full implementation of its objectives. Nevertheless, it has helped to foster trade in North America.

STUDY QUESTIONS

1. Explain the underlying rationale for global trade and explain the difference between comparative and absolute advantage.

2. What are the essential factors for economic growth and increased development of global trade flows? Why are they so important in today's global economy?

3. A number of authors have observed that traditional, hierarchical organizations have changed in the current global economy. How have organizations changed? Why have they changed? What are the impacts of those changes likely to be?

4. What private sector company epitomizes the concept of a global company with a well managed global supply chain? Provide a rationale for your response.

5. What special role do supply chains play in the globalization of organizations? What contributions do successful supply chains make to companies?

6. What is meant by the current description of the global economy that "time and distance have been compressed"? Do you agree? What has been the impact of this compression?

7. Why are customer service and its related strategy so important for companies operating global supply chains? Do you think that customer service is more important than lower cost to the customers?

8. What is meant by the phrase "that supply chain security, especially on a global basis," is a balancing act? Is the pendulum swinging in one direction or the other?

9. Why are regional trade agreements among countries so important in the global economy? What is your evaluation of NAFTA and its impact on the participating countries?

10. What is the role of ports for global commerce and why is that role important? Is our current port infrastructure sufficient? Why or why not?

NOTES

1. Fariborz Ghadar and Erik Peterson, GLOBAL TECTONICS; Penn State Center for Global Business Studies, pp. 14–16.

2. Ibid., pp. 17–19.

3. Ibid. p. 11.

4. Ruchir Sharma, "How the Birth Rate Saps Economic Growth, THE WALL STREET JOURNAL, September 24, 2015.

5. Thomas L, Friedman, THE WORLD IS FLAT (New York: Farrar, Strauss and Giroux, 2005) pp. 6–11.

6. Bruce A. Forster, "A Brief Overview of Selected World Economy Trends: Past and Present" JOURNAL OF APPLIED BUSINESS AND ECONOMICS (12:2 May 2011) 18–26.

7. "Securing the Global Supply Chain," U.S. Customs and Border Protection (Washington, DC: Office of Field Operations, November 2004): 1–25.

8. "America's Ports Today," American Association of Port Authorities (Alexandria, VA: 2014): 1–8.

9. "North American Cruise Statistical Snapshot 2011," Maritime Administration, U.S. Department of Transportation (Office of Policy and Plans, March 2012).

CASE 2.1

Red Fish, Blue Fish, LLP

Two years have elapsed since Fran Fisher, CEO of Red Fish–Blue Fish met with Eric Lynch and Jeff Fisher, Senior Vice President of Supply Chain Management and Vice President of Operations respectively, to discuss increasing their scope and scale of operations. There has been good news and bad news during this period. The good news is that sales have increased domestically as the company expanded into Maryland, New Jersey, Virginia, and Washington, D.C. In fact, the construction and consulting business improved dramatically. Jim Beierlein accepted the position of Vice President, Construction Sales and his experience and contacts had been a real benefit to Red Fish–Blue Fish. However, global sales were disappointing, according to Fran Fisher. European and Canadian Sales were good, but the Asian Market sales were not very good. They developed some new web pages for China, India and Japan. While they had many "hits" on the web page, the sales were not satisfactory. The company relied upon internet sales in the Asian Markets.

Some Additional Background

Red Fish–Blue fish was established in 2007 by Fran Fisher after he decided to make a career change. He was at that time a successful broadcaster specializing in broadcasting athletic events but was also visible in other venues. He had developed an interest in fishes over the years and maintained large fish tanks which were part of the décor in his office. One of his friends Andy Zimmerman, was a dentist who specialized in dental care for children and adolescents. Andy approached Fran when he was remodeling his offices to help use fish tanks for new décor but also he thought that it would help relax and interest his young patients and make their experience less stressful. Fran got interested in the project and spent a considerable amount of time and effort in the design aspects and in the selection of the fish. Andy was so impressed along the way that he insisted on paying Fran a substantial consulting fee and offered to provide financial backing for a new venture which subsequently was named Red Fish–Blue Fish. And as they say, the rest is history. The business took off like it was "shot from a gun" and Fran was able to bring in several additional individuals to help with supply chain issues, construction and overall operations. Now they were at a crossroads with respect to expansion.

Current Challenges and Issues

The company had established a footprint in China through purchasing most of their fish from supplies in china and a Chinese Export Company. Fran hired several students from Penn State's Supply Chain Program to do some studies for him as part of their internship; their analysis agreed with Fran's conclusions, that is, global markets offered the most potential. They based their conclusions on two important developments that they found with their research—the Trans-Pacific Trade—agreement that was in the works between the United States and about a dozen Asian countries and the demographics of the Asian countries!!!

CASE QUESTIONS

1. Explain the advantages of a trade agreement and how it might impact a company like Red Fish–Blue Fish.
2. What makes the demographics of the Asian countries attractive for future trade development?
3. What challenges would Red Fish–Blue Fish likely experience ?
4. What are the options for Red Fish–Blue Fish as far as global intermediaries are concerned? What do you recommend? Why?
5. What other options does Red Fish–Blue Fish have to expand their Asian sales?

Chapter 3

ROLE OF LOGISTICS IN SUPPLY CHAINS

Learning Objectives

After reading this chapter, you should be able to do the following:

- Understand the contributions of logistics in improving organizational supply chains.
- Appreciate how efficient and effective logistics management contributes to the vitality of the economy and improves global competitiveness.
- Discuss the value-added roles of logistics on both a macro and micro level.
- Explain the relationship between logistics and other important functional areas in an organization, including manufacturing, marketing, and finance and their unique contributions to efficiency and effectiveness.
- Discuss the importance of management activities in the logistics function.
- Analyze logistics systems from several different perspectives to meet different objectives.
- Determine the total costs and understand the cost tradeoffs in a logistics system.

Supply Chain Profile   *Small Ports Boxed Out by Big Ships*

Jim O'Halloran had just finished reading the Seattle-Tacoma Herald and exclaimed loudly to those within earshot of his Portland, Washington office, "we are going to be driven out of business by these large "container ships." Jim was the CLO of the Tacoma/Portland Grain and Seed Company which had facilities and offices in both the Seattle-Tacoma metropolitan area and Portland, Oregon. Both locations had port access, but Portland's accessibility was more challenging because of its inland location along the Columbia River. Traditionally, Portland's location was beneficial because the Columbia River provided them access to various agricultural producers and shippers in Idaho. Barge service along the Columbia River from Utah locations to Portland allowed these producers to ship a variety of agriculture products for export including potatoes, lentils, peas, and wheat. In Portland, these farm products would be trans-loaded on to ocean going vessels for export to Asia and Europe. Incoming vessels would bring freight such as steel, autos, and fertilizer. The combination of the imports and exports placed Portland among the top 25 U.S. ports (21st). A position that was economically beneficial to Portland and the states of Washington and Idaho as well as some contiguous locations.

In 2014, Portland handled over 130,000 containers (20'TEU's), but in 2015 there was hardly any container traffic. The new, larger container ships found the 100 mile winding journey along the Columbia River from the Pacific Ocean to Portland to be slow and challenging as well as expensive. Consequently, the shipping companies decided to eliminate service to Portland leaving everyone "high and dry." Portland and its customers were cut off from some parts of the global marketplace for imports and exports unless they were willing to pay much more to truck shipments to Tacoma which was 150 miles away. Portland was not unique in this regard. Other ports along the East Coast and even Seattle and Tacoma are facing similar challenges with the big ships which can carry 8-10,000 TEU's. With the improvements in the Panama and Suez canals to enable them to accommodate these larger ships, it is anticipated that there will an increase in the number of larger vessels for global shipping, particularly from Asia and especially China. Such ships can significantly lower shipping costs if the ports and contiguous waterways can accommodate them. Some ports are spending millions of dollars to dredge and widen the access waterways to the port areas in order to accommodate the larger container ships. They recognize to participate in the broader global market place efficient water transportation is a necessary but not sufficient condition. The port infrastructure is must also be adequate and functional to accommodate the "Super" size container ships.

Jim O' is really frustrated because he sees the opportunities that are possible for export in the larger global markets. His company can still do some exporting with smaller vessels which can navigate the Columbia River, but they will be precluded from the larger more profitable markets unless they can resolve this issue of their port infrastructure. Their situation demonstrates the criticality of efficient and effective logistics service to a supply chain, and also that the transportation infrastructure is a critical ingredient for success. As you read this chapter, consider the possible alternative strategies for the Portland/Tacoma Grain and Seed Company.

3-1 Introduction

Logistics professionals and other knowledgeable managers realize, that in spite of all the hype about the Internet, omni-channels, etc., successful organizations must manage order fulfillment effectively and efficiently for competitive advantage and profitability. The much-noted e-tailing problems of the 1999 Christmas season provide ample proof of the need for good, basic logistics systems and processes. Sophisticated front-end systems cannot stand alone in the competitive global marketplace of today—"back office" execution is critical for customer satisfaction. In fact, the speed of ordering via the Internet and other technologies exacerbates the need for an efficient and effective logistics system that can deploy appropriate levels of inventory, expedite completed orders to customers, and manage any returns. The often-quoted adage "Good logistics is business power" is appropriate because logistics helps to build customer loyalty. If an organization cannot get its products to customers in a timely manner, it will not stay in business very long. This is not to say that quality products and effective marketing are not important, but they must be combined with effective and efficient logistics systems for long-run success and financial viability.

The challenge is to manage the entire logistics system in such a way that order fulfillment meets and perhaps, exceeds customer expectations. At the same time, the competitive marketplace demands efficiency—controlling transportation, inventory, and other logistics-related costs. As will be discussed, cost and service tradeoffs must be considered when evaluating customer service levels and the associated total cost of logistics, but both goals— efficiency and effectiveness—are important to an organization in today's competitive environment.

At this point, it is important to delineate more explicitly the relationship between logistics management and supply chain management. In Chapter 1, supply chain management was defined using a pipeline analogy, with the start of the pipeline representing the initial supplier and the end of the pipeline representing the ultimate customer (see Figure 3.1). In other words, it is an extended set of enterprises from the supplier's supplier to the customer's customer.

Another perspective on supply chain management is to view it as a connecting network of the logistics systems and related activities of all the individual organizations that are a part of a particular supply chain. The collective logistics systems play a role in the success of the overall supply chain. The coordination or integration of the logistics systems in a supply chain can be a challenge.

The focus in this chapter is on the dimensions and roles of logistics systems, but must recognize that no logistics system operates in a vacuum. For example, the outbound part of a manufacturer's logistics system interfaces with the inbound side of its customer's logistics system. Supply chain management encompasses logistics as well as other activities discussed in Chapter 1. Having introduced the concept of logistics and its relationship to the supply chain, the next section will discuss definitions of logistics and the value-adding roles of logistics.

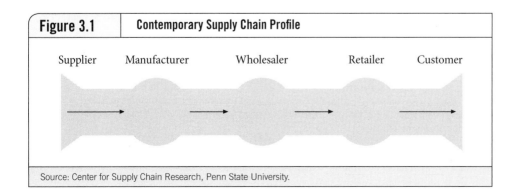

| **Figure 3.1** | **Contemporary Supply Chain Profile** |

| Supplier | Manufacturer | Wholesaler | Retailer | Customer |

Source: Center for Supply Chain Research, Penn State University.

3-2 What Is Logistics?

The term **logistics** has become much more widely recognized by the general public. In the last 20 years, television, radio, and print advertising have lauded the importance of logistics. Transportation firms, such as UPS, DHL, and FedEx, frequently refer to their organizations as logistics companies and stress the importance of their service to overall logistics success. The Persian Gulf War of the 1990s also contributed to increased recognition of logistics because CNN news commentators' frequent mention of the logistics challenges associated with the 7,000-mile long supply pipeline to support the war effort in the Persian Gulf countries. Another factor contributing to the recognition of logistics has been increased customer sensitivity not only to product quality but also to the logistics service quality.

Logistics management, as defined in this text, encompasses logistics systems not only in the private business sector but also in the public/government and nonprofit sectors. In addition, service organizations such as banks, hospitals, restaurants, and hotels have logistics challenges and issues, and *logistics management* is an appropriate and growing activity for service organizations. Consequently, there are different definitions of logistics because of the different perspectives (see Table 3.1).

For the purposes of this text, the definition offered by the Council of Supply Chain Management Professionals (formerly the Council of Logistics Management) is the most appropriate. However, it is important to recognize that logistics owes its origins to the military, which has long recognized the importance of logistics activities for national defense, and that the other definitions are also appropriate for their respective objectives and perspectives.

The military definition of logistics encompasses supply items (food, fuel, spare parts) as well as personnel. The term *logistics* became a part of the military lexicon in the eighteenth century in Europe. The logistics officer was responsible for encamping and quartering the troops as well as for stocking supply depots.

Table 3.1	Logistics Definitions
PERSPECTIVE	**DEFINITION**
Inventory	Management of materials in motion and at rest
Customer	Getting the right product, to the right customer, in the right quantity, in the right condition, at the right place, at the right time, and at the right cost (called the "seven Rs of logistics")
Dictionary	The branch of military science having to do with procuring, maintaining, and transporting material, personnel, and facilities
International Society of Logistics	The art and science of management, engineering, and technical activities concerned with requirements, design, and supplying and maintaining resources to support objectives, plans, and operations
Utility/Value	Providing time and place utility/value of materials and products in support of organization objectives
Council of Supply Chain Management Professionals	That part of the supply chain process that plans, implements, and controls the efficient, effective flow and storage of goods, services, and related information from point of origin to point of consumption in order to meet customer requirements
Component support	Supply management for the plant (inbound logistics) and distribution management for the firm's customers (outbound logistics)

Source: Adapted from Stephen H. Russell, "A General Theory of Logistics Practices," *Air Force Journal of Logistics* 24, no. 4 (2000): 15. Reproduced by permission.

The logistics concept began to appear in the business-related literature in the 1960s under the label of **physical distribution**, which had a focus on the outbound side of the logistics system (plant to market). During the 1960s, military logistics began to focus on engineering dimensions of logistics – reliability, maintainability, configuration, management, life cycle management, and so on – with increased emphasis on modeling the quantitative analysis. In contrast, the business or commercial applications were usually more focused on consumer nondurable goods related to the marketing and physical distribution of finished products. The engineering-related logistics, as practiced by the military, attracted attention among businesses that produced industrial products that had to be maintained with repair parts over the life cycle of the product. For example, heavy machinery manufacturers, such as Komatsu, have developed world-renowned logistics systems for delivering spare parts to repair and maintain their vehicles.

The business sector approach to logistics developed into inbound logistics (materials management to support manufacturing) and outbound logistics (plant distribution to support marketing) during the 1970s and 1980s. Then, in the 1990s, the business sector began to view logistics in the context of a supply or demand chain that linked all of the organizations from the supplier's supplier to the customer's customer. Supply chain management requires a more dynamic, collaborative, and coordinated flow of materials and goods through the logistics systems of all the organizations in the network, as indicated in Chapter 1. Logistics can be viewed as part of organizational management with four major subdivisions:

- **Business logistics** – That part of the supply chain that plans, implements, and controls the efficient, effective, flow and storage of goods, services, and related information from point of origin to point of consumption in order to meet customer requirements.
- **Military logistics** – The design and integration of all aspects of support for the operational capability of the military forces (deployed or in garrison) and their equipment to ensure readiness, reliability, and efficiency.
- **Event logistics** – The network of activities, facilities, and personnel required to organize, schedule, and deploy the resources for an event to take place and to efficiently withdraw after the event.
- **Service logistics** – The acquisition, scheduling, and management of facilities, assets, personnel, and materials to support and sustain a service operation or business.

All four subdivisions have some common characteristics and requirements such as forecasting, scheduling, and transportation, but they also have some differences in their primary purpose. All four, however, can be viewed in a supply chain context; that is, upstream and downstream other organizations play a role in their overall success and long-run viability. Having offered definitions of logistics, it is now appropriate to discuss how logistics adds value to an organization's products.

3-3 Value-Added Roles of Logistics

There are five principal types of economic utility that add value to a product or service: form (transformation), time, place, quantity, and possession and they are interrelated. Generally, production/manufacturing activities are credited with providing form utility; logistics activities with time, place, and quantity utilities; and marketing activities with possession utility. Each will be discussed briefly.

3-3-1 Form Utility

Form or Transformation Utility refers to the value added to the goods through a manufacturing or assembly process. For example, such utility results when raw materials or components are combined in some predetermined manner to produce a finished product. This is the case, for example, when Dell combines components along with software to assemble a computer to a customer's specifications. The process of combining these different components represents a change in the product *form* that adds value to the finished product.

3-3-2 Place Utility

Logistics provides **place utility** by moving goods from production points to markets WHERE demand exits. Logistics extends the physical boundaries of the market area, thus adding economic value to the goods. Logistics creates place utility primarily through transportation. For example, moving Huggies diapers from a Kimberly-Clark manufacturing facility in Wisconsin by motor carrier to markets where consumers need these diapers creates place utility. The market boundary extension, added by place utility, increases competition, which often leads to lower prices and increased profit opportunities through economies of scale.

3-3-3 Time Utility

Not only must goods and services be available *where* customers need them but also at the time *when* customers or need them. **Time utility** is the economic value added to a good or service by having it at a demand point at a specific time when it is needed. Logistics creates time utility through proper inventory maintenance, the strategic location of goods and services, and transportation. For example, having heavily advertised products and sale merchandise available in retail stores at the time promised in the advertisement or being able to supply products when there is an emergency are good examples of time utility. Time utility is much more important today because of the emphasis on reducing lead time and minimizing inventory levels through logistics-related strategies to improve cash flow.

On the Line	*AGE OF THE DRONE: Good News or Bad News???*

The Logistics and Supply Chain publications, newspapers, other media are replete with stories about the information systems and related technology that may be changing the "face" of supply chains in terms of inventory replenishment, warehousing, transportation, order processing and fulfillment, etc. There is no question that we are living in an era of change that is challenging shippers, carriers, customers and others to transform, and become more efficient or get "left in the dust." References are made to driverless vehicles and smart highways, intelligent warehouses, robotics, cloud computing, 3-D printing, transportation and warehouse management systems, etc. However, nothing seems to have captured the attention of so many as the DRONE, especially among the general public. Before answering the question posed above, let's review some background on DRONES.

The Drone is technically classified as a remote controlled device and they were developed during World War II for use by the military. Later, remote controlled model airplanes and boats were developed for outdoor entertainment. These remote controlled devices became more sophisticated and expensive over time. In the last twenty years more commercial uses were envisioned for these pilotless aircraft in agriculture, forestry and in safety and security including traffic control. The military drone was viewed as less costly to develop and replace in case of loss and also would reduce human casualties.

In 2013, Amazon announced that they were going to experiment with the use of drones for delivery of selected items in the San Francisco area. This announcement attracted a lot of attention from both doubters and proponents. The proponents were not surprised since Amazon has frequently pushed the "edge of the envelope" in logistics and supply chain management. As pointed out in a later chapter, transportation provides economic and social benefits including accessibility and connectivity. The so-called "last mile" in congested city areas for delivery has been an on-going challenge. The selective use of drones in such situations could improve effectiveness if it can be accomplished on an efficient basis. The flexibility of the drone and its minimal requirements for infrastructure make such service attractive and of interest.

DHL, a German parcel delivery company, which competes with FEDEX and UPS, has announced that they are going to use drones for the delivery of medication and drugs on a routine basis for delivery to remote, inaccessible locations, such as the Island of JUIST off the German coast. One can readily imagine such service for a variety of needed products to remote, inaccessible areas in such locations as Alaska and many other places. Amazon and also Google have been stymied in their efforts to provide similar service by various regulatory authorities in the U.S. Amazon is offering such a service in Canada and Google is doing the same in in Australia. The rationale appears sound and one can only hope that regulatory barriers will be removed and replaced with reasoned and sound controls for public safety. Such use combined with use for agriculture, forestry, fire protection and traffic safety appears to offer many potential benefits, that is, the "Good News."

What then is the "Bad News? The answer to that question has been publicized by various media reporting the rapidly growing interest and use of drones by the general public and some others. The investment for a drone is relatively modest even for a reasonably sophisticated model with a camera, and this has attracted the public to use them to view various activities like forest fires, accidents sites, civil disorder and riot sites, etc. frequently interfering with police and safety responders. Therein, lies the problem and potential for the Bad News for Drones. The situation is analogous to mobile communication devices and drivers of autos and trucks. The devices themselves can perform a useful service for individuals and groups as well as public agencies, but when used while driving for tweeting and e-mailing, a potential dangerous situation is created as has been demonstrated numerous times in recent years—Good News and Bad News!!! With appropriate controls and public cooperation, we can have the Good News or what could be termed a Win-Win.

3-3-4 Quantity Utility

Today's global competition requires that products not only be delivered on time to the correct destination but also be delivered in the correct quantities to minimize inventory cost and prevent stockouts. The utilities of *when* and *where* must be accompanied by *how much*. Delivering the proper quantities of an item to where it is demanded provides **quantity utility**. For example, assume that General Motors will be assembling 1,000 automobiles on a given day and is using a JIT inventory strategy. This will require that 5,000 tires be delivered to support the automobile production schedule. Assume that tire supplier only delivers 3,500 tires on time at the correct location. Even though the *when* and *where* utilities are created, the *how much* utility is not. Thus, GM will not be able to assemble the 1,000 cars as planned. Logistics must deliver products at the right time, to the right pace, and in the right quantities to add utility and economic value to a product. All three are obviously interrelated.

3-3-5 Possession Utility

Possession utility is primarily created through the basic marketing activities related to the promotion and sales of products and services. **Promotion** can be defined as the effort, through direct and indirect contact with the customer, to increase the desire to possess a good or benefit from a service. The role of logistics in the economy is related to and supports possession utility; time, place, and quantity utilities make sense only if demand for the product of service exists. Marketing also depends on logistics, since possession utility cannot be accomplished unless time, place, and quantity utilities are provided.

3-4 Logistics Activities

The logistics definition discussed previously indicates activities for which the logistics manager could be responsible:

- Transportation
- Warehousing and storage
- Industrial packaging
- Materials handling
- Inventory control
- Order fulfillment
- Inventory forecasting
- Production planning and scheduling
- Procurement
- Customer service
- Facility location
- Return goods handling
- Parts and service support
- Salvage and scrap disposal

The list is quite comprehensive, and some organizations with well-developed logistics functions may not place responsibility for all of these activities within the logistics area. However, decisions regarding these activities impact total logistics costs and requires input from logistics management to evaluate the costs and benefits when changes are made in one or more of the aforementioned activities.

3-4-1 Transportation

Transportation is a very important activity in the logistics system and is often the largest variable logistics cost. A major focus in logistics and supply chains is on the physical movement or flow of goods in the network that moves the product. The network is usually composed of transportation organizations and related service organizations that are evaluated, selected and used in moving raw materials, components, and finished goods or developing private transportation as an alternative. It is important to note that transportation is a very important component of supply since it provides the physical link among the various organizations in a supply chain.

3-4-2 Storage

A second area, which has a tradeoff relationship with transportation, is storage. Storage involves two separate but closely related activities: inventory management and warehousing. A direct relationship exists between transportation and the level of inventory and number of warehouses required. For example, if organizations use a relatively slow mode of transportation, they usually have to hold higher inventory levels and thus have more warehousing space for inventory. An organization might consider using a faster, more expensive mode of transportation to eliminate warehouse space and inventory.

A number of important decisions are related to storage activities (inventory and warehousing), including how many warehouses are needed, how much inventory should be held, where to locate the warehouses, warehouse size, etc. Since transportation affects storage-related decisions, an analytical framework is needed to examine the tradeoffs related to the various alternatives.

3-4-3 Packaging

A third area of interest to logistics is industrial (exterior) packaging. Industrial packaging protects the product during movement and storage and includes materials such as corrugated cardboard boxes, stretch wrap, banding, bags, etc. For example, rail or ocean transportation typically requires additional packaging expenditures because of the greater risk of damage in transit. In analyzing tradeoffs for proposed changes in transportation modes, logistics mangers usually examine how the changes will influence packaging costs. In many instances, changing to a premium transportation mode, such as air, will reduce packaging costs because there is less risk of damage. Packaging has received much more scrutiny in recent years with the increased interest in sustainability. Packaging material often ends up in the landfills. Companies have significantly reduced their packaging waste by using alternate materials.

3-4-4 Materials Handling

A fourth area to be considered is materials handling which may also be of interest to other functions in a typical manufacturing organization. Materials handling is important to consider in warehouse design and warehouse operations. Logistics managers are concerned with the movement of goods into a warehouse from a transportation vehicle, the placement of goods in a warehouse, the movement of goods from storage to order-picking areas and eventually to dock areas for transportation out of the warehouse. Materials handling is concerned with the mechanical equipment used for short-distance movement and includes equipment such as conveyors, forklift trucks, overhead cranes, and automated storage and retrieval systems (ASRS). Materials handling designs should be coordinated in order to ensure congruity between the types of equipment used and the storage devices they are moving.

3-4-5 Inventory Control

A fifth area to examine is inventory control which has two dimensions, namely, assuring adequate inventory levels and certifying inventory accuracy. Assuring adequate inventory levels requires monitoring current inventory levels and placing appropriate replenishment orders from manufacturing or vendors to prevent stockouts. Another dimension of inventory control is certifying inventory accuracy. As inventory is depleted to fill customer orders, a facility's information system should be tracking the status of current inventory levels.

To assure that the actual physical inventory levels match those shown in the information system, cycle counts are taken of selected items every period throughout the year. The use of bar codes and RFID tags has helped to make this process more efficient and effective.

3-4-6 Order Fulfillment

Order fulfillment consists of the activities involved in filling and shipping customer orders. Order fulfillment is important because it directly impacts the time that elapses from when a customer places an order until the customer receives the order. This may also be referred to as order lead time. The four basic processes or activities of order fulfillment or lead time are order transmittal, order processing, order preparation, and order delivery which will be discussed in more detail in a later chapter.

3-4-7 Forecasting

Another important activity is demand forecasting. Reliable forecasting is required to meet inventory requirements for manufacturing efficiency and customer needs. Logistics and supply chain personnel should develop inventory forecasts in conjunction with manufacturing scheduling and marketing forecasts of demand to assure that proper inventory levels are maintained to meet customer requirements.

3-4-8 Production Planning

Another area of interest to logistics is production planning and scheduling for effective inventory control. Once a forecast is developed and the current level of inventory on-hand and the usage rate are determined, production managers can calculate the number of units to manufacture to ensure adequate market coverage. However, in organizations with multiple product lines that require manufacturing-process timing, may require close coordination or actual control of production planning and scheduling by logistics.

3-4-9 Procurement

Procurement is another activity that can be included in logistics. The basic rationale for including procurement in logistics is that transportation and inventory costs are related to the geographic location (distance) of raw materials and other needed items to meet manufacturing needs. The quantities purchased also affect total logistics costs. For example, buying components parts from China for a manufacturing facility located in the United States might require a lead time of 10 to 12 weeks. This would have a direct impact on the inventory levels needed at the manufacturing facility to prevent a plant shutdown. Using a premium mode of transportation to reduce this lead time would reduce inventory levels but would probably increase transportation costs. Procurement decisions also need to be made from a systems perspective.

3-4-10 Customer Service

Two dimensions of customer service are important to this discussion: (1) the process of interacting directly with the customer to influence or take the order and (2) the levels of service an organization offers to its customers. From an order-taking perspective, logistics is concerned with being able to inform the customer, at the time the order is placed, when the order should be delivered. This requires coordination among inventory control, manufacturing, warehousing, and transportation when the order is taken for delivery time and product availability.

The second dimension of customer service relates to the levels of service the organization promises its customers. These service dimensions could include order fill rates and on-time delivery rates. Decisions about inventories, transportation, and warehousing relate to customer service levels. Logistics plays an important role in ensuring that the customer gets the right product at the right time and the right quantity. Logistics decisions impact product availability and lead time, which are critical to customer service.

3-4-11 Facility Location

Another area of interest to logistics is plant and warehouse site location. A site location change could alter time and place relationships between facilities and markets or between supply points and manufacturing facilities. Such changes will affect transportation costs and service, customer service, and inventory requirements. Therefore, the logistics manager is concerned and should provide input for facility location decisions.

3-4-12 Other Activities

Other areas that can be considered a part of logistics include parts and service support, return goods handling, and salvage and scrap disposal. Logistics managers can also provide valuable input for product design as well as to maintenance and supply services, since transportation and storage decisions impact these decisions. These areas may require the development of a reverse logistics system that will allow used, broken, or obsolete products to be returned to the supplier for disposition which is usually managed in the logistics area directly or through a third party logistics service provider.

On the Line	"UPS and Wiley Coyote"

The recently announced acquisition of Coyote Logistics by UPS conjures up memories of the origins of UPS and the strategic journey to their present position in the logistics and supply chain world. Some logistics and supply chain professionals may not be aware of the relatively humble beginnings of United Parcel as a small package delivery service for major retailers in East Coast cities like NYC, Philadelphia and Washington, D.C. Many urban families lived in very modest homes and did not own automobiles. They would use public transportation (bus and trolley cars) to get to the central districts in the city where the large multiple-story department stores were located to shop for non-food items, normally not available in the smaller neighborhood retail stores and/or to see more variety. If they had too many packages or the items were too large for the transit carriers, the items could be delivered by United Parcel. It was an invaluable service "for the times," but "times change."

With the end of World War II, there was pent up demand and increased household savings from the War years. Families started to move from small, urban homes to larger suburban residencies with individual lots and most families acquired an automobile for convenience and shopping. This Post-War phenomenon had serious implications for United Parcel as retail stores started locating in shopping malls with free parking for shoppers which lessened the demand for parcel delivery. United Parcel had to do an evaluation of their business model and strategy, and ask the classic question, viz., "What Business Are We In."

United Parcel essentially answered the question by stating that they were a transportation company that specialized in moving small packages between and among businesses as well as residencies, that is, business-to-business, business-to-residences, and residences-to-residences. This restatement of their mission opened up many new opportunities but presented some major challenges going forward. Intrastate and interstate transportation carriers were highly regulated by the federal government and state agencies where operating authorities had to be approved. It was especially challenging for approval of interstate service. Also, it put them in direct competition with the U.S. Post Office which offered similar service but not direct pick-up at businesses and homes. Over time they mitigated these "roadblocks" and with the elimination of federal regulation of motor carrier transportation at the federal level, they could move ahead more aggressively. However, deregulation of transportation also provided an opportunity for another potential competitor, viz., Federal Express. Initially one could say that UPS provided surface transportation service and FEDEX provided air service. However, that distinction has become blurred over time as both companies moved aggressively to grow and expand.

Both UPS and FedEx have used acquisition of established companies to expand the scope of their services and global geographic reach. The end result has been the development of two successful organizations who started as delivery companies and have become much more comprehensive logistics service companies who offer a variety of services for businesses and individuals. UPS is currently ranked fourth as a 3PL with almost $6 billion in revenue. Both companies have become household names as they have rode the wave of interest and expansion of logistics and supply chain management into the twenty-first century by providing service on a global basis.

Their ability to identify and meet the needs of global organizations has accounted for their growth and expansion, but competition and the need to be more efficient and effective has necessitated a continual effort to improve and stay ahead of their rivals. Coyote Logistics appears to be a "gem" in terms of a "fit" for UPS just as GENCO Distribution was for FEDEX. The latter provided entry into the ever growing product returns or reverse logistics business for FEDEX. UPS is looking to expand aggressively into the freight brokerage which is an important part of Coyote's success and profitability because of their development of a proprietary scheduling technology for managing that service. This same technology should be a major benefit to UPS to handle their fleet of trucks especially during the peak holiday season which has been a serious challenge for UPS during the last several seasons.

The key takeaway here is that UPS has been able to change their internal operations and business model to meet the challenges and changes occurring in the external environment and to recognize the criticality of the "final mile" of the supply chain which is essentially a logistics function. Maybe the title of this piece should be "Coyote Logistics and Wiley UPS"?

3-5 Logistics in the Economy: A Macro Perspective

The overall cost of logistics on a macro basis increases with growth in the economy. In other words, if more goods and services are produced, total logistics costs will increase. To determine the efficiency of the logistics system, the total logistics costs need to be measured in relationship to gross domestic product (GDP), which is a widely accepted barometer used to gauge the rate of growth in the economy. In 2014, logistics related costs accounted for 8.3% of GDP and totaled $1,449 billion. This was an increase of 3.1% from the previous year due to increases in inventory costs, warehousing costs, and transportation cost due to growth in the economy.

As indicated in Figure 3.2, logistics costs have been relatively stable since 2005 with a low point in 2009 due to the recession. Logistics costs were closer to 20% of GDP in the early to mid-1970s.

The reduction in logistics cost as a percent of GDP has resulted from a significant improvement in the overall logistics systems of the organizations operating in the economy. This reduction in relative cost allows organizations to be more competitive since it directly impacts the cost of producing goods. It can be argued that the turnaround that occurred in the U.S. economy in the early 2000s was due in part to the reduction in relative logistics costs.

Some additional understanding of logistics costs can be gained by examining the three major cost categories – warehousing and inventory costs, transportation costs, and other logistical costs. These costs are depicted in Figure 3.3 for 2014. Warehousing costs are those associated with the assets used to hold inventory. Inventory costs are all the expenses associated with holding goods in storage. Carrying costs include interest expense (or the opportunity cost associated with the investment in inventory), risk-related costs (obsolescence, depreciation), and service-related costs (insurance, taxes). Transportation costs are the total national expenditures for the movement of freight in the United States. The third category of logistics costs is the administrative and shipper-related costs associated with managing logistics activities and personnel.

The declining trend for logistics costs relative to GDP started in the early 1980s and was related to the deregulation of transportation, which permitted much more flexibility for shippers to purchase transportation services and allowed more flexibility for carriers to adjust their freight rates and service in response to competition. A second factor contributing to the trend has been the improved management of inventory levels with more attention being focused on inventory investment and the technology available to managers to make more effective inventory decisions. Finally, the focus by many organizations on cash flow resulted in more emphasis on inventory turnover.

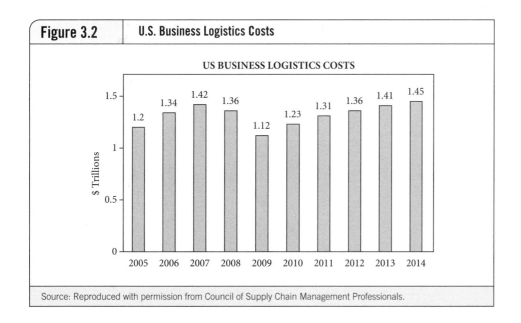

Figure 3.2	**U.S. Business Logistics Costs**

Source: Reproduced with permission from Council of Supply Chain Management Professionals.

Figure 3.3	Total Logistics Costs	
TOTAL LOGISTICS COST - 2014		
CARRYING COSTS - $2.496 TRILLION - ALL BUSINESS INVENTOY		**$ BILLION**
Interest		2
Taxes, obsolescence, depreciation, insurance		331
Warehousing		143
	Subtotal	476
Transportation Costs		
Motor Carriers		
Truck - Intercity		*486*
Truck - Local		*216*
	Subtotal	702
Other Carriers		
Railroads		80
Water (International 31, Domestic 9)		40
Oil Pipelines		17
Air (International 12, Domestic 16)		28
Forwarders		40
	Subtotal	205
Shipper-related costs		10
Logistics administration		56
Total logistics cost		**1449**

Source: Annual State of Logistics Report, http://cscmp.org (2015)
Reproduced with permission from Council of Supply Chain Management Professionals.

Figure 3.4	Inventories Growth Slowed in 2014

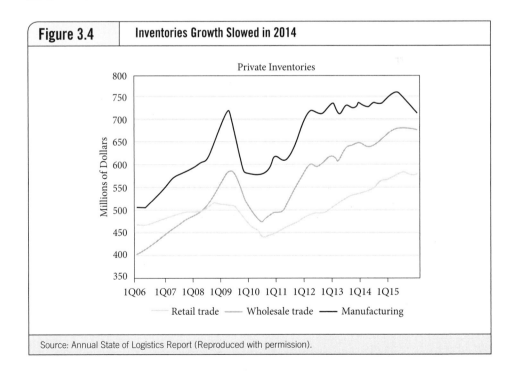

Source: Annual State of Logistics Report (Reproduced with permission).

The two largest cost categories in any organization's logistics system are transportation and inventory costs. As indicated, transportation is usually the single largest variable. Note the magnitude of the motor carrier expenditures relative to other carriers shown in Figure 3.3 ($702 billion versus $205 billion for all other modes). This level of expenditure is not based necessarily on the lowest transportation rates but also reflects the value to shippers of the service provided by motor carriers and importance of LANDED COSTS. This point is discussed in Chapter 11 on transportation, but it is worth noting here because logistics management requires examining the total cost of logistics, not just one cost such as transportation. It is also worth noting that inventory growth slowed in 2014 and that manufacturing inventory continued to decline into 2015 (see Figure 3.4).

3-6 Logistics in the Firm: The Micro Dimension

The micro dimension of logistics examines the relationships between logistics and other functional areas in an organization—marketing, manufacturing or operations, finance and accounting, and others. Logistics focuses on processes that cut across traditional functional boundaries, particularly in today's environment with emphasis on the supply chain. Consequently, logistics interfaces in many important ways with other functional areas since the logistics-related flows, as well as supply chain flows, tend to be horizontal in an organization, cutting across other functions.

3-6-1 Logistics Interfaces with Manufacturing or Operations

A classic interface between logistics and manufacturing relates to the length of the production run. Manufacturing efficiency is often based upon long production runs or scale with infrequent manufacturing line setups or changeovers. The long run can result in higher inventory levels of inventory for some finished products and limited supplies of others. The best or optimal manufacturing decisions require managers to analyze the cost trade-offs of longer production runs and their impact on inventory cost. Shorter production runs with more efficient set-ups can provide flexibility to meet short run changes in demand. The current trend toward "pull" systems where the product is "pulled" in *response* to demand as opposed to be "pushed" in *advance* of demand necessitates such flexibility. This practice lowers inventory levels, which can lower total logistics costs even though production costs may increase.

The production manager is also interested in minimizing the inventory impact of seasonal products. For example, the candy industry is affected by several holidays or events, namely, Valentine's Day, Easter, Back-to School purchases, Halloween, and Christmas. To minimize manufacturing cost and potential stockouts, production managers usually produce in advance of the holiday or event. This strategy requires accumulating inventory and the associated costs. The manufacturing cost savings should be traded off against the inventory costs and other related benefit or costs.

Logistics and manufacturing also interface on the inbound side of production. For example, a shortage or stockout could result in the shutdown of a manufacturing facility and an increase in production costs. The logistics manager should ensure that available quantities of raw materials and components are adequate to meet production schedules yet are conservative in terms of inventory carrying costs. Because of the need for this type of coordination, many organizations today have shifted the responsibility for production scheduling from manufacturing to logistics.

Another activity at the interface of logistics and manufacturing is industrial packaging, which many organizations treat as a logistics responsibility. In the context of manufacturing or logistics, the principal purpose that industrial packaging serves is to protect the product from damage. This is distinct from whatever value the consumer packaging might have for marketing or promotional reasons.

The interface between logistics and manufacturing is becoming more critical, given the growth in procurement of raw materials and components from offshore sources and sustainability issues. Also, many organizations today are making arrangements with third-party manufacturers, "co-packers," or contract manufacturers to produce, assemble, or enhance some or all of the organization's finished products. These arrangements are especially prevalent in the food industry where some manufacturers produce food items to be sold under someone else's label. Management of global supply chains is intensifying the importance of the need for collaboration between logistics and production.

3-6-2 Logistics Interfaces with Marketing

Logistics has an important relationship with marketing that also necessitates collaboration. The rationale for this strong relationship is that physical distribution, or the outbound side of an organization's logistics system, plays an important role in the sale of a product. In some instances, order fulfillment may be the key variable in the continuing sales of products; that is, the ability to provide the right product at the right time to the right place in the right quantities and the right cost can be the critical element in making a sale.

This section discusses the interfaces between logistics and marketing activities in each principal area of the so-called marketing mix – price, product, promotion, and place. In addition, recent trends in the interface between logistics and marketing will be discussed.

3-6-2-1 Price

Organizations selling products often provide a discount schedule for larger purchase quantities. If such discount schedules relate to transportation rate discount schedules in terms of weight, then both the shipper and customer should be able to reduce total transportation cost. In some organizations, entire pricing schedules conform to various quantities that can be shipped by modes of transportation. Under the Robinson-Patman Act and related legislation, transportation cost savings are a valid reason for offering a price discount.

In addition, the logistics manager should be interested in the volume requirements of the price schedule because this impacts inventory requirements, replenishment times, and other aspects of customer service. An organization should consider its ability to provide sufficient volumes within an attractive price schedule. The logistics manager should be notified of pricing specials so that he or she can adjust inventory levels to meet projected demand.

3-6-2-2 Product

Much has been written about the number of new products that come on the market each year. Their size, shape, weight, packaging, and other physical dimensions affect the ability of logistics and supply chain systems to move and store the new products. The logistics manager can offer input when marketing is deciding on the physical dimensions of new products to minimize problems. In addition to new products, organizations frequently change established products to improve or maintain sales. Very often, such changes might take the form of new package design and, perhaps, different package sizes. The physical dimensions of products affect the utilization and costs of warehousing and transportation systems such as equipment needed, damage rates, storage ability, use of materials-handling equipment such as conveyors and pallets, industrial packaging, etc.

Frustration can mount for logistics managers when faced with a change in a product's dimensions that makes use of standard-size pallets uneconomical or that uses trailer or container space inefficiently or in a way that can damage products. These issues may seem mundane and somewhat trivial to sales and marketing executives, but they greatly affect an organization's overall success and profitability in the long run. Collaboration to allow logistics managers to provide input about the impact upon logistics costs in these situations is needed.

Another marketing area that affects logistics is consumer packaging. The marketing manager often regards consumer packaging as a "silent salesperson." At the retail level, the package can be a determining factor in influencing sales. The marketing manager will be concerned about package appearance, information provided, and the other related aspects; for a consumer comparing several products on a retailer's shelf, the consumer package might make the differences. The consumer package is also important to the logistics manager for several reasons. First, the consumer package has to fit into the industrial package, or the external package. The size, shape, and other dimensions of the consumer package will affect the use of the industrial package. Second, the protection offered by the consumer package also concerns the logistics manager. The physical dimensions and the protection aspects of consumer packages affect the logistics system in the areas of transportation, materials handling, and warehousing. Simply stated, consumer packaging can negatively impact logistics costs (efficiency) and customer service if there is damage. Collaboration is a necessary ingredient for efficiency and effectiveness for logistics and marketing.

3-6-2-3 Promotion

Companies may spend millions of dollars on national advertising campaigns and other promotional practices to improve sales. An organization making a promotional effort to stimulate sales should collaborate with the logistics manager so that appropriate levels of inventory will be available for distribution to the customer. Problems can still occur, even with collaboration, because of the difficulty of forecasting the demand for a new product, but frequent interchange of information can mitigate problems, and supply chain collaboration can further improve the situation. Chapter 4 discusses the growth of OMNI-CHANNEL DISTRIBUTION among many large retailers which necessitates even more collaboration between logistics and marketing.

3-6-2-4 Place

The place decision refers to the distribution channel selection and involves both transactional and physical distribution channel decisions. Marketers typically become more involved in making decisions about marketing transactions and in deciding, for example, whether to sell products to wholesalers or to deal directly with retailers. From the logistics manager's perspective, such decisions can affect logistics system requirements. For example, wholesalers purchase in larger quantities with more predictably and consistency, thus lowering their service cost. The emergence of super-size retailers, like Wal-Mart has changed this dynamic, as indicated in Chapter 1.

3-6-2-5 Recent Trends

Perhaps, the most significant trend is that marketers recognize the strategic value of place in the marketing mix and the increased revenues and customer satisfaction that might result from excellent logistics service. As a result, many organizations have recognized

customer service as the interface activity between marketing and logistics and have aggressively and effectively promoted customer service as a key element of the marketing mix. Organizations in such industries as food, chemicals, pharmaceuticals, and technology have reported considerable success with this strategy to improve efficiency and effectiveness.

3-6-3 Logistics Interfaces with Other Areas

While manufacturing and marketing are probably the two most important internal functional interfaces for logistics in a product-oriented organization, there are other important interfaces. The finance area has become increasingly more important during the last decade. In fact, it will be argued in a later chapter that finance is the second language of logistics and supply chain management. The impact that logistics and supply chain management can have upon return on assets (ROA) or return on investment (ROI) is very significant. Logistics can positively impact ROA in several ways. First, inventory is both a current asset on the balance sheet and a variable expense on the income statement. Reducing inventory levels reduces the asset base as well as the corresponding variable expenses, thus having a positive impact on ROA. Second, transportation and warehousing costs can also influence ROA. If an organization owns its warehouses and transportation fleet, they are fixed assets on the balance sheet. If these assets are reduced or eliminated, ROA should increase. Similarly, if an organization utilizes 3PL's for warehousing and transportation, variable expenses and asset levels will usually be impacted. Finally, the focus on customer service (Chapter 9) can increase revenue. As long as the incremental increase in revenue is larger than the incremental increase in the cost of customer service, ROA will increase.

Logistics managers are also expected to justify increased investment in logistics-related assets using acceptable financial tools related to payback periods. Consequently, supply chain and logistics managers must be knowledgeable about financial metrics and standards of performance which will be discussed in detail in a later chapter.

Accounting is also an important interface for logistics. Accounting systems are critical for providing appropriate cost information for analysis of alternative logistics options. Far too often in the past, logistics-related costs were not measured specifically and were often accumulated into an overhead account, which made it extremely difficult to systematically monitor logistics costs. The recent interest in customer profitability and the related cost accounting systems such as activity-based costing (ABC) has been beneficial to improving the quality of logistics data and analyses. Accounting systems are also critical for measuring supply chain tradeoffs and performance.

3-7 Logistics in the Firm: Factors Affecting the Cost and Importance of Logistics

This section deals with specific factors relating to the cost and importance of logistics. Understanding some of the competitive, product and spatial relationships of logistics can help explain the strategic role of an organization's logistics activities.

3-7-1 Competitive Relationships

Frequently, competition is narrowly interpreted only in terms of price competition. While price is certainly important, customer service can also be a very important form of competition. For example, if an organization can reliably provide customers with its products in a relatively short time period, then its customers can reduce their inventory costs. Customers may consider minimizing their inventory costs to be just as important as keeping product prices low, since minimizing such costs will contribute to profit.

3-7-1-1 Order Cycle

Order cycle length directly affects inventory levels. Stated another way, shorter order cycles reduce the inventory required by the customer. Figure 3.5 shows this relationship. **Order cycle** can be defined as the time that elapses from when a customer places an order until the order is received. The order cycle includes activities such as order transmission, order receipt, order processing, order preparation (picking and packing), and order shipment. Figure 3.5 shows that longer order cycle times usually necessitate higher customer inventories. For example, assume that a customer is using 10 units of a product per day and that the supplier's order cycle time is eight days. The customer's average inventory during order cycle time is 40 units (80/2). If the supplier can reduce the order cycle time to four days, the customer's average inventory is reduced to 20 units (40/2). Therefore, such a cost reduction could be as important as a price reduction.

3-7-1-2 Substitutability

Substitutability very often affects the importance of customer service. In other words, if a product is similar to other products, consumers may be willing to substitute a competitive product when a stockout occurs. Therefore, customer service is usually more important for highly substitutable products than for products that customers are willing to wait for or back-order. This is one reason why companies advertise their brands. They want consumers to ask for their brands, and, if their brands are temporarily not available, they would like consumers to wait until they are. As far as logistics managers are concerned, an organization wishing to reduce its lost sales cost, which is a measure of customer service and substitutability, can either spend more on inventory and/or spend more on transportation to reduce the order cycle.

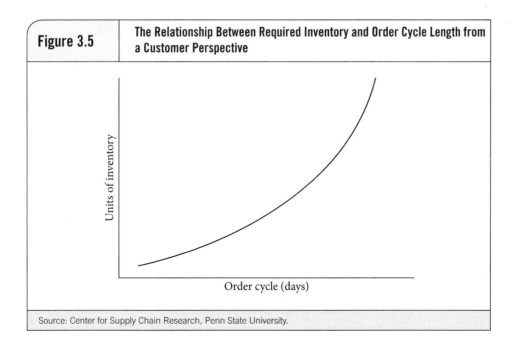

| Figure 3.5 | The Relationship Between Required Inventory and Order Cycle Length from a Customer Perspective |

Source: Center for Supply Chain Research, Penn State University.

3-7-1-3 Inventory Effect

Figure 3.6 shows that by increasing inventory costs (either by increasing the inventory level or by increasing the reorder point), organizations can usually reduce the cost of lost sales. An inverse relationship exists between the cost of lost sales and inventory cost. However, organizations are usually willing to increase the inventory cost only until total costs start to increase or stated in economic terms, to the point at which the marginal savings from reducing lost sales cost equals the marginal cost of carrying additional inventory.

3-7-1-3 Transportation Effect

A similar relationship exists with transportation as can be seen in Figure 3.7. Companies can usually trade off increased transportation costs against decreased lost sales costs. For transportation, this additional expenditure usually involves buying a better service—for example, switching from water to rail, or rail to motor, or motor to air. The higher transportation cost could also result from shipping more frequently in smaller quantities at higher transportation prices. As indicated in Figure 3.7, organizations can reduce the cost of lost sales by spending more on transportation service to improve customer service. Once again, most organizations willingly do this only up to the point where the marginal savings in lost sales cost equals the marginal increment associated with the increased transportation cost.

Organizations can spend more for inventory and transportation simultaneously to reduce the cost of lost sales. Improved transportation will usually result in lower inventory cost, that is, the situation is more interactive and coordinated than is indicated above.

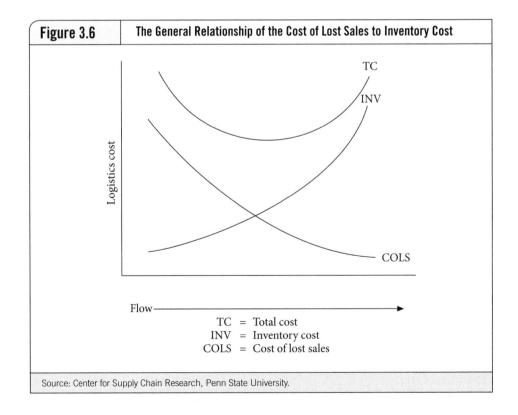

| Figure 3.6 | The General Relationship of the Cost of Lost Sales to Inventory Cost |

TC = Total cost
INV = Inventory cost
COLS = Cost of lost sales

Source: Center for Supply Chain Research, Penn State University.

Figure 3.7	The General Relationship of the Cost of Lost Sales to Transportation Cost

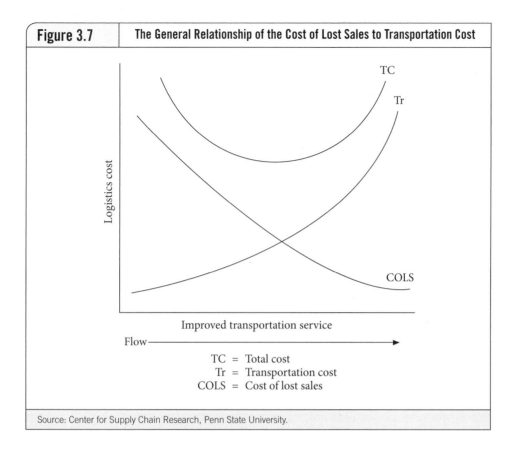

TC = Total cost
Tr = Transportation cost
COLS = Cost of lost sales

3-7-2 Product Relationships

A number of product-related factors affect the cost and importance of logistics. Among the more significant of these are dollar value, density, susceptibility to damage, and the need for special handling.

3-7-2-1 Dollar Value

The product's dollar value typically affects warehousing costs, inventory costs, transportation costs, packaging costs, and even materials-handling costs. As Figure 3.8 indicates, as the product's dollar value increases, the cost in each identified area also increases. The actual slope and level of the cost functions will vary among products.

Transportation prices reflect the risk associated with the movement of goods, and higher value products are often more susceptible to damage and loss and/or require more care in the movement. Transportation providers may also charge higher prices for higher-value products since these customers may be willing to pay higher rates for transportation service.

Warehousing and inventory costs also increase as the dollar value of the product increases. Higher value means more working capital invested in inventory, resulting in higher total capital costs. In addition, the risk factor for storing higher-value products increases the costs of obsolescence and depreciation. Also, since the physical facilities required to store higher-value products are more sophisticated, warehousing costs increase with higher dollar value products.

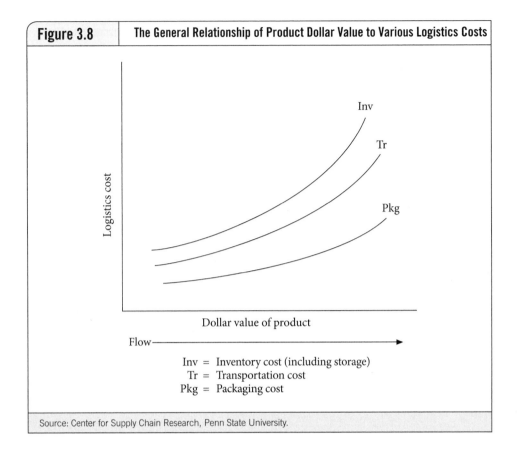

Figure 3.8	The General Relationship of Product Dollar Value to Various Logistics Costs

Inv = Inventory cost (including storage)
Tr = Transportation cost
Pkg = Packaging cost

Source: Center for Supply Chain Research, Penn State University.

Packaging costs also usually increase because the organization uses protective packaging to minimize potential damage to the product. An organization spends more effort in packaging a product to protect it from damage or loss if it has higher value. Finally, materials-handling equipment used to meet the needs of higher-value products is very often more sophisticated. Organizations are usually willing to use more capital-intensive and expensive equipment to speed higher-value goods through the warehouse and to minimize the chance of damage.

3-7-2-2 Density

Another factor that affects logistics cost is product density, which refers to the weight/space ratio of the product. An item that is lightweight compared to the space it occupies—for example, household furniture—has low density. Density affects transportation and warehousing costs, as shown in Figure 3.9. As density increases for a product, its transportation and warehousing costs tend to decrease.

When establishing their prices, transportation providers consider how much weight they can fit into their vehicles, since they quote their prices in dollars and cents per hundred pounds. Therefore, on high-density items, providers can charge a lower price per hundred pounds because they can fit more weight into their vehicle. For example, assume a motor carrier needs $5,000 in revenue from the freight that fills a 53-foot trailer. A low-density product might be able to fit 20,000 pounds into this trailer to fill it completely. The motor carrier would need to charge $25 per hundred pounds for this product. On the other hand, a

Figure 3.9	The General Relationship of Product Weight Density to Logistics Costs

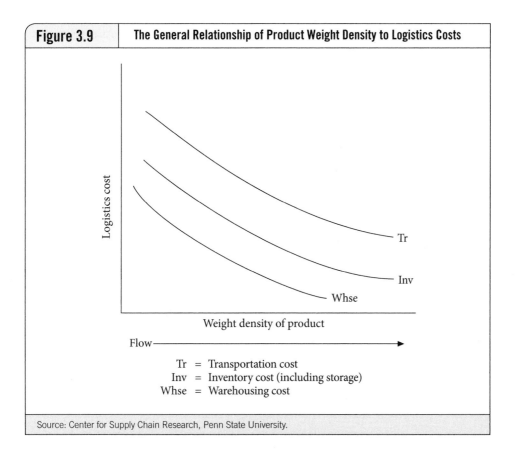

Tr = Transportation cost
Inv = Inventory cost (including storage)
Whse = Warehousing cost

Source: Center for Supply Chain Research, Penn State University.

high-density product might be able to fill the trailer at 40,000 pounds. The resulting price per hundred pounds would be $12.50.

3-7-2-3 Susceptibility to Damage

The third product factor affecting logistics cost is susceptibility to damage (see Figure 3.10). The greater the risk of damage to a product, the higher the transportation and warehousing cost. Because of a higher degree of risk and liability associated with more fragile goods, higher are prices charged by both transportation and warehousing providers. These providers might also charge higher prices because of measures they must take to prevent product damage.

3-7-2-4 Special Handling Requirements

A fourth factor is special handling requirements for products. Some products might require specifically designed equipment, for example, refrigeration, heating, or strapping. These special requirements will usually increase warehousing, transportation, and packaging costs.

3-7-3 Spatial Relationships

A final topic that is extremely significant to logistics is spatial relationships, the location of fixed points in the logistics system with respect to demand and supply points. Spatial relationships are very important to transportation costs, since these costs tend to increase with distance. Consider the following example (see Figure 3.11).

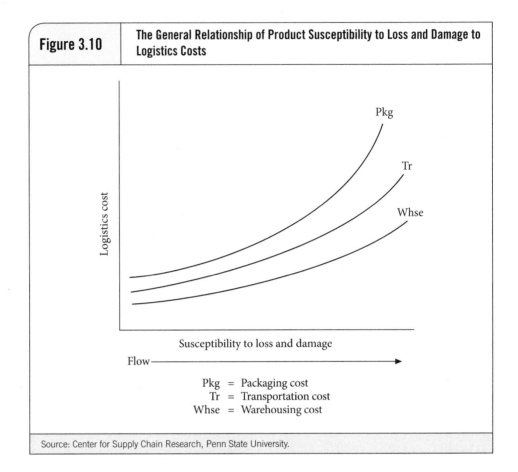

Figure 3.10 | The General Relationship of Product Susceptibility to Loss and Damage to Logistics Costs

Pkg = Packaging cost
Tr = Transportation cost
Whse = Warehousing cost

Source: Center for Supply Chain Research, Penn State University.

3-7-3-1 Example

The firm located at point B has a $1.50 production cost advantage over Firm A, since Firm B produces at $7.00 per unit as opposed to $8.50 per unit for Firm A. However, Firm B pays $1.35 for inbound raw materials ($0.60 + $0.75) and $3.50 for outbound movement to the market (M), for a total of $4.85 in per-unit transportation charges. Firm A pays $0.90 for inbound raw materials and $1.15 for outbound movement, for a total of $2.05 in per-unit transportation charges. Firm A's $2.80 transportation cost advantage offsets the $1.50 production cost disadvantage. Firm B could investigate alternative strategies to compete more effectively at M.

The distance factor or spatial relationships may affect logistics costs in ways other than transportation costs. For example, a firm located far from one or more of its markets might need to use a market-oriented warehouse to make customer deliveries in a satisfactory time period. Therefore, distance can add to warehousing and inventory carrying costs.

Distance or spatial relationships are of such importance to logistics that logistics responsibilities might include site location. For many organizations, warehouse location decisions are made based on distance to market, distance from suppliers, and access to transportation. Location, or site analysis, is considered in some detail later in this text.

Figure 3.11	Logistics and Spatial Relations from attachment

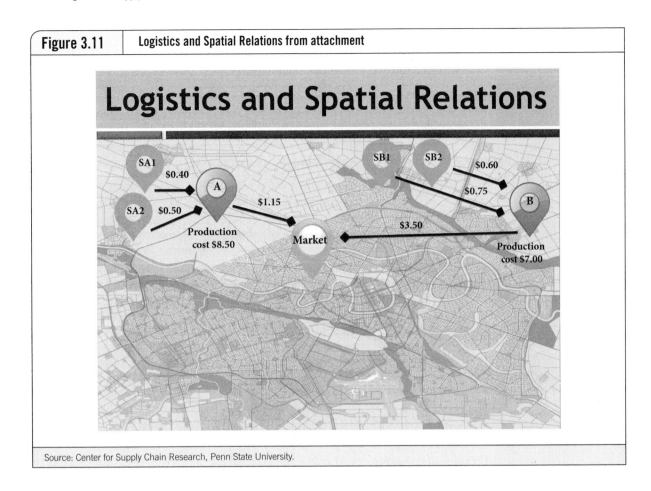

Source: Center for Supply Chain Research, Penn State University.

3-7-4 Logistics and Systems Analysis

An earlier section pointed out that developments in analyses and methodologies have facilitated the development of logistics. One such development was systems analysis, or the systems concept. Essentially, a system is a set of interacting elements, variables, parts, or objects that are functionally related to one another and that form a coherent group. The systems concept is something to which most individuals have been exposed at an early educational stage; for example, in science, students learn about the solar system and how relationships among the planets, the sun, and the moon result in day and night, changing weather, and so forth. In biology, students view the parts of the human body, such as the heart and blood, and their relationships as another system. The general tenet of the systems concept is that the focus is not on individual variables but on how they interact as a whole. The objective is to operate the whole system efficiently and effectively, not just the individual parts. From a supply chain perspective, this is a major challenge.

SUMMARY

- Logistics developed as an important area of business after World War II with several phases of development.

- Logistics has become an important part of supply chain management. The coordination and integration of the logistics systems of the organizations in a supply chain facilitate the successful management of supply chains.

- While there are a number of different definitions for logistics, the definition developed by the Council of Supply Chain Management Professionals is the primary definition used in this text.

- Logistics is an area of management that has four sub-disciplines: business, military, service, and event.

- On a macro basis, logistics-related costs have helped the U.S. economy maintain its competitive position on a global basis.

- Logistics adds place, time, and quantity utilities to products and enhances the form and possession utilities added by manufacturing and marketing.

- Logistics has an important system relationship to manufacturing, marketing, finance, and other areas of the organization which aids in making organizations more efficient and effective.

- Logistics activities, including transportation, inventory, warehousing, materials handling, industrial packaging, customer service, forecasting, and others are important components of supply chains.

- Logistics systems can be viewed or analyzed in several different ways including materials management versus physical distribution, cost centers, nodes versus links, and channels. All four approaches are viable for different purposes.

- Logistics is frequently analyzed from a systems approach, which emphasizes cost and service tradeoffs when changes are proposed. Either a short or a long-run perspective can be used.

- The cost of logistics systems can be affected by a number of major factors, including competition in the market, the spatial relationship of nodes, and product characteristics.

STUDY QUESTIONS

1. Provide a definition of logistics and a rationale for why is it important in private companies and public organizations?

2. Explain the importance of logistics important on a macro level and the contributions of logistics to the economy?

3. How does logistics add value in the economy? How does logistics add value for firms? What, if any are the differences?

4. Explain the relationship between logistics and supply chain management?

5. Compare and contrast the four major subdivisions of logistics discussed in this chapter.

6. Discuss the relationship between manufacturing and logistics. What are the tradeoffs between the two areas?

7. Physical distribution has a special relationship to marketing. What is the nature of the relationship between logistics and marketing? Is the relationship becoming more or less important? Why?

8. Logistics encompasses a relatively large number of managerial activities. Discuss five of these activities and why they are important to logistics systems.

9. Why do companies analyze their logistics systems from perspective of nodes and links?

10. What product characteristics affect logistics costs? Discuss the effects of these characteristics on logistics costs.

NOTES

1. Stephen H. Russell, "Growing World of Logistics," *Air Force Journal of Logistics*, Vol. 24, No. 4 (2000): 13–15.

2. Ibid.

3. Ibid.

4. Peter F. Drucker, "The Economy's Dark Continent," *Fortune* (April 1962): 103.

5. E. Jerome McCarthy and William E. Perrault, Jr., *Basic Marketing: A Managerial Approach*, 9th ed. (Homewood, IL: Richard D. Irwin, 1987): 46–52.

6. Philip Kotler, *Marketing Management: Analysis, Planning, and Control*, 5th ed. (Englewood Cliffs, NJ: Prentice-Hall, 1984): 463–464.

7. J. L. Heskett, Robert M. Ivie, and Nicholas A. Glaskowsky, Jr., *Business Logistics: Management of Physical Supply and Distribution* (New York, NY: Ronald Press, 1973): 454–469.

8. Roy Dale Voorhees and Merrill Kim Sharp, "Principles of Logistics Revisited," *Transportation Journal* (Fall 1978): 69–84.

CASE 3.1

Jordano Food Products

Supply Chain Profile

Jordano Foods

Tracie Shannon, Vice President for Logistics at Jordano Foods (Jordano), had just sent the following e-mail to members of the executive committee of the company:

> *I just returned from a lengthy meeting with Susan Weber, CEO of SAB Distribution. She is under great pressure from her Board of Directors to continue to grow market share and improve profitability. SAB has received a recent tender offer from another larger food distributor to buy the company and several members of their board have recommended that the offer be seriously considered. Susan feels that SAB can continue to improve their "bottom line" with additional changes in service offerings. Ms. Weber is meeting with all of SAB's major suppliers and customers to discuss new services that SAB can offer to enhance the competitiveness of the SAB supply chain.*

Background On Jordano Foods

Jordano Foods was founded in 1950 in Lewistown, Pennsylvania, by two brothers, Luigi and Mario Jordano. Their parents operated a restaurant in Burnham, Pennsylvania, featuring Italian cuisine. Marie Jordano was famous for her culinary skills. She developed her own recipes for pasta sauce, meatballs, fresh and dry pasta, and other Italian food items. Luigi and Mario worked in a restaurant prior to establishing Jordano Foods. The brothers felt that they could capitalize on the family recipes by selling pasta, sauces, and other related Italian food products to other restaurants in nearby communities in central Pennsylvania.

Their initial venture was so successful that they expanded their product line and began selling their products too small to medium-sized wholesalers and distributors throughout Pennsylvania. They built a plant in Lewistown to produce their food products and subsequently built another plant in Elizabethtown, Pennsylvania, and a warehouse in Mechanicsburg, Pennsylvania.

Current Situation

The 1990s and 2000s were times of significant growth for Jordano. Mario and Luigi were still active in the company as president/CEO and chairman of the board, respectively. Revenue now exceeded $600 million per year, and a third plant had been built in the western part of Pennsylvania near Uniontown. A group of professional managers has been developed in the company to head up the major functional areas. Tracie Shannon was hired in 2010 to manage the logistics area which had not received much attention.

Tracie realized that the Jordano brothers had managed and developed the manufacturing and marketing functions during the formative years, and these two areas had been considered as cornerstones of the company's success. Logistics was a relatively new functional area for Jordano, but had received more attention during with Tracie's vision and leadership. The new vision of Susan Weber for SAB had tremendous potential for all members of their supply chain, including Jordano Foods. Now, Tracie has to help orchestrate the transformation of Jordano.

CASE QUESTIONS

1. What is your overall evaluation of the potential for Jordano Foods in this new relationship with SAB? Explain your position.
2. What areas of logistics do you think have the most potential for Jordano and SAB to collaborate for the benefit of SAB's customers? Why?

CASE 3.2

Senco Electronics Company

Senco Electronics Company (Senco) is a U.S.-based manufacturer of personal computers and other electronic equipment. Current assembly operations are still located in the United States and primarily serve the U.S. market. Transportation in the United States from Senco sites to its customers is primarily performed by motor carriers. Rising costs in its U.S. operations caused Senco to evaluate the construction of a new assembly plant in China. Subsequently, Senco decided to also consider Viet Nam. Jim Beierlein, the new executive vice president of supply chain management for Senco, is concerned with how Senco will transport its products from Asia to the United States. "We've had the luxury of a well-developed ground transportation infrastructure in the United States to move our products. Now we will be faced with moving enormous quantities of electronic products across several thousand miles of ocean. We really don't have that much experience with other modes of transportation."

Skip Grenoble, director of logistics for Senco, was called on for his advice. "Obviously, we need to decide on whether to use ocean or air transportation to move our products from the new locations. Air transportation will cost more than ocean but will result in lower inventory costs because of the faster transit times. The opposite is true for ocean transportation. Moving products by air will also result in higher ordering costs since we will be ordering more often for replenishment for our U.S. distribution centers. Using either mode will require some fixed investment in loading/unloading facilities at both the new plant and our U.S. distribution centers. Projected annual demand from the new facility is 2.5 million pounds. However, we expect this demand to grow by 5 percent annually over the next five years. Although the air transportation system appears to be the more expensive option right now, we need to take into consideration our growth and how each mode will help us achieve our profit and service goals." The relevant cost information for each alternative is presented in the following table.

	OCEAN	AIR
Total Transportation costs	$150,000	$290,000
Inventory costs		
Carrying	48,000	23,000
Handling	20,000	22,000
Ordering	7,000	15,000
Fixed cost	600,000	450,000
Total costs	$823,000	$800,000

CASE QUESTIONS

1. If you were Skip Grenoble, which alternative would you advise Jim Beierlein to implement? What criteria would you use to arrive at your decision?
2. At what level of demand (in pounds) per year would these two alternatives be equal?
3. Graphically represent these two alternatives and their tradeoff point.
4. Which alternative would you recommend be in place to accommodate future demand growth? What additional factors should be considered?

APPENDIX 3A

Techniques of Logistics System Analysis

In this section, total cost analysis techniques for logistics are discussed. Only the more basic models are examined; more sophisticated techniques of total cost analysis are discussed later in this text. The basic approaches examined here re-enforce some of the basic concepts discussed thus far and provide a background for much of the material in the remainder of this text.

Short-Run/Static Analysis

One general approach to total cost analysis for logistics is known as **short-run analysis**. In a short-run analysis, a specific point in time or level of production, is chosen and costs are developed for the various logistics cost centers described previously. Multiple short-run analyses would be considered and then the system with the lowest overall cost would be selected, as long as it was consistent with constraints the organization imposed on the logistics area. Some authors refer to this short-run analysis as **static analysis**.

Essentially, they are saying that this method analyzes costs associated with a logistics system's various components at one point in time or one output level.

Example

Table 3A.1 shows an example of static, or short-run, analysis. In this example, an organization is currently using an all-rail route from its plant and the associated plant warehouse to its customers. At the plant warehouse, the chemicals are bagged and palletized and shipped by rail to the customer. A proposed second system would use a market-oriented warehouse. The chemicals would be shipped from the plant to the market warehouse and then packaged and sent to the customer. Instead of shipping all goods by rail, the organization would ship them by barge to the market warehouse, taking advantage of low, bulk transportation prices. Then, after bagging, the chemicals would move by rail from the warehouse to the customer.

In this example, the tradeoff is lower transportation costs versus some increases in storage and warehousing. If the analysis is strictly static (at a specific level of output), the proposed system is more expensive than the current one. So, unless further analysis provided additional information more favorable to the proposed system, the organization would continue with its current system.

However, there are two reasons to favor the proposed system. First, there is no information about customer service requirements. The new market-oriented warehouse might provide better customer service, therefore increasing sales and profits and offsetting some of the higher costs of System 2.

Second, the organization might switch to System 2, even though it is experiencing lower costs with the current system (System 1), because the organization expects System 2 to result in lower costs in the future. This will require the use of dynamic analysis, which is the topic of discussion in the next section.

Table 3A.1	Static Analysis of C&B Chemical Company (50,000 Pounds of Output)	
PLANT LOGISTICS COSTS*	SYSTEM 1	SYSTEM 2
Packaging	$ 500	$ 0
Storage and handling	150	50
Inventory carrying	50	25
Administrative	75	25
Fixed cost	4,200	2,400
Transportation Costs		
To market warehouse	0	150
To customer	800	100
Warehouse Costs		
Packaging	0	500
Storage and handling	0	150
Inventory carrying	0	75
Administrative	0	75
Fixed cost	0	2,400
Total cost	$5,775	$5,950

*All amounts are in thousands of dollars.

Source: Center for Supply Chain Research, Penn State University

Long-Run/Dynamic Analysis

While short-run analysis concentrates on specific time or level of output, **dynamic analysis** examines a logistics system over a long time period or range of output. Using the data from Table 3A.1, a dynamic analysis can be undertaken. The results can be seen in Figure 3A.1. For a mathematical solution, the equation for a straight line is used ($y = a + bx$). In this particular case, a would be the fixed costs of each system, and b would be the variable cost per unit. The x would be the output level. To solve for the output level at which the two systems are equal, an equation for each system is developed and they are set equal to each other in order to solve for x. As shown below, the two systems are equal at 70,588 pounds of output and this becomes the point of indifference. This can also be seen in the graph in Figure 3A.1.

System 1

Total Cost = Fixed Cost + Variable Cost/Unit × Number of Units
$y = \$4,200 + \$0.0315x$

System 2

$y = \$4,800 + \$0.0230x$

Tradeoff point

$\$4,800 + \$0.0230x = \$4,200 + \$0.0315x$
$600 = 0.0085x$
$x = 70,588$ pounds

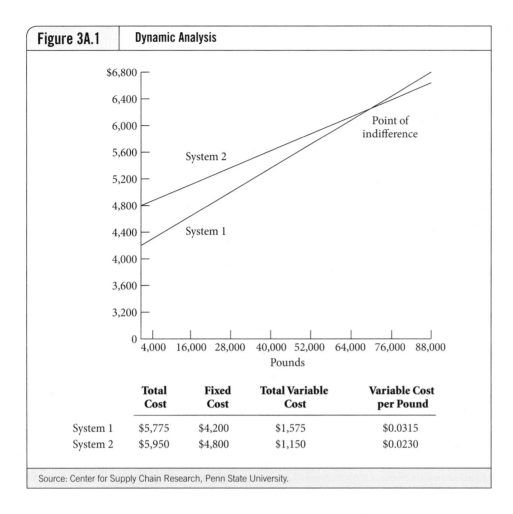

Figure 3A.1 | **Dynamic Analysis**

	Total Cost	Fixed Cost	Total Variable Cost	Variable Cost per Pound
System 1	$5,775	$4,200	$1,575	$0.0315
System 2	$5,950	$4,800	$1,150	$0.0230

Source: Center for Supply Chain Research, Penn State University.

In this case, the organization is better off using System 1 at output levels up to 70,587 pounds. System 2 is less expensive at output levels greater than 70,588. At an output level of 70,588 pounds, both systems produce the same total costs.

A particular organization might consider more than two logistics systems at one time. The same basic methodology can be used for graphing and mathematically solving for the points of indifference regardless of how many systems are analyzed.

APPENDIX 3B

Approaches to Analyzing Logistics Systems

The analysis of logistics systems may require different views or perspectives of logistics activities. The best perspective to take depends on the type of analysis that is needed. For example, if an organization wants to analyze the long-run design of its logistics system, an analysis of logistics that focuses on the network of node and link relationships would probably be most beneficial. On the other hand, if an organization is evaluating a change in a carrier or mode of transportation, it should probably analyze the logistics system in terms of cost centers. In this section, four approaches to analyzing logistics systems are discussed: (1) materials management versus physical distribution, (2) cost centers, (3) nodes versus links, and (4) logistics channels.

Materials Management versus Physical Distribution

The classification of logistics into materials management and physical distribution (inbound and outbound logistics) can be very useful. Frequently, the movement and storage of raw materials is quite different from the movement and storage of finished goods. For example, a drywall manufacturer transports gypsum and other bulk commodities to its plants in rail cars. Storage is very basic and consists of enclosed domes (located outside the plant) with an opening at the top through which the gypsum rock is transferred from the rail cars. Finished goods movement and storage for drywall is different. Transportation is usually provided by specially designed rail cars or flatbed motor carrier vehicles. Storage of the finished drywall product is usually inside the facility where pallets of drywall sheets are stacked and prepared for loading to prevent the drywall from getting wet.

The different logistics requirements that might exist between materials management and physical distribution can have important implications for the logistics system design. Close coordination between materials management and physical distribution is still critical, regardless of the differences.

Cost Centers

Logistics usually includes transportation, warehousing, inventory, materials handling, industrial packaging, etc. By examining these activities as cost centers, tradeoffs between them can be analyzed to determine the overall lowest cost or highest service logistics system, which represents a second approach to logistics system analysis. For example, changing the mode of transportation from rail to motor might result, because of faster, more reliable transit times, and in lower inventory costs that can offset the higher motor carrier price. Table 3B.1 shows that the motor carrier price is higher than rail, but resulting reductions in other costs offsets the higher transportation price. Another example might be increasing the number of warehouses in a logistics system, thereby increasing warehousing and inventory costs but possibly decreasing transportation and lost sales costs. As Table 3B.2 shows, however, this might not result in the lowest cost solution.

Table 3B.1	Analysis of Total Logistics Cost with a Change to a Higher Cost Mode of Transport	
COST CENTERS	RAIL	MOTOR
Transportation	$ 3.00	$ 4.30
Inventory	5.00	3.75
Packaging	3.50	3.20
Warehousing	1.50	0.75
Cost of lost sales	2.00	1.00
Total cost	$15.00*	$13.00*
*Costs per unit.		
Source: Center for Supply Chain Research, Penn State University.		

Table 3B.2	Analysis of Total Logistics Cost with a Change to More Warehouses	
COST CENTERS	SYSTEM 1: THREE WAREHOUSES	SYSTEM 2: FIVE WAREHOUSES
Transportation	$ 850,000	$ 500,000
Inventory	1,500,000	2,000,000
Warehousing	600,000	1,000,000
Cost of lost sales*	350,000	100,000
Total cost	$3,300,000	$3,600,000
*Expected cost based upon probabilities of not having stock/inventory available when customers want it.		
Source: Center for Supply Chain Research, Penn State University.		

Nodes versus Links

A third approach to analyzing logistics systems in an organization is in terms of nodes and links (see Figure 3B.1). The **nodes** are fixed spatial points where goods stop for storage or processing. In other words, nodes are manufacturing/assembling facilities and warehouses where the organization stores materials for conversion into finished products or stores finished products for delivery to the customer (balancing supply and demand).

Links represent the transportation network and connect the nodes in the logistics system. The network can be composed of individual modes of transportation (rail, motor, air, ocean, or pipeline) and of combinations and variations that will be discussed in Chapter 10.

From a node-link perspective, the complexity of logistics systems can vary enormously. A node system might use a simple link from suppliers to a combined plant and warehouse and then to customers in a relatively small market area. At the other end of the spectrum

Figure 3B.1	Nodes and Links in a Logistics System

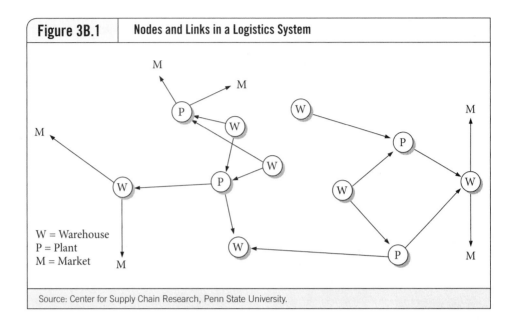

W = Warehouse
P = Plant
M = Market

Source: Center for Supply Chain Research, Penn State University.

are large, multiple-product organizations with multiple plant and warehouse locations. The complex transportation networks of the latter can include three or four different modes and perhaps private as well as for-hire transportation.

The node-link perspective, in allowing analysis of a logistics system's two basic elements, represents a convenient basis for seeking possible system improvements. As has been noted, the complexity of a logistics system often relates directly to the various time and distance relationships between the nodes and the links and to the regularity, predictability, and volume of flow of goods entering, leaving, and moving within the system.

Logistics Channels

A final approach to logistics system analysis is the **logistics channel**, or supply chain of network organizations engaged in transfer, storage, handling, communication, and other functions that contribute to the efficient flow of goods.

The logistics channel can be simple or complex. Figure 3B.2 shows a simple channel in which an individual producer deals directly with a final customer. The control in this channel is relatively simple. The individual manufacturer controls the logistics flow since it deals directly with the customer.

Figure 3B.3 presents a more complex, multi-echelon channel, with a market warehouse and retailers. The market warehouse could be a public warehouse. In this instance, the control is more difficult because of the additional storage and transportation provided by third-party organizations.

Figure 3B.4 illustrates a complex, comprehensive channel. In this instance, the task of achieving an effective logistics flow in the channel is far more challenging. This figure very realistically portrays the situation confronting many large organizations operating globally.

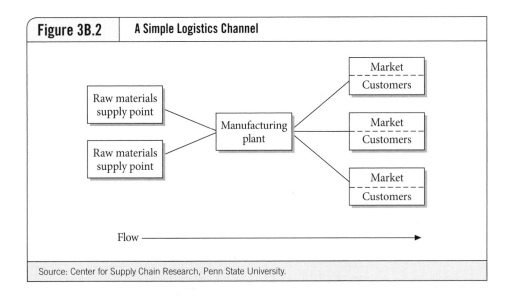

Figure 3B.2 | **A Simple Logistics Channel**

Source: Center for Supply Chain Research, Penn State University.

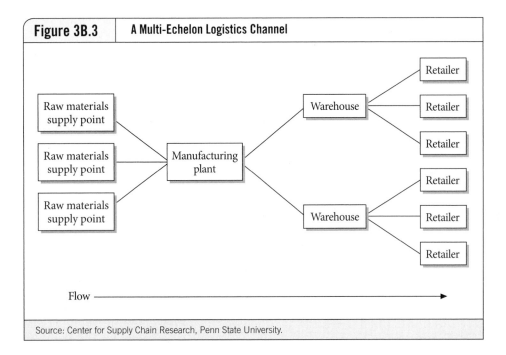

Figure 3B.3 | **A Multi-Echelon Logistics Channel**

Source: Center for Supply Chain Research, Penn State University.

Figure 3B.4 | A Complex Logistics Channel

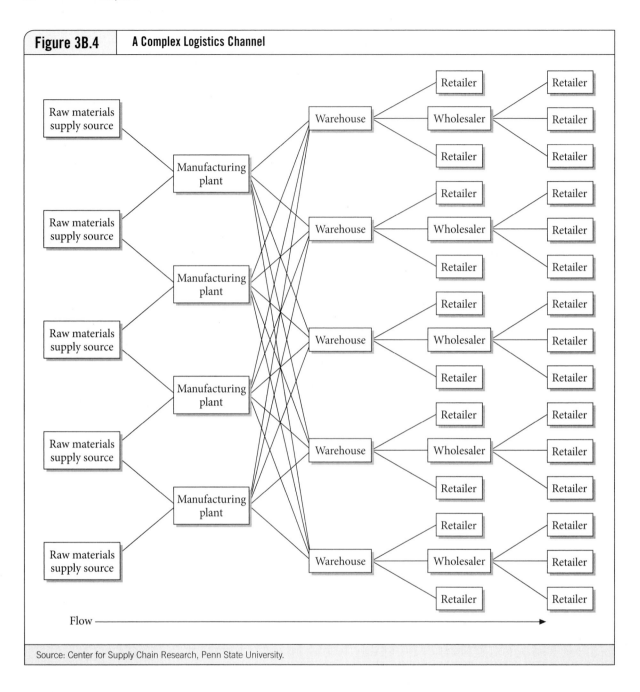

Source: Center for Supply Chain Research, Penn State University.

Some instances involving production of a basic good like steel, aluminum, or chemicals might further complicate the situation because organizations might be a part of more than one supply chain or channel. For example, the steel might be sold to auto manufacturers, container manufacturers, or file cabinet producers. Duplication of storage facilities, small-shipment transportation, conflict over mode choices, and other problems might contribute to inefficiencies in the channel. Communications problems might also exist.

Chapter 4

DISTRIBUTION AND OMNI-CHANNEL NETWORK DESIGN

Learning Objectives

After reading this chapter, you should be able to do the following:

- Recognize the critical need to evaluate the structure and functioning of supply chain networks, and for making changes and improvements as appropriate.

- Utilize an effective process for supply chain network design.

- Be aware of key locational determinants, both regional/national/global and site-specific, and the impacts they may have on prospective location alternatives.

- Understand the different types of modeling approaches that may be used to gain insight into supply chain network design and facility location decision making.

- Apply the simple grid or center-of-gravity approach to facility location, and understand how various factors may affect the location decision.

- Differentiate between a marketing channel and a logistics channel.

- Understand the relevance of "omni-channel" supply chain strategies and their impacts on the structures and functioning of supply chains.

- Become aware of contemporary examples of how firms are responding to the challenges of omni-channel distribution.

Supply Chain Profile — *Why is Tennessee a Hotbed for Manufacturing?*

A lot of big-name companies are flocking to Tennessee. Within the past year, Volkswagen AG opened a $1 billion plant in Chattanooga, and Nissan Motor Company announced it will be building Mercedes-Benz engines for the first time in the United States. Meanwhile, Whirlpool Corp.'s new plant is pursuing LEED Gold certification and Bridgestone Metalpha U.S.A. Inc. expanded to enable a 10% increase in daily output. They join fellow manufacturers Johnson Controls Inc., Dana Holding Corp., Procter & Gamble Co., and others.

The auto sector remains dominant. In fact, Tennessee sits at the No. 8 spot in auto production, and the industry accounts for 34% of manufacturing jobs with 105,000 employees. Adding up original equipment manufacturers (OEMs), suppliers, and ancillary manufacturers, there are 864 auto-related companies in Tennessee.

STRENGTHENING U.S. BASE

Tennessee seems to be cashing in on the trend of non-U.S.-based companies to produce locally for the huge U.S. consumer market. Explaining Volkswagen's decision to locate in Tennessee, back in 2008, Stefan Jacoby, CEO of Volkswagen Group of America, said: "Today's decision is a fundamental part of our new strategic direction in the U.S."

Whirlpool echoed that sentiment last year. "Our $120 million investment in Cleveland, Tenn., is the largest single investment we've ever made anywhere in the world and reinforces our commitment to the competitiveness of U.S. manufacturing," said Jeff Fettig, CEO of Whirlpool Corp.

SUPPORTING EXISTING OPERATIONS

Nissan chose to build upon its past success in the state. "There's no better plant to rise to the challenge than our top-quality manufacturing operations in Smyrna," said Bill Krueger, vice chairman, Nissan Americas.

A contributing factor to the high quality of manufacturing is the level of workforce skills. "My top priority is for Tennessee to be the No. 1 location in the Southeast for high-quality jobs," said Tennessee Gov. Bill Haslam. "Our Jobs4TN plan is a blueprint for doing just that. By leveraging our existing assets in each region, we will be able to attract new businesses to the state while helping our existing businesses expand and remain competitive. We will also be making significant investments in innovation to position Tennessee as a national leader well into the future."

As always, cooperation between private and public enterprises is essential to both attracting and keeping companies. "We need to be competitive, prepared for growth and have the incentive packages ready to bring to the table. Fortunately, we have business and government leaders in this community who understand this," explains James Chavez, CEO of the Clarksville-Montgomery County Economic Development Council.

Source: Adapted from Adrienne Selko, "Why is Tennessee a Hotbed for Manufacturing?", *Industry Week*, June 18, 2012. Reprinted with permission.

4-1 Introduction

As firms continue to search for new ways to lower costs and improve service to their customers, the issue of where to locate logistics and manufacturing facilities has never been more complex or more critical. In addition to enhancing the efficiency and effectiveness of a supply chain operation, the redesign of a firm's overall network can help to differentiate a firm in the marketplace, thus creating a new form of competitive advantage. Considering the increasingly dynamic aspects of today's business world, companies are continually seeking new and improved approaches to network design and operation. Several examples illustrate this type of success:

- A major home improvement retailer created a nationwide network of 18 specialty warehouses. These so-called "rapid deployment centers" were strategically located and were designed to increase the efficiency of restocking store shelves and the delivery of products like generators, snow blowers, and plywood to areas hit hard by damaging weather. The strategy resulted in faster and cheaper supply chain capabilities.

- A leading pharmaceutical distributor with nationwide service significantly reduced its total number of distribution centers, while offering its customers a selection of service responses from which to choose (e.g., same-day delivery, regular service, and so on).

- A prominent office products company shrunk its network of distribution facilities from 11 to 3, while substantially increasing the level of cross-docking activity with its customers and significantly improving logistical customer service.

- As a result of the merger of two large grocery industry manufacturers, the combined logistics network consisted of 54 distribution centers across the United States. Following careful study and analysis, with a look to the future, the company consolidated its network into 15 strategically located facilities. This move significantly reduced the company's overall logistics costs and improved service to its customers.

- A well-known consumer products retailer developed a very large import distribution center to accommodate inbound shipments of products from its global manufacturing sites.

- A major provider of global contract logistics services was tasked with designing a single distribution center that would allow a European manufacturer to consolidate multiple distribution centers into one. The economics of the single, new facility, coupled with significantly enhanced fulfillment of customer orders, resulted in improved market share and improved profitability for the manufacturing client.

- A global semiconductor products manufacturer consolidated its logistics network into a single, global distribution center in Singapore and engaged a third-party supplier of express logistics services to manage its overall distribution activity. The end results included lower cost, improved service, and a new way for the firm to differentiate itself in the marketplace.

As levels of international trade fluctuate, this is accompanied by changing volumes of freight shipped to and from various global port facilities. These variations frequently have significant impacts on the structure and functioning of global supply chains, and the relative roles of various alternative port facilities.

While there are also examples of the opposite situation, in which firms have justifiably expanded their logistics networks and increased the number of distribution facilities, the move to consolidate existing systems is far more prevalent. Assuming that a firm considers the impact of such a decision on total supply chain costs, it is not unusual for the inventory cost savings associated with consolidating facilities to outweigh any additional transportation expense involved with moving product to the customer. Also, the use of currently available information technologies, coupled with the increasingly time-sensitive capabilities of many suppliers of transportation service, can enhance responsiveness and the levels of service experienced by customers.

This chapter first looks at several strategic aspects of supply chain network design. While it may sometimes be that "change for the sake of change" is helpful, a number of prominent factors may suggest that a redesign of the network may be necessary. Next, the process of supply chain network redesign is examined in detail. This content provides a useful framework for understanding the key steps that must be included in a comprehensive approach to network design and facility location.

Following these discussions, attention shifts to several major locational determinants. These factors may be either regionally focused or site-specific. Also included is a summary of current trends governing site selection. The chapter content on network design concludes with coverage of several modeling approaches that can be used to provide insight into the issues of supply chain network design and facility location.

Chapter 4 also provides valuable perspectives on the increasingly-relevant topic of omni-channel supply chain strategies. In addition to details relating to the overall topic of omni-channel, this chapter also considers the network design issues that can facilitate successful implementation of this concept.

4-2 The Need for Long-Range Planning

In the short term, a firm's supply chain network and the locations of its key facilities are relatively fixed, and the logistics managers must operate within the constraints imposed by the facility locations. Site availability, leases, contracts, and investments make changing facility locations impractical in the short term. In the long term, however, the design of the overall network must be thought of as variable. Management decisions can and should be made to change the network to meet the logistics requirements imposed by customers, suppliers, competitive changes, and the realities of the supply chain itself.

In addition, the decisions as to network design and facility location that are made today will have implications far into the future. A facility properly located under today's economic, competitive, and technological conditions may not continue to be at an optimum location as future conditions change. Also, today's facility location decision will have a significant effect on future costs in such areas as logistics, marketing, manufacturing, and finance. Thus, the facility location decision must seriously consider anticipated business conditions and acknowledge a critical need to be flexible and responsive to customer needs as they may change in the future. This latter concern heightens the attractiveness of the third-party logistics option for many logistics operations today.

4-2-1 The Strategic Importance of Supply Chain Network Design

Why analyze the supply chain network? In essence, the answer lies in the fact that all businesses operate in a very dynamic environment in which change is the only constant. Characteristics of consumer and industrial-buyer demand, technology, competition, markets, and suppliers are constantly changing. As a result, businesses must redeploy their resources in response to and in anticipation of this ever-changing environment.

Considering the rate at which change is occurring, it is questionable whether any existing supply chain network can be truly up to date. Any network that has been in existence for a number of years is certainly a candidate for reevaluation and potential redesign. Even if the existing system is not functionally obsolete, an analysis of the existing network will probably uncover new opportunities to reduce cost and/or improve service.

This section focuses on several types of change that may suggest a need to reevaluate and/or redesign a firm's logistics network. While not all of these factors will affect any single firm at the same time, they represent some of the more frequently changing elements of the business environment that affect logistics and supply chain management.

4-2-2 Changes to Global Trade Patterns

With the passage of time, it is easy to see significant changes in the patterns of global trade. This is due to the economies of regions and countries being dynamic and subject to continual change. An example of this would be currency fluctuations that are responsible for products and commodities being at times cheaper in certain parts of the world, and at other times more expensive. This factor alone will have major impacts on global sourcing strategies, as organizations pursue the best value in procuring items to meet their business needs. This factor similarly impacts consumption, as consumers will be attracted to buy certain items where and when they can get the best deal. Some of the factors that need to be considered include:

- Currency exchange rates
- Volumes of commerce between and within regions/countries of the world
- Abilities of regions/countries to have ample availability of needed items for shipment to global locations
- Global transportation infrastructure necessary to physically move items from where they are available to where they are needed
- Balance or lack of balance in global trade lanes (i.e., relates to the issues of supply and demand for global logistics and transportation services)

4-2-3 Changing Customer Service Requirements

The logistical requirements of customers are changing in numerous ways, and so the need to reevaluate and redesign supply chain networks is of great contemporary interest. While some customers have intensified their demands for more efficient and low-cost logistics services, others are seeking relationships with suppliers who can take logistical capabilities and performance to new, unprecedented levels.

While customer service requirements may be subject to change, the types of customers served may also evolve over time. Consider, for example, the case of food manufacturers that have distributed their product to independent stores and regional retail chains for many years and recently added warehouse clubs and online retailers to their list of customers. In these examples, change has occurred at both the customer and supply chain levels, with significant impacts on lead times, order size and frequency, and associated activities such as shipment notification, marking and tagging, and packaging.

One recent development of significance is that of "omni-channel" supply chains, that characteristically make products available to purchasers through multiple supply chains (e.g., traditional retail store, catalog sales, internet sales, etc.). As indicated previously, the concept of omni-channel has become so relevant to the business models of an increasing number of firms, that it is covered in-depth in the latter part of this chapter.

4-2-4 Shifting Locations of Customer and/or Supply Markets

Considering that manufacturing and logistics facilities are positioned in the supply chain between customer and supply markets, any changes in these markets should cause a firm to reevaluate its supply chain. With the increasing globalization of the world's economies, for example, many organizations find it necessary to identify global strategies relating to network design. Essentially, this highlights the need to have multiple facilities at strategic locations around the world, but also to develop operational protocols that will clarify how these disparate facilities need to work together. On the supply side, the service and cost requirements of the automobile industry's movement to just-in-time (JIT)-based manufacturing have forced companies to examine the locations of logistics facilities. Many product suppliers to the automotive industry, for example, have selected nearby points for manufacturing and/or parts distribution facilities. Considering the growing, global nature of parts sourcing, automotive industry firms are also focusing on streamlining their global supply chains to achieve objectives relating to efficiency and effectiveness.

Also on the global scene, there is great interest in leveraging the capabilities of emerging markets to help achieve global supply chain and overall business objectives. In addition to reconfiguring overall supply chain networks, firms doing business in emerging markets have taken steps such as establishing branch operations in these newly popular geographies and entering into joint agreements with companies that are located in and already have a significant business presence in these areas.

4-2-5 Change in Corporate Ownership/Merger and Acquisition Activity

A relatively common occurrence today is for a firm to experience a change-in control of ownership associated with a merger, an acquisition, or a divestiture. In such instances, many companies choose to be proactive and to conduct a formal evaluation of new versus previous supply chain networks in advance of such a change. This is very helpful in terms of making sure that the newly merged or newly independent firm will have fully anticipated the logistics and supply chain impacts of the change in corporate ownership. In other instances, those having management responsibility for logistics and supply chain activities may be the last ones to find out about the impending change, and the role of network design immediately takes on a defensive posture.

Even if these logistics impacts are not part of the planning process, it is critical for firms to reassess their supply chain networks following ownership-related changes such as those identified in the preceding paragraph. Without sufficient advance planning, such changes increase the likelihood that the new operation is duplicating effort and incurring unnecessary logistics expense.

Examples of mergers/acquisitions that over time have had significant implications for supply chain network design include the acquisition of GlaxoSmithKline by Novartis AG.; Reynolds America buying Lorillard; Comcast Acquisition of Time Warner Cable; and previously the merger of two large petroleum-industry companies to form Exxon Mobil Corporation. Also, the spin-off by Kraft Foods of its snack foods product lines into Mondelez International had significant impacts on the supply chains of both of these organizations.

4-2-6 Cost Pressures

A major imperative for many firms today is to figure out new and innovative ways to take cost out of their key business processes, including those relating to logistics and supply chain management. In such instances, a reevaluation of the logistics network and the functioning of the overall supply chain can frequently help to uncover new sources of such savings. Whether the answer lies in reducing cost of transportation, inventory, warehousing, or another area, a detailed examination of the current system versus alternative approaches can be exceptionally useful.

On a global basis, labor wage rates have had a significant impact on the location of manufacturing and logistics operations. In recent history, economic activity has evolved to lower wage rate locations such as the BRIC countries (Brazil, Russia, India, and China), while contemporary areas of global interest include countries such as the VISTA countries (Vietnam, Indonesia, South Africa, Turkey, and Argentina). An interesting example of the movement to new global locations was the opening in 2010 of a billion-dollar plant in Vietnam by U.S.-based chip maker Intel. This facility was the biggest in the world, and expected to create thousands of skilled jobs as Vietnam moves from low-tech to hi-tech.[1]

One of the direct results of successful expansion of economic activity in emerging markets is that wage rates tend to rise due to supply and demand for labor. But with the standard of living rising so quickly and the size of the available labor force shrinking rapidly in low-cost countries like China, wages are rising rapidly. In China specifically, wage growth rates have recently far outpaced the growth rates seen in the United States. As such, portions of the marginal manufacturing capacity are reshoring to the United States.[2] As a caution however, and given the volatility of international business and trade flows, future trends relating to location of manufacturing, sourcing, and marketing-based facilities also may exhibit significant change.

Companies considering plant modernization needs sometimes benefit from a comprehensive cost analysis which might accompany a reevaluation of the logistics network. A firm considering an investment of millions of dollars in an existing plant must ask, "Is this the proper location for a plant, given the current and future customer and vendor locations?"

4-2-7 Competitive Capabilities

Another factor relates to competitive pressures that may force a company to examine its logistics service levels and the costs generated by its network of logistics facilities. To remain competitive in the marketplace or to develop a competitive advantage, a company should frequently examine the relative locations of its facilities toward the goal of improving service and/or lowering costs. Companies often conduct this network review in light of newly developed transportation capabilities that may enhance the ability to serve customers in certain areas.

For example, many firms locate distribution facilities near the hub operations of companies such as FedEx and UPS so that access to time-critical, express transportation services will be facilitated. This strategy is particularly appropriate for inventories of high-value, time-sensitive products that may need to be shipped on a moment's notice. The resulting service levels are higher, and the total cost of the comprehensive, express logistics services is lower than the total cost of warehousing the needed inventories at various locations throughout the company's logistics network. Essentially, the centralization of such inventories at strategically selected locations reduces the overall cost of logistics and significantly improves responsiveness in terms of delivery times. Additionally, the same result may be achieved through the use of a high-quality logistics provider, such as Forward Air Corporation, that specializes in airport-to-airport transportation of service-sensitive shipments and other value-added logistics solutions and logistics services.[3]

4-2-8 Corporate Organizational Change

It is not unusual for supply chain network design to become a topic of discussion at the same time that a firm considers any major corporate organizational change, such as downsizing. In such instances, the strategic functioning of the firm's logistics network is viewed as something that must be protected and even enhanced through the process of organizational change.

4-3 Supply Chain Network Design

An organization must consider many factors as it approaches the task of determining the optimum design of its supply chain network. These factors are identified and discussed at a later point in this chapter. At the outset, however, it is important to realize that the task of designing an appropriate supply chain network should be coordinated closely with the corporate and overall business strategies that may be in place. Since the process of designing or redesigning a firm's supply chain network can be complex, it is discussed in the context of a major supply chain transformation process.

Figure 4.1 identifies the six major steps that are recommended for a comprehensive supply chain network design process. Each of these steps is discussed in detail in the following paragraphs.

Figure 4.1   Supply Chain Network Design Process

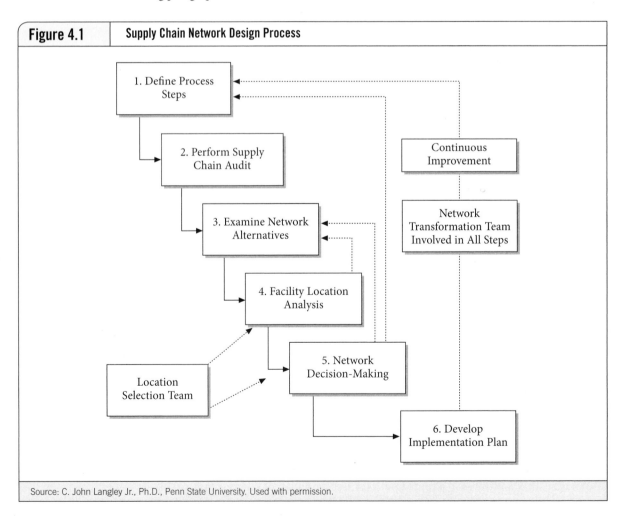

Source: C. John Langley Jr., Ph.D., Penn State University. Used with permission.

4-3-1 Step 1: Define the Supply Chain Network Design Process

Of initial importance is the formation of a supply chain network transformation team to be responsible for all elements of the network design process. This team will first need to become aware of overall corporate and business strategies and the underlying business needs of the firm and the supply chains in which it is a participant.

Also in this step, it is important to establish the parameters and objectives of the network design or redesign process itself. An awareness of the expectations of senior management, for example, is essential to the effective progress of the overall improvement process. Issues pertaining to the availability of needed resources in the areas of funding, people, and systems must be understood at an early stage in the process.

An additional topic to be addressed early on is the potential involvement of third-party suppliers of logistics services as a means of achieving the firm's logistics objectives. This consideration is critical, since it will expand the mindset of the network design team to include a consideration of supply chain network solutions that may involve externally provided as well as internally available logistics resources.

4-3-2 Step 2: Perform a Supply Chain Audit

The supply chain audit provides members of the transformation team with a comprehensive perspective on the firm's logistics process. In addition, it helps to gather essential types of information that will be useful throughout future steps in the redesign process. Figure 4.2 indicates a number of key steps that should be included in a supply chain audit. Listed here are examples of the types of information that should become available as a result of this audit:

- Customer requirements and key environmental factors
- Key logistics goals and objectives
- Profile of the current supply chain network and the firm's positioning in respective supply chain(s)
- Understanding of key supply chain activities and processes
- Benchmark, or target, values for supply chain costs and key performance measurements

Figure 4.2	Key Steps in a Supply Chain Audit

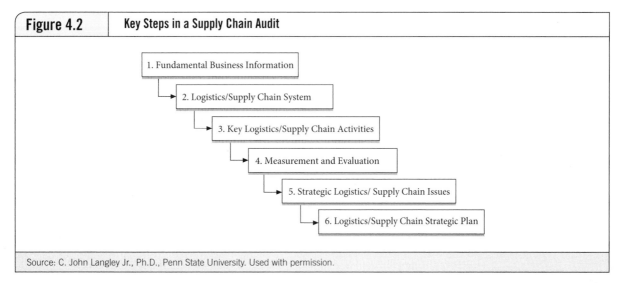

1. Fundamental Business Information
2. Logistics/Supply Chain System
3. Key Logistics/Supply Chain Activities
4. Measurement and Evaluation
5. Strategic Logistics/ Supply Chain Issues
6. Logistics/Supply Chain Strategic Plan

Source: C. John Langley Jr., Ph.D., Penn State University. Used with permission.

- Identification of gaps between current and desired supply chain performance (qualitative and quantitative)
- Key objectives for supply chain network design, expressed in terms that will facilitate measurement

4-3-3 Step 3: Examine the Supply Chain Network Alternatives

The next step is to examine the available alternatives for configuration of the supply chain that includes identifying suitable locations for manufacturing, logistics, and distribution facilities, etc. This involves applying suitable quantitative models to the current logistics system as well as to the alternative systems and approaches under consideration. The use of these models provides considerable insight into the functioning and cost/service effectiveness of the various possible networks. Essentially, the principal modeling approach will be optimization, simulation, heuristic, or some combination of these three approaches that are explored in detail later in this chapter. Briefly, optimization approaches search for "best" solutions, simulation models replicate the functioning of the supply chain network, and heuristic techniques are able to accommodate broad problem definitions but do not provide optimum solutions.

Once an appropriate modeling procedure has been selected, it should be used to help identify a supply chain network that is consistent with the key objectives identified during the audit phase. Although, transformation teams often look to the model to suggest answers to the key questions that have been raised, they quickly realize that the modeling effort is likely to produce more insight than answers, and also additional questions that need to be answered.

Following the identification of preliminary design solutions, subsequent "what-if" types of analysis should be conducted to test the sensitivity of recommended network designs to changes in key variables (e.g., transportation rates, distribution center costs, distances to customer and supplier locations, etc.). The results of this step should provide a useful set of recommendations for the number and general location of logistics facilities that will help to meet the desired objectives.

Also, at this point in the design process, it is critical to understand the geographical parameters of the supply chain under study. Although historically a domestic or regional perspective has been the focus of many network design projects to date, there are an increasing number of projects in which a multinational or global perspective is what is needed. State-of-the-art network design processes are currently capable of dealing with the supply chain needs of this broader geographical setting.

4-3-4 Step 4: Conduct a Facility Location Analysis

Once a general configuration of the desired supply chain network has been recommended, the next task is to carefully analyze the attributes of specific regions and locales that are candidates for sites of logistics facilities, distribution centers, cross-docking operations, etc. These analyses will have both quantitative and qualitative aspects. Many of the quantitative elements have already been incorporated into Step 3 of the modeling effort. The qualitative aspects, to be discussed in a later section of this chapter, include such considerations as labor climate, transportation issues, proximity to markets and customers, quality of life, taxes and industrial development incentives, supplier networks, land costs and utilities, overall supply chain and logistics infrastructure, and company preference.

The effort in this step will be facilitated by the formation of a location selection team that will collect information on specific attributes of acceptable locations such as those identified earlier. In addition, this team should be able to examine potential sites in terms of local factors such as topography, geology, and facility design. To supplement internally available resources, the firm may wish to engage the services of a consulting firm that specializes in assisting clients with the process of selecting a location.

The first screening by the location selection team usually eliminates areas that are uneconomical from a logistics perspective, thereby reducing the number of alternatives. For example, consider the number of potential distribution center sites in the southeastern United States. Applying the supply chain location determinant, the team may find that the optimum location is in the Tennessee/Georgia area. This definitely reduces the number of potential sites and enables the team to direct the location analysis toward a specific area. Or, if the decision situation is in more a global setting, the initial screening may focus attention on potential locations in the South China area, or perhaps Vietnam, with further resolution to be provided through more in-depth analysis.

4-3-5 Step 5: Make Decisions Regarding Network and Facility Location

Next, the network and specific sites for logistics facilities recommended in Steps 3 and 4 should be evaluated for consistency with the design criteria that were identified in Step 1. This step should confirm the types of change that are needed to the firm's logistics network and should do so in the context of overall supply chain positioning. Although the feasibility of involving third-party suppliers should have been incorporated into the alternatives that were evaluated in the two preceding steps, the decision to involve external suppliers will have cost and service implications as well as strategic ones.

4-3-6 Step 6: Develop an Implementation Plan

Once the overall direction has been established, the development of an effective implementation plan, or "blueprint for change," is critical. This plan should serve as a useful road map for moving from the current supply chain network to the desired new one. Since it was known from the beginning that this transformation process was likely to produce recommendations for significant change, it is important that the firm commit the resources necessary to assure a smooth, timely implementation, and the continuous improvement of the network decisions that will have been made.

4-4 Major Locational Determinants

The focus of Step 4 in the supply chain network redesign process is on analyzing the attributes of specific regions and areas that are candidates for sites of logistics facilities. Table 4.1 lists a number of major locational determinants for global/national/regional and site-specific locations. While these factors are listed in general order of importance, the relative weighting applied to each depends on the details of the specific location decision under consideration.

The importance of major locational determinants varies among industries and among individual companies within specific industries. For example, labor-intensive industries such as textiles, furniture, and household appliances place significant emphasis on the

Table 4.1	Major Locational Determinants
BROAD GEOGRAPHIC VS. SITE-SPECIFIC	**LOCATIONAL DETERMINANTS**
Global/National/Regional Determinants	• Labor climate • Transportation services and infrastructure • Proximity to markets and customers • Quality of life • Taxes and industrial development incentives • Supplier networks • Land costs and utilities • IT infrastructure • Company preference

Site-Specific Determinants	• Transportation access
	   — Truck
	   — Air
	   — Rail
	   — Water
	• Inside/outside metropolitan area
	• Availability of workforce and needed skill sets
	• Land costs and taxes
	• Utilities

Source: C. John Langley Jr., Ph.D., Penn State University. Used with permission.

availability and cost of labor in both regional and local market areas. Alternatively, manufacturers of high-tech products such as computers and peripherals, semiconductors, and engineering and scientific instruments place great emphasis on ensuring the availability of a highly qualified workforce with very specific technical skills and, as discussed earlier, proximity to supplier and customer markets. For industries such as drugs, beverages, and printing and publishing, in which competition or logistics costs are significant, other logistics variables are critical.

4-4-1 Key Factors for Consideration

This discussion focuses attention on the regional determinants shown in Table 4.1. Because the site-specific determinants cannot be generalized as readily, this level of detail should be acquired and evaluated through the efforts of the location selection team.

4-4-1-1 Labor Climate

Location decision makers consider a number of factors in determining the labor climate of an area, region, or country. Given the typically labor-intensive nature of many supply chain operations, the cost and availability of labor are major issues of concern. Other factors to be considered include the workforce's degree of unionization, skill level, work ethic, productivity, and the enthusiasm of local public officials. The existence of right-to-work laws in certain states (which prohibit union membership as a condition of employment) and the unionization of major area employers reveal the area workforce's degree of unionization. Government information regarding work stoppages, productivity (value added per employee), and skill levels is available for most areas. Data regarding hourly earnings by industry and occupation are available from governmental agencies.

Another labor-related factor to be considered is the rate of unemployment in the local areas under consideration. While many other factors may seem to be quite acceptable, low levels of unemployment may require a firm to significantly increase its projected hourly wage scales to attract qualified workers. This sometimes unexpected increase may affect the overall attractiveness of a particular local area under consideration. The location study team will need to visit areas of potential interest to gather impressions and study attitudes regarding work ethic, absenteeism, potential labor-management issues, and the cooperativeness of state and local public officials.

4-4-1-2 Transportation Services and Infrastructure

The need by many firms for high-quality, capable transportation services is of great significance in many location decisions. Depending on the product type and industry to be served, a suitable location may require one or more of the following features: interstate highway access, availability of intermodal or local rail facilities, convenience of a major airport facility, proximity to inland or ocean port facilities, and so on. The number of serving carriers and the breadth of overall transport capabilities are factors that may need to be evaluated. Availability of capable transportation services and issues relating to transportation infrastructure may vary widely among regions of the world. In China, for example, investments in transportation infrastructure have been a key priority since they are viewed as being needed to sustain economic development.[4] For this reason, this topic deserves very deliberate and careful consideration in any network design decision.

Considering the significant service improvements that have been made in recent years by many transportation firms, most regional and local areas are strong in at least one or more areas related to transportation. For certain high-value, low-weight products, such as computers, semiconductors, and electronic equipment, the location decision may focus on identifying a single national or international geographical area from which to distribute the company's entire manufactured output. Given the time-sensitive logistics services available today from firms such as FedEx, UPS, DHL, and the postal services of many countries, this strategy is becoming more prevalent.

On a global basis, it is also important to assess the infrastructure capabilities of various geographies and countries. For example, the logistics and transportation road structure in China is continually improving, whereas there are longer-lasting highway deficiencies in parts of India that would be a relevant factor in a supply chain location decision.

4-4-1-3 Proximity to Markets and Customers

The nearness-to-market factor usually considers both logistics and competitive variables. Logistics variables include the availability of transportation, freight cost, and the geographical market size that can be served, for example, on a same-day or next-morning basis. The greater the number of customer firms within the market area, the greater the competitive advantage offered by the proposed location.

Although many companies place a high priority on locating logistics facilities near markets and customers, an overly complex supply chain network can be disadvantageous from a cost perspective. Also, the availability of high-quality transportation services and capable information technologies has resulted in an expansion of the geographical areas that can be served in a timely manner from key logistics facilities. In an extended sense, this has resulted in the enhanced role of global sourcing and global marketing, depending on the service needs of customers. Today's global supply chain capabilities may be enhanced to meet even more rigorous service levels that are established and expected by customers.

4-4-1-4 Quality of Life

A particular region's or area's quality of life is difficult to quantify, but it does affect the well-being of employees and the quality of work they are expected to perform. The quality-of-life factor is more important to companies that must attract and retain a mobile professional and technical workforce capable of moving to any location. Such a situation is common in the high-tech industry, especially in a company's research and development operations. The *Places Rated Almanac*[5] rates the quality of life in metropolitan areas in terms of climate, housing costs, health care and environment, crime, passenger transportation, education, recreation, the arts, and economic opportunities. Another useful source of information is *Cities Ranked and Rated*.[6]

4-4-1-5 Taxes and Industrial Development Incentives

It is important to have advance knowledge of state and local taxes that apply to businesses and individuals. Prevailing business taxes, including revenue or income taxes, inventory taxes, property taxes, and so on, will have a significant impact on the cost of operating a business in the area under consideration. Personal taxes that may affect the attractiveness of a particular region or local area include taxes on income and property, as well as applicable sales taxes, excise taxes, and so forth.

Another significant factor is the availability of industrial development incentives that are used to entice companies to locate in a particular area. Examples include tax incentives (reduced rates or tax abatements on property, inventory, sales, etc.), financing arrangements (state loans or state-guaranteed loans), reduced water and sewage rates, and rent-free buildings that are built by the community to the company's specifications. Most countries, states, provinces, cities, etc., have an industrial development commission that provides information about state and local inducements. In addition, early contact and discussions with representatives of the state and local-area banking institutions and financial communities will provide a wide range of useful information, as well as commitments regarding financing and other services.

A very interesting global example of the use of tax preferences and industrial development incentives is that of the Shanghai Waigaoqiao Free Trade Zone, located in the Northeast of Pudong District, Shanghai, China.[7] This facility was established in 1990, and was the first free trade zone to be established in China. This FTZ, which was incorporated as part of the newly-developed China (Shanghai) pilot free-trade zone on September 29, 2013, includes total space of 10,000 square kilometers. Its customers include companies such as Intel, Hewlett-Packard, Philips, IBM, and Emerson Electric. Interestingly, companies locating in the Waigaoqiao Free Trade Zone were given five years of preferential tax treatment, so instead of paying the corporate tax rate of 15 percent, the tax rate to have been paid started at 8 percent and increased over the five-year period to the full 15 percent.

In 2014, The BMW Group announced plans to build a new plant in San Luis Potosi, Mexico. This decision was in-line with BMW's strategic policy of ensuring globally-balanced growth, and of continuing its practice of "production follows the market." According to BMW, this decision underscores its commitment to the NAFTA region, and involves an investment of $1 billion over the next several years. BMW anticipates opening the plant in 2019, when the workforce is expected to reach 1,500 people. The large numbers of international free trade agreements within the NAFTA area, and with the European Union and the MERCOSUR member states, for example, were decisive factors in the choices of location. Other crucial advantages were the highly-qualified local workforce, a solid network of established suppliers and the well-developed infrastructure.[8]

On the Line
Supply Chain Managers Target U.S. Cities for Onshoring Opportunities

Many mid-size U.S. cities and other areas now make attractive alternatives to India and other offshore locations for companies considering consolidating finance, IT, and other business services operations for shared service or global business services centers, according to new research from The Hackett Group, Inc.

The research found that the diminishing gap in labor costs, combined with factors such as lower turnover rates, greater business knowledge, proximity to customers and headquarters, and state tax incentives has created conditions where many companies are now seriously considering U.S. locations, particularly for centers handling complex and higher-value processes.

Verizon Communications is one of many companies that has made the decision to locate business services operations domestically, consolidating nearly 1,500 finance operations staff into two U.S. service centers over the past two years.

The Hackett Group's Global Business Services Executive Advisory program developed the research that provides detailed rankings for more than 30 cities across the United States, based on a weighted mix of factors. Top 10 cities in the research are Syracuse, NY; Jacksonville, FL; Tampa, FL; Lansing, MI; Grand Rapids, MI; Atlanta, GA; Allentown, PA; Green Bay, WI; Richmond, VA; and Longmont, CO.

Previous research by The Hackett Group has found that while offshoring has led to a dramatic decline in the number of corporate IT, finance, procurement, and HR jobs in the United States, the number of new business services jobs moving offshore has declined steadily over the past few years and will continue to do so, as companies reach the practical limits of the type of work in these areas that can be effectively offshored.

"Companies are realizing that the United States is becoming an increasingly viable option for elements of their service delivery organization, and we're seeing real growth in this sector, with nearly 700 U.S. centers of excellence, shared service centers, and global business services operations now up and running," said The Hackett Group Principal and Global Finance Executive Advisory Practice Leader Jim O'Connor.

He adds that labor and operating costs are still high in the United States compared to eastern Europe, Latin America, and Asia. But the gap is shrinking, and there are significant other benefits.

"In more and more cases, those benefits outweigh the additional cost. In addition, the public response to offshoring has made keeping jobs 'at home' an attractive option for U.S. companies," he says.

Source: Patrick Burnson, Executive Editor, *Logistics Management and Supply Chain Management Review*, May 26, 2015.

4-4-1-6 Supplier Networks

In the case of a manufacturing facility, the availability and cost of raw materials and component parts, as well as the cost of transporting these materials to the proposed plant site are of significance. For a distribution center, it is important to know how the proposed facility sites will fit with the geographic locations of key supplier facilities. To best understand feasible solutions to these types of problems, the cost and service sensitivities of the inbound movements from suppliers must be considered.

As an example, consider the case of Lear Corporation, a company that supplied seats for certain Ford Motor Company truck plants. Essentially, the seats were manufactured in sequence so that they could go right off the delivery vehicle onto the Ford assembly line in the order in which they would be installed. Faced with the need to expand, and knowing that its existing plant was landlocked, Lear chose a new plant site that was 10 minutes away from one plant and 20 minutes from the other. As a result, for 20 hours per day, trucks loaded with seats left the Lear factory every 15 minutes. According to Lear company officials, the location was about as far away from the customer as it can afford and still deliver true, JIT deliveries.

4-4-1-7 Land Costs and Utilities

Depending on the type of facility under consideration, issues relating to the cost of land and the availability of needed utilities are more or less critical. In the case of a manufacturing plant or distribution center, for example, a certain minimum acreage or parcel size may be needed for current use as well as future expansion. This represents a potentially significant expense. Factors such as local building codes and cost of construction are important to consider. Also, the availability and expense of utilities such as electrical power, sewage, and industrial waste disposal need to be factored into the decision-making process.

4-4-1-8 IT Infrastructure

An increasingly relevant issue pertaining to supply chain facility locations is the availability of capable IT infrastructure that refers to the necessary hardware, software, network, and talent resources. Overall, the speed and quality of data transmission will have major impacts on the effectiveness of supply chain operations in various regions and countries of the world. Specific issues may include network enablement, internet connectivity, firewall and security.

One common measure of IT capability is bandwidth, as measured in Mbps (megabytes per second). As reported in Bloomberg Business, among the countries with the fastest average peak speeds were Hong Kong, South Korea, and Japan.[9] Alternatively, examples of other countries that are trying to improve bandwidth capabilities include South Korea, Argentina, India, Egypt, and Indonesia.

4-4-1-9 Company Preferences

Aside from all of the preceding types of factors, a company, or its CEO for that matter, may prefer a certain region and/or local area for the location of a logistics facility. For example, a company may prefer to locate all new facilities in rural areas within 50 miles of a major metropolitan area. Or a company may wish to locate its facilities in areas where competitors already have a presence. In other instances, a firm may wish to locate facilities in an area where it may enjoy common access with other firms to benefits such as a skilled labor supply, excellent marketing resources, or proximity to key supplier industries. This determinant is referred to as **agglomeration**, a phenomenon that sometimes explains why certain firms tend to co-locate facilities. As the trend toward globalization continues to develop in the business world today, it will be interesting to see the growth and expansion of agglomeration to achieve various types of synergies.

4-4-2 Current Trends Governing Site Selection

In addition to focusing on a number of global/national/regional location determinants, Table 4.1 also identifies a number of determinants that are focused more directly on specific sites that may be under consideration. Looking more generally at the topic of site-specific locations, a number of trends in today's supply chain environment may have significant effects on decisions involving logistics facility location. Included among these are the following:

- Strategic positioning of inventories, such that fast-moving, profitable items may be located at "market-facing" logistics facilities. Slower-moving, less-profitable items may be located at more regional, or national facilities. These examples are consistent with implementation of effective inventory segmentation strategies.

- Aside from a general trend toward the elimination of many wholesaler/distributor operations, companies are moving to greater use of "customer-direct" delivery from manufacturing and other upstream supply chain locations. Many times, this bypasses and diminishes the need for complete networks of distribution facilities. Increased use of "drop" shipments provides deliveries of product direct from manufacturing to the customer, thus eliminating the need for intermediate distribution capabilities.

- There is a growing use of and need for strategically located cross-docking facilities that serve as transfer points for consolidated shipments that need to be disaggregated or mixed into typically smaller shipments for delivery to individual customers. An example of this would be the consolidation of multiple-vendor shipments into full trailer loads being shipped to retail stores or points of use. Applied to inbound movements, this concept can significantly reduce the need for inbound consolidation facilities.

- Due diligence for location and site selection decisions is placing great emphasis on access to major airports and/or ocean ports for import and export shipments.

- Greater use of providers of third-party-logistics services, who may assume part or all of the responsibility for moving a firm's products to its customers, and/or moving its inbound parts and materials to its manufacturing process. In the global setting, many of these companies are developing specialized abilities to facilitate the movements of import and export shipments.

- To be discussed later in this chapter, the rising interest in omni-channel capabilities has elevated the importance of not only making good location decisions, but also integrating alternative approaches to fulfilling customer/consumer demand.

4-5 Modeling Approaches

This section focuses broadly on the topic of modeling approaches that can provide insight into the choice of a supply chain network design. As such, the techniques discussed here are applicable to a wide range of issues pertaining to the locations of plants, distribution centers, and customers and to the flows of product and information to support the functioning of the supply chain. These apply to network design decisions that may be made on a domestic and/or global basis. The principal modeling approaches to be covered are optimization, simulation, and heuristic models. Detailed coverage of the grid method for facility location is included as part of the discussion of heuristic modeling approaches.

As indicated previously, the use of appropriate modeling techniques will facilitate a comparison of the functioning and cost/service effectiveness of current versus proposed supply chain networks. Once an appropriate modeling procedure has been selected, it should be used to help identify a network that is consistent with the key objectives identified earlier in the supply chain network redesign process. After preliminary solutions have been identified, subsequent what-if types of analyses should be conducted to test the sensitivity of the recommended network designs to changes in key supply chain variables.

4-5-1 Optimization Models

The **optimization model** is based on precise mathematical procedures that are designed to find the "best," or optimum solution, given the mathematical definition of the problem under evaluation, and any assumptions that have been made. This means that it can be proved mathematically that the resulting solution is the best. The simple EOQ (economic order quantity) model, to be discussed in a later chapter, is an example of a technique that produces an optimum solution.

While recognizing relevant constraints, optimization approaches essentially select an optimal course of action from a number of feasible alternatives. The optimization models in use today incorporate such techniques as mathematical programming (linear, integer, dynamic, mixed-integer linear, etc.), set-partitioning, enumeration, sequencing, and the use of advanced mathematical techniques. Many of these have been incorporated into commercially available software packages.

Figure 4.3 lists example strategic/managerial issues that maybe addressed through the use of optimization techniques. There are several advantages to using this overall type of approach:

- The user is guaranteed to have the best solution possible for a given set of data and assumptions.
- Many complex model structures can be handled correctly.
- The analysis and evaluation of all alternatives that are generated result in a more efficient analysis.
- Reliable run-to-run comparisons can be made since the best solution is guaranteed for each run.
- Cost or profit savings between the optimum and heuristic solutions can be significant.[10]

The classic objective of a network design model has been to establish the number, location, and size of finished goods distribution centers and associated product flows so as to minimize costs and maintain or improve customer service. Now the mandate is to design the *entire supply chain*, from source of raw materials to the final customer. This emerging view encompasses procurement, multiple stages or processes of manufacturing, distribution center functions, and all related transportation flows. The effectiveness of supply chain management is increasingly viewed as a competitive weapon, and concerns about cost minimization are being supplanted by profit maximization (or enhancing shareholder equity). In short, answering network design questions today is virtually impossible without the help of very powerful decision support tools. Databases today are very extensive in terms of size and the combinations of facilities and support patterns number in the trillions. Fortunately, help is readily available for coping with this class of decision problems.[11]

One of the relatively easy-to-understand optimization techniques that has traditionally received significant attention is linear programming (LP). This approach is most useful for linking facilities in a network where supply and demand limitations at plants, distribution centers, or market areas must be treated as constraints. Given an objective function that focuses attention on minimizing total cost, for example, LP defines the optimum facility distribution pattern consistent with the problem's demand-supply constraints. Although

Figure 4.3	Representative Strategic/Managerial Issues Relevant to Supply Chain Network Modeling

I.   *Facility Issues* (types: supplier, manufacturing, DC, cross-dock, pool, port)

   A. Number, size, and location

   B. Ownership

   C. Mission

II. *Facility Mission Issues*

   A. Raw material supplier procurement volumes, costs, and limits

   B. Plant location manufacturing volumes, costs, capacities, and inventory requirements

   C. Distribution center throughput and storage levels, operating costs, throughput and storage capacities, and inventory requirements

   D. Port, cross-dock and pool throughput levels, operating costs and throughput limits

III. *Marketing Issues*

   A. Campaign selection

   B. Market, channel, product

   C. Selection (max profit)

IV. *Major Policy Issues*

   A. Strategic sourcing

   B. Target market expansion

   C. International expansion

   D. Supply chain vulnerability

   E. Mergers and acquisitions

   F. Capacity planning

   G. Transportation policy

   H. Seasonal demand/supply

   I. Long-range planning

   J. Inventory strategy

   K. Customs/channel/product profitability

   L. Product introductions and deletions

   M. Sustainability measurement and objectives

   N. Energy and carbon usage profiles

   O. Customer profitability and cost-to-serve

Source: SAILS: Strategic Analysis of Integrated Logistics Systems (Manassas, VA: Insight, Inc. 2015). Reproduced by permission.

this technique is actually quite useful, its applicability is limited due to the need for the problem formulation to be deterministic and capable of linear approximation. Also, the use of LP itself does not allow for consideration of fixed as well as variable costs of operating logistics facilities. So, while the solution from an application of LP is optimal, it is based typically on a relatively narrow set of assumptions.

On a more advanced scale, the use of mixed-integer linear programming allows consideration of issues such as fixed and variable costs, capacity constraints, economies of scale, cross-product limitations, and unique sourcing requirements. One of the leading models of this type is **strategic analysis of integrated logistics systems (SAILS)**, developed by Insight, Inc. Figure 4.4 illustrates the supply chain complexity that may be addressed by a capable network optimization model such as SAILS. In brief, SAILS is a fully integrated decision support system that can be used to build, modify, solve, and interpret sophisticated strategic supply chain design models. SAILS, has enabled companies to analyze end-to-end operations and to explore how potential changes affect service, costs, asset deployment, sustainability, and risk. SAILS combines a powerful optimization engine with an exceptionally easy to use interface, extensive support databases, powerful data preparation machinery, elaborate scenario generation options, and comprehensive reporting capabilities. SAILS was designed originally to analyze *strategic* issues that involve longer-term resource commitments, but many users have successfully addressed *tactical* issues as well, such as first-level production planning, production line balancing, seasonal pre-build, etc.[12]

Once a modeling database has been created, either simple or complex, the use of SAILS facilitates the rapid generation and evaluation of many alternate scenarios for analysis.[13] Numerous shipment planning controls also permit the user to evaluate the network impact of various shipment planning options such as pooling, stop-offs, pickups, and direct

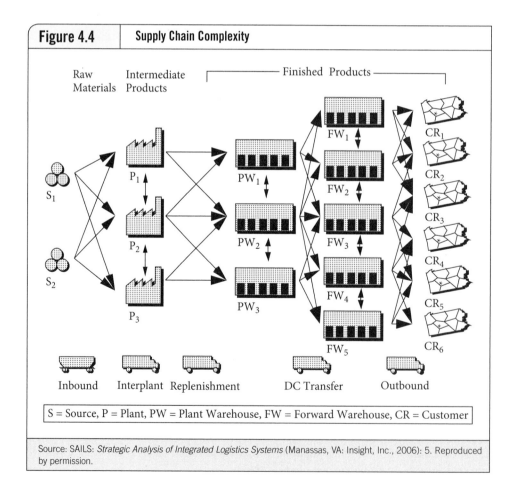

Figure 4.4	Supply Chain Complexity

S = Source, P = Plant, PW = Plant Warehouse, FW = Forward Warehouse, CR = Customer

Source: SAILS: *Strategic Analysis of Integrated Logistics Systems* (Manassas, VA: Insight, Inc., 2006): 5. Reproduced by permission.

plant shipments. SAILS is a highly flexible logistics modeling tool that can be used for a range of problems from the very simple to those in which data may exist in the form of millions of shipment transactions. When a given modeling scenario has been generated, SAILS utilizes mixed-integer linear programming, along with an advanced technique called **network factorization**, to produce an optimum solution. Typical data inputs to SAILS include customer demand (either forecast or historical); aggregated product and customer identification; facility data for plants and DCs; transportation options and rates; and policy considerations such as shipment planning rules, DC inventory constraints, and customer service requirements.

Although optimization approaches typically require significant computer resources, the availability of capable systems today has greatly facilitated their ease of use. Along with improvements in model design and solver technologies, future approaches should be even more convenient for general use by those involved with the design and analysis of supply chains.

In addition to improved analytical techniques, the availability of insightful visual representations of logistics networks has enhanced our ability to gain insight into network alternatives. Figure 4.5 is an example of the types of "geo-mapping" alternatives that are currently available.

4-5-2 Simulation Models

The second approach to supply chain network design includes the development and use of **simulation models**. Simulation is defined as "the process of designing a model of a real system and conducting experiments with this model for the purpose either of understanding the behavior of the system or of evaluating various strategies within the limits imposed by a criterion or set of criteria for the operation of the system."[14] Network simulation involves developing a computer representation of the supply chain network

Figure 4.5	Geographical-Mapping Representations

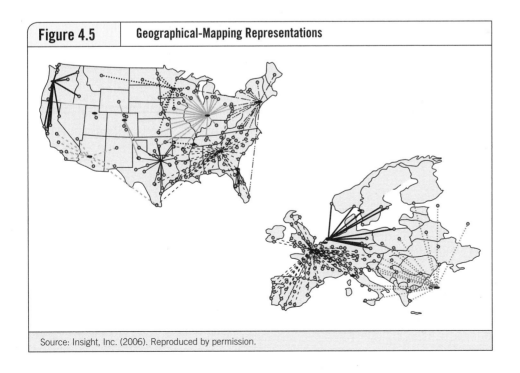

Source: Insight, Inc. (2006). Reproduced by permission.

and then observing the cost and service characteristics of the network as cost structures, constraints, and other factors are varied. It has been stated that the process of simulation is "nothing more or less than the technique of performing *sampling experiments* on the model of the system."[15]

For location analysis, the use of simulation allows the decision maker to test the effect of alternative locations upon costs and service levels. The modeling requires extensive data collection and analysis to determine how system factors such as transportation, warehousing, inventory, materials handling, and labor costs interact. The simulation process evaluates the decision maker's selected sites to determine respective costs. Simulation does not guarantee an optimum solution but simply evaluates the alternatives that are fed into it.[16] A critical characteristic of a simulation tool is whether it is static or dynamic in nature. A dynamic tool will not only incorporate a multiperiod time perspective but also update system status for each time period based on the results of the previous time periods.

Although it is very different from optimization, the use of simulation techniques has great applicability to supply chain network planning. While it does not produce an "optimum" solution, it is very robust in that it easily incorporates a number of assumptions that may closely approximate reality (e.g., transportation costs, labor costs, pricing structures, etc.). Also, simulation approaches are very capable in terms of incorporating relatively comprehensive and detailed problem descriptions. Sometimes an optimization approach is used first to identify and evaluate feasible network design alternatives, and then highly customized simulation models are used to focus on the exact logistics network that will best meet the desired objectives.

4-5-3 Heuristic Models

Heuristic models are able to accommodate broad problem definitions, but they are not designed to provide an optimum solution. The use of a heuristic approach can help to reduce a problem to a manageable size and search automatically through various alternatives in an attempt to find a better solution. As is indicated in the discussion of the grid technique that follows, heuristic approaches can provide a good approximation to the least-cost location in a complex decision problem. To reduce the number of location alternatives, the decision maker should incorporate into the heuristic program site characteristics considered to be optimal.

For example, the location team may consider a desirable warehouse site to be (1) within 20 miles of a major market area, (2) at least 250 miles from other company distribution centers, (3) within three miles of an interstate highway, and (4) within 40 miles of a major airport facility. The heuristic model searches for sites with these characteristics, thus reducing the number of alternative sites to those the decision maker considers practical.

Additionally, heuristic decision rules are sometimes incorporated into the decision-making process in what may appear to be "rules of thumb." Examples may include locating distribution centers so that all customers within a particular area may receive deliveries within one or two days, or making sure plants are co-located in the vicinity of key supplier locations, perhaps selecting suppliers that have locations proximate to your plant locations.

Although the word "heuristics" sometimes is thought to involve a lesser degree of sophistication and rigor than do optimization and simulation approaches, it is not at all unusual for heuristic approaches to be very complex in terms of how they are structured. Also, heuristic approaches are sometimes used in conjunction with sophisticated optimization models, particularly when this results in a more approximate, but solvable model.

4-5-4 Potential Supply Chain Modeling Pitfalls to Avoid

According to Paul Bender, a number of common pitfalls should be avoided in designing and implementing an optimum worldwide supply chain.[17] Recognizing these in advance should help to maximize the value to be achieved through use of appropriate mathematical techniques for supply chain network design.

- **Short-term horizon.** Unless modeling features are designed, implemented, and used with a long-term perspective, significant suboptimization is likely to occur.
- **Too little or too much detail.** Too little detail can make it difficult to implement results due to insufficient information; too much detail can create unnecessary complexity, making it difficult to understand the results and more difficult to implement effectively.
- **Thinking in two dimensions.** While the use of two-dimensional maps certainly helps to provide insight into supply chain problems, the geometry of the networks may ignore cost and geographical dispersions of demand. Over significant distances, and particularly for global supply chain analyses, the curvature of the earth may distort distance calculations, in which case needed adjustments must be made.
- **Using published costs.** Many published costs tend to represent "list" prices that need to be modified to reflect what may result after significant negotiations occur between buyers and sellers of transport services.
- **Inaccurate or incomplete costs.** Analyses based on insufficiently accurate information lead to invalid results; inaccurate cost forecasts result in suboptimal allocations of resources, typically leading to seriously flawed strategies.
- **Fluctuating model inputs.** Given the prevailing uncertainties in many of the relevant inputs to network design models, it is important to conduct sensitivity analyses to be aware of the potential wide swings in key model inputs.
- **Use of erroneous analytical techniques.** The selected techniques and approaches should be matched with the level of precision desired; the identification of modeling objectives is an important forerunner to the selection of the techniques to be utilized.
- **Lack of appropriate robustness analysis.** Since most or all model inputs have at least an element of uncertainty, it is important to understand the consequences that could result from variation in actual behavior of key model inputs; robustness analysis can help to ensure the practicality and validity of the results from the selected analyses.

4-5-5 Example of a Heuristic Modeling Approach: The Grid Technique

Although other factors are also important, the availability and expense of transportation services are commonly included in location analyses. While transportation itself can represent a significant cost, decision makers should strive to make the final decision on the basis of the full range of relevant cost factors, as well as on the customer service implications of the network alternative being evaluated.

The grid technique is a simplistic, but well-known, heuristic approach to help companies with multiple markets and multiple supply points determine a least-cost facility location. Essentially, the grid technique attempts to determine a fixed facility (such as a plant or distribution center) location that represents the least-cost center for moving inbound materials and outbound product within a geographic grid. The technique determines the low-cost "center of gravity" for moving raw materials and finished goods.

This technique assumes that the raw materials sources and finished goods markets are fixed and that a company knows the amount of each product it consumes or sells. The technique then superimposes a grid upon the geographic area containing the raw materials sources and finished goods markets. The grid's zero point corresponds to an exact geographic location, as do the grid's other points. Thus, the company can identify each source and market by its grid coordinates.

Figure 4.6 is an example of a supply source and market environment for a company that is deciding where to locate a plant. The company, which has located supply sources and markets on the map and has superimposed a grid system over the source-market area, purchases raw materials from sources in Buffalo, Memphis, and St. Louis—S_1, S_2, and S_3, respectively.

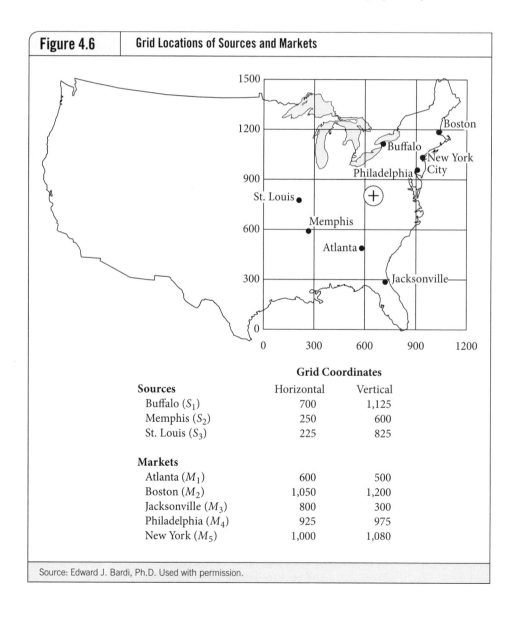

Figure 4.6   **Grid Locations of Sources and Markets**

Grid Coordinates

Sources	Horizontal	Vertical
Buffalo (S_1)	700	1,125
Memphis (S_2)	250	600
St. Louis (S_3)	225	825

Markets		
Atlanta (M_1)	600	500
Boston (M_2)	1,050	1,200
Jacksonville (M_3)	800	300
Philadelphia (M_4)	925	975
New York (M_5)	1,000	1,080

The new plant will serve five markets: Atlanta, Boston, Jacksonville, Philadelphia, and New York—M_1, M_2, M_3, M_4, and M_5, respectively.

The technique defines each source and market location in terms of its horizontal and vertical grid coordinates. For example, the Jacksonville market (M_3) has a horizontal grid coordinate of 800 and a vertical grid coordinate of 300. The Buffalo source is located at grid coordinates 700 horizontal and 1,125 vertical.

We can visualize this technique's underlying concept as a series of strings to which are attached weights corresponding to the weight of raw materials the company consumes at each source and of finished goods the company sells at each market. The strings are threaded through holes in a flat plane; the holes correspond to the source and market locations. The strings' other ends are tied together, and the weights exert their respective pulls on the knot. The strings' knotted ends will finally reach equilibrium; this equilibrium will be the center of mass, or the ton-mile center.

We can compute this concept mathematically, finding the ton-mile center, or center of mass, as follows:

$$C = \frac{\sum\limits_1^m d_i S_i + \sum\limits_1^n D_i M_i}{\sum\limits_1^m S_i + \sum\limits_1^n M_i}$$

where

> C = Center of mass, or ton-mile center
> d_i = Distance from 0 point on grid to the grid location of raw material i
> D_i = Distance from 0 point on grid to the grid location of finished good i
> S_i = Weight (volume) of raw materials purchased at source i
> M_i = Weight (volume) of finished goods sold in market i

This equation will generate the least-cost location if transportation rates for raw materials and finished goods are the same. But transportation rates vary among commodities, and the ton-mile center equation does not reflect differences in the costs of moving commodities. The transportation rate pulls the location toward the location of the commodity with the higher rate. Thus, the higher rates of finished goods will draw the least-cost location toward the finished goods market and thereby reduce the distance the company moves these higher-rated goods. This will increase the distance the company transports lower-rated raw materials.

Thus, we must incorporate into our analysis the transportation rates of different products. This modification is as follows:

$$C = \frac{\sum\limits_1^m r_i d_i S_i + \sum\limits_1^n R_i M_i}{\sum\limits_1^m r_i S_i + \sum\limits_1^n R_i M_i}$$

where

> r_i = Raw materials rate/distance unit for raw material i
> R_i = Finished goods transportation rate/distance unit for finished good i

r_i and R_i are the transportation rates per distance unit, and we assume them to be linear with respect to distance. This assumption does not correspond to the tapering principle of rates (to be discussed later in this chapter), but it does simplify the analysis.

4-5-5-1 Manufacturing Plant Location Example

Table 4.2 presents relevant data for a manufacturing plant location example, as well as the grid technique solution using a computer spreadsheet program. The grid coordinates of the raw materials sources and markets correspond to their locations on the grid in Figure 4.6. For simplicity, we will assume that this company produces only one type of finished good, so that each finished good's transportation rate is the same.

To determine the least-cost center on the grid, we must compute two grid coordinates, one for moving the commodities along the horizontal axis and one for moving them along the vertical axis. We compute the two coordinates by using the grid technique formula for each direction.

Table 4.2 provides this example's computations. The two columns at the far right contain the calculations that the grid technique equation indicates. The first calculations column contains the calculations for the horizontal numerator, or the sum of the rate times the horizontal grid coordinate times the tonnage for each raw materials source and market. The calculations at the bottom of Table 4.2 indicate the numerator and denominator of the grid technique equation.

As Table 4.2 indicates, the plant location's least-cost center in this example is 655 in the horizontal direction and 826 in the vertical direction. We measure both distances from the grid's zero point. Figure 4.6 indicates the least-cost center as point +. The least-cost location for the plant is in southeastern Ohio or northwestern West Virginia in the Wheeling-Parkersburg area.

The preceding example applied the grid technique to a plant location. Companies can use the technique to solve warehousing location problems as well. The company follows the same procedure, but the company's plants are the raw materials sources.

4-5-5-2 Advantages

The grid technique's strengths are in its simplicity and its ability to provide a starting point for location analysis. Computationally, the technique is relatively easy to use. A company can generate the necessary data from sales figures, purchase records, and transportation documents (either the bill of lading or the freight bill). More exact market and source location coding is possible, as is modifying the rate–distance relationship quantification. A computer can easily handle such refinements.

The grid technique also provides a starting point for making a location decision. Although transportation cost is not the only locational determinant, use of the grid technique can help at an early stage in the network design process by helping the decision maker to focus on an area or areas that are logistically advantageous. For example, use of the grid technique may suggest that a distribution center located in The Netherlands may be logistically advantageous to serve as a point of distribution for shipments destined to points of final delivery in western Europe. This is a great step forward in the location decision process, as further steps in the process may help to identify preferred locations within the broader area that is targeted.

4-5-5-3 Limitations

The grid technique has limitations that the decision maker must recognize. First, it is a static approach, and the solution is optimum for only one point in time. Changes in the volumes a company purchases or sells, changes in transportation rates, or changes in raw materials sources or market locations will shift the least-cost location. Second, the

Table 4.2	Grid Technique Analysis of Manufacturing Plant Location Example					
SOURCES/ MARKETS	**RATE $/ TON-MILE (A)**	**TONS (B)**	**GRID COORDINATES**		**CALCULATIONS**	
			HORIZONTAL	**VERTICAL**	**(A) × (B) × HORIZONTAL**	**(A) × (B) × VERTICAL**
Buffalo (S_1)	$0.90	500	700	1,125	315,000	506,250
Memphis (S_2)	$0.95	300	250	600	71,250	171,000
St. Louis (S_3)	$0.85	700	225	825	133,875	490,875
		1,500			520,125	1,168,125
Atlanta (M_1)	$1.50	225	600	500	202,500	168,750
Boston (M_2)	$1.50	150	1,050	1,200	236,250	270,000
Jacksonville (M_3)	$1.50	250	800	300	300,000	112,500
Philadelphia (M_4)	$1.50	175	925	975	242,813	255,938
New York (M_5)	$1.50	300	1,000	1,080	450,000	486,000
TOTALS		1,100			1,431,563	1,293,188
					HORIZONTAL	**VERTICAL**
			Numerator: $\Sigma\,(r \times d \times S) =$		520,125	1,168,125
			$+\Sigma\,(R \times D \times M) =$		1,431,563	1,293,188
			Sum		1,951,688	2,461,313
			Denominator: $\Sigma\,(r \times S) =$		1,330	1,330
			$+\Sigma\,(R \times M) =$		1,650	1,650
			Sum		2,980	2,980
			Grid Center		655	826

Source: Edward J. Bardi, Ph.D. Used with permission.

technique assumes linear transportation rates, whereas actual transportation rates increase with distance but less than proportionally. Third, the technique does not consider the topographic conditions existing at the optimum location; for example, the recommended site may be in the middle of a lake. Fourth, it does not consider the proper direction of movement; most moves occur along a straight line between two points, not "vertically" and then "horizontally."

4-5-5-4 Sensitivity Analysis

As mentioned in the preceding paragraph, the grid technique is a static approach; the computed location is valid only for the situation analyzed. If any of the factors such as transportation rates, market and source locations, and volumes change, the least-cost location changes.

Sensitivity analysis enables the decision maker to ask what-if questions and measure the resulting impact on the least-cost location. For example, the decision maker may examine the least-cost location in light of a five-year sales projection by inserting the estimated market sales volumes into the grid technique equation and determining the least-cost location. Other what-if scenarios could include adding new markets and/or sources, eliminating markets and/or sources, and switching transportation modes, thereby changing rates.

Appendix 4A provides details and explanations of two sensitivity analyses performed for the grid method problem in Table 4.2. The first what-if scenario considers switching from rail to truck to serve the Jacksonville market; the switch entails a 50 percent rate increase. The second what-if sensitivity analysis considers the elimination of a Buffalo supply source and increasing by 500 tons the amount the example company purchases from Memphis. As discussed further in Appendix 4A, we can conclude from these sensitivity analyses that the rates, product volumes, and source/market locations do affect a plant's least-cost location.

Also included in Appendix 4A is a discussion of how the grid method is applicable to the task of determining a distribution center location in a city.

4-5-6 Transportation Pragmatics

There are a number of examples that are representative of the realistic details that need to be considered when conducting network design analyses. These are referred to as transportation pragmatics. A few of these are summarized below, although further details are included in the later chapter in this text on the topic of transportation.

Tapering Rate Principle. The previous discussions highlighted the importance of the transportation factor in the facility location decision. To simplify our analyses, we assumed that transportation costs were represented by a fixed cost per mile. In reality, however, transportation costs per mile tend to decline as the number of miles increases, and so this needs to be included in our modeling approaches to best reflect the actual details of the rate structures. Known as the "tapering rate" principle, this results from the carrier's ability to spread certain fixed shipment costs, such as loading, billing, and handling, over a greater number of miles.

Zone or Blanket Rates. A noted exception to the preceding rate structure is the zone rate or blanket rate. This type of rate does not increase with distance; it remains the same from one origin to all points in the blanket area. Perhaps the most common example is that of zone rates, such as used by UPS, where geographic zones are established, and prices to any points in the same zones are identical. Alternatively, sometimes carriers establish such rates to ensure a competitive price for a product in a given area, thereby ensuring demand for the product and its transportation. An example of a blanket rate would be the same rate of wine traveling from the West Coast to all points east of the Rocky Mountains, enabling the West Coast wine to compete with imported wines entering the East Coast.

Commercial Zones. A specific blanket area is the **commercial zone**, the transportation definition of a particular city or town. It includes the municipality itself plus various surrounding areas. The commercial zone rates that carriers quote to a particular town or city also apply to points in the surrounding area within the commercial zone.

The commercial zone's locational impact appears near the end of the location decision process when a company selects a specific site. If the specific site is beyond the limits of a municipality's commercial zone, rates that apply to the city do not apply to the site. Also, a site outside the commercial zone reduces carrier availability, especially the availability of motor carriers that define their operating scopes in terms of point-to-point operations.

Foreign Trade Zones.[18] A foreign trade zone is a designated area where companies can set up operations with exempted or deferred tariffs on foreign merchandise. FTZs make U.S. manufacturing more competitive by reducing or eliminating unfair tax burdens on companies that make or assemble finished products using foreign components. Some benefits of FTZs are as follows:

- Merchandise may be stored within a foreign trade zone for an unlimited period of time and avoid all duties and excise taxes.
- Merchandise may be opened, examined, assembled, mixed, cleaned, labeled or repackaged within a zone.
- Merchandise may be displayed, sampled or examined within the zone.
- Waste materials and damaged merchandise may be destroyed within the zone to avoid duties.

An example of how a foreign trade zone can help a company is Foreign Trade Zone 50 in Long Beach, California.[19] This involves an electronics company that imports 40,000 electrical capacitors per year from Asia at a value of $200 per unit or 9.6 percent duty rate. The company requested permission to manipulate the merchandise (e.g., open cartons, perform quality control inspections, and repackage cartons) prior to re-exportation to Mexico. The final product then is exported to a free zone within a Mexican maquiladora for manufacturing of the finished goods. The company benefits from duty elimination within Foreign Trade Zone 50 and realizes a yearly zone savings of U.S. $768,000. Overall, there are over 230 foreign trade zone projects and nearly 400 subzones in the United States.[20]

Although the use of foreign trade zones is very prevalent among companies having significant involvement in global commerce, some examples would include Sony Electronics, Daimler Chrysler, Mercedes-Benz, JVC America, PetSmart, Honeywell, Apple, Eastman Kodak, Callaway Golf Company, Black & Decker, Caterpillar, General Electric, etc.[21]

4-6 Omni-Channel Network Design

4-6-1 Introduction

In 1886, Richard Sears began selling watches to supplement his regular income. In 1896, Sears offered its first catalog and in 1925 opened its first retail location in a catalog center on Chicago's west side.[22] This was the first historic attempt by a retailer to offer consumers more than one access point to its products. Today, traditional brick and mortar retailers are turning to the internet to provide an alternative for customers to buy their products. However, a recent study found that nearly one-third of its respondents stated that they are not ready to handle omni-channel retailing, with only two percent rating themselves as high performing in the omni-channel space.[23] One possible reason for this disparity is that many retailers still maintain separate distribution networks for their off-line and online operations. Another reason could be that distribution network operations are different for store replenishment versus internet, or consumer, replenishment.

Regardless of the reason, the definite trend is that traditional retailers are placing a high priority on internet retailing. Amazon has played a significant role in changing the retail landscape for traditional store operations. In fact, Amazon is now the ninth largest retailer in the United States.[24] This is the first time a non-asset retailer has made this list.

On the Line

Keynote: Omni-channel's Impact on Supply Chain Management

In this year's keynote address, Sears' supply chain leaders gave attendees a 30,000 foot view of the state of omni-channel fulfillment from their unique perspectives and offered their insight into best practices and top strategies for logistics managers.

During the keynote, Bill Hutchinson, senior vice president of supply chain for the venerable retailer, and Jeff Starecheski, vice president of logistics services, explore how they implemented an omni-channel fulfillment strategy as a way to improve the overall customer experience.

"Managing a business today is fundamentally different than it was 30 years ago," says Starecheski. "The most profound difference is the level of complexity people have to cope with." For example, he points to the fact that many companies that once functioned within simple, self-contained markets now face competition from unexpected players.

"Retail is now constantly changing, and changing fast," adds Starecheski. "Digitally-enabled customers are empowered with information at their fingertips that wasn't available to them just a few years ago. Today, customers have a mall in their hands and they can shop using finger strokes versus footsteps."

The question remains how does the retailer differentiate its brand in this new, omni-channel environment? "Why should people shop at your store?" asks Starecheski. "Will it be the shopping experience, price, services offered, the assortment, the location, fulfillment options—or all of these—that will attract the digitally empowered consumer to the retail establishment?"

According to Hutchinson, Sears approaches these and other questions by using a simple mission: to serve, delight, and engage members while they shop their way. "The customer is in charge," says Hutchinson. He points to Sears' single pile of inventory, which gives customers access to inventory regardless of its location in the supply chain, its "always-on" network, and the retailers final-mile solution—same-day delivery 6 or 7 days a week—as a few of the company's top omni-channel strategies to meet new, pressing consumer demands.

Going forward, Hutchinson says that the smartest retail supply chains will be those that transform from traditional hierarchical supply chains to omni-channel supply chains, invest in relevant technology platforms, and invest in talent. "Cross-functional skills and leadership are required," says Hutchinson.

Source: Bridget McCrea, *Logistics Management*, January 2015, pp. 58S–60S. Reprinted with permission of Peerless Media, LLC.

So, the concept of providing multiple access points to consumers for retail products is not new. What is new is the concept of omni-channel retailing. Omni-channel will be defined as "a direct to consumer (D2C) business model where all sales channels ranging from online, mobile, telephonic, mail order, self-service, and physical retail establishments are aligned and fulfillment processes integrated to provide consumers with a seamless shopping experience in alignment with the company's brand proposition."[25] This definition highlights three important points. First, omni-channel strategy must align with the firm's "go to market" strategy which dictates how consumers will be able to gain access to the firm's products. Second, the fulfillment processes must be integrated regardless of order entry point. In other words, whether the order is a purchase at a store or is placed through a Web site, the replenishment/fulfillment processes must be integrated to provide rapid and consistent delivery. Finally, "ease of shopping" for the consumer is a priority regardless of where or how the order is placed.

The next section of this chapter will present a discussion on traditional channels of distribution that will address the go to market strategy as discussed earlier. After that, several omni-channel network design options will be presented in an attempt to show how companies are integrating their fulfillment processes to service both store and internet orders.

4-6-2 Channels of Distribution

A channel of distribution consists of one or more organizations or individuals who participate in the flow of goods, services, information, and finances from the production point to the final point of consumption. A channel of distribution can also be thought of as the physical structures and intermediaries through which these flows travel. These channels encompass a variety of intermediary firms, including those that can be classified as distributors, wholesalers, retailers, transportation providers, and brokers. Some of these intermediary firms take physical possession of the goods, some take title to the goods, and some take both. Thus, it is critical in the design of a distribution channel to take into consideration both the logistics channel and the marketing channel.

The logistics channel refers to the means by which products flow physically from place of availability to place of demand. The marketing channel refers to the means by which necessary transactional elements are managed (e.g., customer orders, billing, accounts receivable). An example of a retail marketing and logistics channel can be seen in Figure 4.7.

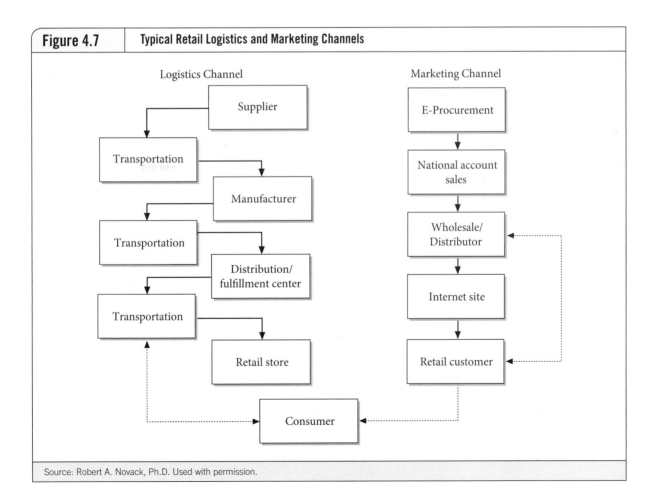

Figure 4.7	Typical Retail Logistics and Marketing Channels

Source: Robert A. Novack, Ph.D. Used with permission.

Effective channel management requires a good grasp of the different alternatives available to deliver a product and the resulting benefits of each. The four basic functions of the logistics channel are (1) sorting out, (2) accumulating, (3) allocating, and (4) assorting. Channel systems can be classified as either direct or indirect and can be further subdivided into traditional and vertical marketing systems (VMS). With the VMS, some degree of implicit or explicit relationship exists among the organizations in the channel and channel members have considerable opportunities to coordinate their activities.

Using the grocery industry as an example, Figure 4.8 shows the numerous channels of distribution that are responsible for delivering products to consumers. While it is true that several of these channels might compete with one another, collectively they provide the consumer with a significant number of choices as to where and how to purchase grocery products. Each individual channel represents a unique path from grocery manufacturer to consumer, and a set of effective logistics strategies must be developed for each channel.

An important observation to note about channel structure involves the elements of fixed costs versus variable costs. Using Figure 4.8 as an example, assume that a food manufacturer uses a traditional channel to deliver its product to a retail store. One channel would include the manufacturer, the manufacturer's distribution center, the retailer's distribution center, and the retailer's store. This channel involves a significant amount of fixed costs in the form of distribution centers and stores. However, variable costs, in the form of transportation, are relatively low since most shipments would be made in large volume quantities between channel members. Assume that the food manufacturer decided to begin Internet fulfillment direct to the consumer (this is the second channel from the right in Figure 4.8). While much of the fixed cost in this channel is significantly reduced (eliminating the need for the retailer's distribution center and stores), the variable transportation

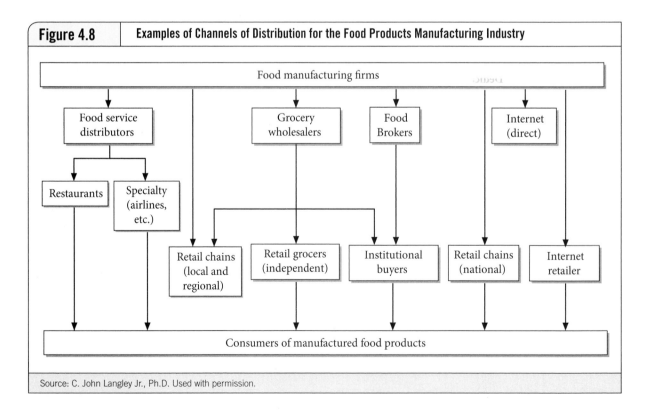

Figure 4.8   **Examples of Channels of Distribution for the Food Products Manufacturing Industry**

Source: C. John Langley Jr., Ph.D. Used with permission.

costs will increase significantly. This occurs because the origin (food manufacturer) and ultimate destination (consumer) in both channels are the same, resulting in approximately the same distance to move product, but the shipment size is reduced significantly. The lower the shipment size the higher the transportation cost per pound, holding constant commodity and distance. So a rule of thumb in channel design is, assuming that the origin and destination remain the same, the more intermediaries used to deliver the product the higher the fixed cost and the lower the variable cost, and vice versa.

4-6-3 Customer Fulfillment Models

The term omni-channel typically refers to retailers that offer products to consumers through both retail stores and Web sites. In the retail sector, both stores and consumers are considered customers. As such, various network designs are used to fulfill the demands of these customers. These networks can be privately owned or outsourced to third party logistics providers. A discussion of these third party providers can be found in Chapter 12. This section will offer a brief discussion of several models that can and are being used in the retail industry to service stores and/or consumers. Figure 4.9 shows several of these networks and will provide the basis for discussion in the remainder of this section.

4-6-3-1 Integrated Fulfillment

Many retailers today maintain both a "bricks-and-mortar" and "clicks-and-mortar" presence to the consumer. That is, retailers have both retail stores as well as Internet sites where consumers can buy direct. One example would be Office Depot/Office Max with

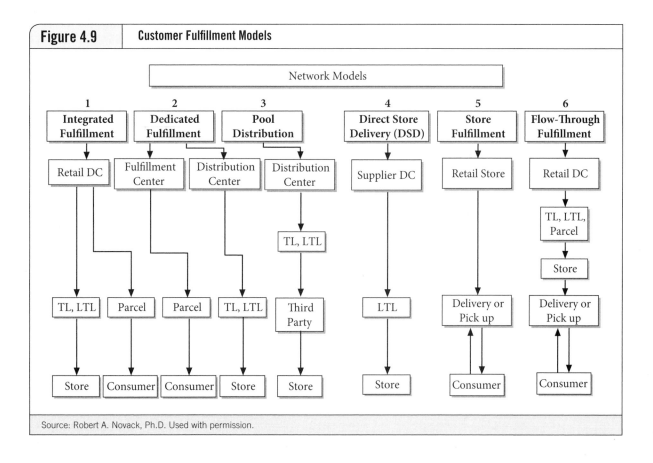

Figure 4.9 | **Customer Fulfillment Models**

Source: Robert A. Novack, Ph.D. Used with permission.

its large number of retail outlets as well as its presence with Office Depot.com. Integrated fulfillment means the retailer operates one distribution network to service both channels.

This fulfillment model can be seen in Figure 4.10. In a typical distribution center for this model, both store orders and consumer orders are received, picked, packed, and shipped. Typically, shipping orders to stores would require full truckload (TL), less-than-truckload (LTL), or pool distribution movements (pool distribution will be discussed later in this section). Shipping to consumers would utilize parcel carriers (like UPS, FedEx, or the U.S. Post Office) or, in some cases, bicycles or some other unconventional mode of transportation. One advantage to this model is low start-up costs. If the retailer has an established distribution network that handles store orders and then decides to develop an Internet presence, the existing network can service both. In other words, new distribution centers need not be built. This would also eliminate the need to have a duplicate inventory to handle the Internet orders. Another advantage to this model is workforce efficiency because of consolidated operations. The existing workforce now has an opportunity to move more volume through a fixed-cost facility. However, this model has several challenges. First, the order profile will change with the addition of consumer Internet orders. While store orders would probably be picked in case and/or pallet quantities, consumer orders would require consumer units (eaches) in smaller order quantities. Second, products might not be available in eaches. While cases and inner packs might be the minimum order quantity for a store, an individual unit (each) might be required for a consumer order. Third, the addition of unit pick (each pick) would require a "fast pick," or broken case, operation to be added to the distribution center. Case pick operations are usually very efficient because of the use of automation in the form of conveyors to move a large volume very quickly. Unit picks are very labor intensive and will not be able to move very much volume. Finally, a conflict might arise between a store order and an Internet order. If both orders want the same item and there is not sufficient inventory to fill both, which gets priority? Some would argue that the Internet order should be filled because the retailer has already received the money for the items. Others might argue that the store should get the inventory since it is also a customer of the distribution center and each store is a separate profit and loss center. So, this model presents some economies because it can use existing resources to satisfy the needs of two channels. However, it presents some operating challenges that must be addressed.

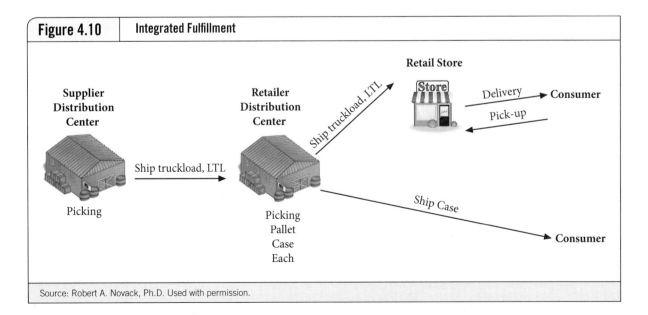

Figure 4.10 | **Integrated Fulfillment**

Source: Robert A. Novack, Ph.D. Used with permission.

4-6-3-2 Dedicated Fulfillment

Another option for the retailer that desires to have both a store and an Internet presence is called dedicated fulfillment that achieves the same delivery goals as integrated fulfillment but with two separate distribution networks. Picking, packing, and shipping in dedicated fulfillment is the same as in integrated fulfillment. So, customers will see no difference between the two networks in how the order is received. An example would be Walmart with separate networks for its stores and Internet orders. This model can be seen in Figure 4.11. Having a separate distribution network for store delivery and consumer delivery eliminates most of the disadvantages of integrated fulfillment. However, now the retailer is faced with duplicate facilities and duplicate inventories. This assumes that the retailer offers exactly the same product offering through both channels. However, many retailers offer many more products on their Internet sites than they offer in their stores. This makes dedicated fulfillment a more logical choice. However, the trend today among omni-channel retailers is moving away from dedicated fulfillment and toward integrated fulfillment.

4-6-3-3 Pool Distribution

Although not considered a traditional omni-channel fulfillment model, pool distribution is a common method used by retailers to replenish their stores. Retailers with high volumes and large store footprints, like Walmart and Target, are able to ship at least one full truckload of merchandise to each store per day. Smaller retailers do not have the volume or store network to be able to capitalize on this efficiency. This is where pool distribution, as shown in Figure 4.12, can be used. Typical delivery schedules to stores in this model are not every day but every second day or possibly a Monday, Wednesday,

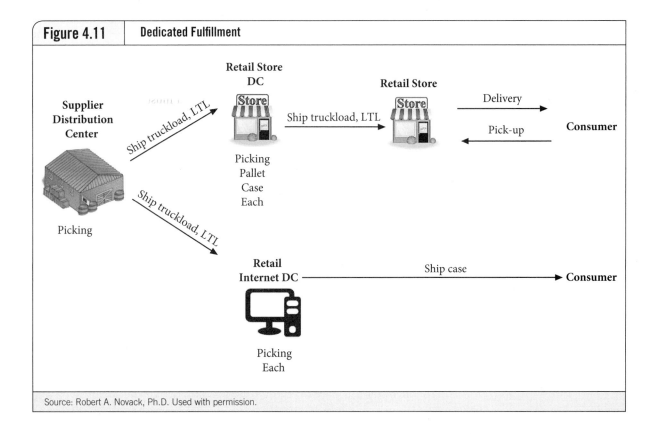

| Figure 4.11 | Dedicated Fulfillment |

Source: Robert A. Novack, Ph.D. Used with permission.

On the Line

Distribution: What does it take to be an Omni-channel Fulfillment DC?

The decision to use retail fulfillment or e-commerce distribution is no longer an either/or question. Driven by the need for flexibility, speed, and maximum uptime, shippers are turning to a new generation of technologies and innovative processes to handle pallet, case, and single-line orders to fulfill both types of orders.

In this session, Bryan Jensen, vice president and principal at St. Onge Company highlights the strategies, technologies, and best practices leading companies are taking to move to omni-channel distribution. Jensen launches the session by explaining that there are several basic network types and configurations for servicing retail, wholesale, and direct-to-consumer customers, including:

- Combination center: Stores, wholesale, and online customers serviced from the same facility.
- Dedicated centers: Stores, wholesale, and online customers serviced from separate locations.
- Store distributed: Online customers are serviced from stores.
- Hybrid: Combination of the above strategies based on geography, stock keeping unit (SKU) segment (type or velocity).

Jensen explains each of the three configurations, highlights how each works, and shows the pros and cons of each. Single fulfillment centers, for example, have the greatest concentration of volume to leverage both economies of scale or technology investment, yet they generally result in longer cycle times to customers. And while multiple locations offer the advantage of lower cycle times, they also give shippers multiple inventories to manage.

Regardless of how an organization's DCs are configured, each must be equipped with the right balance of order entry and the proper warehouse management system (WMS). If, for example, the facility is to function for store replenishment, wholesale, and direct to consumer facility then the WMS must be able to support channels simultaneously and provide the necessary inventory visibility and positioning.

"The system must have an understanding of multiple-site inventory locations and inventory by locations," says Jensen. "This enhances multi-line ordering, enables multiple pick types for a single SKU, and opens up the potential for inventory-sharing among channels."

Source: Bridget McCrea, *Logistics Management*, January 2015, p. 60S. Reprinted with permission of Peerless Media, LLC.

Friday schedule. A "pool" is a grouping of stores and they could be in a specific state (Pennsylvania) or in a geographic area (northeast). Retailers use third party logistics companies, or pool distributors, for store delivery. Trailers are loaded with merchandise at the retailer's DC for all of the stores in a pool. Typically this will be a truckload shipment of multiple LTL orders. The trailer will be sent to the pool distribution site where the merchandise will be mixed and allocated by store in the pool. The pool carrier will then deliver LTL orders to each store in their region in a "milk run" where Store 1 gets the first delivery, then Store 2, and so on. Pool distribution gives the retailer the efficiency of a truckload shipment for the line haul and the effectiveness of allowing stores to receive LTL orders on a regular schedule.

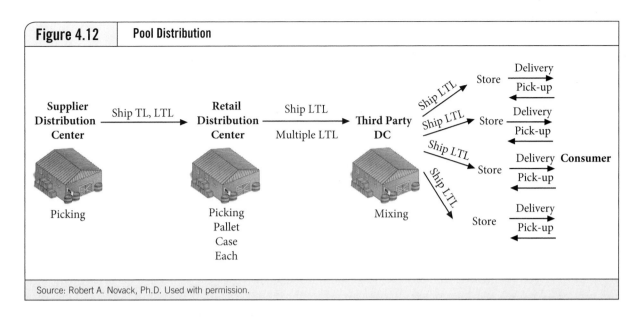

Figure 4.12 | **Pool Distribution**

Source: Robert A. Novack, Ph.D. Used with permission.

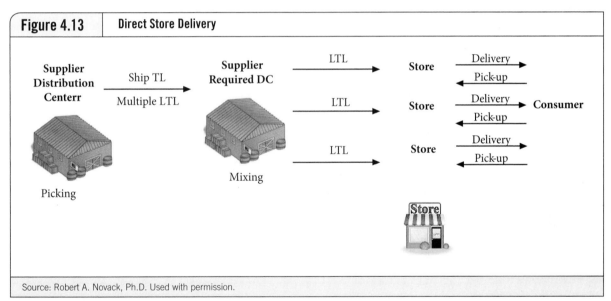

Figure 4.13 | **Direct Store Delivery**

Source: Robert A. Novack, Ph.D. Used with permission.

4-6-3-4 Direct Store Delivery

Another common fulfillment model in the retail industry is called direct store delivery, or DSD. In this network, the manufacturer delivers its product directly to a retailer's stores, bypassing the retailer's distribution network, as illustrated in Figure 4.13. A good example of this type of fulfillment is provided by Frito-Lay, a company that manufactures its products and stores them in its distribution network. From this central distribution network, products flow to regional storage locations where Frito-Lay delivery vehicles are stocked and then make direct store deliveries in a small geographic area. The driver of the vehicle will restock the retailer's shelves, rotate stock, merchandise the inventory, and gather competitive pricing and slotting information at the store level. A major advantage of this model is the reduction of inventory in the distribution network. This occurs because the retailer does not need to stock Frito-Lay's inventory in its distribution centers. Another major advantage to Frito-Lay is the direct control of its inventories at the store level. A disadvantage to the retailer is the possible reduction of inventory visibility of Frito-Lay's products since the retailer does not "touch" these products in its distribution network.

This type of model requires close collaboration and agreement between the manufacturer and retailer for several reasons. First, not every retailer supplier can do drop-shipped fulfillment. From a practical perspective, if every supplier to a store delivered direct on a daily basis, the number of delivery vehicles and manufacturer personnel in a store would cause overwhelming congestion at the store. Second, the retailer and manufacturer need to agree on the types and timing of information shared on inventory levels to provide the retailer with the proper level of inventory visibility. Finally, DSD fulfillment works best for products that have a short shelf life and/or where freshness is a requirement. As such, this model makes sense for a limited number of products sold in a retail store.

4-6-3-5 Store Fulfillment

For a retailer that has both a storefront as well as an Internet presence, store fulfillment can offer several opportunities. In this model, shown in Figure 4.14, the order is placed through the Internet site. The order is sent to the nearest retail store where it is picked and put aside for the customer to pick up or the store can arrange for delivery. This works well for large electronic appliances (such as plasma screen televisions) and is used by firms such as Best Buy. Several advantages exist for this type of fulfillment. First, there is a short lead time to the customer if the item is in stock. Second, there are low start-up costs for the retailer. Inventory is already in place in close proximity to the consumer. Third, returns can be handled in the usual manner through the retail store. Finally, the product will be available in consumer units.

Several disadvantages exist for this type of fulfillment. First, there might be reduced control and consistency over order fill since each store will be responsible for its own order picking. Second, conflict may arise between inventories. Stores hold inventories for the shopper, which can result in impulse buys. Now the store is required to remove the item from the shelf for an Internet order, resulting in a possible out-of-stock at the shelf. One method to alleviate this conflict is to adjust the profit of the store so it also gets credit for the Internet sale. Third, the retailer must have real-time visibility to in-store inventories in order to satisfy the Internet order. Finally, stores lack sufficient space to store product. Staging products for customer pick-ups in any area of the store takes space away to generate additional sales for the store.

Figure 4.14	**Store Fulfillment**

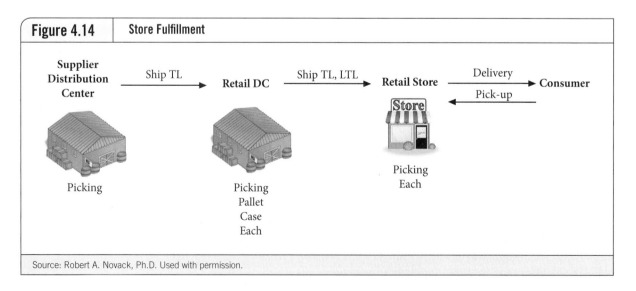

Source: Robert A. Novack, Ph.D. Used with permission.

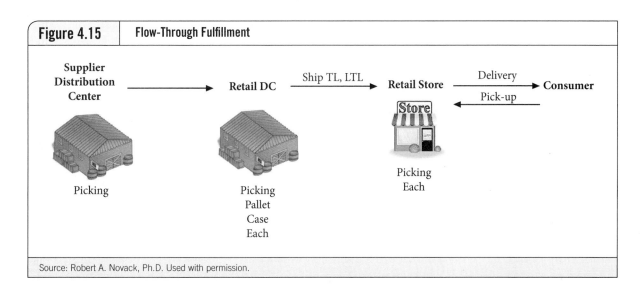

Figure 4.15 | Flow-Through Fulfillment

Source: Robert A. Novack, Ph.D. Used with permission.

4-6-3-6 Flow-Through Fulfillment

The flow-through fulfillment method, illustrated in Figure 4.15, is very similar to store fulfillment. The main difference between the two is that in flow-through fulfillment the product is picked and packed at the retailer's distribution center and then sent to the store for customer pickup or delivery. Again, this is a common method used in the consumer electronics retailing industry. Another example of this practice is Walmart's "Site to Store" option. The flow-through model eliminates the inventory conflict the store might realize between store sales and Internet sales. When the consumer is providing the pickup service, the retailer avoids the cost of the "last mile" transportation. The retailer also does not need store-level inventory status in the flow-through model. Returns can be handled through the existing store network, as in store fulfillment. Storage space at the store for pickup items remains an issue. Whereas store fulfillment can make a product available on the same day the order is received, flow-through fulfillment normally takes longer since the picking is done at the DC and the order must travel with the other store replenishment merchandise.

In conclusion, the retailing industry offers many models of fulfillment to get product into consumers' hands. Each one has advantages and disadvantages. The choice of the proper model(s) will depend on both cost considerations and market influences.

SUMMARY

- The supply chain network design decision is of great strategic importance to the firm as a whole, its supply chain, and logistics functions and processes. This decision is becoming increasingly important due to trends related to the increasing globalization of manufacturing, marketing, sourcing, and procurement.

- A formal, structured process for network design or redesign is preferable; the potential impacts on cost and service justify a significant effort toward following a sound process.

- Numerous factors may affect the design of a logistics network and the location of specific facilities within the context of the network.

- Principal modeling approaches to gain insight into the topic of supply chain network design include optimization, simulation, and heuristic models.

- The grid method represents a useful way to obtain a good, but not necessarily optimal, solution to a logistics facility location problem.
- The availability and cost of transportation affects the location decision in a number of significant and unique ways.
- In an omni-channel environment, many network models exist that can be used to service retail stores and Internet consumers.
- In designing customer fulfillment models, retailers focus on speed of product to and availability of products for the customer (effectiveness) and the cost of providing that service (efficiency).
- The type of product and nature of the order will influence customer fulfillment model design.
- Each type of customer fulfillment model has its advantages and disadvantages; trade-offs must be taken into consideration when deciding which network model to use.

STUDY QUESTIONS

1. In what ways can the design of a firm's supply chain network affect its ability to create value for customers through efficiency, effectiveness, and differentiation?

2. What are the steps in the process of supply chain network design? Of these steps, which are most relevant to the task of selecting a specific location for a logistics facility?

3. Discuss the factors that cause a company to analyze the design of a supply chain network or to reconsider the location of a particular facility.

4. Why are most location decisions analyzed by a team of managers instead of a single person? What types of teams are suggested as being helpful to the task of logistics network redesign?

5. What are the major locational determinants, and how does each affect the location decision?

6. What is the difference between a regional/national location decision, and in what ways do the determinants of each differ?

7. Discuss the role of logistics variables in the decision as to where to locate a plant or distribution center.

8. What are the principal types of modeling techniques that apply to the task of supply chain network design and facility location? What are the strengths and limitations of each?

9. Describe the grid technique. What is its purpose and how does it lead to the making of a decision? What are its strengths and limitations?

10. Using the grid technique, determine the least-cost location for the following problems:
    (a)

	TONS	RATE	GRID COORDINATES (H, V)
S_1	200	0.50	2, 14
S_2	300	0.60	6, 10
M_1	100	1.00	2, 2
M_2	100	2.00	10, 14
M_3	100	1.00	14, 18
M_4	100	2.00	14, 6

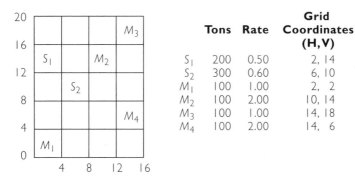

	Tons	Rate	Grid Coordinates (H,V)
S_1	200	0.50	2, 14
S_2	300	0.60	6, 10
M_1	100	1.00	2, 2
M_2	100	2.00	10, 14
M_3	100	1.00	14, 18
M_4	100	2.00	14, 6

(b)

CUSTOMER	TONS	GRID COORDINATES (H, V)
A	100	1, 11
B	300	7, 11
C	200	5, 9
D	500	7, 7
E	1,000	1, 1

Customer	Tons	Grid Coordinates (H,V)
A	100	1, 11
B	300	7, 11
C	200	5, 9
D	500	7, 7
E	1,000	1, 1

11. Explain how tapering rates, blanket rates, commercial zones, foreign trade zones, and in-transit privileges affect the facility location decision.

12. Define omni-channel. How is it different from a typical retail channel?

13. Compare and contrast the concepts of a marketing channel and logistics channel.

14. Pick any three customer fulfillment models from Figure 4.9 and:
    a. Explain how the network operates
    b. Identify its advantages
    c. Identify its disadvantages
    d. Identify the type of market in which this model would work best

CASE 4.1

Johnson & Johnson

Healthcare consumer packaged goods giant Johnson & Johnson's (J&J) European operations were comprised of 12 distribution centers in seven countries. The company's initial analysis showed there was little or no consolidation among facilities. The facilities had high operational costs (U.S. $10 million+), but transportation costs were relatively low (U.S. $6 million+). The distribution centers were geographically located to help meet the specific needs and service expectations of their European customers. Since J&J is always on the lookout for ways to streamline and improve its supply chain practices, it was very interested in ways to improve its manufacturing and distribution activities in Europe.

An initial result of applying the network optimization software was a reduction in the number of distribution centers from 12 to 2. Although this scenario was accompanied by increases in the transportation costs to customer locations, overall systems costs decreased by U.S. $7 million. Given the strategic importance of maintaining acceptably high levels of customer service, however, it was important to incorporate the requirement of retaining reasonable customer service levels (i.e., one-day service for some customers, with two-day service for others) into the formulation of the network optimization model. In addition, it also was necessary for the model to consider factors such as the expense of long-term leases, etc.

Subsequently, a network optimization model that responded to the issues discussed earlier was developed and utilized. The end result included a reduction in the number of distribution centers from 12 to 5, which translated into a decrease in facility costs from U.S. $10.1 million to U.S. $3.9 million. Although transportation costs increased slightly—from U.S. $6.6 million to U.S. $7.6 million, the overall network experienced a system savings of approximately U.S. $5 million. At the same time, the optimized network was able to meet customer service objectives such as those outlined earlier.

CASE QUESTIONS

1. What factors help to explain why J&J historically had as many as 12 distribution centers in Europe?
2. What steps in the supply chain network design process discussed in this chapter would have been most relevant to the task faced by J&J in Europe?
3. Are there other factors that the network optimization study should have considered?
4. This case study focuses on the shipments from distribution centers to customer locations. What factors on the supply side, or inbound-to-DC-side, would be relevant to the analysis that was conducted?

CASE 4.2

Bigelow Stores

Bigelow stores is a general merchandise retailer located in Atlanta, GA. With 250 stores and three distribution centers (DCs) located in the southeast United States, Bigelow has captured a significant market share in the off-price market. Bigelow carries everyday items as well as "one-time" buy specials that it advertises to consumers at special discounted prices. Bigelow also carries food products with expiration dates but none need refrigeration. Because of the density of the market and the size of its stores, Bigelow can ship full truckloads (TL) of its products from its DCs to its stores on a daily basis. Bigelow currently does not have an internet presence.

With a high market penetration in the southeast intact, Bigelow has decided to expand into the northeast and midwest through acquisitions. It has acquired a medium-sized retailer in Pennsylvania, Lions, that specializes in both general merchandise and perishable and non-perishable food items. Lions currently has 100 stores and two distribution centers in the northeast. It utilizes both direct TL shipments to larger stores that are closer to the DCs and pool distribution to the smaller, more distant stores. Lions has an internet presence where consumers can order groceries online and then pick their order up the same day at the store. Bigelow also acquired Spartan Stores, located in Michigan. Spartan is an outdoor recreational sports retailer that has 50 stores and one DC. It is an omni-channel retailer that picks and ships both store and internet orders from its single DC. Spartan utilizes LTL carriers for store deliveries and small package carriers for internet orders.

Bigelow's strategy is to grow these acquired firms, first regionally, then nationally and to incorporate them under the Bigelow name. It also has decided to invest heavily in an internet presence to become an omni-channel retailer.

CASE QUESTIONS

1. The new Bigelow "network" is comprised of different product lines, with different geographies and volumes, with varying customer touch points (stores versus internet). How would you advise the management of Bigelow on how to proceed in implementing their one-brand, omni-channel strategy?
2. What type(s) of customer fulfillment networks would you implement to service the different channels in different geographies?
3. What challenges and opportunities do you see for Bigelow in offering all products to all consumers on a single Web site? Would the current DC network support this strategy? Explain your answer.

NOTES

1. Ian Timberlake, "Intel opens biggest ever chip plant in Vietnam," www.phys.org, Oct 29, 2010.

2. www.businessinsider.com, January 23, 2014

3. For example, see www.forwardair.com

4. Figures relating to the development of transportation infrastructure in China suggest that in the 50 years from 1949 to 1999, road length in China increased 16 times, highway and expressways increased by 15 times, and seaport terminals increased by 7.6 times. By the end of 1999, passenger transportation had increased by 100 times that of 1949 and cargo transportation increased 155 times. Adapted from Charles Guowen Wang, *CSCMP Global Perspectives China* (Oak Brook, IL: Council of Supply Chain Management Professionals, 2006) and the official Web site of the China Ministry of Communications.

5. David Savageau, *Places Rated Almanac* (Washington, DC: Places Rated Books, LLC, 2011).

6. Bert Sperling and Peter Sander, *Cities Ranked and Rated: More Than 400 Metropolitan Areas Evaluated in the US and Canada*, 2nd ed. (Hoboken, NJ: Wiley Publishing Company, 2009).

7. *Investing in Waigaoqiao Free Trade Zone*, Shanghai Waigaoqiao Free Trade Zone United Development Co., Ltd., 2005. Additional information available at www.ftz-shanghai.com/

8. www.bmwgroup.com, Corporate News, Current Articles, "BMW Group to build plant in Mexico," March 7, 2014.

9. *Bloomberg Business*, "Where to Find the World's Fastest Internet," January 23, 2013.

10. Richard F. Powers, "Optimization Models for Logistics Decisions," *Journal of Business Logistics 10*, No 1 (1989): 106.

11. SAILS (Strategic Analysis of Integrated Logistics Systems), Manassas, VA, Insight, Inc. Further information available at www.insight-mss.com

12. Ibid.

13. Ibid.

14. Robert E. Shannon, *Systems Simulation: The Art and Science* (Englewood Cliffs, NJ: Prentice-Hall, 1975): 1.

15. Frederick S. Hillier and Gerald J. Lieberman, *Introduction to Operations Research*, 3rd ed. (San Francisco, CA: Holden-Day, Inc., 1980): 643.

16. For an excellent overview of simulation modeling, see Donald J. Bowersox and David J. Closs, "Simulation in Logistics: A Review of Present Practice and a Look to the Future," *Journal of Business Logistics 10*, No. 1 (1989): 133–148.

17. The content of this section has been adapted from Paul S. Bender, "How to Design an Optimum Supply Chain," *Supply Chain Management Review* (Spring 1997): 79–80.

18. This information available at www.polb.com (Port of Long Beach, CA).

19. Ibid.

20. "A Brief history of the U.S. Foreign-Trade Zones Program," Foreign Trade Zone Resource Center, www.foreign-trade-zone.com/history.htm

21. Op.cit., www.polb.com (Port of Long Beach, CA)

22. Sears Archive, 2015.

23. C. John Langley, Jr. and Capgemini LLC, "2015 19th Annual Third Party Logistics Study", p. 19.

24. National retail Federation, 2015.

25. Deloitte Consulting, "Achieving Assurance of Supply in an Omni-Channel World", 2014.

APPENDIX 4A

Grid Method—Sensitivity Analyses and Application to Warehouse Location In a City

Grid Method—Sensitivity Analysis

Tables 4A.1 and 4A.2 illustrate two sensitivity analyses for the original problem in Table 4.2. The first what-if scenario considers switching from rail to truck to serve the Jacksonville market; the switch entails a 50 percent rate increase. The data in Table 4A.1 show that the rate increase shifts the least-cost location toward Jacksonville; that is, the new location grid coordinates are 664 and 795, or east and south of the original location (655, 826). Therefore, a rate increase will pull the least-cost location toward the market or supply source experiencing the increase.

The second what-if sensitivity analysis considers the elimination of a Buffalo supply source and increasing by 500 tons the amount the example company purchases from Memphis. Table 4A.2 shows the effect of this sourcing change. With Memphis supplying all the material the company formerly purchased from Buffalo, the new least-cost location moves toward Memphis, or south and west of the original location. Similarly, a new market or a market experiencing a sales volume increase will draw the least-cost location.

We can conclude from these sensitivity analyses that the rates, product volumes, and source/market locations do affect a plant's least-cost location. The least-cost location moves toward a market or source experiencing a rate or volume increase, and away from the market or source experiencing a decrease. Introducing a new market or source pulls the location toward the additional market or source.

Grid Method—Application to Distribution Center Location in a City

A special case exists for applying the grid technique to the location of a distribution center in a city. The situation's uniqueness comes from the blanket rate structure, which applies the same rate from an origin to any point within the city or commercial zone. Thus, any location within a city's commercial zone incurs the same inbound transportation cost from a company's mix of suppliers used; that is, the cost of moving supplies to a distribution center within the same city does not affect the location decision.

Since the supply volumes moving into the distribution center do not affect the location decision, the least-cost distribution center location within a city considers the cost of moving finished goods from the distribution center to the customers. We modify the grid technique equation as follows:

$$C = \frac{\sum_{1}^{n} R_i D_i M_i}{\sum_{1}^{n} R_i M_i}$$

Table 4A.1	Impact of Transportation Rate Change on Least-Cost Location					
SOURCES/ MARKETS	**RATE $/ TON-MILE (A)**	**TONS (B)**	**GRID COORDINATES**		**CALCULATIONS**	
			HORIZONTAL	**VERTICAL**	**(A) × (B) × HORIZONTAL**	**(A) × (B) × VERTICAL**
Buffalo (S_1)	$0.90	500	700	1,125	315,000	506,250
Memphis (S_2)	$0.95	300	250	600	71,250	171,000
St. Louis (S_3)	$0.85	700	225	825	133,875	490,875
		1,500			520,125	1,168,125
Atlanta (M_1)	$1.50	225	600	500	202,500	168,750
Boston (M_2)	$1.50	150	1,050	1,200	236,250	270,000
Jacksonville (M_3)	$2.25	250	800	300	450,000	168,750
Philadelphia (M_4)	$1.50	175	925	975	242,813	255,938
New York (M_5)	$1.50	300	1,000	1,080	450,000	486,000
	TOTALS	1,100			1,581,563	1,349,438
					HORIZONTAL	**VERTICAL**
			Numerator: $\Sigma (r \times d \times S) =$		520,125	1,168,125
			$+\Sigma (R \times D \times M) =$		1,581,563	1,349,438
			Sum		2,101,688	2,517,563
			Denominator: $\Sigma (r \times S) =$		1,330	1,330
			$+\Sigma (R \times M) =$		1,838	1,838
			Sum		3,168	3,168
			Grid Center		664	795

Source: Edward J. Bardi, Ph.D. Used with permission.

If we assume that the cost of distributing (.R) the commodity throughout the city is the same, .R cancels out, reducing the equation to a ton-mile center as follows:

$$C = \frac{\sum_{i}^{n} D_i M_i}{\sum_{1}^{n} M_i}$$

Table 4A.2	Impact of Supply Source Change on Least-Cost Location					
SOURCES/ MARKETS	RATE $/ TON-MILE (A)	TONS (B)	GRID COORDINATES		CALCULATIONS	
			HORIZONTAL	VERTICAL	(A) × (B) × HORIZONTAL	(A) × (B) × VERTICAL
Buffalo (S_1)	$0.90	0	700	1,125	0	0
Memphis (S_2)	$0.95	800	250	600	190,000	465,000
St. Louis (S_3)	$0.85	700	225	825	133,875	490,875
		1,500			323,875	946,875
Atlanta (M_1)	$1.50	225	600	500	202,500	168,750
Boston (M_2)	$1.50	150	1,050	1,200	236,250	270,000
Jacksonville (M_3)	$2.25	250	800	300	450,000	168,750
Philadelphia (M_4)	$1.50	175	925	975	242,813	255,938
New York (M_5)	$1.50	300	1,000	1,080	450,000	486,000
	TOTALS	1,100			1,581,563	1,349,438
					HORIZONTAL	VERTICAL
			Numerator: $\Sigma (r \times d \times S) =$		323,875	946,875
			$+\Sigma (R \times D \times M) =$		1,581,563	1,349,438
			Sum		1,905,438	2,296,313
			Denominator: $\Sigma (r \times S) =$		1,335	1,335
			$+\Sigma (R \times M) =$		1,838	1,838
			Sum		3,193	3,193
			Grid Center		597	719

Source: Edward J. Bardi, Ph.D. Used with permission.

As before, this modified grid technique enables the decision maker to eliminate certain areas of the city and to concentrate the analysis upon sites in the general vicinity of the least-cost location's grid coordinates. To determine a specific site for the distribution center, the decision maker must consider land and facility availability, expressway systems, and highway access in this general vicinity.

Aside from providing useful coverage of the foundations of supply chain, the first four chapters included frequent mention of the strategic importance of supply chain management and its role in the competitive success of both public and private organizations in today's increasingly global environment. It is essential that individual organizations do what they can to meet and exceed the needs of their customers and consumers, and to assure that the financial results are sufficient to grow and enhance their market positioning. Also, it is essential for these individual organizations to understand that their overall success is dependent on the success of the supply chains in which they participate. Thus, the old adage that "the (supply) chain is as strong as its weakest link," is alive and well.

Part II focuses on the fundamentals of supply chain management, which includes coverage of four key process areas that must be well-managed, both individually and together, to contribute to the effectiveness and efficiency of the overall supply chain and the organization itself. These areas include: sourcing materials and services; operations – producing goods and services; demand management; and order management and customer service.

Chapter 5 highlights the importance of strategic sourcing and the key steps and considerations to being successful in this area. Of particular significance is the need to recognize the operational and strategic importance of a company's supplier base to the functioning of its overall supply chain. Also, a look at current trends in sourcing includes useful perspectives on this important process in the context of e-Commerce.

Chapter 6 recognizes the strategic role played by operations in the supply chain. Emphasis is placed on the concept of a transformation process and how this is relevant to both production and other types of value-adding processes. Additional detail focuses on the design of assembly and production operations, measurement of productivity and quality, and the ways in which capable information technologies support these key areas.

Chapter 7 considers the importance of outbound-to-customer supply chain needs, and the capabilities needed to satisfy and create value for customers. Included are the need to balance supply and demand, and to investigate factors that affect each of these. In addition, attention is focused on the use of forecasting and demand management, point-of-sale information, and basic collaborative techniques such as sales and operations planning (S&OP). The chapter concludes with coverage of the importance and functioning of capable order fulfillment processes.

Chapter 8 addresses the concepts of customer service and order management, and how they are related and managed within organizations. The basic elements of customer service are identified and discussed from the perspectives of how they affect both buyers and sellers. The use of activity-based costing (ABC) is highlighted, and the concept of calculating stockout costs is introduced. Also included are the major outputs of order management, how they are measured, and their financial impacts on buyers and sellers. The chapter concludes with a discussion of service recovery and its importance to organizations.

Chapter 5

SOURCING MATERIALS AND SERVICES

Learning Objectives

After reading this chapter, you should be able to do the following:

- Understand the role and nature of purchasing, procurement, and strategic sourcing in a supply chain context.
- Consider the importance of types of items and services purchased to the sourcing and procurement processes.
- Understand the strategic sourcing process.
- Recognize principles and approaches for the effective management of sourcing and procurement activities.
- Appreciate the importance of companies having effective relationships with suppliers and for developing meaningful processes for evaluating suppliers.
- Examine the concept of total landed cost (TLC) and its value to the procurement process.
- Be aware of contemporary advances in the areas of e-sourcing and e-procurement, and appreciate the roles played by various types of e-commerce models.

<table>
<tr><td>

Supply Chain Profile

</td><td>

Strategic Sourcing Facilitates Innovation, Transformation, and Cost Reduction

</td></tr>
</table>

Two of the words heard most often at the Institute for Supply Management (ISM) Annual Conference were innovation and transformation. They both were covered by the umbrellas of strategic sourcing and supplier relationship management.

This makes sense, of course, as everyone in the supply chain profession wants to elevate their discipline within the organization. What's more, who doesn't want to automate the mundane transactions associated with issuing a purchase order, arranging a shipment, or scheduling a production run so they can lead an effort to transform their department or have a role in new product or process development and innovation?

So where are we? Certainly headway is being made. In the last two issues of *Supply Chain Management Review* (SCMR), articles have provided details as to how Molson Coors is integrating supply management into its new product development process and how Raytheon is launching a supplier advisory council in its journey to become the customer of choice—the one that gets access to supplier innovation first.

At the same time, there's a long way to go. "When you talk to CFOs, which is where the rubber hits the road, they are still focused on cost reduction," says a principal at The Hackett Group and a proponent of strategic sourcing, transformation and innovation.

So, can we have it all, or will cost-cutting lead the day? This is a very contemporary topic, and one that received significant attention following a presentation on supplier relationship management by executives with Staples Advantage and The Hackett Group.

One interesting comment by a category manager for a CPG company is that she is constantly being asked to innovate. "I'm not very creative," she said with a little frustration. "But when we talk to suppliers, we know they are experts that have solutions that align with our business needs. We really need to learn to listen to them." That led to a great conversation about the challenges of trying to innovate and cut costs that would have continued if time had permitted.

Done right, it seems that procurement can do all three—transform its processes, innovate with suppliers and deliver cost savings to the total cost of a product or service. But it also seems as if the profession, just like our friends in manufacturing, logistics, and distribution, must help to convince the C-suite of the value strategic sourcing can deliver.

Source: Adapted from Bob Trebilcock, Editorial Director, *Supply Chain Management Review,* May 7, 2015. Used with permission.

5-1 Introduction

Logistics and supply chain managers are looking for ways to drive more value from their purchasing and procurement operations. Whether it may be pressure from demanding customers, the emergence of lower-cost competition from global sources, or the complexity of supply chains, executives are finding that the time-honored emphasis on low-cost purchasing just isn't cutting it anymore.

As a result, the topics of purchasing, procurement, and strategic sourcing are all receiving considerable attention as organizations try to improve the overall efficiency and effectiveness of their supply chains. While the following definitions are intended to aid understanding of some of the similarities, differences, and linkages between purchasing, procurement, and strategic sourcing, it is not uncommon at times for these terms to be used somewhat interchangeably.

- **Purchasing:** This function is responsible for managing an organization's acquisition procedures and standards. In a business setting this is a largely transactional activity that consists of the buying of products and services. This is facilitated by the placement and processing of a purchase order. Typically, this activity follows conduct of a formal sourcing process.

- **Procurement:** Essentially, this refers to managing a broad range of processes that are associated with an organization's need to procure goods and services that are needed throughout the supply chain and the overall organization. Examples of activities within the procurement process include product/service sourcing, supplier selection, price negotiation, contract management, transaction management, and supplier performance management.

- **Strategic sourcing:** This is a significantly broader process than procurement, and it represents a very useful means to make sure that procurement priorities are well-aligned with goals and objectives of the supply chain and of the overall organization. Also, reliance on a capable strategic sourcing process facilitates the objective of achieving alignment and collaboration among the supply chain and other areas of the organization such as marketing, manufacturing, R&D, etc.

Based on a review of these definitions, it is important to consider purchasing simply as an activity (albeit an important one), while procurement and strategic sourcing are best described as processes. Figure 5.1 identifies five examples of ways in which strategic

Figure 5.1	Unique Aspects of Strategic Sourcing

1. **Consolidation and Leveraging of Purchasing Power:** If every department or division in an organization were to make independent purchasing decisions, the end result would be more costly than if the purchases were coordinated. Looking broadly at everything purchased by an organization, significant savings may be achieved through the consolidation of purchasing power and leveraging larger volumes of purchases with fewer total suppliers.
2. **Emphasis on Value:** Far too frequently, organizations place the highest priority on trying to procure needed items at the lowest possible cost. In so doing, opportunities may be missed to achieve greater value, for example, through reduced costs over the life cycle of the product. Buying a copier/fax/scan machine on the basis of acquisition cost alone, would effectively neglect the long-term costs that may be associated with toner, repairs, etc.
3. **More Meaningful Supplier Relationships:** Strategic sourcing benefits from developing sound business relationships with many types of suppliers. Depending on the type of purchase being considered, the development of truly "collaborative" relationships can be very effective.
4. **Attention Directed to Process Improvement:** Strategic sourcing looks beyond the need for effective purchasing practices, and focuses attention on the business processes that are related to the particular purchase being considered. Additionally, reformulation and streamlining of purchasing processes are a key element of strategic sourcing.
5. **Enhanced Teamwork and Professionalism:** The concept of teamwork is essential to the success of strategic sourcing. Through the use of cross-functional teams, that may include representatives of supplier and customer organizations, the benefits of strategic sourcing may be realized.

Source: C. John Langley Jr., Ph.D., Penn State University, Used with permission.

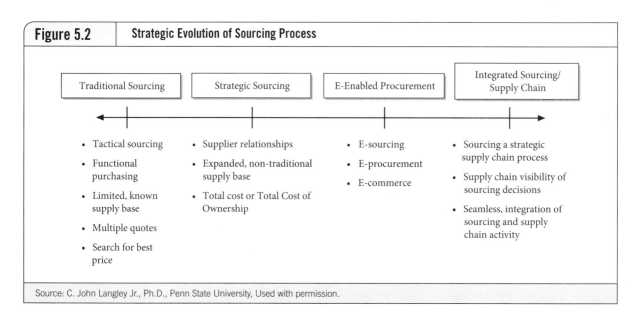

Figure 5.2 | **Strategic Evolution of Sourcing Process**

Traditional Sourcing	Strategic Sourcing	E-Enabled Procurement	Integrated Sourcing/ Supply Chain

- Tactical sourcing
- Functional purchasing
- Limited, known supply base
- Multiple quotes
- Search for best price

- Supplier relationships
- Expanded, non-traditional supply base
- Total cost or Total Cost of Ownership

- E-sourcing
- E-procurement
- E-commerce

- Sourcing a strategic supply chain process
- Supply chain visibility of sourcing decisions
- Seamless, integration of sourcing and supply chain activity

Source: C. John Langley Jr., Ph.D., Penn State University, Used with permission.

sourcing is a more comprehensive concept: (1) consolidation and leveraging of purchasing power—to concentrate larger volumes of purchases into fewer suppliers or fewer purchasing transactions; (2) emphasis on value—rather than acquisition cost alone; (3) more meaningful supplier relationships; (4) attention directed to process improvement; and (5) enhanced teamwork and professionalism—to include suppliers and customers, as appropriate.

Figure 5.2 suggests a strategic evolution to the sourcing process. This diagram highlights not only the trend from traditional/tactical sourcing to strategic sourcing, but ultimately to e-enabled procurement and integration of sourcing and supply chain. Regardless of the terminology used to describe the future state, it is clear there is a high priority on developing and enhancing approaches to procurement and sourcing that create additional value for organizations, their customers, and their suppliers. Michael Porter, in his value chain, identified the strategic importance of procurement, since it includes such activities as qualifying new suppliers, procuring different types of inputs, and monitoring supplier performance.[1] As such, procurement serves as a critical link between members of the supply chain.

5-2 Types and Importance of Items and Services Purchased[2]

Obviously, the products and services purchased by a company are not all the same. Some products are more important and require greater procurement attention. For example, a computer manufacturer would have very different sourcing and procurement strategies, tactics, and resources for semiconductor chips than it would have for office supplies such as paper, notepads, etc. Clearly, the semiconductor chips have a distinctly different criticality than do office supplies.

A widely-used approach known as the quadrant technique enables supply chain managers to assess the importance of each product or service being purchased. This technique utilizes a two-by-two matrix to determine a procured item's relative importance on the basis of value and risk. The criteria used to delineate importance are value or profit potential and risk or uniqueness.

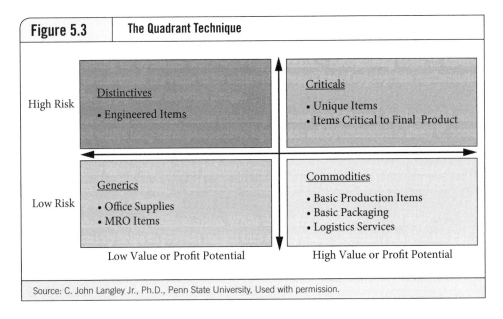

Figure 5.3 | **The Quadrant Technique**

Source: C. John Langley Jr., Ph.D., Penn State University, Used with permission.

The value criterion examines product or service features that enhance profits for the final product and the firm's ability to maintain a competitive advantage in the marketplace. For example, a computer chip that is faster or an operating system that is more user friendly will make the computer more desirable, thereby increasing demand for the product and, consequently, increasing profits. Alternatively, the addition of a gold-plated paper clip to the computer instruction manual probably will not increase computer sales or solidify a competitive advantage in the marketplace.

Risk reflects the chance of failure, nonacceptance in the marketplace, delivery failures, and source nonavailability. The risk of a paper clip failure is really not a significant risk for a computer manufacturer. That is, if a paper clip fails to hold a number of pieces of paper together, the operation of the company's computer should not be affected. However, if a computer chip fails, the computer will not operate, and the marketplace will respond in a negative way. Thus, the computer chip poses a greater risk than the paper clip to a computer manufacturer.

Figure 5.3 depicts the value risk quadrant and categorizes item importance. Items of low risk, low value are identified as generics; those of low risk, high value are commodities. Products or services that are high risk, low value are distinctives; while those of high risk, high value are criticals.

Generics are low-risk, low-value items and services that typically do not enter the final product. Items such as office supplies and maintenance, repair, and operating items (MRO) are examples of generics. The administrative and acquisition processing costs are more significant than the purchase price of generics, and, for some generics, the administration and processing costs may exceed the price paid for the item or service. The strategic procurement thrust for generics is to streamline the procurement process to reduce the cost associated with purchasing generics. For example, the use of purchasing cards (corporate credit cards) reduces the number of checks written and the administrative costs associated with check payment, bank verification, and so on.

Commodities are items or services that are low in risk but high in value. Basic production materials (bolts), basic packaging (exterior box), and transportation services are examples of commodities that enhance the profitability of the company but pose a low risk. These items and services are fundamental to the company's finished product, thus making their value high. Risk is low because commodities are not unique items, and there are many sources of supply. Because commodities are not unique, there is little brand distinction, and price is a significant distinguishing factor. Freight and inventory are major procurement cost considerations for commodities. The procurement strategies used for commodities include volume purchasing to reduce price and just-in-time systems to lower inventory costs.

Distinctives are high-risk, low-value items and services such as engineered items, parts that are available from only a limited number of suppliers, or items that have a long lead time. The company's customers are unaware of or do not care about the uniqueness of distinctives, but these products pose a threat to continued operation and/or high procurement cost. A stockout of distinctives results in stopping the production line or changing the production schedule to work around a stocked-out item; both tactics increase production costs. Alternatively, using premium supply sources or premium transportation will eliminate the stockout, but procurement costs will increase. The strategic focus for distinctives is developing a standardization program to eliminate or reduce the uniqueness of the distinctives, thereby changing these items to generics.

Finally, **criticals** are high-risk, high-value items that give the final product a competitive advantage in the marketplace. As noted earlier, the computer chip used may give the computer a unique speed that differentiates it from all competitors. This unique computer chip increases the computer's value to the customer, and the risk of nonavailability is customer dissatisfaction and reduced sales. Criticals, in part, determine the customer's ultimate cost of using the finished product—in our example, the computer. The procurement strategy for criticals is to strengthen their value through use of new technologies, simplification, close supplier relations, and/or value-added alterations. The focus of critical procurement is on innovation to make the critical item provide greater market value to the finished product.

The preceding discussion of the quadrant technique emphasizes that not all items and services purchased are of equal importance. It also suggests that the supply chain manager must utilize varying procurement strategies based on the value and risk of the item. Greater resources and attention should be directed toward procuring criticals than toward generics. For example, one full-time procurement specialist may be assigned responsibility for the purchase of one critical item—say, a computer chip—whereas one full-time person may be assigned to the purchase of hundreds of generics—office supplies.

Figure 5.4 helps to understand the three types of buy situations that may occur. The first is that of capital goods that may represent a longer-term investment for an organization

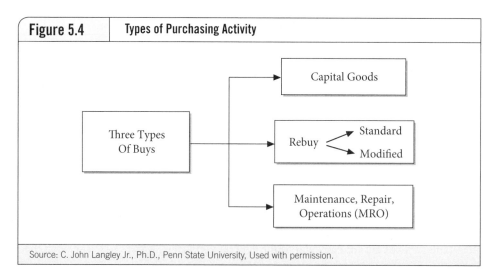

Figure 5.4   **Types of Purchasing Activity**

Source: C. John Langley Jr., Ph.D., Penn State University, Used with permission.

that may require significant financial planning. The second is that of re-buys that are repeat purchases that may either be identical to historical purchases (standard) or some variation thereof (modified). The third is that of MRO items that are needed for the continuing operation of the company and its supply chain activities.

5-3 Strategic Sourcing Process

As indicated previously, strategic sourcing is a much broader and more comprehensive process than procurement or purchasing. Although there are numerous methodologies to describe the strategic sourcing process, Figure 5.5 outlines the elements of one such approach, "Managing Strategic Sourcing Process" (MSSP). Beginning with development of

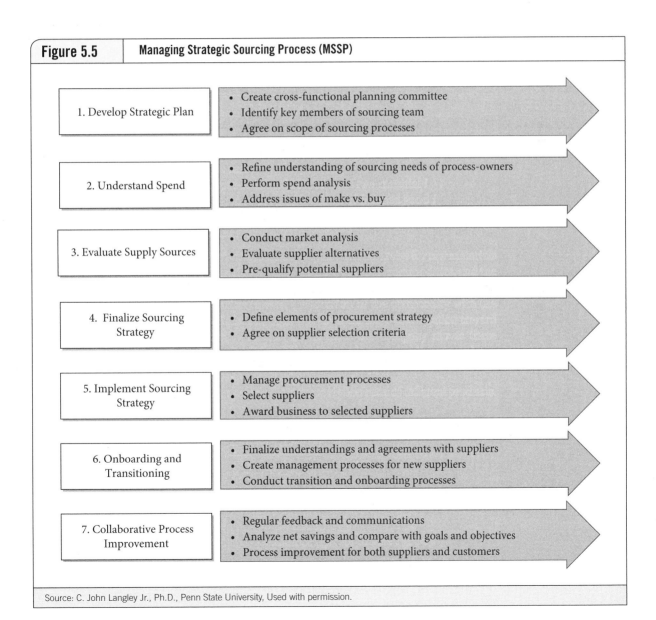

Figure 5.5 — Managing Strategic Sourcing Process (MSSP)

1. Develop Strategic Plan
   - Create cross-functional planning committee
   - Identify key members of sourcing team
   - Agree on scope of sourcing processes

2. Understand Spend
   - Refine understanding of sourcing needs of process-owners
   - Perform spend analysis
   - Address issues of make vs. buy

3. Evaluate Supply Sources
   - Conduct market analysis
   - Evaluate supplier alternatives
   - Pre-qualify potential suppliers

4. Finalize Sourcing Strategy
   - Define elements of procurement strategy
   - Agree on supplier selection criteria

5. Implement Sourcing Strategy
   - Manage procurement processes
   - Select suppliers
   - Award business to selected suppliers

6. Onboarding and Transitioning
   - Finalize understandings and agreements with suppliers
   - Create management processes for new suppliers
   - Conduct transition and onboarding processes

7. Collaborative Process Improvement
   - Regular feedback and communications
   - Analyze net savings and compare with goals and objectives
   - Process improvement for both suppliers and customers

Source: C. John Langley Jr., Ph.D., Penn State University, Used with permission.

a strategic plan for the strategic sourcing process, this model recognizes several elements, each of which contributes significantly to a comprehensive MSSP process. Each of these is discussed in the sections that follow.

To help guide the strategic sourcing process, five core principles are recognized as key drivers to achieve the desired levels of value. These principles are as follows:

- **Assess the total value**—Emphasis must go beyond acquisition cost and evaluate total cost of ownership and the value of the supplier relationship.
- **Develop individual sourcing strategies**—Individual spend categories need customized sourcing strategies.
- **Evaluate internal requirements**—Requirements and specifications must be thoroughly assessed and rationalized as part of the sourcing process.
- **Focus on supplier economics**—Suppliers' economics must be understood before identifying buying tactics such as volume leveraging, price unbundling, or price adjustment mechanisms.
- **Drive continuous improvement**—Strategic sourcing initiatives should be a subset of the continuous improvement process for the procurement and sourcing organizations.

5-3-1 Step 1: Develop Strategic Plan

The most effective way to initiate a MSSP process is to take the time to map out a formal plan for the design and implementation of the process itself. Included here is the creation of a cross-functional planning group to guide and oversee the overall strategic sourcing process, and the identification of key members of the strategic sourcing team. Also, there should be consensus on the scope and design of the MSSP process, which must include a preliminary understanding of what types of products and services may be within the responsibility of this initiative.

5-3-2 Step 2: Understand Spend

Once the direction and cadence of the MSSP process is finalized, the planning group needs to develop a baseline understanding of what products and services are being procured, what purposes they serve, the financial implications of these purchases, etc. This needs to include a formal "spend analysis" that is designed to understand spend by supplier, category, and internal user and to profile current sourcing approaches and areas for improvement.

Included in this step will be the need to refine understanding of the sourcing needs, particularly with the needs and requirements of process owners throughout the supply chain and the broader organization. Once these needs have been determined, the nature of the requirement must be represented by some type of measurable criteria. The criteria may be relatively simple—for example, criteria for copy machine paper could be 8½ by 11-inch white paper of a certain bond weight—or they may be very complex in the instance of a highly technical product. Using these criteria, the sourcing professional can communicate the user's needs to potential suppliers. Last, an evaluation of the "make vs. buy" decision will be critical to the direction of the MSSP process. Even with a "make" decision, however, the buying firm will usually have to purchase some types of inputs from outside suppliers. This step has become much more important today, when more companies are outsourcing in order to focus upon their core activities.

A primary result of this step is to fully understand the scope and scale of these activities at the time the MSSP process is initiated. To do so will provide a meaningful profile of the current, or baseline situation, and will serve as a basis for comparison once progress with the MSSP process has been made. The end result should include recommendations for improvement of the overall sourcing process and likely financial benefits.

5-3-3 Step 3: Evaluate Supply Sources

This is a very critical step in the strategic sourcing process, as it involves making sure that all potential sources of supply are identified and that useful mechanisms are in place for meaningful comparisons of alternative supply sources. A few perspectives on this step are as follows:

- A useful evaluation of supply sources begins with a comprehensive market analysis. Sources of supply can operate in purely competitive markets (many suppliers), oligopolistic markets (a few large suppliers), or monopolistic markets (one supplier). Information related to the type of market will help the sourcing professional determine the number of suppliers in the market, where the power/dependence balance lies, and which method of buying might be most effective—negotiations, competitive bidding, and so on. Specific information about market type is not always easily available, and so some research may be necessary using standard reference sources such as *Moody's*, information from trade associations, and a wide range of information that may be available through use of the internet.

- It is important to identify all possible suppliers that might be able to satisfy the user's needs—including some suppliers that the buying firm may not have worked with previously. Considering the extent to which global markets continue to evolve and expand, this task may be challenging at times. Again, formal research efforts may be needed to uncover the needed information. If the company is small, it may rely on more common secondary sources of such information, such as local buying guides, internet searches, etc.

- Once the effort to identify capable suppliers has largely been completed, the next priority is to identify the pool of possible suppliers that can satisfy the users' demands. This is referred to as pre-qualifying potential suppliers. This may be a relatively straightforward process when the items being procured are relatively common and for which demand is relatively predictable. Alternatively, when needed parts or materials may need custom-manufacturing, or for which usage patterns are not very predictable, the pre-screening process may be more involved.

This step also should recognize the need to simplify purchasing complexity and whenever possible rationalize products. In addition, attention should be directed to developing a detailed understanding and analysis of pricing, identifying opportunities to consolidate buying and create leverage, and redefining and modernizing supplier relationships. Making sure that objectives such as these are met should help to provide a comprehensive and meaningful evaluation of supply sources.

5-3-4 Step 4: Finalize Sourcing Strategy

Prior to embarking on the task of supplier selection, it is important to fully develop a sourcing strategy that defines the parameters of the process and the steps to be followed. Figure 5.6 provides an overview of the supplier portfolio screening process; it spans Steps 3–5 in the MSSP process. Of particular interest in this process are the steps related to initial supplier research and screening, development of a responsive request for information (RFI) and request for proposal (RFP), site visits with follow-up discussions, and supplier selection.

- The purpose of the RFI is to establish whether a supplier has the capabilities and interest to be considered further in the sourcing process and is potentially able to meet the customer's business requirements. Examples of information that may be requested in an RFI include company background, financial stability, markets covered, manufacturing and distribution facilities, research and development, and quality systems. RFIs generally focus attention on non-price information that may be of interest and relevance to the buying organization.

- The RFP provides specific information as to what the buying company would like to source and asks potential suppliers for details as to how they would respond to the request. Included in this response would be substantive information as to the specific products and services to be provided, as well as pricing information.

The strategic sourcing process requires two major types of investments by the firm, time and information. Time is expended by the individuals involved in making the purchase; the more complex and important the purchase, the more time must be spent on it, especially if it is a new buy. Information can be both internal and external to the firm. Internal information is gathered concerning user requirements and the implications that the purchase will have for the firm. External information concerning the input to be purchased may be gathered from supply chain members, potential suppliers, and others. The more complex and important the purchase, the more information is needed for the procurement process to be effective. Determining the level of investment needed in time and information to adequately meet a user's requirements is a firm-specific process. Once the level of investment is decided, the strategic sourcing process can then move forward.

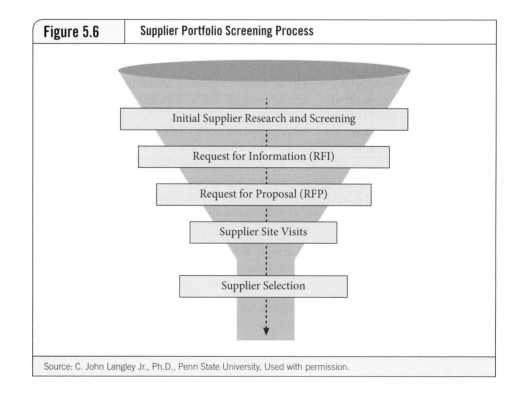

| Figure 5.6 | Supplier Portfolio Screening Process |

Initial Supplier Research and Screening

Request for Information (RFI)

Request for Proposal (RFP)

Supplier Site Visits

Supplier Selection

Source: C. John Langley Jr., Ph.D., Penn State University, Used with permission.

The sourcing strategy also should include supplier selection criteria and a process for evaluating submissions from multiple suppliers. The selection criteria should relate directly to the previously established objectives to be met by the formal strategic sourcing process. Examples of supplier selection criteria are shown in Figure 5.7, and a few additional comments regarding each are as follows:

> **Quality**. Typically the most important factor in supplier selection is **quality**. In today's business environments, quality standards are very high, and suppliers are counted upon to take major responsibility for quality. Over time, several techniques and approaches have been developed that address issues relating to soundness of processes, results achieved, and continuous improvement. Buying organizations need to look closely to make sure that participation in these programs actually produces results that are of real and measurable value, and that benefits and improvements can be documented. A few of the well-recognized approaches are as follows:[3]
>
> - **Total Quality Management**—Arising in the 1980s in response to Japanese competition and the teachings of Dr. W. Edwards Deming, TQM represented a strategy in which entire organizations were focused on an examination of process variability and continuous improvement. This approach was heavily dependent on the use of statistical process control (SPC), and employee involvement to produce desired results.
>
> - **Six Sigma**—Similar to TQM in its focus on techniques for solving problems and using statistical methods to improve processes, the Six Sigma approach involves training experts (known as green belts and black belts) who work on solving important problems while they teach others in the company.
>
> - **ISO 9000**—Started in 1987 by the International Organization for Standardization, a primary objective is to make sure that companies have standard processes in place that follow: "Document what you do and do what you document." ISO 9000 involves a third-party registration program (not dissimilar to Underwriters Laboratories—a very well-known registrar) certifying that companies are following documented processes.

Figure 5.7	Example Supplier Selection Criteria

- **Quality**
  — Technical specifications
  — Design
  — Product life
  — Ease of repair
  — Maintenance
  — Dependability
- **Reliability**
  — On-time delivery
  — Performance history
  — Warranty and replacement policies

- **Risk**
  — Lead time risk and uncertainty
  — Potential for supply uncertainty
  — Cost risk
- **Capability**
  — Production capability
  — Technical capability
  — Management
  — Information
  — Operating controls
  — Labor relations

- **Financial**
  — Prices of products
  — Financial stability
- **Desirable Qualities**
  — Cultural compatibility and supplier attitude
  — Supplier locations
  — Packaging
  — Repair and return capabilities
  — Training aids
- **Sustainability**
  — Commitment to sustainability
  — View sustainability as a potential driver of increased efficiency and effectiveness

Source: C. John Langley Jr., Ph.D., Penn State University. Used with permission.

Reliability. Time-definite and on-time deliveries are among the top-ranked factors relating to reliability. The importance relates to avoiding production line shutdowns, unavailability of finished products due to lack of materials, and ultimately to successfully fulfill customers' orders in the marketplace. When off-shore alternatives are being considered for certain types of supplies and materials, the larger distances involved would suggest greater attention be focused on the reliability factor.

Risk. There are many types of risks, including service reliability as indicated earlier. Other types may include potentials for supply uncertainty, lead time uncertainty, and cost uncertainty. Included may be elements such as variation in availability of needed parts and materials, uncertainty in the availability of needed transportation resources, natural disasters, etc. To minimize exposure to risks, the supplier selection process should exhibit great diligence in identify types of potential risk, their likelihoods, and potential consequences.

Capability. This criterion considers potential suppliers' production facilities and capacity, technical capability, management and organizational capabilities, and operating controls. These factors indicate the supplier's ability to provide a needed quality and quantity of material in a timely manner. One factor that needs to be a subject of inquiry is the labor relations record of suppliers that are being considered. Also, the capabilities of suppliers with regard to information technologies may be very important, particularly as they are needed to manage their own operations and interface with customers.

Financial. In addition to price, buying firms are wise to consider the financial positions of potential suppliers. Financially unstable suppliers pose possible disruptions in a long-run continued supply of material. By declaring bankruptcy, a supplier providing materials critical to a final product could impair the functioning of a customer's manufacturing operations.

Desirable Qualities. The types of concerns here may be extensive, but some of those likely to be relevant include cultural compatibility and supplier attitude; locations of key supplier facilities; packaging capabilities; repair and return services; and others such as availability of training aids, etc.

Sustainability. This factor is "last but not least," in the sense that a commitment to sustainability is regarded as essential in many leading supply chains. Given the priority that businesses and society in general have placed on initiatives relating to sustainability, supply chains are well-positioned to make significant contributions to progress in this area.

All of these criteria are important or can be important in certain procurement situations. However, the one criterion that generates the most discussion and frequently the most frustration for procurement specialists is price or cost. Therefore, Appendix 5A includes additional perspectives and extended discussion relating to the topic of procurement price.

5-3-5 Step 5: Implement Sourcing Strategy

The management of procurement processes begins with an evaluation of the suppliers that remain following the RFI and RFP processes and culminates in the award of a contract. With the pool of suppliers reduced to those viewed as capable of meeting the customer's needs and requirements, this activity may be accomplished through the use of competitive bidding if the procurement item or items are fairly simple or standard and there are a sufficient numbers of potential suppliers. If there are only a few suppliers, then it may be preferable to enter into a negotiation process with those who remain.

Clearly, the most important part of this step is to choose a supplier (or suppliers, depending on the objectives of the sourcing decision). The choice of supplier also determines the relationship that will exist between the buying and supplying firms and how the mechanics of this relationship will be structured and implemented.

In either a competitive bidding or negotiations process, each potential supplier should be evaluated using selection criteria similar to those suggested previously in Figure 5.7. This process should provide a means to weight the importance of each factor, as may be appropriate, and also be sufficiently flexible to supplement the process with any additional relevant factors that may be identified. The concluding element of this step is to award the business to those suppliers that best meet the full range of selection criteria.

5-3-6 Step 6: Onboarding and Transitioning

Important elements of this step are the finalization of the contractual agreement, planning the transition process, and receipt or delivery of the product or service. This activity commences with the first attempt by the supplier or suppliers to satisfy the user's needs. The completion of this activity also begins the generation of performance data to be used for the next step in the strategic sourcing process.

Other key elements of this step include creating and communicating management processes for new suppliers; and conducting transition and onboarding processes. Given the obvious rigor of the overall MSSP process, it sometimes occurs that this onboarding and transitioning responsibility does not receive the attention it deserves. This is unfortunate, as experience has suggested that this step is one of the most important in the overall strategic sourcing process.

5-3-7 Step 7: Collaborative Process Improvement

A very important step in the MSSP process is to establish procedures for regular feedback and communication between suppliers and customers. Once the product has been delivered or the service performed, the supplier's performance must be evaluated to determine whether it has truly satisfied the user's needs. Then, this should facilitate the identification of any areas or ways in which either the supplier or customer needs to improve for the benefit of the overall relationship. Next, it is necessary to analyze net savings and compare with goals and objectives that should have been agreed to with suppliers. This will provide very relevant financial information that may be used to evaluate the overall benefits to the customer organization from the overall MSSP process.

One final comment relating to the strategic sourcing process is that all of the activities identified in this section may be subject to influences beyond the control of the procurement professional. These influences can determine how effectively each activity is performed. They include intra- and inter-organizational factors and external factors such as governmental influences. For example, a change in marketing needs or manufacturing process may require repeating all or some of the activities identified before the first iteration is completed. Financial failure of a potential supplier will also cause problems and necessitate repeated activities.

On the Line

Haworth, Inc. Realizes $1.2 Million in Cross-Border Savings

Haworth, Inc. produces raised floors, movable walls, adaptable technology, lighting, furniture systems, seating, storage, and wood case goods. With over 600 dealers worldwide, this $1.2 billion, Holland, Michigan company designs, manufactures, and ships a significant amount of goods within the North America Free Trade Association (NAFTA) region, representing approximately $200 million annually—about 85 percent of Haworth's overall exports.

To take advantage of NAFTA benefits, Haworth needed to automate the process of qualifying goods for preferential treatment for export from both the U.S. and Canada. This process required the acquisition of NAFTA certification data for over 43,000 purchased parts, from more than 1,000 suppliers worldwide. Previously, this process had been outsourced to a third-party service provider, where the NAFTA analysis was managed separately and results were manually uploaded into the export documentation system. Paper NAFTA certificates were created for parts on transactional shipments and sent via courier to Haworth's brokers and customers daily.

While the process worked to some extent, it proved to be very cumbersome, and the third-party was only able to qualify about 50 percent of Haworth's 16,000-plus export products. The imperative was clear—Haworth needed to take control over the NAFTA compliance system across the company's entire product line.

To address this problem, Haworth implemented a Web portal for automating the solicitation and management of qualification data from suppliers. The solution was integrated into four different, internal legacy systems, including order management, warehouse management, and two manufacturing ERP systems. As a result, Haworth was able to integrate these systems and automatically pull data into one global trade database. This streamlined and automated Haworth's entire compliance and NAFTA qualification process.

In the new system, export transactions are processed daily, parts are inserted based on new customer order data, and orders for NAFTA territories drive the corresponding analysis. Bills of materials (BOM) are automatically captured, thereby creating new records that initiate the supplier selection process. Also, e-mails are automatically created and sent to suppliers who then can respond electronically via the application's Web portal.

Results have been impressive with Haworth having saved $1.2 million in duties and taxes from preferential treatment. Additionally, the company is saving approximately $225,000 annually resulting from elimination of outsourcing costs, and paper, fax, and courier charges.

Source: Adapted from John D. Schultz, "Erasing Cross-Border Complexities," *Logistics Management*, June 2015, pp. 36–39. Used with permission.

5-4 Supplier Evaluation and Relationships

Many successful companies have recognized the key role that sourcing and procurement play in supply chain management and that supplier relationships are a vital part of successful procurement strategies. "Good suppliers do not grow on trees" is an adage that is often quoted by procurement professionals. Although the strategic sourcing process has its complexities, it can be managed effectively as long as there is a systematic process to follow. An important factor in achieving efficiency and effectiveness in this area is the development of successful supplier relationships. In fact, many supply chain executives agree that today's global marketplace requires developing strong supplier relationships in order to create and sustain a competitive advantage. Companies such as NCR and Motorola go so far as to refer to suppliers as partners and/or stakeholders in their company. When suppliers are "partners," companies tend to rely more upon them to provide input into processes such as product design, engineering assistance, quality control, etc.

Evaluation of suppliers should be done regularly and on a formal basis. Essentially, the three most important questions include (1) Did the supplier succeed in meeting the customer's needs? (2) What elements of the relationship, both strategic and tactical/operational may benefit from modification and improvement? (3) Did the investments by both customer and supplier produce measurable benefits that justified the time and effort of the relationship? If the process was not effective, the cause could be traced to not enough investment, not performing the proper activities, or mistakes made in performing one or more of the activities. In any case, when the strategic sourcing process is less effective than would be desired, the cause(s) must be identified and corrective actions taken to make sure that future sourcing strategies will prove to be effective. If the purchase satisfied the user's needs at the proper level of investment, the strategic sourcing process may be deemed to be effective and can serve as a reference for future purchases.

Another important dimension of the supplier relationship is the extent to which the customer–supplier relationship contributes to the competitive advantage of the company, whether the advantage is one of low cost, differentiation, or a niche orientation (using Porter's generic strategies).[4] Therefore, the goals of the strategic sourcing process must be consistent with the overall competitive advantage that a company is seeking to attain in the marketplace. An example of this would be L Brands (Limited, Inc.), which considers its supply chain capabilities to be a key differentiator of the entire organization in the marketplace. L Brands is viewed as a global leader on this capability, and their partnerships with their suppliers of all types focus on achieving the overall goals of the organization.

5-5 Total Landed Cost (TLC)

As indicated in Figure 5.8, purchase or acquisition cost is only the tip of the iceberg when the analysis is broadened to encompass factors that would better relate to the TLC. This concept represents the sum of all costs associated with making and delivering products to the point where they are needed. In effect, this perspective brings into play a few considerations that are helpful to the supplier selection process. Among those that are highlighted are life cycle costs, inventory costs, strategic sourcing costs, transaction costs, quality costs, technology costs, and management costs.

Figure 5.9 illustrates how important it is to consider types of cost that are in addition to the purchase price for needed product. Interestingly, the product prices are lowest in Vietnam and highest in the EU, but after transportation, customs, and VAT costs are included, sourcing from the EU is the least expensive and from Vietnam the most expensive. Although this is a relatively straightforward example, it reinforces the importance of looking beyond the price of the products themselves when trying to make a cost-effective sourcing decision.

As a practical matter, it is essential that sourcing decisions rely on a sound understanding and knowledge of the total costs associated with the individual purchasing decisions. To provide further insight and perspective on this important topic, Appendix 5A, titled "The Special Case of Procurement Price," includes a wide range of relevant details relating to these decisions. Also, various other considerations that are relevant to sourcing and purchasing decisions are discussed at various points in this text, particularly Chapter 2, "Global Dimensions of Supply Chains."

Figure 5.8	Total Landed Cost (TLC)

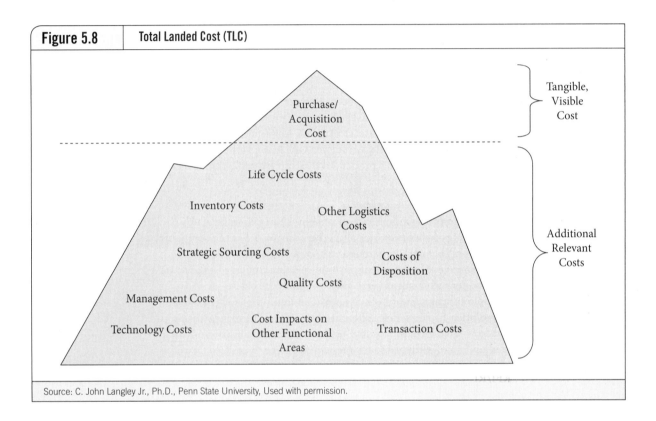

Source: C. John Langley Jr., Ph.D., Penn State University, Used with permission.

Figure 5.9	Cost Comparisons of Example Sourcing Options

Destination Country—Switzerland	Country of Origin		
Price Components—all prices in Euros	China	Vietnam	EU
Net purchasing price for a specific volume of the product from three different suppliers	10,000	8,000	12,000
Total transportation cost to Switzerland – Ocean freight from China/Vietnam—Road freight within Europe	4,000	6,000	1,200
Customs according to trade agreement	1,000	1,500	n.a.
VAT (Switzerland 7.6%) based on value of goods	1,140	1,178	1,003
Total Landed Cost	16,140	16,678	14,203

Source: C. John Langley Jr., Ph.D., Penn State University, Used with permission.

5-6 e-Sourcing and e-Procurement

Obviously, the computer and Internet have created some dramatic changes in the business world and in the everyday activities of consumers. For example, it has become quite common for individual consumers to research products and services, locate retail and e-retail suppliers, purchase goods and services, and track the delivery of shipments—all electronically and in the convenience of their own home. According to a current five-year e-commerce forecast by Forrester Research, U.S. online retail sales were expected to reach $334 billion in 2015 and $480 billion by 2019. At the time of the forecasts, 69% of the U.S. online population regularly purchased products online, with clothing, consumer electronics, and computers generating about a third of all online shopping dollars in the US.[5]

Of great relevance to the topic of this chapter, procurement was found to be the business process that made the greatest early application of e-commerce. Initially, companies utilized electronic data interchange (EDI) technology to connect with their major customers to process purchase orders, send notifications of shipment, and transfer funds. Aside from the significant popularity of EDI over a long period of time, use of the Internet has gained significant traction due to its greater convenience, lower costs, and less need for special technology to implement. This has opened the door to increased application of e-commerce techniques to the areas of procurement and sourcing.

For purposes of this discussion, **e-procurement** and **e-sourcing** will refer to the use of electronic capabilities to conduct activities and processes relating to procurement and sourcing. Figure 5.10 provides a number of common functionalities that relate to e-procurement and e-sourcing.

Figure 5.10	e-Sourcing and e-Procurement Functionality

- **Industry Analysis and Supplier Identification:** Provides useful information on supplier industries and facilitates development of candidate supplier lists for specific commodities, geographies, and product types.
- **Analytical Tools:** Supplier selection, bid, spend, and performance management analytics.
- **Management of RFI/RFP Processes:** Electronic support for the preparation, submission, and evaluation of these repetitive processes.
- **Process Automation:** Provides needed automation of purchase order and of item selection from central resources such as online catalogs.
- **Online Negotiations:** Supports real-time sourcing, e.g., through online bidding or reverse auction.
- **Collaboration Tools:** Used to support collaborative sourcing with other functions and divisions in same organization, with other organizations, and interaction and electronic connections with suppliers.
- **Logistics Procurement:** Responsibility for e-procurement of logistics services such as transportation, forwarding, etc. Utilizes a growing number of tools and technologies, e.g., online bidding, to facilitate and improve efficiency of logistics procurement processes.
- **Project Management:** Standardization and improvements in cost, quality, and time.
- **Knowledge Management:** Provides centralized, computerized availability of past, current, and future information relating to purchasing and sourcing activities. Serves as knowledge resource for those who are involved in e-sourcing and e-procurement.
- **Contract Management:** Fulfilling needs relating to legal contracts or agreements with suppliers.

Source: C. John Langley Jr., Ph.D., Penn State University, Used with permission.

5-6-1 Which of These Solutions Should be Considered[6]

According to Norek and Favre, strategic sourcing solutions should be considered for any entity that has a significant amount of spending with outside suppliers (over $50 million total). The spend should also be segmented into categories (e.g., sheet steel, contractor services) and sorted in descending dollars so only the top dollar spend categories are candidates for a strategic sourcing solution (the number of significant categories will go up for firms with a larger amount of spending). For smaller companies, a hosted solution (software run by the software company, behind their firewall) is less expensive and more manageable. For larger companies with higher usage, the software is typically purchased outright.

Transactional procurement systems are typically used to reduce the time and effort associated with the tactical aspects of procurement, such as requisition and purchase order creation as well as the approval and payment processes. Companies with 10,000 purchase transactions or more per year should consider transactional procurement solutions. Companies with fewer transactions who don't purchase a solution outright can take advantage of supplier Internet sites for business-to-business transactions—for example, ordering office supplies or work gloves directly from a supplier's Web site using a purchasing card.

Data management and analytics are valuable for medium to large companies with a large number of part numbers and supplier information. They are especially valuable for companies with multiple locations and/or divisions where data are not currently managed centrally. With data standardization, companies can find common suppliers and items across divisions and locations, allowing them to aggregate spend volumes and achieve discounts.

5-6-1-1 Advantages

The advantages of e-commerce procurement are shown in Figure 5.11. An obvious advantage is the lowering of procurement operating costs. The reduction of paperwork and the associated cost of paper processing, filing, and storing is a major cost-saving area of e-commerce. Although many companies have made significant progress at becoming paperless, there is still great progress to be made by many others.

Another paper reduction innovation that has become a reality with e-commerce is electronic funds transfer (ETF). Paying supplier invoices electronically eliminates the cost of preparing, mailing, filing, and storage of the checks. Estimates of the cost of writing a check vary from a low of $10 to a high of $85, the majority of this cost being the cost of accounts payable personnel. Experience has shown that the costs of ETF capabilities are significantly less than those of writing checks, and the overall experience is greatly enhanced for both customers and suppliers.

Reduced sourcing time means increased productivity because a procurement specialist spends less time per order and can place more orders in a given time period. Likewise, the seller utilizing e-commerce can increase the productivity of customer service representatives. Many of the questions asked by the buyer can be answered online, thereby saving time for both the buyer and seller personnel.

Given the real-time nature of e-commerce information, sellers have up-to-date information on demand and can adjust production/purchases to meet the current demand level. This same real-time information enables the buyer to establish controls that will

Figure 5.11	Advantages and Concerns of Electronic Procurement

- **Advantages**
  - — Lower operating costs
  - — Improve procurement and sourcing efficiency
  - — Reduce procurement prices
- **Concerns**
  - — Cybersecurity
  - — Lack of face-to-face contact between the buyer and seller
  - — Technology-related concerns

Source: C. John Langley Jr., Ph.D., Penn State University, Used with permission.

coordinate purchase quantities with requirement quantities and monitor spending levels. That is, the buyer is now in the position of monitoring the quantity of an item ordered, received, and on hand; comparing it to the amount needed; and doing this in a real-time mode. The same is true for monitoring spending activities against budgeted amounts.

Electronic procurement affords efficiency in the process by utilizing fewer resources to produce a given level of purchases. With a click of the mouse, a purchasing manager can search the world for alternative supply sources of a product or service. With another click, the manager can then ascertain information about the sources identified through the electronic search. All of this research is done in the office without phone calls, additional personnel, or outside sources.

A significant efficiency factor of e-commerce is improved communications. The buyer can secure information from the supplier's company—product line, prices, and product availability. The seller can obtain information regarding requests for proposals, blueprints, technical specifications, and purchase requirements from the buyer. Also, the seller can improve customer service by communicating the status of the order, giving the buyer advance notice of any delays in order fulfillment such as stockout situations, transportation delays, etc. As noted earlier, e-commerce permits the seller to gain real-time information to more accurately predict demand and anticipate problems before they occur.

Better use of procurement personnel is made possible by relieving them of the clerical tasks associated with processing the order, such as manually preparing purchase orders, mailing them to the supplier, and checking the status of the order via phone. The procurement manager is now free to focus attention on the long-term strategic procurement issues such as long-term item availability, opportunities for supply chain efficiencies, innovative products, and so on.

Reduced procurement prices have resulted from the ability of a buyer to gain access to pricing information from more potential suppliers. With more suppliers bidding for the business, the buyers are finding lower prices forthcoming. In addition, the procurement manager has the ability to view online the qualities of different supplier products and services, making comparison much easier. The overall effect of increased comparison shopping and increased number of potential suppliers is lower prices.

5-6-1-2 Concerns

Although there are some reported concerns about e-commerce, many of them are in the process of being neutralized or eliminated. The most frequently voiced concern about using the Internet for sourcing and procurement activities is that of "cybersecurity." This refers to the increasing threat of the use of electronic technologies to hack into databases and information depositories of all types. Whether it be in the form of cyber attacks that result in the electronic theft of personal information (e.g., credit card numbers, social security numbers, bank transactions, etc.) or disruptions to manufacturing or other supply chain activities, the threat is a real one, and is receiving significant attention by businesses worldwide.

Another problem may be the lack of face-to-face contact between the buyer and seller. Buying and selling via e-commerce many times reduces the ability to build close supplier relationships. This can be overcome by making a concerted effort to develop and enhance personal communications with the supplier.

Other concerns deal with technology. More specifically, there are concerns with the lack of standard protocols, system reliability, and technology problems. Lastly, there is reluctance on the part of some to invest the time and money to learn the new technology. For the most part, these concerns are diminishing daily as new and improved technology is developed and the business community demands the use of e-commerce capabilities.

On the Line

Transportation Sourcing— Innovative Approaches to Bid Optimization

Prevailing business conditions make it essential for shippers to be economical in their selection of specific carriers to serve individual freight lanes in their networks. Thus, new and improved methods for transportation sourcing and lane assignments have been developed and successfully implemented. These approaches assume that if transportation providers have an opportunity to bid simultaneously on multiple lanes, and/or pre-specified packages or combinations of lanes, results will be a significant improvement. Earlier bidding strategies asked providers to state their prices for individual lanes only, and then the shipper's task was to select the "lowest price" carrier for each individual lane. This traditional approach generally resulted overall in higher-costs for transportation than decisions based on use of the newer technologies.

The results of using these enhanced bidding techniques are a win-win for both shippers and carriers. Shippers see improvements in the efficiency and effectiveness of their transportation operations, and cost savings from awarding greater volumes of business to a smaller number of providers. Carriers benefit through improved capacity utilization, more strategic routing of vehicles and drivers, greater opportunities for continuous improvement, and overall improved alignment between carrier business objectives and shippers' transportation needs.

Industry-leading technologies for transportation bid optimization are available from many commercial suppliers such as SciQuest, Inc., which acquired CombineNet.com (www.sciquest.com), Infor (www.infor.com), JDA Software (www.jda.com), Manhattan Associates (www.manh.com), Oracle (www.oracle.com), and Sterling Commerce an IBM Company (www.ibm.com/software/info/sterling-commerce).

Source: C. John Langley Jr., Ph.D., Penn State University. Used with permission.

5-7 e-Commerce Models[7]

The four basic types of e-commerce business models used in procurement and sourcing are **sell-side system**, **electronic marketplace**, **buy-side system**, and **online trading community**. The following comments and examples clarify each of their roles:

- **Sell-side system:** Online businesses selling to individual companies or consumers. Examples include Office Depot and OfficeMax (www.officedepot.com), Staples (www.staples.com), Xpedx (www.xpedx.com), Best Buy (www.bestbuy.com), Walmart (www.walmart.com), and CNET (www.cnet.com). An increasing number of sell-side Web sites provide buyer login capabilities that allow storing of information concerning buying preferences, buying history, etc., for future reference.

- **Electronic marketplace:** A seller-operated service that consists of a number of electronic catalogs from suppliers within a market. The electronic marketplace provides a one-stop sourcing site for buyers who can examine the offerings of multiple suppliers at one Internet location. Examples include Expedia.com (www.expedia.com), PlasticsNet (www.plasticsnet.com), ThomasNet (www.thomasnet.com), Froogle (www.froogle.google.com), Amazon (www.amazon.com), eBay (www.ebay.com), and Hotwire (www.hotwire.com).

- **Buy-side system:** A buyer-controlled e-procurement or e-commerce service that is housed on the buyer's system and is administered by the buyer, who typically pre-approves the suppliers who have access to the system, and the process of the suppliers' products and services that have been prenegotiated. These systems permit tracking and controlling procurement spending and help to reduce unauthorized purchases. However, the cost of buy-side systems is frequently high due to the cost of developing and administering the system with a large number of suppliers. For this reason, most buy-side systems are usually in the domain of large companies. An interesting example of a buy-side system is Elemica (elemica.com), a supply chain operating network that provides integrated messaging, applications, and analytics across a network of trading partners.

- **Online trading community:** A system maintained by a third-party technology supplier where multiple buyers and multiple sellers in a given market can conduct business. The difference between the online trading community and the electronic marketplace is that the electronic marketplace is focused on providing information about sellers, whereas the online community permits the buyers and sellers to conduct business transactions.

  The online trading community also may be viewed as an electronic auction. In such instances, the buyer indicates the type of product, quantity, and so on, desired and the sellers respond. In a downward auction, the buyer states a maximum time period to receive the best bid from potential suppliers. At the end of the time period, the buyer selects the supplier(s) with the lowest price and will conduct negotiations, if necessary, to finalize the transaction. Examples of online trading companies include Travelocity (www.travelocity.com), Priceline (www.priceline.com), eBay (www.ebay.com), and NTE (www.nteinc.com).

  Other examples of online trading communities are E2open (www.e2open.com), which focuses on high-tech and electronics, and AGENTics (www.agentics.com), a global retail industry.

Gartner defines strategic sourcing application suites as a set related, integrated solutions that support "upstream" procurement activities. Used primarily by large companies, there are four main components to these suites: spend analysis; e-sourcing; contract management; and supply base (SBM) applications. Also, Gartner evaluates the strengths and cautions of providers of these types of technologies using the Gartner Magic Quadrant™, which focuses on the ability to execute and the completeness of vision for the companies under consideration.[8]

Overall, electronic procurement is here and is quickly establishing itself as the direction for the future. It will not replace all procurement activities, but it could reach 80 percent or more of a company's total purchase order activity. Electronic procurement focuses on the processing of orders and maintaining a source of real-time information for better decision making. Procurement specialists focus on selecting suppliers, negotiating prices, monitoring quality, and developing supplier relations.

SUMMARY

- Expertise in the areas of purchasing, procurement, and strategic sourcing is essential to the success of supply chain management.
- Different procurement and sourcing strategies are related to the risk and value or profit potential from needed products and services. Not all purchased items are of equal importance. Using the criteria of risk and value, the quadrant technique classifies items into four categories: generics, commodities, distinctives, and criticals. Generics have low risk, low value; commodities have low risk, high value; distinctives have high risk, low value; and criticals have high risk, high value.
- The MSSP focuses on several key elements. Included areas are develop strategic plan; understand spend; evaluate supply sources; finalize sourcing strategy; implement sourcing strategy; transition and onboarding; and collaborative process improvement.
- Keys to effective management of the procurement and sourcing processes include determining the type of purchase, determining the necessary levels of investment, performing the procurement process, and evaluating the effectiveness of the process.
- A number of key factors should be considered in the supplier selection and evaluation process, including certifications and registrations such as TQM, Six Sigma, and ISO 9000.
- Understanding the concept of TLC will be a highly-valuable element of the overall procurement process.
- E-sourcing and e-procurement practices and technologies are helping to enhance the effectiveness and efficiency of traditional buying processes. In addition, a number of e-commerce model types have been developed and are becoming very popular: sell-side, electronic marketplace, buy-side, and online trading community systems. Overall, the advantages of e-sourcing and e-procurement include lower operating costs, improved efficiency, and reduced prices.

STUDY QUESTIONS

1. Describe and discuss the differences and relationships between purchasing, procurement, and strategic sourcing. How have these concepts evolved?

2. Using the quadrant or risk/value technique, categorize the importance of the following items for an automobile manufacturer: engine, tires, gasoline, paper for the employee newsletter, a uniquely designed and engineered muffler, and rail car service to dealers. Describe the rationale you used to ascertain each categorization.

3. The MSSP process can be described in terms of a series of elements that should be used in the purchase of goods and services. Briefly discuss these elements.

4. Maximizing the effectiveness of the procurement process is a major goal of an organization. What steps can be taken to help ensure that the process is maximized?

5. A key part of the procurement process is the selection of suppliers. What criteria are commonly used in this selection process? Which criteria should be given the highest priority? Why?

6. What are the components of TLC? Is it realistic to expect companies to consider all of these components?

7. Discuss the advantages and disadvantages of using e-commerce in the procurement process.

8. Describe the different types of e-commerce business models available for procurement and point out their respective benefits and disadvantages.

NOTES

1. Michael E. Porter, *Competitive Advantage* (New York Free Press, 1985), 16.

2. This section is adapted from Joseph L. Cavinato, "Quadrant Technique Key to Effective Acquisition and Access," *ARDC Spectrum, Report #11* (State College, PA: Acquisition Research and Development Center).

3. Further information on this topic is available at Knowledge@Wharton, December 9, 2005.

4. Porter, 33–34.

5. Further information available at www.forrester.com, April 22, 2015.

6. The content of this section is adapted from Christopher D. Norek and Donavon Favre, "Procurement Solutions: What Might Work for You," *Logistics Quarterly* (March 2006): 25–26.

7. The framework suggested in section is adapted from Mark Vigoroso, "Buyers Prepare for Brave New World of E-Commerce," *Purchasing* (April 22, 1999). The current examples are provided by C. John Langley Jr., Ph.D., Penn State University.

8. Gartner, Inc., "Magic Quadrant for Strategic Sourcing Application Suites," February 4, 2015.

CASE 5.1

Alligator, Inc.

Alligator, Inc. is a shoe designer, manufacturer, and distributor that launched its business in 2012. Although the company operates globally, its headquarters location is in Arteixo, Galicia, Spain, which coincidentally is the central location for Zara, the flagship chain store of the Inditex group, the world's largest apparel retailer. The best-selling brand of Alligator, Inc. is its Gators™ model, which is a market leader in the funky, brightly-colored, lightweight shoe market that has enjoyed unexpectedly high demand in recent years. Made of a highly-resilient, space-age plastics material, Gators™ success is related also to the fact that each pair includes "one-size fits all" orthotics to meet the needs of individual consumers. Alligator, Inc. has patented the processes relating to the manufacture of the orthotics, and the overall value of this product innovation is similar to the way in which the super-secret formula for Coke is valuable to Coca-Cola, Inc.

The Alligator supply chain begins with retail consumers who are located in regions throughout the world. The Gators™ product is available for consumers at a wide variety of department stores, airport kiosks, Internet, and a select number of Alligator stores located primarily in developed countries. In addition to proprietary manufacturing facilities in Spain, Gators™ are produced by contract manufacturers in the Shenzhen area of China and in Brasilia, Brazil. Generally, the manufacturing costs per unit were lower in Shenzhen and Brasilia, and somewhat higher in Spain. Conversely, the quality of Gators™ manufactured in Spain was considerably better than that of the other locations. The markets served by the respective manufacturing facilities were those that were in greatest proximity.

The supply side of the Gators™ supply chain was a little more complicated, as most inputs to the finished product were available from suppliers in the regional markets, but the custom-fit orthotics were all produced in University Park, PA in the United States. This is because the developers of the orthotics technology were professors in the supply chain and information systems and footwear technology departments at Penn State University. Overall, Alligator's relationships with its suppliers could have benefited from better coordination, and more timely and complete exchanges of information. At the time that this case study was published, Alligator was in the process of designing an IT capability that would capture point-of-sale information, for further use in streamlining and aligning supply chain operations. Also, the sales of Gators™ exhibited seasonal variation, but to some extent seasonal sales in the southern hemisphere complemented sales in the northern hemisphere.

To help address some of the supply chain issues facing Alligator, Bryson Wilde has recently been hired as the new SVP Supply Chain, and Molly Walters has been selected as the first chief information officer for Alligator. Collectively, and with the help of consultant Anna Walters, this group has taken time so far to visit the company's global facilities and to become aware of the situation, problems, and concerns that are faced by Alligator, Inc. with regard to the Gators™ product. The following are some of the questions that will need to be addressed by this group.

CASE QUESTIONS

1. Based on your knowledge of the global business environment and the positioning of Alligator with regard to its markets and supply sources, what do you think are some of the major global issues that will be relevant to the area of strategic sourcing?

2. What are the impacts of less-than-perfect demand forecasts for Alligator products, including Gators™, and of volatility in the length and cost the supply chain services needed to move components from suppliers to manufacturing sites, and the subsequent movement of finished products to market? What should be done to mitigate these problem areas?

3. What elements of the strategic sourcing process do you feel are the top candidates for improvement at Alligator, and why?

4. How would you respond to the assertion that some of your contract manufacturers are involved in producing illegal merchandise (i.e., Gators™ "knock-offs") that ends up competing with the branded merchandise of Alligator?

Source: C. John Langley Jr., Ph.D., Penn State University. Used with permission.

CASE 5.2

Trans-Global, Inc.

With corporate headquarters located in Singapore, Trans-Global, Inc. is one of the world's largest sourcing and logistics companies. Although the company owns no fabric mills, manufacturing operations, or logistics-related assets, its primary competitive strength is its network of over 10,000 suppliers in approximately 40 countries that make it possible for the company to be core competent in producing clothing more quickly and inexpensively than otherwise available.

Trans-Global is regarded as one of the major players worldwide in the sourcing, manufacturing, and distribution of clothing and other garments. The company currently has three primary types of product markets in which it competes: (1) proprietary brands, which are sold only through one exclusive retailer; (2) private label merchandise, consisting of in-house brands belonging to individual retailers; and (3) licensed brands that deals with products featuring images of licensed entertainment characters. Although the global marketplace has experienced significant economic volatility in recent years, Trans-Global has been able to maintain its reputation as one of the most impactful, global supply chain players.

According to Tony Tang, CEO of Trans-Global, companies in the supply chain business are looking to expand manufacturing and sourcing operations in more cost-effective areas, and to meaningfully consider new business opportunities in new market areas. Thus, it is no surprise that firms worldwide look to organizations such as Trans-Global to manage a number of key supply chain processes, including sourcing, manufacturing, and distribution. A few of the top global apparel store brands that rely upon the services of Trans-Global include Unlimited Brands, Zaragoza, Femme Fatale, H&B, and Bobby Hilfinger.

Although headquartered in Singapore, major markets for Trans-Global services are in North America, Western Europe, and the Middle East. Most sourcing and manufacturing is centered on China and India, but significant diversification is currently a priority to other countries such as Vietnam, Thailand, Philippines, Indonesia, Turkey, and South Africa.

As Trans-Global prepares for the future as a leader in integrated supply chain management, it's corporate philosophy focuses on "helping our customers to understand their core competencies, and outsource the rest to Trans-Global."

CASE QUESTIONS

1. Assuming that you are SVP supply chain at a leading merchandiser of fashion apparel, what do you feel would be the benefits and drawbacks of developing a business relationship with Trans-Global for the sourcing, manufacturing and distribution of your products?
2. Where does consideration of a relationship with Trans-Global fit into the steps of the MSSP sourcing methodology that was discussed in this chapter?
3. Since a logical objective of a relationship with Trans-Global should be to create benefits to both parties over time, what do you think are some of the very critical "external" factors that could impact the success or failure of this relationship?

Source: C. John Langley Jr., Ph.D., Penn State University. Used with permission.

APPENDIX 5A

The Special Case of Procurement Price

We begin by identifying the four generic sources of prices in procurement situations. This is somewhat basic but important to understand. The discussion of price becomes more complex when one adds an analysis of total acquired cost or value in the procurement process from a supply chain perspective. Total acquired cost and value are discussed after our description of price sources.

Sources of Price

Purchasing managers utilize four basic procedures to determine potential suppliers' prices: (1) commodity markets, (2) price lists, (3) price quotations, and (4) negotiations. Commodity markets exist for basic raw materials such as grain, oil, sugar, and natural resources including coal and lumber. In these markets, the forces of supply and demand determine the price that all potential suppliers will charge. Reductions in the supply of these materials or increases in demand usually result in increased prices; the converse is true for increases in supply or decreases in demand.

Price lists are published prices that are generally used with standardized products such as gasoline or office supplies. The supplier's catalog, electronic or hard copy, describes the items available and lists their prices. Depending on the status, buyers may receive a purchaser discount from the list price. For example, a supplier may give a 10 percent discount to small-volume buyers (less than $1,000 per month) and a 35 percent discount to large-volume buyers (more than $10,000 per month).

Purchasers use the price quotation method for both standard and specially items. It is particularly useful in promoting competition among suppliers. The process begins with the buyer sending potential suppliers requests for quotes (RFQ). An RFQ contains all the necessary information regarding the specifications the purchaser requires and the manner in which potential suppliers are to present their offers. In turn, the suppliers examine the cost they will incur in producing the material, considering the quantity the purchaser will order, the purchase's duration, and other factors that will affect the supplier's profitability. Finally, the purchaser compares the supplier's quoted price and offer specifications with those of other suppliers.

The fourth procedure, negotiation, is useful when the other methods do not apply or have failed. Negotiation is particularly effective when the buyer is interested in a strategic alliance or long-term relationship. The negotiation process can be time consuming, but the potential benefits can be significant in terms of price and quality. Negotiation is becoming more widely used by logistics managers who buy goods and logistics services.

The objective of the procurement process is to purchase goods and services at the "best" price, which may not be the lowest price per unit at the supplier source. This is particularly true from a global supply chain perspective. In all four settings, the base price needs to be evaluated in a total acquired cost context.

A generalized spectrum of expanding procurement approaches to the supply chain concept is presented in Figure 5A.1. At the first level, the firm evaluates procurement and logistics functions simply on the basis of lowest price or lowest cost, without strong regard

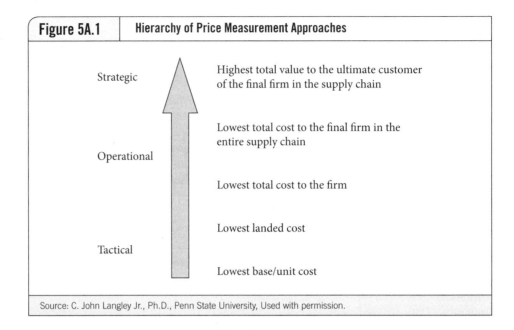

| Figure 5A.1 | Hierarchy of Price Measurement Approaches |

Source: C. John Langley Jr., Ph.D., Penn State University, Used with permission.

to the total costs to the firm. In this context, it is difficult to achieve a total cost savings unless a manager or group becomes directly responsible for the two or more interfacing functions that might offer a total cost savings. As a company attempts to move from the lowest base or unit price to taking a supply chain perspective to create highest value, the procurement function becomes more strategic in nature.

For customer satisfaction, all costs and factors that affect costs and create value should be captured in the total acquired cost. As Figure 5A.1 indicates, a hierarchy of costs and other factors builds upward from raw materials through manufacturing, to distribution, to final marketing and selection and use by the ultimate customer in order to determine total procurement cost and the highest total value.

For the buyer, the total procurement price is more than just the basic purchase price, as indicated in Figure 5A.2. The following discussion starts with the base cost and delineates the additional direct and indirect costs that need to be considered.

Traditional Basic Input Costs

This is the primary price of the product or materials as paid by the firm. It is the traditional price buyers seek through bidding, through negotiating, or in requests for quotes. It is easily measured, and it has long been the hallmark against which buyer performance is measured; but, in a supply chain setting, it is only one factor for the firm to evaluate and consider in the acquisition process.

Direct Transaction Costs

These are the costs of detecting, transmitting the need for, and processing the material flow in order to acquire the goods. They include the process of detecting inventory need, requisitioning, preparing and transmitting the order documentation to the supplier, receiving the acknowledgment, handling shipping documents, and receiving information about

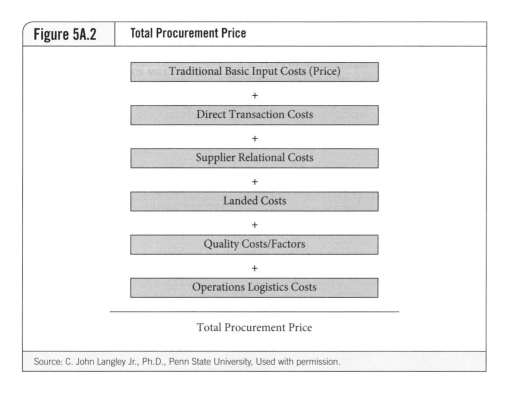

Figure 5A.2 — **Total Procurement Price**

Traditional Basic Input Costs (Price)

+

Direct Transaction Costs

+

Supplier Relational Costs

+

Landed Costs

+

Quality Costs/Factors

+

Operations Logistics Costs

Total Procurement Price

Source: C. John Langley Jr., Ph.D., Penn State University, Used with permission.

input to inventory. This area was made more efficient with the advent of internal electronic mail systems that automated the purchasing requisition and order-transmission process. Users inside the firm use electronic means to transmit their needs to purchasing. EDI and the Internet are extensions of this process outbound to the supplier.

The use of blanket or systems contracting can also reduce transaction costs. These include direct ordering by users to suppliers, single consolidated billing, and user inspection and checking. Direct transaction costs are overhead types of costs that are not easily visible, but they represent time and effort that are not available for more productive value-added activities. Suppliers and interfacing carriers that reduce the need for these activities represent value to the buying firm.

Supplier Relational Costs

These are the costs of creating and maintaining a relationship with a supplier. They include travel, supplier education, and the establishment of planning and operational links between purchasing and the supplier's order-entry operation, as well as other links, including those related to traffic, engineering, research, and product development in both firms. In traditional purchasing settings, this includes the process of evaluating and certifying a supplier for quality and preferred supplier programs.

Landed Costs

The inbound transportation flow includes two key cost elements: the actual transportation cost and the sales/FOB terms. There are four different transportation options with inbound movements—supplier-selected for-hire carrier or private carrier and buyer-selected for-hire carrier or private carrier.

The sales terms define which firm owns the goods during transportation as well as invoice payment requirements. Transportation terms pertain to the carrier in the move between the supplier and the buyer firm. There are nearly a dozen possible transportation terms that include different carrier payment and loss and damage claim options. Each one presents different relative costs to each party in the linkage; for supply chain purposes, the one that can perform the task or own the goods at the lowest overall cost has an advantage that can contribute to the overall chain. Both sales and transportation terms must be considered, and different direct costs, responsibilities, and indirect implicit costs of cash flow are affected by each one of them.

Quality Costs/Factors

Quality pertains to the conformance of goods to a desired specification. It includes the cost of conformance, nonconformance, appraisal, and ultimate use costs. The required quality specification is often balanced against what the supplier can easily provide nearly 100 percent of the time. Often, a product specification that is extremely tight requires extra costs but results in higher quality, which may reduce total cost.

Operations Logistics Costs

This group includes the following four key areas:

- Receiving and make-ready costs are the costs of those flow activities occurring between the inbound transportation delivery of a good and its availability for use by production or other processes. These include the cost of unpacking, inspecting, counting, sorting, grading, removing and disposing of packaging materials (strapping, banding, stretch-shrink wrapping, pallets, etc.), and moving the good to the use point. A streamlined system such as direct forklift delivery to a production line is an example of an efficient receiving/make-ready process. Some leading edge carriers provide information links to the firm that include inspection checks, sequencing of the loads, and final count checks so that receiving processes can be reduced or eliminated.

- Lot-size costs directly affect space requirements, handling flow, unit price, and related cash flows. These are a major cost of inventories.

- Production costs can be affected by suppliers of even seemingly similar goods. Extruded plastic for high-quality towel rods is an example. The plastic is an extruded tube that must be inflated with air and slipped over a metal or wooden rod. Original raw materials quality, differing production processes, and in-transit humidity can cause two suppliers' goods to affect the production line significantly. One might allow assembly of 200 units per hour, while another might split or not form properly, wasting 10 percent of the sleeves and requiring the production line to operate at a slower speed. Thus, each one has a different cost of production operation.

- Logistics costs are also important in both upstream and downstream settings. These are cost factors that are affected by product size, weight, cube, and shape and their resulting impact upon transportation, handling, storage, and damage costs. Purchased goods and packaging materials have a direct bearing on these subsequent process costs.

All firms in the supply chain add cost and, hopefully, value to a product as it moves through the supply chain. Value is added by reducing total acquired cost or by enhancing the function of the product. Each firm in the supply chain can contribute to or detract from these factors. The key is to focus downstream in the supply chain, but it is also important to note the key role that the procurement process can play at each point along the supply chain by being aware of a product's total acquired cost. Ideally, the focus should be upon the total value at the end of the supply chain. Therefore, the analysis should also include indirect financial costs (payment terms), tactical input costs (supplier capabilities), and strategic business factors (factors that cause customers to buy the product).

Source: This section is adapted from J. L. Cavinato, "A Total Cost/Value Model for Supply Chain Competitiveness," *Journal of Business Logistics*, Vol.13, No. 2 (1992): 285–299.

Chapter 6

PRODUCING GOODS AND SERVICES

Learning Objectives

After reading this chapter, you should be able to do the following:

- Discuss the strategic value-adding role operations plays in the supply chain.
- Explain the concept of a transformation process and its application to goods and services.
- Appreciate the tradeoffs and challenges involved in production operations.
- Understand the primary production strategies and types of planning.
- Discuss the primary assembly processes and production methods for goods creation.
- Describe the various production process layouts.
- Explain the role of productivity and quality metrics for improving operations performance.
- Know how information technology supports efficient production of goods and services.

Supply Chain Profile   *Establishing a Production Footprint: The VW Journey*

Establishing a new production facility is no simple task. It requires a great deal of time, money, and land. Government cooperation and incentives are also needed. And, a supply chain must be established with quality suppliers and logistics service providers to support the inventory needs of the facility.

The evolution of the Volkswagen plant in Chattanooga, Tennessee highlights the effort required to establish a manufacturing presence in a new country. The company announced its intention to build the Chattanooga Assembly Plant in July 2008 on a 1,400 acre site. Construction of the facility took nearly 3 years and an investment of $1 billion. Over 2,400 new employees went through a 3-week training program at the Volkswagen Academy, suppliers were selected, and two major railroads were hired to provide rail transportation of finished vehicles.

Designed to be 20 percent more efficient than its existing facilities, the 2 billion square foot Chattanooga plant relies on a "jellyfish" body-shop arrangement that differs from the "fishbone" layout typical of many auto assembly plants. Sub-assemblies flow from individual lines into the body shop, the highlight of which is two enormous robotic framing jigs to attach body sides, which represents the body of the jellyfish, with the sub-assembly lines flowing out from the body.

There are 383 advanced robots in the body shop, where the automation level is about 77 percent. There are 4,730 weld spots and 292 welding guns. The paint shop uses 52 robots and dips cars in paint rather than spraying them. This saves time, water, and chemicals. The time and materials required to change from one color vehicle to another is also greatly reduced. The production output goal is 31 cars per hour.

The plant was the first automotive manufacturing plant in the world to receive Platinum certification from the U.S. Green Building Council's Leadership in Energy and Environmental Design (LEED®) green building certification program. Key features include the use of mineral rock wool insulation, LED exterior lighting, highly reflective white roofing materials, and hydroelectric dam power to reduce energy consumption. Water conservation is provided through the use of collected rainwater and low flow fixtures.

The first Volkswagen Passat finally rolled off the production line on April 18, 2011, the culmination of many years of planning and development. By 2015, the plant had built its 500,000th car.

However, the company is not standing pat at one production line and one vehicle. Volkswagen announced that it is undertaking a $900 million expansion to produce a seven-seat, midsize SUV at the Chattanooga plant. The expansion is expected to add 2,000 jobs and will begin assembly in by the end of 2016.

Sources: Mike Pare, "Chattanooga's Volkswagen Plant Expansion gets Supersized," *TimesFreePress.com* (April 5, 2015). Retrieved August 4, 2015 from http://www.timesfreepress.com/news/local/story/2015/apr/05/vw-plant-expansigets-supersized/297001/; Bill Visnic, "To Become No. 1, Volkswagen Needs to Succeed in Chattanooga," *Edmunds Auto Observer* (December 6, 2010); and, "Volkswagen Chattanooga," *Volkswagengroupofamerica.com*. Retrieved August 4, 2015 from http://www.volkswagengroupamerica.com/facts.html.

6-1 Introduction

Operations focus on the "make/build" portion of the supply chain. They focus on production of goods and services needed to fulfill customer requirements. Production involves the transformation of inputs into outputs that customers demand. For example, a computer manufacturer like Lenovo or Apple assembles a set of components (processor, memory, hard drive, etc.) into the Y50 Touch or MacBook Air, respectively. Likewise, a hospital emergency room has knowledgeable doctors and nurses to transform an injured person (the input) back to a healthy state (the output).

In the execution of these processes, production facilities must interact with supply chain functions that are discussed throughout the book. Both manufacturers and service providers need ready access to inventories of key inputs from their suppliers. Lenovo and Apple need hardware and software to build computers that are functional when they are removed from the box. The doctors and nurses require diagnostic equipment, medical supplies, and pharmaceutical products to evaluate and treat the patient. Hence, there's a critical link between supply management, inventory, inbound transportation, and production operations.

Also, operations create the outputs that are distributed through supply chain networks. Consumer demand for computers cannot be satisfied without production of the physical goods. Production schedules must be coordinated with delivery schedules and transportation methods to ensure that inventory is received when promised. Ambulances and delivery vehicles may be needed to transport treated patients and home care equipment to their residences. Thus, it is easy to understand why production operations are part of the supply chain and cannot be conducted independently. All activities in the purchase, production, and delivery of goods and services need to be synchronized to ensure consistent, efficient product and service flows.

This is no easy task, as highlighted by the Volkswagen example in the Supply Chain Profile. To remain competitive, automobile manufacturers—and all product producers—must design and operate facilities that generate quality output at a reasonable production cost.

This chapter focuses on the need to balance flexibility and responsiveness with efficiency during the transformation process, as well as the critical links between production processes and other supply chain activities. We will discuss the planning and development of production capabilities, as well as the processes, metrics, and technologies that support efficient product and service operations. Throughout the chapter, you will gain an understanding of the roles that production strategies and methods play in the creation of the inventories needed to fulfill customer demand.

6-2 The Role of Production Operations in Supply Chain Management (SCM)

When you think about it, many of the supply chain and logistics activities discussed throughout this book focus on operations—procurement operations that provide access to materials, transportation operations that support the flow of goods, distribution operations that streamline order fulfillment, and so on. Collectively, they create time and place utilities. However, the potential contributions of goods manufacturing and service production to supply chain effectiveness are often overlooked because they focus on a different, but also important, dimension of economic utility called **form utility**. All the activities and processes involved in changing the appearance or composition of a good or service—component fabrication, product assembly, and service request execution—focus on creating form utility. The goal is to make the product or service more attractive to potential and actual users so that demand is created.

Of course, a great product design or form utility is important, but not enough to guarantee success. Form utility drives the need for supply chain capabilities (i.e., time and place utilities).

When Sony introduces a product like the PlayStation 4, they need integrated supply chain processes to fulfill customer demand for the gaming system. It is imperative to procure key materials quickly, marshal production resources and capacity to assemble the components, and move the finished goods to retailers in sufficient quantities to meet demand. Otherwise, the door opens for competitors to hijack potential customers.

It takes a great deal of effort and coordination to run an effective production operation that is supported by and also supports the supply chain. Processes must be effectively designed and flawlessly executed, supply chain tradeoffs must be understood and made, and economies of scale need to be achieved, all while the organization addresses competitive challenges and other problems. Consider the success of the Apple iPhone. A great product design, procurement–assembly–distribution synchronization, and savvy marketing all contributed to the success of this commercial juggernaut. Rapid execution of the "plan/buy/make/move" supply chain processes is essential to meeting global demand for this innovative smartphone.

With the vital connection between production and SCM established, we'll take a deeper look at the details of production operations.

6-2-1 Production Process Functionality

Manufacturers, contract assemblers, and service providers all engage in production processes. Whether they make sandwiches, laser printers, or bank loans, these organizations perform a group of related activities during which inputs are transformed into outputs. This production process, as shown in Figure 6.1, also uses resources such as facilities, equipment, knowledge, labor, and capital to support the transformation. Feedback of key information is used to make adjustments within the process (e.g., speed up or slow down the purchase of inputs and the production of outputs according to changes in demand requirements) in an attempt to synchronize production more closely to demand. Ignoring these

Figure 6.1	The Production Process

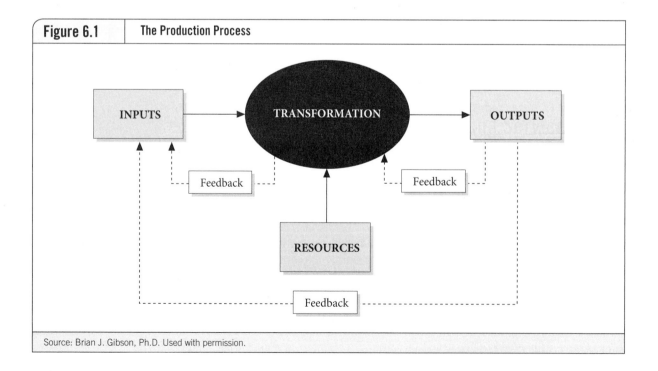

Source: Brian J. Gibson, Ph.D. Used with permission.

feedback signals will lead to excess inventory of unpopular products or inventory shortages of hot items.

While the basic input–transformation–output principle applies to all production processes, no two are organized exactly alike or perform to the same level. For example Dominos, McDonald's, and Subway each make fast food but have slightly different product strategies that drive their process design and assembly methods. Dominos and Subway offer assemble-to-order (ATO) products that are created from a variety of available components (e.g., pre-sliced meats, cheeses, and vegetables) when you place an order. McDonald's produces some products in anticipation of demand using standardized product components. As you might expect, ATO methods tend to be more complex, be more labor intensive, and require longer processing time than the mass-production-oriented, make-to-stock (MTS) operations. Process capacity (how much can be produced) is also impacted by product type and production methods.

Process functionality also plays a role in the success of an organization. The ability to perform different processes from those of competitors to create unique products and services can create a competitive advantage. For example, Amazon became an online powerhouse by developing retail and fulfillment processes that are vastly different from traditional methods. On the other hand, the ability to perform common processes better than the competition can also generate efficiencies and lower costs for the organization. Southwest Airlines is a good example of a company that provides the same basic passenger flight services as its competition, but at a lower operating cost. As long as the level of service and quality of output meets customer expectations, either focus can help the organization reach its goals.

6-2-2 Production Tradeoffs

One of the most important issues for supply chain professionals to understand is the tradeoffs involved within production operations and between production operations, other supply chain functions, and corporate strategy. All decisions are interrelated and can impact costs, productivity, and quality in other areas. In the next few paragraphs, common tradeoffs are discussed.

The volume–variety tradeoff is a primary issue in production. Higher volume leads to lower cost per unit of output, according to the long-established economies of scale principle. In situations where production processes have high fixed costs and equipment like chemical production or paper manufacturing, it makes sense to pursue volume. In contrast, processes that can produce a range of products are said to have **economies of scope**. These flexible capabilities are important in situations where efficient, low-volume production runs of a wide variety of products are required to meet changing customer demand.[1] Organizations should evaluate their product, process, and demand characteristics to determine their relative need for variety versus volume.

Fundamental tradeoffs between responsiveness and efficiency arise when production facility decisions are made. Centralized production facilities provide operating cost and inventory efficiencies, while regional production facilities allow companies to be closer to customers and more responsive. Larger facilities with excess capacity provide the flexibility to respond to demand spikes. In contrast, smaller facilities that are better utilized will be more cost efficient. Finally, the operating methodology used by the facility impacts this tradeoff. Product-focused facilities that perform many processes on a single product type will tend to be more responsive than process-focused facilities that concentrate on a few functions across multiple product types. The latter type of facility will be more efficient at its limited scope of activities.[2]

Tradeoffs between production processes for goods and the costs involved in manufacturing them must also be understood. Production and supply chain costs vary for MTS, ATO, and build-to-order (BTO) products. As Figure 6.2 highlights, BTO products incur the highest total cost of manufacturing due to the lower production economies of scale and higher transportation costs. On the other hand, MTS production processes have lower total costs due to higher volumes and lower transportation costs. One should not forget that while MTS may be cheaper from a total cost of manufacturing standpoint, the method may sacrifice customer service, responsiveness, and variety.[3]

Another consideration is whether to conduct your own production operations or to outsource production to external suppliers. The make-versus-buy decision can be very complex and involves sacrifice whichever way the company chooses to go. Internal production processes are more directly visible and should be easier to control from a quality standpoint. Outsourced production may lead to lower product costs and allow the company to focus its resources on other, more strategic needs.

An organization needs to understand and evaluate the tradeoffs and comparative costs of producing or purchasing goods before making a final decision. Once outsourced, supplier quality and service must be monitored. A high-profile safety recall like the 34-million vehicles recalled for defective airbags produced by a Tier 1 supplier, can wreak havoc across the supply chain. Eleven carmakers and millions of customers were affected by the quality failure.[4]

Finally, traditional wisdom suggests that production operations cannot strive to be all things to all people and tradeoffs must be made. That is, when designing and executing production processes, they should focus on the following competitive dimensions: low cost,

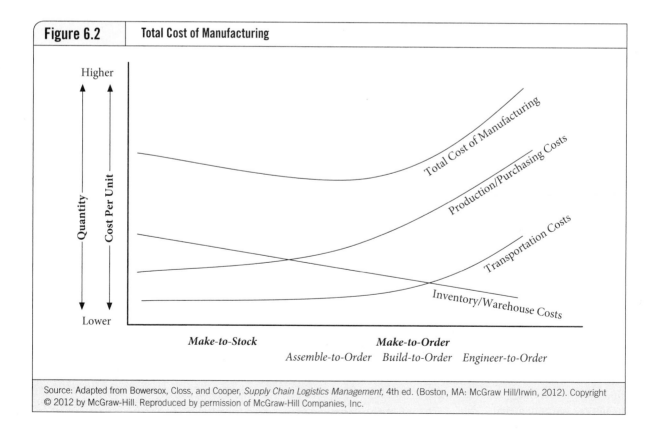

Figure 6.2 **Total Cost of Manufacturing**

high quality (features and reliability), fast delivery speed, high delivery reliability, ability to cope with demand change, or the flexibility to offer variety. Logic would dictate that an operation cannot excel simultaneously on all six competitive dimensions. There are inherent conflicts between the strategies and compromises would be required.

However, world-class organizations are able to improve performance along multiple dimensions without making extensive performance tradeoffs or sacrifices. Procter & Gamble (P&G) is one of these world-class companies. Perennially ranked in the top five of the Gartner Supply Chain Top 25, P&G was honored as a supply chain master in 2015.[5] The company is at the forefront of demand-driven SCM, specialized production operations in emerging markets, commodity hedging upstream for key inputs, and environmental responsibility.

6-2-3 Production Challenges

To say that production is a dynamic field would be a severe understatement. Operations managers face an ever changing set of challenges and tradeoffs that must be managed successfully if the organization and supply chain are to achieve their performance goals. Current challenges include complying with increased regulation and traceability requirements, keeping up with the pace of product innovation, overcoming a shortage of skilled labor, controlling pay and benefits costs, managing environmental concerns; and balancing productivity throughput with maintenance requirements.[6] The long-term growth of manufacturers will depend on their ability to develop and deploy production process innovations.

Competitive pressure is another major challenge for many established manufacturers and service providers. As the global reach of supply chains makes it possible to source product from nearly anywhere in the world, companies need to continually update their production capabilities and develop innovative responses to upstart competitors. The U.S. automobile industry is a prime example. Not only do General Motors and Ford need to compete with Toyota's lean production capabilities and Honda's product quality, but U.S. manufacturers must also develop an effective response to low-cost producers like Hyundai and Kia. A "business as usual" approach will lead to further deterioration of market share and supply chain woes for these organizations.

Customers' demand for choice and rapidly changing tastes make life difficult for product makers. For many products, it is no longer possible to focus on mass production and the Henry Ford approach to customization: "People can have the Model T in any color—so long as it's black." The expectation today of customized products that meet the specifications of individual buyers requires far different production processes than the assembly methods needed for standardized goods. The shrinking life cycle of products today also renders long production runs of these common goods obsolete. In response, technology and apparel companies have developed responsive capabilities by building supply chains around ATO production capabilities. Today, you can design your own Nike shoes at NikeiD.com.

While the use of responsive, small quantity production processes is growing, company executives still demand productivity and efficiency. They expect operations managers to employ processes that are *both* financially efficient and responsive to demand. Leanness and adaptability are requirements for success, though many organizations struggle to make the transition from traditional production methods and strategies to more contemporary ones that can better balance product quality, process flexibility, fulfillment speed, and execution costs.

Certainly, operations managers face many other operations challenges. Labor productivity, synchronization of activities with the supply chain, and capital costs are just a few of the additional obstacles that must be overcome. The next section discusses planning methods and strategies used for product and service operations. Thoughtful, advanced preparation of production processes that consider these difficult challenges and tradeoffs will elevate an organization's prospects for growth and profitability.

6-3 Operations Strategy and Planning

A great deal of planning, preparation, and engagement of multiple parties is required for production operations to make a positive contribution to supply chain effectiveness. Strategies that encompass product/service characteristics, internal capabilities, customer expectations, and competitive issues must be developed. From these strategies, long- to short-range production plans are created, followed by the implementation of product assembly/service delivery processes.

6-3-1 Production Strategies

Over the last 35 years, significant development and shifts have occurred in production strategy. Many organizations have advanced from forecast-driven production strategies to demand-driven approaches. These companies strive to be lean, flexible, or adaptive; wait for customers to pull products to the market; and rely on much smaller stockpiles of inventory. The demand-driven strategies are vastly different from the efficiency-focused, mass-production concepts that dominated production strategies from the early part of the twentieth century until the 1970s. Figure 6.3 provides a general timeline and description of the evolution of production strategies.

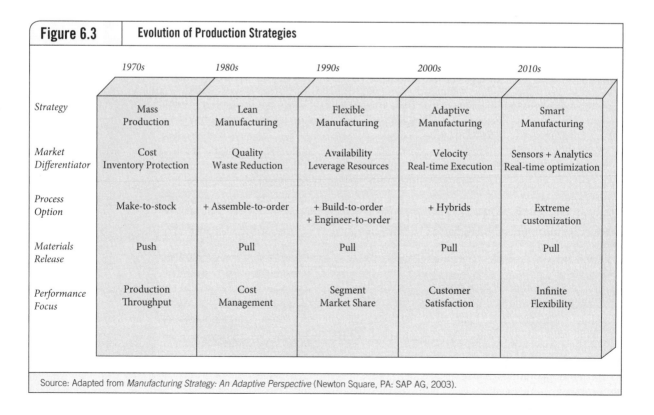

Figure 6.3	Evolution of Production Strategies				
	1970s	*1980s*	*1990s*	*2000s*	*2010s*
Strategy	Mass Production	Lean Manufacturing	Flexible Manufacturing	Adaptive Manufacturing	Smart Manufacturing
Market Differentiator	Cost Inventory Protection	Quality Waste Reduction	Availability Leverage Resources	Velocity Real-time Execution	Sensors + Analytics Real-time optimization
Process Option	Make-to-stock	+ Assemble-to-order	+ Build-to-order + Engineer-to-order	+ Hybrids	Extreme customization
Materials Release	Push	Pull	Pull	Pull	Pull
Performance Focus	Production Throughput	Cost Management	Segment Market Share	Customer Satisfaction	Infinite Flexibility

Source: Adapted from *Manufacturing Strategy: An Adaptive Perspective* (Newton Square, PA: SAP AG, 2003).

In the era of mass production, operations strategy focused on efficiency and scale. The strategy of choice for mass production is a push-based system that relies on long-term forecasts for production planning and decision making. This methodology works well if demand is constant with limited variability throughout the year. Processes can be established to fulfill this stable demand without the need for excess or just-in-case capacity, and production throughput can be maximized.

In reality, few companies enjoy perfectly stable demand for their products and the related opportunity to maintain level of production that is quickly consumed. More often, organizations must deal with demand variation. In these situations, goods are produced to stock according to the forecast and finished goods inventory or production backlogs are used to accommodate variation. Inventories accrue during lower-demand seasons, and the stockpile is reduced during peak seasons. If production can't keep up with demand during these high-demand periods, then a backlog of orders will start to accumulate and be worked down as orders decline.

The push-based strategy works well for supply chains that focus on the immediate delivery of off-the-shelf, low-cost, standardized goods. Monster Energy drinks and Vans Shoes are examples of MTS products that fit these criteria. As long as trading partners seek these low-priced stock items in reasonable volume, the producer can profitably use this production strategy.

Push-based supply chains are not without challenges. Operating from forecasts that are derived from supply chain partners' predictions may limit the producer's responsiveness. Without visibility to actual end-consumer demand, the producer will be slow to react to changes in the marketplace. The result may be continued production of items whose demand is dropping and may soon be obsolete. Alternatively, the producer may fail to recognize changing customer requirements and ramp up production of desired goods. The ultimate impact will be missed opportunities, unrecoverable costs, and/or missed revenues.

The other problem with basing production on supply chain partners' forecasts is the potential for the bullwhip effect to occur. Under this phenomenon, forecast errors are magnified and demand variability increases as orders move upstream from retailers to distributors to producers. The producers have to complete larger and more variable production batches to supply the often-changing downstream orders. This can lead to inefficient resource utilization as production capacity is not consistently engaged—sometimes being overworked, other times being idled.[7]

The 1980s ushered in the era of lean production to address the changing demand environment and the shortcomings of push-based, mass-production strategies. Lean production is an integrated set of activities designed to minimize the movement and use of raw materials, work-in-process, and finished goods inventories during production. The goal is to have materials arrive at the needed location just in time for rapid processing and flow through the system. A principal focus of lean manufacturing is to minimize all forms of waste and to produce quality products without the need for rework. The lean philosophy is largely based on the **Toyota production system (TPS)**, which seeks to develop and redesign production processes to remove overburden (*muri*), smooth production (*mura*), and eliminate waste (*muda*). Table 6.1 describes the seven types of *muda* targeted for elimination in the TPS.

Lean production relies on pull-based systems to coordinate production and distribution with actual customer demand rather than a potentially error-laden forecast of demand. In a pull system, the producer only responds to customer demand. No action is taken until an order is placed or a purchase is made. The order signal sets the production process into

Table 6.1	TPS Seven Deadly Wastes
WASTE	**DESCRIPTION**
Overproduction	Making more parts than you can sell.
Delays	Waiting for processing, parts sitting in storage, etc.
Transporting	Excessive movement of parts to various storage locations, from process to process, etc.
Overprocessing	Doing more "work" to a part than is required.
Inventory	Committing money and storage space to parts not sold.
Motion	Moving parts more than the minimum needed to complete and ship them.
Making defective parts	Creating parts that cannot be sold "as is" or that must be reworked, etc.

Source: Ta'Ichi Ohno, *Toyota Production System: Beyond Large-Scale Production* (New York, NY: Productivity Press, 1988).

motion to quickly assemble the requested item (which may be an ATO product that is tailored to the customer) and move it toward the point of demand. The technology tools discussed in Chapter 14—point-of-sale scanning, electronic data interchange, the Internet, and auto-ID tags—support pull-based systems by providing visibility of demand. This allows quick action to be taken for the purpose of minimizing customer order cycle time.

One of the main benefits of a lean, pull-based system is the reduction of waste. Manufacturers don't have to build inventory in anticipation of demand or without knowledge of customer orders. This will limit the problems of overproduction, excess inventory, and unnecessary processing. The bullwhip effect is also reduced when all supply chain partners function based on customer demand. This helps to reduce variation in the system and shrink lead times. Other benefits include an enhanced ability to manage resources and a reduction in system costs compared to push-based systems.[8]

Some computer assemblers rely on pull-based systems to manufacture desktop computers. Rather than trying to predict what customers will order, these manufacturers wait until specific orders are received via its website or call center. Needed components are rapidly obtained from suppliers and third-party warehouses, assembled to customer specifications, and shipped via a customer's chosen delivery method. The manufacturer does not waste effort building computers and putting them into inventory with the hope of a customer wanting that particular model. Organizations whose products have similar characteristics—higher value, customizable, short life cycle—can also benefit from the pull-based strategy.

A few challenges are inherent in the pull-based strategy. In some cases, customers want immediate access to products and don't want to wait for production and delivery (basic necessities like milk and bread are good examples). Also, it can be difficult to achieve economies of scale in ATO and BTO product operations, making them more expensive to produce. Finally, companies short on technological capabilities would find it difficult to achieve the supply chain visibility and synchronization needed in pull-based systems.

Although many companies have made significant gains during the evolution from mass production to lean production processes, perfection has not been achieved. Industry experts suggest that the shortcomings of lean processes need to be addressed if significant further progress is to be made. Minimal inventory levels, overreliance on sole sourcing arrangements, and the use of common parts across products increase the risk of production shutdowns in the event of a supplier quality problem. The growing technological complexity of products also makes for lean production challenges.[9]

Flexible manufacturing emerged in the early 1990s in response to the production challenges described earlier in this chapter—product proliferation, shorter life cycles, faster competitors, and more sophisticated customers. The purpose of this strategy is to build some flexibility into the production system in order to react effectively to markets characterized by frequent volume changes and rapid product evolution.[10]

One type of reactive capability is **machine flexibility**. Under this strategy, flexible machines and equipment staffed by cross-trained workers provide the ability to produce different types of products as well as change the order of operations executed on a product. In the automobile industry, Honda is a flexibility leader, producing 16 Honda and Acura models on its nine North American auto assembly lines. This flexible manufacturing system provides a competitive advantage for Honda due to the efficient utilization of global production resources and increased stability of local manufacturing operations and employment.[11]

Another type of reactive capability (there are eight in all) is called **routing flexibility**, which provides managers with production options and the ability to adapt to changing needs. In its simplest terms, routing flexibility provides managers with a choice between machines for a part's next operation.[12] This capability is valuable for overcoming machine breakdowns so that production can continue for the given products. It also creates opportunities to flow products through alternate routes within the production facility. Under these scenarios, the system has the ability to absorb large-scale changes, such as in volume, capacity, or capability.

A primary advantage of the flexible manufacturing strategy is the ability to leverage production resources (e.g., time and effort) in support of different transformation processes. It also takes advantage of the capabilities of strong vendors, information technology, and highly trained indirect staff. The desired outcome is the achievement of economies of scope where small batches of a large variety of products can be produced cost effectively. Other benefits include improved productivity, quality, and labor cost due to higher automation, as well as shorter preparation and setup time for new products.

For all its benefits, the flexible strategy is not perfect. Its main flaw is high capital investment, as companies find it expensive to purchase multipurpose or adjustable equipment. Flexible manufacturing is also a complex undertaking. The system can be difficult to understand, highlight skilled technicians are needed, and a disciplined and high level of planning is required.[13]

Given these issues, many organizations have adopted an outsourcing strategy for some or all of their production operations. Business process outsourcing involves the farming out of any internal process—payroll, transportation, or production—to a third party. Contract manufacturers provide outsourced production and assembly services just as a third-party logistics firm provides distribution, warehousing, and transportation services (see Chapter 12). Should the activity be relocated to a contract manufacturer in another country, it is commonly called **offshoring**. Throughout the 1990s and early 2000s, China was the default location for offshore production. However, rising labor rates and production costs have driven manufacturers to look elsewhere.[14]

The business case for outsourcing varies by situation, but the reasons often focus on cost and capacity issues. The outsourcing strategy commonly provides lower cost access to variable capacity versus other manufacturing strategies.[15] Additional reasons for production outsourcing include the following:

- The ability to focus on core competencies by getting rid of peripheral ones
- Lack of in-house resources
- Getting work done more efficiently or effectively
- Increased flexibility to meet changing business and commercial conditions
- Tighter control of budget through predictable costs
- Lower ongoing investment in internal infrastructure
- Access to innovation and thought leadership[16]

While outsourcing has proven to be a valuable strategy whose popularity has grown dramatically, it is important to conduct a full analysis of the benefits and drawbacks of offshoring. Moving production offshore raises transportation costs, inventory carrying costs of goods in transit, customs costs, and some hidden expenses. As production spreads out among multiple facilities in different countries, it becomes more difficult to maintain visibility and synchronize activities. Finally, companies may lose control over quality, intellectual property rights, and customer relationships.

Given these challenges, many manufacturers are pursuing the concepts of on-shoring and nearshoring. On-shoring seeks to return production to the home country while nearshoring focuses on production in nearby or neighboring countries. The On the Line feature identifies a variety of organizations that have decided to bring production back to the United States to reduce dependence on suppliers located in the Far East. North America and Latin America are both popular regions for closer to home production strategies.

On the Line   *A North American Manufacturing Comeback*

North American manufacturers are actively bringing production activities on-shore. The reasons are many and the practice is becoming more prevalent. In fact, a survey by AlixPartners indicates that 42% of senior executives have either already taken steps to near shore manufacturing operations or plan to do so within the next three years.

Why would a company go through the challenges of uprooting current operations and move them across an ocean? A Manufacturing Today article indicates the following factors are making North America a more attractive place to produce goods:

- Chinese labor costs have skyrocketed at a double-digit pace.
- Transportation transit times of 35 to 45 days are no longer acceptable to customers.
- Political instability and environmental catastrophes—ranging from the Arab Spring to the Japanese earthquake and tsunami—demonstrated how vulnerable an Asian-based supply chain can be to external factors.
- Severe time-zone discrepancies make it difficult for U.S.-based managers to communicate with their Asian production facilities.
- Difficulty in monitoring quality control.

The Wall Street Journal also notes that the United States could be in a cost parity situation with Chinese manufacturers as early as 2015. Other concerns include protection of intellectual property rights, the ability to be more responsive to customers, and the opportunity to have a more predictable supply chain.

There are a number of high-profile organizations that have adopted the strategy. Key examples include:

- Apple has moved part of an existing Mac Pro production line to Texas.

- Caterpillar spent $120 million on a new factory in Victoria, Texas for the production of excavator machines.

- Dow Chemical opened an 800,000-square-foot plant located near its Midland, MI, headquarters. The factory produces batteries for hybrid and electric vehicles.

- Whirlpool has relocated its mixer assembly from China to Ohio and has invested $120 million in a new Cleveland, Tennessee factory.

In addition to company benefits, nearshoring and on-shoring benefit the local economy. Dow Chemical estimates that for every new job created in a chemical plant, five more jobs are created at suppliers and related businesses.

Sources: John T. Costanzo, "Near-Shoring Takes Hold," *Manufacturing Today.* Retrieved July 31, 2015 from http://www.manufacturing-today.com/index.php/sections/columns1/801-near-shoring-takes-hold; Rita Gunther McGrath, "Why 'Nearshoring' is Replacing 'Outsourcing'," *The Wall Street Journal,* (June 4, 2014); and, Premium Staffing, "Manufacturing Industry on the Rise in the United States," (November 26, 2013). Retrieved July 31, 2015 from http://www.premiumstaffinginc.com/2013/11/26/manufacturing-industry-rise-united-states/.

Manufacturers and technology suppliers continue to pursue production strategy innovations. Two recent strategies include adaptive manufacturing and smart manufacturing.

Adaptive manufacturing flexibly develops, produces, and delivers products through optimal use of existing resources. The strategy leverages lean manufacturing principles, Six Sigma best practices, and real-time actionable intelligence from the factory floor.[17] The adaptive approach rejects traditional reliance on standard lead times and long-range forecasts in favor of a demand-driven approach in which the supply side quickly senses and responds to customer demand.[18] The result is increased production flexibility and demand fulfillment velocity.

For adaptive manufacturing to happen, manufacturers must seamlessly transfer knowledge for defining, scheduling, and producing products between their enterprise systems and shop-floor systems. These linkages and real-time information are critical for sensing supply chain and manufacturing exceptions and quickly responding with appropriate actions.[19]

Smart manufacturing—or Industrie 4.0 as it is called in Europe—proposes to use robotics, networked data collection, and analytics to drive greater performance. It uses sensors to collect data from every material conversion step to drive quality control and continuous process improvement at the unit level versus the batch level.[20] Positive outcomes include greater labor, material, and energy efficiency, better equipment maintenance and utilization, and higher reliability of processes and products.[21]

To make use of smart manufacturing, at least three capabilities must be in place. These include a network with messaging standards to collect and connect the information, an analytical toolkit to make sense of it, and flexible automation to take action. Smart manufacturing initiatives will incorporate and integrate these digital readings and other outputs into a more disciplined root cause analysis and corrective action capability.

Each of the existing and emerging strategies has a role in today's supply chain, including the traditional mass-production, push-based strategy. Newer manufacturing strategies will not completely replace the older ones. Rather, the goal is to link the strengths of the traditional strategies with the enhanced capabilities of the innovative strategies to meet customer requirements. Manufacturers must develop strategic solutions that are appropriate for the product being made, the volume and variability of demand, and the capabilities of the manufacturer. The wider the range of products and customers is, the more likely the organization will be to run a hybrid system that leverages multiple strategies.

6-3-2 Production Planning[22]

With a strategy or combination of strategies defined, an organization turns its attention toward the planning aspects of production. During the planning process, operations managers continually try to balance inputs, capacity (resources), and outputs so as to not create waste. Excess inputs and outputs create unnecessary inventory, while excess capacity leads to higher than necessary production costs. On the flip side, shortages of inputs will starve the production process and reduce output. Capacity shortages lead to overwork of machines and labor that may result in quality problems.

This section briefly discusses two types of planning: **capacity planning** and **materials planning**. Three planning timeframes are also covered (1) **long-range plans**, which span a year or more, focus on major decisions regarding capacity and aggregate production plans; (2) **medium-range plans**, which span 6 to 18 months and involve tactical decisions regarding employment levels and similar issues; and (3) **short-range plans**, which range from a few days to a few weeks, and deal with specific issues and the details of production—quantities of items to be produced, schedules, and sequences. The major planning activities are identified in Figure 6.4.

Capacity planning focuses on determining the appropriate production levels that the company is capable of completing. **Capacity** is the maximum amount of work that an

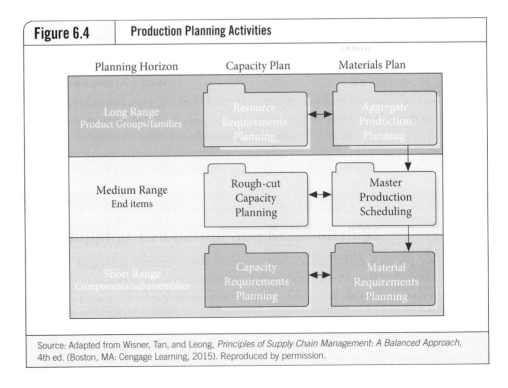

| Figure 6.4 | Production Planning Activities |

Planning Horizon	Capacity Plan	Materials Plan
Long Range Product Groups/families	Resource Requirements Planning	Aggregate Production Planning
Medium Range End items	Rough-cut Capacity Planning	Master Production Scheduling
Short Range Components/subassemblies	Capacity Requirements Planning	Material Requirements Planning

Source: Adapted from Wisner, Tan, and Leong, *Principles of Supply Chain Management: A Balanced Approach,* 4th ed. (Boston, MA: Cengage Learning, 2015). Reproduced by permission.

organization is capable of completing in a given period of time. It will help the company determine if changing customer demand can be met or if a discrepancy exists. A discrepancy between capacity and demands results in an inefficiency, either in underutilized resources or unfulfilled customer requirements. The goal of capacity planning is to minimize this discrepancy.

Resource requirements planning (RRP) is a long-run, macro-level planning tool. It helps the operations leaders determine whether aggregate resources are capable of satisfying the aggregate production plan. Gross labor hours and machine hours are the primary focus at this level of planning. If the RRP reveals inadequate resource levels, capacity expansion may be initiated via new facilities, capital equipment, or contract manufacturer resources. Otherwise, the aggregate production plan must be revised downward to make it feasible within the constraints of the available resources.

The next step is to create a **rough-cut capacity plan (RCCP),** a process that checks the feasibility of the master production schedule. The medium-range RCCP takes the master production schedule and converts it from production to capacity required and then compares it to available capacity for each production period. If the RCCP and master production schedule are in sync, the schedule is set. If not, capacity can be adjusted through the planned use of overtime, subcontracting, resource expansion, or routing flexibility to meet production needs. Alternatively, the schedule can be revised downward.

Finally, **capacity requirements planning (CRP)** is used to check the feasibility of the materials requirement plan. This short-range capacity planning technique determines, in detail, the amount of labor and equipment resources that were needed to accomplish production requirements. Even though RCCP may indicate that sufficient capacity exists to execute the master production schedule, CRP may show that capacity is insufficient during specific time periods.

Materials planning, in general, focuses on balancing of future supply and demand. It involves managing sales forecasts, creating master schedules, and running materials requirement planning tools.

The **aggregate production plan (APP)** is a long-range materials plan that translates annual business plans, marketing plans, and forecasts into a production plan for all products produced by a facility. The anticipated demand is used to set the facility's output rate, workforce size, utilization and inventory, and backlog levels. The planning horizon for the APP is a year or more and is continuously rolled forward to allow the company to analyze future capacity requirements on an ongoing basis. The objective of the APP is to develop a game plan that is capable of producing enough finished goods within product families or groups each period to meet the sales goal. Of course, the APP must work within the production capacity constraints while controlling the use of financial resources for labor costs, machine setup and operating costs, inventory costs, and related expenses.

The **master production schedule (MPS)** is a medium-range plan that is more detailed than the APP. The MPS breaks down the APP, listing the exact end items to be produced within a specific period. That is, the MPS defines the production quantity required to meet demand from all customers and provides the baseline for computing the requirements (production, staffing, inventory, etc.) for all time-phased end items. It also serves as an input to the materials requirement plan, which computes component and subassembly requirements. Thus, effective execution of the MPS helps avoid parts shortages, costly expediting, last-minute scheduling, and inefficient allocation of resources. Additionally, the MPS provides vital information regarding production availability. This information can help the organization use capacity more effectively in handling customer demand changes or accepting additional orders for completion and delivery within specific periods.

The **materials requirement plan (MRP)** is a short-range materials plan that converts information regarding end-items in the MPS into a set of time-phased component and part requirements. MRP focuses on scheduling and placing orders for dependent demand items so that they are available in the exact quantities on the date the independent demand item is to be manufactured. Lead time for ordering and receiving these dependent demand items must also be factored into the MRP process. Dependent demand items are components of finished goods—raw materials, component parts, and subassemblies—for which the amount of inventory needed depends on the level of production of the final product. For example, in a plant that manufactures motorcycles, dependent demand inventory items include aluminum, tires, seats, and exhaust system components.

For MRP to provide effective planning knowledge, the following three sets of information are needed:

1. Independent demand information—The MPS-defined demand for the final product or component.
2. Parent-component relationship—The bill of materials (BOM) inclusive listing of all component parts and assemblies that make up the final product, including the planning factor and lead-time information. The BOM effectively provides the "recipe" of component quantities and assembly sequence for making the final product.
3. Inventory status of the final product and all components—Information regarding net inventory requirements (gross requirements minus on-hand inventory). Orders for needed components are placed to ensure that orders are released on time for creating higher-level components as scheduled.

The goal of all these materials planning tools, especially MRP, is to provide useful information for operations decision makers. Solid production information regarding scheduled receipts, on-hand inventories, net requirements, and planned order releases is necessary for effective execution of assembly operations and timely fulfillment of customer orders. Recall that an understanding of capacity is the other piece of the production puzzle. You need both effective production and capacity planning to put an organization's production strategies to successful use. Otherwise, it will be difficult to meet customer deadlines with quality products that are made in the most cost-efficient manner possible.

6-4 Production Execution Decisions

The production strategy and planning outcomes, along with product characteristics, influence the execution methods used for day-to-day operations. Effective selection of assembly processes can help an organization manage its variability of demand. Products with consistent demand patterns require far different manufacturing methods than do products whose demand is affected by seasonality, short life cycles, and competitors' goods. Organizations must also establish facility layouts and production flows that are well matched to demand volume and manufacturing requirements. And organizations must use proper packaging to safely handle and transport the production outputs. This section will address these three topics that impact day-to-day production performance.

6-4-1 Assembly Processes

Earlier in the chapter, we alluded to products that are built either according to plan or to demand. Their production occurs via either a MTS or a **make-to-order (MTO)** manufacturing process. MTO can be segmented into three variations **ATO**, **BTO**, and

engineer-to-order (ETO). Each process is appropriate for some types of products. Selection is driven by the current state of the business environment, the need for the supply chain to manage demand variation, and the product's level of standardization and production complexity.

MTS is the traditional production method where end-item products are finished before receipt of a customer order. In these mass-production processes, customer orders are filled from finished goods inventories, and production orders are used to replenish finished goods inventories. This generally makes production scheduling easier, supports cost-effective manufacturing with economies of scale, and enables the manufacturer to quickly fill orders from finished goods inventory. Accurate forecasting and inventory control are critical issues in MTS, and warehousing of end products is the norm.

In this build-ahead production approach, production plans are driven by historical demand information in combination with sales forecast information. This approach is good for high-volume products where the demand is predictable or requires production in advance of seasonal demand. MTS is an ideal method for continuous process manufacturing and works well for commodity-based end products such as chemicals, pharmaceuticals, and paper products.

ATO product assembly commences after receipt of a customer's order. The finished ATO product is generally a combination of common components and a limited number of options or accessories made available to the customer. The individual components are often stocked in anticipation of demand, but the finished goods are not assembled until customers place orders for their desired products.

ATO is useful in repetitive manufacturing situations where a large number of end products (based on the selection of options and accessories) can be assembled from common components. Automobiles and personal computers are good examples of ATO products that allow for limited consumer choice. As the On the Line feature below explains, ATO can be applied to a wide range of products. Key benefits of this production process versus MTS include lower finished goods inventory, greater ability to adapt to changing demand, streamlined forecasting for components rather than finished goods, and higher levels of customer engagement.

On the Line   *Have it Your Way*

E-commerce is not limited to retailers selling their wares online. Many manufacturers have seized the opportunity to engage directly with consumers. One aspect of this direct engagement involves the production of customized or semi-customized goods based on the desires of individual consumers. The manufacturer then builds your semi-customized product and delivers it to your location of choice.

Today, it is possible for the individual to go online and design products ranging from chocolate bars to cars. Examples include:

Chocomize.com—Customers select either a chocolate bar or heart shape, flavor of chocolate (dark, milk, or white), and up to five toppings from 100 different options. The potential combinations number 600 million and the bars are made to order and shipped to arrive within four business days.

Hem.com—Customers design their own furniture using a four step process. Custom shelving involves the determination of shelving unit size and configurations, selection of materials and color, and the choice of shelf thickness. The design is priced and an estimated delivery time is generated.

TeslaMotors.com—Customers go to the design studio to create their personal Model S. Customers select the battery size which determines driving range, drivetrain, paint color, wheels, and interior colors. They also can choose a variety of upgrade options. The Web site prices the car as designed by the customer and an estimated production date is provided.

Why do companies strive to support these customer driven products? It is about customer access and revenue growth. Eric Heinbockel, a founder of Chocomize says: "We chose this concept because we think that mass customization is the future for many industries, thanks to the buying power of the Internet."

Sources: "About Chocomize," *Chocomize.com.* Retrieved August 3, 2015 from http://www.chocomize.com/About-chocomize-custom-chocolate; "Custom Furniture," *hem.com.* Retrieved August 3, 2015 from http://hem.com/en/customize/?ref=home.home.cust_sub; and, "Design Studio," *Teslamotors.com.* Retrieved August 3, 2015 from http://my.teslamotors.com/models/design.

The BTO production approach also delays assembly until a confirmed order is received for the product. The end-item finished product is a combination of standard and custom-designed components that meet the unique needs of a specific customer. It differs from ATO in the higher level of customization and lower volume level of production. BTO is considered a good choice for products that require some custom configuration, such as a private jet where the aircraft is a standard model but the customer specifies the avionics and interior design. It is also effective for situations where holding finished goods inventories in anticipation of demand is very expensive.

A primary benefit of the BTO approach is its ability to handle variety and meet customers' product specifications. Like ATO, BTO requires little or no finished goods inventory, which means carrying costs and product obsolescence rates are low. On the other hand, demand fluctuations can cause extreme swings in BTO manufacturing capacity utilization, setup costs can be high, and lead times are relatively long, because orders are not filled from readily available inventory.[23] The manufacturer also faces the challenge of deciding how much capacity to reserve in each production period for BTO products and what lead time should be quoted for each item.

ETO production focuses on the creation of highly tailored products for customers whose specifications require unique engineering design or significant customization. In this manufacturing environment, no two products are identical, and each order requires detailed cost estimates and tailored pricing. Each customer order results in a unique set of part numbers, bill of materials, and routings that tend to be complex with long lead times. Components and raw materials may be stocked but are not assembled into the finished good until a customer order is received and the product is designed.

Also known as *project manufacturing*, successful ETO initiatives depend on effective collaboration between all supply chain participants. Customers must be involved throughout the entire design and production process. Supplier engagement is also a critical aspect of ETO production. The materials required by the manufacturer can be very unique or ordered infrequently. Working together, engineering, purchasing, and suppliers can compress the lead time for these inputs and help keep production on schedule. ETO products include capital equipment, industrial machinery, and complex items in the aerospace and defense industries. Table 6.2 summarizes the role and benefits of ETO relative to the other MTO options.

Some firms rely exclusively on MTO processes, while others employ only the MTS method. Given the widespread proliferation of products, a number of manufacturers take a hybrid approach, where some items are built to stock and others are built to order.

Table 6.2	Comparison of Make-to-Order (MTO) Options		
	ATO	**BTO**	**ETO**
Level of customization	Limited	Moderate	Total
Cost of finished goods	Moderate	High	Very high
Order fulfillment speed	Days to weeks	Weeks to months	Month to years
Production process complexity	Moderate	High	Extreme
Example products	Personal computers Automobiles	Computer servers Private jets	Stadium JumboTron Nuclear power plant

Source: Brian J. Gibson, Ph.D. Used with permission.

Delayed differentiation is a hybrid strategy in which a common product platform is built to stock. It is later differentiated by assigning to it certain customer-specific features, only after demand is realized. Hence, manufacturing occurs in two stages (1) an MTS stage, where one or more undifferentiated platforms are produced and stocked, and (2) an ATO stage, where product differentiation takes place in response to specific customer orders. For example, a technology company like Motorola has all the components for a Moto X on hand but waits until a customer order is placed. Then, the phone is assembled based on the casing color, accent color, memory, and engraving preferences of the customer (ATO stage).

Delayed differentiation carries several benefits. Maintaining stocks of semifinished goods reduces order cycle time relative to BTO or ETO production. Since many different end products have common parts, lower levels of semifinished goods inventory are needed. Furthermore, investment in semifinished inventories is smaller when compared with the option to maintain a similar amount of finished goods inventory. There is also the benefit of having better demand information before committing generic semifinished products to unique end products. Additional benefits from delayed differentiation include streamlining the MTS segment of the production process and simplification of production scheduling, sequencing, and raw materials purchasing. However, implementing delayed differentiation also carries extra materials costs due to the need for redundant or more expensive parts.[24]

6-4-2 Production Process Layout

One of the key drivers of how production activities will be carried out is **facility layout**—the arrangement of machines, storage areas, and other resources within the four walls of a manufacturing or an assembly facility. The layout is influenced by the production strategy and assembly process employed by the organization. Product characteristics (weight, fragility, size) and demand characteristics (volume and variability) also play a role in the layout decision, as do service commitments, production mix issues, and facility costs.

A thorough analysis of these issues will often lead to an obvious and ideal layout choice. The goal of process layout selection is to ensure that production activities are carried out as efficiently and effectively as possible. An appropriate, successful layout is one that does the following:

- Reduces bottlenecks in moving people or materials
- Minimizes materials-handling costs
- Reduces hazards to personnel

- Utilizes labor efficiently
- Increases morale and ease of supervision
- Utilizes available space effectively and efficiently
- Provides flexibility
- Facilitates coordination and face-to-face communication[25]

Production process layouts generally fit into a spectrum of work flow that moves from projects to continuous processes. This spectrum is highlighted in Figure 6.5 according to the product standardization and product volume requirements of each layout. Additionally, as you move from project to continuous process layout, note the following characteristics:

- Labor skill requirements decrease
- Material requirements become better known
- High-capacity utilization becomes more important to controlling costs
- Product flexibility declines
- Ability to adapt rapidly to changing market conditions diminishes

A **project layout** is a fixed location layout where the product remains in place for the duration of production. Materials and labor are moved to this production site. For example, assembly of a cruise ship would take place in a dry dock in which the entire process from construction of the hull to the installation of the propulsion system and on-board facilities would take place. Areas on site will be designated for supporting activities such as materials staging, subassembly construction, site access for specialized equipment, and a project

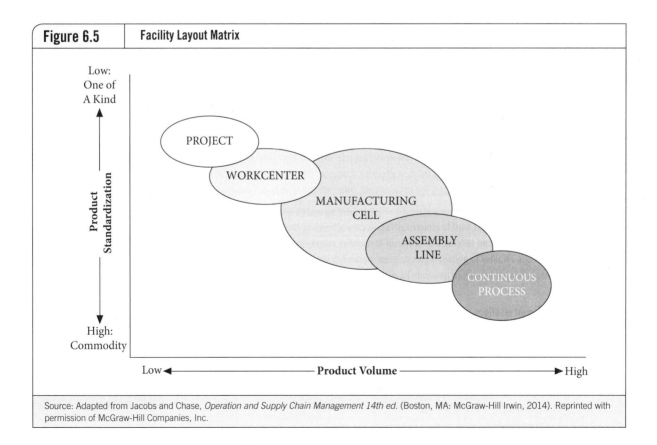

Figure 6.5 **Facility Layout Matrix**

Source: Adapted from Jacobs and Chase, *Operation and Supply Chain Management 14th ed.* (Boston, MA: McGraw-Hill Irwin, 2014). Reprinted with permission of McGraw-Hill Companies, Inc.

management area. Similar layouts are used for road construction, home building, and other major projects.

A **workcenter** is a process-focused layout that groups together similar equipment or functions. The materials move from department to department for completion of similar activities and tasks. For example, a manufacturer of towels may have different departments focused on individual operations related to textile production—yarn spinning, weaving, dyeing, cutting, and sewing. This layout provides flexibility in that equipment and personnel can be used where they are needed, lower equipment investment is needed, and supervisors gain expertise in their functions. The downsides of the workcenter layout are related to the materials handling and movement costs, worker idle time between tasks, and the cost of training and developing a highly skilled workforce that can move between areas.

The **manufacturing cell** is another process-focused layout that dedicates production areas to a narrow range of products that are similar in processing requirements. Setting up a manufacturing cell involves four activities (1) identifying families of parts with similar flow paths, (2) grouping machines into cells based on part families, (3) arranging cells so materials movement is minimized, and (4) locating large shared machines at the point of use. When properly implemented, cellular manufacturing provides higher production efficiency, reduces waste, lowers inventory levels, shortens production cycle times, and improves customer response time. This type of layout is widely used for fabrication operations and production of mobile phones, computer chips, and automotive subassemblies.

An **assembly line** is a product-focused layout in which machines and workers are arranged according to the progressive sequence of operations need to make a product. Often used for mass production of goods, the assembly steps are completed at workstations that are typically linked by materials-handling equipment. An assembly line can begin as many different lines, each devoted to a different component of a product, with the lines converging upon one another, becoming fewer until only one line is left for the final product. The key to success is control, matching the assembly line speed to the skills of the workforce and the complexity of the assembly processes being performed. Assembly lines are cost efficient, eliminate cross flows and backtracking, limit the amount of work in process, and streamline production time. This type of layout is appropriate for appliances, automobiles, and video game consoles.

Continuous process facilities are similar to assembly lines, with product flowing through a predetermined sequence of steps. The main difference is the continuous, rather than discrete, nature of the flow. Widely used for high-volume, standardized products like chemicals, paper products, and soft drink concentrate, these highly automated, capital-intensive facilities need to run almost nonstop to gain maximum efficiency. This layout is not without challenges. The equipment is large and fixed in nature, limiting the flexibility of continuous processes to meet changing requirements. Also, finished goods inventories can be high as companies are likely to continue to run the production line during low-demand periods.

6-4-3 Packaging

As product comes off the assembly line, the handoff from production operations to logistics begins. Packaging plays important roles in the smooth transfer of finished goods from the plant to the distribution center and customer locations. Package design issues can affect labor and facility efficiency. Well-designed packaging facilitates efficient handling and shipping of the products, keeping landed costs in check. Proper packaging protects the integrity and quality of the goods just produced. And customized packaging can provide another level of product differentiation sought by the customer. These packaging-focused links between production operations and logistics, along with the materials used, are worthy of a brief discussion.

Package design impacts an organization's ability to use space and equipment. The design must promote effective space utilization in the production facility and distribution centers. Package shape, strength, and materials impact the ability to use the full cubic capacity (both horizontal and vertical space) of facilities. Hence, it is common to use square or rectangular boxes or containers with adequate strength to support stacking. The physical dimensions of products and packaging must fall within the capabilities of existing materials-handling equipment at the factory, distribution centers, and customer locations. Poor package design leads to costly and potentially dangerous manual handling of products.

A major packaging concern is the ease of handling in relation to materials handling and transportation. Handling ease is quite important to the production manager, whose labor must be used to place the goods in the packages. It is also important to logistics managers who need product to be handled quickly and without wasted effort. Large packages, for example, may be desirable from a production perspective, but the size and weight of the contents might cause problems when transferring product into and out of transportation equipment. Also, packaging design should take pallet and transportation vehicle capacity into account, so as to fully utilize these assets. Failure to do so will lead to the costly consequence of "shipping air" rather than product, driving up the cost of goods.

Another primary concern is protecting the goods in the package. In the production facility, adequate packaging is needed to protect goods as they move through the facility. Products falling off conveyor lines or packages being hit with a forklift are just two examples of dangers that must be factored into the design process. Protection is important when logistics service providers transport products. Protection can also mean protecting products from contamination resulting from contact with other goods, water damage, temperature changes, pilferage, and shocks in handling and transport. Packaging must support the weight of products stacked above it or provide even weight distribution within the package to facilitate manual and automatic materials handling.

With customer service playing an ever-increasing role in the supply chain, companies need to integrate their packages with customers' materials-handling equipment. A special package that can interface with a customer's innovative equipment will help move product quickly through the supply chain, keeping costs down, product availability strong, and customer satisfaction high. In contrast, incompatible packaging and equipment will lead to inefficient receiving and storage. It may also increase the potential for product damage. In these situations, customer service value may be lost.

Also, packaging plays a key role in providing information about the package contents. Information provision is also important to production and logistics personnel in their day-to-day execution responsibilities. Properly identified packages and reusable containers make it easier for production personnel to locate goods needed by the workcenter or assembly line. Goods stored in a distribution center must bear the proper identification so that order pickers can locate them easily and correctly for customer orders. Barcodes, RFID tags, and other auto-ID tools can be attached to or built into the packaging to make product information more readily accessible.

Accomplishing these key goals is dependent upon finding the right materials for exterior packaging and interior cushioning materials. It is important to use materials that are economical, strong, and sustainable. Durable packaging materials like wood and metal— which are expensive and add excess weight to the product—are instead being replaced by softer packaging materials—recycled cardboard, polyethylene bags, and biodegradable cushioning materials made from cornstarch and soy—in an effort to reduce cost and waste. Additional packaging sustainability innovations are discussed in the On the Line box.

The sustainability mantra of reduce, reuse, recycle is not lost on other manufacturers who are embracing these new packaging materials and technologies. In fact, the global market for sustainable packaging is projected to reach $244 billion by 2018. Sustainable packaging programs are viewed as a source of innovation that can help in differentiating a company by appealing to the consciences of consumers.[26]

According to the Sustainable Packaging Coalition, sustainable packaging meets several criteria:

- Is beneficial, safe, and healthy for individuals and communities throughout its life cycle
- Meets market criteria for performance and cost
- Is sourced, manufactured, transported, and recycled using renewable energy
- Optimizes the use of renewable or recycled source materials
- Is manufactured using clean production technologies and best practices
- Is made from materials healthy throughout the life cycle
- Is physically designed to optimize materials and energy
- Is effectively recovered and utilized in biological and/or industrial closed loop cycles[27]

On the Line   *Developing More Sustainable Packaging*

In a perfect world, all packaging would be sourced responsibly, designed to be effective and safe throughout its life cycle, meet market criteria for performance and cost, be made entirely using renewable energy, and once used, be recycled efficiently to provide a valuable resource for subsequent generations. That's the vision of the Sustainable Packaging Coalition® (SPC)—a true closed loop system for all packaging materials that collects and recovers material at the highest value that is economically feasible.

How should companies foster sustainability in the packaging area? The most common sustainable packaging trends include:

- Reduced packaging size and weight
- Increased recycling and waste recovery
- Increased use of recycled content
- Increased use of renewably sourced materials
- Improvements in packaging and logistical efficiency

Examples of these efforts include:

European beer maker Carlsberg recently worked with its global suppliers to develop the next generation of packaging that is optimized for recycling and reuse. One example is using recyclable plastic kegs instead of stainless steel kegs.

Food manufacturers have been working to make product packaging smaller, lighter, and use less material. Heinz introduced a 10-oz pouch of tomato ketchup, lowering both the cost of production and cost to consumers. Coca-Cola and Pepsico reduced the amount of plastic contained in their 16.9-oz water bottles.

Coffee makers sell over 9 billion Keurig coffee pods per year. Hence, there is a growing need to design these single use containers for recycling. Biome Bioplastics is designing coffee pods made of plant-based materials and resources that meet international composting standards.

James Cropper, a paper manufacturer, has developed a process to use the husk of cocoa beans into unbleached cellulose fiber to produce a food-grade paper. With 3.5 million metric tons of cocoa beans used for chocolate production each year, the husk conversion effort will reduce landfill use.

Sources: Mike Hower, "Sustainable Packaging Market to Hit $244 Billion by 2018," *Sustainable Brands* (February 19, 2014). Retrieved August 2, 2015 from http://www.sustainablebrands.com/news_and_views/ packaging/mike_hower/report_sustainable_packaging_market_hit_244_billion_2018; Tom Skzaky, "Blog: 5 Sustainable Packaging Trends to Look Out for in 2014," *Packaging Digest* (March 19, 2014). Retrieved August 2, 2015 from http://www.packagingdigest.com/sustainable-packaging/blog-5-sustainable-packaging-trends-look-out-2014; and, Sustainable Packaging Coalition, *Definition of Sustainable Packaging Version 2.0* (Revised August 2011). Retrieved August 1, 2015, from http://sustainablepackaging. org/uploads/Documents/Definition%20of%20Sustainable%20Packaging.pdf

6-5 Production Metrics[28]

Throughout this chapter, we have discussed the evolution of production operations from assembly-line-focused, mass-production processes to more lean and flexible manufacturing approaches. The problem is that many organizations continue to monitor production performance as if the goal were strictly to make product to stock at the lowest possible labor cost. This has led to the use of measurements and key performance indicators (KPIs) that do not support operational strategies, organizational objectives, or customer requirements. Thus, it is important to avoid three mistakes when establishing production metrics:

- Using KPIs that are too narrow—Avoid metrics that focus on discrete events as indicators of overall success of the process. For example, labor cost is sometimes studied in detail and used as a surrogate for overall cost. It is only one component of total cost and must be combined with other data to be meaningful.

- Encouraging wrong outcomes—Eliminate measurements that promote activity rather than needed output. Be wary of standard cost accounting measures that lead to good direct labor efficiency, high machine utilization, and continuous production. They may also produce unneeded inventory and high overhead expenses.

- Focusing on issues that are not key priorities—Shun narrowly focused, shortsighted production goals that are disconnected from the overall strategy of the organization. For example, the goal of reducing year-over-year manufacturing costs may not be realistic for a lean production environment.

So, what should operations managers do to ensure that they are measuring the right things in the right way? They should align operations metrics with corporate objectives, leading people toward behaviors and goals that are important to the overall success of the organization. They should keep the metrics program straightforward, limiting the number of metrics used to a maximum of five or six per team or function and focus on KPIs that can be easily compiled and updated. They should also measure the performance of individual activities as key inputs to manufacturing and supply chain performance goals. The key is to follow the "five golden metrics" of manufacturing that impact an organization's bottom line: (1) total cost, (2) total cycle time, (3) delivery performance, (4) quality, and (5) safety.

6-5-1 Total Cost

The most meaningful measurement of **total cost** is on a cash basis. All money spent on manufacturing must be summarized and the total compared to the previous period, rather than to a flexible budget or a plan. What matters is whether the total cash spent on manufacturing (including sales, general, and administrative expense) was more or less than it was in the previous period. The cost figure should exclude arbitrary allocations and major capital investment spending and adjust expenses for accounts receivables and payables. This allows manufacturing performance to be evaluated as if payment were made at the time materials and services were delivered and payment were collected at the time finished goods were shipped to an outside customer.

6-5-2 Total Cycle Time

Total cycle time is a measure of manufacturing performance that is calculated by studying major purchased components and determining the total days on hand of each one. The total days on hand is the sum of all of such components in the plant regardless of form, with the only exception being low-cost, bulk items. Components in their original purchased state, embedded in assemblies or subassemblies, in a modified state in work-in-process inventory, or embedded in a finished product should be included in the sum.

The total days on hand figure is divided by the planned shipments per day for all products that require that component. For example, if there are 5,000 of a component in the plant in all its various forms, and it goes into two final products that are each projected to ship 100 per day, the cycle time for that component is 5,000/200 = 25 days. The total cycle time for the plant or for an individual value stream within the plant is the cycle time of the component with the greatest cycle time.

6-5-3 Delivery Performance

Delivery performance is the percentage of customer orders shipped when the customer requested them to be shipped. It should not be modified to accommodate company policies or shipping promises. It is purely a metric of manufacturing's ability to meet customer requirements.

6-5-4 Quality

The definition of **quality** will vary by company, but it must focus on quality from the perspective of the customer. As a result, customer returns or warranty claims are a good basis for this metric rather than a summary of internal quality metrics (e.g., defect rates or first-pass yield). It is important to realize that internal metrics are only important to the extent that they provide information that management can use to minimize cost, improve flow, and pursue customer quality requirements.

6-5-5 Safety

The standard metrics of accident/incident frequency, severity, and cost are important to monitor, with continuous improvement (i.e., reduction) as the goal. Frequency can be measured in the number of accidents and the number of OSHA-recordable accidents.

Severity involves the number of lost workdays or the number of days of workers' compensation paid. Financial impact can be evaluated via the cost of injuries and injuries as a percentage of manufacturing cost.

To gain maximum results, these production cost, timeliness, delivery, quality, and safety metrics must be in sync with company goals. Before beginning to establish supply chain metrics, managers must ensure that they fully understand key organizational objectives. Once these are understood, they can be translated into specific facility, process, functional, or business unit objectives, which can then be defined in terms of metrics.[29] World-class manufacturers continually track process performance factors that impact success. They work to gain balanced improvement of the five golden metrics of production while supporting overall supply chain KPIs (e.g., order-to-delivery cycle time, throughput, inventory levels, operating expenses, and customer satisfaction).

6-6 Production Technology

As production operations become more and more complex—receiving inputs from a wider variety of suppliers, producing goods in smaller batches, and delivering a larger range of outputs—technology is needed to keep the facility running at peak performance. The enterprise resource planning systems and supply chain technologies discussed in Chapter 14 and other chapters help improve operational efficiency and support basic plant scheduling for production, material use, inventory levels, and delivery. However, they don't always effectively link the factory to the supply chain or ensure that operations are being managed proactively. Other tools must be linked to these systems to create flexible and adaptive production processes that are capable of responding in real time to changing market dynamics.

Manufacturers across all industries understand the importance of sharing real-time information across their extended manufacturing and supply chain network. Enhanced manufacturing visibility helps an organization improve its operations, synchronize processes with suppliers, and provide better customer service.[30] These organizations are using **manufacturing execution systems (MES)** to link ERP systems and supply chain applications to ensure that operations are being managed in real time. The MES is a control system for managing and monitoring work-in-process on a factory floor. It keeps track of all manufacturing information in real time, receiving up-to-the-minute data from robots, machine monitors, and employees.[31]

MES derives its name from its inherent purpose of providing intelligent process control through an electronic system designed to execute instructions to control manufacturing operations. The goal is to supply a continuous flow of meaningful instructions, and most importantly, for those instructions to be carried out correctly and reliably. An effective MES provides manufacturing planning information, supports the day-to-day execution of operations, and provides production process control. The primary functions of MES include:

- Resource allocation and status
- Operation/detail scheduling
- Dispatching production unit
- Document control
- Data collection
- Labor management
- Quality management

- Process management
- Exception management
- Maintenance
- Management
- Product tracking and genealogy
- Performance analysis[32]

The MES functions as follows: the system receives an order from the ERP system and then makes an intelligent decision on where to produce the orders. This decision is based on facility capabilities, capacity, and price. Next, the MES publishes the instructions for the best way to manufacture the product for the parties involved in the manufacturing process. Finally, the details of production performance are tracked via KPIs and dashboards in real time, allowing managers or the system to react to changes and problems in a timely fashion.

Although MES has been in existence for years, the market for these software systems is growing at 12.6% per year. MarketsandMarkets estimates that the global MES market will be worth $13.59 billion by 2020.[33] Table 6.3 highlights the short- and long-term benefits that are driving MES adoption.

What is the future roadmap for MES? A supply chain solutions provider suggests that MES can make strategic contributions to the organization beyond the factory floor. This will only occur if the following improvements are achieved in the near future:

- MES must become more agile and capable of dealing with product and process customization to the shop floor level than is possible today.
- MES must be capable of orchestrating suppliers across a global industry landscape.
- MES must optimize resources and constraints far beyond the four walls of the manufacturing plant to drive more rapid time-to-market and better cost controls.
- MES needs to scale up and support multi-site, globally deployed production planning, supplier coordination, compliance and quality management initiatives that span the entire value chain.
- The MES-level data must support the extraction of metrics that drive overall business performance and profitability.[34]

Table 6.3	Manufacturing Execution Systems (MES) Benefits Over Time	
INITIAL 3-12 MONTHS	**NEXT 12-36 MONTHS**	**36 MONTHS AND BEYOND**
Efficiency gains	Process improvements	Accelerated new product development
Cost reductions	Shortened cycles/work flows	Reduced indirect labor costs
Improved quality	Reduced inventory carrying costs	Increased organizational agility
		Improved asset utilization

Source: Oliver Dean, "Manufacturing Execution Systems—the Investment that Keeps on Giving," *Manufacturing Transformation*, (May 20, 2015). Retrieved July 31, 2015 from http://www.apriso.com/blog/2015/05/manufacturing-execution-systems-the-investment-that-keeps-on-giving/

SUMMARY

The key concept from this chapter is the critical and codependent link between production operations and logistics. Just as your heart and arteries need to work together to move blood through your circulatory system, production and logistics must work in concert to move product through the supply chain. For their part, production managers must coordinate demand information, inputs, and resources to transform them into outputs (products and materials) that are desired by customers. The faster and more flexible the transformation processes are, the more responsive the production operation can be to changing conditions and disruptions. This in turn makes the supply chain more dynamic and competitive.

Additional topics from the chapter include the following:

- Production operations include all activities and processes involved in changing the composition of a good or service—component fabrication, product assembly, and service request execution—for the purpose of creating form utility.

- Numerous tradeoffs must be made regarding production: volume versus variety, responsiveness, or efficiency; make or outsource; and focusing on a few versus many competitive dimensions.

- Intensified competition, more demanding customers, and relentless pressure for efficiency as well as adaptability are driving significant changes across many manufacturing industry settings.

- There have been significant developments and shifts in production strategy. Organizations have advanced from forecast-driven mass production to demand-driven, lean, flexible, adaptive, and smart manufacturing approaches.

- Capacity planning and materials planning are used to balance inputs, capacity (resources), and outputs so that customer demand can be fulfilled without creating waste.

- Most manufacturers use a combination of MTS and MTO production methods to satisfy demand for their products.

- Within the MTO method, companies can leverage ATO, BTO, or ETO options, based on product complexity and uniqueness.

- Facility layout involves the arrangement of machines, storage areas, and other resources within the four walls of a manufacturing or an assembly facility.

- Facility layout is influenced by the product characteristics, production strategy, and assembly process employed by the organization.

- Packaging plays important roles in the smooth, safe, and economical transfer of finished goods from the plant to the distribution center and customer locations.

- Sustainability is a key consideration in packaging selection, and companies are turning to recyclable and reusable materials for exterior and interior packaging.

- Production KPIs must be linked to corporate goals and objectives, customer requirements, and overall performance of the production operation.

- Critical production KPIs address total cost, total cycle time, delivery performance, quality, and safety.

- MES software solutions improve an organization's ability to manage production operations and make them more responsive to disruptions, challenges, and changing marketplace conditions.

STUDY QUESTIONS

1. Discuss the role of production operations in the supply chain. Provide examples of how effective/ineffective production operations impact supply chain performance.

2. Describe the major challenges faced by production managers in the current environment.

3. Compare and contrast push-based production strategies with pull-based production strategies. What are the primary capabilities, advantages, and disadvantages of each?

4. Outsourcing has been a popular supply chain strategy. Discuss the reasons for and against an organization outsourcing its production processes.

5. Discuss the reasons why U.S.-based organizations are considering a nearshoring or re-shoring strategy.

6. Describe the differences between capacity planning and materials planning.

7. Discuss the concept of delayed differentiation and why it is considered to be a hybrid approach to product assembly. What types of products can benefit from delayed differentiation?

8. Using the company Web sites, compare the supply chain and contract manufacturing services provided by the following organizations:
   a. Flextronics (http://www.flextronics.com) and Cinram Group (http://www.cinram-group.com)
   b. Accupac (http://www.accupac.com) and Jabil Circuit (http://www.jabil.com)
   c. ModusLink (http://www.moduslink.com) and Cott Corporation (http://www.cott.com)

9. Identify and discuss the most appropriate assembly process and facility layout for each of the following products:
   a. Coke Zero concentrate
   b. Harley-Davidson motorcycle
   c. Apple iPhone

10. Discuss how packaging affects manufacturing and supply chain operations.

11. Describe how organizations can be more environmentally conscious in their use of packaging.

12. Describe the characteristics of good production metrics and the types of KPIs that companies should monitor.

13. Using Internet search engines, identify two MES solutions providers. Describe the capabilities and supply chain impact that their tools promise.

NOTES

1. Donald J. Bowersox, David J. Closs, and M. Bixby Cooper, *Supply Chain Logistics Management,* 4th ed. (Boston, MA: McGraw-Hill, 2012).

2. Sunil Chopra and Peter Meindl, *Supply Chain Management, Strategy, Planning, and Operations,* 5th ed. (Upper Saddle River, NJ: Pearson Prentice Hall, 2012).

3. Donald J. Bowersox, David J. Closs, and M. Bixby Cooper, *Supply Chain Logistics Management,* 4th ed. (Boston, MA: McGraw-Hill, 2012).

4. Howard Mustoe, "Takata Doubles Faulty Airbag Recall to 34 Million," *BBC News* (May 19, 2015). Retrieved August 1, 2015, from http://www.bbc.com/news/business-32806056.

5. Stan Aronow, "Gartner Announces Rankings of Its 2015 Supply Chain Top 25," *Gartner.com* (May 14, 2015). Retrieved July 31, 2015, from http://www.gartner.com/newsroom/id/3053118.

6. Abigail Phillips, "6 Challenges Facing the Global Manufacturing Sector in 2015," *Manufacturing Global* (November 11, 2014). Retrieved August 1, 2015, from http://www.manufacturingglobal.com/leadership/226/6-challenges-facing-the-global-manufacturing-sector-in-2015.

7. David Simchi-Levi, Philip Kaminsky, and Edith Simchi-Levi, *Designing and Managing the Supply Chain: Concepts, Strategies, and Case Studies*, 3rd ed. (Boston, MA: McGraw-Hill Irwin, 2008), 153–154.

8. Ibid., 188–89.

9. Daisuke Wakabayashi, "How Lean Manufacturing Can Backfire," *The Wall Street Journal* (January 30, 2010). Retrieved August 2, 2015, from http://www.wsj.com/articles/SB10001424052748704343104575032910217257240.

10. Tullio Tolio, ed., *Design of Flexible Production Systems: Methodologies and Tools* (Berlin, Germany: Springer-Verlag, 2009), 1.

11. Honda, "Advanced Manufacturing Flexibility in North America" *News & Views* (March 11, 2015). Retrieved August 2, 2015, from http://www.hondainamerica.com/news/advanced-manufacturing-flexibility-north-america.

12. Felix S. Chan, "The Effects of Routing Flexibility on a Flexible Manufacturing System," *International Journal of Computer Integrated Manufacturing*, Vol. *14*, No. 5 (2001).

13. Gaurav Akrani, "Disadvantages of Flexible Manufacturing System FMS," *Kalyan City Life* (February 18, 2012). Retrieved August 2, 2015, from http://kalyan-city.blogspot.com/2012/02/disadvantages-of-flexible-manufacturing.html

14. Darin Buelow, Doug Gish & Josh Timberlake, "Manufacturing Beyond China," *Deloite University Press* (March 23, 2013). Retrieved August 2, 2015, from http://dupress.com/articles/manufacturing-beyond-china/.

15. Laura Cole, "The Art of Manufacturing: Is Outsourcing or Insourcing Better for Your Business," *Monster* (May 21, 2015). Retrieved August 2, 2015, from http://news.monster.com/a/business/the-art-of-manufacturing-is-outsourcing-or-insourcing-better-for-your-business-af87a2.

16. Stephanie Overby, "Tutorial: Outsourcing Definitions and Solutions," *CIO.com* (May 9, 2007). Retrieved August 2, 2015, from http://www.cio.com/article/2439495/outsourcing/outsourcing-definition-and-solutions.html#2.

17. Tesha Harvey, "Adaptive Manufacturing," SAP Community Network (September 8, 2006). Retrieved August 1, 2015, from http://wiki.scn.sap.com/wiki/display/ESpackages/Adaptive+manufacturing.

18. Roberto Michel, "Adaptive Manufacturing Moves In," *Modern Materials Handling* (September 2006): 29–31.

19. Andy Dé, "Adaptive Manufacturing," *SAP Info* (October 2005): 30–32.

20. Kevin O'Marah, "Smart Manufacturing is Ready to Pop." SCM World (July 24, 2015). Retrieved August 1, 2015, from http://www.scmworld.com/columns/beyond-supply-chain/smart-manufacturing-is-ready-to-pop/.

21. Bob Parker, "Making the Business Case for Smart Manufacturing," *IndustryWeek* (February 27, 2015). Retrieved August 1, 2015, from http://www.industryweek.com/smart-manufacturing?page=2.

22. This section is adapted from Joel D. Wisner, Keah-Choon Tan, and G. Keong Leong, *Principles of Supply Chain Management: A Balanced Approach*, 4th ed. (Boston, MA: Cengage Learning, 2015), chap. 6.

23. MIT Center for Transportation and Logistics, "Solving Production Puzzles," *Supply Chain Frontiers* (July 2007). Retrieved August 1, 2015, from http://ctl.mit.edu/library/solving_production_puzzles.

24. Saif Benjaafar, "Make-to-Order, Make-to-Stock, or Delay Product Differentiation? A Common Framework for Modeling and Analysis," *IIE Transactions* (June 2004), pp. 529–546.

25. Henry C. Co, "Facility Design and Layout." Retrieved August 1, 2015, from http://www.slidefinder.net/f/facility_design_layout_henry_technology/05faciltydesignlayout/7173422.

26. Mike Hower, "Sustainable Packaging Market to Hit $244 Billion by 2018," *Sustainable Brands* (February 19, 2014). Retrieved August 1, 2015, from http://www.sustainablebrands.com/news_and_views/packaging/mike_hower/ report_sustainable_packaging_market_hit_244_billion_2018.

27. Sustainable Packaging Coalition, *Definition of Sustainable Packaging Version 2.0* (Revised August 2011). Retrieved August 1, 2015, from http://sustainablepackaging.org/uploads/Documents/Definition%20of%20Sustainable%20Packaging.pdf

28. Unless noted otherwise, information in this section is adapted from Bill Waddell, *Manufacturing's Five Golden Metrics*. Retrieved August 1, 2015, from http://s189494.gridserver.com/manufacturing-leadership/wp-content/uploads/sites/ 2/2013/01/Manufacturing-5-Golden-Metrics.pdf.

29. Robert Handfield, "Supply Chain Metrics: Make Sure They Are Aligned with Your Strategy!" *Supply Chain View from the Field* (April 1, 2015). Retrieved August 2, 2015 from http://scm.ncsu.edu/blog/2015/04/01/supply-chain-metrics-make-sure-they-are-aligned-with-your-strategy/.

30. Andy Vabulas, "Turning Manufacturing Visibility into a Competitive Advantage." *Manufacturing.net* (December 7, 2012). Retrieved July 31, 2015, from http://www.manufacturing.net/articles/2012/12/turning-manufacturing-visibility-into-a-competitive-advantage.

31. Margaret Rouse, "Manufacturing Execution System (MES)," *TechTarget*, (2008). Retrieved July 31, 2015, from http://search-manufacturingerp.techtarget.com/definition/manufacturing-execution-system-MES.

32. WorkWise ERP Team, "What is MES?" WorkWise (September 26, 2013). Retrieved July 31, 2015, from http://www.work-wisellc.com/what-is-mes/.

33. MarketsandMarkets, "Manufacturing Execution System market worth $13.59 Billion by 2020," (May 2014). Retrieved July 31, 2015, from http://www.marketsandmarkets.com/PressReleases/mes.asp.

34. ibasetsolumina, "Predicting the Future of Manufacturing Execution Systems in Aerospace and Defense," (July 1, 2014). Retrieved July 31, 2015, from http://www.ibaset.com/blog/p-manufacturing-execution-systems/.

CASE 6.1

Hudson Guitars

Saul Hudson was walking around the empty building that would soon house his guitar factory. Accompanying him were an architect and the recently hired vice president (VP) of manufacturing.

A rock and roll virtuoso, Saul has been building custom guitars for his band for more than 20 years. On a break from those grinding world tours, Saul is launching a line of electric guitars. Rather than outsource production to Mexico or China, Saul has decided to hire his own team to produce the guitars.

During the building tour, Saul and his team discuss ideas for facility layout, production methods, and technology requirements.

"How we set it up is a function of volume, variety, and product pricing," notes the VP. "We can go anywhere from master craftsmen making one guitar at a time to an automated production line cranking them out by the hundreds per day."

"We are in this to make money so I can't sit in this huge space and make them one at a time," Saul replies. "But, I don't want to produce a $300 guitar for the mass market. We want a great product that customers will see as an investment in a quality guitar that will last for decades."

A brief discussion ensues in which Saul shares his vision for selling three models in five stock colors. They will be sold through music stores. He also wants customers to have the option of configuring their own sound package and adding a custom paint job for a higher price. These semi-custom guitars will be sold via the company's website.

"You also need to think about what part of the production will be done in-house versus outsourced," noted the architect. "That will influence how I modify the building."

Saul adds "if we want to do it right, we need to do the major work in-house. Cutting the bodies and necks, painting, assembly and testing will happen right here. We can purchase the humbuckers, strings, knobs, jacks, and other components from trusted suppliers."

"Hmm, parts coming in from multiple suppliers, fifteen different combinations of guitars plus semi-custom orders, and serious manufacturing activity," the VP recaps. "I think that we will need some technology support to keep everything coordinated."

"That's why I hired you—to make those important decisions," replies Saul. "Remember we're here to deliver stunning guitars that will launch the career of the next B.B. King, Keith Richards, or that guy called Slash."

As he walked toward the door, Saul adds: "and, don't forget that we need profits. Tell me how you are going to measure our success."

CASE QUESTIONS

1. Given the description of the product and the work that will occur in the guitar factory, which production process layouts could be considered? Which do you recommend? Explain.
2. What types of software should be used to help manage the scheduling and operations of the guitar factory? What benefits will they provide?
3. How should the VP evaluate performance of the factory? Discuss the metrics that must be balanced to achieve Saul's goals.
4. What roles will packaging play in the success of Saul's guitar company?

Source: Brian J. Gibson, Ph.D. Used with permission.

CASE 6.2

Elvis Golf Ltd.

Elvis Golf Ltd. (EGL) manufactures the King 460cc driver, a $79 copycat of a far more expensive golf club from a well-known brand. The King is manufactured at the company's small Memphis, Tennessee, factory and is shipped to major sporting goods retailers. EGL uses a mass production strategy to gain economies of scale and high labor productivity. This strategy is coupled with a MTS assembly process, and goods are produced in anticipation of demand.

The company has experienced a sales slump over the last three quarters. In response, EGL sent their sales team to the World Golf Expo, a major trade show. The goal of this trip to the Expo was to boost awareness of the King, gain retailer feedback, and generate orders. The sales team set up a display booth and had plenty of literature to distribute.

The trip wasn't successful from an order standpoint, but the sales team gained valuable insights from the Expo attendees. At a post-trip meeting, the following information was shared with EGL executive management:

- Retailers liked the novelty and price of our product but having only one model available—a right-handed, 43-inch, 10-degree loft, steel shaft driver with a tacky grip—limits the market appeal.
- Competitors at the event were offering semi-customizable clubs similar to the King at a $119 price point. Options included left-handed clubs, a choice of three different grips, steel or graphite shaft, and six shaft length/flex combinations.
- A few retailers commented that sales would explode if EGL offered an optional package deal—the King, a blue suede head cover, and a golf hat with "Elvis" written on it.

Tom Parker, the company CEO, was intrigued by the customization angle. He liked the higher price and believed that the input component costs wouldn't be much higher than the current model of the King. "Let's get started right away," he said.

"But that will add great complexity to our supply chain and production operations," replied Pat Boone, vice president of manufacturing. He noted that the company would now have to manufacture 72 different models based on all the possible configurations of club heads, shaft types, shaft length/flex options, and grips. "Creating a forecast will be a nightmare and we'll have to hold finished goods inventory of every model," he added. "And don't get me started on that package deal mess either. Blue suede head covers, how tacky is that?"

"Well, Mr. Boone, you'd better figure it out," replied Parker. He went on to talk about the need for EGL to adopt a more modern and agile manufacturing strategy. "We need to respond to our customers, and offering semi-customized clubs sounds like a good idea to me," he added. "If that is too much to ask, then I may need to think about outsourcing our manufacturing and your job!"

"I want your production plan on my desk in one week," said Parker as he walked out of the meeting.

CASE QUESTIONS

1. In terms of production strategy, should Boone stick with mass production or try something else? Explain.
2. Is the make-to-stock assembly process well-suited to Parker's desire to make semi-customized clubs? What other assembly options could be considered?
3. What do you think of Parker's idea to outsource the manufacturing of the King?
4. Develop a brief proposal for the production plan requested by Parker. Discuss your recommended production strategy, assembly process, other considerations, and the benefits/drawbacks of your proposal.

Source: Brian J. Gibson, Ph.D. Used with permission.

Chapter 7

DEMAND MANAGEMENT

Learning Objectives

After reading this chapter, you should be able to do the following:

- Understand the critical importance of outbound-to-customer logistics systems.
- Appreciate the growing need for effective demand management as part of an organization's overall logistics and supply chain expertise.
- Know the types of forecasts that might be needed and understand how collaboration among trading partners will help the overall forecasting and demand management processes.
- Understand the basic principles underlying the sales and operations planning process.
- Identify the key steps in the order fulfillment process and appreciate the various channel structures that might be used in the fulfillment process.

Supply Chain Profile   *The Great Convergence*

The terms "convergence" and "collaboration" have been popping up recently in discussions about improving logistics and supply chain management processes and the collection and synchronization of the data that can foster those improvements.

When we discuss collaboration in terms of end-to-end logistics and supply chain processes, we refer to basics such as real-time contact with carriers, sharing long-term plans with our 3PLs, clearly communicating data through our own organizations, and improving freight visibility and inventory management through collaborative planning with our suppliers—but that just scratches the surface.

Putting these practices in place can reduce transportation rates and improve service and communication for all supply chain stakeholders. However, our 2014 panel says that the majority of logistics and supply chain operations are simply not built to truly collaborate and achieve these benefits.

In fact, a recent Gartner survey found that the inability to synchronize end-to-end business processes was named as the second biggest obstacle to reaching supply chain goals. As Gartner's Dwight Klappich shares in this year's roundtable, to get there, supply chain organizations need to do a better job of orchestrating and synchronizing the data and activities across warehousing, transportation, and manufacturing functions—a concept he calls "supply chain execution convergence."

"Look at the way most supply chain organizations were traditionally organized: They were broken down into functional silos like planning, sourcing, manufacturing, warehousing, and transportation and at best they were loosely connected," says Klappich. "Companies pass data back and forth between applications, but coordinating end-to-end processes across application silos remains elusive."

To remedy that, Klappich sees the market evolving toward platforms that optimize end-to-end processes, and this will happen over time in phases that include rolling up data into a common analytical system, achieving tighter integration between supply chain applications, and achieving bidirectional communication between systems that will synchronize activities.

Capgemini's Belinda Griffin takes that concept one step further. She uses the term "supply chain collaboration" for the next step in the technological evolution.

"Supply chain collaboration is a broader concept that includes not only supply chain execution, but also encompasses forward looking planning and forecasting activities," says Griffin. For example, supply chain execution convergence brings shippers, 3PLs, and other partners together at the same time of shipment to promote shipping efficiencies. "Supply chain collaboration is about going beyond this and allowing providers to see what capacity is going to be demanded of them during a key future shipping window so that they can develop mitigation strategies for inadequate capacity," she says.

Chances are high that you have a full range of supply chain software and enabling hardware at your fingertips, yet you're facing significant execution issues. So, while the concepts our analysts share this month may seem more theoretical that practical, it's time to give some thought to how you define collaboration and convergence in your operations.

Source: Adapted from Michael Levins, *Logistics Management*, May 2014, p. 9. Reprinted with permission of Peerless Media, LLC.

7-1 Introduction

In an effort to better serve their customers, many organizations place significant emphasis on what might be termed their outbound-to-customer logistics systems. Also referred to as *physical distribution*, this essentially refers to the processes, systems, and capabilities that enhance an organization's ability to serve its customers. For example, the ways in which retailers such as Walmart, Target, and Amazon fulfill their customers' orders are examples of outbound logistics. This topic has been of significant historical interest in the study of logistics and supply chain management. This chapter will highlight key areas of concern related to this general topic.

Correspondingly, the topic of inbound-to-operations logistics systems refers to the activities and processes that precede and facilitate value-adding activities such as procurement (see Chapter 5), operations (see Chapter 6), and assembly. Other terms that focus on these elements of the supply chain include materials management and physical supply. A typical example would be movements of automotive parts and accessories that need to move from supplier locations to automotive assembly plants. Although many of the principles of inbound logistics are conceptually similar to those of outbound logistics, some important differences must be recognized. Thus, the topic of inbound logistics systems will be the focus of Chapter 5, which is titled "Sourcing Materials and Services."

Considering the complexity of the topic at hand, this chapter has a relatively aggressive agenda of topics to be discussed. First, a discussion of demand management provides an overview of the importance of effectively managing outbound-to-customer processes. Second, the topic of forecasting is addressed. Third, an introduction to the sales and operations planning (S&OP) process is provided. Finally, the recent emphasis on collaborative forecasting approaches is covered.

7-2 Demand Management

According to Blackwell and Blackwell, demand management might be thought of as "focused efforts to estimate and manage customers' demand, with the intention of using this information to shape operating decisions."[1] Traditional supply chains typically begin at the point of manufacture or assembly and end with the sale of product to consumers or business buyers. Much of the focus and attention has been related to the topic of product flow, with significant concern for matters such as technology, information exchange, inventory turnover, delivery speed and consistency, and transportation. This notwithstanding, it is the manufacturers—many times far removed from the end user or consumer market—who determine what will be available for sale, where, when, and how many. If this seems to reflect a disconnect between manufacturing and demand at the point of consumption, that is exactly what it is. Thus, any attention paid to demand management will produce benefits throughout the supply chain.

The essence of demand management is to further the ability of firms throughout the supply chain—particularly manufacturing through the customer—to collaborate on activities related to the flow of products, services, information, and capital. The desired end result should be to create greater value for the end user or consumer. There are a number of ways in which effective demand management will help to unify channel members with the common goals of satisfying customers and solving customer problems:[2]

- Gathering and analyzing knowledge about consumers, their problems, and their unmet needs
- Identifying partners to perform the functions needed in the demand chain

- Moving the functions that need to be done to the channel member that can perform them most effectively and efficiently
- Sharing with other supply chain members knowledge about consumers and customers, available technology, and logistics challenges and opportunities
- Developing products and services that solve customers' problems
- Developing and executing the best logistics, transportation, and distribution methods to deliver products and services to consumers in the desired format

As organizations identify the need for improved demand management, several problems occur. First, the lack of coordination between departments (i.e., the existence of "functional silos") results in little or no coordinated response to demand information. Second, too much emphasis is placed on forecasts of demand, with less attention on the collaborative efforts and the strategic and operational plans that need to be developed from the forecasts. Third, demand information is used more for tactical and operational purposes than for strategic ones. In essence, since in many cases historical performance is not a very good predictor of the future, demand information should be used to create collective and realistic scenarios for the future. Primary emphasis should be on understanding likely demand scenarios and mapping their relationships to product supply alternatives. The end result will be to better match demand as it occurs with appropriate availability of needed product in the marketplace.

Figure 7.1 provides an overview of how supply and demand misalignment might impact overall supply chain effectiveness. Using the personal computer (PC) industry as an example, this figure charts production, channel orders, and true end-user demand over the life cycle of a product. Ignoring the early adopters, end-user demand for PCs typically is at its highest level at the time new products are launched, which is also the time that availability is most precarious. As new, competing products become available, end-user demand begins to taper off, eventually reaching a modest level, at which time the product, now much more available, is generally phased out.

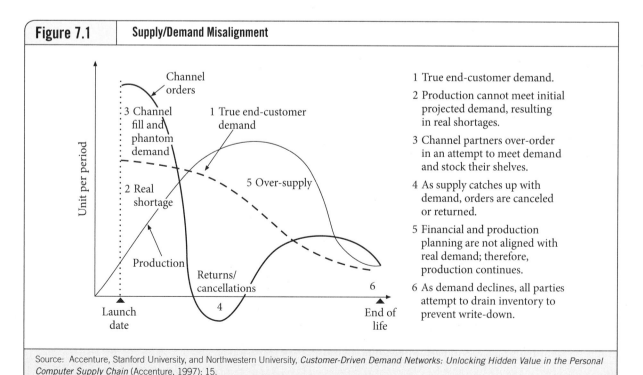

| Figure 7.1 | Supply/Demand Misalignment |

1 True end-customer demand.

2 Production cannot meet initial projected demand, resulting in real shortages.

3 Channel partners over-order in an attempt to meet demand and stock their shelves.

4 As supply catches up with demand, orders are canceled or returned.

5 Financial and production planning are not aligned with real demand; therefore, production continues.

6 As demand declines, all parties attempt to drain inventory to prevent write-down.

Source: Accenture, Stanford University, and Northwestern University, *Customer-Driven Demand Networks: Unlocking Hidden Value in the Personal Computer Supply Chain* (Accenture, 1997): 15.

Looking more closely at Figure 7.1, we see that in the first phase of a new product launch, when end-user demand is at its peak and opportunities for profit margins are greatest, PC assemblers are not able to supply product in quantities sufficient to meet demand—thus creating true product shortages. Also during this time, distributors and resellers tend to "over-order," often creating substantial "phantom" demand. In the next phase, as production begins to increase, assemblers ship product against this inflated order situation and book sales at the premium, high-level launch price. As channel inventories begin to grow, price competition sets in, as do product overages returns. This further depresses demand for the PC product, and the PC assemblers are the hardest hit.

In the final phase noted in Figure 7.1, as end-user demand begins to decline, the situation clearly has shifted to one of oversupply. This is largely due to the industry's planning processes and systems, which are primarily designed to use previous period demand as a gauge. Since much of the previous period's demand was represented by the previously mentioned phantom demand, forecasts are distorted. The net result of aligning supply and demand is that a large majority of product is sold during the declining period of profit opportunity, thereby diminishing substantial value creation opportunities for industry participants. Adding insult to injury, substantial amounts of inventory are held throughout the supply chain as a hedge against supply uncertainty.

According to Langabeer, there is growing and persuasive evidence that understanding and managing market demand are central determinants of business success.[3] Aside from this observation, relatively few companies have successfully linked demand management with strategy. Table 7.1 provides a view of how demand data might be used strategically

Table 7.1	**How Demand Management Supports Business Strategy**
STRATEGY	**EXAMPLES OF HOW TO USE DEMAND MANAGEMENT**
Growth strategy	• Perform "what if" analyses on total industry volume to gauge how specific mergers and acquisitions might leverage market share. • Analyze industry supply/demand to predict changes in product pricing structure and market economics based on mergers and acquisitions. • Build staffing models for merged company using demand data.
Portfolio strategy	• Manage maturity of products in current portfolio to optimally time overlapping life cycles. • Create new product development/introduction plans based on life cycle. • Balance combination of demand and risk for consistent "cash cows" with demand for new products. • Ensure diversification of product portfolio through demand forecasts.
Positioning strategy	• Manage product sales through each channel based on demand and product economics. • Manage positioning of finished goods at appropriate distribution centers, to reduce working capital, based on demand. • Define capability to supply for each channel.
Investment strategy	• Manage capital investments, marketing expenditures, and research and development budgets based on demand forecasts of potential products and maturity of current products. • Determine whether to add manufacturing capacity.

Source: Jim R. Langabeer II, "Aligning Demand Management with Human Strategy," *Supply Chain Management Review* (May/June 2000): 58. Copyright © 2000 Reed Business Information, a division of Reed Elsevier. Reproduced by permission.

to enhance an organization's growth, portfolio, positioning, and investment strategies. As suggested, effective use of demand data can help organizations to guide strategic resources in a number of important ways.

7-3 Balancing Supply and Demand

The essence of demand management, as previously stated, is to estimate and manage customer demand and use this information to make operating decisions. However, demand and supply in an organization will more than likely never be balanced to allow for zero stockouts and zero safety stocks. Many methods to manage this imbalance exist. However, there are four methods that are commonly used across many industries. Two of those, price and lead time, are referred to as external balancing methods. The other two, inventory and production flexibility, are called internal balancing methods.

External balancing methods are used in an attempt to change the manner in which the customer orders in an attempt to balance the supply-demand gap. Dell has found these methods to be relatively effective in smoothing demand to meet supply. For example, Dell frequently refreshes its Web site with price changes and availability changes based on the demand for an item and its supply. If customer demand exceeds the current supply, Dell can increase the lead time for that item for customer delivery. By doing so, one of two results can occur. First, if the customer finds the increased lead time unacceptable, she or he might decide to specify an alternative item from Dell for which there is sufficient inventory. Second, if the customer decides the increased lead time is acceptable, Dell now has the opportunity to wait for the next delivery of that item from suppliers. If customer demand is less than current inventory levels for a particular item, a price reduction for that item will appear on the Web site, hopefully increasing demand for the item. Using both methods allows Dell to manage stockouts while minimizing safety stock inventories.

Internal balancing methods utilize an organization's internal processes to manage the supply-demand gap. Production flexibility allows an organization to quickly and efficiently change its production lines from one product to another. This is one principle of lean manufacturing. Being able to react quickly to changing demand by altering production schedules will allow for a minimum of safety stocks while reducing the possibility of a

On the Line   *Volatility in Demand has Become the Norm*

In today's business environment, companies remain "cautiously optimistic," observes Ted Fernandez, chairman and CEO of global business advisory firm, The Hackett Group. "Most companies in the S&P 500 beat their guidance for the first quarter," he says. But mixed guidance has been the issue as companies continue to struggle to meet growth objectives." Fernandez added that many companies have been quick to turn to productivity initiatives to hit earnings targets. "This should improve as the U.S. economy continues to show better signals, but for now there remains cautious optimism across the globe." According to Fernandez, finding sustainable demand continues to be more challenging than expected as we now approach the sixth anniversary of the financial crisis. "Volatility in demand has become the norm, and companies understand that they need the ability to quickly recalibrate."

Source: Logistics Management, June 2014, p. 3. Reprinted with permission of Peerless Media, LLC.

stockout. The tradeoff here is between production changeover costs and safety stock costs. Inventory is probably the most common, and maybe the most expensive, method used to manage the imbalance between supply and demand. Many organizations produce product to a forecast that includes safety stock to smooth the effects of both demand and lead time variability. This allows an organization to minimize the number of changeovers it needs to make in production but also results in high inventory levels. In these cases, stockout costs are usually high as are production changeover costs.

These four methods are not mutually exclusive in most organizations. Some combination of all of them is used to manage safety stocks and stockouts. Their use and level of implementation will be determined by the nature of the product and the cost of stocking out. Also affecting their use will be the organization's ability to properly forecast customer demand. Forecasting will be the topic of the next section.

7-4 Traditional Forecasting

A major component of demand management is forecasting the amount of product that will be purchased, when it will be purchased, and where it will be purchased by customers. Although various statistical techniques exist to forecast demand, the common thread for all forecasts is that they will ultimately be wrong. The key to successful forecasting is to minimize the error between actual demand and forecasted demand. Although this sounds simple, many factors can arise in the marketplace that will change demand contrary to the forecast. However, forecasts are necessary because they serve as a plan for both marketing and operations to set goals and develop execution strategies. These goals and strategies are developed through the sales and operations planning (S&OP) process. This concept will be covered in a later section in this chapter. The remainder of this section will focus on the various basic types of forecasting techniques used throughout industry.

7-4-1 Factors Affecting Demand

Two types of demand exist: (1) independent demand, which is the demand for the primary item, and (2) dependent demand, which is directly influenced by the demand for the independent item. For example, the demand for bicycles would be called *independent*. It is the demand for the primary, or finished, product and is directly created by the customer. The demand for bicycle tires would be called *dependent*, because the number of tires demanded is determined by the number of bicycles demanded. Most forecasting techniques focus on independent demand. For example, a bicycle manufacturer will forecast the demand for bicycles during a given period. Given that level of demand, the manufacturer knows that two tires will be required for each bicycle demanded. As such, there is no need for the bicycle manufacturer to forecast the demand for tires. From a different perspective, the tire manufacturer will need to forecast the demand for tires, because these are its independent demand items. However, the tire manufacturer will not need to forecast the demand for rims since each tire requires one rim. So, each organization in a particular supply chain will have different definitions for independent and dependent demand items. Forecasting, however, will still usually be done at the independent demand item level.

Normally, the demand for independent demand items is known as base demand, that is, *normal demand*. However, all demand is subject to certain fluctuations. One type of demand fluctuation is caused by random variation, a development that cannot be anticipated and is usually the cause to hold safety stocks to avoid stockouts. For example, the hurricanes that devastated parts of Louisiana caused an unexpected surge in the demand for building supplies in that region. A second type of demand fluctuation is caused by trend—the gradual increase or decrease in demand over time for an organization. The demand for advanced electronic components in the consumer market (e.g., iPods and DVD players) is trending upwards. The demand for VCR players is trending downwards. A third type of demand fluctuation is caused by seasonal patterns, which will normally repeat themselves during a year for most organizations. For example, chocolate manufacturers are normally faced with several seasonal patterns during the year, such as Valentine's Day, Easter, and Halloween. Finally, demand fluctuations can be caused by normal business cycles. These are usually driven by the nation's economy and can be growing, stagnant, or declining. These patterns usually occur over periods of more than one year. Almost every firm is subject to all of these demand influences, making forecasting an even more challenging task. The next section will briefly examine the concept of forecast error and discuss some of the more popular forecasting methods and will show how some of these demand variations can be included in an organization's forecasts.

7-5 Forecast Errors

As previously mentioned, almost all forecasts will be wrong. Some forecasts will be higher than demand, and some will be lower. Managing the forecasting process requires minimizing the errors between actual demand and forecasted demand. The key to successful forecasting is to choose the technique that provides the least amount of forecast error. To determine which forecasting technique is best for a set of data, the forecast error must be measured.

Four types of forecast error measures can be used. The first is called the cumulative sum of forecast errors (CFE) and can be calculated using Formula 7.1.

$$\text{CFE} = \sum_{n}^{t-1} e_t \qquad\qquad 7.1$$

CFE calculates the total forecast error for a set of data, taking into consideration both negative and positive errors. This is also referred to as *bias* and was used in Tables 7.2 through 7.4. This gives an overall measure of forecast error. However, taking into consideration both negative and positive errors, this method can produce an overall low error total although individual period forecasts can either be much higher or much lower than actual demand.

The second measure of forecast error is mean squared error (MSE). This measure can be calculated using Formula 7.2.

$$\text{MSE} = \frac{\sum E_t^2}{n} \qquad\qquad 7.2$$

This measure squares each period error so the negative and positive errors do not cancel each other out. MSE also provides a good indication of the average error per period over a set of demand data. Closely related to MSE is the third type of forecast error measure, mean absolute deviation (MAD). It can be calculated using Formula 7.3.

$$\text{MAD} = \frac{\sum |E_t|}{n} \qquad\qquad 7.3$$

Table 7.2	Forecast Calculation			
	FORECASTS			
PERIOD	D_t DEMAND	FOUR-PERIOD MOVING AVERAGE	FOUR- PERIOD WEIGHTED MOVING AVERAGE	EXPONENTIAL SMOOTHING
2014				
September	8,299			
October	11,619			
November	7,304			
December	5,976			
2015				
January	10,210	8,300	7,204	10,500
February	9,226	8,777	8,998	9,863
March	9,717	8,179	8,839	9,790
April	11,226	8,782	9,506	10,508
May	9,718	10,095	10,573	10,113
June	9,135	9,972	9,995	9,624
July	10,702	9,949	9,594	10,163
August	11,289	10,195	10,267	10,726
September	10,210	10,211	10,770	10,468
November	12,179	10,726	10,692	11,382
December	11,683	11,095	11,544	11,533
Total	125,998			
x	10,500			
Source: Robert A. Novack, Ph.D. Used with permission.				

This measure is also calculated in Tables 7.2 through 7.4. By taking the absolute value of each error, the negative and positive signs are removed and a good indication of average error per period is calculated. This measure is popular because it is easy to understand and provides a good indication of the accuracy of the forecast.

Another measure of forecast error is mean absolute percent error (MAPE). MAPE can be calculated using Formula 7.4.

$$\text{MAPE} = \frac{\Sigma(|E_t|/D_t)100}{n} \qquad 7.4$$

Finally, tracking signal can be used to measure forecast error. It is especially good at identifying if a bias exists in the forecast errors and can be calculated using Formula 7.5.

Tracking signal = Cumulative forecast error (CFE)/Mean absolute deviation (MAD)   7.5

The next section will examine three common forecasting techniques and will generate these five error terms for each. As will be seen, the closer each error term is to zero, the better the forecast.

7-6 Forecasting Techniques

There are many different statistical techniques companies use to generate forecasts. All of these techniques require accurate data and rely on the assumption that the future will repeat the past. However, these requirements are usually violated and the forecast will be generating a forecast error. The key to good forecasting is to minimize forecast error by utilizing a forecasting technique that best fits the nature of the data. This section will briefly discuss three of the more popular forecasting techniques: simple moving average, weighted moving average, and exponential smoothing. All three will use the same historical data to develop a forecast to see which technique best fits the data.

7-6-1 Simple Moving Average

The simple moving average is probably the simplest to develop method in basic time series forecasting. It makes forecasts based on recent demand history and allows for the removal of random effects. The simple moving average method does not accommodate seasonal, trend, or business cycle influences. This method simply averages a predetermined number of periods and uses this average as the demand for the next period. Each time the average is computed, the oldest demand is dropped and the most recent demand is included. A weakness of this method is that it forgets the past quickly. A strength is that it is quick and easy to use.

Table 7.2 presents an example of using the simple moving average technique on the historical demand shown in column 2 for the end of 2014 and all of 2015. This example will use a four-period moving average. To determine the forecast for January, the demand for September, October, November, and December are averaged. This calculation is shown in Formula 7.6.

$$A_t = \frac{\text{Sum of last } n \text{ demands}}{n}$$
$$= D_t + D_{t-1} + D_{t-2} + \ldots D_{t-n+1} \qquad 7.6$$

Where

$$D_t = \text{Actual demand in period } t$$
$$n = \text{Total number of periods in the average}$$
$$A_t = \text{Average for period } t$$

This would result in the following calculation:

$$(8{,}299 + 11{,}619 + 7{,}304 + 5{,}976)/4 = 8{,}300$$

The forecast for February drops the demand for September from its calculation and adds the demand for January. The calculation is as follows:

$$(11{,}619 + 7{,}304 + 5{,}976 + 10{,}210)/4 = 8{,}777$$

This process repeats itself until all forecasts are made. The four-period moving average is shown in column 3 in Table 7.2. Having created a forecast using historical data from 2014 and 2015, the next step is to apply this forecast to future demand for 2016. This example will take some liberties and assume that we have gone through the year 2016. Table 7.3 shows the actual demand by month for 2016 in column 2 and the forecast generated in Table 7.2 is shown in column 3. The error term is simply the difference between the forecast

Table 7.3	**Simple Moving Average**					
(1) **PERIOD**	**(2)** D_t **DEMAND**	**(3)** F_t **FORECAST**	**(4)** E_t $D_t - F_t$ **ERROR**	**(5)** $\mid D_t - F_t \mid$ **ABSOLUTE DEVIATION**	**(6)** e_t^2	**(7)** $(\mid e_t \mid \div D_t) \times 100$ **ABSOLUTE % DEVIATION**
2016						
January	9,700	8,300	+ 1,400	1,400	1,960,000	14.43
February	8,765	8,777	− 12	12	144	.1369
March	9,231	8,179	+ 1,052	1,052	1,106,704	11.40
April	10,664	8,782	+ 1,882	1,882	3,541,924	17.65
May	9,233	10,095	− 862	862	743, 044	9.34
June	8,679	9,972	− 1,293	1,293	1,671,849	14.90
July	10,166	9,949	+ 217	217	47,089	2.13
August	10,725	10,195	+ 530	530	280,900	4.94
September	9,700	10,211	− 511	511	261,121	5.27
October	10,169	10,334	− 165	165	27,225	1.62
November	11,570	10,726	+ 844	844	712,336	7.29
December	11,100	11,095	+ 5	5	25	.045
Total	119,702					
X	9,975.2					
Bias (total CFE)			+ 3,087			
Bias x			+ 257.25			
Absolute Deviation Total				8,773		
Absolute Deviation x (MAD)				731.08		
Squared Error Total					10,352,361	
Squared Error x (MSE)					862,696.75	
Absolute % Error Total						89.15
Absolute % error x (MAPE)						7.43

and the actual demand and can be seen in column 4. Adding together the error terms for the forecasts results in what can be called bias or CFE—a measure of how accurate the forecast is compared to actual demand. A positive bias means that the demand was higher than forecast during the forecast period, resulting in stockouts; a negative bias means the demand was lower than the forecast, resulting in excess inventories. The closer the bias term is to zero, the better the forecast. In this example, the bias is +3,087 units or +257.25 units per forecast period (+3,087/12 periods). This means that the forecast was lower than actual demand by 3,087 cases in total and lower than actual demand per month by 257.25 cases. Absolute deviation removes the positive and negative signs from the error terms and is a measure of how accurate the overall forecast is. The closer to zero, the better the forecast is at estimating demand. The absolute deviation is shown in column 5 of Table 7.3. Adding this column results in a total absolute deviation of 8,773 units or a MAD of 731.08 (8,773/12). Squared error is shown in column 6. Adding this column results in a total squared error of 10,352,361 or a MSE of 862,696.75 (10,352,361/12). Column 7 represents the percent absolute deviation of the forecast. The total for this column is 89.15 and the MAPE is 7.43 (89.15/12). Finally, Table 7.3 calculates the tracking signal which is CFE/MAD and results in a tracking signal of 4.2. Except for bias, the magnitude of the other error terms in absolute numbers might not make intuitive sense. However, error terms are meant to be compared to each other to see which technique is best. The next technique will attempt to improve on this forecast accuracy.

7-6-2 Weighted Moving Average

In the simple moving average method, each previous demand period was given an equal weight. The weighted moving average method assigns a weight to each previous period with higher weights usually given to more recent demand. The weights must be equal to one. The weighted moving average method allows emphasis to be placed on more recent demand as a predictor of future demand. The data in Table 7.2 will be used again to develop a weighted moving average forecast. Assume that the weights to be used will be 0.60 for the most recent period, 0.20 for the second most recent, 0.15 for the third most recent, and 0.05 for the fourth most recent period. The average for the next period will be calculated using Formula 7.7.

$$A_t = 0.60D_t + 0.20D_{t-1} + 0.15D_{t-2} + 0.05D_{t-3} \qquad 7.7$$

Column 4 in Table 7.2 shows the results of this formula. The weighted moving average for January would be calculated as follows:

$$(0.60 \times 5,976) + (0.20 \times 7,304) + (0.15 \times 11,619) + (0.05 \times 8,299) = 7.204$$

These forecasts were rounded up or down using a 0.05 cutoff since neither a demand nor a forecast can be in partial units. This becomes the forecast for January. These forecasts can be seen in column 4. Once again, the error term is calculated and shown in column 4 in Table 7.4. The bias term for this method is +1,274 units with an average bias per period of +106.2 units. The other error terms are MAD = 886.2; MSE = 1,169,415.5; MAPE = 9.03; and tracking signal = 1.44. The bias and tracking signal shown for this method are better than those found by using the simple moving average method. However, the other three error terms are not. This is primarily because the weighted moving average method does not assume equal weights for each period in the calculation. However, the results from the weighted moving average method are still not very good forecasts of demand. There are three possible causes for this. First, the weights assigned to the four periods might not accurately reflect the patterns in demand. Second, using four periods to develop the forecast might not be the appropriate number of periods. Finally, the weighted moving average technique does not easily accommodate demand patterns with seasonal influences. In an attempt to improve on this forecast, another technique will be applied to the historical demand data.

Table 7.4	Weighted Moving Average					
(1) PERIOD	(2) D_t DEMAND	(3) F_t FORECAST	(4) E_t $D_t - F_t$ ERROR	(5) $\lvert D_t - F_t \rvert$ ABSOLUTE DEVIATION	(6) e_t^2	(7) $(\lvert e_t \rvert \div D_t) \times 100$ ABSOLUTE % DEVIATION
2016						
January	9,700	7,204	+ 2,496	2,496	6,230,016	25.73
February	8,765	8,998	– 233	233	54,289	2.66
March	9,231	8,839	+ 392	392	153,664	4.25
April	10,664	9,506	+ 1,158	1,158	1,340,964	10.86
May	9,233	10,573	– 1,340	1,340	1,795,600	14.51
June	8,679	9,995	– 1,316	1,316	1,731,856	15.16
July	10,166	9,594	+ 572	572	327,184	5.63
August	10,725	10,267	+ 458	458	209,764	4.27
September	9,700	10,770	– 1,070	1070	1,144,900	11.03
October	10,169	10,446	– 277	277	76,729	2.72
November	11,570	10,692	+ 878	878	770,884	7.59
December	11,100	11,544	– 444	444	197,136	4.00
Total	119,702					
X	9,975.2					
Bias (total CFE)			+ 1,274			
Bias x			+ 106.2			
Absolute Deviation Total				10,634		
Absolute Deviation x (MAD)				886.2		
Squared Error Total					14,032,986	
Squared Error x (MSE)					1,169,415.5	
Absolute % Error Total						108.41
Absolute % error x (MAPE)						9.03
Tracking signal: CFE ÷ MAD = + 1,274 ÷ 886.2 = 1.44 $\alpha D_t = 0.6,\ \alpha D_{t-1} = 0.2,\ \alpha D_{t-2} = 0.15,\ \alpha D_{t-3} = 0.05$						
Source: Robert A. Novack, Ph.D. Used with permission.						

7-6-3 Exponential Smoothing

Exponential smoothing is one of the most commonly used techniques because of its simplicity and its limited requirements for data. Exponential smoothing needs three types of data: (1) an average of previous demand, (2) the most recent demand, and (3) a smoothing constant. The smoothing constant must be between 0 and 1. Using a higher constant assumes that the most recent demand is a better predictor of future demand. Formula 7.8 is used to calculate the forecast.

$$A_t = \alpha(\text{Demand this period}) + (1-\alpha)(\text{Forecast calculated last period})$$
$$= \alpha D_t + (1-\alpha)A_{t-1}$$

7.8

Using the data contained in Table 7.2, the forecast using exponential smoothing is generated and can be seen in column 5. Assume that the average for the previous period (the average of the 12 periods was used for convenience) is 10,500 units. Alpha will be 0.50 in this example. The forecast for January is simply the average from the previous period (10,500 cases). The forecast for February is calculated as follows:

$$\text{Forecast} = (0.5 \times 9,226) + (0.5 \times 10,500) = 9,863$$

The forecast for March follows the same calculation.

$$\text{Forecast} = (0.5 \times 9,717) + (0.5 \times 9,863) = 9,790$$

Again, 0.50 was used for rounding. Table 7.5 shows the results of using the exponential smoothing forecast seen in Table 7.2. The error terms are CFE (bias) = −5,554; MAD = 520.67; MSE = 403,033.5; MAPE = 5.52; and, tracking signal = 10.67. Exponential smoothing forecasts will lag actual demand. If demand is relatively constant, exponential smoothing will produce a relatively accurate forecast. However, highly seasonal demand patterns or patterns with trends can cause inaccurate forecasts using exponential smoothing.

Table 7.6 summarizes the error terms for the three different forecasting techniques. While none of the three techniques were accurate, exponential smoothing scored best on three of the five error terms MAD, MSE, and MAPE with weighted moving average scoring best on CFE and tracking signal. As such it is reasonable to conclude that exponential smoothing is

Table 7.5	**Exponential Smoothing**					
(1) PERIOD	(2) D_t DEMAND	(3) F_t FORECAST	(4) E_t Dt − Ft ERROR	(5) $\lvert D_t - F_t \rvert$ ABSOLUTE DEVIATION	(6) e_t^2	(7) $(\lvert e_t \rvert \div D_t) \times 100$ ABSOLUTE % DEVIATION
2016						
January	9,700	10,500	− 800	800	640,000	8.25
February	8,765	9,863	− 1,098	1,098	1,205,604	12.53
March	9,231	9,790	− 559	559	312,481	6.06
April	10,664	10,508	+ 156	156	24,336	1.46
May	9,233	10,113	− 880	880	774,400	9.53
June	8,679	9,624	− 945	945	893,025	10.89

Table 7.5	Continued					
July	10,166	10,163	+ 3	3	9	0.0295
August	10,725	10,776	− 1	1	1	0.00932
September	9,700	10,468	− 768	768	589,824	7.92
October	10,169	10,586	− 417	417	173,889	4.10
November	11,570	11,382	+ 188	188	35,344	1.62
December	11,100	11,533	− 433	433	187,489	3.90
Total	119,702					
X	9,975.2					
Bias (total CFE)			−5,554			
Bias x			−462.83			
Absolute Deviation Total				6,248		
Absolute Deviation x (MAD)				520.67		
Squared Error Total					4,836,402	
Squared Error x (MSE)					403,033.5	
Absolute % Error Total						66.30
Absolute % error x (MAPE)						5.52

Tracking signal: CFE ÷ MAD = −5,554 ÷ 520.67 = −10.67
Assume F_{Jan} = 10,500
$\quad\quad\alpha = 0.5$

Source: Robert A. Novack, Ph.D. Used with permission.

Table 7.6	Forecast Accuracy Summary				
	(1) BIAS (CFE)	(2) MAD	(3) MSE	(4) MAPE	(5) TRACKING SIGNAL
Simple moving average	+ 3,087	731.08	862,696.75	7.43	4.2
Weighted moving average	+ 1,274	886.2	1,169,415.5	9.03	1.44
Experimental Smoothing	− 5,554	520.67	403,033.5	5.52	− 10.67

the best fit for the data. This is why multiple error terms should be used to assess the accuracy of a forecast. If only CFE were used to determine accuracy, a sub-optimal technique would be used to develop future forecasts.

On the Line   *Practice Change*

It's much easier to identify an inventory management problem than it is to fix one overnight. That's not what you want to hear, but it's the truth in most situations. However, there are valid factors that can lead to more warehouse inventory than you need, which can be studied and altered.

However, one of the largest factors contributing to excess inventories in recent years is marketing's challenge to drive sales. This is the dreaded "marketing versus logistics" scenario that you've probably experienced. It typically goes like this: The logistics/warehouse manager says, "Why are we receiving all of these green toys when we have a thousand of the yellow ones in inventory that haven't moved in six months." The marketing manager then says, "We need the green toys which our survey shows will increase our sales, which could also increase the sales of the yellow toys."

It's easy to get frustrated with the situation described above, but what needs to happen is a collaborated effort to discuss the cost impact of high or obsolete inventory versus marketing activities. Each is trying to perform their jobs effectively, but both need to understand the impact of these decisions across the network, including inventory levels and warehouse performance.

For example, if additional inventory takes your facility from 85 percent to 95 percent storage utilization, the results can negatively impact customer orders getting shipped. Consider these questions: If more inventory results in a required expansion or use of a satellite warehouse, is the cost warranted? Is the management of inventory in the warehouse resulting in poor use of storage space and unidentified obsolete inventory that could free-up space?

What's important is to collaborate on these topics and help management understand the cost implications of marketing decisions. A way to remove the emotion and impact of personalities from the situation described above is to conduct an operations research based inventory and sales simulation model. This will provide analysis-based answers to the inventory issues and the related costs/benefits.

Source: Adapted from Norm Saenz and Don Derewecki, *Logistics Management,* January 2014, p. 44. Reprinted with permission of Peerless Media, LLC.

This section analyzed the mathematical development of forecasts. The next section, Sales and Operations Planning (S&OP) will discuss how companies take this mathematical forecast and adjust it for sales and operations changes.

7-7 Sales and Operations Planning

The previous section discussed statistical methods for arriving at a preliminary demand forecast for an organization. Historically, many organizations developed several functional forecasts for the same products during the same time period. It would not be unusual for a manufacturer to have a financial forecast, a manufacturing forecast, a marketing forecast, and a distribution forecast. What compounds the complexity of having multiple forecasts is that most times these functional forecasts did not agree. Marketing would forecast higher demands that neither manufacturing nor distribution could execute. Finance forecasts would be higher than marketing would be able to meet. It is necessary for an organization to arrive at a forecast internally that all functional areas agree upon and can execute. A process that can be used to arrive at this consensus forecast is called sales and operations planning (S&OP). The S&OP Benchmarking Consortium in the Center for Supply Chain Research adopted a five-step process in arriving at this consensus forecast.[4] Figure 7.2 illustrates this process. Step 1 (Run sales forecast reports) requires the development of a statistical forecast of future sales. This would be done using one or more of the forecasting techniques discussed in the previous section.

Step 2 (Demand planning phase) requires the sales and/or marketing departments to review the forecast and make adjustments based on promotions of existing products, the introductions of new products, or the elimination of products. This revised forecast is usually stated in terms of both units and dollars since operations are concerned with units and finance is concerned with dollars.

Step 3 (Supply planning phase) requires operations (manufacturing, warehousing, and transportation) to analyze the sales forecast to determine if existing capacity is adequate to handle the forecasted volumes. This requires analyzing not only the total volumes but also the timing of those volumes. For example, existing manufacturing capacity might be adequate if demand is stable over the forecast period. However, heavy promotions might produce a "spike" in demand that might exceed existing capacity. Two options to solve this capacity constraint are available. First, the promotional activity could be curtailed to bring demand to a more stable level. This could result in lost revenue. Second, additional manufacturing could be secured either by investing in more manufacturing capacity internally or securing contract manufacturing capacity externally. This would result in additional costs. The same types of capacity issues would need to be considered for both warehousing space and transportation vehicle capacity with similar resulting options if capacity does not meet demand: either curtail demand or invest in additional capacity. The decisions to these capacity issues are addressed in the next step.

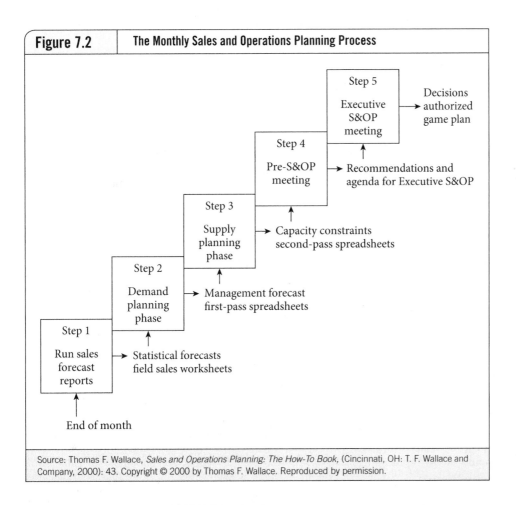

| Figure 7.2 | The Monthly Sales and Operations Planning Process |

Source: Thomas F. Wallace, *Sales and Operations Planning: The How-To Book,* (Cincinnati, OH: T. F. Wallace and Company, 2000): 43. Copyright © 2000 by Thomas F. Wallace. Reproduced by permission.

Step 4 (Pre-S&OP meeting) asks individuals from sales, marketing, operations, and finance to attend a meeting that reviews the initial forecast and any capacity issues that might have emerged during Step 3. Initial attempts will be made during this meeting to solve capacity issues by attempting to balance supply and demand. Alternative scenarios are usually developed to present at the executive S&OP meeting (Step 5) for consideration. These alternatives would identify potential lost sales and increased costs associated with balancing supply and demand. The sales forecast is also converted to dollars to see if the demand/supply plan meets the financial plan of the organization.

Step 5 (Executive S&OP meeting) is where final decisions are made regarding sales forecasts and capacity issues. This is where the top executives from the various functional areas agree to the forecast and convert it into the operating plan for the organization. Consensus among the various functional areas is critical in this meeting. Decisions regarding tradeoffs between revenue and costs are made here. Once the final plan is approved, it is important that the appropriate metrics are in place for each functional area to encourage compliance to the plan. For example, assume that the traditional operating metric for manufacturing is cost per pound manufactured. The lower the cost per pound, the better is the performance of the manufacturing group. However, the S&OP plan requires additional investment in capacity for manufacturing, which raises the cost per manufactured pound. This would make manufacturing performance unacceptable. While low cost is important, manufacturing has little or no control over the increased cost. A revised metric of compliance to schedule might be more appropriate. This new metric would reward manufacturing for making the planned quantities at the planned times. The point here is that the appropriate metrics must be in place for each functional area so that it is encouraged and rewarded for achieving the business plan.

7-8 Collaborative Planning, Forecasting, and Replenishment

The S&OP process described how organizations are structuring their planning processes to arrive at a consensus forecast internally. The next logical step would be for members of a supply chain to also agree upon a consensus forecast. Many industry initiatives have attempted to create efficiency and effectiveness through the integration of supply chain activities and processes. They have been identified by such names as quick response (QR), vendor-managed inventory (VMI), continuous replenishment planning (CRP), and efficient consumer response (ECR). All of these have had some success at integrating replenishment between supply chain members. However, they were all somewhat deficient in that they did not include a strong incentive for collaborative planning among supply chain members.

One of the most recent initiatives aimed at achieving true supply chain integration is collaborative planning, forecasting, and replenishment (CPFR).[5] CPFR has become recognized as a breakthrough business model for planning, forecasting, and replenishment. Using this approach, retailers, distributors, and manufacturers can utilize available Internet-based technologies to collaborate on operational planning through execution. Transportation providers have now been included with the concept of collaborative transportation management (CTM). Simply put, CPFR allows trading partners to agree to a single forecast for an item where each partner translates this forecast into a single execution plan. This replaces the traditional method of forecasting where each trading partner developed its own forecast for an item and each forecast was different for each partner.

The first attempt at CPFR was between Walmart and Warner-Lambert (now a part of Johnson & Johnson) in 1995 for its Listerine product line. In addition to rationalizing inventories of specific line items and addressing out-of-stock occurrences, these two organizations collaborated to increase their forecast accuracy, so as to have the right amount of inventory where it was needed, when it was needed. The three-month pilot produced significant results and improvements for both organizations. This resulted in the adoption of CPFR by both Walmart and many of its other suppliers to manage inventories through collaborative plans and forecasts.

Figure 7.3 shows the CPFR model as a sequence of several business processes that include the consumer, retailer, and manufacturer. The four major processes are (1) strategy and planning, (2) demand and supply management, (3) execution, and (4) analysis. Two aspects of this model are important to note. First, it includes the cooperation and exchange of data among business partners. Second, it is a continuous, closed-loop process that uses feedback (analysis) as input for strategy and planning.

Figure 7.4 demonstrates how the process shown in Figure 7.3 is executed. As shown in Figure 7.4, CPFR emphasizes a sharing of consumer purchasing data (or point-of-sale data)

Figure 7.3	The CPFR Model

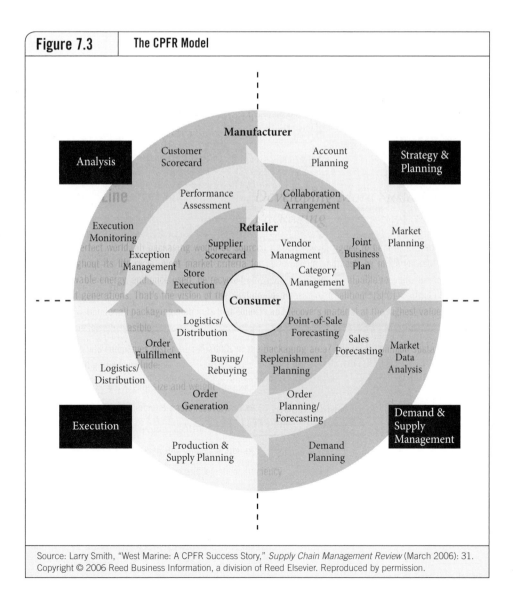

Source: Larry Smith, "West Marine: A CPFR Success Story," *Supply Chain Management Review* (March 2006): 31. Copyright © 2006 Reed Business Information, a division of Reed Elsevier. Reproduced by permission.

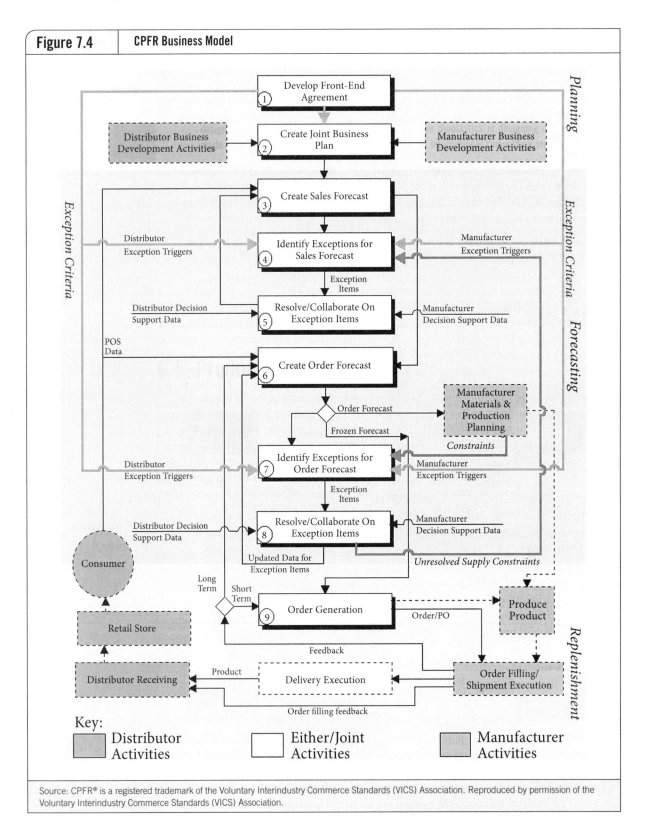

Figure 7.4 | **CPFR Business Model**

Source: CPFR® is a registered trademark of the Voluntary Interindustry Commerce Standards (VICS) Association. Reproduced by permission of the Voluntary Interindustry Commerce Standards (VICS) Association.

as well as forecasts at retail among and between trading partners for the purpose of helping to manage supply chain activities. From these data, the manufacturer analyzes its ability to meet the forecasted demand. If it cannot meet the demand, a collaborative effort is undertaken between the retailer and manufacturer to arrive at a mutually agreed-upon forecast from which execution plans are developed. The strength of CPFR is that it provides a single forecast from which trading partners can develop manufacturing strategies, replenishment strategies, and merchandising strategies.

The CPFR process begins with the sharing of marketing plans between trading partners. Once an agreement is reached on the timing and planned sales of specific products, and a commitment is made to follow that plan closely, the plan is then used to create a forecast, by stock-keeping unit (SKU), by week, and by quantity. The planning period can be for 13, 26, or 52 weeks. A typical forecast is for seasonal or promotional items that represent approximately 15 percent of sales in each category. The regular turn items, or the remainder of the products in the category, are forecast statistically. Then the forecast is entered into a system that is accessible through the Internet by either trading partner. Either partner may change the forecast within established parameters.

Theoretically, an accurate CPFR forecast could be translated directly into a production and replenishment schedule by the manufacturer since both quantity and timing are included in the CPFR forecast. This would allow the manufacturer to make the products to order (based on the quantity and timing of demand) rather than making them to inventory, thus reducing total inventories for the manufacturer. The retailer would enjoy fewer out-of-stocks at the retail shelf. Although CPFR has not yet fully developed into a make-to-order environment, it has enjoyed the benefits of reduced supply chain inventories and out-of-stocks. West Marine employed the CPFR model with its suppliers and reaped some amazing results. More than 70 of its top suppliers are loading West Marine order forecasts directly into their production planning systems. In-stock rates at stores are close to 96 percent, forecast accuracy has risen to 85 percent, and on-time shipments are better than 80 percent.[6] So, the use of collaborative efforts among supply chain partners can have positive results on the service and cost performance of these partners.

SUMMARY

- Outbound-to-customer logistics systems have received the most attention in many companies; but even in today's customer service environment, outbound and inbound logistics systems must be coordinated.

- Demand management may be thought of as "focused efforts to estimate and manage customers' demand, with the intention of using this information to shape operating decisions."

- Although many forecasts are made throughout the supply chain, the forecast of primary demand from the end user or consumer will be the most important. It is essential that this demand information be shared with trading partners throughout the supply chain and be the basis for collaborative decision making.

- Various approaches to forecasting are available, each serving different purposes. The S&OP process has gained much attention in industry today. It serves the purpose of allowing a firm to operate from a single forecast.

- The S&OP process is a continual loop involving participation from sales, operations, and finance to arrive at an internal consensus forecast.

- CPFR is a method to allow trading partners in the supply chain to collaboratively develop and agree upon a forecast of sales. This allows for the elimination of inventories held because of uncertainty in the supply chain.

STUDY QUESTIONS

1. What are the differences and similarities between outbound and inbound logistics systems? Which types of industries would place heavier emphasis on outbound systems? On inbound systems? Explain your choices.

2. How do outbound logistics systems relate directly to the needs of the customer?

3. How can demand management help to unify channel members, satisfy customers, and solve customer problems?

4. What are some of the logistics problems that might arise when supply and demand for a product are not aligned properly? What are some of the methods used to soften the effects of this imbalance?

5. What are the basic types of forecasts? What are their strengths and weaknesses?

6. What are the basic elements of the S&OP process? How do marketing, logistics, finance, and manufacturing contribute to each element?

7. What are the critical elements of collaborative planning? What benefits do they provide for the supply chain?

8. What are the similarities between the CPFR and S&OP processes? What are the differences?

NOTES

1. Roger D. Blackwell and Kristina Blackwell, "The Century of the Consumer: Converting Supply Chains into Demand Chains," *Supply Chain Management Review*, No. 3 (Fall 1999): 22–32.

2. Ibid., 32.

3. Jim R. Langabeer, "Aligning Demand Management with Business Strategy," *Supply Chain Management Review* (May/June 2000): 66–72.

4. Adapted from Tom Wallace, *Sales and Operations Planning: The "How-To" Handbook* (Cincinnati, OH: T. F. Wallace, 1999), 43–50. This process will be briefly described in this section.

5. CPFR® is a registered trademark of the Voluntary Interindustry Commerce Standards (VICS) Association.

6. Larry Smith, "West Marine: A CPFR Success Story," *Supply Chain Management Review* (March 2006): 20–36.

CASE 7.1

Tires for You, Inc.

Tires for You, Inc. (TFY), founded in 1987, is an automotive repair shop specializing in replacement tires. Located in Altoona, Pennsylvania, TFY has grown successfully over the past few years because of the addition of a new general manager, Ian Overbaugh. Since tire replacement is a major portion of TFY's business (it also performs oil changes, small mechanical repairs, etc.), Ian was surprised at the lack of forecasts for tire consumption for the company. His senior mechanic, Skip Grenoble, told him that they usually stocked for this year what they sold last year. He readily admitted that several times throughout the season stockouts occurred and customers had to go elsewhere for tires.

Although many tire replacements were for defective or destroyed tires, most tires were installed on cars whose original tires had worn out. Most often, four tires were installed at the same time. Ian was determined to get a better idea of how many tires to hold in stock during the various months of the year. Listed below is a summary of individual tire sales by month:

PERIOD	TIRES USED
2014	
October	9,797
November	11,134
December	10,687
2015	
January	9,724
February	8,786
March	9,254
April	10,691
May	9,256
June	8,700
July	10,192
August	10,751
September	9,724
October	10,193
November	11,599
December	11,130

Ian has hired you to determine the best technique for forecasting TFY demand based on the given data.

CASE QUESTIONS

1. Calculate a forecast using a simple three-month moving average.
2. Calculate a forecast using a three-period weighted moving average. Use weights of 0.60, 0.30, and 0.10 for the most recent period, the second most recent period, and the third most recent period, respectively.
3. Calculate a forecast using the exponential smoothing method. Assume the forecast for period 1 is 9,500. Use alpha = 0.40.
4. Once you have calculated the forecasts based on the above data, determine the error terms by comparing them to the actual sales for 2012 given below:

PERIOD	TIRES USED
2016	
January	10,696
February	9,665
March	10,179
April	11,760
May	9,150
June	9,571
July	8,375
August	11,826
September	10,696
October	11,212
November	9,750
December	9,380

5. Based on the three methods used to calculate a forecast for TFY, which method produced the best forecast? Why? What measures of forecast error did you use? How could you improve upon this forecast?

Source: Robert A. Novack, Ph.D. Used with permission.

CASE 7.2

Playtime, Inc.

Playtime, Inc. manufactures toys for children under the age of 12 and has been in business for 50 years. While Playtime does not hold a major share of the toy market, it has experienced significant growth over the last five years because of its collaboration with major movie studios to introduce action figures to coincide with new movie releases. Playtime is a publicly held company.

Playtime's executive council consists of vice presidents of marketing (includes sales), operations (manufacturing), supply chain (procurement, inventory, warehousing, and transportation), and finance. This group is ultimately responsible for approving the forecast for the upcoming year.

The forecast is developed using last year's sales as historical data. This forecast is then given to the supply chain and operations groups to determine if capacity is sufficient to accommodate the new volumes. If capacity is sufficient, the forecast is then moved to finance where it is analyzed to determine if volumes are sufficient to satisfy the needs of the investors.

Jim Thomas, manager of supply chain, and Gail Jones, manager of operations, had a meeting to discuss the first version of the forecast. "I know we use last year's sales to project for next year, but this forecast has me worried," said Jim. "One of our major movie studio partners is coming out with a blockbuster movie next year and we have no idea what the impact of that might be on our distribution capacity." Gail agreed, saying "I know. We have the capacity right now based on this forecast, but if volumes surge we are in trouble from a manufacturing perspective." Jim and Gail also know that if the projected volume does not satisfy the needs of inventors, finance will send the forecast back to marketing to increase volumes until financial goals will be met.

This forecast process has resulted in a disconnect among the supply chain, operations, and marketing functions within Playtime. The managers in these functions typically end up developing their own forecasts based on what they think demand will really be, regardless of what finance presents to the investors. Over the last several years, this has presented some problems for the operations and supply chain areas because of manufacturing capacity issues (toys are very seasonal) and inventory issues. Although Playtime has been able to handle these issues, Jim and Gail are very concerned about next year because of the uncertainty the new movie release will have on the demand for their toys.

CASE QUESTIONS

1. What are the issues associated with Playtime's current forecasting process? What impacts, negative or positive, does this process have on the marketing, operations, supply chain, and finance functions?
2. Using the S&OP process discussed in this chapter, design a more effective and efficient forecasting process that will mitigate the negative impacts you identified in question 1.

Source: Robert A. Novack, Ph.D. Used with permission.

Chapter 8

ORDER MANAGEMENT AND CUSTOMER SERVICE

Learning Objectives

After reading this chapter, you should be able to do the following:

- Understand the relationships between order management and customer service.

- Appreciate how organizations influence customers' ordering patterns as well as how they execute customers' orders.

- Realize that activity-based costing (ABC) plays a critical role in order management and customer service.

- Identify the various activities in the SCOR process D1 (deliver stocked product) and how it relates to the order-to-cash cycle.

- Know the various elements of customer service and how they impact both buyers and sellers.

- Calculate the cost of a stockout.

- Understand the major outputs of order management, how they are measured, and how their financial impacts on buyers and sellers are calculated.

- Be familiar with the concept of service recovery and how it is being implemented in organizations today.

E-Commerce Survey Asks   *Need for Green or Need for Speed?*

A recent survey has found that more than half of e-commerce consumers (54 percent) are willing to pay at least 5 percent higher prices for products ordered online if they are delivered sustainably, and 76 percent would wait at least one extra day for climate-friendly transport.

These are among the findings of the *Need for Green or Need for Speed Survey* commissioned by consulting firm West Monroe Partners. The survey went on to reveal that although consumers seem positive about greener delivery, they're largely unaware such delivery options exist. Further, retailers supply virtually no green shipping choices in the course of e-commerce transactions.

In a recent interview, Yves Leclerc, managing director of supply chain for West Monroe, said that the results were surprising and challenge the assumption that same-day delivery is the "holy grail" of e-commerce.

"This would lead us to believe that, if presented with the option, consumers would pay a premium or wait longer," said Leclerc. "The challenge today is for businesses to present the option and some visibility into the carbon footprint of various shipping methods. Based on the survey, if those options exist they will drive consumer behaviors."

Leclerc said that previous research has suggested that the carbon footprint of picking, packing, and shipping an item next day is as much as 30 times greater than if the consumer simply drove to the store to buy the same item. Inside a distribution facility, the benefits of being able to postpone fulfillment enables consolidation resulting in fewer miles per stop.

"Green shipping or sustainable shipping is just not about five-day versus next-day shipping," Leclerc clarified. "It's the total logistics transaction from the consumer order to delivery. Packaging, returnable containers, inventory holding strategy, consolidation, last-mile methodologies, all of it is folded into the concept of green shipping."

Leclerc went on to suggest that regulatory impacts in coming years will likely force corporations to pursue greener logistics, perhaps including electric- or natural gas-powered vehicles for last-mile delivery.

"And now we know what the consumer actually wants as opposed to assuming they want next- or same-day shipping," Leclerc said. "We might now be facing the perfect storm where consumers, businesses, and lawmakers are on the same page. I would expect to see a lot of improvement in corporate America's approach to green and sustainable efforts."

In addition, the survey sought to understand how price tolerance varies across different demographics like age, income, educational level, and geography. Interestingly, annual income was not an influential factor in consumers' willingness to pay more for sustainable delivery.

In fact, respondents who earn more than $100,000 a year were slightly less likely to accept higher prices for climate-friendly transport. "Just because consumers may have more disposable income," he said, "they are not necessarily willing to part with it in the interests of sustainability."

Source: Josh Bond, *Logistics Management,* August 2014, pp. 19–20. Reprinted with permission of Peerless Media, LLC.

8-1 Introduction

Chapter 7 (Demand Management) discussed how organizations develop forecasts from which marketing, production, finance, and logistics plans are created. These plans are used to align the resources of the organization to meet organization and market goals.

Chapter 8 will discuss the concepts of order management and customer service, which serve as the mechanisms to *execute* the plans. Order management defines and sets in motion the logistics infrastructure of the organization. In other words, how an organization receives an order (electronically versus manually), how it fills an order (inventory policy and number and location of warehouses), and how it ships an order (mode choice and its impacts on delivery times) are all dictated by how an organization manages an order. This chapter will present two phases of order management. First, the concept of **influencing the order** will be presented. This is the phase where an organization attempts to change the manner by which its customers place orders. Second, the concept of **order execution** will be discussed. This phase occurs after the organization receives the order.

Customer service, on the other hand, is *anything that touches the customer*. This includes all activities that impact information flow, product flow, and cash flow between the organization and its customers. Customer service can be described as a *philosophy*, as *performance measures*, or as an *activity*.[1] Customer service as a *philosophy* elevates customer service to an organization-wide commitment to providing customer satisfaction through superior customer service. This view of customer service is entirely consistent with many organizations' emphasis on value management, elevates it to the strategic level within an organization, and makes it visible to top executives. Customer service as *performance measures* emphasizes customer service as specific performance measures, such as on-time delivery and percentage of orders filled complete. These customer service measures pervade all three definitions of customer service and address strategic, tactical, and operational aspects of order management. Finally, customer service as an *activity* treats customer service as a particular task that an organization must perform to satisfy a customer's order requirements. Order processing, invoicing, product returns, and claims handling are all typical examples of this definition of customer service.

Most organizations employ all three definitions of customer service in their order management process. Figure 8.1 shows one way in which order management and customer

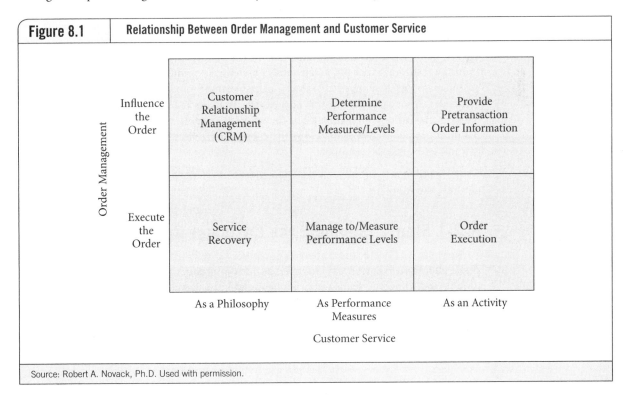

| Figure 8.1 | Relationship Between Order Management and Customer Service |

Source: Robert A. Novack, Ph.D. Used with permission.

service are related. As this figure shows, customer service is involved in both influencing a customer's order as well as in executing the customer's order. The topics in this figure will be discussed in more detail in this chapter.

The remainder of this chapter will be organized as follows. First, the concept of **customer relationship management (CRM)** will be explored. Second, the concepts of **activity-based costing** and **customer profitability** will be discussed. Third, **customer segmentation** will be introduced. Fourth, the **order execution process** will be presented. Fifth, **customer service** will be discussed. Finally, the concept of **service recovery** will be explained.

8-2 Influencing the Order—Customer Relationship Management

Customer relationship management is the art and science of strategically positioning customers to improve the profitability of the organization and enhance its relationships with its customer base. CRM is not a new concept. It has been used for many years in service industries, such as banking, credit cards, hotels, and airline travel. Frequent-flier programs, used by the airline industry, are typical examples of the use of CRM to segment and reward an airline's best customers based on number of miles traveled. Similarly, the hotel industry segments its customers by the number of nights stayed and the amount of money spent at a particular hotel. Both CRM strategies target customers that are low in cost to service and who are very profitable. Normally, business travelers would earn a "best" rating in both industries because of the amount of travel and hotel stays involved.

The concept of CRM, however, has not been widely used in the business-to-business environment until lately. Traditionally, manufacturers and distributors are more adept at and actively involved in order execution, which involves filling and shipping *what* their customers order. Today, more manufacturers and distributors are becoming adept at and actively involved in influencing *how* their customers order. This shift in philosophy comes from the realization that not all customers are equally profitable for an organization. *How* customers order, *how much* customers order, *what* customers order, and *when* customers order all impact an organization's cost of executing an order. Customers whose ordering patterns maximize the efficiencies of the shipping organization's logistics network will be the most profitable customers. Using the CRM philosophy allows an organization to identify and reward those customers.

There are four basic steps in the implementation of the CRM process in a business-to-business environment.[2]

8-2-1 Step 1: Segment the Customer Base by Profitability

Most firms allocate direct materials, labor, and overhead costs to customers using a single allocation criterion, for example, pounds of product purchased during a particular time period. However, firms today are beginning to use techniques such as activity-based costing (to be discussed in the next section) to more accurately allocate costs to customers based on the specific costs of servicing a customer's orders based on how, how much, what, and when a customer orders. Normally, a **cost-to-serve (CTS) model** is developed for each customer. These CTS models are very much like an income statement for the customer.

8-2-2 Step 2: Identify the Product/Service Package for Each Customer Segment

This step presents one of the most challenging activities in the CRM process. The goal of this step is to determine what each customer segment values in its relationship with the supplier. This decision is usually based on feedback from customers and sales representatives. The challenge here is how to "package" the value-adding products and services for each customer segment. One solution is to offer the same product/service offering to each customer segment, while varying the product quality or service levels. For example, Table 8.1 presents a scenario where the offerings for each customer segment do not change, but the level of the offering does. In this table, assume that Customer Segment A is the most profitable and Customer Segment C is the least profitable. As is shown, Customer Segment A receives the best product and the best service, while the other two customer segments receive less quality in product and service. This type of package assumes that all customer segments value the same types of supplier offerings. This could be a disadvantage for this approach. The advantage to this approach is that it is easy for the supplier to manage.

Another solution to this part of the CRM process is to vary the service offerings for each customer segment. An example of this approach can be seen in Table 8.2. In Table 8.2, the offerings for each segment are different, with the top customer segment (A) receiving the most differentiation. The basis for this package is that each segment values different services. The advantage to this method is that it meets the needs of each segment. The disadvantage is that it is much more difficult for the supplier to manage. Of the two methods shown in Tables 8.1 and 8.2, Option A (see Table 8.1) is most commonly found in industry today.

8-2-3 Step 3: Develop and Execute the Best Processes

In Step 2, customer expectations were determined and set. Step 3 delivers on those expectations. Organizations many times go through elaborate processes to determine customer needs and set target performance levels, only to fail when it comes to executing on those customer promises. One cause for this might be that organizations fail to recognize that process reengineering might be necessary to meet expected performance targets. For example, the order fill rate promised to Customer Segment A in Table 8.1 might not be possible given the current inventory policy of the supplier's organization. So, inventory levels and

Table 8.1	Hypothetical Product/Service Offerings: Option A		
PRODUCT/SERVICE OFFERING	CUSTOMER SEGMENT A	CUSTOMER SEGMENT B	CUSTOMER SEGMENT C
Product quality (% defects)	Less than 1%	5%–10%	10%–15%
Order fill	98%	92%	88%
Lead time	3 days	7 days	14 days
Delivery time	Within 1 hour of request	On day requested	During week requested
Payment terms	4/10 net 30	3/10 net 30	2/10 net 30
Customer service support	Dedicated rep	Next available rep	Through Web site
Source: Robert A. Novack, Ph.D. Used with permission.			

Table 8.2	Hypothetical Product/Service Offerings: Option B
CUSTOMER SEGMENT A	
Product quality (% defects)	Less than 1%
Order fill	98%
Lead time	3 days
Delivery time	Within 1 hour of request
Payment terms	4/10 net 30
Customer service support	Dedicated rep
CUSTOMER SEGMENT B	
Product quality (% defects)	5%–10%
Credit hold	Less than 48 hours
Return policy	Up to 10 days after delivery
CUSTOMER SEGMENT C	
Order fill	88%
Ordering process	Through Web site
Source: Robert A. Novack, Ph.D. Used with permission.	

locations might have to be reconsidered given a target performance rate for order fill of 98 percent. The higher the expectations of the customer are, the more the dissatisfaction if they are not achieved.

8-2-4 Step 4: Measure Performance and Continuously Improve

The goal of CRM is to better serve the different customer segments of the supplier organization, while at the same time improving the profitability of the supplier. Once the CRM program has been implemented, it must be evaluated to determine if (1) the different customer segments are satisfied and (2) the supplier's overall profitability has improved. Remember, the goal of CRM is to identify those customers who provide the most profit by ordering product in a manner that minimizes the supplier's costs. So, another measure of the CRM program might be the number of customers who have moved from one customer segment to another by changing their ordering patterns. The goal of CRM is not to eliminate customers; rather, it is to satisfy the customer while maximizing profits for the supplier. If the CRM program is not achieving these goals, it must be reevaluated and/or repositioned to bring it into alignment with performance targets.

The concept behind CRM is simple: align the supplier's resources with its customers in a manner that increases both customer satisfaction and supplier profits. The execution of a CRM program presents many challenges. CRM implementation is not so much a destination as it is a journey. CRM is a strategic initiative by a supplier organization that requires changes in resource allocation, organizational structure, and market perception.

This section presented a general overview of CRM. The next section will delve deeper into the details of how customers are segmented using activity-based costing and customer profitability.

8-2-5 Activity-Based Costing and Customer Profitability

Traditional cost accounting is well suited to situations where an output and an allocation process are highly correlated. Take, for example, a warehouse that receives product in pallet quantities, stores product in pallets, picks product in pallets, and ships product in pallets. Also, assume that the same amount of labor expense, machine expense, and space expense are consumed for each pallet regardless of the type of product on the pallet. In this scenario, cost accounts such as direct labor, direct machine expense, and direct overhead (space) can be allocated to each product based on the number of pallets moved through the warehouse for a particular time period.

On the other hand, traditional cost accounting is not very effective in situations where the output is not correlated with the allocation base. This is the more likely scenario in logistics. For example, assume that the warehouse just described will need to start picking and shipping in case quantities and in inner-pack quantities as well as in pallet quantities. Using an allocation base of pallets, products shipped in pallets will burden a majority of the direct costs incurred in the warehouse. However, the case pick and inner-pack pick, being very labor intensive, are driving most of the costs in the warehouse. As such, traditional cost accounting in this case would be penalizing the most cost effective method of moving product through the warehouse and subsidizing the least cost effective method of moving product. This is where we can see the effectiveness of activity-based costing (ABC), which can be defined as, "A methodology that measures the cost and performance of activities, resources, and cost objects. Resources are assigned to activities, then activities are assigned to cost objects based on their use. ABC recognizes the causal relationships of cost drivers to activities."[3] Using the ABC methodology in the warehouse example previously discussed would more accurately assign costs to those activities that absorbed the most resources. In other words, ABC would identify that picking and shipping inner-packs is more expensive than picking and shipping pallets.

Another way to look at the difference between traditional cost accounting and ABC can be seen in Figure 8.2. As this figure shows, conventional accounting assigns resources to department cost centers (e.g., warehouse labor is assigned to the warehousing department), then allocates a particular cost to a product (e.g., labor dollars per pallet). ABC assigns resources to an activity (e.g., labor cost for picking product), identifies the cost drivers (e.g., labor cost for picking a pallet versus picking an inner-pack), and then allocates those costs to products, customers, markets, or business units. ABC more accurately reflects the actual cost of performing an activity than does traditional cost accounting.

An example of how ABC works might be beneficial here. Assume that a consumer goods distribution center (DC) always receives and stores product in pallet quantities but picks and ships in pallets, tiers, cases, and eaches (individual consumer units). The product flow can be seen in Figure 8.3. The DC receives pallets for both storage and returns from customers. The returns process is separate and will not be discussed here. Once the pallet is received, it is put away (stored) until product is ready to be picked. Customers are allowed to order in quantities from eaches to full pallets. Shipping can be done from eaches to full pallets. After the pallet is stored, ten separate processes can be used to pick and ship product to comply with the customer's order. Intuitively, the most cost efficient method in this figure is obviously pallet pick and pallet ship. The most expensive method in this figure is each pick and each ship. Tier picking means a customer orders a product in "tier" quantities—the number

Figure 8.2 | **Traditional Accounting Versus Activity-Based Costing**

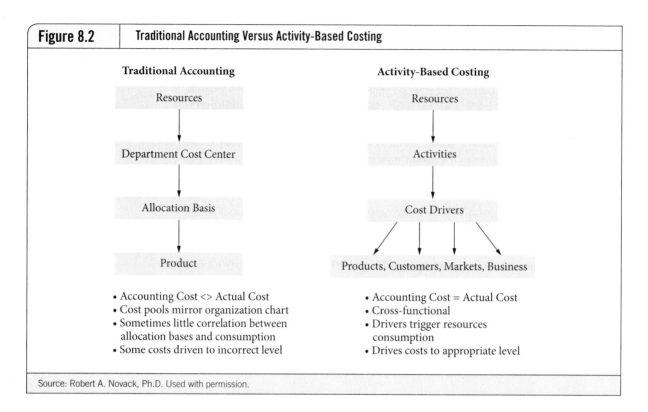

Source: Robert A. Novack, Ph.D. Used with permission.

Figure 8.3 | **Distribution Center Process Flow Chart**

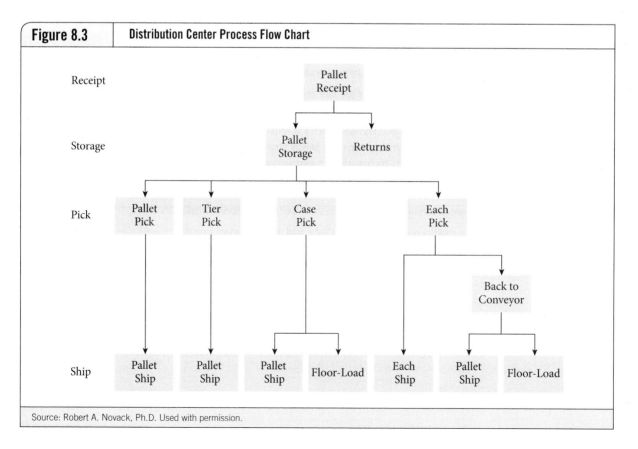

Source: Robert A. Novack, Ph.D. Used with permission.

of cases of a product that fits onto a single layer on a pallet. This number is also called "tie." "High" is the number of layers of products on a pallet. Usually, tier picking results in a "rainbow" pallet, which is a pallet that contains several layers of different products. In case picking, the case can be picked and assembled onto a pallet for shipping or the case can put onto the conveyor system and eventually floor-loaded (each case loaded separately) in the trailer. In each picking, the each can be combined with other eaches into a reusable shipping case, put back onto the conveyor with other cases, and either floor-loaded or palletized. Each picks can also be shipped as eaches.

With the numerous methods that product can flow through the DC identified, the next step is to identify the activities that absorb the two main costs in a DC: space and labor. Space consumption by activity can be seen in Table 8.3. This table shows that storage absorbs 73 percent of the DC overhead cost. So products that require excess storage space will be allocated more of the direct overhead (facility) costs. Table 8.4 shows the number of full-time equivalent employees (FTEs) required to perform the different types of activities shown in Figure 8.3. Picking cases to be placed onto the conveyor requires the most FTEs (19.54).

Combining the costs from these two tables with the product flows identified in Figure 8.3 results in the costs to perform these activities and can be seen in Figure 8.4. Using equivalent case quantities as the allocation basis, it is easy to understand that receiving, storing, picking, and shipping products in pallets results in the lowest cost per case for the DC. Alternatively, receiving and storing products in pallets and picking and shipping eaches results in the highest cost per case. This ABC methodology, then, can be used to determine the costs of the various customer ordering policies and may be used to influence how the customer orders.

Distribution center expenses are but one cost that a shipper incurs in dealing with a customer. Traditional customer profitability analyses would start with gross sales less returns and allowances (net sales) and subtract the cost of goods sold to arrive at a gross margin figure. Although this number might provide a general guideline for the profitability of a customer, it falls short on capturing the real costs of serving a customer. A broader approach to determining customer profitability can be seen in Table 8.5. This is an actual example from a company that shall remain anonymous. This example identifies many other

Table 8.3	Distribution Center Space Allocation
ACTIVITY	**PERCENTAGE OF TOTAL NET SQUARE FEET**
Storage	73.0
Case pick	10.0
Receiving	5.0
Each pick	4.0
Test location	3.0
Staging	3.0
Returns	2.0
Total	100.0
Source: Robert A. Novack, Ph.D. Used with permission.	

Table 8.4	Distribution Center Labor Allocation
ACTIVITY	**FTEs***
Receiving	17.73
Storage	6.90
Case pick	19.54
Floor-loading	6.90
Test area	6.90
Each pick	6.90
Back to conveyor	1.28
Courier delivery	1.28
Pallet pick	5.49
Returns	9.71
Total FTEs	82.63

*Full-time equivalent employees.

Source: Robert A. Novack, Ph.D. Used with permission.

Figure 8.4	Flow-Through Costing for a Distribution Center

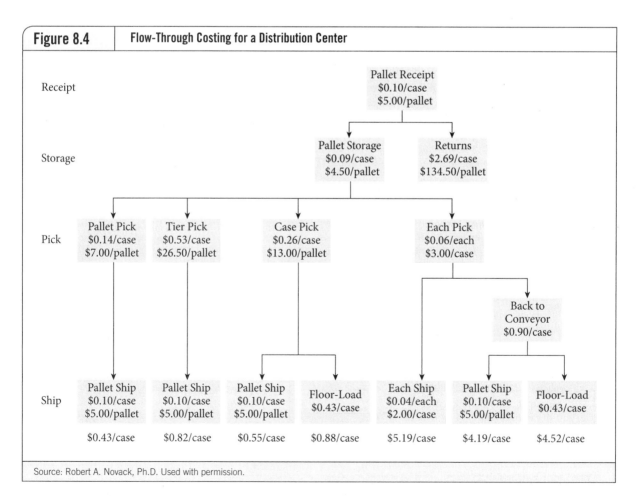

Source: Robert A. Novack, Ph.D. Used with permission.

| Table 8.5 | Customer Profitability Analysis |

CUSTOMER P&L STATEMENT							CUSTOMER A TOTAL U.S. CONSOLIDATED		
MAC CODE: 123456	1997 ACTUALS	% TO SALES	1998 QUARTER 1	1998 QUARTER 2	1998 QUARTER 3	1998 QUARTER 4	1998 YTD ACTUALS	% TO SALES
Gross Sales			$17,439,088	$15,488,645	$17,382,277	$16,632,060	$66,942,069	102.6%
Returns			78,383	60,150	66,828	143,225	348,587	100.5%
Cash Discounts			348,782	309,773	347,646	332,641	1,338,841	102.1%
Net Sales			$17,011,923	$15,118,722	$16,967,803	$16,156,194	$65,254,641	100.0%
Cost of Goods Sold:			$ 4,392,341	$ 3,686,569	$ 4,170,382	$ 3,959,373	$16,208,665	24.8%
Standard Costs			$ 4,279,660	$ 3,615,837	$ 4,070,518	$ 3,830,855	$15,796,870	24.2%
Royalties			$ 112,681	$ 70,732	$ 99,864	$ 128,518	$ 411,795	0.6%
Gross Margin			$12,619,582	$11,432,153	$12,797,421	$12,196,820	$49,045,976	75.2%
Promotional Costs:			$ 1,366,220	$ 1,476,337	$ 1,624,152	$ 2,210,575	$ 6,677,284	10.2%
Allowances			$ 299,893	$ 85,025	$ 110,627	$ 0	$ 495,544	0.8%
Off Invoice			$ 957,617	$ 885,877	$ 1,054,432	$ 1,115,520	$ 4,013,447	6.2%
Trade Promotion Funds			$ 108,710	$ 505,435	$ 459,093	$ 1,095,055	$ 2,168,293	3.3%
Racks			$ 0	$ 0	$ 0	$ 0	$ 0	0.0%
Other			$ 0	$ 0	$ 0	$ 0	$ 0	0.0%
Advertising:			$ 0	$ 0	$ 0	$ 0	$ 0	0.0%
Market Research			$ 0	$ 0	$ 0	$ 0	$ 0	0.0%
Other Variable Expenses:			$ 576,922	$ 396,040	$ 464,740	$ 474,752	$ 1,912,454	2.9%
Bracket Pricing			$ 373,099	$ 256,242	$ 300,028	$ 320,522	$ 1,249,892	1.9%
Freight			$ 203,822	$ 139,798	$ 164,712	$ 154,229	$ 662,562	1.0%
Direct Profit Contribution			$10,676,440	$ 9,559,776	$10,708,529	$ 9,511,494	$40,456,238	62.0%
Selling Expenses:			$ 277,303	$ 288,458	$ 320,217	$ 377,591	$ 1,263,569	1.9%
Headquarters Selling			$ 59,690	$ 59,690	$ 59,690	$ 59,690	$ 238,762	0.4%
Retail Selling			$ 45,481	$ 45,481	$ 46,843	$ 75,246	$ 213,052	0.3%
Category Management			$ 50,238	$ 50,238	$ 50,238	$ 50,238	$ 200,953	0.3%
CBT's			$ 121,893	$ 133,048	$ 163,446	$ 192,416	$ 610,802	0.9%

(continued)

Table 8.5   Continued

CUSTOMER P&L STATEMENT				CUSTOMER A TOTAL U.S. CONSOLIDATED					
MAC CODE: 123456	1997 ACTUALS	% TO SALES	1998 QUARTER 1	1998 QUARTER 2	1998 QUARTER 3	1998 QUARTER 4	1998 YTD ACTUALS	% TO SALES
Operations:			$ 192,555	$ 266,837	$ 269,382	$ 269,673	$ 998,447	1.5%
Warehousing			$ 100,632	$ 145,456	$ 142,890	$ 153,564	$ 542,541	0.8%
Order Processing			$ 91,923	$ 121,381	$ 126,492	$ 116,109	$ 455,905	0.7%
Operating Profit			$10,206,582	$ 9,004,481	$10,118,929	$ 8,864,230	$38,194,223	58.5%
Write Offs:			$ 15,791	$ 4,701	$ (820)	$ 18,433	$ 38,105	0.1%
Allowance Reserve				$ 310	$ 2,939	$ 7,792	$ 10,953	0.0%
Claims Reserve			$ 15,481	$ 2,688	$ 1,365	$ 6,641	$ 26,175	0.0%
Handling Charges			$ 0	$ (926)	$ (2,097)	$ 4,000	$ 977	0.0%
Adjusted Operating Profit			$10,190,791	$ 8,999,780	$10,119,749	$ 8,845,797	$38,156,118	58.5%
Footnotes:								
Items Journaled Requiring Further Investigation			$ 1,034	$ 2,223	$ 2,492	$ 9,125	$ 14,875	0.0%
Unearned Cash Discounts Written Off			$ 0	$ 809	$ 0	$ 30,213	$ 31,022	0.0%

Source: Robert A. Novack, Ph.D. Used with permission.

cost drivers that are impacted by customers and how they interact with the shipper. Notice that the DC example just covered falls under the "Operations" section of this customer profitability formula. As can be seen with this example, using gross margin alone as the indicator of profitability understates the costs incurred with serving this customer. Every line item under gross margin is represented by a process model as shown in Figure 8.4. With this information on how a customer's interaction drives a shippers costs, the shipper can then segment its customers by profitability.

Figure 8.5 shows one method to classify customers by profitability. The vertical axis measures the net sales value of the customer, while the horizontal axis represents the cost to serve. Those customers who fall into the "Protect" segment are the most profitable. Their interactions with the shipper provide the shipper with the most cost efficiencies. Those customers who are in the "Danger Zone" segment are the least profitable and are more than likely incurring a loss for the shipper. For these customers, the shipper has three alternatives: (1) change the manner in which the customer interacts with the shipper so the customer can move to another segment; (2) charge the customer the actual cost of doing business (this would more than likely make the customer stop doing business with the shipper—this is usually not an acceptable strategy employed by most shippers); or (3) switch the customer to an alternative distribution channel (e.g., the shipper might encourage the customer to order through a distributor or wholesaler rather than buying direct from the shipper). The customers who fall into the "Build" segment have a low cost to serve and a low net sales value. The strategy here is to maintain the cost to serve but build net sales value to help

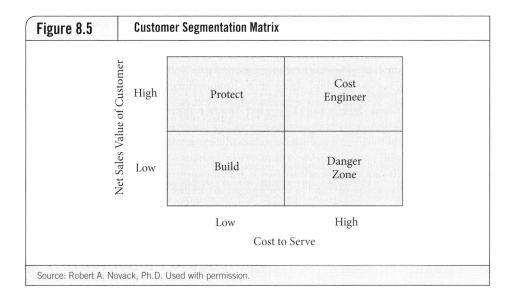

Figure 8.5 | **Customer Segmentation Matrix**

Net Sales Value of Customer

High — Protect | Cost Engineer

Low — Build | Danger Zone

Low   High
Cost to Serve

Source: Robert A. Novack, Ph.D. Used with permission.

drive the customer into the "Protect" segment. Finally, the customers who are in the "Cost Engineer" segment have a high net sales value and a high cost to serve. The strategy here is to find more efficient ways for the customer to interact with the shipper. This might include encouraging the customer to order in tier quantities rather than in case quantities. This switch in ordering policy would reduce the operating cost of the shipper and possibly move the customer into the "Protect" segment.

Combining ABC, customer profitability, and customer segmentation to build profitable revenue is a strategy being utilized by an increasing number of organizations today. This strategy helps define the true cost of dealing with customers and helps the shipper influence how the customer interacts with the shipper to provide the highest level of cost efficiency for the shipper. Combining these three tools with CRM allows the shipper to differentiate its offerings to its different customer segments, resulting in maximum profit for the shipper and maximum satisfaction for the customer.

This section discussed the methods organizations use to influence how a customer orders. The next section will discuss the methods used by shippers to execute the order once it is received.

8-3 Executing the Order—Order Management and Order Fulfillment

The order management system represents the principal means by which buyers and sellers communicate information relating to individual orders of product. Effective order management is a key to operational efficiency and customer satisfaction. To the extent that an organization conducts all activities relating to order management in a timely, accurate, and thorough manner, it follows that other areas of company activity can be similarly coordinated. In addition, both present and potential customers will take a positive view of consistent and predictable order cycle length and acceptable response times. By starting the process with an understanding of customer needs, organizations can design order management systems that will be viewed as superior to competitor firms.

The logistics area needs timely and accurate information relating to individual customer orders; thus, more and more organizations are placing the corporate order management function within the logistics area. The move is good not only from the perspective of the logistics process but also from that of the overall organization.

8-3-1 Order-to-Cash (OTC) and Replenishment Cycles

When referring to outbound-to-customer shipments, the term **order to cash** (or **order cycle**) is typically used. The difference between these two terms will be discussed shortly. The term **replenishment cycle** is used more frequently when referring to the acquisition of additional inventory, as in materials management. Basically, one organization's order cycle is another's replenishment cycle. For the remainder of this discussion, the term *order to cash* (OTC) will be used. Traditionally, organizations viewed order management as all of those activities that occur from when an order is received by a seller until the product is received by the buyer. This is called the *order cycle*. The OTC cycle is all of those activities included in the order cycle plus the flow of funds back to the seller based on the invoice. The OTC concept is being adopted by many organizations today and more accurately reflects the effectiveness of the order management process.

Figure 8.6 is a representation of the OTC cycle. This figure is also referred to as Process D1: Deliver Stocked Product in the Supply Chain Council's SCOR Model. It will be used as

Figure 8.6	SCOR Model Process D1: Deliver Stocked Product

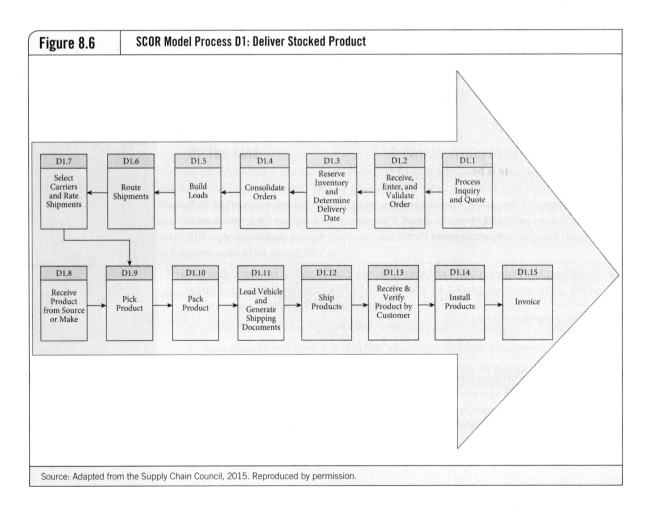

Source: Adapted from the Supply Chain Council, 2015. Reproduced by permission.

the basis of discussion for this session. This process represents not only the lead time for delivery of product to the customer but also the flow of funds back to the seller. Thirteen principal activities constitute the OTC cycle. The first seven (D1.1 through D1.7) represent information flows; the next seven (D1.8 through D1.14) represent product flows; and the last activity (D1.15) represents cash flow. Each of these will be discussed in the following section.

D1.1: Process Inquiry and Quote

This step in the process precedes the actual placement of the order by the customer. In D1.1, the customer is looking for product, pricing, or availability information from the supplier to determine whether or not to place an order. This step in the process requires that the seller have up-to-date information in a single location to provide quickly and accurately to the prospective buyer. Information availability is critical in this step.

D1.2: Receive, Enter, and Validate Order

This step involves the placement and receipt of the order. In many organizations, this step is accomplished through the application of technology such as electronic data interchange (EDI) or the Internet. In some organizations, the order is called in to a customer service representative (CSR) who then enters the order into the seller's order management system. The application of technology to this step has significantly reduced order errors as well as the OTC cycle. Step D1.2 "captures" the order and prepares it for the next step, order processing.

D1.3: Reserve Inventory and Determine Delivery Date

This step in the process has traditionally been referred to as **order processing**. In the buyer/seller relationship, this might be the most critical step because it sets delivery expectations for the customer. Once the order has been "captured" in the seller's order management system, current inventory levels are checked to determine availability and location. If inventory is available in the seller's distribution network, it is reserved for the order and a delivery date is given to the customer. In the case where the seller has inventory to fill the order, the delivery date is based on the concept of **available to deliver (ATD)**. This means that the seller has the inventory and can promise a delivery date.

In some instances, the seller does not have the inventory but knows when it will be produced internally or delivered from a supplier to the seller's distribution centers. In this case, the delivery date is based on the concept of **available to promise (ATP)**. This means that even though the seller does not have physical possession of the inventory to fill the order, it can still promise a delivery date. In either case, the customer has no need to know whether the delivery date is based on ATD or ATP. Implementing the ATP concept requires upstream coordination of information systems between the seller and its manufacturing facilities and/or the seller and its supplier's manufacturing facilities or distribution centers. For example, assume that an order for 40 cases of Product A is ordered from the seller. The seller currently has 20 cases of this product in inventory but knows that its manufacturing facility will be producing another 20 cases tomorrow. The seller can now set an ATP delivery date because it knows that by tomorrow, 40 cases of Product A will be available for the order. Similarly, if the seller has only 20 cases of Product A in inventory but knows that its supplier will deliver another 20 cases this afternoon, it can still set an ATP delivery date. Critical to the success of the ATP concept is the assurance that the upstream suppliers (internal manufacturing facilities or supplier facilities) will keep their promise of delivery of the additional 20 cases. If they cannot meet this promise, either order fill or on-time delivery performance for the seller will suffer.

Once the delivery date is set with the customer, this step will usually transmit the order to the warehouse management system (WMS) for pick scheduling and to the financial system for invoice generation. So this step determines the order execution plan that the seller has determined and communicated to the customer. Its successful completion is critical to internal efficiencies for the supplier (e.g., order fill rate and on-time delivery rate) and external effectiveness for the customer (customer satisfaction).

D1.4: Consolidate Orders

This step examines customer orders to determine opportunities for freight consolidation as well as for batch warehouse picking schedules. Both of these consolidation opportunities offer cost efficiencies for the seller. However, consolidation plans will normally add time to the delivery cycle of the order to the customer. These opportunities, then, need to be examined taking into consideration the ATD or ATP delivery dates specified in the previous step.

D1.5: Build Loads

This step takes the freight consolidation opportunities identified in D1.4 and the delivery date given in D1.3 and develops a transportation plan. Many times, this step is used with less-than-truckload (LTL), small package, stop-off, or pool freight operations. The concept is to designate the order to a specific carrier or transportation vehicle to optimize transportation efficiencies while maintaining customer delivery requirements. Many organizations use transportation management systems (TMS) to build loads for customer deliveries.

D1.6: Route Shipments

This step can follow or be concurrent with D1.5. Here, the "load" (usually a transportation vehicle) is assigned to a specific route for delivery to the customer. Again, many organizations use a TMS to complete this step.

D1.7: Select Carriers and Rate Shipments

Following or concurrent with D1.5 and D1.6, this step will assign a specific carrier to deliver an order or a consolidation of orders. This is usually based on the seller's routing guide that is often contained in the TMS. For example, a seller has 2,000 pounds of freight to be delivered from its distribution center to a destination 1,500 miles away with a two-day delivery window. The routing guide might suggest that a small package air freight carrier (e.g., UPS or FedEx) handle this load. If the delivery window is five days, the routing guide might suggest an LTL carrier (e.g., Yellow/Roadway, FedEx Ground). Once the carrier has been designated, the seller predetermines the freight costs for the shipment based on agreements with the individual carrier. In any situation, this step takes into consideration size of shipment (load), destination (route), and delivery (ATD or ATP) to determine the appropriate carrier and freight costs.

D1.8: Receive Product from Source or Make

This step gains importance when an ATP has been given to a customer's order. In this step, product is received at the distribution center and the order management system is checked to see if there are any orders outstanding that need this particular product. If so, the product is immediately combined with the on-hand inventory in preparation to be picked for the order. If the product is not immediately needed to fill an open order, it is put into storage to await the picking process.

D1.9: Pick Product

This step uses the outputs from D1.3, D1.4, and D1.5 to determine the order picking schedules in the distribution center. With the many order picking strategies that can be used at distribution centers, this step is critical to route orders through the distribution center to optimize order picking efficiency while maintaining delivery schedules.

D1.10: Pack Product

Once the order has been processed, it must be packed. Packing can take several forms. First, individual "eaches" from an internet order can be packed into a specific box. Second, cases picked for the order can be built into a multi-item (rainbow) pallet. Third, cases picked for an order can be built into a single-item (straight) pallet. Regardless of the type of packing, this step readies the order to be loaded onto a transportation vehicle for delivery.

D1.11: Load Vehicle and Generate Shipping Documents

Based on the output from D1.5 and D1.6, the transportation vehicle is loaded in this step. In some cases, the sequencing of the order or orders in a transportation vehicle might not be important. For example, in a full truckload shipment where there is one order with one destination, the sequencing of the products in the vehicle takes on less importance. However, in an LTL or stop-off transportation vehicle where there are multiple orders with multiple destinations, the sequence is important. In this case, the last delivery would be loaded in the "nose" or front of the vehicle, while the first delivery is located on the rear of the vehicle. The proper loading sequence is critical in delivery efficiencies as well as in meeting delivery requirements.

Although some organizations do a credit check on the buyer in this step, credit checks are normally done in D1.2. "Ability to pay" on the part of the buyer is required by many organizations to set the order fulfillment process in motion.

Finally, this step will generate shipment documents to provide to the carrier to execute the shipment. These documents might include bills of lading, freight bills, waybills, and manifests for domestic shipments as well as customs clearance documents for international shipments. When the shipment is legally turned over to the carrier, the shipment process can begin. This is also the step where sellers will officially invoice the customer.

D1.12: Ship Products

With the vehicle properly loaded and all shipping documents generated, the vehicle is now dispatched from the loading facility to begin its movement to the customer. Some shippers will generate an electronic data interchange (EDI) message, referred to as an ASN (advance ship notice), and send it to the customer (business to business transaction) to notify them of shipment date and shipment contents. In a business to customer environment, many times the shipper will send an e-mail message to the consumer that their order has shipped.

D1.13: Receive and Verify Product by Customer

Once the shipment is delivered to the customer location, the receiving location will determine whether or not the delivered product is what was ordered. This verification is important because it is at this point in the process where the buyer will begin processing the seller's invoice if the delivered order is correct. If it is not correct, the buyer and seller need to agree on how to solve any discrepancies. This step also concludes the traditional order cycle. So the seller's success in completing all steps in the process up to this point determines the speed at which the seller will receive payment for the order.

D1.14: Install Product

If an order involves a product that must be installed at the customer location, it is at this point in the OTC cycle where installation takes place. An example might be where a buyer ordered a palletizing machine from a seller that required the seller to provide for installation. The success of the installation could also have an impact on the speed of cash flow back to the seller.

D1.15: Invoice

This step is the culmination of the OTC cycle for the buyer and seller. This is where the buyer is satisfied with the order cycle performance and has initiated payment to the seller. This cash flow represents the final flow of the three critical flows in the supply chain: information, product, and cash.

Process D1, the OTC cycle, represents those activities necessary in both order management and order fulfillment. The absolute time and reliability of the OTC cycle have implications on both the buyer and seller. This will be discussed in the next section.

8-3-2 Length and Variability of the Order-to-Cash Cycle

While interest has traditionally focused more on the overall length of the OTC cycle, recent attention has been centered on the variability or consistency of this process. Industry practices have shown that while the absolute length of time is important, variability is more important. A driving force behind the attention to OTC cycle variability is safety stock. The absolute length of the order cycle will influence demand inventory. The concept of the order cycle is used here because the focus is on the delivery of product to the buyer and not on the flow of cash to the supplier. For example, assume that the order cycle (time from order placement to order receipt) takes 10 days to complete and the buyer needs five units per day for its manufacturing process. Assuming the basic economic order quantity (EOQ) (this will be discussed at length in the next chapter) model is being used by the buyer, the buyer will place an order when it has 50 units of demand inventory on hand. Assuming that the supplier has been able to reduce the order cycle to eight days, the buyer will now place an order when it has 40 units of demand inventory on hand. This is a reduction of 10 units of demand inventory on hand during lead time for the buyer.

Now assume that the 10-day order cycle time has a variability of +/−3 days, producing a range of 7 to 13 days for the order cycle. If the buyer wants to ensure that no stockouts occur for its manufacturing process, it must place an order when it has 65 units of inventory on hand (5 units per day × 13 days). So, the variability of this order cycle has added 15 units of inventory at the buyer's location when compared to the specific 10-day order cycle time. Figure 8.7 is a good representation of how the variability of the order cycle components impacts inventories. In the "Before System Change," the average order cycle time is 13 days with a range of 4 to 22 days. If the supplier is to guarantee delivery to the buyer in 13 days every time, the buyer would need to have 65 units of demand inventory on hand when placing an order (5 units per day × 13 days). The 18-day variability (4–22 days) now requires that the buyer maintain 45 units of safety stock on hand if it wants to avoid any stockouts [5 units per day × 22 days − (65 units)], resulting in a total inventory of 110 units. In the "After System Change," the buyer would order when it had 55 units of demand inventory on hand if the supplier could guarantee an 11-day order cycle time (5 units per day × 11 days).

Figure 8.7	Order Cycle Length and Variability

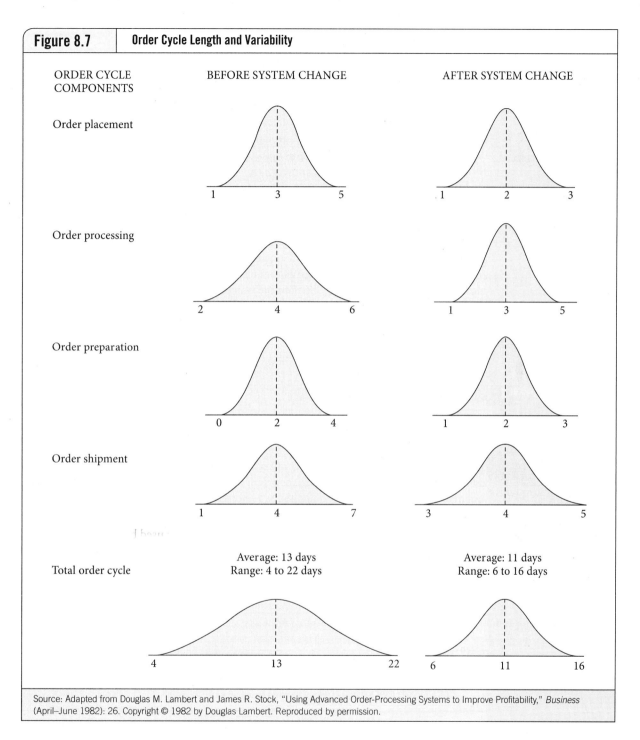

Source: Adapted from Douglas M. Lambert and James R. Stock, "Using Advanced Order-Processing Systems to Improve Profitability," *Business* (April–June 1982): 26. Copyright © 1982 by Douglas Lambert. Reproduced by permission.

The variability of 10 days (6–16 days) would require the buyer to maintain 25 units of safety stock if it wants to avoid any stockouts [5 units per day × 16 days – (55 units)]. This is a reduction of 10 units of demand inventory and 25 units of safety stock resulting from a reduction in order cycle time length and variability.

The concepts of absolute time and variability of time will be covered more in depth in Chapter 9 (Inventory Management). However, it is important to note here that the time and variability associated with order management affects not only customer satisfaction but also a customer's inventories. These cost and service implications of order management are critical to a seller's competitive advantage in the marketplace.

8-4 E-Commerce Order Fulfillment Strategies

This discussion on order management would not be complete without a brief discussion on how the Internet has affected how the OTC cycle is designed and managed. Many organizations are using Internet technology as a means to capture order information and transmit it to their "back end" systems for picking, packing, and shipping. What the Internet is now allowing is the faster collection of cash by the seller organizations. As can be seen in the D1 process shown in Figure 8.6, cash is collected by the seller in the last step of the process. This figure shows the traditional "buy-make-sell" business model used by many organizations that produce product to inventory to wait for an order. Obviously, the longer it takes the selling organization to complete the order management process, the longer it takes to collect its cash. Probably, the most notable example of an organization managing its cash flow is Dell, a company that employs the "sell-buy-make" business model. A large percentage of orders (both consumer and business) received by Dell for its products are placed through its Web site. Once the order is received and confirmed (sell), Dell will process the buyer's credit card or purchasing card to begin the flow of funds before it owns the components that will go into building the customer's order. So Dell has the customer's money before it owns the components for the final product. If we use Process D1 from Figure 8.6 as an example, Step D1.13 now comes after D1.3. Dell estimates that it has a +40-day negative working capital balance. In other words, it has its customers' cash for an average of 40 days before it must pay its suppliers for the components.

Applying Internet technology to the order management process has allowed organizations to not only take time out of the process but also to increase the velocity of cash back to the selling organization. These two benefits have added strategic importance to the order management process.

8-5 Customer Service

No discussion of outbound logistics systems would be complete without the inclusion of customer service, since customer service is the output of the logistics engine. Having the right product, at the right time, in the right quantity, without damage or loss, to the right customer are underlying principles of logistics systems that recognize the importance of customer service.

Another aspect of customer service that deserves mention is the consumer awareness of the price/quality ratio and the special needs of today's consumers, who are time conscious and demand flexibility. Today's consumers also have high standards for quality, and brand loyalty is not necessarily something they always support. Essentially, they want products at the best price, with the best levels of service, and at times convenient to their schedules. Successful companies, such as Walmart and Dell, have adopted customer service strategies that recognize the importance of speed, flexibility, customization, and reliability.

8-5-1 The Logistics/Marketing Interface

Customer service is often the key link between logistics and marketing within an organization. If the logistics system, particularly outbound logistics, is not functioning properly and a customer does not receive a delivery as promised, the organization could lose both current and future revenue. Manufacturing can produce a quality product at the right cost and marketing can sell it, but if logistics does not deliver it when and where promised, the customer will not be satisfied.

Figure 8.8 represents the traditional role of customer service at the interface between marketing and logistics. This relationship manifests itself in this perspective through the "place" dimension of the marketing mix, which is often used synonymously with channel-of-distribution decisions and the associated customer service levels provided. In this context, logistics plays a static role that is based upon minimizing the total cost of the various logistics activities within a given set of service levels, most likely determined by marketing.

However, as Chapter 13 and examples in this chapter illustrate, logistics today is taking on a more dynamic role in influencing customer service levels as well as in impacting an organization's financial position. Again, appropriate examples here would include both Dell and Walmart that have both used logistics and customer service to reduce product prices, increase product availability, and reduce lead times to customers. These two organizations have gained an appreciation for the impact of dynamic logistics systems on their financial positions.

8-5-2 Defining Customer Service

Attempting to define the concept of customer service can be a difficult task. The beginning of this chapter offered three different perspectives on customer service: (1) as a philosophy, (2) as a set of performance measures, and (3) as an activity. However, customer service needs to be put into perspective as including *anything that touches the customer*. From a marketing perspective, there are three levels of a product that an organization provides to its customers: (1) the core benefit or service, which constitutes what the buyer is really buying; (2) the tangible product, or the physical product or service itself; and (3) the augmented product, which includes benefits that are secondary, but an integral enhancement to, the tangible product the customer is purchasing. In this context, logistics customer service can be thought of as a feature of the augmented product that adds value for the customer.[4] However, the product and logistics customer service are not the only outputs by which a seller "touches" the customer. Customer service also includes how a seller interfaces with a customer and provides information about the product. This would include providing information about product availability, pricing, delivery dates, product tracking, installation, post-sale support, and so on. Customer service is really an all-encompassing strategy for how a seller interacts with its customers. Customer service is an activity, a set of performance measures, a philosophy, a core benefit, a tangible product, and an augmented product. Customer service focuses on how a seller interacts with its customers on information flows, product flows, and cash flows.

| Figure 8.8 | The Traditional Logistics/Marketing Interface |

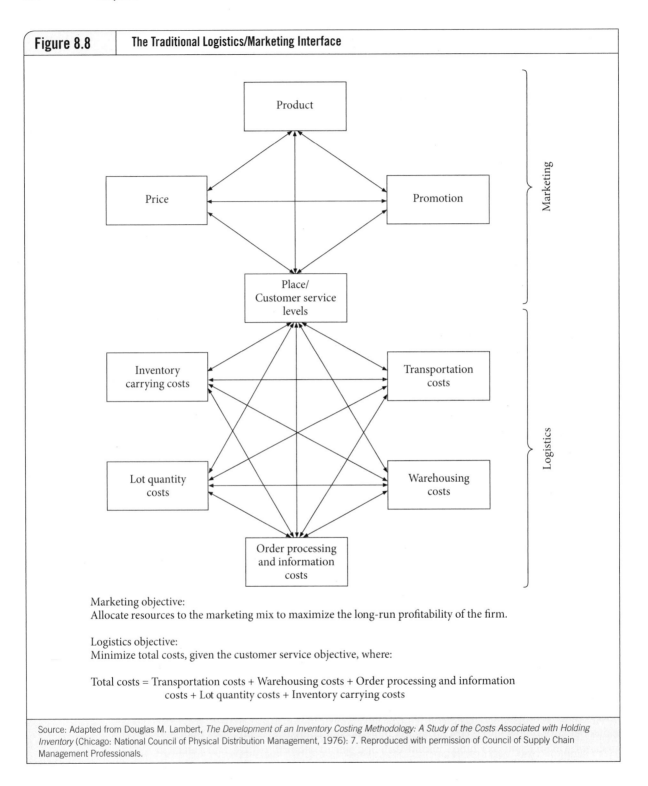

Marketing objective:
Allocate resources to the marketing mix to maximize the long-run profitability of the firm.

Logistics objective:
Minimize total costs, given the customer service objective, where:

Total costs = Transportation costs + Warehousing costs + Order processing and information
              costs + Lot quantity costs + Inventory carrying costs

8-5-3 Elements of Customer Service

Customer service is an important reason for incurring logistics costs. Economic advantages generally accrue to the customer through better supplier service. As an example, a supplier can lower customer inventories by utilizing air transportation rather than motor carrier transportation. Lower inventory costs result from air transportation's lower and more reliable transit time, which will decrease order cycle time but result in higher transportation costs than those incurred by using motor carriage. The supplier's logistics analysis must balance the improved service level the customer desires and the benefits the supplier might gain from possible increased revenue versus the cost of providing that service.

Figure 8.9 is an attempt to show the relationship between service levels and the cost of providing that service. Every incremental improvement in service (e.g., on-time delivery) will require some incremental level of investment from the supplier. This investment could be in faster and more reliable transportation or in additional inventories. An assumption is that for every incremental improvement in service there is an incremental increase in revenue for the supplier from the customer. With the cost and revenue parameters identified, a return on investment (ROI) can be calculated. Figure 8.9 attempts to illustrate that the ROI from service improvement increases at a decreasing rate. In other words, as service continues to improve, the marginal cost of providing the improved service increases, while the marginal increase in revenue decreases. At some point, the cost of service will far outweigh the incremental revenue gained from that service, providing a negative ROI. This is why it is impractical for most firms to provide 100 percent service levels. Therefore, suppliers must recognize the importance of balancing the tradeoffs between service and cost.

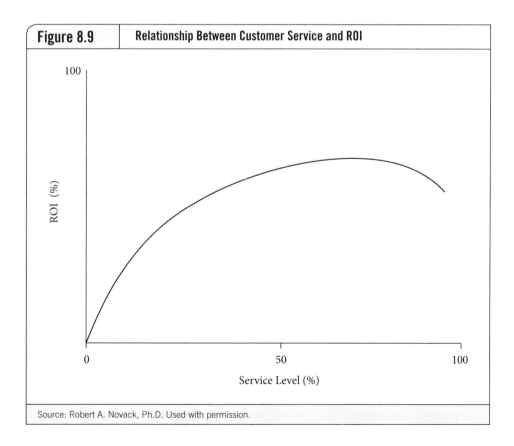

| Figure 8.9 | Relationship Between Customer Service and ROI |

Source: Robert A. Novack, Ph.D. Used with permission.

As previously discussed, customer service is an all-encompassing concept for an organization. From the perspective of logistics, however, customer service can be viewed as having four distinct dimensions: (1) time, (2) dependability, (3) communications, and (4) convenience. The next section will discuss ways in which these elements affect the cost centers of both buying and selling organizations.

8-5-3-1 Time

The *time* factor is usually order to cash, particularly from the seller's perspective. On the other hand, the buyer usually refers to the time dimension as the order cycle time, lead time, or replenishment time. Regardless of the perspective or the terminology, several basic components or variables affect the time factor.

Successful logistics operations today have a high degree of control over most, if not all, of the basic elements of lead time including order processing, order picking, and order shipping. By effectively managing activities such as these, thus ensuring that order cycles will be of reasonable length and consistent duration, seller organizations have improved the customer service levels that they provide to buyers. Remember, inconsistent and long order cycle times adversely impact buyer inventories.

Modifying all of the elements that contribute to lead time might be too costly. The seller organization might therefore make modifications in one area and permit others to operate at existing levels. For example, investing in an Internet-based ordering system for buyers would allow the seller to reduce order receipt and order processing time as well as reduce the number of errors on manually generated orders. This would permit the seller to offset the investment in technology with a reduction in the cost of human "touches" to the order.

Being able to guarantee a given lead time is an important advancement in order management. Efficiencies might accrue to both the buyer (lower inventories) and the seller (productivity improvements) with consistent lead times. However, the concept of time, by itself, means little without dependability.

8-5-3-2 Dependability

To many buyers, *dependability* can be more important than the absolute length of lead time. The buyer can minimize its inventory levels if lead time is constant. That is, a buyer who knows with 100 percent assurance that lead time is 10 days could adjust its inventory levels to correspond to the average demand during the 10 days and would have no need for safety stock to guard against stockouts resulting from inconsistent lead times.

8-5-3-2-1 Cycle Time

Lead time dependability, then, directly affects the buyer's inventory levels and stockout costs. Providing a dependable lead time reduces some of the uncertainty faced by the buyer. A seller who can assure the buyer of a given level of lead time, plus some tolerance, distinctly differentiates its product from that of its competitors.

Figure 8.10 graphs a frequency distribution pertaining to overall lead time, measured in days. The graph is bimodal and indicates that lead time tends to be in the vicinity of either four days or 12 days. The buyer typically receives within four days orders that the seller can fill from existing inventory. Orders that the seller cannot fill from available inventory, and for which the buyer must place a back order, typically result in a total order cycle time of approximately 12 days.

| Figure 8.10 | Example of the Frequency Distribution of Lead Time |

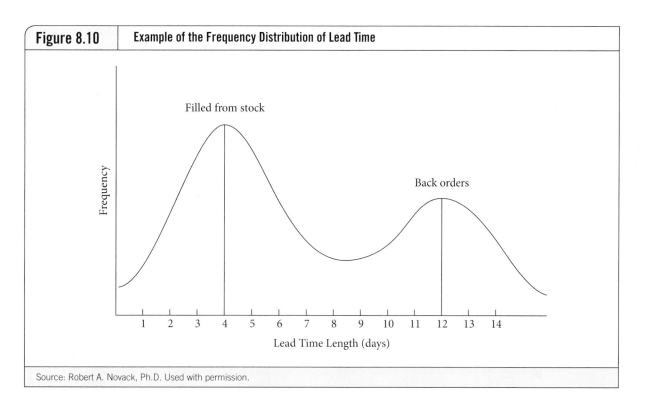

Source: Robert A. Novack, Ph.D. Used with permission.

Inconsistent lead times can result in stockouts, delays, and lost production for the buyer. The seller might incur the costs of claims, lost revenue, and expedited delivery for missing promised delivery dates. These possible outcomes reinforce the importance of dependable order cycle times between buyers and sellers.

8-5-3-2-2 Safe Delivery

The safe delivery of an order is the ultimate goal of any logistics system. As was noted earlier, the logistics process is the culmination of the selling process. If product arrives damaged or is lost in transit, the buyer cannot use the product as intended. A shipment containing damaged product impacts several buyer cost centers—inventory, production, and marketing.

Receiving damaged product deprives the buyer of items for sale, production, or personal consumption. This might increase stockout costs in the form of foregone profits or production. To guard against these costs, the buyer must increase safety stock inventory levels. Thus, unsafe delivery would be unacceptable for a buyer interested in minimizing or eliminating inventories through some form of just-in-time program.

8-5-3-2-3 Correct Orders

Finally, dependability embraces filling orders correctly. A buyer who is awaiting the arrival of an urgently needed shipment might discover upon receiving the shipment that the seller made an error in filling the order. The buyer who has not received what was requested might face potential lost sales, production, or satisfaction. An incorrectly filled order might force the buyer to reorder, if the buyer is not dissatisfied enough to buy from another seller.

8-5-3-3 Communications

Three types of communication exist between the buyer and the seller: (1) pretransaction, (2) transaction, and (3) posttransaction. Pretransaction communication includes current product availability and the determination of delivery dates. These can be communicated either electronically or manually. In either case, pretransaction communication provides the buyer with information upon which the buying decision is made.

Transaction information has both a buyer-seller component as well as what can be called a seller-seller component. The seller-seller component involves the communication of customer order information to the seller's order filling area and the actual process of picking the items ordered out of inventory. If during this process the seller discovers that the promised inventory is not available, then buyer-seller communication is necessary to inform the buyer of the situation. Another buyer-seller communication here involves shipment status and tracking. Many times, buyers need to know if the order is proceeding as planned and will contact the seller for status information.

Finally, posttransaction communication involves repair, assembly, or returns. After a shipment is delivered, the buyer might have questions about its use or assembly. Being able to provide this information quickly and accurately to the buyer allows the seller to differentiate its product from that of its competitors. Buyers might also want to return part of, or the entire, shipment. The returns process, especially for Internet-based operations, is critical. Allowing a dissatisfied buyer to return product to the seller in an easy manner is another differentiating factor for the seller.

8-5-3-4 Convenience

Convenience is another way of saying that the logistics service level must be flexible. From the logistics operation perspective, having one or a few standard service levels that apply to all buyers would be ideal; but this assumes that all buyers' logistics requirements are alike. In reality, this is not the situation. For example, one buyer might require the seller to palletize and ship all shipments by rail; another might require motor carrier delivery only, with no palletization; still others might request special delivery times. Basically, logistics requirements differ with regard to packaging, the mode of transportation and carrier the buyer requires, routing, and delivery times.

The need for convenience in logistics service levels can be attributed to the different consequences these service levels have for different buyers. More specifically, the cost of lost sales will differ among the buyer groups. For example, a buyer purchasing 30 percent of a seller's output loses more revenue for the seller than a buyer purchasing less than 0.01 percent of the seller's output does. Also, the degree of competitiveness in market areas will differ; highly competitive market areas will require a higher service level than less-competitive markets will. The profitability of different product lines in a seller's product portfolio will influence the service levels the seller can offer; that is, a seller might provide a lower service level for low-profit product lines.

However, the logistics manager must place the convenience factor in proper operational perspective. At the extreme, meeting the convenience needs of buyers would mean providing a specific service level policy for each buyer. Such a situation would set the stage for operational chaos; the unlimited offerings of service-level policies would prevent the logistics manager from optimizing the logistics process. The need for flexibility in service-level policies is warranted and is a factor in determining how the buyer perceives the "ease of doing business" with the seller. However, the logistics manager should carefully restrict this flexibility to easily identifiable buyer groups and must examine the tradeoffs between the benefits (improved revenue and profits or elimination of lost profits) and the costs associated with unique service levels in each specific situation.

On the Line — *Timely Delivery Matters Most*

Current consumer behavior indicates that most of us are more concerned with how well retailers are able to deliver goods according to our preferences than we are about ordering via social media channels. Despite the hype surrounding the retail industry's need to focus investment on new shopping channels such as mobile and social media, a GT Nexus online survey, conducted in association with global polling company YouGov, tells a different story. Looking at consumer retail habits, preferences and pain points in the United States, United Kingdom, Germany, and France shows that while 3 percent of respondents say that they've purchased goods using social media channels, consumers generally cite the inclusion of delivery options as being important to them when ordering a product either online or in-store (75 percent). Further interrogation of these numbers shows that consumers consider it important that their expectations of delivery times are filled.

Source: Logistics Management, January 2014, pp. 1–2. Reprinted with permission of Peerless Media, LLC.

8-5-4 Performance Measures for Customer Service

The four traditional dimensions of customer service from a logistics perspective—time, dependability, convenience, and communications—are essential considerations in developing a sound and effective customer service program. These dimensions of customer service also provide the underlying basis for establishing standards of performance for customer service in the logistics area.

Organizations have expanded these four elements into the basic outputs of logistics: product availability, order cycle time, logistics operations responsiveness, logistics system information, and postsale product support. Traditionally, organizations have developed metrics for these five outputs based on the seller's perspective—for example, orders shipped on time and orders shipped complete. Using Figure 8.6 as a reference, traditional logistics metrics would measure performance after the completion of Step D1.12 in the SCOR model.

The new supply chain environment for customer service has resulted in much more rigorous standards of performance. Logistics performance metrics today are now stated from the buyer's point of view:

- Orders received on time
- Orders received complete
- Orders received damage free
- Orders filled accurately
- Orders billed accurately

Again, using Figure 8.6, the supply chain perspective would measure performance after the completion of Step D1.12 in the SCOR model. If the seller is concerned only with customer service prior to shipping, as per traditional metrics, the buyer might not be satisfied and the seller might not know it, because of problems occurring during the delivery process. Furthermore, the seller using traditional metrics would have no basis upon which to evaluate the extent and magnitude of the problem. The supply chain approach, focusing on measurement at the delivery level, not only provides the database to make an evaluation, but it also, and perhaps more importantly, provides an early warning of problems as they are developing. For example, if the standard for on-time delivery is 98 percent and it decreases during a given month to 95 percent, an investigation might show that a carrier is not following instructions or even that the buyer is at fault by not being ready to accept shipments.

Another perspective on supply chain metrics can be seen in Figure 8.11 (this was also referenced in Figure 13.5). The SCOR model provides suggested metrics across multiple dimensions for each of the five Level One processes in the model. Figure 8.11 contains the

Figure 8.11	SCOR Model: Process D1 Metrics

PROCESS CATEGORY: DELIVER STOCKED PRODUCT	PROCESS NUMBER: D1

Process Category Definition

The process of delivering product that is sourced or made based on aggregated customer order/demand and inventory re-ordering parameters. The intention of Deliver Stocked Product is to have the product available when a customer order arrives (to prevent the customer from looking elsewhere). For services industries, these are the services that are pre-defined and off-the-shelf (e.g. standard training). Products or services that are "configurable" cannot be delivered through the Deliver Stocked Product process, as configurable products require customer reference or customer order details.

Performance Attributes	Metric
Supply Chain Reliability	Product Order Fulfillment
Supply Chain Responsiveness	Order Fulfillment Cycle Time
	Delivery Cycle Time
	Current logistics order cycle time
Supply Chain Agility	Upside Deliver Flexibility
	Upside Deliver Adaptability
	Downside Deliver Adaptability
	Additional Delivery Volume
	Current Delivery Volume
Supply Chain Costs	Order Management Cost
	Order Management Labor Cost
	Order Management Automation Cost
	Order Management Property, Plant and Equipment Cost
	Order Management GRC and Overhead Cost
	Fulfillment Cost
	Transportation Cost
	Fulfillment Customs, Duties, Taxes, and Tariffs Cost
	Fulfillment Labor Cost
	Fulfillment Automation Cost
	Fulfillment Property, Plant and Equipment Cost
	Fulfillment GRC, Inventory and Overhead Cost
Supply Chain Asset Management	Cash-To-Cycle Time
	Return on Supply Chain Fixed Assets
	Return on Working Capital
	Inventory Days of Supply – WIP
	Inventory Days of Supply – Finished Goods

suggested metrics for Process D1 as shown in Figure 8.6. Notice that "reliability," "responsiveness," and "agility" are all customer service dimensions. In other words, these three dimensions measure the impact of a seller's service on the buyer. "Costs" are internally focused dimensions and provide the seller with an indication of the resources it is expending to provide service to its buyers.

Figure 8.11 suggests the concept of "perfect order fulfillment" as the metric for reliability. Many organizations today are using multiple metrics simultaneously to measure how well they are serving their customers. The concept of the perfect order combines multiple metrics into an index that attempts to capture the entire customer experience. For example, a simple perfect order index might include the percentage of orders delivered on time, percentage of orders filled complete, and percentage of correct invoices. Assume that the current performance by a seller on each of the three metrics is 90 percent, 90 percent, and 90 percent, respectively. Given that each metric is normally distributed and that none of the metrics are correlated, the perfect order index for this level of performance is 73 percent (90% × 90% × 90%). Therefore, what traditionally might be thought of as an average 90 percent service level is actually a 73 percent service level. However, the 73 percent perfect order index is a more accurate reflection of the true service level experienced by the customer. The number and determination of which metrics to be included in the perfect order index will depend on the seller and its market requirements. However, the development and management of the perfect order index can be challenging for the seller, yet rewarding for the buyer.[5]

8-6 Expected Cost of Stockouts

A principal benefit of inventory availability is to reduce the number of stockouts. Once a convenient method is determined to calculate the cost of a stockout, stockout probability information can be used to determine the total expected stockout cost. Finally, alternative customer service levels can be analyzed by directly comparing the expected cost of stockouts with the revenue-producing benefits of improved customer service.

This section examines stockout issues that relate more to finished goods inventories than to inventories of raw materials or component parts. Calculating stockout costs for finished goods is generally more challenging than calculating these costs for raw material stockouts. The main reason for this is that finished goods stockouts might result in lost current and/or future customer revenue. Raw material stockouts might result in production shutdowns. Both types of stockouts need to be addressed when determining inventory levels.

A **stockout** occurs when desired quantities of finished goods are not available when or where a customer needs them. When a seller is unable to satisfy demand with available inventory, one of four possible events might occur: (1) the buyer waits until the product is available; (2) the buyer back-orders the product; (3) the seller loses current revenue; or (4) the seller loses a buyer and future revenue. From the perspective of most organizations, these four outcomes are ranked from best to worst in terms of desirability and cost impact. Theoretically, scenario 1 (customer waits) should cost nothing; this situation is more likely to occur where product substitutability is very low. Scenario 2 would increase the seller's variable costs. Scenario 3 would result in the buyer canceling a portion of or the entire order, thus negatively impacting the current revenue of the seller. Scenario 4 is the worst situation for the seller and the most difficult to calculate because it results in the loss of future revenue from the buyer.

8-6-1 Back Orders

As previously mentioned, a **back order** occurs when a seller has only a portion of the products ordered by the buyer. The back order is created to secure the portion of the inventory that is currently not available. For example, a buyer orders 100 units of Product A from the seller. However, the seller has only 60 units of Product A available to send to the buyer. A back order for 40 units of Product A is created so when the additional 40 units become available, they are shipped to the buyer. In this simple example, there is usually no major cost disadvantage to the buyer. By placing the back order, the buyer is indicating that it is willing to wait for the additional inventory. However, after experiencing multiple back orders with a seller, a buyer might decide to switch to another seller. This example will assume that switching sellers is not an option for the buyer. Although the buyer incurs minimal or no cost in this situation, the seller experiences an increase in its variable costs (this concept will be introduced in Chapter 13). A back order creates a second order document internal to the seller's order management system. It also requires the generation of another pick list for the distribution center. Labor costs in the seller's distribution center will also increase for that order. For example, had the 100 units of Product A been available to fill the original order, the order picker would have made one trip to the location of Product A to pick 100 units. With the back order situation, the order picker needs to make two trips to the same location: the first trip to pick 60 units and the second trip to pick the remaining 40 units. Transportation costs might also increase for the seller. The complete order of 100 units might have qualified for standard transportation service (e.g., three-day delivery). While the original 60 units still might qualify for standard transportation, the back-ordered 40 units might need more expensive expedited transportation (e.g., next day). For every incremental increase of variable expense for a seller on a particular order, there is a corresponding incremental decrease in operating profit for that order. As such, a seller can estimate the cost of a back order by calculating the incremental variable expenses it incurs for each back order and then compare it with the cost of preventing a back order (e.g., an increase in inventories).

8-6-2 Lost Sales

Most organizations find that although some customers might prefer a back order, others will turn to alternative supply sources. Much of the decision here is based on the level of substitutability for the product. In such a case, the buyer has decided that if the entire order cannot be delivered at the same time, it will cancel the order and place it with another seller. As such, the stockout has resulted in a lost sale for the seller. The seller's direct loss is either the revenue or profit (depending on how the seller wants to account for a lost sale) on the items(s) that was not available when the buyer wanted it. With this information, the seller can calculate the cost of a lost sale. For example, assume that the seller accounts for lost sales with a resulting loss in profit. The buyer orders 100 units of Product A, but the seller has only 60 units available. Operating profit (pretax) for each unit is $10. If the buyer accepts the 60 units and cancels the remaining 40 units, the lost sale cost to the seller is $400. If the buyer decides to cancel the entire order, the lost sale cost to the seller is $1,000.

In the likely event that the seller will sustain lost sales with inventory stockouts, the seller will have to assign a cost to these stockouts as suggested earlier. Then the seller should analyze the number of stockouts it could expect with different inventory levels. The seller should then multiply the expected number of lost sales by the profit (revenue) lost and compare the result with the cost of carrying additional inventory.

8-6-3 Lost Customer

The third possible event that can occur because of a stockout is the loss of a customer; that is, the customer permanently switches to another supplier. A supplier who loses a customer loses a future stream of income. Estimating the profit (revenue) loss that stockouts can cause is difficult. Marketing researchers have attempted to analyze brand switching for some time. Such analysis often uses management science techniques along with more qualitative marketing research methods. This is usually the most difficult loss to estimate because of the need to estimate the number of units the customer might have purchased in the future.

8-6-4 Determining the Expected Cost of Stockouts

To make an informed decision as to how much inventory to carry, an organization must determine the expected cost it will incur due to a stockout. That is, how much money will an organization lose if a stockout occurs?

The first step is to identify a stockout's potential consequences. These include a back order, a lost sale, and a lost customer. The second step is to calculate each result's expense or lost profit (revenue) and then to estimate the cost of a single stockout. For the purposes of this discussion, assume the following: 70 percent of all stockouts result in a back order, and a back order requires the seller to spend an additional $75; 20 percent result in a lost sale for the order, and this loss equals $400 in lost profit; and 10 percent result in a lost customer, or a loss of $20,000.

Calculate the overall impact as follows:

$$70\% \text{ of } \$75 = \$52.50$$
$$20\% \text{ of } \$400 = \$80.00$$
$$10\% \text{ of } \$20,000 = \$2,000.00$$
$$\text{Total estimated cost per stockout} = \$2,132.50$$

Since $2,132.50 is the average dollar amount the organization can save (or avoid losing) by averting a stockout, it should carry additional inventory to protect against stockouts only as long as carrying the additional inventory costs are equal to or less than $2,132.50.

An organization can easily use this information when formally evaluating two or more logistics system alternatives. For each alternative, the organization would need to estimate the potential number of stockouts and multiply those numbers by the estimated cost of a single stockout. This would represent a way to include stockout costs in the overall decision-making process. This concept will be demonstrated more fully in the next section.

8-7 Order Management Influences on Customer Service

A major portion of this chapter has discussed the concepts of order management and customer service as somewhat mutually exclusive. However, the beginning of this chapter explained that these two concepts are, in fact, related to one another. This section of the chapter will introduce and explain the five major outputs of order management that influence customer service: (1) product availability, (2) order cycle time, (3) logistics operations responsiveness, (4) logistics system information, and (5) postsale logistics support. Each of these outputs impacts customer service/satisfaction, and the performance of each is determined by the seller's order management and logistics systems. When examining these five outputs, the question might arise as to which is most important to the buyer and the seller. The answer is that they are all important because they are all related. For example, product availability will impact order cycle time; order cycle time will influence postsale product support; logistics system information will impact logistics operations responsiveness. Figure 8.12 is an attempt to highlight how interrelated these outputs really are. They cannot be managed as single outputs. Synchronizing the order management and logistics systems provides the seller the opportunity to achieve acceptable performance in all of these outputs. As previously mentioned, however, there are costs associated with delivering these outputs. These costs must be weighed against the benefits of providing acceptable levels of performance to the customer.

8-7-1 Product Availability

As Figure 8.12 shows, *product availability* is at the top of the outputs. Although not the most important, product availability is usually the most basic output of an organization's order management and logistics systems. This is true because product availability can be measured by asking the simple question: Did I get what I wanted, when I wanted it, and in the quantity I wanted? As such, product availability is the ultimate measure of logistics and supply chain performance. Product availability influences both the seller's and buyer's inventories. Sellers will normally hold more inventory to increase product availability.

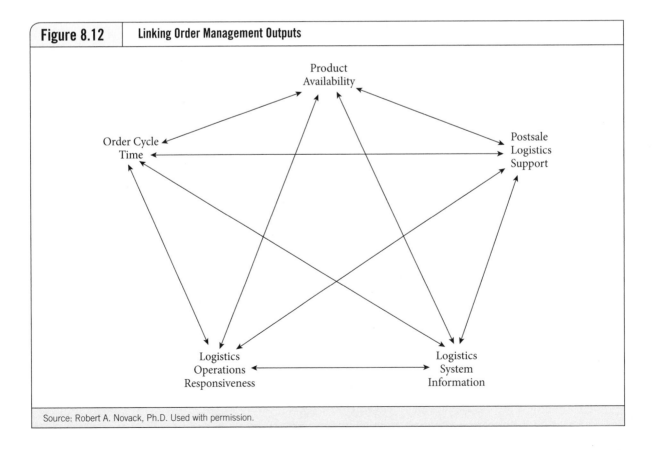

| Figure 8.12 | Linking Order Management Outputs |

Source: Robert A. Novack, Ph.D. Used with permission.

Buyers will hold more inventory to reduce stockouts, thus increasing product availability. Product availability can also influence seller and buyer revenues and profits. If a seller fails to make a product available to a buyer, the buyer might cancel the order and thus reduce revenue to the buyer. If the buyer, for example a retailer, fails to have product on its store shelves, consumers will not have the opportunity to purchase the item.

An important aspect of product availability is defining where in the supply chain it is being measured. As an example to demonstrate this point, the consumer market for processed peanuts will be used. Most peanuts are purchased by consumers on impulse. In other words, consumers normally don't go to a store with the specific intention of buying peanuts. Rather, peanuts are purchased as the consumer walks through the salted snack food aisle to get to where the "destination" items (e.g., meat, milk, eggs) are located. If the peanuts are not available on the store shelf, the sale is missed. So in the case of peanuts, product availability is critical to all members of this supply chain. Assume that the peanut farmer makes raw peanuts available to the processing plant 90 percent of the time; the processing plant makes packaged peanuts available to its distribution center 90 percent of the time; the distribution center makes cases of peanuts available to the retailer's distribution center 90 percent of the time; and the retailer's distribution center makes peanuts available to the store 90 percent of the time. While a 90 percent product availability for each segment of this supply chain might be acceptable, the cumulative effect at the shelf is not. Assuming statistical normality, the probability of having peanuts available at the store shelf is only 65.6 percent ($0.9 \times 0.9 \times 0.9 \times 09$), resulting in a stockout and lost sale 34.4 percent of the time. Hence, it is important to understand and identify where in the supply chain product availability should be measured.

Another important aspect of product availability is determining whether or not all products should be made available at the same level. Some organizations strive to have 100 percent product availability across all products. The cost associated with achieving this goal would be prohibitive and unnecessary as discussed previously in this chapter. Product availability levels for products can be determined by examining the level of substitutability and related stockout costs for a product as well as the demand profile for that product. If a product has a high level of substitutability, and therefore a high stockout cost, inventory levels must be adequate to provide high levels of availability, and vice versa. If the demand for a product is low, the decision might be made to minimize inventory levels to maintain some minimally acceptable level of availability. The point here is that not all products require the same level of availability to the buyer. Sellers must examine their product profile and determine the market requirements for each product or product family. Maintaining high levels of inventory where they are not required results in excess costs for the seller and provides little, if no, benefit to the buyer.

8-7-1-1 Metrics

Many methods exist to measure the efficiency and effectiveness of product availability. However, four metrics are widely used across multiple industries: (1) item fill rate, (2) line fill rate, (3) order fill rate, and (4) perfect order. Item fill rate and line fill rate are considered **internal metrics**; that is, they are designed to measure the efficiency of how well the seller is setting its inventories to fill items or lines on an order. Order fill rates and perfect order rates are **external metrics**; that is, they are designed to capture the buyer experience with product availability. An "item" might be a case of product, an inner-pack, or an "each" on an order. A "line" represents a single product on a multiple product order. Item fill rate is defined as the percentage of items in stock available to fill an order. Line fill rate is defined as the percentage of total lines filled complete on a multiple line order. Order fill rate is the percentage of orders filled complete. Finally, perfect order rate is the percentage of orders filled completely, received on time, billed accurately, etc. (the nature and number of items in the perfect order are determined by the organization that is measuring the perfect order). Typically, the item fill rate is higher than the line fill rate, which is higher than the order fill rate, which is greater than the perfect order rate.

Table 8.6 represents a hypothetical multiple line order. Each line is a different product that the buyer is ordering from the seller. For example, Line A might be laundry detergent, Line B might be hair shampoo, and so on. This order contains a request for 10 separate lines containing 200 items (an item here might be a case of product). In Scenario 1, the buyer is able to completely fill 9 out of the 10 lines requested (A through I) but has no product available to fill the 10th line (J). The line fill rate is 90 percent (9 divided by 10), the item fill rate is 45 percent (90 items divided by 200 items), the order fill rate is zero, and the perfect order rate is zero (both are zero because the order was not completely filled). In this case, line fill > item fill > order fill and perfect order fill. In Scenario 2, Lines A, D, and J are filled completely, while the other lines have no inventory available. In this scenario, line fill is 30 percent (3 divided by 10), item fill is 65 percent (130 divided by 200), and both order fill and perfect order are zero. In this case, item fill > line fill > order fill and perfect order. Whenever line fill or item fill is less than 100 percent, order fill and perfect order rates will be zero. The selling firm needs to measure item fill and line fill rates to determine inventory policy and where corrections in inventories need to be made. The selling firm also needs to measure order fill and perfect order rates because these directly impact the satisfaction and operations of the buyer. However, increasing fill rates has a direct effect on a seller's inventories.

This relationship can be seen in Figure 8.13. As fill rates increase, a seller's inventories will tend to increase at an increasing rate. This will usually result in marginally decreasing profits for the seller as the fill rate increases. Figures 8.13 and 8.9 show the same relationship in different terms. As service levels increase (in this case it would be fill rate), a seller's ROI

Table 8.6	Multiple Line Order			
	LINE	ITEMS ORDERED	SCENARIO 1 ITEMS FILLED	SCENARIO 2 ITEMS FILLED
	A	10	10	10
	B	10	10	0
	C	10	10	0
	D	10	10	10
	E	10	10	0
	F	10	10	0
	G	10	10	0
	H	10	10	0
	I	10	10	0
	J	110	0	110
Total	10	200	90	130

Source: Robert A. Novack, Ph.D. Used with permission.

Figure 8.13 | **Fill Rate and Inventory Investment**

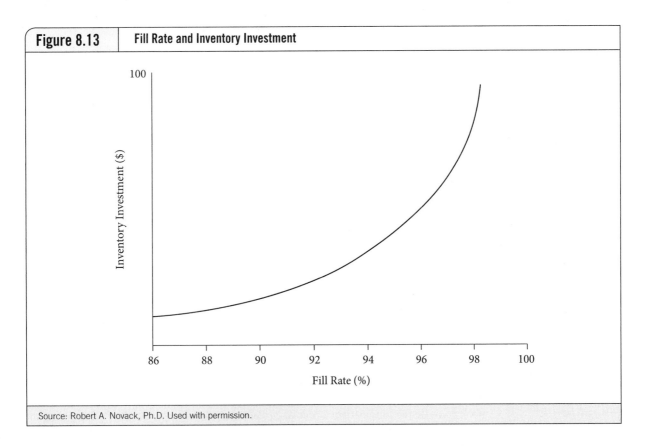

Source: Robert A. Novack, Ph.D. Used with permission.

---

would decrease because the increase in inventory costs would increase at a rate greater than that of additional revenues. So, it is important to understand the relationship between costs and revenues when determining fill rate goals.

8-7-2 Financial Impact

Calculating the financial impact of fill rates will be introduced in Chapter 13. However, it is important to offer another example of the financial impacts of order fill on a seller's firm. Assume that a seller has the following order profile:

- 100 units per order (average)
- 25,000 orders per year
- Pretax profit per unit is $100
- Pretax profit per order is $10,000
- Invoice deduction per order is $250
- Percentage of incomplete orders back-ordered is 70%
- Back order costs per order: administrative = $25.00; rehandling = $50.00; redelivery = $100.00
- Percentage of incomplete orders cancelled is 30%

Assume that the seller's current order fill rate is 80 percent, meaning that 80 percent of all orders received are filled completely. The calculation for lost cash flow is as follows:

$$\text{Cash Flow Lost} = (\text{Number of Incomplete Orders Back-Ordered} \times \text{Back Order Cost per Order}) + (\text{Number of Incomplete Orders Cancelled} \times \text{Lost Pretax Profit per Order}) + (\text{Number of Incomplete Back-Ordered} \times \text{Invoice Deduction per Order})$$

This would result in the following calculation:

$$\text{Cash Flow Lost} = [(20\% \times 25{,}000 \times 70\%) \times \$175] + [(20\% \times 25{,}000 \times 30\%) \times \$10{,}000] + [(20\% \times 25{,}000 \times 70\%) \times \$250] = \$16{,}487{,}500$$

Assume that the seller is able to improve its order fill rate to 85 percent. The new cash flow lost calculation would be as follows:

$$\text{Cash Flow Lost} = [(15\% \times 25{,}000 \times 70\%) \times \$175] + [(15\% \times 25{,}000 \times 30\%) \times \$10{,}000] + [(15\% \times 25{,}000 \times 70\%) \times \$250] = \$12{,}365{,}625$$

The result of improving the order fill rate by 5 percent results in a cash flow lost avoidance of $4,121,875. In other words, a 5 percent improvement in order fill results in a 25 percent improvement in cash flow. Obviously, increasing the order fill rate might require some type of investment in inventories and/or technology. So a strategic profit model calculation would be required to determine the change in ROI as a result of the improvement in order fill rate.

The next step would require the seller to determine the break-even point between order fill rates and inventory costs as shown in Figure 8.13. Assume that the stockout costs identified in this example (back order costs per order of $175, cancelled order cost of $10,000, and invoice deduction cost per order of $250) are inclusive of all stockout costs. In other words, no other stockout costs are incurred. Assume that the most minimal service level (product availability) of 50 percent requires an inventory investment of $5 million. Also assume that the seller has calculated approximate inventory investments for various service levels. This can be seen in Table 8.7. Also seen in this table is the resulting cash flow lost for service levels between 50 percent and 99 percent (the assumption here is that a 100 percent service level is not possible in the long run). These cash flow calculations were made using the numbers from the previous paragraph. Figure 8.14 shows the results of plotting the cash flow lost and inventory investment figures for each service level. As can be seen, the break-even point is at a service level of approximately 83 percent with a resulting inventory

Table 8.7	Cash Flow Lost and Inventory Investment	
SERVICE LEVEL	CASH FLOW LOST	INVENTORY
50%	$41,218,750	$ 5,000,000
60	32,975,000	6,250,000
70	24,731,250	8,750,000
80	16,487,500	12,500,000
90	8,243,750	17,500,000
95	4,121,875	23,750,000
99	824,375	31,250,000

Source: Robert A. Novack, Ph.D. Used with permission.

Figure 8.14	Cash Flow Lost/Inventory Investment Tradeoff

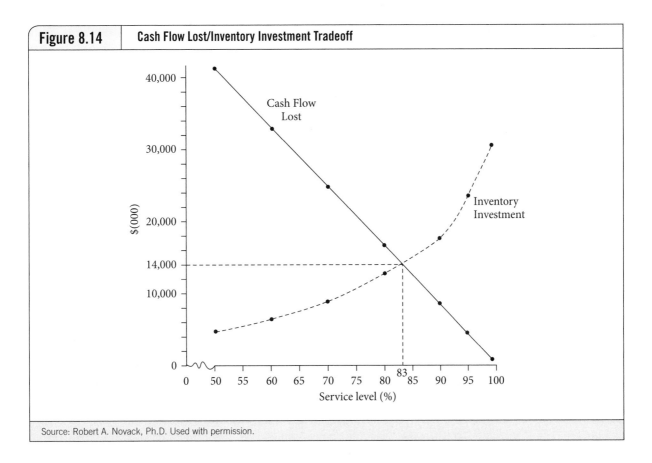

Source: Robert A. Novack, Ph.D. Used with permission.

investment of $14 million. At an 83 percent service level, the cash flow lost is $14,014,375. This figure suggests that the seller should invest no more than $14 million in inventory to provide service to the customer. Investments above this amount would result in decreasing returns in the form of lost cash flow avoided. This is a very simple example and is used to show the basic tradeoffs between cost and service. Obviously, additional factors must be taken into consideration when setting service levels. However, it is important to understand every service level and its associated costs and benefits.

8-7-3 Order Cycle Time

As previously discussed, order cycle time is the time that elapses from when a buyer places an order with a seller until the buyer receives the order. The absolute length and reliability of order cycle time influences both seller and buyer inventories and will have resulting impacts on both revenues and profits for both organizations. Normally, the shorter the order cycle time is, the more inventory that must be held by the seller and the less inventory that must be held by the buyer, and vice versa. For example, assume that an appliance retailer maintains floor models of various washing machines in its stores with no additional inventory for consumer pickup or delivery. In a normal situation, a consumer will decide which model of washing machine to buy and place an order with the store. The store will give the consumer an expected delivery date for the appliance. If consumers demand rapid delivery (e.g., one to two days), then the retailer will need to hold demand inventory in its own distribution network. If the consumer is not sensitive to delivery times and allows the retailer to dictate terms (e.g., a seven-day or more delivery window), the retailer might not have to carry any demand inventory in its network and could rely on the manufacturer to absorb the inventory. In fact, given enough lead time, the manufacturer might not have to carry any inventory if it can produce the appliance for delivery within the stated service window. In this example, a short order cycle time results in additional inventories for the retailer and vice versa. Hypothetically, it might be stated that order cycle times do not eliminate inventories from the supply chain but rather shift them from one supply chain member to the next.

8-7-3-1 Metrics

As previously mentioned, order cycle time, or lead time, includes all activities and related time from when an order is placed by a buyer until the order is received by the buyer. This definition can be viewed as the buyer's perception of lead time because this time ends when the buyer receives the ordered goods. A seller might look at lead time from the perspective of order-to-cash cycle time. This definition of lead time for the seller is important because the receipt of payment for the shipment ends this process for the seller.

Another, often overlooked, definition of order cycle time is **customer wait time (CWT)**. Used in both the private and public sectors, CWT includes not only order cycle time but also maintenance time. CWT is a popular metric when a customer needs a vehicle repaired. CWT is basically the time that elapses from when a vehicle breaks down until it is ready to be used again. Figure 8.15 is an example of what CWT might look like. CWT can be used

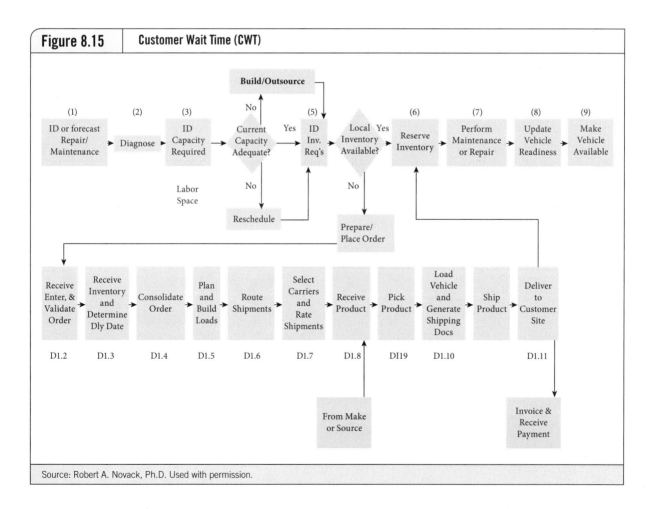

Figure 8.15 | **Customer Wait Time (CWT)**

Source: Robert A. Novack, Ph.D. Used with permission.

for two types of vehicle repair. First, it can be used to measure the time needed for scheduled maintenance such as an oil change. Second, it can be used to measure the time needed for unscheduled maintenance such as repairs related to a vehicle breakdown. The process shown on top in Figure 8.15 is for maintenance; the bottom process is the order cycle time needed to get parts delivered to be able to conduct the maintenance. (This is Process D1 of the SCOR model, introduced earlier.) Thus, order cycle time can be measured in different ways depending on the perspective of who is providing the measurement.

8-7-3-2 Financial Impact

Order cycle time can also have an impact on a buyer's or seller's financial position, depending on who owns the inventories in the supply chain. Inventory costs have an impact on both the balance sheet and income statement. Balance sheet impacts reflect ownership of inventory as an asset and liability; income statement impacts reflect the cost of holding inventory as an expense and therefore a reduction in cash flow. This discussion will focus on the income statement impact. Order cycle time influences two types of inventory: demand, or cycle, stock and safety stock. An example is appropriate here. From the data presented below, assume that a buyer and a seller have a current relationship with the stated performance levels and the seller is proposing a shorter, more reliable order cycle time.

	CURRENT	PROPOSED
Average order cycle time	10 days	5 days
Standard deviation of OCT	3 days	1 day
Demand per day (units)	1,377	1,377
Service level	97.7%	97.7%

Also assume that the delivered cost of each unit to the buyer costs the seller $449 and the inventory carrying cost (to be discussed in more detail in the next chapter) is 28 percent. The proposed order cycle time offers not only a reduced absolute length (10 days to 5 days) but also an improved reliability (reduction in standard deviation from 3 days to 1 day). So two inventory cost reduction calculations are necessary. The first calculation will look at the effects of a reduced standard deviation of order cycle time on safety stocks. The formula for this calculation is as follows:

$$\text{Safety Stock} = \{\text{Demand per Day} \times [\text{OCT} + (z \times \text{Standard Deviation of OCT})]\} - (\text{Demand per Day} \times \text{OCT})$$

This formula focuses on safety stocks since the amount of demand stock is included in the first part of the formula (Demand per Day × OCT) and is subtracted out in the second part of the formula. The z is the z-transformation for the required service level. In this case, the service level of 97.7 percent requires a z-transformation of two standard deviations to capture 97.7 percent of all observations under the normal distribution. To calculate the required safety stock levels between the buyer and the seller under the current order cycle time, the calculation is as follows:

$$\text{Current Safety Stock} = \{1,377 \times [10 + (2 \times 3)]\} - (1,377 \times 10)$$
$$= (1,377 \times 16) - 13,770$$
$$= 8,262 \text{ units}$$

This means that 8,262 units of safety stock need to be held, normally, at the buyer's location to prevent stockouts 97.7 percent of the time. To determine the safety stock levels needed under the proposed order cycle time, the calculation is as follows:

$$\text{Proposed Safety Stock} = \{1,377 \times [5 + (2 \times 1)]\} - (1,377 \times 5)$$
$$= (1,377 \times 7) - 6,885$$
$$= 2,754 \text{ units}$$

The difference between the two order cycle times is a reduction in safety stock levels of 5,508 units. Given the delivered cost of $449 per unit and a 28 percent inventory carrying cost, the net reduction in safety stock cost is calculated as follows:

$$\text{Safety Stock Cost Reduction} = \text{Reduction in Safety Units} \times \text{Cost per Unit} \times \text{Inventory Carrying Cost Percentage}$$

The resulting calculation is as follows:

$$\text{Safety Stock Cost Reduction} = 5,508 \times \$449 \times 28\% = \$692,465.76$$

This has the impact of reducing the variable expense of holding safety stock inventory, thereby increasing the cash flow of the inventory owner (the buyer in this case) by almost $700,000.

A second calculation is needed to determine the impact of the reduction of absolute order cycle time on demand inventories. The formula here is quite simple:

$$\text{Demand Inventory Cost Reduction} = \text{Difference in Absolute OCT} \times \text{Demand per Day} \times \text{Cost per Unit} \times \text{Inventory Carrying Cost Percentage}$$

This results in the following calculation:

$$\text{Demand Inventory Cost Reduction} = 5 \text{ days} \times 1,377 \text{ units} \times \$449 \times 28\%$$
$$= \$865,582.20$$

Adding together the cost reductions (or in this case a possible cost avoidance) for both safety stock and demand stock results in an improvement in cash flow of $1,558,047.96. While this is a simple example, it highlights the dramatic effects of order cycle time on supply chain inventories and their associated costs. The financial impact will be felt by the party that owns the inventories.

8-7-4 Logistics Operations Responsiveness

The concept of **logistics operations responsiveness (LOR)** examines how well a seller can respond to a buyer's needs. This "response" can take two forms: (1) how well a seller can customize its service offerings to the unique requirements of a buyer or (2) how quickly a seller can respond to a sudden change in a buyer's demand pattern. In either case, LOR is a concept that involves value-adding activities that are above and beyond basic logistics services. As such, LOR does not have a specific, generalizable definition that can apply to all buyer-seller interactions. For example, Buyer A might define LOR with a seller as how well the seller can customize end-of-aisle display pallets for in-store delivery. Buyer B might define LOR with the same seller as how long it takes the seller to respond to a rapid increase in demand. As such, developing metrics for LOR will be based on both what to measure and the level of performance required.

8-7-4-1 Metrics

Usually, LOR metrics will measure performance above and beyond basic on-time delivery or order fill rates. Examples of LOR metrics can be found in Process D1 of the SCOR model (see again Figure 8.11) under agility. Three metrics are involved: (1) upside deliver adaptability, (2) downside deliver adaptability, and (3) upside deliver flexibility. These metrics address how well the seller can adapt its deliver capabilities in a situation where buyer demand fluctuates either up or down. Corresponding metrics for manufacturing could also be identified as (1) upside make adaptability, (2) downside make adaptability, and (3) upside make flexibility.

Another dimension of LOR metrics is one that addresses a seller's ability to customize a product or its packaging. In the consumer-packaged goods (CPG) industry, manufacturers routinely offer special packaging of products through the use of co-packers. So a metric that could be used to address customization might be one that measures the time it takes the seller to offer a new package for sale in the retailers' stores. Metrics for LOR, then, address both flexibility/adaptability of process and customization of product/service.

8-7-4-2 Financial Impact

An excellent example of measuring the financial impacts of LOR activities was first identified and used by Procter & Gamble (P&G) during its implementation of the efficient consumer response (ECR) initiative in the grocery industry.[6] P&G developed a menu of value-adding activities that it was willing to offer to its customers in an attempt to customize its products/services to meet the unique needs of customers. One of these customized products was store-built pallets. P&G was willing to build "rainbow" (multiple-product) pallets for its grocery customers that would flow through, or cross-dock, the customer's distribution center and be delivered directly to a store where they could be taken onto the store floor where shelves could be restocked. This would save the customer money by eliminating touches and inventory. Building these pallets would require an investment from P&G. Table 8.8 is an example of the analysis that P&G undertook to determine the savings to the customer as a result of this cross-docking activity. In this table, it can be seen that the customer would incur a one-time savings of $21,747.50 as a result of this cross-docking initiative. So the financial impact of this LOR activity to the customer is evident. But what about savings for P&G? P&G would partner with the customer to determine a "reinvestment ratio," which is the percentage of the customer's savings that would be reinvested in P&G products. This reinvestment would take one of two forms: (1) buy more P&G products, or (2) lower the price to the consumer on P&G products. For example, assume that in the case of the cross-docked pallets, the reinvestment ratio is 40 percent and the cost to P&G for building the pallets is $15,000. The reinvestment amount would be $8,699 for the customer and assume that the customer will reinvest that amount by buying more P&G products. A simple ROI calculation would show that the return for the $15,000 made by P&G would be approximately 58 percent ($8,699/$15,000). So, the customer saves money and P&G revenues increase. In this case, LOR activities require an investment by the seller to create a savings for the buyer. However, both parties enjoy a favorable financial impact from this LOR activity.

Table 8.8	Logistics Operations Responsiveness Financial Impact		
PROCTER & GAMBLE CROSS-DOCK ANALYSIS SAMPLE CUSTOMER			
Base Service: Normal Warehouse Delivery			
Option Service: Cross-Dock Delivery			
Variables in Calculation	Base	Option	Change
A: Event Cases	50,000	50,000	0
B: Daily Customer Sales A/7	$7,142.90	$7,142.90	0
C: Days in Main Warehouse	20	11	9
D: Days in Outside Warehouse	0	0	0
E: Event WHSE Inventory Cases	50,000	50,000	0
F: Cases per Unit Load	100	100	0
G: Unit Loads in Inventory E/F	500	500	0
H: Net Days Credit	10	10	0
I: Transit Time in Days	2	2	0
J: Days Inventory Paid C+D+I–H	12	3	9
Acquisition Cost			
Net Acquisition Cost/case	$50.00	$50.00	$0.00
× Event Volume	50,000	50,000	0
= Event Net Acquisition Costs	$2,500,000	$2,500,000	$0
Main Warehouse Costs			
Handling Cost/case	$0.270	$0.120	$0.150
+ Occupancy Cost/case	$0.300	$0.200	$0.100
= Total Cost/case	$0.570	$0.320	$0.250
× Event Volume	50,000	50,000	0
= Event Main Warehouse Cost	$28,500	$16,000	$12,500
Outside Warehouse Costs	$0	$0	$0
Interest on Inventory			
Event WHSE Inventory Cases	50,000	50,000	0
× Net Acquisition Cost/case	$50.00	$50.00	$0
× Daily Interest Rate	.0411%	.0411%	.0411%
× Days of Inventory Paid (J)	12	3	9
= Event Interest on Inventory	$12,330	$3,082.50	$9,247.50
Total Costs			

Table 8.8	Continued		
Net Acquisition Costs	$2,500,000	$2,500,000	$0
+ Main Warehouse Costs	$28,500	$16,000	$12,500
+ Outside Warehouse Costs	$0	$0	$0
+ Interest on Inventory Costs	$12,330	$3,082.50	$9,247.50
= Total Event Costs of Saving	$2,540,830	$2,519,082.50	$21,747.50

All numbers are disguised.

Source: *Creating Logistics Value: Themes for the Future* (Oak Brook, IL: Council of Logistics Management, 1995): 153. Reproduced with permission of Council of Supply Chain Management Professionals.

8-7-5 Logistics System Information

Logistics system information (LSI) is critical to the logistics and order management processes. It underlies an organization's ability to provide quality product availability, order cycle time, logistics operations responsiveness, and postsale logistics support. Timely and accurate information can reduce inventories in the supply chain and improve cash flow to all supply chain partners. For example, improving forecast accuracy by using point-of-sale data could reduce safety stocks, improve product availability, and increase manufacturing efficiency. Today's technology allows for the accurate capture (barcodes, RFID tags) and transmission (radio frequency, EDI, Internet) of data among trading partners. The challenge is for organizations to determine how they are going to use these data to improve operations.

The beginning of this chapter identified three types of information that must be captured and shared to execute the order management process: (1) pretransaction information, which includes all information that is needed by the buyer and seller before the order is placed; (2) transaction information, which includes all information that is required to execute the order; and (3) posttransaction information, which includes all information that is needed after the order is delivered. An example of the types of information needed for each category to execute a transportation move can be seen in Table 8.9. All three parties involved in a transportation move need information across all three categories. What is also important here is that the information must be timely and accurate. Pretransaction information is needed before transaction information. Another way to think about these three categories of information might be that pretransaction information is used for planning, transaction information is used for execution, and posttransaction information is used for evaluation. So LSI is critical to successful order management and customer service.

8-7-5-1 Metrics

Most metrics involved with LSI address how accurate and timely the data are to allow a decision to be made or an activity to be performed. For example, forecast accuracy is the result of accurate data on past consumption as well as on good predictions on future consumption. Another example would be inventory accuracy. The accuracy of the inventory counts in a distribution center is the result of capturing consumption data from that facility

Table 8.9	Information Needed to Manage the Transportation Process		
	INFORMATION USER		
TRANSPORTATION ACTIVITY	SHIPPER	CARRIER	RECEIVER
Pretransaction	P.O. Information Forecasts Equipment Availability	BOL Information Forecasts Pickup/Delivery Time	Advance Advance Ship Notice
Transaction	Shipment Status	Shipment Status	Shipment Status
Posttransaction	Freight Bill Carrier Performance Proof of Delivery Claim Information	Payment Claim Information	Carrier Performance Proof of Delivery Claim Information

Source: Robert A. Novack, Ph.D. Used with permission.

in an accurate and timely manner. Data integrity is another metric that can be used to measure the quality of outputs from an LSI. Data integrity is a measure of the quality/accuracy of *inputs* to an LSI. Finally, EDI compliance is used by many organizations to measure how well their trading partners are complying with EDI standards when sharing data.

8-7-5-2 Financial Impact

As previously mentioned, LSI is usually not directly measured. What is measured are the results of how an organization uses the information generated by an LSI. Similarly, the financial impacts of an LSI are usually not measured but its results are. An actual example involved a computer manufacturer that had suppliers and customers all around the world. Most component shipments to their plants and finished goods shipments from their distribution centers were completed using air freight. Because of the high value of this manufacturer's finished products, their global customers required a proof of delivery (POD) to begin processing the invoice. The old procedure for generating and delivering the POD was very manual, involving the delivering ground carrier, the air freight company, and the air freight forwarder. This process resulted in an average order-to-cash cycle of 50 days for the manufacturer. The manufacturer analyzed an investment in an electronic global freight tracking system that would use barcodes and EDI for shipment status and well as the generation of electronic advance shipment notices (ASNs) and PODs. Using this new system, the manufacturer could send a POD electronically to a customer, resulting in a reduction of 20 days in the order-to-cash cycle. The new system would cost approximately $1 million to purchase and install. Multiple factors were taken into consideration by the manufacturer when analyzing the investment in this new tracking system.

This example will highlight the analysis performed on using information to reduce the order-to-cash cycle. Three months of shipment data over three global trade lanes were used as the basis for the analysis. Obviously, all numbers used here are disguised. Assume that the average invoice value for each shipment during this period was $648,000. Also assume that the cost of capital for the manufacturer was 10 percent. The calculation used to measure the result on cash flow for decreasing the order-to-cash cycle was as follows:

$$\text{Cash Flow Increase} = \text{Invoice Value} \times (\text{Cost of Captial} / 365) \times \text{Difference in Days in the order-to-Cash Cycle}$$

Using the numbers above, a sample calculation is as follows:

$$\text{Cash Flow Increase} = \$648{,}000 \times (10\% / 365) \times 20 \text{ days}$$
$$= \$3{,}550.68 \text{ per order}$$

During the three-month time period, the manufacturer shipped 344 of these orders, resulting in a combined cash flow increase of $1,221,434. Because the customers began processing the invoice when the POD was received, receiving the POD 20 days sooner using the new system allowed the manufacturer, theoretically, to invest its money at 10 percent for 20 days longer, resulting in an improved cash flow. The ROI for the new system was obviously very favorable. So, while measuring the financial impact of an LSI is challenging, measuring the financial impacts of how it is used is not.

8-7-6 Postsale Logistics Support

Many organizations focus primarily on outbound logistics—getting the product to the customer. For some organizations, supporting a product after it is delivered is a competitive advantage. **Postsale logistics support (PLS)** can take two forms. First, PLS can be the management of product returns from the customer to the supplier. Organizations such as GENCO have established their core competencies on managing product returns for suppliers. The importance of this form of PLS was discovered too late by many Internet sites during the late 1990s. During the dot-com boom, many Web sites were just "front ends," delivering superior customer interfaces on the computer but having no "back end" or physical delivery capability. Their focus was on taking the order and passing it on to a manufacturer or distributor for delivery. What was not considered successfully was what to do for product returns. This was very evident for some Web sites during the Christmas season of 1999. Because these sites had no physical retail presence or physical distribution capability, consumers found it very difficult to return unwanted products. This proved disastrous for many Web sites. Amazon.com, started as a front end-only Web site, quickly discovered the importance of product returns as a competitive weapon. Today, Amazon.com has a physical distribution network not only to provide initial product delivery but also to allow for the efficient return of unwanted product.

The second form of PLS is product support through the delivery and installation of spare parts. This is critical in the very competitive heavy equipment industry as well as in the U.S. military. Firms such as Caterpillar, New Holland, and Ingersoll-Rand have developed core competencies in making spare parts available for their equipment to keep that equipment running while it is at a job site. For firms such as these, it has become increasingly difficult to compete solely on the quality of their heavy equipment. These pieces of machinery can cost thousands or millions of dollars to purchase and thousands more per hour if they are disabled. As such, the accurate and timely delivery of spare parts to dealers and job sites to keep these machines running has become a competitive advantage.

8-7-6-1 Metrics

For the most part, the PLS that manages product returns is measured by the ease with which a customer can return a product. A metric such as time to return a product to a seller is usually not important to a customer. Remember, a product return usually involves some level of dissatisfaction by a customer for a seller's product. So making it easy for a customer to return a product is a critical metric. Walmart, for example, allows a consumer to bring a product back to a store, drop it off at the customer service desk, and get a replacement product with no questions asked. Craftsman Tools allows a 100 percent refund policy at any

Sears store for its products. Web sites, such as Easton Sports, allow a customer to receive a replacement product (e.g., a baseball bat), repackage the return product in the replacement shipping package, and send the product back (usually by UPS or FedEx) to an Easton facility for disposition. All of these firms have made the returns process easy for the consumer, resulting in a competitive advantage.

Metrics for a PLS that manages spare parts are the same as those used for all products: order fill, inventory availability, order cycle time, and so on. These metrics are used to measure the performance of a manufacturer's ability to deliver a bulldozer as well as its ability to deliver a water pump for that bulldozer. So the metrics used to measure the performance of spare parts logistics are those usually found in all other industries providing outbound logistics for customers. However, because of the large stockout costs to the customer for a disabled piece of equipment, availability and time become even more critical for spare parts logistics.

8-7-6-2 Financial Impact

Of the two types of PLS, spare parts logistics provides an easier methodology for calculating financial impacts. As such, the example in this section will focus on spare parts logistics. Assume that a heavy equipment manufacturer knows that its product rebuy life cycle is five years; that is, customers usually will replace a piece of equipment after five years of use. Also assume that the customer bases the rebuy decision on both initial machine quality as well as on spare parts availability. The average revenue per machine for the manufacturer is $25,000, with a pretax profit of $5,000. The average support revenue (parts/labor) for each machine for the manufacturer is $2,000 per year, with a pretax profit of $800 per year. Assume that the manufacturer sells 5,000 machines per year. The current level of spare parts support is 70 percent (the part is available 70 percent of the time). The manufacturer also knows that 80 percent of the time when a spare part is not available, a customer will not switch brands when the rebuy decision is made and 20 percent of the time the customer will buy another brand. When a spare part is not available, the expediting costs per machine per year are $1,000 for the manufacturer. The calculation to determine the spare part service cost is as follows:

$$\text{Service Cost} = \text{Penalty Cost} + \text{Lost Purchase Margin} + \text{Lost Support Margin}$$

As in the previous example examining the cost of not filling an order, not having spare parts inventory available when a customer wants it has two components: (1) a penalty, or expediting cost and (2) a lost profit cost. At a 70 percent service level, spare parts were not available for 1,500 machines (30% × 5,000 machines). For those customers who would still rebuy from the manufacturer, the manufacturer would incur an expediting cost of $1,000 per year of machine life (five years) for each of the 1,500 machines. For those customers who switch to another manufacturer because of the lack of spare part support, the manufacturer would lose the initial purchase pretax profit on those machines ($5,000) and the support pretax profit on those machines ($800 per year for five years). At a 70 percent service level, then, the calculation would be as follows:

70 percent service level

$$\text{Service Cost} = (80\% \times 1{,}500 \text{ units} \times \$1{,}000 \times 5 \text{ years}) + (20\% \times 1{,}500 \text{ units} \times \$5{,}000) + (20\% \times 1{,}500 \text{ units} \times \$800 \times 5 \text{ years}) = \$8{,}700\,000$$

At a 70 percent service level, then, the manufacturer would incur an expediting cost of $6,000,000, a lost initial pretax profit of $1,500,000, plus a lost support pretax profit of $1,200,000.

Assume that the manufacturer was able to increase spare parts availability to 85 percent. The resulting calculation would be as follows (remember, now only 750 machines will not have spare parts available):

85 percent service level

$$\text{Service Cost} = (80\% \times 750 \text{ units} \times \$1,000 \times 5 \text{ years}) + (20\% \times 750 \text{ units} \times \$5,000) + (20\% \times 750 \text{ units} \times \$800 \times 5 \text{ years})$$
$$= \$4,350,000$$

On the Line

After-Sales Service: The Forgotten Supply Chain

Today's digitally empowered customers are just as demanding about after-sales service as they are about the products and services they buy. While customer expectations for after-sales service are growing, surveys consistently find that today's customers are mostly disappointed and frustrated with the customer service they receive.

In fact, two-thirds of respondents to a recent Accenture survey called *The Global Consumer Pulse Research (GCPR) Initiative* said that, within the last year, they switched providers due to poor service. Among that group, more than 80 percent cited broken promises as the reason.

In another survey conducted by Accenture, 43 percent of interviewees observed that, in the previous 12 months, at least one company they dealt with "reneged on a service-related promise." The implications are clear: Many companies aren't providing the quality of service and support that today's more demanding customers expect.

Results from the GCPR survey further revealed that, although call centers are the channel customers use most for service and support, only about 50% of callers are satisfied with their call-center experiences. In turn, companies are falling short in the precise service and support area customers turn to most.

Why are companies finding it so difficult to offer after-sales service that can keep such customers happy? The reason is partly historical. Often called the "forgotten supply chain," service operations tend to suffer from understaffing and underinvestment. More fundamentally, traditional service and support models are still heavily dependent on the availability of human interface—call center personnel or field technicians—to respond to customer requests. This hinders the ability to scale up and meet the digital customers' service expectations.

Traditional service models are also often tied to departmental organizations with their own sets of rules having little or nothing to do with customers' schedules and preferences. With this, front-end customer service organizations and back-end service operations are often siloed service functions that seriously compromise execution.

Many companies lose track of the customer once he or she leaves their call center. The vast majority of call centers also use measures and incentives designed to get a customer off the phone as quickly as possible, for example, average handle time, which has absolutely nothing to do with customer issue resolution.

Similarly, in-home service execution, resource planning (parts, labor), and field execution (schedule, dispatch, routing) remain almost totally unintegrated. All too often, technicians show up without the right part, can't fix the particular equipment, or miss the appointment window altogether.

To get in sync with the digital customer, service operations must build "digital-relevant" speed and agility into its DNA. This is the only way companies can deliver after-sales service experiences that leave a mark on the customers' minds and earn their loyalty.

Source: Adapted from Mark Pearson, *Logistics Management,* March 2015, pp. 20–21. Reprinted with permission of Peerless Media, LLC.

So, a 15 percent increase in spare parts availability would improve the pretax cash flow to the manufacturer by $4,350,000, or a 50 percent increase in cash flow. While this is a simple example, it shows that the lack of spare parts, as in the lack of original product for order fill rates, can have a significant impact on an organization's cash flow. Also, remember that the investment needed by the manufacturer to provide this increase in spare parts availability must be taken into consideration in light of the resulting improvement in cash flow to determine an ROI.

8-8 Service Recovery[7]

No matter how well an organization plans to provide excellent service, mistakes will occur. Even in a Six Sigma statistical environment, 100 percent performance will not happen. High performance organizations today realize this and are using the concept of *service recovery*. Basically, service recovery requires an organization to realize that mistakes will occur and to have plans in place to fix them. Although many ways for an organization to practice service recovery are available, a few warrant discussion here.

A major portion of this chapter has focused on *measuring the costs* of poor service. Not being able to fill an order completely or delivering an order late can result in back orders, lost sales, and/or lost revenue for the selling firm. Understanding the costs of poor service is critical for an organization because it dictates investment in resources, such as inventories. If there is no cost associated with poor service, then little or no additional investment is necessary. However, this is hardly ever the case. Most organizations will suffer financially for not meeting customer expectations.

Another aspect of service recovery is *anticipating the needs for recovery*. In any organization, certain areas of operations will present higher than normal opportunities for failures to occur. These areas need to be identified, and corrective action plans need to be developed *before* the error occurs. A good example of this can be seen in the passenger airline industry. Delayed and/or cancelled flights leave many passengers stranded at airports throughout the United States every day. Airlines have developed plans to accommodate these passengers either through rebooking on another flight or through providing a hotel room until the next flight is available. In this chapter, the concept of the order-to-cash cycle was introduced through SCOR model D1. This model provides an excellent framework for an organization to identify where service failures might occur and to develop plans to mitigate those failures, subject to the cost of failure.

Another principle of service recovery requires an organization to *act fast*. The longer a dissatisfied customer waits for a problem to be solved, the higher the level of dissatisfaction will grow. Being able to fix service failures quickly relies on the ability of the organization to know where a failure is likely to occur and have plans in place to fix them. Included in this concept is the need to communicate with the dissatisfied customer as to how and when the failure will be fixed. For example, a seller has determined that it does not have adequate inventory to fill a buyer's order. This is a common occurrence for which a seller needs to have alternative plans because of the potential high stockout costs. In a service recovery mode, the seller notifies the buyer immediately (usually by phone or e-mail) that current inventory levels are not adequate but additional inventory will become available within, say, two days to fill the order completely. With this action, the seller has acted fast to identify the problem as well as taken steps to communicate with the buyer the actions that will be taken to remedy the situation.

Finally, service recovery requires that *employees be trained and empowered* to be able to identify potential service failure areas and take actions to satisfy the customer. Remember, however, that this must be done considering the cost of a service failure. Frontline employees, usually customer service representatives, need to understand the cost of failure to the entire organization, must be given the appropriate tools for addressing the failure, and must be given a sense of ownership of the failure and the resulting loss of customer satisfaction. Nothing can be more frustrating to a dissatisfied customer than to wait for resolution while recovery actions are being discussed through multiple echelons of an organization's management structure. Granted, some failures will be so large as to require upper management intervention. However, customer contact personnel need to be given the authority to handle service failures quickly and appropriately.

SUMMARY

- Order management and customer service are not mutually exclusive; there is a direct and critical relationship between these two concepts.
- There are two distinct, yet related, aspects of order management: influencing the customer's order and executing the customer's order.
- Customer relationship management (CRM) is a concept being used today by organizations to help them better understand their customers' requirements and understand how these requirements integrate back into their internal operations processes.
- Activity-based costing (ABC) is being used today to help organizations develop customer profitability profiles that allow for customer segmentation strategies.
- Order management, or order execution, is the interface between buyers and sellers in the market and directly influences customer service.
- Order management can be measured in various ways. Traditionally, however, buyers will assess the effectiveness of order management using order cycle time and dependability as the metric, while sellers will use the order-to-cash cycle as their metric.
- Customer service is considered the interface between logistics and marketing in seller organizations.
- Customer service may be defined in three ways: (1) as an activity, (2) as a set of performance metrics, and (3) as a philosophy.
- The major elements of customer service are time, dependability, communications, and convenience.
- Stockout costs can be calculated as back order costs, the cost of lost sales, and/or the cost of a lost customer.
- The five outputs from order management that influence customer service, customer satisfaction, and profitability are (1) product availability, (2) order cycle time, (3) logistics operations responsiveness, (4) logistics system information, and (5) postsale logistics support.
- The concept of service recovery is being used by organizations today to help identify service failure areas in their order management process and to develop plans to address them quickly and accurately.

STUDY QUESTIONS

1. Explain how order management and customer service are related.

2. Describe the two approaches to order management. How are they different? How are they related?

3. What is the role of activity-based costing in customer relationship management? In customer segmentation?

4. Compare and contrast the concepts of order-to-cash cycle time and order cycle time.

5. Explain the impacts of order cycle time length and variability on both buyers and sellers.

6. Customer service is often viewed as the primary interface between logistics and marketing. Discuss the nature of this interface and how it might be changing.

7. Organizations can have three levels of involvement with respect to customer service. What are these, and what is the importance of each?

8. Explain the relationship between customer service levels and the costs associated with providing those service levels.

9. Discuss the nature and importance of the four logistics-related elements of customer service.

10. Effective management of customer service requires measurement. Discuss the nature of performance measurement in the customer service area.

11. What events might occur when an organization is out of stock of a needed product? How might the cost of a stockout be calculated?

12. Assume an organization's current service level on order fill is as follows:

    Current order fill = 80%
    Number of orders per year = 5,000
    Percentage of unfilled orders back-ordered = 70%
    Percentage of unfilled orders cancelled = 30%
    Back order costs per order = $150
    Lost pretax profit per cancelled order = $12,500

    a. What is the lost cash flow to the seller at this 80 percent service level?
    b. What would be the resulting increase in cash flow if the seller improved order fill to 92 percent?
    c. If the seller invested $2 million to produce this increased service level, would the investment be justified financially?

NOTES

1. Bernard J. LaLonde, "Customer Service," in *The Distribution Handbook* (New York: Free Press, 1985), 243.

2. The steps discussed in the process were adapted from a real CRM implementation by a large, global manufacturer during 2005–2006.

3. Norm Raffish and Peter B. Turney, "Glossary of Activity-Based Management," *Journal of Cost Management*, *5*, No. 3 (1991): 53–64.

4. Philip Kotler, *Marketing Management,* 5th ed. (Englewood Cliffs, NJ: Prentice Hall, 1990), 225–226.

5. For a further discussion of the perfect order concept, see Robert A. Novack and Douglas J. Thomas, "The Challenges of Implementing the Perfect Order Concept," *Transportation Journal, 43*, No. 1 (Winter 2004): 5–16.

6. For a full discussion of this analysis, see Robert A. Novack, C. John Langley, Jr., and Lloyd M. Rinehart, *Creating Logistics Value: Themes for the Future* (Oak Brook, IL: Council of Logistics Management, 1995), 148–153.

7. This discussion is adapted from Christopher W. L. Hart, James L. Heskett, and W. Earl Sasser, Jr., "The Profitable Art of Service Recovery," *Harvard Business Review* (July–August 1990): 148–154.

CASE 8.1

Telco Corporation

Telco Corporation (Telco) is a $25 billion global manufacturer of industrial products, with its global headquarters located in Bloomington, Indiana. Telco is comprised of six major divisions: (1) electrical generators, (2) turbines, (3) industrial air conditioners, (4) machine tools (e.g., drill presses and lathes), (5) fork trucks and skid loaders, and (6) air compressors. Each division is managed as a separate profit center, and each has its own sales force, manufacturing facilities, and logistics network. Telco has approximately 15,000 customers worldwide, with 40 percent buying from more than one Telco division.

At a recent operating council meeting, Jean Beierlein, CFO, was lamenting to the other council members the fact that pretax profits were falling even though revenues were growing. "We're in a perplexing situation. The stock market likes us because revenues are growing. However, I don't see how we are going to make our dividend objectives this year because our operating profits are decreasing from last quarter. Our service levels to customers are at an all-time high and our sales forces are consistently meeting their revenue objectives."

Troy Landry, vice president of supply chain for the compressor division, added his observation on this dilemma. "I'll tell you what the problem is. We are constantly exceeding our logistics budget to provide this outstanding service for customers who shouldn't be getting it. Sales is constantly promising expedited delivery or special production runs for customers who generate very little revenue for us. One of these customers, Byline Industries, only spends $1 million per year with us and yet our logistics costs as a percent of revenue for them is 25 percent. Compare this with our average logistics costs as a percent of revenue across our customer base of 11 percent and you can see where the problem lies." Tom Novack, president of the generator division, disagreed with Troy's observation of Byline. "Wait a minute, Troy. Byline is one of my best customers. They buy 15 percent of my revenue at a logistics cost of 8 percent. We need to make sure they are happy."

Listening to this exchange was the new Telco president, Nick Martin, who recently joined Telco after spending 15 years as COO of a global agricultural products manufacturer. This problem was not new to Nick. His former employer was also structured across business lines with common customers across the globe and found that a similar service strategy for all customers was not a viable alternative. Nick added, "I've seen this before. The problem is that we are treating all customers alike and we are not taking into consideration those customers who buy from more than one division. Before the meeting, I asked Jean to run some profitability numbers across our customer base. The results are amazing. Thirty-three percent of all of our customers account for 71 percent of our operating profits. Another 27 percent account for approximately $100 million in losses. Obviously, we have some customers who are more profitable than others. We need to develop a strategy to segment our customers and offer each segment the suite of services they are willing to pay for."

"Wait a minute," exclaimed Chris Sills, vice president of corporate sales. "You're asking us to take some services away from our customers. Who is going to break the news? What about the sales commissions for my reps? This is not going to be received well by the customer base."

You have been hired as an expert on customer relationship management. Telco's current service offerings to its entire customer base include product quality, order fill rates, lead time, delivery time, payment terms, and customer service support. You have been asked to prepare a report outlining how Telco could adopt the CRM approach to its customers. Specifically, this report should address the following:

CASE QUESTIONS

1. How should Telco approach segmenting its customers? That is, on what basis (cost to service, profitability, etc.) should the customers be segmented?
2. How should Telco tailor its service offerings to each customer segment?
3. Should certain customers be asked to take their business elsewhere?
4. How should the revised service packages to each segment be introduced to that segment? By the sales force? Should all segments be done at the same time?
5. Each division has its own sales force, manufacturing facilities, and logistics network. As such, common customers (those who buy from more than one division) place separate orders with each division, receive multiple shipments, and receive multiple invoices. Would it make sense for Telco to organize around customer rather than around product? If so, how would this be done? What would the new organizational metrics look like?

CASE 8.2

Webers, Inc.

Webers is an omni-channel retailer with 250 stores throughout the United States and six distribution/fulfillment centers. Webers specializes in men's and women's clothing across numerous designers and styles. Previously, Webers had relatively no competition for its line of clothing and, as such, was focused more on its productivity rather than on service to its internet customers.

Under the current order management process, a consumer would place an order on-line with Webers and receive a notification that the order was received. The order management system (OMS) would then check the availability of inventory for the order. If inventory was not available, the consumer would receive a notice for a backorder. If inventory was available, the OMS would send the order to the warehouse management system (WMS) to be scheduled for picking. Orders were picked in the order in which they were received. Once picked, the WMS would send the order to the transportation management system (TMS) to be scheduled for shipment. Once shipped, the consumer would be sent a notice of ship date. Under this process, the consumer could not pick delivery times when ordering. Although this has a negative impact on Webers customer service, it allowed Webers to increase productivity in its fulfillment operations.

Under increasing pressure from competitors, Webers decided to now allow the consumer to choose delivery times, e.g., next-day, two-day, etc. This was going to have a major impact on how the three systems (OMS, WMS, TMS) operated and exchanged information to facilitate the order management process. While the consumer is ordering, inventory availability is checked in real-time. When the consumer chooses a delivery option, the OMS must communicate with the TMS to determine when the order needs to be tendered to the carrier at the fulfillment center to meet that delivery window. The TMS then communicates with the WMS to determine when the order needs to be picked.

CASE QUESTIONS

1. Create process maps for the "before" and "after" order management processes. Use Figure 8.15 as a guide. Start from when the consumer places the order and end when the shipment is made.
2. From these process maps, identify where the major changes to the order management process occur.
3. Develop a new set of metrics that Webers can use to measure the performance of the new process. Use Figure 8.11 as a guide.

Source: Robert A. Novack, Ph.D. Used with permission.

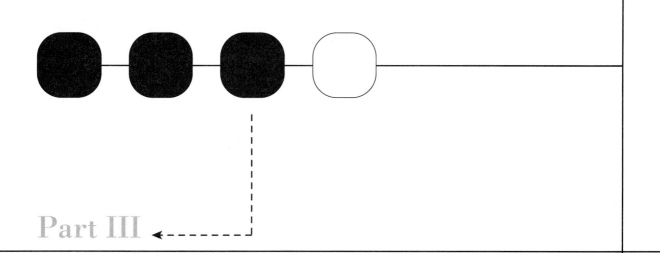

Part III

The first two segments of the book have laid the foundation for product to flow across the supply chain. Cohesive supply chain strategies and design, sourcing, production, and demand management make it possible to accept customer orders. Part III focuses on the fulfillment of those orders through cross-chain logistics processes. Appropriate inventory, distribution, and transportation management processes satisfy demand for raw materials, components, and finished goods. When executed as planned, logistics maximizes customer satisfaction while minimizing costs and supporting rapid order to cash cycles.

The effective management of inventories in the supply chain is one of the key factors for success in any organization. **Chapter 9** offers a comprehensive view of this important process. The chapter begins with a discussion of the economic and organizational importance of inventory and the reasons for carrying inventory. Next, the major types of inventory, their costs, and relationships to decision-making are covered. In-depth coverage of major inventory management approaches is also provided, with emphasis on economic order quantity (EOQ), just-in-time (JIT), materials requirements planning (MRP), distribution require-ments planning (DRP), and vendor-managed inventory (VMI). Finally, **Chapter 9** addresses how inventory can be classified and how inventory levels vary with changes in the number of stocking points. A chapter appendix offers four transportation-related adjustments to the basic EOQ approach

Decisions related to inventory volume and locations affect fulfill-ment operations and warehousing activities. **Chapter 10** focuses on the importance of distribution in meeting customer needs across the supply chain. The chapter opens with coverage of the strategic roles of distribution, particularly in an increasingly omni-channel world.

Important discussions of distribution-transportation-inventory tradeoffs are provided, as well as fulfillment strategy and methods. Next, primary fulfillment processes and support functions are detailed, along with the metrics used to evaluate performance. Finally, **Chapter 10** reveals the role of information technology in providing accurate, timely, and efficient fulfillment. A chapter appendix offers a primer on materials handling objectives, principles, and equipment.

After the distribution team has assembled the customer orders, they must be delivered to the designated location. **Chapter 11** discusses the role of the transportation system in linking geographically separated supply chain partners and facilities for the purpose of creating time and place utilities. The chapter opens with the role of transportation in an organization's supply chain design, strategic planning, and total cost management. Potential role inhibitors are also revealed. Primary chapter coverage is dedicated to the characteristics, costs, and relative capabilities the transportation modes. Next, important transportation planning and decision processes are addressed, followed by key aspects of transportation execution and control. The topics range from mode selection to carrier performance management. Finally, **Chapter 11** identifies technology resources that support transportation planning, execution, and analysis. Chapter appendices provide insights regarding transportation regulation and costing.

Chapter 9

MANAGING INVENTORY IN THE SUPPLY CHAIN

Learning Objectives

After reading this chapter, you should be able to do the following:

- Appreciate the role and importance of inventory in the economy.
- List the major reasons for carrying inventory.
- Discuss the major types of inventory, their costs, and their relationships to inventory decisions.
- Understand the fundamental differences among approaches to managing inventory.
- Describe the rationale and logic behind the economic order quantity (EOQ) approach to inventory decision making, and be able to solve some problems of a simple nature.
- Understand alternative approaches to managing inventory—just-in-time (JIT), materials requirement planning (MRP), distribution requirements planning (DRP), and vendor-managed inventory (VMI).
- Explain how inventory items can be classified.
- Know how inventory will vary as the number of stocking points change.
- Make needed adjustments to the basic EOQ approach to respond to several special types of applications.

Supply Chain Profile   *Inventory Management Requires an End-to-End Approach*

At the operational level, key logistics capabilities, including order management, inventory visibility, and inventory allocation, play an important role in the effective use of inventory. Assuming a simple, make-to-stock scenario, customers orders are received, inventory is allocated, and orders are fulfilled to arrive in full at the customer by the promised date.

However, in spite of diligent planning at the tactical level, inventory may still not be available at the right time, place, and quantity to achieve perfect order fulfillment. Having real-time visibility to inventory, whether in-transit or at stocking locations, helps to manage potential issues.

For example, knowing the position and estimated arrival time of an inventory replenishment shipment can enable expedited fulfillment of the customer order once inventory arrives. Alternatively, a replenishment order could be diverted while in transit from its original destination to a higher-priority location.

In the case of distributed order management (DOM), orders can be fulfilled from alternative stocking locations, which that could include a different distribution center, a vendor or even a retail store location, depending on the situation. A sophisticated technology, DOM leverages visibility across the extended supply chain network and business rules to determine how best to fulfill customer orders across multiple channels from multiple inventory sources.

Its embedded business rules consider inventory availability across stocking locations, fulfillment costs, and capacity constraints to make the appropriate fulfillment decisions. These business rules also help manage decisions regarding inventory allocation by customer segment, so the decisions are aligned with strategic priorities.

Ultimately, having real-time visibility to inventory and the means to fulfill orders from multiple nodes in the extended supply chain can help to reduce safety stock requirements across the network.

Source: Adapted from Jim Morton, Rodrigo Cambiaghi, and Nicole Radcliffe, *Logistics Management*, March 2015, p. 44. Reprinted with permission of Peerless Media, LLC.

9-1 Introduction

As discussed in Chapter 1, the effective management of inventories in the supply chain is one of the key factors for success in any organization. Inventory as an asset on the balance sheet and as a variable expense on the income statement has taken on greater importance as organizations attempt to more effectively manage assets and working capital. As discussed in Chapter 8, however, inventory takes on added importance because of its direct impact on service levels. As such, inventory management has taken a strategic position in many firms today.

Inventories also have an impact on return on investment (ROI) for an organization, which will be discussed as return on net worth in Chapter 13. ROI is an important financial metric from both internal and external perspectives. Reducing inventories usually causes a short-term improvement in ROI because it reduces assets and increases available working capital. Inventory increases have the opposite effect on assets and working capital. Important here is the fact that inventory consumes an organization's resources and is also responsible for generating revenues. Thus, decisions regarding inventories must take into consideration the tradeoffs between costs and service.

The ultimate challenge in managing inventories is balancing the supply of inventory with the demand for inventory. This was presented in Chapter 7. In other words, an organization ideally wants to have enough inventory to satisfy the demands of its customers for its products with no lost revenue because of stockouts. However, the organization does not want to have too much inventory on hand because it consumes valuable working capital. Balancing supply and demand is a constant challenge for organizations to master but is a necessity to compete in the marketplace.

This chapter will offer a comprehensive view of managing inventories in the supply chain. Special importance will be placed on discussing why inventory is important, the nature of inventory costs, and the various approaches to managing inventories. The next section will offer an overview of the importance of inventory in the U.S. economy.

9-2 Inventory in the U.S. Economy

The influence of information technology during the late 1990s and its impact on inventories was reflected in the U.S. economy's ability to grow dramatically while holding inflation in check. This exchange of "information for inventory" showed the impact that inventories have on our economy. With information technology advances escalating in the early twenty-first century, organizations are still implementing programs to take inventories out of the supply chain.

The results of this aggressive management of inventories can be seen in Table 9.1, which shows inventory investment as a percent of U.S. gross domestic product (GDP) from 1996 through 2014. As would be expected, the level or value of inventory increases with growth in the U.S. economy. However, the important question is whether total inventory in the economy grows at the same rate as GDP. Obviously, it is best for inventory to increase at a slower rate than GDP. This means that the economy is generating more revenue with less assets and working capital investment.

Table 9.1 shows that the nominal GDP grew by 135 percent in the time period between 1996 and 2014. Similarly, the value of business inventory increased by 101.3 percent during the same time period. However, inventory costs as a percent of GDP declined from 16.3 percent in 1996 to 14.3 percent in 2014. So, even though the absolute value of inventory increased during this time period, it decreased as a percent of GDP. This declining trend indicates that the economy is producing more revenue with less assets and working capital. While the trend is down, the year-to-year changes indicate the element of volatility faced by many organizations.

The focus of these data should be on the trend, which clearly indicates a relative decline in inventory value and inventory carrying cost as a percent of GDP—a positive metric for the economy and business organizations in general. Inventories represent a cost of doing business and are included in the prices of products and services. Reductions in inventory costs, especially if there is no decline in customer service, are beneficial to both buyers and sellers.

As discussed in Chapter 2, the major cost tradeoff in logistics is between transportation and inventory. That is, the faster and more reliable (and more expensive) the transportation, the less the cost of inventories. Like inventory costs, transportation costs as a percent of GDP declined during the 1990s. However, the cost of fuel today, coupled with capacity constraints in the transportation industry, has escalated the costs of transportation. The economics of this rapid rise in transportation costs have not yet been determined. However, it will be interesting to see if the traditional tradeoffs between transportation and inventory costs will remain the same in this new environment.

| | Table 9.1 | | Macro Inventory in Relation to U.S. Gross Domestic Product | | | |

YEAR	ALL VALUE BUSINESS INVENTORY ($ BILLION)	INVENTORY CARRYING RATE (PERCENT)	INVENTORY CARRYING COSTS ($ BILLION)	NOMINAL GDP ($ TRILLION)	INVENTORY CARRYING AS A PERCENT OF GDP	INVENTORY COSTS AS A PERCENT OF GDP
1996	$1,240	24.4	303	7.41	4.1	16.3
1997	1,280	24.5	314	8.33	3.8	15.4
1998	1,317	24.4	321	8.79	3.7	15.0
1999	1,381	24.1	333	9.35	3.6	14.8
2000	1,478	25.3	374	9.95	3.8	14.9
2001	1,403	22.8	320	10.29	3.1	13.6
2002	1,451	20.7	300	10.64	2.8	13.6
2003	1,508	20.1	304	11.14	2.7	13.5
2004	1,650	20.4	337	11.87	2.8	13.9
2005	1,782	22.3	397	12.64	3.1	14.1
2006	1,859	24.0	446	13.40	3.3	13.9
2007	2,015	24.1	485	14.06	3.4	14.3
2008	1,962	21.4	419	14.37	2.9	13.7
2009	1,865	19.3	359	14.12	2.5	13.2
2010	2,064	19.2	396	14.66	2.7	14.1
2011	2,301	19.1	440	15.52	2.8	14.8
2012	2,392	19.1	457	16.16	2.8	14.8
2013	2,444	19.1	466	16.77	2.8	14.6
2014	2,496	19.1	476	17.42	2.7	14.3

Source: *Freight Moves the Economy in 2014*, CSCMP's Annual State of Logistics Report, 20145. Reproduced with permission of Council of Supply Chain Management Professionals.

9-3 Inventory in the Firm: Rationale for Inventory

As indicated previously, inventory plays a dual role in organizations. Inventory impacts the cost of goods sold as well as supporting order fulfillment (customer service). Table 9.2 reports total logistics costs for the economy and shows that inventory carrying costs are on average about 33 percent of total logistics costs for organizations. Transportation costs comprise about 62.8 percent of all logistics costs.

Consumer packaged goods (CPG) firms and the wholesalers and retailers that are a part of their distribution channels face a special challenge in keeping inventories at acceptable levels because of the difficulty of forecasting demand and the increasing expectations from customers concerning product availability. Both of these factors are magnified by these firms increasing the complexity of their product offerings. For example, if Hershey forecasted aggregate demand for Kisses™ for the first quarter next year to be 1 million cases, it would have to break this number down by stock-keeping unit (SKU), packaging,

Table 9.2	Total Logistics Costs – 2014	
		$ BILLION
Carrying Costs—$2.496 Trillion All Business Inventory		
Interest		2
Taxes, Obsolescence, Depreciation, Insurance		331
Warehousing		143
	SUBTOTAL	476
Transportation Costs—Motor Carriers		
Truck—Intercity		486
Truck—Local		216
	SUBTOTAL	702
Transportation Costs—Other Carriers		
Railroads		80
Water (international 31, domestic 9)		40
Oil Pipelines		17
Air (international 12, domestic 16)		28
Forwarders		40
	SUBTOTAL	205
Shipper-Related Costs		10
Logistics Administration		56
	TOTAL LOGISTICS COST	1,449

Source: *Freight Moves the Economy in 2014*, CSCMP's Annual State of Logistics Report, 2014. Reproduced with permission of Council of Supply Chain Management Professionals.

geography, and so on. This could result in hundreds or thousands of SKUs that require some level of inventory and safety stock. Consumer preferences can change quickly, which makes managing inventory levels a special challenge.

To illustrate the cost side of the challenge, assume that Hershey expects to carry an average monthly inventory during the first quarter of the year of 250,000 cases of Kisses. If each case is valued at $25, the value of the inventory would be $6.25 million (250,000 cases × $25). If its cost of carrying inventory (to be explained later in this chapter) is 25 percent, its cost of carrying inventory during this period would be $1,562,500. If the average inventory increased to 350,000 cases, this would result in an additional $2.5 million of inventory cost. If the increase in inventory was not accompanied by an equal or greater increase in revenue, Hershey would face a reduction in pretax profit.

Hopefully, the point has been made that managing inventory is a critical factor for success in many organizations. Many organizations have responded to this challenge—as indicated by the macro data presented in the previous section—and have reduced inventory levels while maintaining appropriate customer service levels. Their ability to achieve the twin goals of lower inventory (efficiency) and acceptable customer service levels (effectiveness) is based on a number of factors discussed in this chapter. A good starting point is an understanding of why organizations usually have to carry inventories and the resulting tradeoffs and relationships.

9-2-1 Batching Economies or Cycle Stocks

Batching economies or **cycle stocks** usually arise from three sources—procurement, production, and transportation. Scale economies are often associated with all three, which can result in the accumulation of inventory that will not be used or sold immediately—which means some cycle stock or inventory will be used up or sold over some period of time.

In the procurement area, it is not unusual for a seller to have a schedule of prices that reflects the quantity purchased. In other words, larger purchased volumes result in lower prices per unit and vice versa. Purchase discounts are also prevalent for personal consumption items. For example, buying a package of 12 rolls of paper towels at Sam's Club would result in a lower price per roll than if the 12 rolls were bought separately. When the larger package is purchased, cycle stock is created. What is not consumed immediately will have to be stored. When organizations buy raw materials and supplies, particularly in our global economy, they are often offered price discounts for larger quantities. The tradeoff logic that was mentioned earlier suggests that the price discount savings have to be compared to the additional cost of carrying inventory. This is a relatively straightforward analysis, which is discussed later in this chapter. In spite of the framework available for analyzing discount tradeoffs, sometimes organizations just focus on the price savings and do not justify the discount against the additional inventory carrying cost.

A related discount situation occurs with transportation services. Transportation firms usually offer rate or price discounts for shipping larger quantities. In the motor carrier industry, a common example is the lower rate or price per pound for shipping truckload quantities versus less-than-truckload quantities. The motor carrier saves money in pick-up, handling, and delivery costs with the truckload shipment, and these are reflected in a lower rate or price to the shipper. The larger shipment quantities to justify the discount have the same effect as the purchase quantities—that is, cycle stocks. The tradeoff requirement is the same. Do the costs savings from the larger shipment offset the additional inventory carrying cost?

Note that purchase economies and transportation economies are complementary. That is, when organizations buy larger quantities of raw materials or supplies, they can ship larger quantities, which can result in transportation discounts. Therefore, they are frequently the recipients of two discounts for the same item purchased, which can make the tradeoff evaluation positive. One of the big challenges, discussed later in this chapter, is that many organizations might not calculate their carrying costs accurately.

The third batching economy is associated with production. Many organizations feel that their production costs per unit are substantially lower when they have long production runs of the same product. Long production runs decrease the number of changeovers to a production line but increase the amount of cycle stock that must be stored until sold. Traditionally, organizations rationalized long productions runs to lower unit costs without really evaluating the resulting inventory carrying costs, which can be high for finished goods. There is also a related concern about obsolescence of finished goods when high inventories are kept.

Most organizations have cycle stocks, even if they do not purchase products, because of the purchase of supplies. Obviously, cycle stocks can be beneficial as long as the appropriate analysis is done to justify the cost of the inventory.

9-2-2 Uncertainty and Safety Stocks

All organizations are faced with uncertainty. On the demand or customer side, there is usually uncertainty in how much customers will buy and when they will buy it. Forecasting demand (discussed in Chapter 7) is a common approach to resolving demand uncertainty, but it is never completely accurate. On the supply side, there might be uncertainty about obtaining what is needed from suppliers and how long it will take for the fulfillment of the order. Uncertainty can also arise from transportation providers in terms of receiving reliable delivery. The net result of uncertainty is usually the same: organizations accumulate safety stock to buffer themselves against stockouts. The challenge and analysis are different for safety stock than for cycle stock; safety stock is much more complex and challenging to manage because it is redundant inventory.

If a production line shuts down because of a supply shortage or a customer does not receive a delivery, problems will arise. Tradeoff analysis is appropriate and can be accomplished using the appropriate tools to assess the risk and measure the inventory cost. In addition, organizations today are taking a more proactive approach to reducing uncertainty by using the power of information to help reduce the need for safety stocks. A previous discussion noted that information can be used to replace inventory. There has literally been an information revolution because of the technology now available to transmit and receive timely and accurate information between trading partners. Collaboration in the sharing of information in some supply chains has yielded significant results in reducing inventories and improving service at the same time. Collaborative planning, forecasting, and replenishment (CPFR) is an excellent example of such an approach. Sophisticated barcodes, RFID tags, electronic data interchange (EDI), the Internet, and so on have enabled organizations to reduce uncertainty. However, it is not possible to eliminate uncertainty completely so analyses need to be performed to measure the tradeoffs.

Setting safety stock levels for an organization is both an art and a science. As with forecasting, setting safety stock levels assumes that the past will repeat itself in the future. If this assumption holds true, then setting safety stock levels is purely science. However, the future rarely replicates the past exactly. This is when setting safety stock levels becomes an art. And, as with forecasting, it is usually wrong. However, statistical techniques are available to represent the science of setting safety stock levels. This will be discussed in a later section in this chapter.

9-2-3 Time/In-Transit and Work-in-Process Stocks

The time associated with transportation (e.g., supplier to manufacturing plant) and with the manufacture or assembly of a complex product (e.g., automobile) means that even while goods are in motion, an inventory cost is associated with the time period. The longer the time period, the higher the cost.

The time period for in-transit inventory and work-in-process (WIP) inventory should be evaluated in terms of the appropriate tradeoffs. The various transportation modes available for shipping freight have different transit time lengths, transit time variability, and damage rates. The rates or prices charged by carriers in the different modes reflect these differences in service. For example, air freight service is usually the fastest and often the most reliable, but the price charged for this service is considerably higher than that charged by motor carriers, railroads, or ocean carriers. However, air freight should result in less inventory in transit. As an example, assume that ABC Power Tools currently ships 40-foot containers from its manufacturing plant in Europe to a customer's distribution center in California. Currently, ABC uses a mix of motor carrier, railroad, and ocean carriers to complete this move. What would the cost impact be if ABC replaced the ocean and railroad carriers with an air freight carrier? Figure 9.1 is a summary of the current mode mix, proposed mode mix, and relevant cost data. Table 9.3 shows the analysis of the relevant costs associated with the current mode mix. Inventory value is calculated by multiplying the number of units in the container times the manufactured cost of each item divided by 365 days. The value of the inventory is considered an annual valuation. As such, the value of each day's worth of inventory takes the annual value divided by 365. As Table 9.3 shows, the current mode mix takes 22 days from origin to destination with an inventory value of $13,531.54 and a freight cost of $2,050. Table 9.4 shows the cost analysis for the proposed mode mix that replaces the ocean and rail moves with an air freight move. As this table shows, the new inventory value decreased by $10,456.19, but the freight cost increased by $750. The reduction in time through the supply chain from the proposed mode mix resulted in a positive variance for ABC Power Tools. Although this is a simple example, it shows the financial impact of reducing transit time on inventory and transportation costs. The cash flow impacts of this example will be discussed further after the introduction to inventory carrying costs in this chapter.

Finally, WIP inventories are associated with manufacturing. Significant amounts of inventory can be accumulated in manufacturing facilities, particularly in assembly operations such as automobiles and computers. The length of time WIP inventory sits in a manufacturing facility waiting to be included in a particular product should be carefully evaluated in relationship to scheduling techniques and the actual manufacturing or assembly technology. Similar to the transportation example earlier, if an investment in technology reduces the amount of time WIP sits in the facility, a positive variance could result to the manufacturer. As always, a tradeoff analysis of the costs needs to be performed.

Figure 9.1	ABC Power Tools—In-Transit Inventory Analysis

ABC ships product in 40-foot containers from Europe to a customer in California Current mode mix:

- Plant to European port: motor carrier drayage
- European port to U.S port (East Coast): ocean carrier
- Eastern U.S port to rail siding: motor carrier drayage
- Eastern U.S rail siding to California rail siding: rail
- California rail siding to customer DC: motor carrier drayage

Assume that one 40-foot container holds 500 units of Product A:

- Manufactured cost per unit of Product A = $449

Assume ABC owns the inventory to delivery at customer DC.

Assume ABC ships 100 containers per year to this customer. Transportation costs (per container):

- Motor carrier drayage: $150
- Ocean: $700
- Rail: $900
- Air: $2,500

Change modes: Replace ocean and rail with air

Table 9.3	ABC Power Tools-In-Transit Inventory Analysis—Current			
SUPPLY CHAIN MOVE	**DAYS**	**INVENTORY VALUE**	**TRANSPORTATION MODE**	**FREIGHT COST**
ABC plant to European port	1	$ 615.07	Drayage	$ 150.00
Through European port	2	1,230.14	—	—
European port to East Coast U.S. port	5	3,075.35	Ocean	700.00
Through U.S. port	2	1,230.14	—	—
U.S. port to rail siding	1	615.07	Drayage	150.00
East Coast U.S. to California	10	6,150.70	Rail	900.00
California rail to customer	1	615.07	Drayage	150.00
Total	22	$13,531.54		$2,050.00
Source: Robert A. Novack, Ph.D. Used with permission.				

Table 9.4	ABC Power Tools—In-Transit Inventory Analysis (Proposed)			
SUPPLY CHAIN MOVE	**DAYS**	**INVENTORY VALUE**	**TRANSPORTATION MODE**	**FREIGHT COST**
ABC plant to European airport	1	$ 615.07	Drayage	$ 150.00
Through European airport	1	615.07	—	—
European airport to California airport	1	615.07	Air	2,500.00
Through California airport	1	615.07	—	—
California airport to customer	1	615.07	Drayage	150.00
Total	5	$3,075.35		$2,800.00
Source: Robert A. Novack, Ph.D. Used with permission.				

9-2-4 Seasonal Stocks

Seasonality can occur in the supply of raw materials, in the demand for finished product, or in both. Organizations that are faced with seasonality issues are constantly challenged when determining how much inventory to accumulate. Organizations that process agriculture products are a good example of supply seasonality. While the supply of the raw material is available during only one part of the year, demand is stable throughout the year. Therefore, the finished product usually has to be stored until it is sold. That is, when the raw material is available, it needs to be converted to finished product. This scenario often involves high storage costs and high obsolescence costs. An alternative scenario might be to store the raw material, or some preprocessed version of it, and use it to make the finished product as the demand dictates.

Sometimes seasonality can affect transportation, particularly if domestic water transportation is used. Rivers and lakes can freeze during the winter, which might interrupt the shipment of basic raw materials and cause organizations to accumulate raw materials before the freeze to avoid interruption. Another example would be the seasonality of the construction industry in the United States and its impact on the availability of flatbed tractor trailers. Although construction takes place in many areas of the United States year round, the northern states experience a slowdown in construction activity during the winter months. As spring approaches in the north, construction activity increases dramatically. The peak springtime construction season places a heavy demand on a fixed capacity of flatbed trailers to move construction supplies.

Many organizations are faced with seasonality in their product demand. As noted in the forecasting discussion in Chapter 7, Hershey is one of these organizations. A majority of Hershey's demand falls into five events throughout the year: Valentine's Day, Easter, Back-to-School, Halloween, and Christmas. The challenge for an organization like Hershey is multifaceted: meet wide swings in demand, keep production running at a fairly constant level, and avoid excessive inventories. The main tradeoff here is between manufacturing cost per unit and inventory costs.

9-2-5 Anticipatory Stocks

A fifth reason to hold inventory arises when an organization anticipates that an unusual event might occur that will negatively impact its source of supply. Examples of these events would include strikes, significant raw materials or finished goods price increase, a major shortage of supply because of political unrest or weather, and so on. In such situations, organizations might accumulate inventory to hedge against the risk associated with the unusual event. Again, an analysis should be undertaken to assess the risk, probability, and cost of inventory. Obviously, the analysis is more challenging because of the degree of uncertainty. However, analytical techniques are available to help mitigate these challenges.

9-2-6 Summary of Inventory Accumulation

Most organizations will accumulate some level of inventory for very good reasons. In many instances, the inventory cost might be more than offset by savings in other areas. The basic principle is that decisions to accumulate inventory need to be evaluated using a tradeoff framework. In addition to the five reasons just discussed, there are other reasons for accumulating inventory such as maintaining suppliers or employees. For example, during periods of low demand, an organization might continue to purchase from some suppliers to maintain the relationship or keep employees by producing to inventory. Again, an evaluation of the tradeoffs is necessary.

As already discussed, several functional areas in most organizations have a vested interest in decisions that determine how much inventory should be held and related issues regarding timing and location. The next section examines some of the contrasting viewpoints of these functional areas.

9-2-7 The Importance of Inventory in Other Functional Areas

As discussed in Chapter 2, logistics interfaces with an organization's other functional areas, such as marketing and manufacturing. The interface is usually more prominent in the inventory area. As background for analyzing the importance of inventory in the logistics system, several aspects of how logistics relates to other functional business areas with respect to inventory must be discussed.

9-2-7-1 Marketing

The primary mission of marketing is to identify, create, and help satisfy demand for an organization's products or services. In a product-oriented environment, the presence of the correct levels and types of inventory is crucial to fulfilling this mission. As such, marketing tends to have a favorable view on holding sufficient, or extra, inventory to ensure product availability to meet customer needs. Marketing's desire to hold inventory is also driven by new product offerings and continued market growth objectives.

9-2-7-2 Manufacturing

In many organizations, manufacturing operations are measured by how efficiently they can produce each unit of output. This situation typically means that manufacturing operations tend to be optimized when they have long production runs of a single product while minimizing the number of changeovers. These long productions runs will result in high inventory levels but low labor and machine costs per unit. Within industries faced with seasonal demand patterns, manufacturing is optimized by producing product even though demand for the product does not exist at the time of production. Adding the complexity of production scheduling to accommodate product line growth and brand extensions to this seasonality can result in significantly high inventories to create low manufacturing costs.

9-2-7-3 Finance

Inventories impact both the income statement and balance sheet of an organization. Inventories create both an asset and liability on the balance sheet as well as a cash flow impact on the income statement. As such, finance usually looks favorably at low inventories to increase inventory turns, reduce liabilities and assets, and increase cash flow to the organization.

The preceding discussion highlights why other functional areas within an organization are interested in inventory. Objectives of the finance area might obviously conflict with marketing and manufacturing objectives. A more subtle conflict sometimes arises between marketing and manufacturing. The long production runs that manufacturing might desire could cause shortages of some products needed by marketing to satisfy customer demand. For example, manufacturing might want to run 5,000 units of a particular product, while marketing needs another product currently in short supply.

Many companies can make a case for using a formal logistics organization to help resolve these inventory objective conflicts. Inventory is a critical decision area for logistics, and the logistics manager is in an excellent position to analyze inventory tradeoffs not only within logistics but also with the other functional areas discussed here.

Proper inventory management and control affects customers, suppliers, and an organization's functional areas. In spite of the many possible advantages to holding inventory in a logistics system, the costs of holding this inventory are a major expense. So, in making decisions about inventory levels, an organization needs to assess the tradeoffs between costs and the resulting service.

9-3 Inventory Costs

Inventory costs are important for three reasons. First, inventory costs represent a significant component of logistics costs in many organizations. Second, the inventory levels that an organization maintains at nodes in its logistics network will affect the level of service the organization can offer its customers. Third, cost tradeoff decisions in logistics frequently depend on and ultimately impact inventory carrying costs.

The following section provides basic information concerning the costs that logistics managers should consider when making inventory policy decisions. The major types of costs include inventory carrying cost, order and setup cost, expected stockout cost, and inventory in-transit carrying cost.

9-3-1 Inventory Carrying Cost

Inventory carrying costs are those that are incurred by inventory at rest and waiting to be used. From a finished goods inventory perspective, inventory carrying costs represent those costs associated with manufacturing and moving inventory from a plant to a distribution center to await an order. There are four major components of inventory carrying cost: capital cost, storage space cost, inventory service cost, and inventory risk cost.[1]

9-3-1-1 Capital Cost

Sometimes called the **interest** or **opportunity cost**, this cost type focuses on the cost of capital tied up in inventory and the resulting lost opportunity from investing that capital elsewhere. For example, all organizations borrow money from external sources to fund operations. This money might be in the form of equity (from stock issues) or debt (borrowing from banks). In either case, borrowed money has a cost associated with it. For equity, it is dividends; for debt, it is interest payments. In either case, an organization incurs a cost for borrowing money. If an organization decides to use this money to buy raw materials, build manufacturing plants, and hire labor to produce finished products for storage, then this inventory carries this "borrowed money" cost while sitting waiting to be sold. As such, capital tied up in inventory still requires dividend or interest payments to the funding source. The opportunity cost of this inventory is the return on capital the organization might have realized if it had invested in another opportunity rather than in raw materials, plants, and labor.

The capital cost is frequently the largest component of inventory carrying cost. An organization usually expresses it as a percentage of the dollar value of the inventory held. For example, a capital cost expressed as 20 percent of a product's value of $100 equals a capital cost of $20 ($100 × 20%).

In practice, determining an acceptable number to use for capital cost is not an easy task. One way of calculating capital cost for inventory decision making might use an organization's **hurdle rate**, the minimum rate of return on new investments. In this way, the organization makes inventory decisions in the same way that it does for investing in new facilities, advertising, and so on. Another way of calculating capital cost is for an organization to use its **weighted average cost of capital (WACC)**. WACC is the weighted average percent of debt service of all external sources of funding, including both equity and debt. This method reflects the direct debt service costs of having capital tied up in inventory.

The inventory valuation method used is critical to accurately determining capital cost and is subsequently critical to determining overall inventory carrying cost. According to Stock and Lambert, "the opportunity cost of capital should be applied only to the out-of-pocket investment in inventory.... This is the direct variable expense incurred up to the point at which inventory is held in storage."[2] Thus, the commonly accepted accounting practice of valuing inventory at fully allocated manufacturing cost is unacceptable in inventory decision making because raising or lowering inventory levels financially affects only the variable portion of inventory value and not the fixed portion of allocated cost. Thus only direct materials, direct labor, and direct plant cost are normally included in the out-of-pocket investment in inventory. Including inbound transportation costs to a distribution center in inventory value is consistent with this notion of including variable costs in inventory value.

9-3-1-2 Storage Space Cost

Storage space cost includes handling costs associated with moving products into and out of inventory as well as storage costs such as rent, heating, and lighting. Such costs might vary considerably from one circumstance to the next. For example, organizations often unload raw materials from rail cars and store them outside, whereas finished goods typically require covered and more sophisticated storage facilities.

Storage space costs are relevant to the extent that they either increase or decrease as inventory levels rise or fall. Thus, organizations should include variable, rather than fixed, expenses when estimating space costs as well as capital costs. This can be illustrated by contrasting the use of public warehousing versus private warehousing. When an organization uses public warehousing, almost all handling and storage costs vary directly with the level of stored inventory. As a result, these variable costs are relevant to decisions regarding inventory. When an organization uses private warehousing, however, many storage space costs (such as depreciation on the building) are fixed and are not relevant to inventory carrying costs. However, the opposite might be the case in the use of private warehousing where the organization is allocating all costs to products based on their activity levels. As such, each product would be allocated a portion of the fixed costs in the inventory carrying cost calculation.

9-3-1-3 Inventory Service Cost

Another component of inventory carrying cost includes insurance and taxes. Depending on the product value and type, the risk of loss or damage might require high insurance premiums. Also, many states impose a tax on inventory value, sometimes on a monthly basis. High inventory levels resulting in high tax costs can be significant in determining specific locations where organizations store products. Insurance and taxes might vary considerably from product to product, and organizations must consider this when calculating inventory carrying costs.

9-3-1-4 Inventory Risk Cost

The final major component of inventory carrying cost reflects the very real possibility that inventory dollar value might decline for reasons beyond an organization's control. For example, goods held in storage for long periods of time might become obsolete and thus decrease in value. This situation is commonly found in the computer and electronics industries. Also, fashion apparel might rapidly deteriorate in value once the selling season is over. This situation also occurs with fresh fruits and vegetables when quality deteriorates or the price falls over time. Manufactured products might face similar risks, although typically not to the same degree. A box of breakfast cereal has a relatively long shelf life with little risk of depreciating in value over a reasonable amount of time.

Any calculation of inventory risk costs should include the costs associated with obsolescence, damage, pilferage, and other risks to stored products. The extent to which inventoried items are subject to such risks will affect the inventory value and thus the carrying cost.

9-3-1-5 Calculating the Cost of Carrying Inventory

Calculating the cost to carry (or hold) a particular item in inventory involves three steps. First, determine the value of the item stored in inventory. Each organization has predetermined accounting practices to determine the value of inventory for balance sheet purposes.

The most relevant value measure for determining carrying costs is the cost of goods sold or the direct labor, materials, and overhead consumed by that item plus the direct costs of moving that item from the manufacturing facility into a distribution center for storage.

Second, determine the cost of each individual carrying cost component and add them together to determine the total direct costs consumed by the item while being held in inventory. Two types of costs should be considered here: variable-based costs and value-based costs. Variable-based costs are those that are specifically out-of-pocket expenditures, for example, inbound freight expense to the distribution center. Value-based costs are those that use the total value (or total direct costs consumed) of the item at the location where carrying costs are being determined, for example, taxes. Normally, inventory carrying costs are calculated on an annual basis. This assumes that the item will be held in storage for a one-year time period. These two costs must be adjusted for the actual length of time the item will be in storage. One word of caution when calculating inventory carrying costs: a decision must be made (in accordance with the organization's accounting standards) as to which costs are "one-time" and which costs are recurring. This will be especially true when the length of time an item is stored will be greater than one year.

Third, divide the total costs calculated in the second step by the value of the item determined in the first step. This will determine the annual inventory carrying cost for that item.

9-3-1-6 Example

Assume that ABC Power Tools assembles industrial machine tools and handheld tools for the construction industry. Item 1 is a heavy-duty band saw that is assembled at the plant and shipped to an ABC distribution center for storage, waiting for an order to be placed. Table 9.5 summarizes the cost of holding Item 1 in storage for a one-year time period. The direct materials, labor, and overhead incurred at the plant to assemble this item is $614.65. Moving Item 1 to the distribution center incurs a direct transportation cost of $32.35. Receiving this item into the distribution center and labor used for this item while in storage consumes a direct labor expense of $22.00. Direct space cost allocated to storing Item 1 is $28.80 per year. The direct insurance cost for holding Item 1 in storage for one year is $2.00. Interest, taxes, loss and damage, and obsolescence costs are based on the value of Item 1 ($614.65) and are $61.47, $6.15, $23.97, and $6.15, respectively. The interest is assumed to be an opportunity cost incurred for the investment of $614.65 of capital into Item 1. Therefore, the total cost to hold Item 1 in storage for one year is $182.89, or 29.8 percent of the value of Item 1.

Assume that ABC Power Tools sells this item through a typical home improvement retailer like Lowe's or Home Depot. Calculating the cost to hold Item 1 in inventory would be slightly different in this situation compared to the previous example since Item 1 would not be in storage for an entire year before it would be sold to a consumer. Table 9.6 shows how the cost to hold and move Item 1 would be calculated. This example makes two assumptions: (1) inventory carrying costs begin to accrue at the ABC distribution center and (2) all value-based costs must be prorated for each supply chain location based on the days of supply for that location. As can be seen from Line 2, the manufactured cost of Item 1 does not change as it moves through the supply chain. What does change are the cumulative variable-based costs (Line 4) and the cumulative value-based costs (Line 7). This occurs because additional costs are incurred each time Item 1 moves further down the supply chain. Variable-based costs increase every time Item 1 is moved and stored. This increases the value (costs consumed, shown in Line 5) of Item 1. The value-based costs increase because the value of Item 1 increases as it moves further to the point of consumption. Although this is a simple example, it shows that as an item receives multiple "touches"

Table 9.5	ABC Power Tools—Inventory Carrying Cost for Item 1	
COST CATEGORY	COMPUTATION	ANNUAL COST
1. Direct materials, labor, overhead		$614.65
2. Inbound freight to DC		$ 32.35
3. Labor	$10 per unit received plus $1 per unit per month × 2 months	$ 22.00
4. Space	$0.30/sq. ft./month × 8 sq. ft. × 12 months	$ 28.80
5. Insurance	$2.00 per unit per year	$ 2.00
6. Interest	10% @ $614.65	$ 61.47
7. Taxes	$5 per $100 value @ 20%	$ 6.15
8. Loss and damage	3.9% per year @ $614.65	$ 23.97
9. Obsolescence	1% per year @ $614.65	$ 6.15
10. Total inventory carrying costs		$182.89
11. Inventory carrying cost percent	$182.89/$614.65	$ 29.8%

Source: Robert A. Novack, Ph.D. Used with permission.

in the supply chain, the cumulative cost of doing so increases dramatically. As Table 9.6 illustrates, the cost of moving and storing Item 1 increases almost three times from the ABC distribution center to the retail store. This is a good example of how adding "touch points" to inventory drastically increases the cost of holding that inventory.

9-3-1-7 Nature of Carrying Cost

Items with basically similar carrying costs should use the same estimate of carrying cost per dollar value. However, items subject to rapid obsolescence or items that require servicing to prevent deterioration might require separate cost estimates. The estimate of carrying cost per inventory dollar value expressed as a percent of the inventory value carried during the year will reflect how carrying costs change with average inventory value. Table 9.7 shows that as average inventory increases for ABC Power Tools for Item 1 at its distribution center, annual carrying costs increase, and vice versa. In other words, carrying cost is variable and is directly proportional to the average number of items in inventory or the average inventory value.

9-3-2 Ordering and Setup Cost

A second cost affecting total inventory cost is **ordering cost** or **setup cost**. Ordering cost refers to the expense of placing an order for additional inventory and does not include the cost or expense of the product itself. Setup cost refers more specifically to the expense of changing or modifying a production or assembly process to facilitate line changeovers.

9-3-2-1 Ordering Cost

The costs associated with ordering inventory have both fixed and variable components. The fixed element might refer to the cost of the information system, facilities, and technology

Table 9.6	ABC Power Tools—Inventory Carrying Costs for Item 1 to Customer			
CATEGORY	ABC Plant →	ABC DC →	Retail DC →	Retail Store
1. Days of supply	0	60	45	30
2. Direct manufactured cost	$614.65	$614.65	$614.65	$614.65
3. Variable-based costs:				
a. Freight	$ 0	$ 32.35	$ 32.35	$ 32.35
b. Labor	0	12.00	11.50	11.00
c. Space	0	4.80	3.60	2.40
d. Insurance	0	0.33	0.25	0.17
4. Total variable-based costs (cumulative)	$ 0	$ 49.48	$ 97.18	$143.10
5. Total value Item 1 (Line 2 + Line 4)	$614.65	$664.13	$711.83	$757.75
6. Value-based costs (based on Line 5):				
a. Interest (10% per year)	$ 0	$ 11.07	$ 8.90	$ 6.31
b. Taxes	0	6.64	7.12	7.58
c. Loss and damage	0	4.32	3.47	2.46
d. Obsolescence	0	1.11	0.89	0.63
7. Total value-based costs (cumulative)	$ 0	$ 23.14	$ 43.52	$ 60.50
8. Total costs (Line 4 + Line 7)	$ 0	$ 72.62	$140.70	$203.60
9. Carrying cost percent (Line 8/$614.65)	0	11.8%	22.9%	33.1%

Source: Robert A. Novack, Ph.D. Used with permission.

Table 9.7	Inventory and Carrying Costs for ABC Power Tools			
ORDER PERIOD (WEEKS)	NUMBER OF ORDERS PER YEAR	AVERAGE INVENTORY*		TOTAL ANNUAL INVENTORY CARRYING COST†
		Units	Value**	
1	52	25	$ 15,366.25	$ 4,440.85
2	26	50	30,732.50	8,881.69
4	13	100	614,650.00	17,763.39
13	4	325	199,761.25	57,731.00
26	2	650	399,522.50	115,462.00
52	1	1,300	799,045.00	230,924.00

*One week's inventory supply is 50 items. Average Inventory = Beginning Inventory (units) – Ending Inventory (assumed to be zero) ÷ 2.
**Value per unit is $614.65.
†Carrying Cost = 28.9%75

Source: C. John Langley Jr., Ph.D. Used with permission.

available to facilitate order-placement activities. This fixed cost remains constant in relation to the number of orders placed.

There are also a number of costs that vary in relation to the number of orders that are placed to acquire additional inventory. Some types of activities that might be responsible for these costs include (1) reviewing inventory stock levels, (2) preparing and processing order requisitions or purchase orders, (3) preparing and processing receiving reports, (4) checking and inspecting stock prior to placement in inventory, and (5) preparing and processing payment. While the roles played by people and processes might seem trivial, they become very important when considering the total range of activities associated with placing and receiving orders.

9-3-2-2 Setup Cost

Production setup costs might be more obvious than ordering costs. Setup costs are expenses incurred each time an organization modifies a production or assembly line to produce a different item for inventory. The fixed portion of setup cost might include the use of capital equipment needed to change over production or assembly facilities, while the variable expense might include the personnel costs incurred in the process of modifying or changing the production or assembly line.

9-3-2-3 Nature of Ordering and Setup Cost

Separating the fixed and variable portions of ordering and setup cost is essential. Just as calculations should emphasize the variable components of inventory carrying costs, calculations of ordering and setup costs should emphasize the variable portion of these expenses. As discussed later in this chapter, this emphasis becomes central to developing meaningful inventory strategies.

When calculating annual ordering costs, organizations usually start with the cost or charge associated with each individual order or setup. Correspondingly, the annual number of orders or setups affects the total order cost per year; this number is inversely related to individual order size or to the number of units manufactured (production run length) within a simple setup or changeover. Table 9.8 shows this general relationship. As can be seen in Table 9.8, more frequent order placement results in customers placing a larger number of smaller orders per year. Since both small and large orders incur the variable expense of placing an order, total annual order cost will increase in direct proportion to the

Table 9.8	Order Frequency and Order Cost for Computer Hard Disks	
ORDER FREQUENCY (WEEKS)	NUMBER OF ORDERS PER YEAR	TOTAL ANNUAL ORDER COST*
1	52	$10,400
2	26	5,200
4	13	2,600
13	4	800
26	2	400
52	1	200

*Assuming a cost per order of $200.75

Source: C. John Langley Jr., Ph.D. Used with permission.

number of orders placed per year. As long as annual sales and demand remain the same, total annual order or setup cost will relate directly to the number of orders or setups per year and will relate inversely to individual order size or individual production run length.

9-3-2-4 Future Perspectives

Although an accurate, comprehensive statement of inventory cost must include the portion related to ordering and setup activities, the magnitude of these costs is likely to decrease in the future. Considering the move to highly automated systems for order management and order processing and the streamlining of inventory receiving practices, the variable cost of handling individual orders is certain to decrease significantly. In organizations where **vendor-managed inventory (VMI)** programs are being utilized, the concept of placing orders itself loses significance, and therefore the concept of ordering cost loses relevance.

9-3-3 Carrying Cost Versus Ordering Cost

As shown in Table 9.9, ordering cost and carrying cost respond in opposite ways to changes in the number of orders or size of individual orders. Total cost also responds to changes in order size. Close examination indicates that ordering costs initially decrease more rapidly than carrying costs increase, which decreases total costs. In other words, a positive tradeoff occurs since the marginal savings in ordering costs exceed the marginal increase in inventory carrying costs. However, at a certain point, this relationship begins to change and total costs start to increase. A negative tradeoff occurs here because the marginal ordering cost savings are less than the marginal carrying cost increase. Figure 9.2 shows this set of relationships in terms of cost curves.

Table 9.9		Summary of Inventory and Order Cost					
ORDER PERIOD (WEEKS)	NUMBER OF ORDERS PER YEAR	AVERAGE INVENTORY* (UNITS)	TOTAL ANNUAL ORDER COST**	CHANGE IN TOTAL ORDER COST	TOTAL ANNUAL INVENTORY CARRYING COST†	CHANGE IN TOTAL CARRYING COST	TOTAL COST
1	52	50	$10,400		$1,250		$11,650
				−$5,200		$+1,250	
2	26	100	5,200		2,500		7,700
				−2,600		+2,500	
4	13	200	2,600		5,000		7,600
				−1,800		+11,250	
13	4	650	800		16,250		17,050
				−400		+16,250	
26	2	1,300	400		32,500		32,900
				−200		+32,500	
52	1	2,600	200		65,000		65,200

*Assume sales or usage at 100 units per week. Average Inventory = (Beginning Inventory − Ending Inventory) ÷ 2
**Cost per order is $200.
†Value is $100 and carrying cost is 25%.75

Source: C. John Langley Jr., Ph.D. Used with permission.

Figure 9.2	Inventory Costs

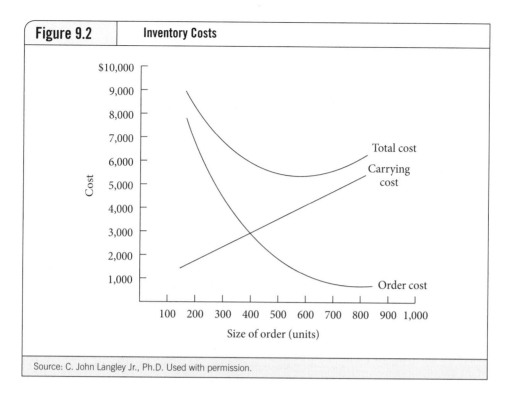

Source: C. John Langley Jr., Ph.D. Used with permission.

9-3-4 Expected Stockout Cost

Another critical cost to making inventory decisions is **stockout cost**—the cost associated with not having a product available to meet demand. When a product is unavailable to meet demand, several consequences might occur. First, the customer might be willing to wait and accept a later shipment (back order). This usually results in the shipping firm incurring incremental variable costs associated with processing and making the extra shipment. This also might result in a less-than-satisfied customer. Second, the customer might decide to purchase a competitor's product in this instance, resulting in a direct loss of profit and revenue for the supplier. Third, the customer might decide to permanently switch to a competitor's product, thus resulting in the loss of future profits and revenues for the supplier. If a stockout occurs on the physical supply side, manufacturing might have to shut down a machine or the entire facility until the material is available.

Stockout costs can be difficult to determine because of the uncertainty of future consequences (e.g., future lost revenue) that might occur. Most organizations hold safety stock to prevent or minimize product stockouts. However, this increases inventory costs. Therefore, a tradeoff exists between the cost of holding safety stock versus the cost of a stockout. Accurate inventory levels cannot be determined without calculating the cost of a stockout. However, many organizations still set inventory levels without knowing the cost of a stockout because of the challenging nature of identifying true stockout costs. Chapter 8 offers a detailed example of how to determine the tradeoffs between safety stock and stockout costs.

9-3-4-1 Safety Stock

As previously stated, most organizations will hold **safety stock**, or **buffer stock**, to minimize the possibility of a stockout. Stockouts occur because of the uncertainties in both demand and lead time. Many techniques exist for setting safety stock levels to accommodate uncertainties in demand and lead time. An example will now be presented.

Assuming that both demand and lead time are normally distributed around the mean, Formula 9.1 can be used to calculate safety stocks.

$$\sigma_C = \sqrt{R\sigma_S^2 + S^2\sigma_R^2}$$ 9.1

where:

σ_C = Units of safety stock needed to satisfy 68% of all probable observations
R = Average replenishment cycle (days)
σ_R = Standard deviation of the replenishment cycle (days)
S = Average daily demand (units)
σ_S = Standard deviation of daily demand (units)

Assume that ABC Power Tools has a monthly demand for Item 1 as shown in Table 9.10.

From this table, the average daily demand of 1,315 units and the standard deviation of demand of 271 units can be calculated. Table 9.11 shows the distribution of lead time being anywhere from 7 to 13 days, with a mean of 10 days and a standard deviation of 1.63 days. Given these data, safety stock requirements can be calculated using Formula 9.2.

$$\begin{aligned}
\sigma_C &= \sqrt{R\sigma_D^2 + D^2\sigma_R^2} \\
&= \sqrt{(10)(271)^2 + (1,315)^2(1.63)^2} \\
&= \sqrt{734,410 + 4,594,378} \\
&= 2,308.42 \approx 2,308 \text{ units}
\end{aligned}$$ 9.2

Using this safety stock requirement from the calculation, relevant safety stock levels for varying service levels can be calculated and are shown in Table 9.12. Figure 9.3 shows the relationship between service levels and safety stocks graphically. As can be expected, as service level requirements increase, safety stocks increase at an increasing rate. The curve

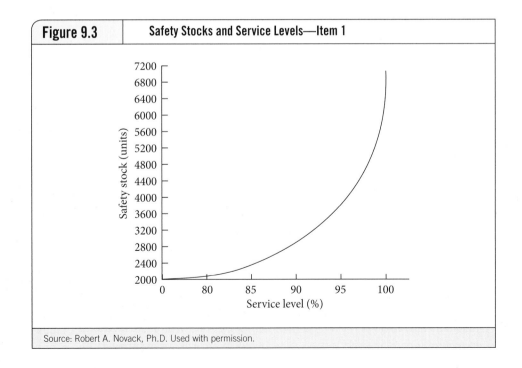

Figure 9.3 | **Safety Stocks and Service Levels—Item 1**

Safety stock (units) vs. Service level (%)

Source: Robert A. Novack, Ph.D. Used with permission.

Table 9.10	Average Daily Demand for Item 1
DAY	**DEMAND (UNITS)**
1	1,294
2	1,035
3	906
4	777
5	1,035
6	1,165
7	1,563
8	1,424
9	1,424
10	1,424
11	1,682
12	1,553
13	1,682
14	1,035
15	1,165
16	1,165
17	1,294
18	1,812
19	1,424
20	1,553
21	906
22	1,294
23	1,682
24	1,424
25	1,165

Average daily demand (D) = 1,314.92 ≈ 1,315

Standard deviation of daily demand (σ_D) = 270.6 ≈ 271

So,

- 68% of the time, daily demand is between 1,044 and 1,586 units.
- 95% of the time, daily demand is between 773 and 1,857 units.
- 99% of the time, daily demand is between 502 and 2,128 units.

Source: Robert A. Novack, Ph.D. Used with permission.

Table 9.11	Lead Time Distribution for Item 1			
LEAD TIME (DAYS)	FREQUENCY (f)	DEVIATION FROM MEAN (d)	DEVIATION SQUARED (d²)	fd²
7	1	−3	9	9
8	2	−2	4	8
9	3	−1	1	3
10	4	0	0	0
11	3	+1	1	3
12	2	+2	4	8
13	1	+3	9	9
$\bar{x} = 10$	$n = 16$			$\Sigma fd^2 = 40$

Average replenishment cycle (R) = 10 days

Standard deviation of replenishment cycle (σ_R) = 1.63 days

$$\sigma_R = \sqrt{\frac{\Sigma fd^2}{n-1}}$$
$$= 1.63$$

Source: Robert A. Novack, Ph.D. Used with permission.

Table 9.12	Safety Stock Levels for Various Service Levels—Item 1	
SERVICE LEVEL	STANDARD DEVIATIONS	SAFETY STOCK (UNITS)
84.1%	1.0	2,308
90.3	1.3	3,000
94.5	1.6	3,693
97.7	2.0	4,616
98.9	2.3	5,308
99.5	2.6	6,001
99.9	3.0	6,924

Source: Robert A. Novack, Ph.D. Used with permission.

approaches the 100 percent service level but will not statistically reach it, even at three standard deviations from the mean. So, the higher the service level requirement (thus, the lower the stockout rate), the higher the inventory level requirement. As the example in Chapter 8 explained, there is a tradeoff between holding this extra inventory and avoiding the cost of a stockout.

Supply Chain Profile   *Is RFID Ready for a Reinvention?*

With iTRAK, cases now have a passive RFID tag affixed to them in the plant, making the receipt of finished goods into the warehouse an almost instant process as finished goods pass through a RFID portal-style reader station. Likewise, in the shipping area, pallets that have been picked and are ready to ship are moved by lift truck into a reader portal, where all the case-level data is automatically captured and cross-referenced against the order data in iTRAK.

Kimble Chase's products ship in cases, but some of them ship with smaller "inner packs," which also need to be tracked for order accuracy. Some orders might have 1,000 different cases or inner packs on each pallet. The previous method of verifying outbound orders was to hand scan and repack each case or pack on outbound pallets, which made the process time-consuming and error prone. With RFID, the picked pallet is simply moved to an RFID portal reader, the scan captures the data for all the cases and smaller inner packs within seconds, cross referencing it against the order data in iTRAK. As a result, the RFID-enabled WMS has dramatically improved the accuracy of outbound orders and of finished goods in the warehouse pick bins.

A key driver of internal benefits is RFID's ability to accurately and quickly scan many items at once without having to institute processes such as picking items to a conveyor and passing them through a fixed-position scanner. "The more touches involved in data capture, the more inefficient the process is and the more potential you have for errors and damage," says Nick Beedles, president of SATO America and SATO Global Solutions.

RFID's accuracy also leads to fewer stock outs in retail supply chains, notes Beedles, but in the retail industry, use of RFID is evolving to allow retailers to provide a better customer experience and drive additional sales. For example, he says, SATO is working on an RFID-enabled store application that can track the items a shopper is trying on in a dressing room.

The tablet app is interactive for shoppers and store associates, explains Beedles. If the fit or color for an item isn't right, the customer can access a screen in the dressing room to see optional sizes or colors which are in stock in the store and select to have that item brought to the dressing room by a store associate. Such store applications could also let a customer know about accessories or other garments that complement an item, or that are on sale and are related to the items the customer is trying on.

Such next generation apps will build off the potential value of having RFID tags on most items, and reader infrastructure within the store that pinpoints where everything is, says Beedles. "So now that I have all the garments in a store tagged, it's about adding value through upselling and cross-selling, and providing a better customer experience," Beedles says. "Retailers will be able to provide a concierge-type of shopping experience."

Source: Adapted from Roberto Michel, *Logistics Management*, October 2015, p. 43. Reprinted with permission of Peerless Media, LLC.

9-3-4-2 Cost of Lost Sales

Although this concept was introduced in Chapter 8, a quick review in this chapter is necessary. Determining safety stock levels and the related inventory carrying costs might be relatively straightforward, but not so for determining the cost of a lost sale. Likewise, determining the cost of a production shutdown for lack of raw materials is also a challenge. For example, assume that a manufacturing line has an hourly production rate of 1,000 units and a pretax profit of $100 per unit. Also assume that the total labor costs per hour for that line are $500. If the line is shut down for lack of raw materials for a total of four hours, the cost of the shutdown would be $402,000 [(1,000 units × $100 × 4 hours) + ($500/hour × 4 hours)].

This figure is probably conservative because it does not include overhead costs or the costs to start the line up again. However, it does give an indication of the out-of-pocket expense of a shutdown and provides a basis for determining raw materials inventory levels.

9-3-5 In-Transit Inventory Carrying Cost

Another inventory carrying cost that many organizations ignore is that of carrying inventory in transit. This cost might be less apparent than those discussed earlier. However, under certain circumstances, it might represent a significant expense. Remember, someone will own the inventory while it is in transit and will incur the resulting carrying costs. For example, an organization selling its products free-on-board (FOB) destination is responsible for transporting the products to its customers since title does not pass until the products reach the customer's facility. Financially, the product remains under the ownership of the shipper until it is unloaded from the transportation vehicle at the customer's location. In-transit inventory carrying cost becomes especially important on global moves since both distance and time from the shipping location increase.

Since this moving inventory is shipper-owned until delivered to the customer, the shipper should consider its delivery time part of its inventory carrying cost. The faster delivery occurs, the sooner the transaction is completed and the faster the shipper receives payment for the shipment. This also means the shipper owns the product in transit for a shorter period of time. Since faster transportation typically means higher transportation cost, the shipper might want to analyze the tradeoff between transportation cost and the cost of carrying inventory in transit. Appendix 9A specifically addresses this situation.

9-3-5-1 Determining the Cost of In-Transit Inventory

An important question at this point is how to calculate the cost of carrying inventory in transit—that is, what variables should an organization consider? An earlier discussion in this chapter focused on four major components of inventory carrying cost: capital cost, storage space cost, inventory service cost, and inventory risk cost. While these categories are still all valid, they apply differently to the cost of carrying inventory in transit.

First, the capital cost of carrying inventory in transit generally equals that of carrying inventory in a warehouse. If the organization owns the inventory in transit, the capital cost will be the same.

Second, storage space cost generally will not be relevant to inventory in transit since the transportation service provider typically includes equipment (space) and necessary loading and handling costs within its overall transportation price.

Third, while taxes generally are not relevant to inventory service costs, the need for insurance requires special analysis. For example, liability provisions when using common carriers are specific, and shippers might not need to consider additional insurance for their products. However, some transportation providers offer limited liability for the products they carry, thus requiring additional insurance while the products are in transit. This is particularly true for U.S. domestic small package transportation and international ocean transportation.

Fourth, obsolescence or deterioration costs are lesser risks for inventory in transit because the transportation service typically takes only a short time. Also, the fact that inventory is moving to the next node in the supply chain assumes that there is a demand for that inventory, lessening the probability that it will not be sold. Thus, this inventory cost is less relevant here than it is for inventory in the warehouse.

Generally, carrying inventory in transit usually costs less than carrying inventory in the warehouse. However, an organization seeking to determine actual cost differences more accurately should examine the details of each inventory cost in depth.

9-4 Fundamental Approaches to Managing Inventory

Historically, managing inventory involved two fundamental questions: *how much* to order and *when* to order. By performing a few simple calculations, an inventory manager could easily determine acceptable solutions to these questions. Today, questions regarding *where* inventory should be held and *what* specific line items should be available at specific locations pose more interesting challenges to inventory decision makers.

Today, organizations are faced with product line extensions, new product introductions, global markets, higher service requirements, and a constant pressure to minimize costs. This dynamic operating environment has caused organizations to examine their inventory policies as well as their customer service policies and find the optimal solution that balances both service and cost. Many approaches exist to identify and analyze this tradeoff. Organizations will choose the approach that serves them best as defined by their markets and corporate goals.

Regardless of the approach selected, inventory decisions must consider the basic tradeoff between cost and service. Figure 9.4, which illustrates this tradeoff, suggests that increasing investments in inventory will probably result in higher levels of customer service. While there is evidence that this relationship exists in industry, a priority today is on identifying logistics solutions that will result in higher levels of customer service while reducing inventory investments. Several factors make this objective achievable: (1) real-time order management systems, (2) improved technologies to manage logistics information, (3) more flexible and reliable transportation resources, and (4) improvements in the ability to position inventories so that they will be available *when* and *where* they are needed. Thus, organizations have been able to avail themselves of these improvements to shift the curve shown in Figure 9.4, which shows how less inventory is needed today to drive improvements in customer service.

9-4-1 Key Differences Among Approaches to Managing Inventory

Given the various approaches to managing inventory that are available and used today, it is important to know how they differ. These differences include dependent versus independent demand, pull versus push, and system-wide versus single-facility solutions to inventory management decisions.

9-4-1-1 Dependent Versus Independent Demand

Demand for a given inventory item is termed *independent* when such demand is unrelated to the demand for other items. Conversely, demand is defined as *dependent* when it is directly related to, or derives from, the demand for another inventory item or product. For example, the demand for a laptop computer is independent, while the demand for its computer chip is dependent. This dependency can be *vertical* (the laptop needs the chip

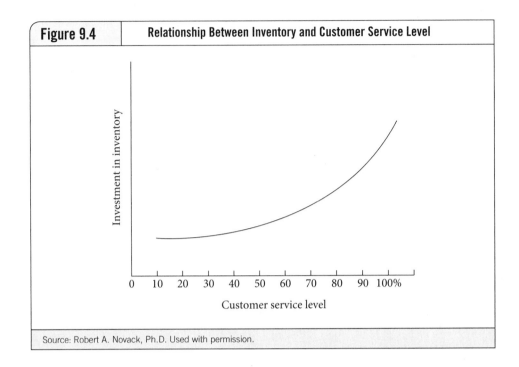

| Figure 9.4 | Relationship Between Inventory and Customer Service Level |

Source: Robert A. Novack, Ph.D. Used with permission.

for assembly) or horizontal (the laptop needs an instruction manual for final delivery to customer).

So, for many manufacturing processes, basic demand for raw materials, component parts, and subassemblies depends on the demand for the finished product. In contrast, the demand for the end-use items, which are typically sold to a customer, is independent of the demand for any other higher-order manufactured item.

An important point to remember is that developing inventory policies for items exhibiting independent demand requires that forecasts be developed for these items. Alternatively, forecasting is less relevant for items having dependent demand since the required quantities for these items depend entirely on the demand for the end-use product. So, once the difficult task of forecasting demand for end-use items is completed, determining the demand for dependent items requires simple calculations based on the bill of materials for that item.

Of the approaches to inventory management that will be discussed, JIT, MRP, and manufacturing resource planning (MRP II) are usually associated with items having dependent demand. Alternatively, DRP generally involves the movement of items having independent demand. The EOQ and vendor-managed inventory approaches apply to both independent and dependent demand items.

9-4-1-2 Pull Versus Push

The "pull" approach relies on customer orders to move product through a logistics system, while the "push" approach uses inventory replenishment techniques in anticipation of demand to move products. For example, Dell has traditionally used the pull approach for the assembly of its computers. With little or no finished goods inventory for computers, Dell waits for a customer order for a computer before it begins assembly. Recently, however, Dell began selling a limited line of its computers through Walmart retail stores. To do this, Dell employs the push model to anticipate future demand, assemble computers to inventory, and move them through its logistics system into Walmart stores.

A principal attribute of pull systems is that they can respond quickly to sudden or abrupt changes in demand because they produce to an order and have very little, if any, finished goods inventory. This is especially true for products where the final addition of value can be postponed. Alternatively, push systems produce to inventory in anticipation of demand, thus making their ability to adapt to changing demand volumes and preferences limited.

Pull systems usually run on short-term forecasts, allowing them the flexibility to adapt to swings in demand. On the other hand, push systems use longer-term forecasts that allow for scale economies in manufacturing but result in high finished goods inventories. These high levels of finished goods inventories can make shelf life a problem in push systems, while this is not an issue for pull systems.

Characteristically, JIT is a pull system since organizations place orders for more inventory only when the amount on hand reaches a certain minimum level, thus "pulling" inventory through the logistics system as needed. Having established a master production schedule, MRP develops a time-phased approach to inventory scheduling receipt. Because they generate a list of required materials in order to assemble or manufacture a specific amount of finished products, MRP and MRP II approaches are push based. Similar to these, but on the outbound or physical distribution side of logistics, DRP involves the allocation of available inventory to meet market demands. Thus, DRP is also a push-based strategy. VMI uses preset reorder points and economic order quantities along with on-hand inventory levels in customers' warehouses to generate replenishment orders. Because the customer is not placing a replenishment order, VMI can be considered a push approach. Finally, the EOQ approach is generally a pull approach, but applications today include elements of the push approach as well. While this permits the EOQ technique to be reactive when necessary, it also allows the preplanning of certain inventory decisions in a proactive, or push, manner. In fact, many EOQ-based systems in evidence today are hybrid approaches that include elements of both pull- and push-based strategies.

9-4-1-3 System-Wide Versus Single-Facility Solutions

A final inventory management issue is whether the selected approach represents a system-wide solution or whether it is specific to a single facility, such as a distribution center. Basically, a system-wide approach plans and executes inventory decisions across multiple nodes in the logistics system. MRP and DRP are typically system-wide approaches to managing inventory. Both approaches plan inventory releases and receipts between multiple shipping and receiving points in the network. On the other hand, a single-facility approach plans and executes shipments and receipts between a single shipping point and receiving point. EOQ and JIT are normally considered single-facility solutions. Both release orders from a single facility to a specific supplier for inventory replenishment. Usually, MRP and DRP are employed to plan system inventory movements, and EOQ and JIT are used to execute these plans at a single-facility level. VMI can be used to plan system-wide replenishment as well as execute replenishment on a single-facility basis.

9-4-2 Principal Approaches and Techniques for Inventory Management

In many business situations, the variables affecting the decision regarding the approach to inventory management are almost overwhelming. Therefore, models developed to aid in the decision process are frequently abstract or represent a simplified reality. In other words, models generally make simplifying assumptions about the real world they attempt to represent.

The complexity and accuracy of a model relate to the assumptions the model makes. Often, the more the model assumes, the easier the model is to work with and understand; however, simple model output is often less accurate. The model developer or user must decide on the proper balance between simplicity and accuracy.

The next several sections of this chapter contain an in-depth treatment of the inventory approaches previously mentioned: the fixed order quantity under conditions of certain and uncertain demand and lead time (also known as the economic order quantity approach), the fixed order interval approach, JIT, MRP, DRP, and VMI.

9-4-3 Fixed Order Quantity Approach (Condition of Certainty)

As its name implies, the **fixed order quantity** model involves ordering a fixed amount of product each time reordering takes place. The exact amount of product to be ordered depends on the product's cost and demand characteristics and on relevant inventory carrying and reordering costs.

Organizations using this approach generally needs to develop a minimum stock level to determine when to reorder the fixed quantity. This is called the **reorder point**. When the number of units of an item in inventory reaches the reorder point, the fixed order quantity (the EOQ) is ordered. The reorder point, then, triggers the next order.

The fixed order quantity model is often referred to as the **two-bin** model. When the first bin is empty, the organization places an order. The amount of inventory in the second bin represents the quantity needed until the new order arrives. Both notions (trigger and bin) imply that an organization will reorder inventory when the amount on hand reaches the reorder point. The reorder point quantity depends on the time it takes to get the new order and on the demand for the item during this lead time. For example, if a new order takes 10 days to arrive and the organization sells or uses 10 units per day, the reorder point will be 100 units (10 days × 10 units/day).

9-4-3-1 Inventory Cycles

Figure 9.5 shows the fixed order quantity model. It shows three inventory cycles, or periods. Each cycle begins with 4,000 units, the fixed quantity ordered or produced. Reordering occurs when the inventory on hand falls to a level of 1,500 units (reorder point). Assuming that the demand or usage rate and the lead time length are constant and known in advance, the length of each cycle will be a constant five weeks. This is an example of the application of the fixed order quantity model under conditions of certainty.

As suggested earlier, establishing a reorder point provides a trigger or signal for reordering the fixed quantity. For example, many consumers have reorder points for personal purchases such as gasoline. When the fuel gauge reaches a certain level, such as one-eighth of a tank, the driver will pull into a gas station to refill the tank. This reorder point also serves the purpose of guaranteeing that a gasoline stockout (running out) does not occur during a trip.

Business inventory situations base the reorder point on lead time and the demand during lead time. The constant monitoring necessary to determine when inventory has reached the reorder point makes the fixed order quantity model a **perpetual inventory system**. Most inventory management systems today are automated with real-time consumption data to make this potentially time-consuming approach more easily achievable.

Figure 9.5	Fixed Order Quantity Model Under the Condition of Certainty

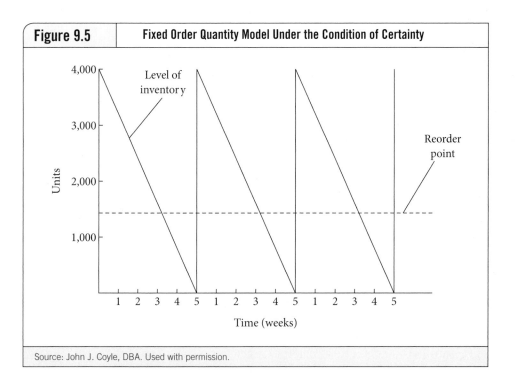

Source: John J. Coyle, DBA. Used with permission.

9-4-3-2 Simple EOQ Model

The following are the basic assumptions of the simple EOQ model:

1. A continuous, constant, and known rate of demand
2. A constant and known replenishment or lead time
3. All demand is satisfied
4. A constant price or cost that is independent of the order quantity (i.e., no quantity discounts)
5. No inventory in transit
6. One item of inventory or no interaction between items
7. Infinite planning horizon
8. Unlimited capital

The first three assumptions are closely related and basically mean that conditions of certainty exist. Demand in each relevant time period (daily, weekly, monthly) is known, and the usage rate is linear over time. The organization uses or depletes inventory on hand at a constant rate and knows the time needed to replenish stock. In other words, the lead time between order placement and order receipt is constant with no variability. As a result, the organization has no need to be concerned about stockouts and safety stock.

There is some concern that these three assumptions of certainty make the basic model too simplistic and, consequently, the outputs too inaccurate. Although this might be true in certain situations, several important reasons justify using the simple model. First, in some organizations, demand variation is so small that making the model more complex is too costly for the incremental accuracy achieved. Second, organizations just beginning to develop inventory models frequently find the simple EOQ model convenient and necessary because of the limited data available to them. Third, the simple EOQ model results are somewhat insensitive to changes in input variables. That is, variables such as demand, inventory carrying cost, and ordering cost can change without significantly affecting the calculated value of the economic order quantity.

The fourth assumption (constant costs) essentially means that quantity discounts do not exist. That is, the price of each unit remains the same, regardless of how much is ordered.

Assuming that there is no inventory in transit means that the organization purchases goods on a delivered price basis (purchase price includes transportation costs) and sells the goods FOB origin (the buyer pays the transportation costs). On the inbound side, this means that title to the goods does not pass until the buyer receives them. On the outbound side, title passes when the product leaves the shipping point. Under these assumptions, the organization has no responsibility for inventory in transit.

The sixth assumption means that the simple model is used to order one item of inventory at each order placement. The basic model easily handles the demand for a single, independent demand item with a single price. Introducing the calculation of an economic order quantity for more than one item into the simple model compounds the difficulty of the mathematics.

Assumptions seven and eight are most often decisions made outside the logistics area. An infinite planning horizon assumes that constraints are not imposed on the length of the time periods that are included in the basic model. Unlimited capital means that there are no financial reasons to limit the quantity ordered.

Given the assumptions listed, the simple EOQ model considers only two basic types of cost: inventory carrying cost and ordering cost. The simple model arrives at an optimum decision that analyzes the tradeoffs between these two costs. If the model focused only on inventory carrying cost, which varies directly with changes in order quantity, the order quantity would be as small as possible (see Figure 9.6). If the model considered

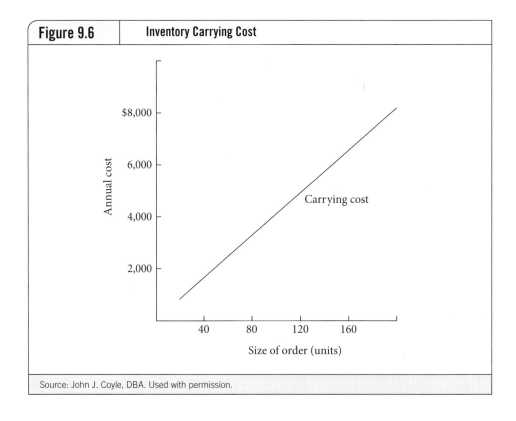

Figure 9.6 | **Inventory Carrying Cost**

Source: John J. Coyle, DBA. Used with permission.

only ordering cost, large orders would decrease total order costs, and small orders would increase total order costs (see Figure 9.7). The lot size decision attempts to minimize total cost by reaching a compromise between these two costs (see Figure 9.8).

9-4-3-3 Mathematical Formulation

The EOQ model can be developed in standard mathematical form, using the following variables:

R = Annual rate of demand (units)

Q = Quantity ordered (units)

A = Cost of placing an order ($ per order)

V = Value or cost of one unit of inventory ($ per order)

W = Carrying cost per dollar value of inventory per year (% of product value)

S = VW = Inventory carrying cost per unit per year ($ per unit per year)

t = Time (days)

TAC = Total annual cost ($ per year)

Given these variables, the total annual cost for a specific economic order quantity can be expressed as either Formula 9.3 or Formula 9.4.

$$\text{TAC} = \frac{1}{2}QVW + A\frac{R}{Q} \qquad\qquad 9.3$$

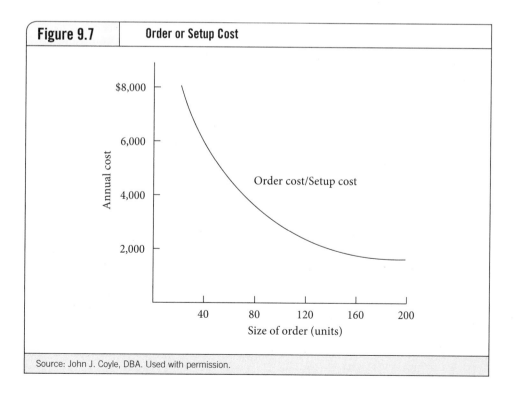

| Figure 9.7 | Order or Setup Cost |

Order cost/Setup cost

Annual cost

Size of order (units)

Source: John J. Coyle, DBA. Used with permission.

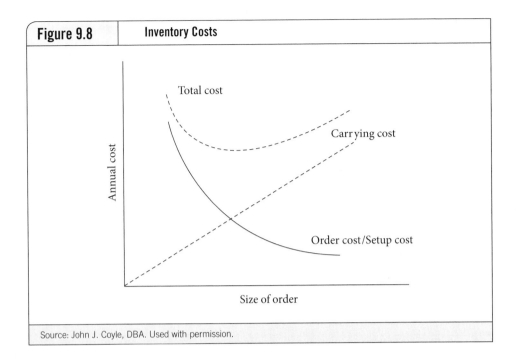

Figure 9.8   **Inventory Costs**

Source: John J. Coyle, DBA. Used with permission.

or

$$\text{TAC} = \frac{1}{2} QS + A\frac{R}{Q}$$ 9.4

The first term on the right-hand side of the equation refers to annual inventory carrying cost; it states that these costs equal the average number of units in the economic order quantity during the order cycle (½Q) multiplied by the value per unit (V) multiplied by the carrying cost percentage (W). In Figure 9.9, called the **sawtooth model**, the equation's logic becomes more apparent. The vertical line labeled Q represents the amount ordered at a given time and the amount of inventory on hand at the beginning of each order cycle. During the order cycle (t), an organization depletes the amount of inventory on hand at a known and constant rate (represented by the slanted line). The average number of units on hand during the order cycle is simply one-half of the economic order quantity (Q). The broken horizontal line in Figure 9.9 represents average inventory. The logic is very simple. Assuming that Q equals 100 units and that daily demand is 10 units, 100 units would last 10 days (t). At the period's midpoint, the end of the fifth day, 50 units would still be left,

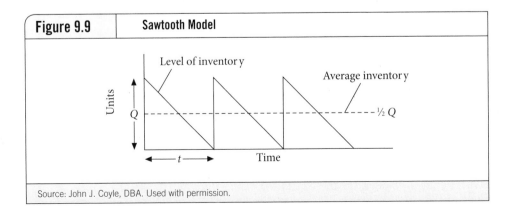

Figure 9.9   **Sawtooth Model**

Source: John J. Coyle, DBA. Used with permission.

which is one-half of Q (½ × 100). Another way to examine this is to assume that average inventory during a period is beginning inventory minus ending inventory divided by 2. Since the beginning inventory equals 100 units and the ending inventory equals zero units, 100 minus zero divided by 2 results in 50 units of average inventory.

Determining the average number of units is only part of the equation. Knowing the value per unit and the percentage carrying cost is still necessary. The larger the Q, the higher the inventory carrying cost will be. This relationship was described earlier: as the order size increases, inventory carrying costs increase. Given constant demand, average inventory will increase as the economic order quantity increases (see Figures 9.10a and 9.10b).

The second terms in Formulas 9.3 and 9.4 refer to annual ordering cost. Again, the cost to place an order is assumed to be constant, regardless of how much is ordered. Therefore, if Q increases, the number of orders placed per year will decrease since annual demand is known and constant. Larger order quantities, then, will reduce annual ordering costs.

The discussion so far has focused on the general nature of annual inventory cost and annual ordering cost. The next step is to discuss the calculation of Q, the economic order

Figure 9.10	Sawtooth Models

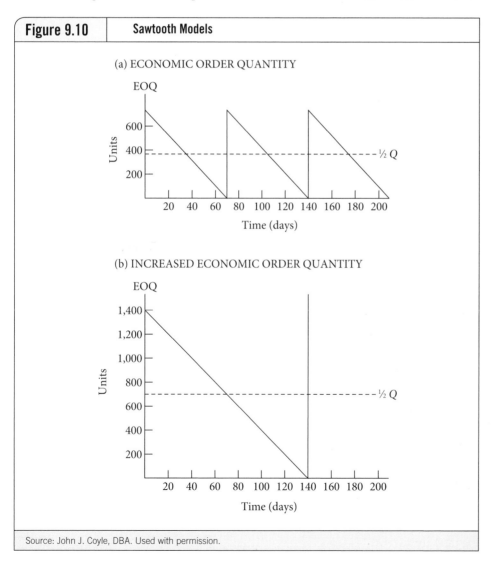

Source: John J. Coyle, DBA. Used with permission.

quantity. As indicated previously, this involves a tradeoff between inventory carrying cost and ordering cost. Determining Q can be accomplished by differentiating the TAC function with respect to Q, as shown in Formula 9.5.

$$\text{TAC} = \frac{1}{2}QVW + A\frac{R}{Q}$$

$$\frac{d(\text{TAC})}{dQ} = \frac{VW}{2} - \frac{AR}{Q^2}$$

9.5

Setting $d(\text{TAC})/dQ$ equal to zero and solving for Q gives:

$$Q^2 = \frac{2RA}{VW}$$

or

$$Q = \sqrt{\frac{2RA}{VW}}$$

or

$$Q = \sqrt{\frac{2RA}{S}}$$

The following example illustrates how Formula 9.5 works:

V = $100 per unit

$W = 25\%$

S = $25 per unit per year

A = $200 per order

R = 3,600 units

To solve for Q, the example proceeds as shown in Formula 9.6.

$$Q = \sqrt{\frac{2RA}{VW}} \qquad\qquad Q = \sqrt{\frac{2RA}{S}}$$

$$Q = \sqrt{\frac{(2)(3{,}600)(\$200)}{(\$100)(25\%)}} \qquad Q = \sqrt{\frac{(2)(3{,}600)(\$200)}{\$25}}$$

9.6

$$Q = 240\,\text{units} \qquad\qquad Q = 240\,\text{units}$$

9-4-3-4 Analysis

Table 9.13 and Figure 9.11 show the proceeding solution's tradeoffs and logic. These illustrations show how inventory carrying cost, ordering cost, and total cost vary as Q ranges from a low of 100 units to a high of 500 units.

As Table 9.13 shows, the lower quantities of Q result in higher annual ordering costs but result in lower annual inventory carrying costs, as expected. As Q increases from 100 to 240 units, annual ordering costs decrease because the number of orders placed per year decreases while annual inventory carrying costs increase because of the higher average inventories. Beyond 240 units, the incremental increase in annual inventory carrying cost exceeds the incremental decrease in annual ordering cost, thereby increasing total annual cost.

Table 9.13	Total Costs for Various EOQ Amounts		
Q	ORDERING COST *AR/Q*	CARRYING COST *½QVW*	TOTAL COST
100	$7,200	$1,250	$8,450
140	5,143	1,750	6,893
180	4,000	2,250	6,250
220	3,273	2,750	6,023
240	3,000	3,000	6,000
260	2,769	3,250	6,019
300	2,400	3,750	6,150
340	2,118	4,250	6,368
400	1,800	5,000	6,800
500	1,440	6,250	7,690

Source: C. John Langley Jr., Ph.D. Used with permission.

Figure 9.11	Graphical Representation of the EOQ Example

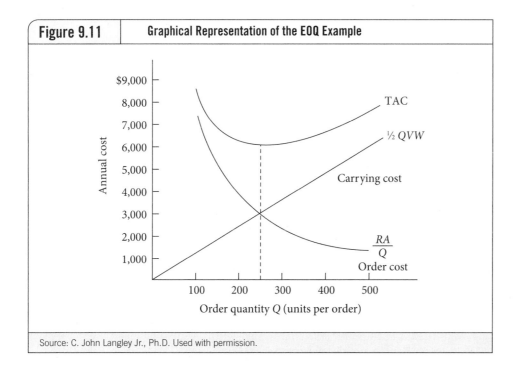

Source: C. John Langley Jr., Ph.D. Used with permission.

By defining the optimum Q in total cost terms, the data in Table 9.13 show that a Q of 240 units is optimal (least total cost). Figure 9.11 also demonstrates this optimum level. Note, however, that the TAC curve between EOQ values of 180 to 200 units and 300 to 320 units is quite shallow. This means that the inventory manager can alter the EOQ considerably without significantly affecting TAC.

9-4-3-5 Reorder Point

A previous discussion indicated that knowing when to order was as necessary as knowing how much to order. The *when*, called the reorder point, depends on the inventory level on hand. Under the assumptions of certainty, an organization needs only enough inventory to last during the replenishment time or lead time. Therefore, given a known lead time, multiplying lead time length by daily demand determines the reorder point.

Replenishment time consists of several components: order transmittal, order processing, order preparation, and order delivery. The time for each depends on factors such as the means used to transmit the order (electronic versus manual), the inventory availability at the supplier, and the transportation mode used for delivery. Factors affecting lead time will be discussed later in this chapter.

Using the previous example, assume that order transmittal takes one day, order processing and preparation take two days, and order delivery takes five days. This results in a replenishment or lead time of eight days. Given that demand is 10 units per day (3,600 units/360 days), the reorder point will be 80 units (8 days × 10 units per day).

9-4-3-6 A Note Concerning the Min-Max Approach

One widely used adaptation of the fixed order quantity approach is the **min-max inventory management approach**. With the traditional approach, inventory will deplete in small increments, allowing an organization to initiate a replenishment order exactly when inventory reaches the reorder point.

The min-max approach applies when demand might be larger and when the amount on hand might fall below the reorder point before the organization initiates a replenishment order. In this case, the min-max approach increments the amount ordered by the difference between the reorder point and the amount on hand. In effect, this technique identifies the minimum amount that an organization should order so that inventory on hand will reach a predetermined maximum level when the organization receives the order. While the min-max approach is very similar to the EOQ approach, individual order amounts will tend to vary under the min-max approach.

9-4-3-7 Summary and Evaluation of the Fixed Order Quantity Approach

Traditionally, the EOQ approach has been a cornerstone of effective inventory management. While not always the fastest way to respond to customer demand, the fixed order quantity approach has been a widely used technique.

Recently, however, many organizations have become more sophisticated in their use of EOQ-based approaches, adapting them to include a push as well as a pull orientation. As a result, many EOQ-based systems effectively blend both push and pull concepts. As indicated earlier, push, or proactive, inventory management approaches are far more prevalent in organizations having greater logistics sophistication.

One principal shortcoming of the EOQ-based approach is that it suits inventory decision making at a single facility more than it suits decision making at multiple locations in a logistics network. Also, the EOQ approach sometimes encounters problems when parallel points in the same logistics system experience peak demands simultaneously. This happens, for example, when many consumers simultaneously stock up on groceries before a major snowstorm. The EOQ approach alone, reacting to demand levels only as they occur, would respond too slowly to replenish needed inventory.

As stated at the outset, the simple EOQ approach, though somewhat unrealistic because of the number of assumptions it requires, is still useful because it illustrates the logic of inventory models in general. Actually, organizations can adjust the simple model to handle more complex situations. Appendix 9A covers applications of the EOQ approach in four special instances: (1) when an organization must consider the cost of inventory in transit, (2) when volume transportation rates are available, (3) when an organization uses private transportation, and (4) when an organization utilizes in-excess freight rates.

Typically, organizations associate EOQ-based approaches with independent, rather than dependent, demand. However, the EOQ approach can also be used for dependent demand items. The overall approach explicitly involves carrying calculated average inventory amounts; the tradeoffs among inventory, order, and expected stockout costs justify carrying these amounts.

9-4-4 Fixed Order Quantity Approach (Condition of Uncertainty)

Under the assumptions used until now, the reorder point was based on the amount of inventory on hand and demand was known and constant. When inventory on hand reached zero, a new order was received in an economic order quantity and stockout costs were not incurred. Although assuming such conditions of certainty might be useful to simplify inventory models, these conditions do not represent the normal situations faced by most organizations today.

Most organizations would not operate under conditions of certainty for a variety of reasons. First, consumers usually purchase products somewhat sporadically. The demand rates for many products vary depending on weather, social needs, physical needs, and a whole host of other factors. As a result, the demand for most products varies by day, week, and season.

In addition, several factors can affect lead time. For example, transit times can and do change, particularly over long distances, despite transportation provider efforts. Factors such as weather, highway congestion, port congestion, and border stops can make transit times very unreliable. In fact, transit time reliability is a major factor used by organizations when they are making both mode and carrier decisions.

Other factors that can cause variations in lead time are order transmittal and processing. Although a significant number of orders today are transmitted electronically, many are still sent through the U.S. Post Office. Mailed orders can be subject to the same unreliability in transit time as mentioned previously. During order processing, factors such as credit blocks and inventory unavailability can cause delays in orders proceeding through the system.

Because of all the potential factors that can influence the reliability of demand and lead time, inventory models need to be adjusted to account for this uncertainty. Figure 9.12 shows the fixed order quantity model adjusted for uncertainty in demand and lead time. This figure varies from the model introduced in Figure 9.5 in three ways. First, demand (affecting on-hand inventory levels) in Figure 9.5 was known and constant. This is why the on-hand inventory line in Figure 9.5 always begins the period at the EOQ amount and ends the period at zero units. This same line in Figure 9.12 fluctuates above the EOQ amount and below zero units because demand is not known or constant. Second, the lead time (or cycle) in Figure 9.5 is known and constant at five weeks, resulting in a very uniform "sawtooth" pattern. When lead time is not known or constant, as shown in Figure 9.12, the length of the period (or lead time) varies resulting in an uneven spacing between orders. Finally, Figure 9.5 makes no allowances for stockouts since its assumptions present conditions of certainty. In Figure 9.12, the uncertainty of demand and lead time makes necessary the addition of

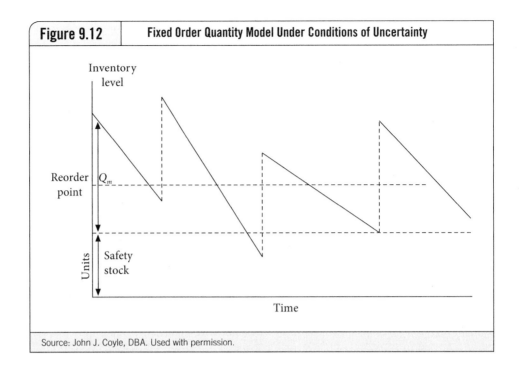

Figure 9.12 | **Fixed Order Quantity Model Under Conditions of Uncertainty**

Source: John J. Coyle, DBA. Used with permission.

safety stock to prevent stockouts. The amount of safety stock to be held will depend on the variability around demand and lead time and the service customers require.

9-4-4-1 Reorder Point—A Special Note

As noted previously, the reorder point under the basic model is the on-hand inventory level needed to satisfy demand during lead time. Calculating the reorder point is relatively easy since demand and lead time are constant. Under uncertainty, an organization must reformulate the reorder point to allow for safety stock. In effect, the reorder point becomes the average daily demand during lead time plus the safety stock, as Figure 9.12 shows. The following discussion clarifies this recalculation.

9-4-4-2 Uncertainty of Demand

The first factor that might cause uncertainty deals with demand or usage rate. While focusing on this variable, the following assumptions concerning EOQ still apply:

1. A constant and known replenishment or lead time
2. A constant price or cost that is independent of order quantity or time
3. No inventory in transit
4. One item of inventory or no interaction between items
5. Infinite planning horizon
6. No limit on capital availability

In discussing demand, logistics managers emphasize balancing the cost of carrying safety stock against the cost of a stockout (lost sales).

In a fixed quantity model with an established reorder point, introducing uncertainty into the analysis initially affects the inventory level needed to cover demand during lead time. Recall that in the previous example, conditions of certainty resulted in an EOQ of 240 units and a reorder point of 100 units. In other words, the inventory period began with 240 units on hand, and reordering occurred when inventory reached a level of 100 units.

The fact that demand will vary—and that the time that elapses between a level of 240 units and 100 units might vary—is not critical to the inventory problem when conditions of uncertainty exist. Determining whether 100 units is the best amount to have on hand at the start of the lead time cycle *is* critical. Thus, raising the reorder level accounts for safety stock. However, raising it too high will leave too much stock on hand when the next order arrives. Setting it too low will result in a stockout.

Using the previous problem, assume that the organization's demand during lead time ranges from 100 units to 160 units, with an average of 130 units. Also assume that demand has a discrete distribution varying in 10-unit blocks and that the organization has established probabilities for these demand levels (see Table 9.14).

In effect, the organization must consider seven different reorder points, each corresponding to a possible demand level as shown in Table 9.14. Using these reorder points, the matrix in Table 9.15 can be developed.

Table 9.14	Probability Distribution of Demand During Lead Time
DEMAND (UNITS)	PROBABILITIES
100	0.01
110	0.06
120	0.24
130	0.38
140	0.24
150	0.06
160	0.01
Source: C. John Langley Jr., Ph.D. Used with permission.	

Table 9.15	Possible Units of Inventory Short or in Excess During Lead Time with Various Reorder Points						
	REORDER POINTS						
ACTUAL DEMAND	100	110	120	130	140	150	160
100	0	10	20	30	40	50	60
110	−10	0	10	20	30	40	50
120	−20	−10	0	10	20	30	40
130	−30	−20	−10	0	10	20	30
140	−40	−30	−20	−10	0	10	20
150	−50	−40	−30	−20	−10	0	10
160	−60	−50	−40	−30	−20	−10	0
Source: C. John Langley Jr., Ph.D. Used with permission.							

While Table 9.15 shows many of the possible situations confronting the organization, it does not use information from the probability distribution of demand. Using the probability of demand would allow the organization with seven possible reorder points to determine the expected units short or in excess at each point during lead time.

Assume that the organization incurs a stockout cost (k) of \$10 per unit whenever a customer demands a unit that is not in inventory. The profit lost on the immediate sale and future sales is an opportunity cost.

Inventory carrying cost associated with safety stock is calculated the same way as it was for calculating carrying cost for the simple EOQ model. The value per unit is still assumed to be \$100, and the percentage annual inventory carrying cost is still 25 percent. Remember that the percentage figure is for the annual cost of inventory stored in the warehouse. Therefore, the \$25 derived by multiplying 25 percent by \$100 is the annual cost per unit of inventory in the warehouse. The \$25 contrasts with the \$10 stockout cost, which is a unit cost per cycle of order period. Therefore, as Table 9.16 shows, multiplying \$10 by the number of cycles or orders per year translates this cost into an annual basis.

Table 9.16 develops expected units short or in excess by multiplying the number of units short or in excess by the probabilities associated with each demand level. The numbers below (shorts) and above (in excess) the horizontal line are added, as the lower portion of Table 9.16 shows, to find the number of units the organization expects to be short or in excess at each of the seven possible reorder points. The variables for this calculation are as follows:

e = Expected excess in units

g = Expected shorts in units

k = Stockout cost in dollars per unit stocked out

$G = gk$ = Expected stockout cost per cycle

$G(\dfrac{R}{Q})$ = Expected stockout cost per year

eVW = Expected carrying cost per year for excess inventory

After performing the calculations indicated in Table 9.16, the total cost for each of the seven reorder points may be calculated. In this instance, the lowest total cost corresponds to the reorder point of 140 units. Although this number does not guarantee an excess or shortage in any particular period, it gives the overall lowest total cost per year: \$390.

Note that the number of orders used in Step 5 of Table 9.16 came from the preceding problem with conditions of certainty. This number was the only information available at that point. Now the total cost model can be expanded to include the safety stock and stockout cost. Formula 9.7 represents the expanded equation.

$$\text{TAC} = \frac{1}{2}QVW + A\frac{R}{Q} + (eVW) + \left(G\frac{R}{Q}\right) \qquad 9.7$$

Solving for the lowest total cost gives Formula 9.8.

$$\frac{d(\text{TAC})}{dQ} = \left[\frac{1}{2}VW\right] - \left[\frac{R(A+G)}{Q^2}\right] \qquad 9.8$$

Table 9.16	Expected Number of Units Short or in Excess							
		REORDER POINTS						
ACTUAL DEMAND	**PROBABILITIES**	**100**	**110**	**120**	**130**	**140**	**150**	**160**
100	0.01	**0.0**	0.1	0.2	0.3	0.4	0.5	0.6
110	0.06	−0.6	**0.0**	0.6	1.2	1.8	2.4	3.0
120	0.24	−4.8	−2.4	**0.0**	2.4	4.8	7.2	9.6
130	0.38	−11.4	−7.6	−3.8	**0.0**	3.8	7.6	11.4
140	0.24	−9.6	−7.2	−4.8	−2.4	**0.0**	2.4	4.8
150	0.06	−3.0	−2.4	−1.8	−1.2	−0.6	**0.0**	0.6
160	0.01	−0.6	−0.5	−0.4	−0.3	−0.2	−0.1	**0.0**
CALCULATION OF LOWEST COST REORDER POINT								
1. Expected excess per cycle (of values above diagonal line) (e)		0.0	0.1	0.8	3.9	10.8	20.1	30.0
2. Expected carrying cost per year (VW)		$0	$2.50	$20.00	$97.50	$270	$502.50	$750
3. Expected shorts per cycle (of values below diagonal line) (g)		30.0	20.1	10.8	3.9	0.8	0.1	0.0
4. Expected stockout cost per cycle (gK) = G		$300	$201	$108	$39	$8	$1	$0
5. Expected stockout cost per year ($G\dfrac{R}{Q}$)		$4,500	$3,015	$1,620	$585	$120	$15	$0
6. Expected total cost per year (2 + 5)		$4,500	$3,017.50	$1,640	$682.50	$390	$517.50	$750

Source: C. John Langley Jr., Ph.D. Used with permission.

Setting this equal to zero and solving for Q results in Formula 9.9.

$$Q = \sqrt{\frac{2R(A+G)}{VW}} \qquad\qquad 9.9$$

Using the expanded model and the computed reorder point of 140 units, a new value for Q can be calculated as shown in Formula 9.10.

$$Q = \sqrt{\frac{2 \times 3{,}600 \times (200 + 8)}{\$100 \times 25\%}} \qquad\qquad 9.10$$
$$= 245 \text{ units approximately}$$

Note that Q is now 245 units with conditions of uncertainty. Technically, this would change the expected stockout cost for the various reorder points in Table 9.16. However, the change is small enough to ignore in this instance. In other cases, recalculations might be necessary. The optimum solution to the problem with conditions of uncertainty is a fixed order quantity of 245 units, and the organization will reorder this amount when inventory reaches a level of 140 units (the calculated reorder point).

Finally, this situation requires a recalculation of total annual cost as shown in Formula 9.11.

$$
\begin{aligned}
\text{TAC} &= \frac{1}{2}QVW + A\frac{R}{Q} + eVW + G\frac{R}{Q} \\
&= \left(\frac{1}{2}\times 245\times \$100\times 25\%\right) + \left(200\times \frac{3,600}{245}\right) \\
&\quad + (10.8\times \$100\times 25\%) + \left(8\times \frac{3,600}{245}\right) \\
&= \$3,062.50 + \$2,938.78 + \$270 + \$117.55 \\
&= \$6,389
\end{aligned}
\tag{9.11}
$$

The $6,389 figure indicates what happens to total annual cost when conditions of uncertainty with respect to demand are introduced into the model. Introducing other factors, such as the lead time factor, would increase costs even more.

9-4-4-3 Uncertainty of Demand and Lead Time Length

This section considers the possibility that both demand and lead time might vary and builds on the preceding section in attempting to make this inventory approach more realistic. As expected, however, determining how much safety stock to carry will be noticeably more complex now than when only demand varied (the mathematical determination of safety stock when both demand and lead time vary was covered at the beginning of this chapter).

As in the previous section, the critical issue is just how much product customers will demand during the lead time. If demand and lead time are constant and known, calculating the reorder point (as was done in the section covering the case of certainty) would be easy. Now that both demand and lead time might vary, the first step is to identify the likely distribution of demand during the lead time. Specifically, the mean and standard deviation of demand during lead time must be estimated.

Figure 9.13 illustrates two key properties of a normal distribution. These concepts were covered earlier in this chapter, but it is important to revisit them here in the context of the fixed order quantity model under uncertainty. First, the normal distribution is symmetrical, with approximately 68.26 percent of all observations within one standard deviation around the mean, 95.44 percent within two standard deviations, and 99.73 percent within three standard deviations. Second, in the normal distribution, the mode (highest point or most observations) equals the mean (average).

After calculating values for the mean and standard deviation of demand during lead time, the stockout probability for each particular reorder point can be described. For example, assume that Figure 9.13 represents the demand distribution during lead time. Setting the reorder point equal to $\bar{X} + 1\sigma$ will result in an 84.13 percent probability that lead time demand will not exceed the inventory amount available. Increasing the reorder point to $\bar{X} + 2\sigma$ raises the probability of not incurring a stockout to 97.72 percent; reordering at $\bar{X} + 3\sigma$ raises this probability to 99.87 percent. Note that in the case of uncertainty, increasing the reorder point has the same effect as increasing the safety stock commitment. An organization must ultimately find some means to justify carrying this additional inventory.

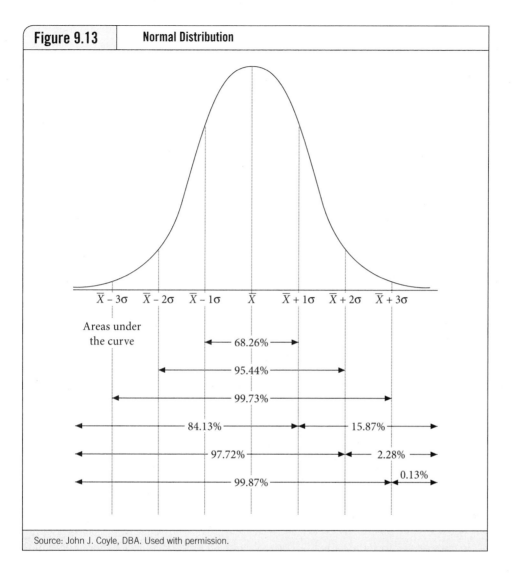

Figure 9.13	Normal Distribution

Source: John J. Coyle, DBA. Used with permission.

Borrowing Formula 9.1, the mean and standard deviation for demand during lead time can be calculated as shown in Formulas 9.12 and 9.13.

$$\bar{X} = SR \tag{9.12}$$

$$\sigma = \sqrt{R(\sigma_S)^2 + S^2(\sigma_R)^2} \tag{9.13}$$

where:

$\bar{X}$ = Average demand during lead time (units)

σ = Standard deviation of demand during lead time (units)

R = Average replenishment cycle (days)

σ_R = Standard deviation of replenishment cycle (days)

S = Average daily demand (units)

σ_S = Standard deviation of daily demand (units)

For example, if the mean and standard deviation of daily demand are 20 and four units, respectively, and if the mean and standard deviation of lead time are eight and two days, respectively, then the mean and standard deviation of demand during lead time can be calculated as shown in Formula 9.14.

$$\begin{aligned}\bar{X} &= SR \\ &= 20(8) \\ &= 160\,\text{units}\end{aligned} \qquad 9.14$$

$$\begin{aligned}\sigma &= \sqrt{R(\sigma_S)^2 + S^2(\sigma_R)^2} \\ &= \sqrt{(8)(4)^2 + (20)^2(2)^2} \\ &= \sqrt{1{,}728} \\ &= 41.57\,\text{or}\ 42\ \text{units}\end{aligned}$$

Using the procedure suggested earlier, setting the reorder point at $X + 1\sigma$, or 202 units, reveals an 84.13 percent probability that demand during lead time will not exceed the inventory available. Stated differently, the probability of a stockout is only 15.87 percent (100%–84.13%) when the reorder point is set at one standard deviation from the mean. Table 9.17 shows these figures and the ones computed for setting the reorder point at two and three standard deviations from the mean. An organization should thoroughly compare the financial and customer service benefits of avoiding stockouts with the cost of carrying additional safety stock before choosing a reorder point.

9-4-5 Fixed Order Interval Approach

The second form of the basic approach is the **fixed order interval** approach to inventory management, also called the **fixed period** or **fixed review period** approach. In essence, this technique involves ordering inventory at fixed or regular intervals; generally, the amount ordered depends on how much is in stock and available at the time of review. Organizations usually count inventory near the interval's end and base orders on the amount on hand at that time.

In comparison with the basic EOQ approach, the fixed interval model does not require close surveillance of inventory levels; thus, the monitoring is less expensive. This approach is best used for inventory items that have a relatively stable demand. Using this approach for volatile demand items might quickly result in a stockout since time rather than inventory level triggers orders.

Table 9.17	Reorder Point Alternatives and Stockout Possibilities	
REORDER POINT	**PROBABILITY OF NO STOCKOUT OCCURRING**	**PROBABILITY OF A STOCKOUT SITUATION**
$\bar{X} + 1\sigma = 202$	84.13%	15.87%
$\bar{X} + 2\sigma = 244$	97.72%	2.28%
$\bar{X} + 3\sigma = 286$	99.87%	0.13%
Source: John J. Coyle, DBA. Used with permission.		

If demand and lead time are constant and known in advance, then an organization using the fixed order interval approach will periodically reorder exactly the same amount of inventory. If either demand or lead time varies, however, the amount ordered each time will vary, becoming a result of demand as well as lead time length. For example, as Figure 9.14 indicates, an organization starting each period with 4,000 units and selling 2,500 units before its next order will have to reorder 2,500 units plus the units it anticipates selling during the lead time to bring inventory up to the desired beginning level of 4,000 units. Figure 9.14 shows an instance in which the amount ordered differs from one five-week period to the next.

Like the fixed order quantity approach to inventory management, the fixed order interval approach typically combines elements of both the pull and push philosophies. This shows again how organizations, in an effort to anticipate demand rather than simply react to it, are developing systems that incorporate the push philosophy.

9-4-6 Summary and Evaluation of EOQ Approaches to Inventory Management

Arguments exist that there are really four basic forms of the EOQ inventory model: fixed quantity/fixed interval, fixed quantity/irregular interval, irregular quantity/fixed interval, and irregular quantity/irregular interval. In an organization that knows demand and lead time with certainty, either the basic EOQ or the fixed order interval approaches will be the best choices (and would produce the same results). If either demand or lead time varies, however, approach selection must consider the potential consequences of a stockout. In instances involving A (high importance) items, a fixed quantity/irregular interval approach might be the best. The irregular quantity/fixed interval approach might be the best when C (low importance) items are involved. Only under very restrictive circumstances could an organization justify using the irregular quantity/irregular interval approach to inventory management.

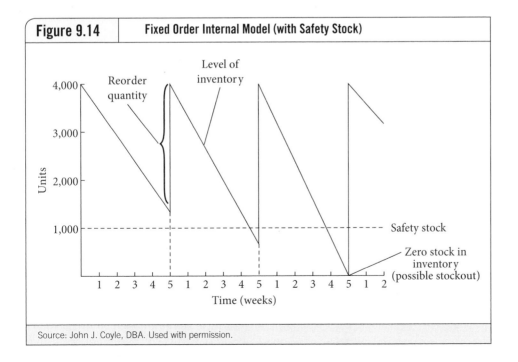

| Figure 9.14 | Fixed Order Internal Model (with Safety Stock) |

Source: John J. Coyle, DBA. Used with permission.

The fixed order quantity (EOQ) and fixed order interval approaches have proven to be effective inventory management tools when demand and lead time are relatively stable as well as when significant variability and uncertainty exist. Most importantly, using these approaches requires that the inherent logistics tradeoffs be considered when making inventory decisions.

Organizations today that are expanding beyond the basic order quantity and order interval approaches have had considerable success with concepts such as JIT, MRP, MRP II, and DRP, which are the next topics of discussion. Keep in mind that all of these techniques for managing inventory incorporate some version of the basic EOQ model into their philosophies.

9-5 Additional Approaches to Inventory Management

The management of inventory levels in the supply chain has often been the underlying rationale for the focus on supply chain management. The interest in reducing inventory levels along the supply chain is indicative of the importance of inventory as a cost of doing business. In many organizations, inventory is the first or second largest asset on the balance sheet.

Organizations, therefore, can reduce their costs of doing business and improve their return on investment or assets (ROI/ROA) by decreasing inventory levels. Keep in mind that service levels are important constraints when decreasing inventories. It should also be noted that the investment in inventory can add value by reducing costs in other areas, such as manufacturing and transportation, or enhance revenue through better service levels. Therefore, the cost and benefit tradeoffs of maintaining inventory in the supply chain must be considered when striving to achieve a balanced view of inventory.

In the following sections, several approaches to inventory management that have special relevance to supply chain management will be examined: JIT, MRP, and DRP.

Supply Chain Technology *Distributor of Education Supplies Passes Inventory Exam*

Asset Education is a distributor of professional development to educators, specializing in the kitting, delivery, and management of hands-on curricula and leased supplies.

Reverse logistics and quality control are essential to the company, which often receives returned kits with missing, damaged, or extraneous items. After deploying a series of custom software applications, the company was able to manage inventory on an item-level —, rather than kit-level, — basis.

The company operates a 20,000 square-foot warehouse on the south side of Pittsburgh. Its 3,000 SKUs include equipment and consumables for science, technology, engineering, and math (STEM) lessons. SKUs are assembled into at least 100 different modules, with 12 lessons in each unit.

"We don't want teachers to have to shop for supplies, so we provide everything they need," says Cynthia Pulkowski, executive director of Asset STEM Education. "But if one item is missing or damaged, they have to make a trip to the store, and we've missed that goal."

Previously, the system assumed that if a kit came back it did so with all components intact. Because that was rarely the case, an accurate inventory count was impossible. Associates often borrowed from one module to complete another.

"It created a nightmare," says Frank Arzenti, director of materials support center. "It was frustrating because we considered continuing to use our existing WMS or look at a new one, which probably would be too costly and big for what we need."

A custom-engineered assortment of functional "apps" (DMLogic) now works with the existing system to provide item-level tracking and management of workflows in returns, picking, and packing. The company executed the changeover to the new apps without any shutdown, while working to add all inventory to the system.

When orders are released to the floor, it creates a unique license plate for specific totes, each representing a module or portion thereof. One person can now pick to six totes at the same time, instead of six people picking to one module each. Last year the company shipped about 10,000 totes containing a total of 3.6 million eaches.

The project reduced space needed for materials, so last year the company was able to give 10,000 square feet back to the landlord while also bringing materials back in-house from off-site storage. After reconfiguring the warehouse to store components instead of pallets of totes, it went from 1,000 linear feet of storage to 4,000 linear feet without breaking a wall.

"Item level has been tremendous improvement to inventory," Pulkowski says. "One of the most important things was that the supplier always listened to the staff as they were developing. They never just gave us something and said, 'use this.' It was what we asked for and they checked at every step of the way."

Source: Josh Bond, *Logistics Management*, February 2015, p. 37. Reprinted with permission of Peerless Media, LLC.

9-5-2 Just-in-Time Approach

One of the most common approaches to inventory management is the just-in-time approach. In today's business environment, discussions focus on JIT manufacturing processes, JIT inventories, or JIT delivery systems. The underlying theme of the phrase *just-in-time* suggests that inventories should be available when an organization needs them—not any earlier or later. This section emphasizes additional factors that characterize a true just-in-time system.

9-5-2-1 Definition and Components of JIT Systems

Generally, JIT systems are designed to manage lead times and to eliminate waste. Ideally, product should arrive exactly when an organization needs it, with no tolerance for late or early deliveries. Many JIT systems place a high priority on short, consistent lead times. However, in a true JIT system, the length of the lead time is not as important as the reliability of the lead time.

The JIT concept is an Americanized version of the **Kanban** system, which the Toyota Motor Company developed in Japan. *Kanban* refers to the cards attached to carts delivering small amounts of needed components and other materials to locations within manufacturing facilities. Each card precisely details the necessary replenishment quantities and the exact time when the replenishment activity must take place.

Production cards (*kan* cards) establish and authorize the amount of product to be manufactured; requisition cards (*ban* cards) authorize the withdrawal of needed materials from the supply operation. Given knowledge of daily output volumes, these activities can be accomplished manually, without the need for computer assistance. Finally, an **Andon system**, or light system, is used as a means to notify plant personnel of existing problems—a yellow light for a small problem and a red light for a major problem. Either light can be seen by personnel throughout the plant. In this way, workers are advised of the possibility of an interruption to the manufacturing process, if the problem warrants such action.[3]

Experience indicates that effectively implementing the JIT concept can dramatically reduce parts and materials inventories, work-in-process inventories, and finished product. In addition, the Kanban and JIT concepts rely heavily on the quality of the manufactured product and components and on a capable and precise logistics system to manage materials and physical distribution.

Four major elements underlie the JIT concept: zero inventories; short, consistent lead times; small, frequent replenishment quantities; and high quality, or zero defects. JIT is an operating concept based on delivering materials in exact amounts and at the precise times that organizations need them—thus minimizing inventory costs. JIT can improve quality and minimize waste and completely change the way an organization performs its logistics activities. JIT, as practiced by many organizations, is more comprehensive than an inventory management system. It includes a comprehensive culture of quality, supplier partnerships, and employee teams.

The JIT system operates in a manner very similar to the two-bin or reorder point system. The system uses one bin to fill demand for a part; when that bin is empty (the signal to replenish the part), the second bin supplies the part. Toyota, among other organizations, has been very successful with this system because of its master production schedule, which aims to schedule every product, every day, in a sequence that intermixes all parts. Manufacturing products in small quantities through short production runs also creates a relatively continuous demand for supplies and component parts. In theory, the ideal lot size or order size for a JIT-based system is one unit. Obviously, this encourages organizations to reduce or eliminate setup costs and incremental ordering costs.

By adhering to extremely small lot sizes and very short lead times, the JIT approach can dramatically reduce lead times. For example, when manufacturing forklift trucks, Toyota experienced a cumulative material lead time of one month, including final assembly, subassembly, fabrication, and procurement. Other manufacturers of forklift trucks cited lead times ranging from six to nine months.[4]

9-5-2-2 JIT Versus EOQ Approaches to Inventory Management

Table 9.18 highlights key ways in which the JIT philosophy differs from customary inventory management in many organizations. The next section discusses these differences.

First, JIT attempts to eliminate excess inventories for both the buyer and the seller. Some feeling exists that the JIT concept simply forces the seller to carry inventory previously held by the buyer. However, successful JIT applications will significantly reduce inventories for both parties.

Second, JIT systems typically involve short production runs and require production activities to change frequently from one product to another. This approach minimizes the economies of scale that are generated from long production runs of a single product. It also

Table 9.18	EOQ Versus JIT Attitudes and Behaviors	
FACTOR	EOQ	JIT
Inventory	Asset	Liability
Safety stock	Yes	No
Production runs	Long	Short
Setup times	Amortize	Minimize
Lot sizes	EOQ	1 for 1
Queues	Eliminate	Necessary
Lead times	Tolerate	Shorten
Quality inspection	Important parts	100% process
Suppliers/customers	Adversaries	Partners
Supply sources	Multiple	Single
Employees	Instruct	Involve

Source: Adapted from William M. Boyst, III, "JIT American Style," *Proceedings of the 1988 Conference of the American Production & Inventory Control Society* (APICS, 1988): 468. Reproduced by permission.

results in higher changeover costs, assuming that the cost of each changeover is constant. However, shorter production runs will result in lower finished goods inventory levels. So, the tradeoff here is between changeover costs and finished goods inventory levels. Many organizations have been successful at reducing changeover costs, thus taking advantage of lower inventory costs.

Third, JIT minimizes wait times by delivering materials and products when and where an organization needs them. Automobile manufacturers, using JIT, have components and parts delivered to the assembly line when needed, where needed, and in the exact quantity needed.

Fourth, the JIT concept uses short, consistent lead times to satisfy the need for inventory in a timely manner. This is why many suppliers tend to locate their facilities close to their customers who are planning to use the JIT approach. Short lead times reduce cycle stock inventories; consistent lead times reduce safety stock inventories. Of the two components of lead time, consistency is more important. That is, a short lead time for JIT success is not as important as a consistent lead time.

Fifth, JIT-based systems rely on high-quality incoming parts and components and on exceptionally high-quality inbound logistics systems. The fact that JIT systems synchronize manufacturing and assembly with timely, predictable receipt of inbound materials reinforces this need.

Sixth, the JIT concept requires a strong, mutual commitment between the buyer and the seller, one that emphasizes quality and seeks win-win decisions for both parties. JIT success requires a concern for minimizing inventory throughout the distribution channel (or the supply channel); JIT will not succeed if organizations only push inventory back to another channel partner.

9-5-2-3 Summary and Evaluation of JIT

The just-in-time concept can enable logistics managers to reduce unit costs and to enhance customer service. A close examination of JIT-based approaches shows that they resemble the more reactive systems such as the EOQ and fixed order quantity approaches since JIT is demand responsive.

The principal difference between JIT and the more traditional approaches is the JIT commitment to short, consistent lead times and to minimizing or eliminating inventories. In effect, JIT saves money on downstream inventories by placing greater reliance on improved responsiveness and flexibility. Ideally, the use of JIT helps to synchronize the logistics system so thoroughly that its operation does not depend on inventories strategically located at points throughout the logistics system.

Successful JIT applications also place a high priority on efficient and dependable manufacturing processes. Since JIT systems require the delivery of parts and materials when and where the demand arises, they rely heavily on the accuracy of the forecasting process used to anticipate finished product demand. In addition, timely JIT system operation demands effective and dependable communications and information systems as well as high-quality, consistent transportation services.

9-5-3 Materials Requirements Planning

Another inventory and scheduling approach that has gained wide acceptance is **materials requirements planning**. Originally popularized by Joseph Orlicky, MRP deals specifically with supplying materials and component parts whose demand depends on the demand for a specific end product. MRP's underlying concepts have existed for many years, but only recently have technology and information systems permitted organizations to benefit fully from MRP and to implement such an approach.

9-5-3-1 Definition and Operation of MRP Systems

An MRP system consists of a set of logically related procedures, decision rules, and records designed to translate a master production schedule into time-phased net inventory requirements and the planned coverage of such requirements for each component item needed to implement this schedule. An MRP system recalculates net requirements and coverage as a result of changes in the master production schedule, demand, inventory status, or product composition. MRP systems meet their objectives by computing net requirements for each inventory item, time-phasing them, and determining their proper coverage.[5]

The goals of an MRP system are to (1) ensure the availability of materials, components, and products for planned production and for customer delivery; (2) maintain the lowest possible inventory levels that support service objectives; and (3) plan manufacturing activities, delivery schedules, and purchasing activities. In doing so, an MRP system considers current and planned quantities of parts and products in inventory as well as the timing needed for these parts and products.

MRP begins by determining how much end products (independent-demand items) customers desire and when they are needed. Then MRP disaggregates the timing and need for components based on the end-product demand. Figure 9.15 shows how an MRP system operates by using the following key elements:

- **Master production schedule (MPS)**—Based on actual customer orders as well as on demand forecasts, the master production schedule drives the entire MRP system. The MPS details exactly what independent demand items an organization

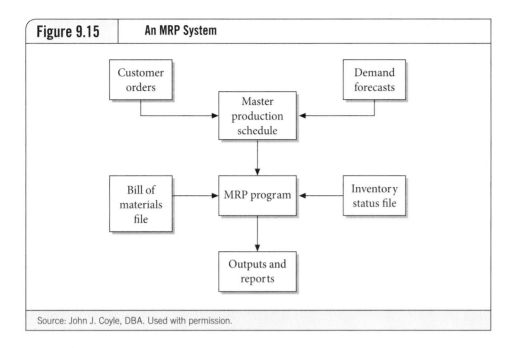

Figure 9.15   **An MRP System**

Source: John J. Coyle, DBA. Used with permission.

must produce and when they are needed. In other words, the MPS provides a detailed schedule of the production timing and quantities for various products.

- **Bill of materials file (BOM)**—Just as a recipe specifies the ingredients needed to bake a cake, the bill of materials file specifies the exact amount of raw materials, components, and subassemblies needed to produce an independent-demand item. Besides identifying gross requirements as needed quantities, the BOM specifies when the individual inputs must be available for the production process. This file also identifies how the various inputs relate to one another and shows their relative importance to producing the end product. Therefore, if several components with different lead times need to be combined as a subassembly, the BOM will indicate this relationship.

- **Inventory status file (ISF)**—This file maintains inventory records so that the organization may subtract the amount on hand from the gross requirements, thus identifying the net requirements at any point in time. The inventory status file also contains important information on specifics such as safety stock and lead time requirements. The ISF plays a critical role in maintaining the MPS and helping to minimize inventory.

- **MRP program**—Based on the independent item need specified in the MPS and on information from the BOM, the MRP program first disaggregates the end-product demand into gross requirements for individual parts and other materials. Then the program calculates net requirements based on ISF information and places orders for the inputs necessary for the production process. The orders respond to needs for specific quantities of materials and to the timing of those needs. The example in the next section clarifies these MRP program activities.

- **Outputs and reports**—After an organization runs the MRP program, several basic outputs and reports will help managers involved in logistics and manufacturing. Included are records and information related to the following:

(1) quantities the organization should order and when they should be ordered, (2) any need to expedite or reschedule arrival dates of needed input quantities, (3) canceled need for product, and (4) MRP system status. These reports are key to controlling the MRP system and in complex environments are reviewed every day to make appropriate modifications and provide information.

9-5-3-2 Example of an MRP System

To understand the MRP approach more fully, consider an organization that assembles egg timers. Assume that according to the MPS, the organization desires to assemble a single, finished egg timer for delivery to a customer at the end of eight weeks. The MRP application would proceed as follows.

Figure 9.16 shows the BOM for assembling a single egg timer. The gross requirements for one finished product include two ends, one bulb, three supports, and one gram of sand. Figure 9.16 also shows that the organization must add the gram of sand to the bulb before assembling the finished egg timer.

Table 9.19 displays the ISF for the egg timer example and calculates the net requirements as the difference between gross requirements and the amount of inventory on hand. The table also notes the lead time for each component. For example, the lead time needed to procure supports and bulbs is one week, whereas sand needs four weeks and ends require five. Once all components are available, the time needed to assemble the finished egg timer is one week.

Figure 9.16	Relationship of Parts to Finished Product: MRP Egg Timer Example

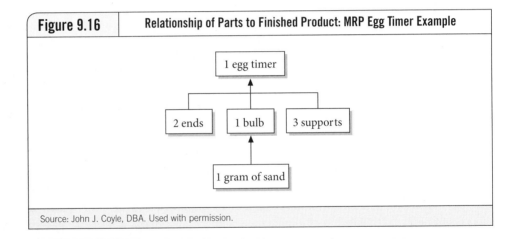

Source: John J. Coyle, DBA. Used with permission.

Table 9.19	Inventory Status File: MRP Egg Timer Example

PRODUCT	GROSS REQUIREMENTS	INVENTORY ON HAND	NET REQUIREMENTS	LEAD TIME (IN WEEKS)
Egg timers	1	0	1	1
Ends	2	0	2	5
Supports	3	2	1	1
Bulbs	1	0	1	1
Sand	1	0	1	4

Source: John J. Coyle, DBA. Used with permission.

Finally, Figure 9.17 is the master schedule for all activities relating to ordering and receiving components and assembling the finished egg timer. Because the organization must have the single egg timer assembled and ready for customer delivery at the end of eight weeks, appropriate parts quantities must be available in the seventh week. The upper portion of Figure 9.17 shows this requirement.

| Figure 9.17 | Master Schedule: MRP Egg Timer Example |

EGG TIMERS (LT=1)	1	2	3	4	5	6	7	8
Quantity needed								1
Production schedule							1	

ENDS (LT=5)	1	2	3	4	5	6	7	8
Gross requirements							2	
Inventory on hand	0	0	0	0	0	0	0	
Scheduled receipts							2	
Planned order releases		2						

SUPPORTS (LT=1)	1	2	3	4	5	6	7	8
Gross requirements							3	
Inventory on hand	2	2	2	2	2	2	2	
Scheduled receipts							1	
Planned order releases						1		

BULBS (LT=1)	1	2	3	4	5	6	7	8
Gross requirements							1	
Inventory on hand	0	0	0	0	0	0	0	
Scheduled receipts							1	
Planned order releases						1		

SAND (LT=4)	1	2	3	4	5	6	7	8
Gross requirements						1		
Inventory on hand	0	0	0	0	0	0		
Scheduled receipts						1		
Planned order releases		1						

Working backward from the need for parts in the seventh week, the lower portions of Figure 9.17 identify strategies for ordering and receiving component inventories. For example, for two ends requiring a lead time of five weeks, the organization must place an order in the second week. For the one additional support requiring a lead time of a single week, the organization should release an order during the sixth week. Finally, the organization must order the bulb in the sixth week for delivery in the seventh and order the sand in the second week for delivery in the sixth.

This example illustrates how the MRP-based approach relates to inventory scheduling and inventory control. In effect, the MRP program itself would perform the calculations involved in Figure 9.17. Once the program develops the master schedule, reports present this information in a format suitable for a manager's use.

In practice, MRP is exceptionally suitable for planning and controlling the ordering and receipt of large numbers of parts and products that might interact during assembly or manufacture. Organizations such as Dell and Boeing use the MRP approach to assembling computers and aircraft, respectively. With the exception of very simple problems such as the egg timer example, computer technology is virtually a prerequisite to using MRP-based applications.

9-5-3-3 Summary and Evaluation of MRP Systems

Having established the MPS, the MRP program develops a time-phased approach to inventory scheduling and inventory receipt. Because it generates a list of required materials in order to assemble or manufacture a specified number of independent demand items, MRP represents a push approach. Correspondingly, this encourages purchase order and production order development. Typically, MRP applies primarily when the demand for parts and materials depends on the demand for some specific end product.

Since actual demand is key to the establishment of production schedules, MRP systems can react quickly to changing demand for finished products. Although some JIT proponents feel that a pull approach is inherently more responsive than a push approach such as MRP, the reverse is sometimes true. MRP systems can also help organizations to achieve other typical JIT objectives, such as those pertaining to lead time management and elimination of waste. In short, MRP can achieve objectives more commonly associated with the JIT-based approaches while at times decisions made through the pull concept do not reflect the future events for which the JIT policies are intended.

The principal advantages of most MRP-based systems include the following:

- They attempt to maintain reasonable safety stock levels and to minimize or eliminate inventories whenever possible.
- They can identify process problems and potential supply chain disruptions long before they occur and take the necessary corrective actions.
- Production schedules are based on actual demand as well as on forecasts of independent demand items.
- They coordinate materials ordering across multiple points in an organization's logistics network.
- They are more suitable for batch, intermittent assembly, or project processes.

Shortcomings of MRP-based approaches include the following:

- Their application is computer intensive, and making changes is sometimes difficult once the system is in operation.

- Both ordering and transportation costs might rise as an organization reduces inventory levels and possibly moves toward a more coordinated system of ordering product in smaller amounts to arrive when the organization needs it.

- They are not usually as sensitive to short-term fluctuations in demand as are order point approaches (although they are not as inventory intensive, either).

- They frequently become quite complex and sometimes do not work exactly as intended.[6]

9-5-3-4 A Note Concerning MRP II Systems

Manufacturing resource planning has a far more comprehensive set of tools than MRP alone. Although MRP is a key step in MRP II, MRP II allows an organization to integrate financial planning with operations and logistics.

MRP II serves as an excellent planning tool and helps describe the likely results of implementing strategies in areas such as logistics, manufacturing, marketing, and finance. Thus, it helps an organization to conduct "what if?" analyses and to determine appropriate product movement and storage strategies at and between points in the logistics system.

MRP II is a technique used to plan and manage all of the organization's resources and reaches far beyond inventory or even production control to all planning functions of an organization.[7] MRP II is a holistic planning technique that can draw together all of the corporate functional areas into an integrated whole. The ultimate benefits of MRP II include improved customer service through fewer shortages and stockouts, better delivery performance, and responsiveness to changes in demand. Successfully implementing MRP II should also help to reduce inventory costs, reduce the frequency of production line stoppages, and create more planning flexibility.[8]

9-5-4 Distribution Requirements Planning

Distribution requirements planning is a widely used and potentially powerful technique for outbound logistics systems to help determine the appropriate level of inventory to be held to meet both cost and service objectives. DRP determines replenishment schedules between an organization's manufacturing facilities and its distribution centers. The success stories involving DRP indicate that organizations can improve service (decrease stockouts), reduce the overall level of finished goods inventories, reduce transportation costs, and improve distribution center operations. With this potential, it is no wonder that manufacturers are interested in the capabilities of DRP systems.

DRP is usually coupled with MRP systems in an attempt to manage the flow and timing of both inbound materials and outbound finished goods. This is particularly true in industries where numerous inbound items are needed to produce a finished product, as is the case in the automobile industry. Items that need to be combined and used in the assembly of a finished product usually have varying lead times. Therefore, MRP is tied to the master production schedule, which indicates what items are to be produced each day and the sequence in which they will be produced. This schedule is then used as the basis to forecast the number of parts needed and when they will be needed.

The underlying rationale for DRP is to more accurately forecast demand and to explode that information back for use in developing production schedules. In that way, an organization can minimize inbound inventory by using MRP in conjunction with production schedules. Outbound (finished goods) inventory is minimized through the use of DRP.

DRP develops a projection for each SKU and requires the following:[9]

- Forecast of demand for each SKU
- Current inventory level of the SKU (balance on hand, BOH)
- Target safety stock
- Recommended replenishment quantity
- Lead time for replenishment

This information is used to develop replenishment requirements at each distribution center. One of the key elements of a DRP system is the development of a DRP table, which consists of a variety of elements including the SKU, BOH, scheduled receipt, planned orders, and so on. Table 9.20 illustrates the DRP table for chicken noodle soup at the Columbus distribution center. The table shows only nine weeks, but a DRP table would typically show 52 weeks and be a dynamic document that undergoes continual change as the data, especially demand, changed. Individual tables provide useful information, but combining tables can produce an increased advantage. For example, combining all of the individual SKU tables of items shipped from one source can provide useful information about transportation consolidation opportunities and when to expect orders to arrive at a distribution center. Combining the demand tables by item by distribution center helps to develop efficient production plans and shipping plans, as illustrated in Figure 9.18.

9-5-4-1 Summary and Evaluation of DRP

DRP systems accomplish for outbound shipments what MRP accomplishes for inbound shipments. The focal point for combining these two systems is the manufacturing facility, where the optimum flow of material is critical. DRP is an example of a push approach and can be used for both single-facility and system-wide applications. The key to a successful DRP approach is having accurate demand forecasts by SKU by distribution center. Consolidating this demand by SKU and incorporating lead times and safety stock requirements allows the manufacturing facility to determine the master production schedule. Once the

Table 9.20	DRP Table for Chicken Noodle Soup								
COLUMBUS DISTRIBUTION CENTER—DISTRIBUTION RESOURCE PLANNING									
WEEK	**JAN. 1**	**2**	**3**	**4**	**FEB. 5**	**6**	**7**	**8**	**MAR. 9**
CHICKEN NOODLE: Current BOH = 4,314; Q = 3,800; SS = 1,956; LT = 1									
Forecast	974	974	974	974	989	1,002	1,002	1,002	1,061
Sched. Receipt	0	0	3,800	0	0	0	3,800	0	0
BOH—Ending	3,340	2,366	5,192	4,218	3,229	2,227	5,025	4,023	2,962
Planned Order	0	3,800	0	0	0	3,800	0	0	3,800
Actual Order				Q = Quantity					
				SS = Safety stock					
				LT = Lead time					
Source: A. J. Stenger, "Distribution Resources Planning," Penn State University, class example.									

Figure 9.18	Combining DRP Tables

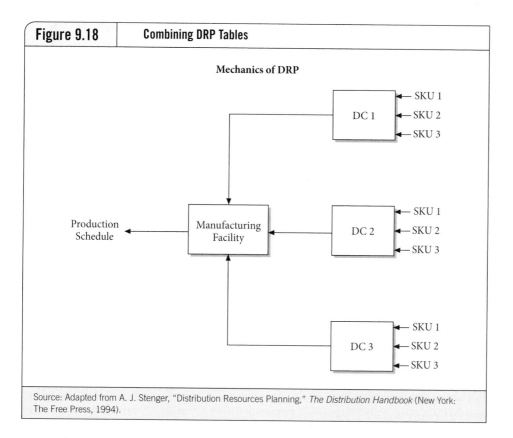

Mechanics of DRP

Source: Adapted from A. J. Stenger, "Distribution Resources Planning," *The Distribution Handbook* (New York: The Free Press, 1994).

MPS is determined, MRP can be used to coordinate the flow and timing of material into the manufacturing facility so it can meet the desired shipments to the distribution centers. So, combining MRP with DRP results in an approach that coordinates the flow of materials from raw materials suppliers through the manufacturing facility (where finished goods are produced) and on to the distribution centers to meet the shipment demands of customers.

9-5-5 Vendor-Managed Inventory

The inventory techniques discussed so far are usually used to manage inventories *within* an organization's logistics network. JIT and MRP manage raw materials and component inventories on the inbound side of a manufacturing facility. DRP manages finished goods inventories between the manufacturing facility and its distribution centers. A relatively new inventory management technique, vendor-managed inventory, manages inventories *outside* an organization's logistics network. In other words, VMI is used by an organization to manage its inventories held in its customer's distribution centers.

The concept of VMI was initiated by Walmart so its suppliers could manage their inventories within Walmart distribution centers. The basis of this concept was that suppliers could manage their inventories better than Walmart could. As such, suppliers took responsibility for making sure that their products were always available in Walmart distribution centers when stores demanded them. VMI has since been adopted by many other organizations across multiple industries.

The basic principles underlying the concept of VMI are relatively simple. First, the supplier and its customer agree on which products are to be managed using VMI in the customer's distribution centers. Second, an agreement is made on reorder points and economic order quantities for each of these products. Third, as these products are shipped from the customer's distribution center, the customer notifies the supplier, by SKU, of the volumes shipped on a real-time basis. This notification is also called "pull data." That is, as the customer "pulls" a product from storage to be shipped to a store or other facility, the supplier is notified that the product has been pulled for shipment, thus diminishing on-hand inventories. Fourth, the supplier monitors on-hand inventories in the customer's distribution center, and when the on-hand inventory reaches the agreed-upon reorder point, the supplier creates an order for replenishment, notifies the customer's distribution center of the quantity and time of arrival, and ships the order to replenish the distribution center. Thus, the customer has no need to place an order for replenishment; through real-time information sharing, the supplier has knowledge of product demand and "pushes" inventory to the customer's location.

VMI was traditionally used for independent-demand items between suppliers and retailers. However, organizations like Dell are allowing component suppliers to use VMI to manage their inventories in third-party warehouses located near Dell assembly plants. So, VMI can be used for both independent- and dependent-demand items.

Many organizations are now using VMI in conjunction with CPFR (discussed in Chapter 7) to manage system-wide inventories. Remember that CPFR is a concept that allows suppliers and their customers to mutually agree upon system-wide demand for products. Since CPFR is used to develop the system-wide plan, organizations need a technique to execute those plans on a system-wide and facility basis. This is where VMI plays a role. VMI can be used to monitor system inventories as well as facility inventories and use these data to help validate the CPFR plan.

The use of VMI to manage inventories is not affected by which organization *owns* those inventories. Traditionally, suppliers using VMI shipped products to customer distribution centers under the FOB destination concept. That is, the supplier owned the inventory in transit, but ownership transferred once the product was received by the customer's distribution center. So the supplier was managing its inventories, but the customer maintained ownership. Some customers have been investigating the use of what can be called **almost consignment inventory** in their distribution centers. In this scenario, the supplier manages and owns the inventory in the customer's distribution centers until that inventory is pulled for shipment. Under the almost consignment concept, suppliers have the challenge of minimizing their inventory investment in their customer's distribution centers while making sure that a sufficient amount of inventory is available to meet demand.

A major benefit of VMI is the knowledge gained by the supplier of real-time inventory levels of its products at its customer locations. This allows the shipper more time to react to sudden swings in demand to assure that stockouts do not occur. A drawback of VMI is that sometimes suppliers use VMI to push excess inventory to a customer distribution center at the end of the month in order to meet monthly sales quotas. This results in the customer holding extra inventory, adding costs to its operations.

All of the inventory techniques discussed to this point have subtle differences and similarities. However, they all use some form of the EOQ and reorder point techniques. Remember that the EOQ and reorder point techniques answer the questions of *how much* and *when*. JIT, MRP, DRP, and VMI all strive to ship the proper quantity at the proper time. As such, all use the EOQ and reorder point techniques. Figure 9.19 is an attempt to show where all these inventory techniques fit into the logistics network. In this figure, a retail network is used. As an inventory technique manages inventory closer to the point of

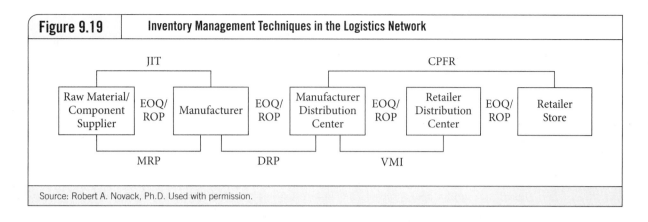

Figure 9.19 Inventory Management Techniques in the Logistics Network

Source: Robert A. Novack, Ph.D. Used with permission.

real demand (e.g., VMI and CPFR), forecast accuracy increases, forecast cycles decrease, and product availability increases. Many organizations today use all of these techniques in managing inventories in their logistics networks.

The discussion so far has focused on techniques for managing raw material, component, and finished goods inventories in a logistics network. One assumption that has been made is that all items are held at all stocking points, thus simplifying the use of these techniques. However, demand levels and variability, as well as lead time levels and variability, are not consistent among items produced by an organization. The next section will address the concept of inventory evaluation, which requires an organization to assess not only which items are most important but also where they will be stored to meet demand.

9-6 Classifying Inventory

Multiple product lines and inventory control require organizations to focus on more important inventory items and to utilize more sophisticated and effective approaches to inventory management. Inventory classification is usually a first step toward efficient inventory management. Many techniques exist that can be used to classify inventory. However, the discussion in the following section will focus on one of the more basic and popular techniques.

9-6-1 ABC Analysis

The need to rank inventory items in terms of importance was first recognized in 1951 by H. Ford Dicky of General Electric (GE).[10] He suggested that GE classify items according to relative sales volume, cash flows, lead time, or stockout costs. He used what is now referred to as **ABC analysis**. This classification technique assigns inventory items to one of three groups according to the relative impact or value of the items that make up the group. A items are considered to be the most important, with B items being of lesser importance, and C items being the least important. Remember that the criteria used to evaluate an item will determine the group to which it is assigned. Using revenue per item as the criterion might assign Item 1 to the A group, while using profit per item as the criterion might assign Item 1 to the C group. Determining which criteria to use for inventory classification will depend on the goals the organization is trying to achieve. Also remember that an organization might determine that it needs more or less than three groupings.

9-6-1-1 Pareto's Law, or the "80–20 Rule"

Actually, ABC analysis is rooted in Pareto's law, which separates the "trivial many" from the "vital few."[11] In inventory terms, this suggests that a relatively small number of items or SKUs might account for a considerable impact on, or value to, the organization. A nineteenth-century Renaissance man, Vilfredo Pareto, suggested that many situations were dominated by a relatively few vital elements and that the relative characteristics of members of a population were not uniform.[12] His principle that a relatively small percentage of a population might account for a large percentage of the overall impact or value has been referred to as the "80–20 rule," which has been found to exist in many practical situations.

For example, marketing research might find that 20 percent of an organization's customers account for 80 percent of its revenues; a university might find that 20 percent of its courses generate 80 percent of its student credit hours; or a study might find that 20 percent of a city's population account for 80 percent of its crime. Although the actual percentages might differ somewhat from example to example, some variation of the 80–20 rule usually applies.

9-6-1-2 Inventory Illustration

Figure 9.20 demonstrates ABC analysis as it applies to inventory management. The diagram indicates that only 20 percent of the items in the product line account for 80 percent of total sales. The items that make up this 20 percent are referred to as A items because of the significant portion of sales for which they are responsible. The items in the B category account for approximately 50 percent of the items in the product line yet contribute only an additional 15 percent of total sales. Finally, the C items are represented by the remaining 30 percent of the items which account for approximately 5 percent of total sales.

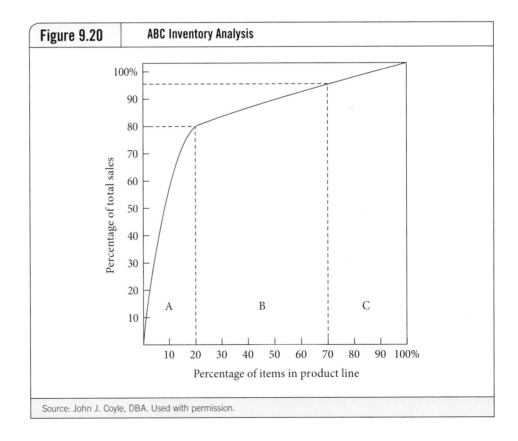

| Figure 9.20 | ABC Inventory Analysis |

Source: John J. Coyle, DBA. Used with permission.

In many ABC analyses, a common mistake is to think of the B and C items as being far less important than the A items and, subsequently, to focus most or all of management's attention on the A items. For example, a decision might be made to assure very high in-stock levels for A items and little or no availability for the B and C items. The fallacy here relates to the fact that all items in the A, B, and C categories are important to some extent and that each category of items deserves its own strategy to assure availability at an appropriate level of cost (stockout cost versus inventory carrying cost). This thinking has led some organizations to differentiate inventory stocking policies by ABC category, making sure that the A items are available either immediately or through the use of express logistics services. The B and C items, while perhaps available at an upstream location in the logistics channel, could be available in a timely manner when needed.

The importance of the B and C items should not be overlooked for a number of additional reasons. Sometimes, the use of B and C items might be complementary to the use of A items, meaning the availability of B and C items might be necessary for the sale of A items; or, in some instances, the C items might be new products that are expected to be successful in the future.

9-6-1-3 Performing an ABC Classification

ABC classification is relatively simple. The first step is to select some criterion, such as revenue, for developing the ranking. The next step is to rank items in descending order of importance according to this criterion and to calculate actual and cumulative total revenue percentages for each item. This calculation will allow the items to be grouped into the ABC categories.

Table 9.21 shows how to base an ABC inventory analysis on revenue generated per line item. The first column identifies the 10 items in the Big Orange product line. The second and third columns show the annual revenue and percentage of total annual revenue

Table 9.21	ABC Analysis for Big Orange Products, Inc.				
ITEM CODE	ANNUAL REVENUE	PERCENTAGE OF ANNUAL REVENUE	CUMULATIVE REVENUE	PERCENTAGE OF ITEMS	CLASSIFICATION CATEGORY
64R	$ 6,800	68.0%	68.0%	10.0%	A
89Q	1,200	12.0	80.0	20.0	A
68I	500	5.0	85.0	30.0	B
37S	400	4.0	89.0	40.0	B
12G	200	2.0	91.0	50.0	B
35B	200	2.0	93.0	60.0	B
61P	200	2.0	95.0	70.0	B
94L	200	2.0	97.0	80.0	C
11T	150	1.5	98.5	90.0	C
20G	150	1.5	100.0	100.0	C
	$10,000	100.0%			

Source: John J. Coyle, DBA. Used with permission.

represented by each item. The fourth and fifth columns show revenue and items, respectively, as percentages of the total. From these columns, it is simple to identify what percentage of items makes up what percentage of revenue. The last column places each item into the ABC classification on the basis of annual revenue.

The last step assigns the items into ABC groups. This step is the most difficult, and no simple technique is available. While the analysis is supported by data inputs, the ultimate decisions will require subjective judgment on the part of the decision maker. As the item rankings are examined, significant natural "breaks" sometimes appear. This is not always the case, and the decision maker will have to consider other variables such as the item's importance and the cost of managing that item.

ABC analysis can also be used in various situations using various criteria to group items. A warehouse manager might assign inventory items to groups using item velocity as the criterion. A marketing manager might assign customers to groups using customer profitability as the criterion. A sales manager might assign sales representatives to groups using gross revenue generated as the criterion. Other classification schemes using ABC analysis might use multiple criteria to rank items, such as profit per item times item turnover. The point here is that items can be classified in many ways, using various criteria, resulting in various groupings. The use of ABC analysis to rank items will depend on the goals management needs to accomplish.

9-6-2 Quadrant Model

Another technique used to classify inventory is called the **quadrant model**. Typically used to classify raw materials, parts, or components for a manufacturing firm, the quadrant model can also be used to classify finished goods inventories using value and risk to the firm as the criteria. Value is measured as the value contribution to profit; risk is the negative impact of not having the product available when it is needed. Figure 9.21 shows an example of a quadrant model. When needed, items with high value and high risk (critical items) need to be managed carefully to ensure adequate supply. Items with low risk and low value (generic or routine items) can be managed much less carefully. Each particular classification in the quadrant model not only suggests stocking policies but also production policies.

Figure 9.21	Quadrant Model

		Low Value	High Value
Risk	**High**	**Distinctives** • High safety stocks • More than one stocking location • Produce to inventory	**Criticals** • High safety stocks • Multiple stocking location • Produce to inventory
	Low	**Generics** • Low/no safety stock • Single stocking location • Produce to order	**Commodities** • Adequate safety stocks • More than one stocking location • Produce to inventory/produce to order

Value

Source: Robert A. Novack, Ph.D. Used with permission.

For example, items in the commodities group (low value, high risk) might be stored in only one location or might be produced only when an order exists. Items in the criticals group might have high levels of safety stock and are always produced to inventory. The quadrant model combines more than one criterion to group items into a category. From that grouping, decisions concerning logistics and manufacturing can be made. The impact of inventory classification on stocking decisions will be the topic of the next section.

9-6-3 Inventory at Multiple Locations— The Square-Root Rule

In their aggressive efforts to take costs out of logistics networks, organizations are searching for new ways to reduce inventory levels without adversely affecting customer service. One current approach is to consolidate inventories into fewer stocking locations in order to reduce overall inventories and their associated costs. This strategy requires the involvement of capable transportation and information resources to assure that customer service is held at existing levels and improved whenever possible.

The **square-root rule** helps determine the extent to which inventories might be reduced through such a consolidation strategy. Assuming that total customer demand remains the same, the square-root rule estimates the extent to which aggregate inventory need will change as an organization increases or decreases the number of stocking locations. In general, the greater the number of stocking locations, the greater the amount of inventory needed to maintain customer service levels. Conversely, as inventories are consolidated into fewer stocking locations, aggregate inventories will decrease.

The square-root rule states that total safety stock inventories in a future number of facilities can be approximated by multiplying the total amount of inventory in existing facilities by the square root of the number of future facilities divided by the number of existing facilities. Mathematically, this relationship can be stated as shown in Formula 9.15.

$$X_2 = (X_1)\sqrt{n_2 / n_1}$$ 9.15

where:

n_1 = Number of existing facilities

n_2 = Number of future facilities

X_1 = Total inventory in existing facilities

X_2 = Total inventory in future facilities

To illustrate, consider an organization that currently distributes 40,000 units of product to its customers from a total of eight facilities located throughout the United States. Current distribution centers are located in Boston, Chicago, San Francisco, Los Angeles, Dallas, Orlando, Charlotte, and Baltimore. The organization is evaluating an opportunity to consolidate its operations into two facilities, one in Memphis, Tennessee, and the other in Reno/Sparks, Nevada. Using the square-root rule, the total amount of inventory in the two future facilities is computed as shown in Formula 9.16.

$n_1 = 8$ existing facilities

$n_2 = 2$ future facilities   9.16

$X_1 = 40,000$ total units of product in the 8 existing facilities thus,

X_2 = total units of product in the 2 future facilities

$\quad = (40{,}000)\sqrt{2/8}$

$\quad = (40{,}000)(0.5)$

$\quad = 20{,}000$ units

Based on the results of this analysis, the two future facilities would carry a total inventory of 20,000 units to satisfy existing demand. If the organization designed these facilities to be of equal size, and if market demand was equal for the geographic areas, each of these distribution centers would carry one-half of this total, or 10,000 units each. Conversely, if the organization considered increasing the number of distribution centers from 8 to, say 32, total inventory needs would double from 40,000 to 80,000 units.

Using data from an actual organization, Table 9.22 shows the total average units of inventory implied by specific numbers of distribution centers in the logistics network. For example, as stocking locations increase from 1 to 25, the total average number of units in inventory increases from 3,885 units to 19,425 units. This is consistent with the rationale underlying the square-root rule. Table 9.22 also shows the percentage change in inventories as the number of distribution centers in the network increases.

Although the square-root rule is simply stated, the model is based on several reasonable assumptions: (1) inventory transfers between stocking locations are not common practice; (2) lead times do not vary, and thus inventory centralization is not affected by inbound supply uncertainty; (3) customer service levels, as measured by inventory availability, are constant regardless of the number of stocking locations; and (4) demand at each location is normally distributed.[13] In addition, it has been shown that the potential for aggregate inventory reduction through consolidation of facilities will be greater when the correlation sales between stocking locations is small to negative and when there is less sales variability at each of the stocking locations.[14]

Table 9.22	Example Impacts of Square-Root Rule on Logistics Inventories		
NUMBER OF WAREHOUSES (n)	$\sqrt{n}$	TOTAL AVERAGE INVENTORY (UNITS)	PERCENT CHANGE
1	1.0000	3,885	—
2	1.4142	5,494	141%
3	1.7321	6,729	173%
4	2.0000	7,770	200%
5	2.2361	8,687	224%
10	3.1623	12,285	316%
15	3.8730	15,047	387%
20	4.4721	17,374	447%
23	4.7958	18,632	480%
25	5.0000	19,425	500%

Source: Robert A. Novack, Ph.D. Used with permission.

Combining the square-root rule with ABC analysis further explains why aggregate inventories are reduced when stocking locations are reduced. Using the example above, assume all eight distribution centers carry A, B, and C items with their associated safety stocks. Reducing the number of stocking points to two has two results: (1) redundant safety stocks are eliminated because now there are two quantities of safety stocks rather than eight, and (2) the organization has the option of further reducing inventories by consolidating C items into one of the two future facilities. In other words, both safety stocks and cycle stocks can be reduced by consolidating facilities as well as by consolidating inventories. So facility, as well as inventory, consolidation can result in significant reductions in inventories for organizations.

SUMMARY

- Inventory as a percent of overall business activity continues to decline. Explanatory factors include greater expertise in managing inventory, innovations in information technology, greater competitiveness in markets for transportation services, and emphasis on reducing cost through the elimination of non-value-adding activities.

- As product lines proliferate and the number of SKUs increases, the cost of carrying inventory becomes a significant expense of doing business.

- There are a number of principal reasons for carrying inventories. Types of inventory include cycle stock, work-in-process, inventory in transit, safety stock, seasonal stock, and anticipatory stock.

- Principal types of inventory cost are inventory carrying cost, ordering and setup cost, expected stockout cost, and in-transit inventory carrying cost.

- Inventory carrying cost is composed of capital cost, storage space cost, inventory service cost, and inventory risk cost. There are precise methods to calculate each of these costs.

- Choosing the appropriate inventory model or technique should include an analysis of key differences that affect the inventory decision. These differences are determined by the following questions: (1) Is the demand for the item independent or dependent? (2) Is the distribution system based upon a push or pull approach? (3) Do the inventory decisions apply to one facility or to multiple facilities?

- Traditionally, inventory managers focused on two important questions to improve efficiency, namely, how much to reorder from suppliers and when to reorder.

- The two aforementioned questions were frequently answered using the EOQ model, trading inventory carrying cost against ordering costs, and then calculating a reorder point based on demand or usage rates.

- The two basic forms of the EOQ model are the fixed quantity model and the fixed interval model. The former is the most widely used. Essentially, the relevant costs are analyzed (traded off), and an optimum quantity is decided. This reorder quantity will remain fixed unless costs change, but the intervals between orders will vary depending on demand.

- The basic EOQ model can be varied or adapted to focus more specifically on decisions that are impacted by inventory-related costs, such as shipment quantities where price discounts are involved.

- Just-in-time inventory management captured the attention of many U.S. organizations during the 1970s, especially the automobile industry. As the name implies, the basic goal is to minimize inventory levels with an emphasis on frequent deliveries of smaller quantities and alliances with suppliers or customers. To be most effective, JIT should also include quality management.

- Materials requirements planning and distribution requirements planning are typically used in conjunction with each other. In addition, a master production schedule is utilized to help balance demand and supply of inventory. DRP is used on the outbound side of a logistics system. Demand forecasts of individual SKUs are developed to drive the DRP model. Then, an MPS schedule is developed to meet the scheduled demand replenishment requirements.

- VMI is used to manage an organization's inventories in its customers' distribution centers. Using pull data, suppliers monitor inventory levels and create orders to ship product to bring inventory levels up to an economic order quantity in the customers' distribution centers.

- ABC analysis is a useful tool to improve the effectiveness of inventory management. Another useful tool is the quadrant model.

- When organizations are adding warehouses to their logistics networks, a frequently asked question is, "How much additional inventory will be required?" The square-root rule is a technique that can be used to help answer this question.

STUDY QUESTIONS

1. Explain why inventory costs and inventory levels have declined relative to GDP over the last 20 years. Is this beneficial to the economy? Why or why not?

2. What are the major components of inventory carrying cost? How would you measure capital cost for making inventory policy decisions?

3. How can inventory carrying cost be calculated for a specific product? What suggestions would you offer for determining the measure of product value to be used in this calculation?

4. Explain the differences between inventory carrying costs and ordering costs.

5. Why is it usually more difficult to determine the cost of lost sales for finished goods than it is for raw materials inventories?

6. How does inventory carrying cost for inventory in transit differ from the cost of inventory at rest?

7. What is the difference between independent and dependent demand items? Why is this distinction important to inventory managers?

8. Compare and contrast the fixed quantity version of EOQ with the fixed interval version. In which situations would each be used?

9. Why has the JIT approach to inventory control become popular in some industries? How does the JIT approach compare to the EOQ approach to inventory management? Should JIT be adopted by all inventory managers? Why or why not?

10. Explain the essential characteristics of MRP, DRP, and VMI. How do they operate with each other to provide a systematic approach to managing supply chain inventories?

11. What are the benefits of classifying inventory using ABC analysis? What are the different types of criteria that could be used to classify inventory?

12. What is the underlying principle of the square-root rule? How do inventories change as the number of warehouses in a logistics network changes?

NOTES

1. Douglas M. Lambert, *The Development of an Inventory Costing Methodology: A Study of the Costs Associated with Holding Inventory* (Oak Brook, IL: National Council of Physical Distribution Management, 1976).

2. Douglas M. Lambert and James R. Stock, *Strategic Logistics Management*, 3rd ed. (Homewood, IL: Irwin, 1993): 378–379.

3. Walter E. Goddard, "Kanban or MRP II—Which Is Best for You?" *Modern Materials Handling* (November 5, 1982): 42.

4. Ibid., 45–46.

5. Joseph Orlicky, *Materials Requirements Planning* (New York, NY: McGraw-Hill, 1975): 22.

6. Denis J. Davis, "Transportation and Inventory Management: Bridging the Gap," *Distribution* (June 1985): 11.

7. John Gatorna and Abby Day, "Strategic Issues in Logistics," *International Journal of Physical Distribution and Materials Management 16* (1986): 29.

8. For additional information regarding MRP II, see Oliver W. Wright, "MRP II," *Modern Materials Handling* (September 12, 1980): 28.

9. Alan J. Stenger, "Materials Resources Planning," *The Distribution Handbook* (New York, NY: The Free Press, 1994): 89–97.

10. Robert Goodell Brown, *Advanced Service Parts Inventory Control*, 2nd ed. (Norwich, VT: Materials Management Systems, 1982): 155.

11. Thomas E. Hendrick and Franklin G. Moore, *Production/Operations Management*, 9th ed. (Homewood, IL: Irwin, 1985): 173.

12. Lambert and Stock, *Strategic Logistics Management*, 426–429; Jay U. Sterling, "Measuring the Performance of Logistics Operations," in James F. Robeson and William C. Copacino, eds., *The Logistics Handbook*, Chapter 10 (New York, NY: The Free Press, 1994): 226–230.

13. Walter Zinn, Michael Levy, and Donald J. Bowersox, "Measuring the Effect of Inventory Centralization/Decentralization on Aggregate Safety Stock: The 'Square Root Law' Revisited," *Journal of Business Logistics 10*, No. 1 (1989): 14.

14. Ibid., 14.

CASE 9.1

MAQ Corporation

MAQ Corporation, a major producer of consumer electronics equipment, is currently faced with a rapidly growing product line and its associated inventory problems. MAQ's president, Mary Semerod, has decided to initiate a program to analyze the company's inventory requirements utilizing different inventory techniques. The first phase of this program consists of an ABC analysis of the company's product line (shown in the following table). Ms. Semerod has encountered difficulties in deciding on the appropriate criteria to use in the classification and in developing appropriate cutoff levels for each class of inventory. To solve her dilemma, Ms. Semerod has contracted the services of a logistics consulting firm to perform the inventory analysis.

SALES DATA (ONE-YEAR PERIOD)

PRODUCT #	UNITS SOLD	PRICE PER UNIT	PROFIT PER UNIT
SR101	15,000	$250	$50.50
SR103	750	1,500	330.00
SR105	1,600	600	90.00
SR201	45	2,250	877.50
SR203	10	3,500	1,750.00
SR205	9,250	500	125.00
SR301	700	650	195.00
SR303	550	700	196.00
SR305	3,000	920	303.60
SR500	100	1,100	440.00

CASE QUESTIONS

1. If you were employed by the consulting firm, how would you construct your method of analysis?
2. What criteria would you use?
3. What would the cutoff levels be? Be sure to provide explanations of the reasoning supporting your decisions.

Source: Robert A. Novack, Ph.D. Used with permission.

CASE 9.2

Baseball Card Emporium

Baseball Card Emporium (BBE) of Lewistown, Pennsylvania, is a distributor of baseball cards to sports card retailers. Its market area encompasses most of Pennsylvania, eastern Ohio, and New Jersey. The cards are printed in Neenah, Wisconsin, and currently shipped to Lewistown via motor carrier transportation. Kenny Craig, vice president of logistics, has asked his staff to evaluate using air carrier service to ship the cards.

Nick Gingher, director of distribution, has collected the following information:

- Annual demand: 6,000 cases of cards
- Case value (price): $96 each
- Inventory carrying cost (annual): 30%
- Cost per order to replenish inventory: $75
- In-transit inventory carrying cost: 18%
- Transit time using motor carrier (parcel ground: 4 days
- Cycle time using motor carrier (parcel ground): 7 days
- Transit time using air carrier: 1 day
- Cycle time using air carrier:2 days
- Motor carrier rate: $1.20 per cwt. (100 lbs.)
- Air carrier rate: $2.50 per cwt.
- Unit weight: 50 lbs. per case

CASE QUESTIONS

1. What is the economic order quantity for BBE in units? In pounds?
2. What is the total cost (not considering transportation-related costs) of the EOQ?
3. What is the total cost for using motor carrier transportation?
4. What is the total cost for using air carrier transportation?
5. Which alternative should BBE use?

Source: Robert A. Novack, Ph.D. Used with permission.

APPENDIX 9A

Special Applications of the EOQ Approach

Adjusting the Simple EOQ Model for Modal Choice Decisions—The Cost of Inventory in Transit

Chapter 1 mentioned the tradeoff possibilities between inventory costs and transportation decisions regarding choice of mode. Implied in this discussion was the idea that longer transit times resulted in higher inventory costs. This is because in-transit inventory carrying costs will be incurred by the firms having ownership of the goods while they are being transported. In effect, the carrying costs of inventory in transit will be similar to the carrying costs of inventory in the warehouse. There are differences between inventory in transit and inventory in the warehouse, but basically the company is responsible for inventory in both instances. There is always some cost attached to having inventory, whether it is sitting in a warehouse or plant or moving to another point. Therefore, if modes of transportation have different transit times and different rates (prices), with other variables being equal, the tradeoff between transportation rates and the inventory cost associated with the transit times should be examined. The transportation rates are usually easy to obtain. However, to calculate the cost of carrying inventory in transit, it will be necessary to modify the basic or simple EOQ model.

Recall that the simple EOQ model essentially considered only the tradeoff between order or setup costs and the carrying cost associated with holding inventory in a warehouse. To consider how different transit times affect transportation and its cost, the company must relax one basic assumption of the EOQ model and adapt the model accordingly.

One assumption of the simple EOQ model was that inventory incurred no cost in transit, because the company either purchased inventory on a delivered-price basis or sold it FOB plant. If conditions change so that the company makes purchases FOB origin or sells products on a delivered-price basis, then it will be necessary to consider the cost of carrying inventory in transit. Figure 9A.1 depicts a modified sawtooth inventory model; the lower half shows the inventory in transit.

The Sawtooth Model Adjusted

Comparing the lower half of Figure 9A.1 with the upper half, which depicts inventory in the warehouse, we can see two differences relevant for calculating the appropriate costs. First, inventory is usually in transit for only part of the cycle. Typically, the number of inventory shipping days would be less than the number of days that inventory from the preceding EOQ replenishment would be in the warehouse. Second, inventory in transit is not used up or sold; warehouse inventory may be used up or sold.

Since inventory in transit has these two distinctive characteristics, the cost of carrying inventory in transit will differ from that of storing inventory in the warehouse. We can calculate this cost in several ways. If a daily inventory-in-transit carrying cost were available, we could multiply it by the number of days in transit. We could calculate this daily cost by multiplying the inventory-in-transit value by a daily opportunity cost. After multiplying this cost by the number of transit days, we could multiply it by the number of orders per year or cycles per year. This would give an annual cost of inventory in transit. In effect, this resembles the procedure we followed when calculating the cost of inventory in the warehouse.

Figure 9A.1	Sawtooth Model Modified for Inventory in Transit

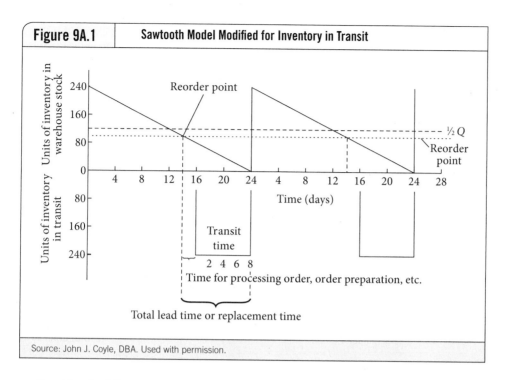

Source: John J. Coyle, DBA. Used with permission.

Consider the following:

Y = Cost of carrying inventory in transit

V = Value = unit of inventory

t = Order cycle time

t_m = Inventory transit time

M = Average number of units of inventory in transit

We calculate the value of M as follows:

$$\frac{t_m}{t} = \text{Percentage of time inventory is in transit per cycle period}$$

Therefore,

$$M = \frac{t_m}{t} Q$$

We could rewrite this as follows:

$$t(\text{days in cycle}) = \frac{360(\text{days in year})}{R/Q \ (\text{cycles per year})}$$

$$t = 360 \frac{Q}{R}$$

$$M = \frac{(t_m Q)}{360} \frac{Q}{R}$$

$$M = \frac{t_m}{360} R$$

The two approaches to calculating M give the same result, given the preceding assumptions. The second equation for M, however, is frequently more useful, since the variables are given in the problem.

Now that we have developed a way of calculating the average number of units in transit, all that remains is to multiply this figure by the value per unit and the percentage annual carrying cost of inventory in transit. The result will be a dollar cost for inventory in transit that compares to the dollar cost of inventory in the warehouse:

$$\frac{t_m}{t}QVY$$

We could write the new total inventory cost equation in either of the following forms:

$$\text{TAC} = \frac{1}{2}QVW + A\frac{R}{Q} + \frac{t_m}{t}QVY$$

or

$$\text{TAC} = \frac{1}{2}QVW + A\frac{R}{Q} + \frac{t_m}{360}RVY^*$$

*Differentiating this equation and solving for Q with the expanded total cost formula results in the same equation as the previous one since the last term added is not a function of Q; that is, $Q = \sqrt{\dfrac{2RA}{VW}}$

Example of Modal Selection

We can measure the tradeoff between transit times and transportation cost using the total cost formula developed in the preceding section. First review the information provided in the example in Chapter 9 to demonstrate the simple EOQ model:

R = 3,600 units (annual demand)

A = $200 (cost of one order or setup)

W = 25% (cost of carrying inventory in warehouse)

V = $100 (value per unit)

Q = 240 units (this would remain the same)

Now consider that a hypothetical company is choosing between two transportation modes (rail or motor) and that the following information is available:

Rail: 8 days in transit time; $3 per hundred pounds

Motor: 6 days transit time; $4 per hundred pounds

Next assume that the company will ship the same amount, 240 units, regardless of mode. If each unit weighs 100 pounds, this represents 24,000 pounds, or 240 hundred-weight (cwt). The cost of carrying inventory in transit (Y) is 10 percent. Given the preceding variables, we may examine the two alternatives using the formula developed previously.

The first step is to look at the product's total inventory cost if the company decides to ship by rail:

$$\text{Total Inventory Cost (rail)} = \left(\frac{1}{2} \times 240 \times \$100 \times 25\%\right) + \left(\$200 \times \frac{3,600}{240}\right)$$

$$+ \left(\frac{8}{24} \times 240 \times \$100 \times 10\%\right)$$

$$= \$3,000 + \$3,000 + \$800$$

$$= \$6,800$$

If we add the transportation cost to the inventory cost, the total cost would be as follows:

$$\text{Total Cost (rail)} = \$6,800 + \left(\$3 \times 240 \times \frac{3,600}{240}\right)$$

$$= \$6,800 + \$10,800$$

$$= \$17,600$$

The next step is to determine the total inventory cost if the company ships the items by motor as shown:

$$\text{Total Inventory Cost (motor)} = \left(\frac{1}{2} \times 240 \times \$100 \times 25\%\right) + \left(\$200 \times \frac{3,600}{240}\right)$$

$$+ \left(\frac{6}{24} \times 240 \times \$100 \times 10\%\right)$$

$$= \$3,000 + \$3,000 + \$600$$

$$= \$6,600$$

Once again, we should add the transportation cost to the inventory costs as follows:

$$\text{Total Cost (motor)} = \$6,600 + \left(\$4 \times 240 \times \frac{3,600}{240}\right)$$

$$= \$6,600 + \$14,400$$

$$= \$21,000 \text{ by motor}$$

Given these calculations, the rail alternative would be less costly and thus preferable. Before leaving this section, we should examine the tradeoffs more closely. As you can see, the rail alternative has a higher inventory cost because of the slower transit time, but the transportation cost savings offset this. The net effect is an overall savings by rail.

Finally, we should note that the procedure suggested in this section is based on conditions of certainty. If transit times varied, we would need to establish probabilities and approach the solution in a more sophisticated manner.

Adjusting the Simple EOQ Model for Volume Transportation Rates

The basic EOQ model discussed previously did not consider the possible reductions in transportation rates per hundredweight associated with larger-volume shipments. For example, the hypothetical company in the previous illustration decided that 240 units was the appropriate quantity to order or produce. If we assume again that each unit weighed 100 pounds, this would imply a shipment of 24,000 pounds. If the rate on a shipment of

24,000 pounds (240 cwt) was $3 per hundred pounds (cwt) and the rate for a 40,000-pound shipment was $2 per cwt, knowing whether to ship 400 units (40,000 pounds) instead of the customary 240 units would be worthwhile.

Shippers transport a specified minimum quantity (weight) or more commonly publish volume rates on carload (rail) and truckload (motor carrier)* quantities. Therefore, in inventory situations, the decision maker responsible for transporting goods should consider how the lower-volume rate affects total cost. In other words, in addition to considering storage (holding) cost and order or setup cost, the decision maker should consider how lower transportation costs affect total cost.

*Motor carriers often publish different LTL rates and TL rates on quantities of 500, 2,000, and 5,000 pounds.

Cost Relationships

Sometimes the economic order quantity suggested by the basic model may be less than the quantity necessary for a volume rate. We can adjust the model to consider the following cost relationships associated with shipping a volume larger than the one determined by the basic EOQ approach.

- **Increased inventory carrying cost for inventory in the warehouse**—The larger quantity required for the volume rate means a larger average inventory ($\frac{1}{2}Q$) and consequently an increased inventory carrying cost.

- **Decreased order or setup costs**—The larger quantity will reduce the number of orders placed and the ordinary costs of order placement and order setup.

- **Decreased transportation costs**—The larger quantity will reduce the cost per hundredweight of transporting the goods, consequently lowering transportation costs.

- **Decreased in-transit inventory carrying cost**—Carload (CL) and truckload (TL) shipments usually have shorter transit times than less-than-carload (LCL) or less-than-truckload (LTL) shipments, and the faster time generally means a lower cost for inventory in transit.

Figure 9A.2 represents the cost relationships and considers possible transportation rate discounts (volume rates versus less-than-volume rates). The total cost function "breaks," or is discontinuous, at the quantity that permits a company to use the volume rate. Therefore, we cannot use the cost function for the transportation rate discount or discounts in the original EOQ formulation. Rather, we must use sensitivity analysis, or a sensitivity test, to determine whether total annual costs are lower if the company purchases a quantity larger than the basic EOQ amount. Note that although Figure 9A.2 indicates that using the volume rate will lower total cost, this does not necessarily have to be the case. For example, if the inventory dollar value was very high, then the increased storage (holding) costs could more than offset reductions in order and transport cost.

Mathematical Formulation

Although there are several ways to analyze opportunities for using volume transportation rates, a useful method is to calculate and compare the total annual costs of the EOQ-based approach with those of the volume-rate-based approach. The following symbols will be useful in this analysis:

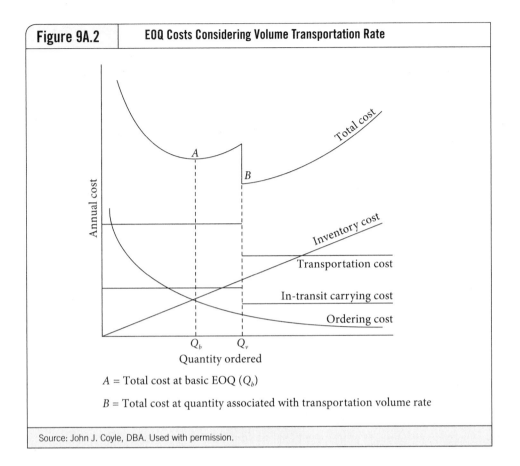

| Figure 9A.2 | EOQ Costs Considering Volume Transportation Rate |

A = Total cost at basic EOQ (Q_b)

B = Total cost at quantity associated with transportation volume rate

Source: John J. Coyle, DBA. Used with permission.

TAC = inventory carrying cost + order cost + transportation cost + in-transit inventory carrying cost

TAC_b = total annual cost at basic EOQ

TAC_v = total annual cost at volume rate quantity

Q_b = basic EOQ

Q_v = volume rate quantity

t_m = time in transit for less-than-volume shipment

t_n = time in transit for volume shipment

H = less-than-volume rate (high rate)

L = volume rate (low rate)

We calculate each total annual cost as follows:

$$TAC_b = \frac{1}{2}Q_bVW + A\frac{R}{Q_b} + HQ_b\frac{R}{Q_b} + \frac{t_m}{t}Q_bVY$$

$$TAC_v = \frac{1}{2}Q_vVW + A\frac{R}{Q_v} + LQ_v\frac{R}{Q_v} + \frac{t_m}{t}Q_vVY$$

Noting that $HQ_b \dfrac{R}{Q_b}$ can be written simply as HR and that $LQ_b \dfrac{R}{Q_b}$ can be written simply as LR, we can reduce these equations to the following:

$$TAC_b = \frac{1}{2}Q_bVW + A\frac{R}{Q_b} + HR + \frac{t_m}{t}Q_bVY$$

$$TAC_v = \frac{1}{2}Q_vVW + A\frac{R}{Q_v} + LR + \frac{t_n}{t}Q_vVY$$

Transportation Rate Discount Example

An example that builds on the previous problem will illustrate in this section how transportation rate discounts produce possible annual cost savings.

For this new example, assume the following variables:

H = \$3:00 = cwt (assume each unit weighs 100 pounds)

L = \$2:00 = cwt with a minimum of 40,000 pounds (with each unit weighing 100 pounds; this would be 400 units, or 400 cwt)

t_n = 6 days (time in transit for volume movement)

Y = 10% (carrying cost of inventory while in transit)

Q_v = 400 units

t_v = 40 days (length of a single inventory cycle for Qv = 400 units)

From the previous problem, we know the following:

R = 3,600 units (3,600 cwt) (annual sales)

A = \$200 (cost of placing an order or cost of setup)

V = \$100 = cwt = unit (value per unit)

W = 25%

Q_b = 240 units (240 cwt, or 240,000 pounds)

t_m = 8 days (time in transit for LTL movement)

t = 24 days (length of a single inventory cycle or period)

Solving for TAC_b and TAC_v, we get the following result:

$$TAC_b = \left[\frac{1}{2} \times 240 \times \$100 \times 25\%\right] + \left[\$200 \times \frac{3,600}{240}\right]$$

$$+ [\$3 \times \$3,600] + \left[\frac{8}{24} \times 240 \times \$100 \times 10\%\right]$$

$$= \$17,600$$

$$TAC_v = \left[\frac{1}{2} \times 400 \times \$100 \times 25\%\right] + \left[\$200 \times \frac{3,600}{500}\right]$$

$$+ [\$2 \times \$3,600] + \left[\frac{6}{40} \times 400 \times \$100 \times 10\%\right]$$

$$= \$14,240$$

Since TAC_b exceeds TAC_v by \$3,360, the most economical solution is to purchase the larger quantity, 400 cwt. Reductions in ordering, transportation, and in-transit inventory carrying costs offset the increased cost of holding the larger quantity.

We may modify this analysis to consider potential volume discounts for purchasing in larger quantities. The same procedure of calculating and comparing total annual costs under the various alternatives applies, providing we make minor modifications to the equations.

Adjusting the Simple EOQ Model for Private Carriage

Many companies that use their own truck fleet or that lease trucks for private use assess a fixed charge per mile or per trip, no matter how much the company ships at any one time. In other words, since operating costs such as driver expense and fuel do not vary significantly with weight, and since fixed costs do not change with weight, many companies charge a flat amount per trip rather than differentiate on a weight basis. Therefore, since additional weight costs nothing extra, it is logical to ask what quantity the company should ship.

The basic EOQ model can handle this analysis since the fixed trip charge is comparable to the order cost or setup cost. Therefore, the decision maker must trade off the prospect of a smaller number of larger shipments against the increased cost of carrying larger average inventory amounts.

If T_c represents the trip charge, we can write the formula as follows:

$$TAC = \frac{1}{2}QVW + \frac{R}{Q}A + \frac{R}{Q}T_c$$

We can derive the basic model as follows:

$$EOQ = \sqrt{\frac{2R(A+T_c)}{VW}}$$

From the previous example, we can add a charge of \$100 per trip.

$$EOQ = \frac{\sqrt{2\times\$3,600\times(\$200+\$100)}}{\$100\times25\%}$$

$$= \frac{\sqrt{\$2,160,000}}{\$25}$$

$$= \sqrt{86,400}$$

$$= 293.94$$

The EOQ size has been increased to 293.94 units because of additional fixed charges associated with private trucking costs.

Adjusting the Simple EOQ Model for the Establishment and Application of In-Excess Rates[*]

We can adjust the basic inventory analysis framework discussed in Chapter 9 to utilize an in-excess rate. Through in-excess rates, carriers encourage heavier shipper loadings.

[*]This section is adapted from James L. Heskett, Robert M. Ivie, and Nicholas A. Glaskowsky, *Business Logistics* (New York: Ronald Press, 1964): 516–520.

The carrier offers a lower rate for weight shipped in excess of a specified minimum weight. A logistics manager must decide whether the company should use the in-excess rate and, if so, the amount the company should include in each shipment.

Consider the following example: CBL Railroad has just published a new in-excess rate on items that XYZ Company ships quite often. CBL's present rate is $4/cwt with a 40,000-pound minimum (400 cwt). The in-excess rate just published is $3/cwt on shipment weight in excess of 40,000 pounds up to 80,000 pounds. The XYZ logistics manager presently ships in 400 cwt lots. The manager wants to know whether XYZ should use the in-excess rate, and, if so, what quantity the company should ship per shipment.

XYZ supplied the following data:

R = 3;200;000 pounds (32,000 cwt)(annual shipments)

V = $200 (value of item per cwt)

W = 25% of value (inventory carrying cost = unit value = year)

Each item weighs 100 pounds.

XYZ should use the in-excess rate as long as the annual transportation cost savings offset the added cost of holding a larger inventory associated with heavier shipments. That is, realizing the transportation cost savings of the in-excess rate will increase XYZ's inventory carrying cost. The optimum shipment size occurs when annual net savings are maximal, that is, when annual transport savings minus the annual added inventory carrying cost are the greatest.

In developing the savings and cost functions, we will use the following symbols:

S_r = Savings per cwt between present rate and new in-excess rate

Q = Optimum shipment quantity in cwt

Q_m = Old minimum shipment quantity in cwt

The annual net savings equals the annual transport savings minus the annual added inventory carrying cost, or $N_s = S_y - C_y$.

The annual transport savings equals the number of shipments per year times the savings per shipment, or:

$$S_y = \frac{R}{Q} S_r (Q - Q_m)$$

where R/Q is the number of shipments per year, $Q - Q_m$ is the amount of shipment weight the company will ship at the lower in-excess rate, and $S_r(Q - Q_m)$ is the transportation savings per shipment. Rewriting the equation for S_r results in the following:

$$S_y = RS_r (1 - \frac{Q_m}{Q})$$

The annual added inventory carrying cost, C_y, equals the added inventory carrying costs of the consignor (shipper or seller) and the consignee (receiver or buyer). The calculations must consider the consignee's added inventory since the seller must pass these savings on as a price discount to encourage the buyer to purchase in larger quantities, or the seller will incur this cost if the shipment goes to the seller's warehouse or distribution center, for example.

Table 9A.1	Annual Savings, Annual Cost, and Net Savings by Various Quantities Using Incentive Rates		
Q	SY	CY	N_s
400	0	0	0
410	781	500	281
420	1,524	1,000	524
430	2,233	1,500	733
440	2,909	2,000	909
450	3,556	2,500	1,056
460	4,174	3,000	1,174
470	4,766	3,500	1,266
480	5,333	4,000	1,333
490	5,878	4,500	1,378
500	6,400	5,000	1,400
505	6,654	5,250	1,404
510	6,902	5,500	1,402
520	7,385	6,000	1,385
530	7,849	6,500	1,349
540	8,296	7,000	1,296
550	8,727	7,500	1,227
560	9,143	8,000	1,143
570	9,544	8,500	1,044
580	9,931	9,000	931
590	10,305	9,500	805
600	10,667	10,000	667
610	11,017	10,500	517
620	11,355	11,000	355

Source: John J. Coyle, DBA. Used with permission.

We calculate the added average inventory—the difference between the average inventories with the larger shipment quantity and the smaller (present) shipment quantity—as follows:

$$\text{Consignor's added inventory} = \frac{1}{2}Q - \frac{1}{2}Q_m$$

$$\text{Consignee's added inventory} = \frac{1}{2}Q - \frac{1}{2}Q_m$$

$$\text{Total added inventory} = 2(\frac{1}{2}Q - \frac{1}{2}Q_m) = Q - Q_m$$

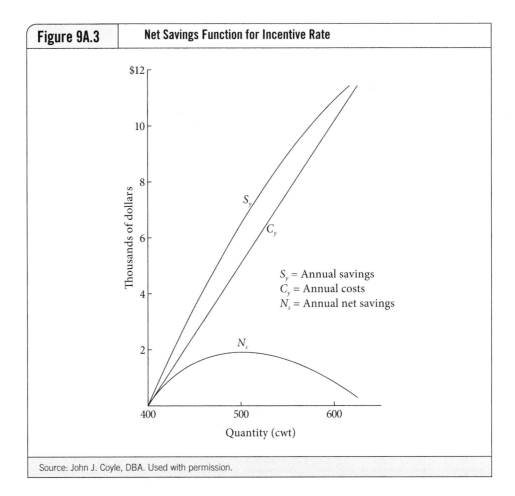

Figure 9A.3	Net Savings Function for Incentive Rate

S_y = Annual savings
C_y = Annual costs
N_s = Annual net savings

Source: John J. Coyle, DBA. Used with permission.

$C_y = WV(Q - Q_m)$, where $V(Q - Q_m)$ equals the value of added inventory and W equals the inventory carrying cost per dollar value. Table 9A.1 and Figure 9A.3 show the savings and cost relationships developed here.

The function that maximizes annual net savings is as follows:

$$N_s = S_y - C_y = RS_r(1 - \frac{Q_m}{Q}) - WV(Q - Q_m)$$

Taking the first derivative, setting it equal to zero, and solving for Q results in the following:

$$\frac{d(N_s)}{dQ} = RS_r\frac{Q_m}{Q^2} - WV = 0$$

$$WV = \frac{RS_rQ_m}{Q^2}$$

$$Q^2 = \frac{RS_rQ_m}{WV}$$

$$Q = \sqrt{\frac{RS_rQ_m}{WV}}$$

Now, taking the data from the problem posed in this example, we find the solution as follows:

$$Q = \sqrt{\frac{(32,000)(\$1.00)(400)}{(0.25)(\$200)}} = \sqrt{256,000} = 506\,\text{cwt}$$

The conclusion is that XYZ Company should use the in-excess rate and should ship 50,600 pounds in each shipment.

SUMMARY

The four adjustments to the basic EOQ approach discussed in this appendix all relate to decisions important to the logistics manager—modal choice, volume rates, private trucking, and in-excess rates. We could include other adjustments, but these four should be sufficient in most cases. While all of the adjustments discussed here assume a condition of certainty, other adjustments may require modifying the model for conditions for uncertainty.

Chapter 10

DISTRIBUTION—MANAGING FULFILLMENT OPERATIONS

Learning Objectives

After reading this chapter, you should be able to do the following:

- Discuss the strategic value-adding role distribution plays in the supply chain.
- Recognize the tradeoffs between distribution and other supply chain functions.
- Understand the analytical framework for distribution planning decisions.
- Evaluate fulfillment strategies and distribution methods.
- Describe the primary fulfillment processes and support functions in distribution center operations.
- Use productivity and quality metrics to analyze fulfillment performance.
- Describe how information technology supports distribution operations.
- Discuss materials handling objectives, principles, and equipment uses.

Supply Chain Profile   *The Changing Face of Distribution*

More than 20 years ago, Jeff Bezos quit his job at a Wall Street investment firm to start a new business. That company, which would become Amazon.com, has fundamentally disrupted retailing and affected the distribution strategies involved in moving products through consumer channels.

In the subsequent two decades, supply chain professionals have had to rapidly adapt to omni-channel commerce initiatives and escalating customer expectations. Traditional distribution centers (DC) and warehouses have morphed into much more agile fulfillment facilities to support the buy anywhere, ship anywhere, and return anywhere habits of increasingly demanding shoppers. Essential fulfillment capabilities and characteristics include:

- Speed to market – to increase order velocity, organizations must look beyond expedited transportation. Orders first need to be prioritized for fulfillment based on customers' delivery or pickup deadlines. Companies like Staples and Walgreens use warehouse automation and control technologies to quickly, accurately, and efficiently serve demand in the proper sequence.

- Customer proximity – to improve customer access at a reasonable cost, it is necessary to locate facilities near major markets or leverage existing stores as distribution points. To gain critical proximity, Amazon has grown from two distribution centers in 1997 to more than 167 facilities with 101 million square feet of capacity by the end of 2014.

- Facility flexibility – to fully leverage facility investments across multiple order types, manufacturer and retailer DC processes must be able to handle multiple order types. Bass Pro Shops and other retailers use integrated DCs to adeptly fulfill high volume, case quantity orders for stores and unit quantity orders for end users.

- Store fulfillment – to optimize inventory and improve customer service, orders must be filled from multiple locations. Target, Sears, and other retailers use their stores as mini fulfillment centers to pick orders from existing inventory for customer pickup or home delivery.

- Inventory accuracy – to ensure that inventory quantities listed on the customer-facing website truly reflect reality, DCs and stores must periodically validate their on-hand quantities. Retailers like Macy's and BCBGMAXAZRIA have adopted RFID technology to ensure high item-level accuracy and rapid inventory retrieval.

- Technology upgrades – legacy order management systems and warehouse management systems are often not up to the "fulfill from anywhere" task. Walmart and other major retailers are turning to distributed order management systems to aggregate orders from multiple channels, access inventory locations, and determine the best DC, store, or vendor location to fill the order.

Without question, omni-channel commerce has forever changed the roles of DCs and executives' perspectives about their importance to the organization. Those dusty old facilities that warehouse outdated product have given way to fast-paced, technology-driven activity hubs with the necessary capabilities to support store and end-customer requirements. Customers can thank Mr. Bezos and omni-channel innovators for prodding DCs and fulfillment practices into the twenty-first century.

Source: MWPVL International, *Amazon Global Fulfillment Center Network* (October 2015). Retrieved October 27, 2015 from http://www.mwpvl.com/html/amazon_com.html; Caroline Baldwin, "Single Inventory Accuracy: The Holy Grail of Retail," *ComputerWeekly.com* (February 2015). Retrieved October 27, 2015 from http://www.computerweekly.com/feature/Single-inventory-accuracy-the-Holy-Grail-of-retail; and, Clint Reiser, "Warehouse Automation Makes e-Commerce Viable," *Logistics Viewpoints* (January 21, 2015). Retrieved October 27, 2015 from http://logisticsviewpoints.com/2015/01/21/warehouse-automation-makes-e-commerce-viable/.

10-1 Introduction

Distribution in the twenty-first century focuses on the continuous flows of product to fulfill customer requirements at the lowest possible cost. No longer focused on long-term storage of inventory in static warehouses, distribution operations provide a variety of capabilities for the supply chain. Whether the cross-docks production parts for an automobile assembly plant, supports manufacturer to retailer replenishment, or fulfills omni-channel demand as outlined in the Supply Chain Profile, the goal is to serve the supply chain quickly, accurately, and cost efficiently.

While speed is of the essence, running efficient distribution facilities and networks is also critical. With U.S. warehousing and distribution-related expenses accounting for $143 billion of the $476 billion in inventory related costs, there is a great need to focus on fulfillment expenses in the supply chain.[1] Cost-reducing opportunities such as limiting product handling, consolidating facilities, and streamlining inventories must be leveraged for supply chains to be competitive.

This chapter focuses on the importance of distribution in meeting customer needs across the supply chain. We will discuss the planning and development of distribution capabilities, as well as the operations, processes, and technologies involved in efficient demand fulfillment. Throughout the chapter, you will gain an understanding of the roles that distribution strategies, facilities, and tools play in the effective management of inventory and the creation of customer value through improved product availability.

10-2 The Role of Distribution Operations in SCM

In a perfect world, supply and demand would be balanced, with desired products being assembled when needed and delivered directly to the point of use. However, this goal is not feasible for most consumer products because production and consumption are not perfectly synchronized, transportation of individual units is very costly, and coordination of activities between such a large number of origin and destination points is complex. To overcome such issues, distribution operations—distribution centers, warehouses, cross-docks, and retail stores—are established within the supply chain.

These inventory handling, storage, and processing facilities help supply chains create time and place utility. By positioning raw materials, components, and finished goods in production and market-facing positions, goods are available when and where they are needed. Shorter lead times can be achieved, product availability increased, and delivery costs reduced, increasing both the effectiveness and efficiency of the distribution operations. In highly contested markets, these responsive capabilities can help a supply chain enhance its competitive position.

Enhanced customer service is not the sole rationale for inserting distribution operations into the supply chain. Such facilities also help organizations overcome challenges, support other processes, and take advantage of economies of scale. These roles involve several factors:

- **Balancing supply and demand**—Whether seasonal production must service year-round demand (e.g., corn) or year-round production is needed to meet seasonal demand (e.g., holiday decorations), distribution facilities can stockpile inventory to buffer supply and demand.

- **Protecting against uncertainty**—Distribution facilities can hold inventory for protection against forecast errors, supply disruptions, and demand spikes.

- **Allowing quantity purchase discounts**—Suppliers often provide incentives to purchase product in larger quantities. Distribution facilities can hold the additional quantities until needed, reducing the purchase cost per unit.

- **Supporting production requirements**—If a manufacturing operation can reduce costs via long production runs or if outputs need to properly age (e.g., wine and cheese), the output can be warehoused prior to distribution.

- **Fulfilling omni-channel demand**—Strategically located distribution facilities near key demand areas improve access to customers at a more reasonable cost for same-day, next-day, and second-day home delivery service.

- **Promoting transportation economies**—Fully utilizing container capacity and moving product in larger quantities is less expensive per unit than shipping "air" and moving small quantities at a time. Distribution facilities can be used to receive and hold the larger deliveries of inventory for future requirements.

10-2-1 Distribution Facility Functionality

Distribution facilities can provide numerous services, depending on the requirements of the supply chain. In traditional distribution operations, four primary functions are carried out: (1) accumulation, (2) sortation, (3) allocation, and (4) assortment.[2]

Accumulation involves the receipt of goods from a variety of sources. The DC serves as a collection point for product coming from multiple origins and provides required transfer, storage, or processing services. The accumulation function allows organizations to consolidate orders and shipments for production and fulfillment processes. As Figure 10.1 demonstrates, with accumulation there are fewer deliveries to schedule and manage. Also, significant transportation cost savings are achieved through larger, more cost-efficient deliveries.

Figure 10.1	The Distribution Center's Accumulation Role

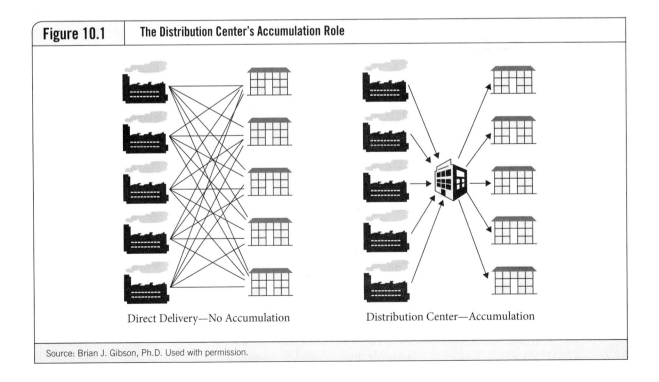

Direct Delivery—No Accumulation   Distribution Center—Accumulation

Source: Brian J. Gibson, Ph.D. Used with permission.

Sortation focuses on assembling like products together for storage in the distribution facility, processing or transfer to customers. During the receiving process, goods are segmented according to their key characteristics—production lot number, stock-keeping unit (SKU) number, case pack size, expiration date, etc.—and prepared for safe storage in the facility or immediate distribution. Proper sortation is essential for the effective management of inventory and fulfillment of customer orders. For example, mixing cases of fresh chicken with two different expiration dates on a single pallet can lead to improper inventory rotation and some product spoilage. Likewise, improper sortation of SKUs may result in shipping the wrong products to customers.

Allocation focuses on matching available inventory to customer orders for a SKU. The order is compared to inventory levels, and available units are retrieved from storage according to the quantity requested by the customer. This break-bulk capacity promotes product availability for multiple customers and allows them to purchase needed quantities rather than excess volume that is not desired. For example, rather than distributing chewing gum only by the pallet (36 cases × 12 display boxes × 24 selling units = 10,368 packs of gum), a DC can allocate product on a case or individual display box basis.

Assortment involves the assembly of customer orders for multiple SKUs held in the distribution facility. As Figure 10.2 highlights, the facility provides a product mixing capability, allowing customers to quickly order a variety of items from a single location. This avoids the expenses related to placing numerous orders and having them shipped from a variety of locations. Just as companies benefit from the assortment function, individuals gain from the assortment/product mixing concept when shopping for food. Rather than traveling to the butcher shop, bakery, dairy store, and produce market, we make a single trip to the grocery store, saving us time and transportation costs. Given the congestion, capacity, and fuel costs faced by industry today, this product mixing role is a key distribution facility capability.

While these four roles are key to the success of a distribution facility, other functions and capabilities are needed. Many distribution facilities are taking on a number of value-adding

Figure 10.2	The Distribution Center's Mixing Capability

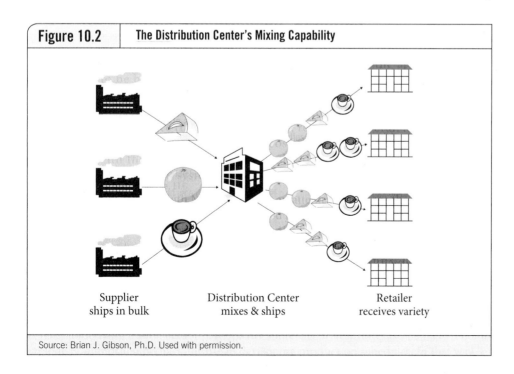

Supplier   Distribution Center   Retailer
ships in bulk   mixes & ships   receives variety

Source: Brian J. Gibson, Ph.D. Used with permission.

Table 10.1	Value-Adding Roles of Distribution Operations

- **Assembly services**—Handle limited/light assembly of products such as building and filling in-store display units.
- **Inventory management and visibility**—Provide consignment and vendor-managed inventory programs.
- **Product kitting, bundling, and unbundling**—Build customized combinations of products to meet specific customer requirements such as all components needed for a customized smartphone bundle or repacking a combination of goods for retail promotion (gift with purchase or multipack goods).
- **Product postponement**—Conduct specific activities (assembly, sizing, packaging, and/or labeling) that have been delayed until customer places order.
- **Production sequencing**—Prepare inventory for just-in-time line-side delivery to manufacturing facilities. Components are picked, loaded, and delivered in the precise sequence needed for assembly.
- **Quality control**—Verify the product quality, condition, and count before it is delivered to the customer.
- **Recycling, repair, and returns management**—Provide services related to reverse flows of products from customers such as inspection, disposal, refurbishment, or credit.

Source: Brian J. Gibson, Ph.D. Used with permission.

roles to complement their basic functionality and to support evolving supply chain needs. Most distribution facilities are no longer viewed as places to store products but as activity centers with flexible space and labor that can be leveraged for a variety of customer needs ranging from product labeling to light manufacturing. The value-added activities highlighted in Table 10.1 help organizations handle special customer requirements, create supply chain efficiencies, and differentiate themselves from their competition.

10-2-2 Distribution Tradeoffs

To this point, we have focused on the value-adding roles and functionality of distribution operations. Although many organizations tout the importance of distribution operations, others do not see it the same way. They view distribution facilities as costly operations that interrupt the flow of goods. Both perspectives are realistic, and it is up to supply chain professionals to determine how to best balance customer service and costs. This requires an understanding of the functional tradeoffs highlighted in Figure 10.3.

Figure 10.3	Functional Tradeoffs

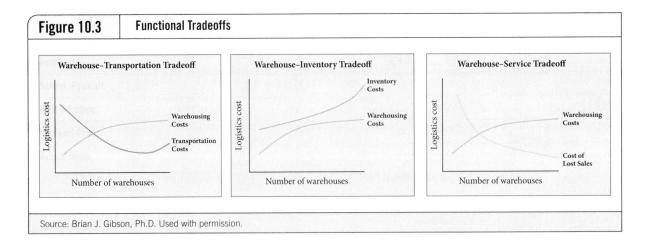

Source: Brian J. Gibson, Ph.D. Used with permission.

One important interaction that must be considered is the tradeoff between distribution and transportation operations. When a manufacturer ships product directly from its plants to customers, the transportation costs will be very high. Organizations may benefit substantially from the establishment of one or several warehouses to reduce transportation costs. Why? Large shipments can be transported over long distances from plants to distribution facilities via truckload carriers; then the smaller shipments are delivered to regional customers. However, a saturation point can be reached where too many DCs are built and total costs increase. Why is this so? With so many facilities, operating costs will increase and transportation expenses will rise. For example, inbound shipments will become less-than-truckload shipments, which are more expensive than shipping full truckloads.

Another key tradeoff must be made between distribution and inventory. Generally, the more DCs and warehouses, the higher the total inventory carrying costs. As facilities are added to a fulfillment system, the amount of inventory will increase in total, but at a decreasing rate. This move toward decentralized inventory inhibits the ability to adopt a **risk pooling** strategy as each facility must hold additional safety stock. Supply chain leaders must be mindful of this interaction and regularly evaluate the tradeoff between inventory levels and the number of facilities.

A common fulfillment strategy of many firms is to use its distribution network for mid- to high-velocity items and maintain one centralized facility for their low-velocity items. These slow movers may be replacement parts, items that are needed only by a few customers, or costly products. Maintaining a central inventory rather than holding the goods in multiple facilities creates inventory carrying cost savings that offset the increased expenses of longer delivery distances.

The tradeoff between distribution operations and customer service is another important issue. Having a larger number of distribution facilities in the supply chain creates better service for customers. Buyers are more comfortable if they know the supplier has a DC within a day's drive from their operations. They don't feel as comfortable if the facility is two thousand miles away. Decision makers must balance the value of better service levels with the additional costs of operating facilities and carrying inventory.

Tradeoffs must also be made at the facility level between the primary resources available to distribution managers—space, equipment, and people. Space allows for the storage of goods when supply and demand are imbalanced. Warehouse equipment, including materials-handling devices ranging from racks to conveyor lines, supports the efficient movement and storage of product within the distribution facility. People are the most critical distribution resource, playing multiple roles in the facility over different schedules. Their capabilities can be increased through training, while their numbers can be quickly increased to handle demand surges.

For internal efficiency targets to be met, it is necessary to make conscientious financial and performance tradeoffs between resources. The primary tradeoffs and relationships include the following:

- **Space vs. equipment**—The larger the facility and the more space used for distribution operations, the more equipment will be needed in the facility. Proper equipment allows organizations to leverage space by using the vertical capacity in the facility and improving the speed by which products travel through the facility.

- **Equipment vs. people**—The greater the use of equipment to automate materials handling and distribution activity, the lower the labor requirements of a facility. Conversely, the more manual the operation, the more people are needed to complete distribution activities.

- **People vs. space**—The larger the facility workforce, the larger the facility size and throughput possible. It is difficult for a small team to operate a sizable facility unless there is significant use of materials handling and flow automation. Thus, it is critical to hire and schedule enough labor to effectively use the facility and serve customers.

Distribution goals also impact resource requirements. Demands for faster order cycle times or increased facility throughput will require a larger workforce or use of more materials-handling equipment. High safety stock requirements will require more facility capacity to handle the additional inventory. Increased order accuracy requirements will promote the use of equipment, as automated systems are not prone to the errors commonly found in labor-focused operations. Finally, increased demand will necessitate more space, people, and/or equipment.

While there are other tradeoffs to consider in distribution, these cross-organizational and cross-functional tradeoffs are among the most important. They highlight the need for advanced planning, communication, and collaboration among supply chain partners and within organizations. A failure to plan, communicate, and collaborate will lead to ineffective decision making and poor utilization of resources.

10-2-3 Distribution Challenges

Distribution is a dynamic component of the supply chain. Each day in a distribution facility brings new challenges, additional customer orders, and expectations for perfect order fulfillment. Chief among these challenges are labor availability issues, demand variation, and increasing customer requirements. DC management must be flexible and creative in addressing these issues, which often impact each other. Failure to do so leads to higher costs and service problems for the organization, as well as disruptions of the supply chain.

In most organizations, distribution is a people-intensive activity. Unfortunately, it is growing increasingly difficult to find and train high-quality personnel for DC operations. From an hourly position perspective, DC work is physically demanding and often occurs around the clock, seven days a week. Wages are typically competitive with other hourly positions, but there is limited opportunity for salary growth. Add this all up, and the result is an industry with an ongoing turnover challenge. Compounding the problem is the demographic trend toward the graying of labor forces in Europe and the United States. The result of an aging population is a smaller labor pool from which to find quality DC employees. Given the difficulty and cost of finding, training, and retaining DC talent, some organizations are moving to automated DCs. Automation is discussed in Appendix 10A, as well as the On the Line feature.

Demand variation is another supply chain challenge that affects distribution operations. Many products are seasonal in nature, with high demand during some periods and low demand during others. Sunscreen lotion and related products have a much higher demand in the spring and summer seasons than the fall and winter, though some demand will occur year round as people prepare for warm weather vacations. The DC handling this product may be short on space capacity as inventory builds up in advance of the primary selling season but be nearly empty during the off-season. Labor issues also arise—for example, not enough help is available to fulfill orders during the peak season but little work is available at other times. Without some ability to smooth out demand, it is difficult to effectively utilize the space and equipment resources and retain labor throughout the year. Thus, it is critical to balance the DC requirements of seasonal products with products that have alternate primary selling seasons and/or stable year-round demand.

Expanding the role of DCs to include value-adding activities (see Table 10.1) can create both benefits and challenges for organizations. As customers have learned that DCs are more than just storage facilities, the desire for additional capabilities and service has grown. Also, lean strategies have prompted many customers to reduce inventory. They expect suppliers to provide smaller, more frequent, and faster fulfillment of orders. Together, these trends place a great deal of pressure on DCs to maximize speed and service while keeping costs under control. The solution is to build flexible fulfillment processes that can handle the varying requirements of different customer segments.

On the Line

DC Automation: Solving the Labor Dilemma (and more)

It's not easy being a distribution manager in the current operating environment. "Order fulfillment is a more complex process than ever," notes Staci Cretu of Westfalia Technologies in a recent article. "In today's fast-paced business environment, customers demand and expect more, as their orders are more frequent, contain more diverse stock-keeping units (SKUs) and require more customized solutions. There is no room for delay, error, or delivery of low-quality products."

Couple these challenges with the growing labor shortage, a proliferation of slow moving SKUs, and shorter lead times for processing orders and you have real problems. Traditional processing methods that depend on manual picking and the operator-to-goods principle just won't work. They are too labor intensive and require too much travel time in the DC to rapidly serve demand.

DC automation has been widely used in Europe to offset land constraints, high labor costs, and low labor availability. Increasingly, North American companies are deploying DC automation for their receiving, putaway, picking, and shipping processes. Significant capital investments are being made in automated storage and retrieval systems (AS/RS), automated case picking systems, robotic palletizing systems, and conveyor systems.

Grocery wholesalers and retailers were early U.S. adopters of AS/RS. Manufacturers and omni-channel retailers are joining the automation trend. For example, Buffalo Trace Distillery recently invested $20 million in an AS/RS that occupies 46,574 square feet inside the company's new DC. The AS/RS has three storage and retrieval cranes that serve five-deep storage lanes and store pallets six levels high. Each crane can induct/output 55 pallets of finished goods per hour for a total of 165 pallets moving within the system per hour.

The goal of this capital investment is to reduce labor requirements, improve speed, and save money. "We look forward to being able to serve our customers in a more efficient manner and having the capacity for even further growth in the future," said Mark Brown, president and chief executive officer of Buffalo Trace.

Source: Carrie Mantey, "The Era of Automated Storage and Retrieval," *Supply+Demand+Chain Executive,* (September 11, 2015). Retrieved October 29, 2015 from http://www.sdcexec.com/article/12108015/the-era-of-the-automated-storage-and-retrieval-system-september-2015-on-the-floor; "Buffalo Trace Distillery Opens New High Tech Distribution Center," *BEVNET* (July 21, 2015). Retrieved October 29, 2015 from http://www.bevnet.com/news/spirits/2015/buffalo-trace-distillery-opens-new-high-tech-distribution-center/; and, Cliff Holste, "Logistics News: When it Comes to DC Auomation – The Questions are: When, What, and How Much," *Supply Chain Digest* (January 28, 2015). Retrieved October 29, 2015 from http://www.scdigest.com/experts/Holste_15-01-28.php?cid=8931.

10-3 Distribution Planning and Strategy

Understanding the role of distribution in the supply chain is the foundation of effective fulfillment processes. The next step is to develop distribution strategies that are tailored to the products being handled, customer requirements, and available internal expertise and resources. A series of interrelated distribution planning decisions must be made to ensure that the strategy can be executed at a reasonable cost while supporting supply chain demands. These planning issues, highlighted in Figure 10.4, are discussed next.

10-3-1 Capability Requirements

When establishing a distribution strategy, the first and most obvious consideration is the product. Product characteristics must drive the design of the distribution process. Issues such as product value, durability, temperature sensitivity, obsolescence, volume, and other factors must be considered just as they are in transportation decision making. For example, raw materials (coal and timber) can often be held in outdoor stockpiles and transferred as needed to the production facility. The same distribution process would be inappropriate for manufactured goods (pharmaceutical products and iPhones), which need to be distributed quickly, shielded from the environment, and protected against theft and damage. Hence, it is critical to align distribution processes with the products involved to protect product integrity, promote customer service and satisfaction, and improve inventory control.

Another issue that has a major impact on the distribution strategy and network structure is the product flow requirements of the supply chain. Two options are available: (1) direct shipment of goods from the manufacturer to retailer or retailer to consumer or (2) movement of goods through distribution facilities to customers.

Direct shipping operations bypass distribution facilities, fulfilling retail store and end user requests from the primary production point (manufacturer's factory or warehouse)

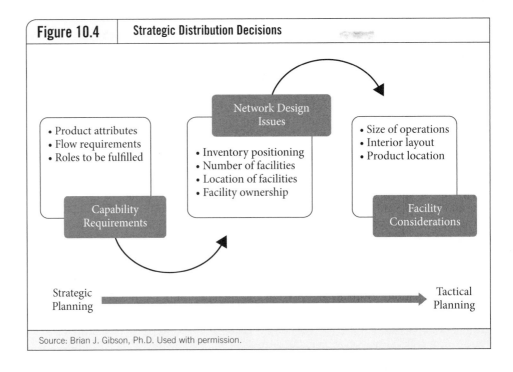

Figure 10.4   Strategic Distribution Decisions

- Product attributes
- Flow requirements
- Roles to be fulfilled

Capability Requirements

Network Design Issues

- Inventory positioning
- Number of facilities
- Location of facilities
- Facility ownership

- Size of operations
- Interior layout
- Product location

Facility Considerations

Strategic Planning   Tactical Planning

Source: Brian J. Gibson, Ph.D. Used with permission.

rather than interim facilities that hold inventory. Similarly, Internet retailers directly distribute goods to consumers without the need for retail outlets. Direct shipping avoids the need to build and operate distribution facilities, reduces inventory in the system, and often compresses order cycle time. Direct shipping works particularly well when customers place orders for truckload quantities or when product perishability is an issue. For example, it is better to have bread and milk delivered directly to a grocery store than to a DC as they are high-volume products and direct shipping maximizes product shelf life.

On the downside, it is expensive to deliver small quantities to buyers (reduced transportation efficiencies), and there is limited safety stock available to protect against demand surges. Furthermore, many companies struggle to fulfill orders for case and individual unit quantities. Thus, it is important to consider product characteristics, demand volume and variability, and related issues before making the decision to establish a direct shipping strategy.

Properly planned distribution facilities can address the shortcomings of direct shipping. These facilities – including DCs, traditional warehouses, and cross-docking facilities– provide the supply chain with additional capabilities. Warehouses and related distribution facilities can hold goods in anticipation of customer orders, provide a buffer of safety stock to protect against contingencies, and handle small quantity orders efficiently from transportation and fulfillment standpoints. Cross-docks can provide a high-velocity alternative to direct shipping at lower transportation cost with product mixing capabilities. Figure 10.5 provides additional insight on cross-docking.

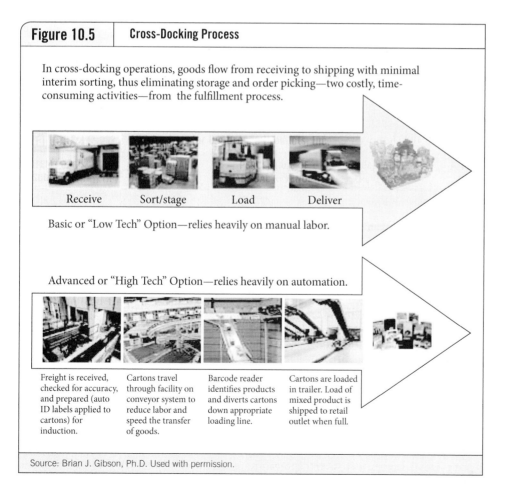

| Figure 10.5 | Cross-Docking Process |

In cross-docking operations, goods flow from receiving to shipping with minimal interim sorting, thus eliminating storage and order picking—two costly, time-consuming activities—from the fulfillment process.

Receive   Sort/stage   Load   Deliver

Basic or "Low Tech" Option—relies heavily on manual labor.

Advanced or "High Tech" Option—relies heavily on automation.

Freight is received, checked for accuracy, and prepared (auto ID labels applied to cartons) for induction.

Cartons travel through facility on conveyor system to reduce labor and speed the transfer of goods.

Barcode reader identifies products and diverts cartons down appropriate loading line.

Cartons are loaded in trailer. Load of mixed product is shipped to retail outlet when full.

Source: Brian J. Gibson, Ph.D. Used with permission.

Of course, it is necessary to analyze the inventory, transportation, and service tradeoffs before choosing between direct shipping, warehousing, and cross-docking facilities. The logical answer may be to employ a combination of the strategies to ensure distribution efficiency and customer satisfaction. A grocery chain will use multiple methods to address variation in product volume, product perishability, and supplier proximity.

The role being played by the distribution facility also influences required capabilities. For example, the need for accumulation, sortation, allocation, and assortment functionalities portend the use of traditional DCs and warehouse facilities. On the other hand, a need for value-added, nontraditional roles such as product customization or repackaging will drive the development of assembly capabilities in the facility.

10-3-2 Network Design Issues

Understanding the distribution capabilities required by a supply chain takes much of the guesswork out of the network design phase. If you know the types of activities that must be completed, the volume of product flows, and the expectations of customers, it is far easier to create a network that will perform well. This phase of strategic planning involves the determination of inventory positioning, the number and location of distribution facilities, and the ownership of facilities in the network.

Inventory positioning addresses where to locate stock within the supply chain. One strategy is to hold a centralized stock of inventory at a single location such as the origin point or some other advantageous location in the supply chain. Product is distributed to customers across the network from this central stocking point. The benefit of this consolidation strategy is greater control over the inventory and reduced demand variability due to risk pooling. The central or national inventory pool supports higher in-stock availability, though there is a need for less safety stock.[3]

The drawback of centralized inventory is the longer distances to customers, which extend lead times and result in higher transportation costs. Despite these drawbacks, manufacturers of high-value, low-weight products such as prescription pharmaceuticals often rely on a centralized inventory pool. The transportation costs associated with next-day and second-day order delivery are offset by the reductions in inventory carrying costs, the enhanced visibility of product flows, and the improved control over order-filling processes, product pedigree issues, and recall events.

The alternate inventory positioning strategy is to hold product in customer-facing locations. Stocking inventory regionally or locally helps to reduce customer delivery costs and order cycle time as product can be readily dispatched to meet customer requirements. This decentralized inventory strategy works well for high-volume, low-cost products with low demand uncertainty such as laundry detergent, pet food, and cereal.

The decentralized inventory strategy is not without challenges. First, more facilities are required to stock the product, leading to higher handling costs, the risk of product damage, and the potential for product pilferage, not to mention the additional expenses of running the facilities. Also, average inventory levels will rise as each facility will have to hold safety stock to cover demand variation within the region.

Which inventory positioning strategy is best? There is no single answer, and many organizations use both strategies. For example, Amazon.com decentralizes inventories of books on the best seller list but centralizes slow-moving, out-of-print books. Ultimately, this strategy is based on product demand, customer expectations and power, and competitors' actions. Other factors such as transportation prices, inventory carrying costs, and other supply chain expenses also affect inventory positioning strategy.

The second and third network design issues focus on the number and locations of distribution facilities within the supply chain. The required number of facilities will be driven by inventory positioning strategy. The greater the centralization of the inventory, the fewer the number of facilities needed to distribute the product. Market scope also impacts the decision. Small- and medium-sized companies with a regional market area often will need only one distribution facility, whereas large companies with national or global market areas need to consider using multiple facilities, some of which may have different distribution roles.

Determining the number of facilities needed for a supply chain involves the evaluation of cost tradeoffs with other functional areas. Figure 10.6 depicts the impact of increasing the number of warehouses on other logistics functional costs. As the number of warehouses increases, transportation cost and the cost of lost sales decline, though inventory and warehousing costs increase. At the optimal number of warehouses, the lowest total cost will be reached. However, total costs begin to rise when additional facilities are opened. The increasing inventory and warehousing costs offset decreasing transportation costs and the cost of lost sales. Of course, the total cost curve and the range of warehouses it reflects will be different for each company.

- **Transportation costs**—An increase in the number of warehouses brings the warehouses closer to the customer and market area, reducing outbound transportation distance and costs.

- **Cost of lost sales**—An increase in the number of facilities improves inventory availability and order fill rates. Fewer customers will be compelled to find substitute products or suppliers, thus reducing defections and lost sales.

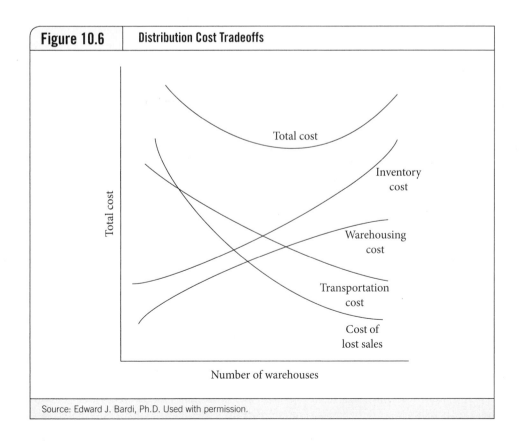

| **Figure 10.6** | **Distribution Cost Tradeoffs** |

Source: Edward J. Bardi, Ph.D. Used with permission.

- **Inventory costs**—As discussed previously, a higher number of stocking points increases the overall safety stock levels and inventory carrying costs in the supply chain.
- **Warehousing costs**—A larger number of facilities increases administrative and operational costs. Each warehouse will require its own leadership team, support personnel, technology, and administrative space which drives expenses upward.

After settling on the number of distribution facilities, the issue of facility location arises. Though general heuristics (rules of thumb) such as locating high-service facilities near markets and raw materials mixing centers close to suppliers are valuable, it is important to pursue a desired level of customer service at the least possible logistics cost. Analyzing the DC's intended function, sources and volume of supply, customer locations and demand patterns, and related fulfillment costs will lead to more effective location selection than rules of thumb alone. Similar to other strategic distribution issues, this analysis should consider functional tradeoffs and leverage network design models and software tools. Chapter 4 provides a detailed discussion of facility location analysis.

The final piece of a network design strategy is the facility ownership question—should an organization own and operate private distribution facilities or contract with third-party logistics providers for distribution services? Based on the organization's expertise versus the scope of tasks required and their financial resources relative to the number and size of facilities needed, they can strategically analyze the question. There are three possible solutions: (1) private facilities, (2) public facilities, and (3) contract facilities.

Private DCs are company operated facilities that are owned or leased from a commercial real estate company. Owning and operating facilities provide the organization with greater control over fulfillment processes and inventory. Also, economies of scale can be achieved if the activity levels are high enough. If so, the cost per unit delivered to the customer is less, and the retailer can charge a lower price or maintain a higher profit margin. Company owned facilities are assets that can be depreciated and can also provide a source of income by renting or leasing excess space to those who need storage facilities.

In order to make a private distribution cost-effective, the facility needs high product throughput, requires stable demand, and should be located in or near a dense market area. Additionally, the organization must have distribution expertise, the resources to build facilities, and the desire to operate them. If these attributes are not present, the firm should look to third party logistics (3PL) service providers to handle distribution and warehousing.

Public warehousing is the traditional external distribution option. A public warehouse rents out space to individuals or firms needing storage capacity on a short-term, transactional basis. These companies may focus on specific product types—refrigerated goods, household goods, and bulk storage.

Contract warehousing is a customized version of public warehousing in which the 3PL provides a combination of distribution services. They dedicate space, labor, and equipment to a client's specific product needs with the goal of providing integrated, accurate distribution services. These facilities can address the specialized handling requirements for critical products such as pharmaceuticals, electronics, and high-value manufactured goods. The customized nature of contract facilities leads to strong relationships between the 3PLs and its key clients.

These external distribution services should be considered for several reasons. First, contracting for services alleviates capital investment in private distribution facilities. Second, short-term commitments for capacity allow distribution network flexibility. If demand shifts to another region, you simply lease the needed capacity in the new market. Another benefit of outsourcing distribution responsibilities is that you do not have to hire

---

Figure 10.7 | **Distribution Cost Comparison**

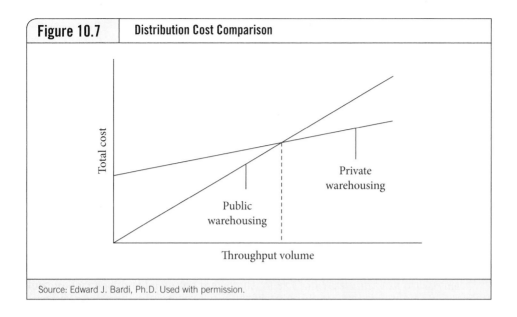

Source: Edward J. Bardi, Ph.D. Used with permission.

---

and manage operations personnel. Essentially, distribution becomes a variable cost activity that is run by 3PL experts who can leverage their investments, expertise, and capacity across multiple customers.

Choosing between private and 3PL distribution options requires significant planning and analysis. On a financial basis, the selection decision boils down to the volume of product being moved through the supply chain. Figure 10.7 highlights the variable-cost-only nature of purchased 3PL distribution services versus the fixed-cost-plus-lower-variable-cost structure of private operations. At low throughput volumes, the 3PL cost structure has a distinct advantage but eventually loses out to the private distribution cost structure as throughput volume increases.

Cost is not the only consideration in this warehouse "make versus buy" decision. Service factors and demand characteristics must be also be analyzed. The primary issues are summarized in Table 10.2.

Table 10.2 | **Factors Affecting Distribution Facility Ownership**

FIRM CHARACTERISTICS	FAVORS PRIVATE DISTRIBUTION	FAVORS 3PL DISTRIBUTION
Throughput volume	Higher	Lower
Demand variability	Stable	Fluctuating
Market density	Higher	Lower
Special physical control needs	Yes	No
Security requirements	Higher	Lower
Customer service requirements	Higher	Lower
Multiple use needs	Yes	No

Source: Brian J. Gibson, Ph.D. Used with permission.

10-3-3 Facility Considerations

When an organization chooses to outsource the distribution function to 3PL providers, facility design strategies shift to these service suppliers. However, when the facilities are privately owned and operated, a great deal of planning is required. The organization must determine the size of each facility in the distribution network, the interior layout of the facilities, and product locations within the facility.

It is important to carefully assess the situation and make competent decisions regarding these three issues before facilities are built. Once completed, it is expensive and operationally disruptive to modify structures, layouts, and flows.

The first facility consideration is to determine the size of each operation within the network. This decision is driven by decisions made during the network design phase. Typically, the more facilities in the distribution network, the smaller they need to be. Note that facilities do not have to be the exact same size, function, or layout.

Each facility must be large enough to accommodate the distribution activities that will be performed within the four walls. Traditional warehouses require storage space. It is important to use the cubic storage space as efficiently as possible. This means making use of the vertical and horizontal capacity within the facility.

Space is also needed to interface with the transportation network. Most inbound goods are unloaded directly from trailers into the facility and received prior to storage. An area is needed to receive and inspect the goods, as well as stage pallets of product before storage. Outbound goods may need to be sorted, staged, and consolidated prior to loading. The volume and frequency of orders moving through the facility are critical in determining receiving and shipping space needs.

Additional space is required for order picking and assembly. The amount needed depends on order volume and the product's nature, along with the materials-handling equipment used in the facility. Proper layout of the space used for these activities is critical to efficient operations and customer service.

Space may need to be allocated to three additional functions. First, an area may be needed for processing rework and returns. Second, office space is needed for administrative and clerical activities. Finally, break rooms, locker rooms, meeting rooms, equipment storage, and maintenance area spaces are needed.

Demand forecasts for the facility can be used to create a rough estimate of space requirements as follows:

1. Develop a demand forecast; prepare an estimate in units for a relevant sales period (usually 30 days) by product category. Then the company will need to determine each item's order quantity, usually including some allowance for safety stock.
2. Convert the demand into cubic capacity requirements based on product case sizes. Also, add 10 to 15 percent to the capacity needs for volume growth. This provides a basic estimate of storage space requirements.
3. Add space needs for aisles and other fulfillment activities (receiving, shipping, order picking, assembly, etc.). Traditional distribution facilities devote up to one-third of total space to these non-storage functions.

The rough estimate should be validated through the use of technology. Computer simulations allow companies to analyze a vast number of variables and future growth forecasts when projecting space requirements.

After the facility size is determined, attention shifts to the layout of the operations within the distribution operation. The company must make decisions regarding aisle space, shelving, materials-handling equipment, and the interior dimensions of the facility. Table 10.3 highlights general principles for designing the interior of a facility.

Using these general principles as a guide, organizations design the interior of the distribution facility to support timely, accurate, and efficient customer order fulfillment. A number of objectives must be kept in mind during the planning process, with utilization of the facility's cubic capacity being first and foremost on the list. Effective use of storage capacity can be achieved by matching storage bay size to product velocity. For low turnover products, the bays can be wide and deep, with limited access, and the aisles can be narrow. Increased turnover necessitates quick access for better customer service and, consequently, smaller bays and wider aisles.

Product protection is another key objective. The layout must accommodate the physical characteristics of the products being handled. For example, hazardous materials such as explosives, flammable items, and oxidizing items must be separated from other items so as to eliminate the possibility of damage. Also, high-value goods must be safeguarded against pilferage, and temperature-sensitive products must receive proper refrigeration or heat. Finally, distribution personnel should avoid stacking or storing light or fragile items near other items that could cause damage.

Proper use of automation and materials-handling equipment is an important goal. Both offer great potential to improve distribution efficiency. Careful planning should include consideration of the risks of investing in automation—obsolescence due to rapid technological change, market fluctuations, and return on investment. Mechanized materials-handling equipment makes sense when products are shipped in cases or totes, and when flow through volume is consistently high. A detailed discussion of materials-handling principles and tools is provided in Appendix 10A.

Another objective is process flexibility. The facility design should not be so permanent as to limit the facility from handling new product lines and providing value added services when new requests emerge. For example, configurable racking and multifunctional materials-handling equipment can prevent the building from becoming obsolete if demand patterns change significantly. Such capabilities make the layout more dynamic.

Table 10.3	Facility Layout Principles
PRINCIPLE	**BENEFITS**
Use a one-story facility	• Provides more usable space per investment dollar • Results in lower construction costs
Use vertical capacity	• Reduces building footprint and land requirements
Minimize aisle space	• Provides more storage and processing capacity
Use direct product flows	• Avoids backtracking and costly travel time
Deploy warehouse automation solutions	• Improves facility productivity and safety • Reduces travel time • Reduces labor needs
Use an appropriate product storage plan	• Maximizes space utilization and product protection
Source: Brian J. Gibson, Ph.D. Used with permission.	

Continuous improvement is the ultimate facility objective. An organization should not design an initial layout and then assume that it will work perfectly forever. Goals and standards for costs, order-handling efficiency, and customer service must be set and monitored on a regular basis. If measurements reveal that optimal facility performance is not being achieved, steps must be taken to improve productivity.

The final facility consideration is product placement within the facility. Before order fulfillment operations begin, goods must be located or slotted in the facility. **Slotting** is defined as the placement of product in a facility for the purpose of optimizing materials-handling and space efficiency. The main objective of slotting is to minimize product handling and employee travel in the building. This is important because travel and other nonproductive tasks can account for up to 60 percent of distribution labor hours.

Three criteria are commonly used to slot product within a distribution facility: (1) popularity, (2) unit size, and (3) cube. The popularity criterion locates high volume (popular) items near the shipping area and the low volume (unpopular) items away from the shipping area. Reduced order-picking time and effort are achieved.

The unit size criterion suggests that small-size items (cubic dimensions) be located near the shipping area and larger-size items be placed farther away from the shipping area. By locating smaller-size items near the shipping area, proximity is improved. This reduces travel distance and order-picking time. The cube criterion is a variation of unit size in that the items with smaller total cubic space requirements (item cube multiplied by the number of items held) are located near the shipping area. The logic is the same as that used for unit size.

Why focus on slotting criteria and strategy? Proper product slotting can improve labor productivity and generate other advantages for the organization and its customers. Several benefits will be generated by effective product slotting:

- **Picking productivity**—Travel time is a significant portion of a picker's daily activity. A good product slotting strategy can reduce travel time, thereby reducing picking labor.
- **Efficient replenishment**—By sizing the pick face location based upon a standard unit of measure (case, pallet) for the product in question, you can significantly reduce the labor required to replenish the location.
- **Work balancing**—By balancing activity across multiple pick zones you reduce congestion in the zones, improve material flow, and reduce the total response time for a given order or batch of orders.
- **Load building**—To minimize product damage, heavy product is located at the beginning of the pick path ahead of crushable product. Product may also be located based on case size to facilitate pallet building.
- **Accuracy**—Similar products are separated to minimize the opportunity for picking errors.
- **Ergonomics**—High velocity products are placed in easy to reach locations which reduce bending and reaching. Heavy or oversized items are placed on lower levels or in a separate area where material handling equipment can be utilized.
- **Pre-consolidation**—Storing and picking product by family group can reduce downstream sorting and consolidation activity. For example, grocery DCs may slot products according to store aisle location to facilitate rapid restocking.

On the Line

Efficient and Environmentally Friendly DCs

With mounting pressure from regulators, clients, and consumers to reduce carbon emissions and energy use, companies must develop strategies to improve their supply chains. The risk of not doing so is the potential loss of customers who are offered more sustainable and cost-efficient options elsewhere.

In response, organizations are adding environmentally friendly features to their DCs and warehouses. The investments range from simple solutions like the installation of energy-efficient lighting to major initiatives like the pursuit of zero facility waste. Three ambitious recent initiatives include:

- **Turning garbage into energy.** Kroger, the largest U.S. grocery chain, is converting food waste into energy for its 650,000 square foot DC in Compton, California. An anaerobic digester at the facility will process more than 55,000 tons of food waste a year, about 150 tons a day, providing 20 percent of the DC's energy. The initiative will reduce truck travel by more than 500,000 miles each year. Rather than making special trips to haul food waste to landfills or waste-to-energy plants, the trucks that deliver food to supermarkets from the DC will make their return trip with food waste from the supermarkets to feed the anaerobic digester.

- **Keeping the cold in the building**. Partner Logistics provides 3PL services to the frozen food supply chain. Its Wisbech DC is the largest cold storage facility in the United Kingdom. To reduce the resources required to maintain a consistent temperature of -24 degrees in this facility, the company has invested in important energy-saving features. A specially designed foundation, external cladding made of thick insulated panels and a thermal barrier between the low bay and high bay prevent cold leakage. Also, a much higher volume to surface area ratio considerably reduces energy consumption per pallet. Overall, the facility uses 50 percent less energy than the best-in-class standards set by the European Cold Storage and Logistics Association.

- **Achieving green construction leadership.** Golden State Foods, a major supplier to McDonalds, opened a 158,000 square foot distribution center that received Leadership in Energy & Environmental Design (LEED) designation. LEED gold-certification was achieved through a concerted effort to create an environmentally sustainable DC. Key facility features include: an ammonia CO_2 cascade refrigeration system that uses non-ozone-damaging chemicals, forklifts powered by efficient and environmentally friendly hydrogen fuel cells rather than lead-acid batteries, a variable air ventilation system that improves air quality and promotes a dust-free environment, and a rooftop rainwater collection system that irrigates the facility's natural landscaping.

Although these sustainability initiatives sound costly, the rewards far outweigh the expense and effort. A "green DC" alleviates harmful environmental effects of DC operations, improves worker safety, earns respect from customers, and lowers operating costs. Thus, companies can make green (money) while being green (sustainable).

Source: "GSF Opens LEED-Certified Distribution Center," *Food Engineering* (February 24, 2015). Retrieved October 29, 2015 from http://www.foodengineeringmag.com/articles/93563-gsf-opens-leed-certified-distribution-center, "Sustainable Warehousing: Making the Supply Chain Greener," Partner Logistics (January 5, 2015). Retrieved October 29, 2015 from http://www.partnerlogistics.eu/sustainable-warehousing-making-the-supply-chain-greener; "Kroger to Power Distribution Center with Spoiled Food," GreenBiz (May 21, 2013). Retrieved October 29, 2015 from http://www.greenbiz.com/news/2013/05/21/kroger-power-distribution-center-spoiled-food.

As this list suggests, proper product slotting is a foundation of facility productivity and sets the stage for a variety of other benefits. However, slotting is not a one-time, start-up event. Changing business environments and product demand fluctuation may eventually lead to disorganization and improperly slotted product. Hence, it is important for organizations to regularly monitor and adjust product locations as needed to maintain optimal facility performance.

Beyond these operational issues, leading organizations are also bringing sustainability considerations into the facility design process. The On the Line feature describes how three organizations are gaining efficiencies while doing their part to support the environment.

10-4 Distribution Execution

Distribution strategy and planning activities set the stage for day-to-day operation of the facility. They facilitate effective execution of product movement and storage, order fulfillment, and value-added customer services. This section will focus on the processes that take place within DCs, warehouses, and cross-dock facilities. The discussion is segmented into two topics—product-handling functions and support functions.

10-4-1 Product-Handling Functions

The primary facility operations focus on the movement and storage of product. Storage is the more traditional function, while movement may seem unimportant. However, maintaining proper product flows through efficient short-distance moves within the facility is a critical aspect of distribution. Goods arriving at DCs and cross-docks move through the building rapidly to fulfill customer orders and maintain high inventory turnover. Hence, effective in-facility movement supports strong customer service and high inventory velocity, which reduces holding costs; lowers loss, damage, or obsolescence risks; and holds storage capacity requirements in check.

As shown in Figure 10.8, product handling involves five primary processes: (1) receiving—transferring goods into the facility from the transport network, (2) put-away—moving goods into storage locations, (3) order picking—selecting goods for customer orders, (4) replenishment—moving product from storage locations to picking slots, and (5) shipping—loading goods for delivery to the customer. All five involve short-distance movement of product, while put-away also focuses on the storage activity.

At the receiving operation, the inbound carrier is scheduled to deliver the goods at a specific time so as to improve labor productivity and unloading efficiency. The goods are unloaded from the delivery vehicle onto the receiving dock. During the process, receiving clerks inspect the delivery to ensure that the goods match the purchase order and packing slips, the quantity received is accurate, and no damage is found. Problems are noted on the carrier's delivery receipt, and the receipt is signed.

Once on the dock, the goods are sorted by SKU, stacked on pallets to the correct ti-hi (*ti* is the number of cartons stored on a layer and *hi* is the number of layers on the pallet), and secured using tape or shrink-wrap. Prior to transfer, the items are tagged with pallet labels that assign storage locations in the facility or designate the goods for direct transfer to the shipping dock if immediately needed to fill a customer order.

The put-away operation focuses on the physical movement of product from the receiving dock to assigned storage locations in the facility. Forklift operators check the pallet

Figure 10.8	Primary Distribution Center Processes

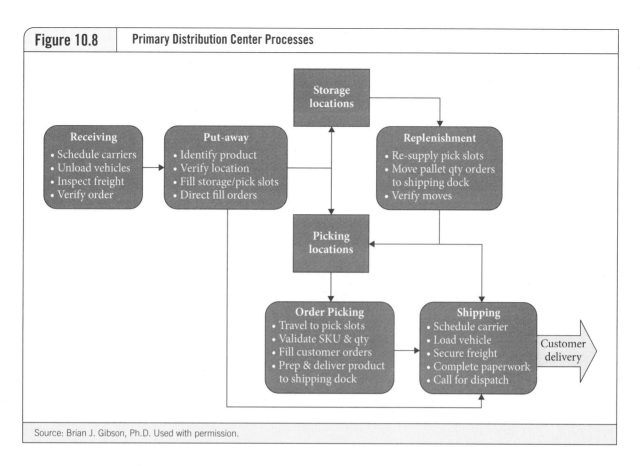

Source: Brian J. Gibson, Ph.D. Used with permission.

configuration to validate product safety, verify the storage location, pick up the pallet, and scan the bar code on the pallet label. The product is moved to the proper storage location or picking location and placed in the rack. It is critical that the forklift operator verify that product is being put in the correct location or it may become lost among the vast number of pallet locations and similar looking boxes. After the process is completed, inventory records are updated to reflect receipt of the item, its storage location, and availability for customer order.

There are two keys to achieving an accurate, productive flow of goods into the facility. First, receiving clerks must be well trained to evaluate incoming goods and match product with carrier counts, vendor documentation, and the purchase order. Failure to do so will lead to a mismatch between the physical inventory and what is recorded in the system. This will subsequently lead to order-filling problems. Second, coordination of the receiving and put-away operations is needed. Most receiving docks have limited floor capacity, so pallets must be cleared away quickly to ensure that there is space to unload additional deliveries. One way to achieve coordination is to cross-train workers so that they can be shifted back and forth between receiving clerk and put-away forklift operator functions. Another option is to stagger the shift start time so that the receiving process is started early and work is generated for the later start time of the put-away function.

The order-picking process focuses on the selection of goods to fulfill customer orders. Order fulfillment personnel travel through the facility from pick slot to pick slot and pull the requested quantity of each product identified on the pick list. The pick list may be generated as a paper checklist, labels that are placed on the carton, a computer display, or a voice-activated picking system. Once picked, the items may be labeled and put on a conveyor system for transfer to the shipping area or assembled on a pallet or cart designated for the customer. If the latter method is used, the order fulfillment personnel transfer the order to the shipment staging area and prepare it for delivery. The completed customer order is staged in a predesignated area for loading onto the appropriate outbound delivery vehicle.

For many organizations, order picking is the most labor-intensive and expensive distribution activity, often accounting for more than half of DC operating costs. This function requires a great deal of travel throughout the facility and the handling of individual cases or units within cases. Thus, it is important for managers to focus on creating a productive, safe, and accurate order-picking operation, if the function is to be done correctly and at the lowest possible cost.[4] Table 10.4 highlights a variety of industry practices that are used to improve picking productivity.

The replenishment operation plays an important supporting role for order picking, moving product from storage locations in the facility to the designated pick slots. These storage locations are often inaccessible to the order fulfillment personnel, and specialized equipment is needed to retrieve the product. Replenishment forklift operators focus on

Table 10.4	Best Practices in Order Picking
PRINCIPLE	**BEST PRACTICES**
Minimize travel time	• Sequence pick patterns and pick lists so that order fillers make one trip through the facility without backtracking. • Use batch picking. Order fillers select multiple orders during a single pass through the facility. • Use zone picking. Order fillers work in a limited area, selecting the parts of orders within their zone.
Maximize time spent picking product	• Reduce or eliminate paperwork to keep order fillers on task. Use voice or light-directed picking systems instead of paper orders. • Keep like items together to facilitate fast pallet building, reduce order rehandling, and avoid product damage. • Have necessary tools and equipment readily available.
Facilitate accurate order picking	• Provide clean and well-lighted picking areas with ample space for order pickers to perform tasks. • Clearly identify all pick locations with labels or placards that can be read from a distance. • Use systems that require validation of order-picking location and quantity before order filler is directed to next location.
Leverage materials-handling equipment	• Use carousels and automated storage/retrieval solutions lines to move product to the picker, reducing search and travel time. • Use conveyor lines to move product from picking areas to shipping area, eliminating back and forth travel. • Use forklifts and pallet jacks to handle bulk items and large quantities. This will promote safety and reduce picking time.
Minimize idle time	• Deploy inventory based on activity profiles, spreading out fast-moving products to facilitate access and reduce congestion. • Develop and enforce time standards for order-picking operation. • Maintain adequate inventory levels in pick slots so that product is available for order fillers to grab on their initial pass.

Source: Adapted from *The Journey to Warehousing Excellence,* (Raleigh NC: Tompkins Press, 1999), Section 2.

keeping an adequate supply of product in each pick slot. When a pick slot is empty, the order pickers will have to make a second trip to retrieve the required quantity of product. These additional trips are labor intensive and may cause split deliveries or delay the dispatch of customer orders. Hence, it is critical to synchronize order-picking and replenishment activities, shifting personnel back and forth between the functions as needed.

The final movement process occurs at the shipping operation. In some facilities, empty trailers are dropped at shipping dock doors and loaded as orders arrive from the picking operation. In other operations, a "live" loading process takes place when the outbound carrier arrives at the shipping dock. The goods are moved from the staging area to the loading dock, counted and inspected as required, and loaded into the carrier's vehicle. The carrier signs the bill of lading that has been prepared by the shipper, indicating receipt of the goods, and departs from the facility.

Though it appears to be more of a transportation-related activity, the shipping operation has a major impact on the success of distribution facilities. The shipping personnel must take steps to protect the freight from in-transit damage, accurately load orders into trailers, and complete work in a timely fashion to meet dispatch deadlines. They also need to utilize trailer space completely to reduce the cost of each trip. Collectively, these efforts augment the customer service and cost efficiency efforts of the other distribution operations.

10-4-2 Support Functions

While the product-handling functions account for the vast majority of the activity, labor, and cost in distribution facilities, a number of other administrative and management activities facilitate the successful execution of day-to-day operations. These support functions provide coordination between key processes and across the supply chain, protect the organization's inventory investment, and improve working conditions within the facility. Chief among these support functions are (1) inventory control; (2) safety, maintenance, and sanitation; (3) security; (4) performance analysis; and (5) information technology.

One of the most challenging activities in a distribution operation is to maintain control over the inventory. With product flowing in and out of the facility on a daily basis, it is critical to ensure that the inventory database accurately reflects what is actually inside the facility. Inventory control specialists and analysts resolve stock discrepancies, search for misplaced product, conduct cycle counts and quality audits, and make inventory adjustments. Their efforts improve the reliability of inventory reports so that when customers place product orders, the right quantities of the right products are available and accessible to the order fulfillment personnel. Additional discussion of inventory control is provided in Chapter 9.

Establishing a safe, clean, working environment is not only a management obligation but also a distribution productivity booster. The safety function focuses on preserving the health and welfare of distribution employees via an ergonomically sound working environment. Training employees on proper techniques for lifting, requiring industrial equipment training and licensing, and creating awareness of potential hazards will reduce costly workplace accidents and injuries. Preventive maintenance of equipment and timely repairs of problems also promote safe working conditions in the distribution facility. Finally, the sanitation function focuses on complying with regulatory standards and maintaining worker morale. Also, all three functions help keep product damage in check.

The security function seeks to protect the organization from merchandise theft and fraud. Numerous techniques can be used in the distribution facility to prevent losses. Physical tools such as trailer seals, security tags, and monitored processing areas are used to reduce inventory losses. Personnel procedures can also be effective deterrents against theft. Prescreening potential employees, conducting inspections and audits, and limiting access to the facility can be helpful. Finally, a security staff can monitor facility activity and investigate problems.

The management team is also responsible for evaluating and improving facility performance. Some organizations will have distribution analysts or software measure productivity, quality, utilization, and costs for each aspect of the distribution process. A failure to monitor the performance of individual employees using labor standards and the accuracy of their work can lead to poor facility performance. Distribution measures are discussed in the next section.

Organizations rely heavily on information technology to receive, fill, and distribute customer orders. Access to a strong team of internal or external technology experts is needed to build stronger information-sharing processes and enhance visibility of inventory and orders. Specific software tools for distribution execution are discussed in an upcoming section of the chapter.

Together, these support functions facilitate product movement and storage within the distribution operation and the fulfillment of perfect orders. Without them, it would be difficult to protect workers and product from a host of challenges, maintain precise inventory records, or know how well the operation is performing. In short, the operation would quickly fall into disarray without the team of specialists behind the frontline managers and labor.

10-5 Distribution Metrics

The activities performed in the distribution function can be readily evaluated through the measurement and analysis of key performance indicators (KPIs). Customers use distribution KPIs to objectively assess the quality of service provided by the distribution operation. Management uses KPIs to appraise the operational costs and productivity of company and 3PL fulfillment processes. KPI performance can be analyzed versus past history, current goals, and industry benchmarks.

Many aspects of distribution performance can be evaluated across customer service and DC order fulfillment activities. The challenge lies in narrowing down the vast array of metrics that can be rapidly generated by information systems to a manageable number of KPIs that address important distribution requirements of a supply chain. Properly chosen KPIs focus personnel on fulfillment objectives, evaluate the impact of distribution process improvements, and keep distribution priorities in line with corporate and supply chain goals.

Customers focus on KPIs that address fulfillment service quality. When you place an order from your favorite website, your goal is clear—to get the right product in the quantity ordered at the expected time. Thus, customer-facing KPIs must target reliability of the distribution processes to provide accurate, complete, and timely fulfillment of orders. Table 10.5 reveals how the most common service quality metrics are calculated.

Order accuracy and **order completeness** are important service quality KPIs that influence customer satisfaction and retention. Accurate and complete fulfillment occurs when the products selected and shipped from the DC match the customer's order. Doing so avoids costly problems like customer returns of incorrect products, expedited fulfillment of backordered products, and inventory discrepancies at the DC. Hence, continuous monitoring of these KPIs is important for detecting and resolving order fulfillment errors, shortages, and overages.

Table 10.5	Example Distribution Service Quality Metrics
METRIC	**FORMULA**
Unit Fill Rate	Total units shipped / Total units ordered
Case Fill Rate	Total cases shipped / Total cases ordered
Order Value Fill Rate	Total value shipped / Total value ordered
Order Accuracy	Total correct units shipped / Total units shipped
Document Accuracy	Total correct customer invoices / Total customer invoices
On Time Dispatch	Total orders ready by deadline / Total orders dispatched
Perfect Order Index	Complete Order % x Damage-Free % x Billing Accuracy % x On-Time Dispatch %
Source: Brian J. Gibson, Ph.D. Used with permission.	

Timeliness is a critical component of fulfillment customer service. Typically, timeliness is considered a transportation issue, but the distribution operation facilitates on-time performance. An order must be picked, packed, and made available for loading by a shipping deadline. Otherwise, the order will not be dispatched as planned and will have to wait for the next carrier pickup, voyage, or flight. KPIs related to order processing time average and percentage of orders completed by shipping deadlines direct attention toward improvement of order fulfillment velocity.

Of course, the goal is to meet customer expectations across all KPIs to support perfect order fulfillment. The DC plays a key role in achieving perfect orders by picking the right products in the right quantities for the right customer order. The DC must also ensure that the products are in the right condition (damage-free) and the orders meet the ship-by deadlines, respectively. Perfect execution avoids customer frustration, customer service intervention, and DC rework to correct the order.

Companies can also evaluate the combined impact of these KPIs via a metric called the **perfect order index (POI)**. The Perfect Order Index (POI) is established by multiplying the results of four KPI measurements: complete orders (100% fill rate), damage-free condition, documentation accuracy, and on-time dispatch. Rather than look at each component separately, the metric highlights the total impact of an incorrect order.[5]

While service quality is the foundation of customer satisfaction with the fulfillment process, internal performance is also critical. Organizations must balance order fulfillment expenses with customer service requirements. To achieve low fulfillment costs relative to product value, effective utilization of assets and productive execution of distribution processes are needed. Table 10.6 identifies common DC operations metrics and how they are calculated.

Distribution cost efficiency of internal and 3PL operations is critical, given the magnitude of U.S. warehousing and distribution-related costs—$143 billion in 2014.[6] **Aggregate cost efficiency** measures focus on the total distribution spending versus goal or the cost of goods sold. Item-level KPIs focus on the distribution expense per unit of measure (e.g., cost per pallet, case, or order). These metrics highlight the impact of distribution on supply chain costs and provide a baseline for cost reduction initiatives.

Asset utilization is important as organizations spend significant sums of money on distribution facilities, materials-handling equipment, and technology. All must be utilized

Table 10.6	Example Distribution Operation Metrics
METRIC	**FORMULA**
Distribution cost per unit	Total distribution cost / Total number of units processed
Distribution cost ratio	Total distribution cost / Total cost of goods sold
Capacity utilization	Total storage slots used / Total storage slots available
Equipment utilization	Total operational time / Total time available
Labor productivity	Total number of cases processed / Total hours paid
Distribution efficiency	Task completion time / Standard time allowed
Source: Brian J. Gibson, Ph.D. Used with permission.	

regularly to justify current and future investment. If the facility is half empty, if equipment sits unused during operating hours or is idled due to maintenance issues, then these critical DC assets are not being effectively deployed. Utilization KPIs provide an objective assessment of how intensively DC managers are working their resources.

Resource productivity affects distribution cost and the ability of the DC to maximize throughput on a consistent basis. Productivity is measured as the ratio of real output to real input. With distribution costs averaging nearly 10 percent of a sales dollar, productivity improvements will contribute to an organization's financial success. Productivity KPIs help distribution managers evaluate facility performance versus goals, estimate a DC's maximum daily throughput, and schedule labor. Declining productivity results are early warning signals of distribution problems that must be addressed.

Resource efficiency measures compare distribution activity completion time versus engineered time standards. Time and motion studies are used to observe how much time employees require to complete key operations and establish appropriate time standards.[7] These expected completion times include allowances for task complexity, fatigue, travel, and safe work practices. Efficiency can be measured at individual, functional, shift, or facility levels to evaluate completion of key tasks within the allowable amounts of time.

Consistent measurement and review of relevant distribution service quality and operational KPIs generates valuable insights. KPIs help organizations take a proactive, knowledge-based approach to managing fulfillment activities and resolving issues before they can negatively affect the supply chain. KPIs also help organizations pinpoint distribution inefficiencies and develop strategies for supply chain cost reduction. Finally, KPI data can be used to analyze cost–service level tradeoffs for decisions regarding distribution outsourcing, fulfillment process modification, and cost reduction initiatives.

10-6 Distribution Technology

While the distribution environment is dependent upon effective product flows, it also requires timely, accurate flows of information within distribution facilities and across the supply chain. Information must be shared regarding customer order status, inventory levels and location within the facility, labor performance, and more. Virtually every distribution strategy and process discussed in this chapter is easier to plan, execute, and evaluate with ready access to relevant information. Fortunately, distribution managers no longer need to manually track vast amounts of distribution information. Software and information technology tools are available to support distribution control and decision making. In this final section of the chapter, the primary technologies are presented.

10-6-1 Warehouse Management Systems

The core software used to manage fulfillment processes is called warehouse management systems (WMS), a mature technology dating back to the 1970s.[8] Widely used to support all types of distribution operations, WMS primarily functions as a software control system that improves product movement and storage operations through efficient management of information and completion of distribution tasks. The fundamental goals are to achieve high levels of control, inventory accuracy, and productivity through directed picking, directed replenishment, and directed put-away.

A WMS is more than a simple database that provides stock location information. Instead, it is an integrated package whose components often include radio-frequency (RF) communications, dedicated localized computer hardware, and the necessary applications software. The detailed setup and processing within a WMS can vary significantly from one software vendor to another; however, the basic logic will use a combination of item, location, quantity, unit of measure, and order information to determine where to stock, where to pick, and in what sequence to perform these operations.[9]

Beyond the main functionalities, WMS can also provide value-added capabilities and support a variety of supply chain activities. These features include:

- **Labor management**—The ability to link WMS with a related labor tracking module allows the organization to create assignments based on engineered time standards, monitor the productivity of each employee, and audit the quality of their work. Performance analysis, incentive programs, and productivity improvement initiatives are supported by labor management tools.

- **Automated data collection**—Powerful WMS use automatic identification (Auto-ID) tools, to accurately capture data, provide visibility of product flows in the DC, and automate activities. Once data have been collected, it is transmitted to the WMS for decision processing, report generation, and performance analysis. The next section and Chapter 14 provide extended coverage of auto-ID technologies.

- **Task interleaving**—This process involves mixing dissimilar tasks such as put-away and replenishment. In large warehouses, WMS-based task interleaving can greatly reduce travel time, not only increasing productivity but also reducing wear on the lift trucks and saving on energy costs by reducing lift truck fuel consumption.

- **Fulfillment flexibility**—A robust WMS will support multiple order types, including omni-channel orders for single units and commercial orders for full cases or pallets of product. It will also facilitate case pick distribution and cross-dock fulfillment, support light assembly and kitting operations, and allow various order picking patterns to be used in the DC.

- **Systems convergence**—The ability to interface the WMS with the enterprise resource planning (ERP) system, order management systems, and transportation management will provide a strong flow of information across the organization and the supply chain. Convergence of these systems, which supports orchestration and synchronization of execution processes, is the focus of the On the Line feature.

On the Line   *Convergence is the Word in WMS*

A WMS is an excellent tool for managing operations inside the four walls of a DC, cross-dock, or fulfillment center. The problem is that these facilities are not remote islands of activity that operate independently. Distribution facilities are integral nodes in the supply chain and it is imperative that the WMS connects with other supply chain systems to generate rapid, accurate fulfillment and delivery of customer orders as efficiently as possible.

To accomplish this objective, organizations need to better orchestrate and synchronize execution processes across functional areas. That is, they need to achieve convergence of their systems—WMS, transportation management systems (TMS), distributed order management systems (DOM), order management systems (OMS), and related supply chain software.

Gartner, a supply chain research firm, notes that convergence is only possible when these SCM software systems have a common technical architecture with a shared user interface, data model, and business logic. Leading SCM software vendors offer WMS with convergence capabilities today, though the competition is striving to catch up.

Supply chain convergence gives shippers a way to break through the "difficulty or inability to coordinate and synchronize end-to-end supply chain processes barrier and better synchronize their processes across different functions," according to Dwight Klappich, research vice president for Gartner. By eliminating the functional silos that existed among warehousing, transportation, procurement, yard management, and global shipping activities, for example, shippers can optimize activities across previously siloed functions that didn't communicate or work with one another.

Having convergence between WMS and other software tools is especially important for omni-channel supply chains that must support commerce everywhere to anywhere strategies. No longer do we have days to coordinate information from disparate systems, it all has to occur in the matter of minutes. For example, a retailer must be able to capture a customer order, identify inventory locations (DC, store, supplier's warehouse), commit that inventory to the order, and produce the transaction that

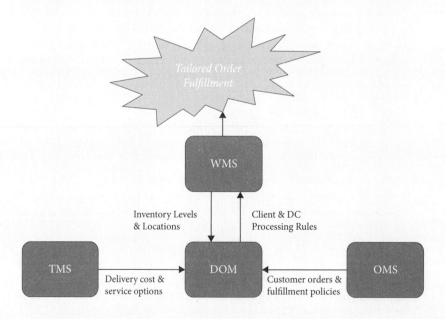

indicates that the chosen location needs to fill and ship the order. This requires synchronization of the retailer's WMS, TMS, OMS, and DOM software as highlighted in the diagram.

To support the expedited fulfillment and delivery requirements of omni-channel commerce, a software vendor must offer a supply chain execution system with the necessary functionality—WMS, TMS, DOM, and more. The functionality within each software module must be rich. And, the modules must be highly integrated and capable of supporting multiple workflows. That is how vendors help organizations break down functional (and software) silos to support supply chain convergence and optimization.

Source: Bridget McCrea, "Supply Chain and Logistics Technology: Convergence Gaining Momentum," *Logistics Management* (June 2015). Retrieved November 10, 2015 from http://www.logisticsmgmt.com/ article/supply_chain_and_logistics_technology_convergence_gaining_momentum; Dan Gilmore and Dinesh Dongre, *The Changing Role of WMS in an Era of Supply Chain Convergence* (Charlotte, NC: Material Handling Institute, 2015). Retrieved November 10, 2015 from http://cdn.promatshow.com/seminars/ assets/932.pdf; and SC Digest Editorial Staff, "Supply Chain News: Insights from the Gartner Warehouse Management System Magic Quadrant," On-Target (October 20, 2014). Retrieved November 10, 2015 from http://www.scdigest.com/ontarget/14-10-20-1.php?cid=8606.

An advanced WMS may also feature performance reporting capabilities; support paperless processes; enable integration of materials-handling equipment, picking systems, and sorting systems; facilitate inventory cycle counting; and capacity planning.

An effective WMS implementation that leverages the capabilities listed earlier should generate multiple benefits. Increases in inventory accuracy and order picking quality will boost customer service. Greater labor control and reduced travel time will boost facility productivity. And, faster processing of orders in the proper sequence will reduce order cycle time. The WMS also provides essential information for managers to analyze operations, perform what-if scenario planning, and make informed decisions that are based on current conditions. In addition, these systems can improve space utilization by determining the optimal storage patterns to maximize space utilization.

Given these benefits, it is not surprising WMS is used by 85 percent of the companies responding to a 2015 *Logistics Management* survey. That is up from 76 percent usage in 2012. Among the users, 41 percent operate a legacy WMS (internally developed), 40 percent license a WMS as part of an enterprise resource planning (ERP) system, and 19 percent license software from a best-of-breed WMS vendor.[10] Legacy systems and best-of-breed solutions are lauded for their ability to support customization requirements. In contrast, ERP-based WMS integrate quickly with other modules to support straightforward distribution operations.

10-6-2 Automatic Identification Tools

Auto-ID technologies help machines identify objects. Bar codes, radio-frequency identification (RFID), smart cards, voice recognition, and biometric technologies are available to supply chain managers.

Barcodes and RFID are the auto-ID tools of choice in distribution to help track, locate, and move product quickly—with near perfect accuracy rates to consumers. Barcodes have been used in distribution applications for more than three decades. The barcode sequence provides relevant data that scanners can translate into important information such as a shipment's origin, the product type, the place of manufacture, and the product's price.

This improves data collection speed, facilitates rapid receiving and order fulfillment, and helps to integrate data collection with other areas. This creates stronger information flows and inventory control. Items can be moved more quickly into the DC, and personnel can select and prepare orders much more rapidly.

Basic EAN/UPC barcodes are printed on virtually every consumer product in the world. These 8 to 13 digit one-dimensional (1D) barcodes are used to scan goods at point of sale. Other types of 1D barcodes such at the Code 128 barcodes and the GS1 Databar can hold a much larger number of digits which expands the informational capabilities of the labels. Two-dimensional (2D) barcodes systematically represent data using symbols and shapes. A QR code and DataMatrix code has capacity for thousands of alphanumeric characters, allowing the barcode to store a significant amount of information.[11] Figure 10.9 provides sample barcode types.

RFID tags, which consist of silicon chips and an antenna that can transmit data to a wireless receiver, are being used to track everything from jeans to cars. Unlike barcodes, which need to be scanned manually and read individually, RFID tags do not require line-of-sight for reading. There is a resurgence of interest in RFID due to the growth of omni-channel retailing. RFID is viewed as an excellent tool for improving inventory accuracy and visibility which support store-based order fulfillment methods.[12]

In the distribution environment, it is possible to automatically read hundreds of RFID tags per second as the product travels within the field of a wireless reading device. Not only can these tags be read faster than barcodes, but they also contain more information so they can recall items more efficiently.[13] Chapter 14 provides additional details regarding RFID.

New WMS and auto-ID functionalities are continuously being developed. Before buying new tools, it is important for an organization to assess its distribution technology requirements. The goal is to deploy distribution technologies that help distribution managers make better decisions, achieve maximum throughput, and support customer requirements. Sometimes, a low-cost WMS and auto-ID solutions can provide needed capabilities without great expense or complexity.

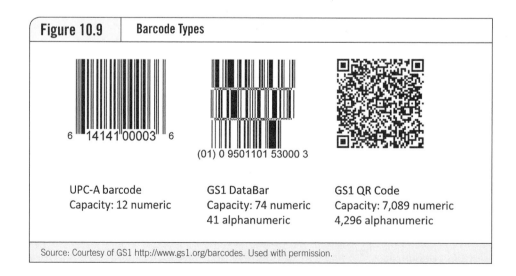

Figure 10.9	Barcode Types

UPC-A barcode
Capacity: 12 numeric

6 14141 00003 6

GS1 DataBar
Capacity: 74 numeric
41 alphanumeric

(01) 0 9501101 53000 3

GS1 QR Code
Capacity: 7,089 numeric
4,296 alphanumeric

Source: Courtesy of GS1 http://www.gs1.org/barcodes. Used with permission.

SUMMARY

Distribution managers play a critical role in the supply chain, facilitating product flows to manufacturing facilities, retailers, and directly to consumers. Fulfilling these orders accurately and quickly while achieving the lowest possible cost is a balancing game that distribution managers must play daily. They must coordinate people, processes, capacity, and technology to achieve customer satisfaction, meet internal goals, and provide value-added services to the supply chain.

Managing the distribution system for maximum supply chain impact requires considerable planning, coordination of fulfillment strategy with the execution of distribution operations, analysis of key metrics, and information sharing. Additional concepts from this chapter include the following:

- Distribution operations perform inventory handling, storage, and processing activities to create time and place utility for the supply chain.

- A variety of supply chain challenges—balancing supply and demand, protecting against uncertainty, and promoting transportation economies, among others—can be addressed by distribution facilities.

- Four primary functions are carried out by traditional distribution facilities: (1) accumulation, (2) sortation, (3) allocation, and (4) assortment.

- Distribution operations are taking on value-adding roles—assembly, kitting, product postponement, sequencing, etc.—to complement their basic functionality and to support evolving supply chain needs.

- Tradeoffs must be made between space, equipment, and people—the primary resources available to distribution managers.

- It is critical to match distribution processes to the items being handled to protect product integrity, promote customer service and satisfaction, and provide greater control of the inventory.

- Distribution network design issues involve centralization/decentralization of inventory, the number and location of facilities, and facility ownership.

- Effective facility planning—operational size, layout, and product placement—positively impacts labor productivity and response time.

- Distribution execution involves five primary processes related to the handling and storage of product: (1) receiving, (2) put-away, (3) order picking, (4) replenishment, and (5) shipping.

- Fulfillment support functions provide coordination between key processes and across the supply chain, protect the organization's inventory investment, and improve working conditions within the facility.

- Distribution KPIs address asset utilization, labor productivity, and cost efficiency of the operation, as well as customer service quality issues and the ultimate goal of perfect order fulfillment.

- Warehouse management systems software solutions improve product movement and storage operations through efficient management of information and completion of distribution tasks.

- Barcodes and RFID are the auto-ID tools of choice in distribution for product control, visibility, and flow—with great accuracy rates.

STUDY QUESTIONS

1. Discuss the role of distribution in the supply chain. Provide examples of how distribution operations can positively and negatively impact supply chain performance.

2. Compare and contrast the four primary functions of a DC: accumulation, sortation, allocation, and assortment.

3. Discuss the primary tradeoffs that must be made between distribution and other logistics activities.

4. Describe the major challenges faced by distribution managers in the current environment.

5. What are the primary capabilities, advantages, and disadvantages of direct distribution, DCs, and cross-docks?

6. Why would a company such as Unilever, which produces a wide variety of consumer goods, use 3PL distribution services?

7. Using company Web sites, compare the distribution service offerings for the following 3PL organizations:

    a. Kane is Able (http://kaneisable.com) and AmeriCold Logistics (http://www
       .americold.com)

    b. GENCO (http://www.genco.com) and Neovia Logistics Services (http://www
       .neovialogistics.com/)

8. When designing a DC, what interior layout objectives and slotting principles must be considered? Why?

9. Identify and describe the five primary product-handling functions in a DC.

10. What are the key support functions in a DC? Why are they important?

11. How would a distribution operation monitor its service quality? What types of metrics would be used to evaluate operating performance of a DC?

12. Using Internet search engines, identify three WMS solutions providers. Describe the capabilities and supply chain impact that their tools promise.

NOTES

1. Rosalyn Wilson, *26th Annual State of Logistics Report* (Oak Brook, IL: Council of Supply Chain Management Professionals, 2015).

2. Scott B. Keller and Brian C. Keller, *The Definitive Guide to Warehousing: Managing the Storage and Handling of Materials and Products in the Supply Chain* (Upper Saddle River, NJ: Pearson Education, 2014), 16–17.

3. Matthew A. Waller and Terry L. Esper, *The Definitive Guide to Inventory Management,* (Upper Saddle River, NJ: Pearson Education, 2014), 155–158.

4. Marc Wulfraat, "5 Ways to Improve Order Picking Productivity," *Supply Chain 24/7,* (May 15, 2013). Retrieved October 29, 2015 from http://www.supplychain247.com/article/5_ways_to_improve_order_picking_productivity/MWPVL_International.

5. Kate Vitasek and Karl Manrodt, *Benchmarking the Perfect Order* (Sugar Land, TX: Compliance Networks, 2008). Retrieved November 8, 2015 from http://www.compliancenetworks.com/jdownloads/2008_perfect_order_index_study.pdf.

6. Rosalyn Wilson, *26th Annual State of Logistics Report* (Oak Brook, IL: Council of Supply Chain Management Professionals, 2015).

7. Martin Murray, "Measures of Warehouse Productivity," *About.com: Logistics/Supply Chain*. Retrieved November 9, 2015 from http://logistics.about.com/od/supplychainmodels/a/measures.htm

8. Joan Nystrom and Dan Gilmore, "WMS: Core of the Integrated Logistics Suite," *Supply Chain Digest Letter* (July 2010), pp. 1–9.

9. Dave Piasecki, "Warehouse Management Systems," *Inventoryops.com*. Retrieved November 10, 2015 from http://www.inventoryops.com/warehouse_management_systems.htm

10. Roberto Michel, "2015 Warehouse & DC Operations Survey Results," *Supply Chain 24/7* (November 9, 2015). Retrieved November 11, 2015 from http://www.supplychain247.com/article/2015_warehouse_dc_operations_survey_results/viastore_systems

11. Scandit, *Types of Barcodes: Choosing the Right Barcode* (January 27, 2015). Retrieved November 11, 2015 from http://www.scandit.com/2015/01/27/types-barcodes-choosing-right-barcode/

12. MH&L Staff, "RFID Demand Up with Rise of Omni-Channel Retailing," *Material Handling & Logistics* (June 1, 2015). Retrieved November 11, 2015 from http://mhlnews.com/technology-automation/rfid-demand-rise-omni-channel-retailing

13. Jessica Säilä, "6 Most Common FAQs of Barcode vs RFID," *RFID Arena* (December 2, 2013). Retrieved November 11, 2015 from http://www.rfidarena.com/2013/12/2/6-most-common-faqs-of-barcode-vs-rfid.aspx

CASE 10.1

Power Force Corporation

Kip Himmer, executive vice president of operations of Power Force Corporation (PFC), is feeling stressed out. The producer of power tools for the do-it-yourself market is experiencing higher fulfillment costs as retailers change their buying patterns. They all seem to want smaller, more frequent shipments to a larger number of locations. And, the retailers' service expectations are on the rise. They are demanding advanced shipping notification, RFID tags on all products, and improved inventory visibility.

Gone are the days when the retailers bought power tools by the truckload for delivery to a few regionally dispersed DCs. Instead, they are asking for smaller shipments to multiple DCs and direct delivery to stores. Some retailers are also inquiring about PFC's ability to deliver orders for individual customers direct to their homes. This drop-shipping strategy is completely new to PFC and Himmer worries that it could create major bottlenecks at the company's centralized DC that sits next to the factory in Louisville, Kentucky. And, all of these new requirements are accompanied by shorter order cycle time goals.

Himmer feels that he is stuck between a rock and a hard place as the major home improvement chain stores (Home Depot, Lowe's, and True Value) account for more than 80 percent of PFC's sales. Although compliance is proving to be very expensive, PFC cannot afford to deny the requests. Doing so would have an unwelcome effect on revenues.

After consulting with his fulfillment team, Himmer has come to the conclusion that he has three reasonable options to address the emerging marketplace requirements:

Option 1 – Upgrade the existing PFC DC in Kentucky to handle multiple order types and smaller shipments. Deploy warehouse automation to improve order fulfillment speed and efficiency.

Option 2 – Expand the PFC fulfillment network. Add regional DCs in Nevada and New Jersey to the existing Kentucky DC. Modify operational processes and flows so that orders for DCs, stores, and individual consumers can be fulfilled.

Option 3 – Outsource fulfillment to a capable third party logistics company so that PFC can focus its efforts on quality production, accurate demand planning, and lean inventory management.

Himmer's next step is to fully evaluate the three options and choose a path forward before his upcoming meeting with Marcia Avis, the owner of PFC. Avis will ask tough questions and Himmer must be confident in his recommendation.

CASE QUESTIONS

1. Compare and contrast the three options from the perspective of customer service. Which do you believe will provide the best level of service? Why?
2. Compare and contrast the three options from the perspective of cost. Which one do you believe will provide the most economical solution for PFC? Why?
3. What types of functional and cost trade-offs will Himmer need to analyze?
4. Which distribution option do feel gives PFC the best opportunity for future success? Why?

Source: Brian J. Gibson, Ph.D. Used with permission.

CASE 10.2

TV Gadgetry

TV Gadgetry (TVG)—a distributor of inexpensive kitchen tools and small appliances that are promoted on late-night infomercials—is facing challenges in its DC operations. Compared to the previous month, both the numbers of orders and customer complaints regarding service quality have increased dramatically in September. The company's manual picking systems and paper-based order management methods seem to be affecting performance, as is the heavy labor turnover occurring in the DC.

Dylan Larking, the company's vice president of logistics is determined to uncover the source of these complaints. He asks the new intern, Connor McDavis, to collect data and evaluate a variety of KPIs. McDavis jumps on the task and captures the information needed to evaluate order fill rate, fulfillment accuracy, invoice accuracy, and on-time dispatch. These metrics, McDavis believes, will help him identify the real problems so that changes can be made.

His effort generates the following data:

FULFILLMENT DATA	SEPTEMBER	AUGUST
Customer Orders Processed	50,000	40,000
Units Ordered	300,000	200,000
Units Shipped	287,333	192,507
Correct Units Shipped	247,385	188,263
Correct Customer Invoices	46,310	39,124
Orders Ready by Deadline	49,188	38,791
Total Labor Hours Paid	2,000	1,500

After thanking McDavis for the collecting the data, Larking asks the intern to do three things: (a) Calculate relevant distribution KPIs; (b) Compare the results to the TVG fulfillment goals; and (c) Identify the major problem areas and potential solutions.

"Get busy with this," says Larking. "I want you to investigate the situation and report back to me on Monday."

CASE QUESTIONS

1. Help McDavis with the analysis by calculating KPIs for: (a) Unit fill rate; (b) Fulfillment accuracy; (c) Document accuracy; (d) On-time dispatch; and (e) Productivity.
2. Compare your KPIs to the following TVG goals and comment on the problem areas:

KPI	GOAL
Unit Fill Rate	95%
Fulfillment Accuracy	98%
Document Accuracy	99%
On-Time Dispatch	95%
Productivity	135 units shipped per labor hour

3. Based on your KPI calculations, what is the perfect order index for TVG?
4. What actions should TVG management take to address the problems that you identified?
5. What benefits could TVG gain by adopting a warehouse management system?

Source: Brian J. Gibson, Ph.D. Used with permission.

APPENDIX 10A

Materials Handling

Distribution centers (DCs), cross docks, and other flow through facilities are under intense pressure to process and handle orders rapidly, accurately, safely, and economically. You can't do it by physical labor alone. Just imagine if Amazon tried to manually pick and ship the 34.4 million items purchased during its 24-hour Prime Day sale.[1] Or if FedEx did not have "The Matrix," a sortation system with 300 miles of conveyor belts, diverters, scanners, and technology to process a half million packages per hour.[2] You'd be waiting weeks for your expedited order to arrive and that's just not acceptable today.

The need for speed and efficiency makes it imperative that organizations use material handling equipment, automation, and technology to complete the key distribution functions of accumulation, sortation, allocation, and assortment. This equipment can be used to improve speed to market and reduce manual labor in fulfillment operations.

Generally speaking, materials handling focuses on the activities, equipment, and procedures related to the movement, storage, protection, and control of materials in a system. In logistics, the focus of materials handling is efficient short-distance movement of products and materials within the confines of a DC, factory, cross-dock, transportation terminal, or store. Adapting the customer-oriented "seven Rs" definition of logistics yields the following:

> *Materials handling uses the right method to provide the right amount of the right material at the right place, at the right time, in the right sequence, in the right position, in the right condition, and at the right cost.*

To achieve the seven Rs of materials handling within a DC, specially designed equipment is used. Properly selected, this equipment improves labor productivity for receiving, put-away, replenishment, order picking, and shipping activities; increases space utilization; and improves DC order cycle time.

Objectives and Principles of Materials Handling

The objective of materials handling is to create a more productive, efficient, and safe operation. To achieve a proper balance between service and cost, safety and productivity, and volume and capacity, logistics professionals must effectively manage four critical dimensions of materials handling: (1) movement, (2) time, (3) quantity, and (4) space.

The *movement* dimension of materials handling involves the conveyance of goods into, through, and out of DCs. Logistics professionals must select the proper combination of labor and equipment to achieve efficient flows.

The *time* dimension of materials handling is concerned with preparing goods for production or for order fulfillment. The longer it takes to get raw materials to production, the greater the chance of work stoppage, excess inventories, and increased storage space. Likewise, the longer it takes to move finished goods to the shipping area, the longer the order cycle time and the lower the customer service.

The *quantity* dimension addresses the varying usage and delivery rate of raw materials and finished goods, respectively. Materials-handling systems are designed to ensure that the correct quantity of product is moved to meet the needs of production and customers.

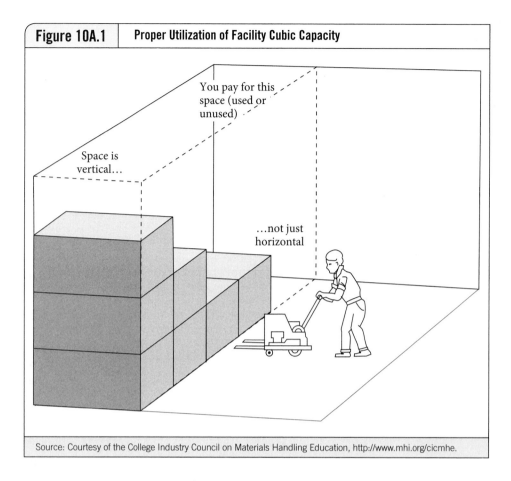

Figure 10A.1 | **Proper Utilization of Facility Cubic Capacity**

You pay for this space (used or unused)

Space is vertical...

...not just horizontal

Source: Courtesy of the College Industry Council on Materials Handling Education, http://www.mhi.org/cicmhe.

The *space* dimension of the DC focuses on the capacity constraints of the facility. Properly chosen materials handling equipment and systems allow an organization to use both the horizontal and vertical space effectively. For example, high reach forklifts can extend to heights of 25 to 30 feet, thereby increasing the vertical capacity utilization of the DC. Figure 10A.1 illustrates the importance of vertical space.

Balancing these interrelated dimensions requires significant analysis of the many options for mixing space, equipment, and people. Fortunately, these challenges have been addressed by the Material Handling Industry of America in a set of guidelines called the *Ten Principles of Materials Handling*. Table 10A.1 identifies and summarizes the key points of these standards. Supply chain professionals apply them on a daily basis when designing and managing DC operations.

These principles are important and interrelated. In the twenty-first century, materials handling helps companies minimize distribution facility investment, reduce expenses, and support supply chain requirements. It also helps organizations overcome some of the labor challenges associated with an aging workforce.

Materials-Handling Equipment[3]

Effective materials handling requires the effective use of different types of mechanical and automated equipment to move goods whenever the requirements, volume, and cost tradeoffs justify the investment. The recent warehouse automation and control market

Table 10A.1	The Ten Principles of Material Handling

1. **Planning Principle**. All material handling should be the result of a deliberate plan where the needs, performance objectives, and functional specifications of the proposed methods are completely defined at the outset.

2. **Standardization Principle**. Material handling methods, equipment, controls, and software should be standardized within the limits of achieving overall performance objectives and without sacrificing needed flexibility, modularity, and throughput.

3. **Work Principle.** Material handling work should be minimized without sacrificing productivity or the level of service required of the operation.

4. **Ergonomic Principle.** Human capabilities and limitations must be recognized and respected in the design of material handling tasks and equipment to ensure safe and effective operations.

5. **Unit Load Principle.** Unit loads shall be appropriately sized and configured in a way which achieves the material flow and inventory objectives at each stage in the supply chain.

6. **Space Utilization Principle.** Effective and efficient use must be made of all available space.

7. **System Principle.** Material movement and storage activities should be fully integrated to form a coordinated, operational system which spans receiving, inspection, storage, production, assembly, packaging, unitizing, order selection, shipping, transportation and the handling of returns.

8. **Automation Principle.** Material handling operations should be mechanized and/or automated where feasible to improve operational efficiency, increase responsiveness, improve consistency and predictability, decrease operating costs, and eliminate repetitive or potentially unsafe manual labor.

9. **Environmental Principle.** Environmental impact and energy consumption should be considered as criteria when designing or selecting alternative equipment and materials-handling systems.

10. **Life Cycle Cost Principle.** A thorough economic analysis should account for the entire life cycle of all material handling equipment and resulting systems.

Source: Material Handling Institute, *The Ten Principles of Material Handling*. Retrieved November 14, 2015 from http://www.mhi.org/downloads/learning/cicmhe/guidelines/10_principles.pdf. Reproduced by permission.

study by ARC Advisory Group points toward significant capital investments in material handling equipment and automation, largely due to the e-commerce boom.[4]

Choosing the right equipment is a multifaceted task. To reduce purchase, maintenance, and operating costs, materials-handling equipment should be standardized. It is also important to employ flexible equipment that accomplishes a variety of tasks. Finally, the equipment must be properly suited to the goods flowing through the DC and should have a minimal environmental impact.

The College-Industry Council of Material Handling Education classifies materials-handling equipment into five major categories: (1) transport equipment, (2) positioning equipment, (3) unit load formation equipment, (4) storage equipment, and (5) identification and control equipment. This taxonomy includes the equipment commonly used in distribution centers. Each category of equipment is briefly described below, with examples provided.

Transport equipment moves material from one location to another within a DC. This type of equipment improves product flows through the facility, minimizes labor effort and reduces dwell time. Figure 10A.2 presents different types of transport equipment.

Forklifts and other industrial trucks are used to move materials over variable paths, with no restrictions on the area covered by the movement. For example, personnel use industrial trucks to unload arriving freight from trailers, move product from dock to various storage areas, and load outbound vehicles. Pallet jacks allow order pickers to assemble orders directly on pallets and efficiently move to subsequent pick locations.

Figure 10A.2	Materials Transport Equipment

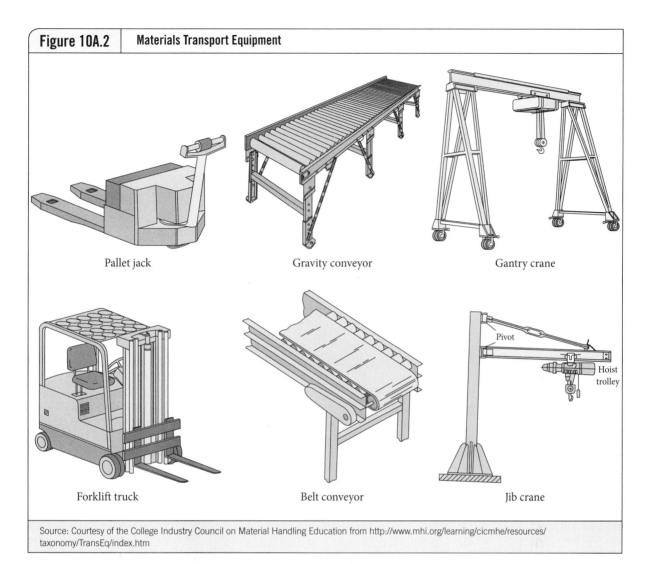

Pallet jack   Gravity conveyor   Gantry crane

Forklift truck   Belt conveyor   Jib crane

Source: Courtesy of the College Industry Council on Material Handling Education from http://www.mhi.org/learning/cicmhe/resources/taxonomy/TransEq/index.htm

Automatic guided vehicles (AGVs) are machines that connect receiving, storing, manufacturing, and shipping. AGVs can either roam freely or move on a fixed path, with computers that make traffic control decisions. Essentially, AGVs travel around the warehouse or manufacturing plant carrying items to a particular programmed destination. Since these AGVs do not require a driver, labor costs are reduced.

Conveyors are used to move materials over a fixed path between specific points in a DC. They are beneficial when there is adequate volume and frequency of movement between points to warrant the investment. Numerous types of conveyors are used to accomplish labor-free flows. Primary classifications include unit load or bulk load conveyors; overhead, on-floor, or in-floor location; and gravity or motorized power. A variety of automated sortation conveyors also ease labor requirements in the DC.

Cranes are used to move loads over variable paths within a restricted area of the DC or factory. They are more flexible than conveyors, have the ability to move goods both vertically and horizontally, and can handle oddly shaped loads. Cranes make sense when there is limited volume and the cost of installing conveyors is not feasible.

| Figure 10A.3 | Product Positioning Equipment |

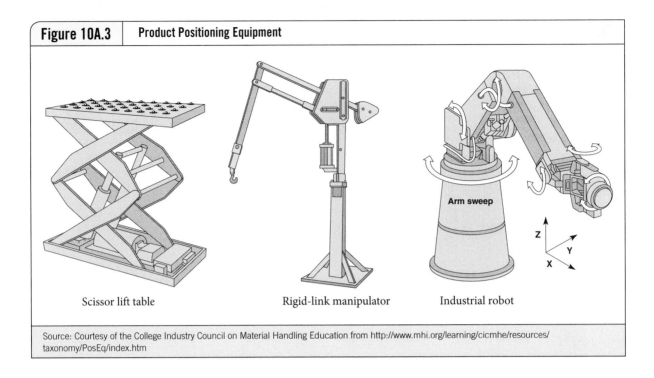

Scissor lift table   Rigid-link manipulator   Industrial robot

Positioning equipment is used to handle material at a single location so that it is in the correct position for subsequent handling, machining, transport, or storage. Unlike transport equipment, positioning equipment is usually used for materials handling at a single workstation. Examples of positioning equipment include lift/turn/tilt tables, manipulators, hoists, and industrial robots. Figure 10A.3 presents different types of positioning equipment.

This equipment boosts productivity by moving, lifting, and positioning goods with limited manual labor. It also protects quality and limits damage to heavy products by reducing the need for manual handling and the potential for worker fatigue and injuries.

Unit load formation equipment restricts materials so that they maintain their integrity when being moved or stored as a single load. Pallets are one type of unit load formation equipment that enables a DC to leverage standardized transport equipment such as forklifts. Also, more items can be handled at the same time, thereby reducing the number of trips required. This reduces handling costs, loading and unloading times, and product damage. Crates, bags, bins, slipsheets, and stretch-wrap are also used to create unit loads. Figure 10A.4 presents common examples of unit load formation equipment.

Storage equipment allows companies to hold materials economically over a period of time. Racks, automatic storage/retrieval systems (AS/RS), carousels, and mezzanines allow use of the vertical and horizontal space in the DC. Storage capacity also gives the company an opportunity to buy goods in bulk for purchase quantity and transportation discounts, hedge against anticipated price increases, and provide a buffer against demand spikes. Properly laid out storage systems can enhance the speed, accuracy, and cost-effectiveness of the order-picking process.

Storage equipment can be segmented into two types: picker-to-part and part-to-picker. Picker-to-part storage systems require the order picker to travel to the product storage location. Examples of picker-to-part storage equipment include bin shelving, modular

| Figure 10A.4 | Unit Load Formation Equipment |

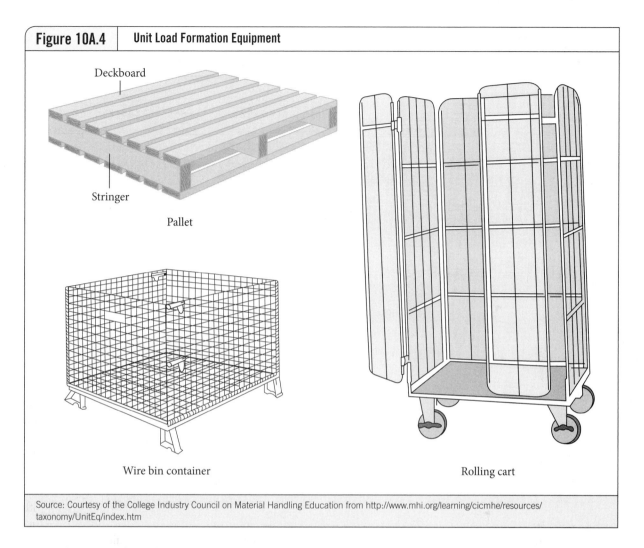

Source: Courtesy of the College Industry Council on Material Handling Education from http://www.mhi.org/learning/cicmhe/resources/ taxonomy/UnitEq/index.htm

storage drawers, racks, and mezzanines. Figure 10A.5 displays various types of picker-to-part storage equipment.

Racks are made up of rails and load-supporting upright beams. Pallets of product are placed on the beams and held until needed. Multiple rack options exist: selective (single-deep, narrow aisle, or double-deep), flow-through, drive-in, drive-through, push-back, and cantilever are most commonly used in DCs.

Mezzanines are double-layered storage systems that utilize a second level of bin shelving, modular storage cabinets, flow racks, or carousels above the first storage level. A mezzanine adds a second level to efficiently utilize DC cubic capacity and allow order picking to take place on both levels. Steel grating usually divides the two levels, which workers access by stairs. Because the mezzanine is not part of the building's actual construction, its location is flexible.

In part-to-picker storage systems, the pick location travels through an automated machine to the picker. Examples include carousels and AS/RS. These systems have a higher initial cost than picker-to-part systems, but automation equipment speeds up order-picking operations, improves inventory control, and increases profits. Part-to-picker systems minimize travel time. Figure 10A.6 displays various types of part-to-picker storage equipment.

Figure 10A.5 | Picker-to-Part Storage Systems

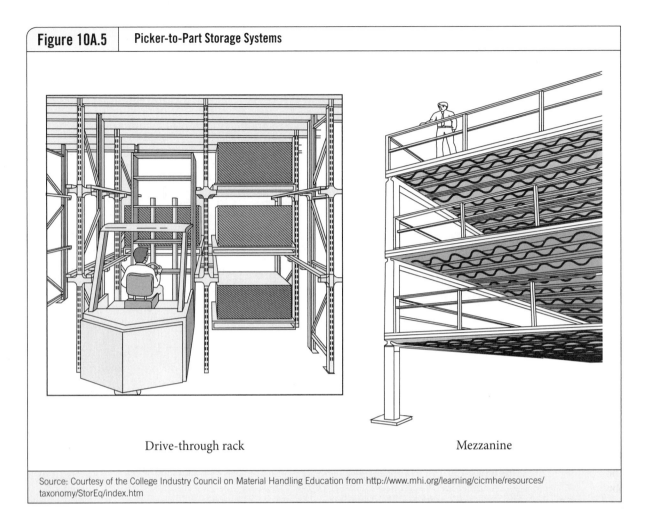

Drive-through rack   Mezzanine

Carousels are shelves or bins linked together by a mechanical device that stores and rotates items for order picking. Horizontal carousels are a linked series of bins that rotate around a vertical axis. A computer locates a needed part and rotates the carousel until the part location stops in front of the order picker's fixed position. Automated systems attempt to minimize wait times and maximize order-picking times. Industries that use horizontal carousels include aviation, electronic, paper, and pharmaceutical.

Vertical carousels are enclosed for cleanliness and security and the carousel rotates around a horizontal axis. The vertical carousel operates on a continuous lift principle, rotating the necessary items to the order picker's work station. This vertical storage approach cuts floor space use by 60 percent and increases picking productivity by up to 300 percent over racks and shelving of equal capacity. Some industries that use vertical carousels include electronics, automotive, aerospace, and computer.

AS/RS are technically advanced storage and order-picking equipment for distribution. They efficiently use storage space and achieve the highest accuracy rate in order picking. The AS/RS machine travels both horizontally and vertically to storage locations in an aisle, carrying item storage containers to and from an order-picking station at the end of the aisle.

Figure 10A.6	Part-to-Picker Storage Systems

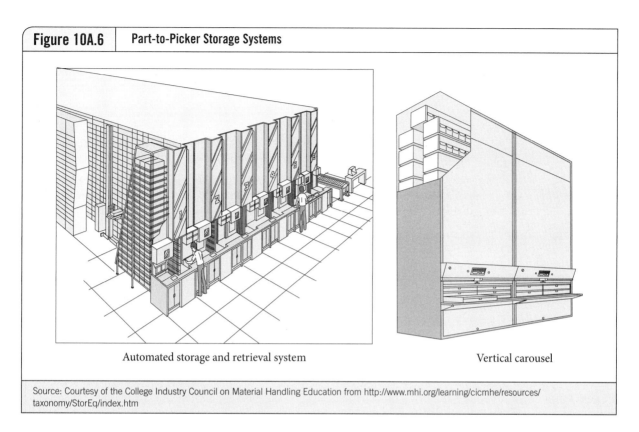

Automated storage and retrieval system   Vertical carousel

Source: Courtesy of the College Industry Council on Material Handling Education from http://www.mhi.org/learning/cicmhe/resources/taxonomy/StorEq/index.htm

At the order-picking station, the order picker programs the correct item-picking sequence. The AS/RS machine retrieves the next container in the sequence, while the order picker obtains items from the present container. AS/RS are space and labor efficient but are very expensive to purchase and install.

Identification and control equipment collects and communicates information that is used to coordinate the flow of materials within a facility and between a facility and its suppliers and customers. Automatic identification tools—bar codes, magnetic stripes, and radio frequency identification tags—capture data with little or no human intervention. These tools are discussed in Chapter 10 and Chapter 14. Other critical control tools include portable data terminals and rugged tablets to capture and store information, as well as electronic data interchange tools and supply chain software that facilitate the transfer of information.

SUMMARY

Materials handling drives efficient operation of DCs and other logistics facilities. The equipment and tools discussed in this appendix facilitate internal flows of goods from receiving to shipping. The key to success is selecting the appropriate equipment for the type and volume of product being distributed by the facility. Ultimately, effective selection and application of materials-handling principles to daily operations will improve capacity utilization, employee productivity, and fulfillment speed.

NOTES

1. "Amazon's First Ever Prime Day Breaks Global Records, Sales Exceed Black Friday," *Business Wire* (July 16, 2015). Retrieved November 14, 2015 from http://phoenix.corporate-ir.net/phoenix.zhtml?c=176060&p=irol-newsArticle&ID=2068444

2. "Success for FedEx Express as Memphis Hub Wins Prestigious Award," *FedEx Newsroom* (July 19, 2010). Retrieved November 14, 2015 from http://about.van.fedex.com/newsroom/global-english/success-for-fedex-express-as-memphis-hub-wins-prestigious-award/

3. This section is based on the College-Industry Council of Material Handling Education's *Material Handling Equipment Taxonomy.* Retrieved November 14, 2015 from http://www.mhi.org/cicmhe/resources/taxonomy

4. Clinte Reiser, "Would've, Could've, Should've Invested in Warehouse Automation," *Logistics Viewpoints,* (March 11, 2015). Retrieved November 14, 2015 from http://logisticsviewpoints.com/2015/03/11/wouldve-couldve-shouldve-invested-in-warehouse-automation/

Chapter 11

TRANSPORTATION—MANAGING THE FLOW OF THE SUPPLY CHAIN

Learning Objectives

After reading this chapter, you should be able to do the following:

- Explain the role transportation plays in the supply chain.
- Discuss the service and cost characteristics of the primary transportation modes.
- Discuss the key activities involved in transportation planning and execution.
- Explain current transportation management strategies used to improve supply chain performance.
- Use service and cost metrics to analyze transportation performance.
- Describe how information technology supports transportation planning and execution.

Supply Chain Profile   *A Transportation "Perfect Storm"*

If inventory is the life blood of supply chains, then transportation is the pumping heart that moves products throughout the system. Effective product movement is essential for the success of manufacturers, distributors, and retailers.

Retailers, in particular are challenged to maintain consistent product flows from global suppliers to retail distribution centers, stores, and customers' homes. The flow of products can be disrupted by facility congestion, equipment shortages, and labor availability issues. All three problems become acute prior to peak selling season as retailers seek to fill their shelves for holiday customers.

In 2014, a "perfect storm" hit the industry as a confluence of negative factors hit the transportation industry. Many months of labor contract negotiations and disputes at 29 U.S. Pacific Coast ports led to massive work slowdowns and several days of operation suspension. This led to a backlog of work that hampered 2014 holiday sales. Also, trucking industry capacity was stretched very thin as the number of available drivers and trucks continued to shrink. Finally, intermodal congestion grew significantly as retailers and other shippers shifted freight to gain cost advantages and to avoid trucking industry capacity problems. During 2014, intermodal transit times nearly doubled in many key corridors.

Although the freight backlog at Pacific coast port operations was finally cleared in May 2015, many of the "perfect storm" challenges are here to stay. Retail supply chain executives worry that their transportation capacity issues will increase over time. They believe that port labor challenges will occur with every contract negotiation, that few viable solutions exist for the truck driver shortage, and that rail infrastructure will remain stressed.

Rather than passively ride out the "perfect storm," retailers are taking steps to mitigate their transportation problems. These strategies, which can be leveraged by any type of freight shipper, include:

- **Re-route freight flows** – Retailers are moving more imported freight through ports on the Atlantic and Gulf coasts to reduce reliance on often congested Ports of Los Angeles and Long Beach in California.

- **Ship product earlier** – Retailers are moving more freight prior to the late summer and early fall peak seasons. This avoids some port congestion and peak pricing but forces the retailer to hold inventory for longer time periods.

- **Use technologically advanced port** – By moving freight through ports that are highly automated, retailers can avoid some congestion problems and minimize the risks associated with labor disputes.

- **Provide "driver friendly" freight** – With more work than they can handle, carriers avoid retailers who are costly to serve. Their freight must be easy to handle and retailers must quickly turnover equipment to cut carrier wait time.

- **Become a "carrier friendly" customer** – To secure the services of quality carriers, retailers must prioritize service over price, collaborate on capacity requirements, and properly compensate carriers.

Retail supply chain executives realize that transportation is a dynamic function and that new challenges will emerge. Today's innovative strategies will be tomorrow's standard operating practices. The best performing retailers will be those who continuously monitor the transportation environment, adapt their processes to changing conditions, and have the foresight to mitigate disruptions.

Source: Brian J. Gibson, C. Clifford Defee, and Rafay Ishfaq, *State of the Retail Supply Chain: Essential Findings of the Fifth Annual Report* (Auburn, AL: Auburn University Center for Supply Chain Innovation, 2015): 13–17.

11-1 Introduction

Transportation involves the movement of people and goods between origin and destination points. As individuals, we rely on transportation to get to work, school, and home, to bring us the products that we need, and to increase our access to society. From a business standpoint, the transportation system links geographically separated partners and facilities in a company's supply chain. Be it movement of products by truck, train, plane, ship, pipeline, or fiber optic wire, transportation facilitates time and place utility.

Transportation also has a major economic impact on the financial performance of businesses. In 2014, more than $907 billion was spent on freight transportation in the United States.[1] This figure represents nearly 63 percent of total logistics expenditures, far exceeding the amount of money spent on warehousing, inventory management, order processing, and other fulfillment. Thus, transportation costs must be taken into account during the development of supply chain management (SCM) strategies and processes.

This chapter focuses on the role of transportation in the supply chain. We focus on the key methods, strategies, and decisions required for the cost-efficient, effective flow of goods between sellers and buyers. As you will learn, proper management of these transportation issues is vital to the fulfillment of customer demand and the ultimate success of an organization.

11-2 The Role of Transportation in Supply Chain Management

Conceptually, a supply chain is a network of organizations that are separated by distance and time. Transportation provides the critical links between these organizations, permitting goods to flow between their facilities. Through transportation, organizations can extend the reach of their supply chains beyond local supplier capabilities and market demand. With efficient, effective transportation capabilities, organizations can build global supply chains that leverage low-cost sourcing opportunities and allow them to compete in new markets.

Transportation service availability is critical to demand fulfillment in the supply chain. The need for transportation is derived from customer demand. As the Supply Chain Profile points out, a shortage of transportation capacity can strand inventory in the system, leading to empty shelves and lost sales. Retailers like Hennes & Mauritz (H & M), a multinational fast-fashion clothing retailer, must work effectively with financially solvent carriers who can handle peak demand for freight services. A transportation capacity shortage would negate H & M's efforts to drive and fulfill customer demand because their trend-inspired apparel would not reach stores in a timely fashion.

Transportation efficiency promotes supply chain competitiveness. On the supply side, cost-effective transportation provides access to higher-quality, lower-priced materials and promotes production economies of scale. Likewise, low-cost transportation improves demand fulfillment opportunities. By keeping transportation expenses reasonable, the total landed cost of a product (its production costs plus transportation costs and related fulfillment costs) can be competitive in multiple markets. If a Berlin, Germany manufacturer can sell beer steins for $20 plus $5 for order processing and delivery versus $26 for a similar-quality domestic beer stein, then the German company can compete effectively in U.S. markets.

Availability and efficiency are not enough; transportation service must also be effective. Inexpensive transportation is of little value to a supply chain if the product does not arrive as scheduled and damage-free to the correct location. High-quality, customer-focused transportation has a direct impact on an organization's success as it **delivers** the right product at the right time, in the right quantity and quality, at the right cost, and to the right destination. Additionally, transportation can create supply chain flexibility. By working with carriers that offer a range of transit times and service options, organizations can satisfy supply chain demands for expedited and standard delivery speeds.

Transportation also influences supply chain design, strategy development, and total cost management.

- Transportation service availability, capacity, and costs affect the number and location of supply chain facilities in a network. For example, many organizations attempt to avoid locating distribution facilities in the state of Florida due to transportation costs. With little freight originating in the state, carriers compensate for the empty outbound trips by charging higher rates to move freight into Florida.
- Transportation capabilities must align with the company's goals. As Amazon.com expands Sunday delivery service to satisfy its customer base, partnerships with capable carriers are needed. To support the expansion strategies of Amazon, the United States Postal Service has invested in real-time package tracking technologies, changed employee schedules, and began to replace its aging fleet of delivery vehicles.[2]
- Intentional tradeoffs should be made between transportation and related activities to optimize supply chain efficiency. For example, retailers can hold lower safety stock levels if the cost of more frequent, faster deliveries does not exceed the inventory carrying cost savings. Similarly, manufacturers can employ lean production strategies if lot sizes can be minimized without creating excessive transportation costs.

Given these critical roles, it is clear that proper management of transportation processes is needed to efficiently and effectively operate an organization's supply chain. Company leadership must not treat transportation as a "necessary evil" or an afterthought to production and marketing. Instead, they must include transportation considerations when developing organizational strategies, integrate transportation into supply chain processes, and optimize total supply chain cost rather than minimize transportation costs. Leading organizations from Apple to Unilever have already moved in this direction. They understand that time and place utilities are achievable only when effective transportation processes exist.

11-2-1 Role Inhibitors

While transportation can provide valuable support to an organization's supply chain, it is a mistake to assume that these roles can be easily accomplished. There are numerous issues—supply chain complexity, competing goals among supply chain partners, changing customer requirements, and limited information availability—that inhibit the synchronization of transportation with other supply chain activities. Further compounding the challenge is a variety of supply chain trends and external issues that must be addressed by the organization.

Offshore manufacturing creates major transportation challenges. The reliance on global supply chains that extend from China, India, and other countries to your hometown leads to greater expenses, longer transit times, and higher risk of supply chain disruptions. One response is to hold higher levels of inventory. Another response is to shift manufacturing operations closer to markets. "On-shoring" and "near-shoring" strategies minimize the risk and expense of transporting goods vast distances.

Changing customer requirements also affect the transportation function. Growing demand for smaller, more frequent deliveries will limit opportunities to move product in economical container load quantities. Compression of order cycle times results in higher delivery costs and extended fulfillment operation hours. Also, the desire for real-time shipment visibility requires technological strength. To meet these customer expectations, organizations must align their operations with high-quality carriers that support capacity, speed, and consistency requirements at a reasonable cost.

Transportation capacity constraints pose another challenge to organizations needing to move freight through the supply chain. As the Supply Chain Profile indicated, major bottlenecks and delays occur when transportation demand outstrips carrier and facility capacity. During peak delivery season, port facilities must grapple with a surge of containers and highways are clogged with truck traffic. Carriers are also struggling to keep pace with freight growth, whether it be hiring and retaining enough truck drivers or putting enough locomotives into service. The outcomes of a capacity crunch include higher freight rates, shipment delays, and difficulty finding new carriers.

Transportation rate variation adds to the complexity of the transportation function. Capacity, freight volume, and fuel costs each influence the rates charged by carriers. As volume increases and capacity becomes constrained, rate increases become a real possibility. Conversely, when freight volume decreases due to an economic slowdown or demand shifts, excess capacity results and rates tend to decrease. Realize that modal rates may not move in tandem. For example, air cargo rates may decline at the same time that truckload rates are on the rise. Transportation managers must monitor the changes and may need to shift freight between modes if the rates are dramatically different.

The transportation industry is also impacted by governmental requirements that affect cost structures and service capabilities. Historically, government regulation of transportation has focused on competition and pricing. For decades, these rules limited opportunities and incentives for carriers to develop unique service offerings and tailored pricing. Economic deregulation of most modes by 1980 and ocean shipping in 1998 gave carriers the freedom to operate with little governmental intrusion, sparking much-needed competition based on services, price, and performance. Additional coverage of economic and safety regulation can be found in Appendix 11A.

In contrast, regulation is growing in areas where the transportation industry has the potential to impact the safety of citizens, quality of life, and protection of commerce.

- Protection of the traveling public is a primary driver of transportation safety regulation. Federal and state laws limit the size of transportation equipment, combined freight and equipment weight, and travel speed. Regulations also exist to ensure that commercial carriers operate safely. For example, the Compliance, Safety, Accountability (CSA) initiative seeks to reduce crashes, injuries and fatalities related to commercial motor carrier vehicles. Using a new enforcement and operational model, the Federal Motor Carrier Safety Administration (FMCSA) measures carrier safety performance, evaluates high-risk behaviors, and intervenes with corrective actions and penalties as needed.[3] Likewise, reductions in the commercial vehicle driver hours of service (HOS) rules seek to minimize the number of fatigued truck drivers on the roads. Drivers can no longer be on duty more than 14 consecutive hours followed by 10 hours off duty.[4]

- Environmental sustainability is also addressed by governmental regulation. Laws aimed at reducing noise, air, and water pollution from the transportation sector have long been the focus of federal and state regulators. Additionally, governmental agencies have initiated campaigns to promote environmental stewardship among freight and passenger transportation companies. The National Clean Diesel Campaign and SmartWay are two voluntary programs that help businesses create more sustainable supply chains by moving freight in the cleanest most-fuel efficient ways possible.[5]

- The ongoing threat of terrorism has led to security-focused legislation that directly impacts the transportation industry. Enhanced border security initiatives improve security but require increased cargo inspection, greater paperwork requirements, and longer Customs clearance times across all modes of transportation. Additionally, voluntary government-industry transportation security initiatives such as Customs-Trade Partnership Against Terrorism (C-TPAT) and Free and Secure Trade (FAST) seek to enhance transportation security and foster international trade.

When making legislative moves that benefit society, lawmakers and government agencies must also work to mitigate the negative impact on commerce. Compliance costs must not be burdensome and the flow of legitimate trade must not be restricted.

Ultimately, the inhibitors discussed above make it difficult to develop transportation processes that mesh well with supply chain requirements. Individual organizations must make a concerted effort to overcome these constraints to move freight in the most cost-efficient, customer-supportive manner possible. They must strategically leverage the mode and carrier options available.

11-3 Modes of Transportation

When the need to move freight arises, supply chain managers can choose from among five modes of transportation: truck, rail, air, water, and pipeline. Additionally, intermodal transportation combines the use of two or more of the basic modes to move freight from its origin to destination.

Each mode has different economic and technical structures, and each provides different level of service quality. This section provides an overview of each mode's service characteristics, volume and type of freight handled, cost structure, carrier types and service offerings, equipment variety, and current industry trends. Comparisons of the service capabilities, freight rates, and tradeoffs between the modes are provided in the discussion of modal selection later in the chapter.

Collectively, 19.7 billion tons of goods valued at nearly $17.4 trillion move through the U.S transportation system.[6] Table 11.1 provides key data for each mode of transportation. The trucking industry dominates freight flows in terms of the value and volume of goods moved. The results are less skewed on the basis of **ton-miles** (an output measurement combining weight and distance, or tonnage multiplied by miles transported). Trucks tend to focus on local and regional markets while the other modes provide long distance moves of larger freight quantities.

In terms of freight expense, organizations spent $907 billion for transportation services in 2014. More than 77 percent of the total was spent on trucking services at $702 billion. Rail followed with 8.8 percent; water, 4.4 percent; forwarders, 4.4 percent; air, 3.1 percent;

Table 11.1	Freight Shipments Within the U.S.		
MODE OF TRANSPORTATION	VALUE OF GOODS	TONS (MILLIONS)	TON-MILES (BILLIONS)
Truck	72.9%	70.2%	40.2%
Rail	3.6%	11.1%	26.4%
Water	1.3%	3.6%	8.2%
Air	2.2%	<1%	<1%
Pipeline	4.8%	8.7%	15.0%
Multiple modes	11.5%	3.2%	8.4%
Other/Unknown	3.6%	3.1%	1.6%

Source: U.S. Department of Transportation Bureau of Transportation Statistics, *2015 Pocket Guide to Transportation* (2015):17.

and, pipeline, 1.9 percent.[7] Collective consideration of freight value, volume, and spending indicate that rail, water, and pipelines provide economically priced services for lower-value commodities. Truck, multimodal, and air transportation are premium-priced services for moving higher-value goods.

11-3-1 Motor Carriers

Motor carriage is the most widely used mode of transportation in the U.S. domestic supply chain. From small delivery vans to large tractor-trailer combinations, trucks move freight in local, regional, and national supply chains. The sophisticated U.S. highway network facilitates these flows, giving motor carriers excellent accessibility to virtually all freight shipping and receiving locations. This accessibility, combined with the industry's excellent service capabilities, makes trucking a popular mode to move high-value, time-sensitive goods.

The trucking industry is highly competitive. It is made up of 532,024 interstate motor carriers and intrastate hazardous materials motor carriers.[8] These companies range in size from single-truck, owner-operator service providers to UPS, a $58 billion transportation conglomerate. Its UPS Freight division provides domestic U.S trucking service via 5,733 tractors and 19,880 trailers.[9]

The economic structure of the motor carrier industry contributes to the vast number of carriers in the industry. First, there are no significant barriers to entry that make it impossible for small carriers to compete. The equipment and licensing costs are within the reach of most organizations. Second, most expenses are related to freight movement, making trucking a high-variable-cost, low-fixed-cost business. Wages and benefits, fuel, maintenance, and tires drive the cost structure of trucking companies. Third, fixed costs are minimal as most trucking companies do not have extensive terminal and equipment needs. Also, the U.S. government builds and maintains the highways, and motor carriers pay for highway use through fuel taxes, licenses, and other user fees.

Much of the freight moved by the trucking industry is regional in nature, moving within a 500-mile radius of the origin. Some of the primary commodities handled by this mode include consumer-packaged goods, electronics, electrical machinery, furniture, textiles, and automotive parts. Shippers rely on the trucking industry to transport these time sensitive and valuable goods that require superior protection while in transit.

The trucking industry is comprised of for-hire and private fleet operations. For-hire trucking companies move freight for other organizations. Private fleets transport freight that is owned by the organization that is operating the trucks. Roughly 48 percent of trucking companies are for-hire carriers, 42 percent are private carriers, 8 percent are hybrid for-hire/private carriers, and the balance are other types of carriers.[10] The average distance per shipment is 508 miles via for-hire trucks and 58 miles via private truck.[11]

The three general types of for-hire carriers include the following:

- **Truckload (TL) carriers** handle single shipments that use the full cubic capacity of the trailer or exceed 15,000 pounds. TL carriers provide direct service, picking up the load at the origin point and delivering it directly to the destination without stopping at freight-handling terminals.
- **Less-than-truckload (LTL) carriers** move multiple shipments ranging from 150 pounds up to 15,000 pounds in each trailer. National LTL carriers use a hub-and-spoke network of local and regional terminal facilities to sort and consolidate shipments moving to a particular market area. Regional LTL carriers focus their efforts on a particular area of the country.
- **Small package carriers** handle shipments up to 150 pounds and move multiple shipments on a single van or truck. They use networks similar to LTL carriers to move freight efficiently throughout the country. UPS, FedEx Ground, and the United States Postal Service are the primary U.S. small package ground carriers.

Over time, the lines between carrier types have blurred. Customers prefer to work with motor carriers that can provide multiple capabilities. In response, FedEx and UPS transitioned from small package carriers to full service trucking companies with TL and LTL divisions. Additionally, regional LTL carriers offer some direct TL-like services, and TL carriers are providing multi-stop deliveries for their customers.

Multiple equipment types and sizes allow motor carriers to transport a wide variety of commodities and shipment sizes. Single trailers up to 53 feet long and twin 28-foot trailers are allowed nationwide. In a limited number of states, specially trained truck drivers are allowed to move longer combination vehicles on designated highways. Figure 11.1 highlights the variety of equipment combinations used in the trucking industry.

While motor carriers are the primary force in domestic transportation, trucking is useful for shipping goods to an adjacent country—between the United States and Mexico or Canada, for example. It is very common in Europe, where transport distances are relatively short. Motor carriers also play a major role in intermodal shipments, moving freight to airports and ports and picking up freight for delivery at the destination airports and ports. To minimize paperwork and border crossing delays, international truck shipments are often made **in bond**—the carrier seals the trailer at its origin and does not open it again until it reaches its destination country.

The trucking industry faces key challenges related to labor, costs, and competition. The American Trucking Association estimates that the current shortage of 48,000 drivers could rise to 175,000 by 2024.[12] Though trucking companies use fuel surcharges to pass along rising energy costs, they are not always able to recoup rising labor, insurance, and maintenance expenses. Finally, competition continues to be fierce within the trucking industry as well as with other modes of transportation. Customers expect near-perfect performance and will look for different options if service disruptions occur or rates spike.

Figure 11.1	Motor Carrier Equipment Options

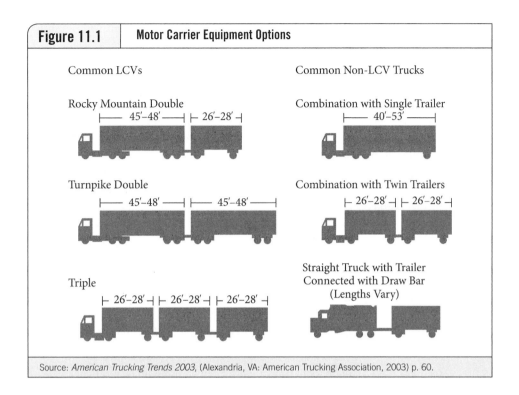

Source: *American Trucking Trends 2003*, (Alexandria, VA: American Trucking Association, 2003) p. 60.

11-3-2 Railroads

Railroads transport a significant volume of freight in the United States, moving nearly 2.2 billion tons of freight annually. The combination of volume and the average shipment length of 805 miles make rail a high ton-mile mode of transportation.[13] These activity levels have been achieved despite a lack of direct accessibility to all parts of the supply chain. Nagging perceptions of rail being a slow, inflexible, and inconsistent mode are challenges that must be overcome if the industry is to compete for higher-value, more profitable freight.

Although there are 575 railroads in the United States, the industry is dominated by seven Class I railroads (linehaul railroads with revenues in excess of $467 million). The Class I carriers generated $70.5 billion of freight revenue and handled 28.8 million carloads and 12.8 million intermodal trailers and containers.[14] BNSF Railway, CSX Transportation, Norfolk Southern Railway, and Union Pacific Railroad are the dominant carriers in the industry. No single rail carrier services the entire country. Carriers use interline agreements to provide coast-to-coast rail service.

The economic structure largely accounts for the limited number of rail carriers. Railroads require a large investment in terminals, equipment, and trackage to begin operation; the accompanying huge capacity allows railroads to be a decreasing cost industry. As output (ton-miles) increases, the average per-unit production cost decreases. Thus, having fewer railroads in operation in a given area and permitting those few firms to realize inherent large-scale output economies are beneficial to society.

Railroad transportation is primarily used for the long-distance movement of low-value goods. Primary commodities handled include coal, chemicals, farm products, minerals, food, and other basic materials. These products tend to be shipped in large quantities and stockpiled by customers to gain transportation efficiencies. Railroads also handle some high-value goods, primarily automobiles and intermodal containers filled with imported finished goods. The intermodal volume is growing at a faster rate than railcar traffic. Their respective volumes were up 10.6% and 4.8% in 2014.[15]

The rail industry is comprised of the following two carrier types:

- **Linehaul freight carriers** provide service between major markets and customers within those markets. These carriers move freight in container, carload, and unit train quantities. This group includes the seven Class I railroads that provide a full array of interregional or regional services.
- **Shortline carriers** provide the local and regional links between individual customers and the national rail network of the Class I railroads. They serve smaller markets, handle local delivery service, and facilitate the interline process—activities that the long-haul carriers no longer find profitable.

Railroads move almost any type of freight—liquid or gas, slurry or solid, hazardous or harmless—in very large quantities. From tri-level auto racks with capacity of 15 vehicles to tank cars that hold nearly 20,000 gallons of corn syrup, equipment exists to move the customer's freight. Hopper cars, boxcars, intermodal well cars, and other specialized equipment are available from railroads, railcar leasing companies, or private owners.

Rail equipment can be organized into loads and transported in one of the three following primary ways:

- Manifest trains contain a mixture of equipment and freight for multiple customers. These mixed trains travel through multiple rail yards where railcars may be added to or removed from the train, depending on their destination. This time-consuming assembling and disassembling of trains, called **classification**, can add more than 24 hours to the delivery process.
- Unit trains move an entire block of railcars carrying a single commodity (e.g., coal) from the origin to a single destination. This eliminates the need to stop for time-consuming rail yard classification activities. Unit trains also have priority on the rail network. Thus, they can provide service that competes effectively with trucks, especially on cross-country moves.
- Intermodal trains are special types of unit trains that focus on the long-distance or linehaul movement of intermodal containers and trailers. These trains move products from ports and other high-volume locations to markets where the containers are offloaded and transferred to customers via trucks.

Rail is primarily a domestic mode of transportation, though it can be valuable for cross-border movement of commodities and containers. The constraints on international rail transport include limited border crossing points and differing track gauges between countries.

One unique international strategy is the use of land bridge routing that combines ocean and rail modes. For example, a container travels from Tokyo to Seattle via ocean vessel, from Seattle to New York via train, and onward to Rotterdam via ocean vessel. The strategy can reduce transit time by a week or more versus all-water service.

The rail industry faces a number of challenges moving forward. Captive shippers served by a single railroad want rate relief. External factors such as fluctuating economic conditions and severe weather events are potential concerns. And, capacity is an ongoing problem. Railroad companies have responded with massive capital expenditures for infrastructure improvements, equipment purchases, and new employees.[16]

11-3-3 Air Carriers

Historically, air cargo transportation was viewed as an expensive, emergency mode. The growth of e-commerce, global supply chains, and lean inventory initiatives changed this perspective and spurred demand for air transportation. The speed of airplanes combined with frequent scheduled flights can reduce global transit times from as many as 30 days by water carrier to one or two days by air carrier. Faster delivery leads to reduced inventory carrying costs, stockout risks, and packaging requirements that can be traded off against high air cargo freight costs. The result is a lower total logistics cost, as illustrated in Chapter 2.

Air cargo transportation is specialized mode in terms of tonnage with U.S. spending at $28 billion in 2014 of which $12 billion is international cargo.[17] Global air cargo revenue is expected to reach $63 billion in 2015 and the mode moves 35 percent of the value of world trade by value of goods.[18] The top air cargo service provider groups are identified in Table 11.2.

The air carrier cost structure consists of high variable costs in proportion to fixed costs. Similar to motor and water carriers, air carriers do not invest heavily in facility infrastructure or byways. The government builds terminals and provides traffic control of the airways. Air carriers pay variable lease payments and landing fees for their use. Equipment costs, though quite high, are still a small part of the total cost.

Air transportation is used to ship small quantities of high-value, low-weight goods. Primary commodities handled by this mode include electronics, pharmaceuticals, perishable seafood and flowers, and designer apparel. Companies are willing to pay a high premium to transport these goods because they are time sensitive and need superior protection while in transit.

Two carrier types dominate this mode:

Table 11.2	Top 10 Cargo Air Carriers
AIR CARRIER	**CARGO TRAFFIC (MILLIONS OF FREIGHT TONNE-KILOMETRES)**
Federal Express	16,072
Emirates	11,326
UPS Airlines	10,923
Lufthansa	10,897
Cathay Pacific Group	10,044
Air France-KLM	9,817
Korean Air	8,254
DHL Express	7,850
Cargolux	6,364
Singapore Airlines	6,151

Source: Randy Woods, "Freight 50: Top 50 Cargo Airlines/Groups by FTK," *Air Cargo World* (August 26, 2015). Retrieved October 21, 2015 from http://aircargoworld.com/freight-50-top-50-cargo-airlinesgroups-by-ftk/

- **Combination carriers** move freight and passengers, with cargo loaded in the belly of the aircraft. As demand has grown, some of the larger international carriers have dedicated equipment specifically for scheduled cargo service to meet the demands of global commerce. United, Delta, and American are the largest U.S. combination carriers, handling the most freight ton-kilometers each year.

- **Air cargo carriers** move freight, packages, letters, and envelopes. Some carriers provide scheduled daily service through highly coordinated networks, while others provide on-demand service for customers who need immediate, direct transportation or the full capacity of the aircraft. Air carriers can also be separated on the basis of service capabilities.

  - **Integrated carriers** like FedEx and UPS provide door-to-door service, scheduled pickup and delivery windows, and expedited service through their hub-and-spoke networks. Ease of use and service quality makes these carriers the logical choice for domestic next-day and second-day delivery.

  - **Nonintegrated carriers** provide on-demand, air-only service from airport to airport. Movement to and from the airport is handled by other service providers or the customers. Direct service speed, flexibility, and same-day cargo movement are key capabilities of these carriers.

A wide variety of aircraft is used to move air freight domestically and around the world. Propeller planes move letters and small packages from smaller markets to consolidation points and sort operations. Jets ranging in size up to the largest Boeing 747–400 freighter (capacity of nearly 27,500 cubic feet and 124 tons of freight) are used for long-range domestic and international service. Unique aircraft like the Anatov 225 can transport massive products as large as 45,900 cubic feet and 220 tons. Whatever the shipment requirement may be, an aircraft with an appropriate combination of payload, range, and speed is likely available.

The air cargo industry faces numerous obstacles to profitable growth. First, demand is waning for products, such as notebook computers and boxed software, which previously moved in large volume via air. Second, mode-shifting of freight from air to ocean and new rail connections in Asia is limiting air freight growth. Finally, the strategies of near-shoring and on-shoring reduce the need for long-distance international air cargo service. Despite these challenges, industry advocates believe that international air cargo can reach annual revenues of $100 billion.[19]

11-3-4 Water Carriers

Water transportation has played a significant role in the development of many countries and is a major facilitator of international trade. In the United States, $302 billion worth of freight and 6.5 percent of the total ton-miles annually is moved via water transportation.[20] The industry generated $40 billion in revenue, $31 billion for the movement of international goods, and $9 billion for domestic coastal, inland, and Great Lakes traffic.[21] Globally, water carriers dominate all other modes, garnering approximately half of the international freight revenue and handling nearly all tonnage.

The U.S. flagged fleet moves 2.2% percent of the nation's freight value via 8,918 self-propelled vessels and 31,081 barges.[22] The international ocean fleet includes approximately 50,000 merchant ships including 16,800 bulk carriers, 11,651 tankers, 10,381 general cargo ships, and 5,106 containerships.[23] There are more than 20 million TEU (20-foot equivalent unit containers) and 252 million tons (deadweight) of capacity in active liner trades.[24] Table 11.3 highlights the primary global container shipping companies.

Table 11.3	Top 10 Containership Operators	
OPERATOR	TEU TRANSPORTED	TOTAL SHIPS (OWNED + CHARTERED)
APM-Maersk	16,072	594
Mediterranean Shipping Co	11,326	497
CMA CGM Group	10,923	467
Evergreen Line	10,897	199
Hapag-Lloyd	10,044	174
COSCO Container L.	9,817	164
CSCL	8,254	133
Hamburg Süd Group	7,850	137
Hanjin Shipping	6,364	104
MOL	6,151	98

Source: *Alphaliner – Top 100*. Retrieved October 21, 2015 from http://www.alphaliner.com/top100/

Water transportation is a high variable cost business. To begin operation, carriers require no investment for the right-of-way. Nature provides the "highway," and port authorities provide terminals with unloading and loading services, storage areas, and freight transfer facilities. The water carriers pay user fees for these port services only when used. Large oceangoing ships require significant capital investments, but cost is spread over a large volume of freight transported during the lengthy lifespan of most ships.

Domestic water carriers compete with railroads for long-distance movement of low-value, high-density, bulk cargoes that mechanical devices can easily load and unload. Primary commodities moved include: petroleum, coal, iron ore, chemicals, forest products, and other commodities. However, international water carriers handle a wider variety of goods. Every conceivable type of cargo is transported via ocean carrier, from low-value commodities to imported automobiles. Many imported consumer goods flow to the United States in ocean shipping containers.

Two primary carrier types dominate the for-hire portion of the water industry, as follows:

- **Liner services** employ a wide variety of ships in their fixed-route, published-schedule service. These carriers transport individual shipments for their customers, including containers, pallets, and other unit loads.

- **Charter services** lease ships to customers on a voyage or time basis and follow routes of the customer's choosing. The charter customer normally uses the entire capacity of the ship for large-volume freight. Contracts for charter services are facilitated by ship brokers who negotiate the price with ship owners.

Charter services operate similarly to taxicab service with customer-specified route and tailored services. In contrast, liner service is much like a scheduled bus service with fixed routes and standard service levels. A third, though less frequently used option, is private transportation. Large companies may establish a private fleet of ships to achieve greater control and reduce cost for the movement of unique commodities.

Ocean transportation of goods ranging from crude oil to electronics is facilitated by a wide range of specialized ships. The most widely used options include the following:

- **Containerships** are critical to the globalization of trade. These ships are specially designed to carry standardized TEU or FEU (40-foot equivalent unit) containers. Containerships vary considerably in size, from small ships that hold fewer than 400 TEUs to the latest ultra-large containerships (ULCS) with capacities of 18,000 or more TEUs.
- **Bulk carriers** carry cargoes with low value-to-weight ratios, such as ores, grain, coal, and scrap metal. Very large openings on these ships' holds allow easy loading and unloading. Watertight walls dividing the holds allow a ship to carry more than one commodity at a time.
- **Tankers** carry the largest amount of cargo by tonnage, usually on a charter basis. These ships range in capacity from 18,000 tons to very large crude carriers (VLCCs), some of which top 500,000 tons. Tankers are constructed in much the same way as bulk carriers but with smaller deck openings. New tankers are required to be double-hulled to protect the environment in case of a collision.
- **General cargo ships** transport shipload cargoes on a charter basis. They have large cargo holds and freight-handling equipment to facilitate loading and unloading of a large variety of freight. The self-sufficiency of these ships allows them to load and discharge cargo at ports in less-developed countries that lack modern cargo-handling equipment.
- **Roll-on, roll-off (RO–RO) vessels** are basically large ferry ships. Cargo is driven directly onto the ship using built-in ramps and driven or towed off the ship at the destination port. Large RO–ROs can transport 2,000 or more automobiles, as well as freight trailers, farm and construction equipment, and other wheeled vehicles.

Water carriers operate in a highly competitive marketplace and face significant financial challenges. First, there is significant overcapacity in the container shipping sector due to the number of mega-vessels that are being put into service. This is occurring at a time when the strategies of near-shoring and on-shoring reduce the need for trans-Pacific service. Second, congestion at major ports and transfer points for containers disrupt freight flows. New technologies and infrastructure is needed to alleviate these chokepoints. Finally, the schedule reliability of liner service continues to lag other modes. Though service improvements are being achieved, much work remains.[25]

11-3-5 Pipelines

Pipelines are the "hidden giant" of the transportation modes, quietly handling 5.6 percent of U.S. freight tonnage. This unique mode uses equipment that is fixed in place and the product moves through it in high volume. Pipelines effectively protect the product from contamination and also provide a warehousing function. Pipelines provide the most economical form of transportation with the lowest cost per ton of any mode.

The United States has the largest network of energy pipelines of any nation in the world—more than 10 times larger than the European network. The network, owned by pipeline companies and large oil companies, contains 55,000 miles of crude oil trunk lines, 95,000 miles of refined products pipeline, more than 190,000 miles of liquid petroleum pipelines, and 2.4 million miles of natural gas pipelines.[26] From remote oilfields in Alaska to individual homes, the goal of the pipeline network is to safely and efficiently deliver raw materials and energy products in support of the economy.

Pipeline costs are predominantly fixed. Pipeline operators must build their own right-of-way, which is a rather expensive proposition. Variable costs in the industry are very low as little labor is required to operate the pipelines and limited fuel is needed to run pumps. The construction of a pipeline becomes cost effective when product flows continuously, allowing the fixed costs to be spread over a high volume of goods.

The vast majority of products moved by pipeline are liquids and gases, the economically feasible products to flow via this mode. Common liquid products include crude oil and petroleum-based fuels for transportation and home heating. Widely distributed gaseous products include natural gas for home heating and propane, anhydrous ammonia, and carbon dioxide used in agricultural and industrial applications. In the past, attempts have been made to move solid product in a slurry form, but this has not proved to be competitive with water and rail transportation.

The pipeline industry is comprised of for-hire and private carriers that maintain their own infrastructures. For-hire carriers of liquid products can move different products through their system at the same time, separated by a batching plug that maintains the integrity of individual products. Private carriers include petroleum and natural gas companies that use pipelines to move product to and from their refineries, processing plants, and storage facilities. Companies, like a power plant or a chemical plant, may operate a small pipeline system to bring fuel to the plant or to move feed-stocks from one plant to another.

The oil system is made up of the following three primary types of pipelines:

- **Gathering lines** are very small pipelines, usually from 2 to 8 inches in diameter. They are used together and move oil from both onshore and offshore oil wells to trunk lines.
- **Trunk lines**, measuring from 8 to 24 inches in diameter, bring crude oil from extraction points to refineries. This network includes the well-known Trans-Alaska Pipeline System, an 800-mile long, 48-inch diameter pipeline that connects Prudhoe Bay on Alaska's North Slope to Valdez, the northernmost ice-free port in North America.
- **Refined product pipelines** carry petroleum products—gasoline, jet fuel, home heating oil, and diesel fuel—from refineries to large fuel terminals with storage tanks in almost every state in the country. These pipelines vary in size from relatively small 8- to 12-inch diameter lines up to 42-inch diameter lines.

Natural gas pipelines use similar networks of gathering lines, transmission lines, and main distribution lines to move product closer to the market. The major difference is the direct delivery of natural gas to homes and businesses using local distribution lines. These distribution lines, found below street level in almost every city and town, account for the vast majority of pipeline mileage in the United States.

The growth of the U.S. oil industry is creating pipeline transportation challenges. Network capacity is stretched thin in areas where new oil fields are operated but it takes significant time, money, and regulatory approval to build new pipelines. Safety is also an ongoing issue. Though pipelines have enviable safety and environmental records with spills amounting to only one gallon per million barrel-miles, the age and condition of the existing network is a concern. Any spill or accident creates fire, environmental, and health risks.

11-3-6 Intermodal Transportation

While the five primary modes give supply chain managers numerous transportation options, an alternative exists. **Intermodal transportation service** refers to the use of two or more carriers of different modes in the origin-to-destination movement of freight. Shifting freight between modes may seem inefficient and time consuming, but the improved reach and combined service advantages created by intermodal transportation offset these issues. These primary benefits of intermodalism include the following:

- Greater accessibility is created by linking the individual modes. The road infrastructure allows trucks to reach locations that are inaccessible to other modes, especially air transportation, water transportation, and pipelines. Likewise, railroads can work with domestic river carriers and international ocean carriers to effectively transport commodities.

- Overall cost efficiency can be achieved without sacrificing service quality or accessibility. Intermodal transportation allows supply chains to utilize the inherent capabilities of multiple modes to control cost and fulfill customer requirements.

- Intermodal transportation facilitates global trade. The capacity and efficiency of ocean transportation allow containers to be transported between continents at relatively low per-unit costs with final delivery by truck or rail. The speed of air transportation allows perishable goods to flow quickly between countries with trucks handling airport to customer deliveries.

Although no universal statistics are kept on intermodal transportation, there is strong evidence that intermodal transportation has grown in importance and volume. The number of containers flowing through North American ports more than doubled in 20 years; from 24.7 million TEUs in 1995 to 56.9 million TEUs in 2014.[27] Domestic flows of intermodal freight have also risen. The U.S. rail system moved 13.5 million containers in 2014.[28]

Intermodal growth is largely attributable to the development of standardized containers that are compatible with multiple modes. A standard dry box container looks much like a truck trailer without the chassis; can be lifted, stacked, and moved from one piece of equipment to another; and is built to standard dimensional height and width specifications in a variety of lengths (10-, 20-, and 40-foot marine containers for international transportation and 40-, 48-, and 53-foot containers for domestic truck and rail transportation). Specialized containers are also available for handling temperature-sensitive goods, commodities, and other unique cargoes.

Other factors have contributed to the growth of intermodal transportation. They include better information systems to track freight as it moves through the supply chain and the development of intermodal terminals to facilitate efficient freight transfers between modes. In addition, new generations of ocean vessels, railcars, and truck trailers are being built specifically to handle intermodal freight in greater quantity and with greater ease.

Ocean carriers are continually developing larger containerships to handle international intermodal traffic, improve fuel efficiency, and reduce carbon emissions per container transported. In response, the Panama Canal Authority is completing an eight-year, $5.25 billion expansion project to handle these ships. The expanded locks, scheduled to open in April 2016, will allow 12,000 TEU ships to move through the Canal.

The rail industry can move both trailers and containers in their intermodal operations. "Piggy-back" service or trailer-on-flatcar (TOFC) service has been largely replaced by container-on-flatcar (COFC) service and double-stack container services. These methods allow rail companies to carry a wider variety of containers—everything from 10-foot ocean containers to 53-foot domestic freight containers—in nearly any combination. Double-stack service is especially efficient.

The freight services provided by intermodal transportation can be viewed in terms of product-handling characteristics as follows:

- **Containerized freight** is loaded into or onto storage equipment (a container or pallet) at the origin and delivered to the destination in or on that same piece of equipment with no additional handling.

- **Transload freight** involves goods that are handled and transferred between transportation equipment multiple times. Transload freight primarily consists of bulk-oriented raw materials that must be scooped, pumped, lifted, or conveyed from one container to another when transferred from one mode to another.

Another way to look at the intermodal option is based on the type of service used. Figure 11.2 depicts the most prevalent forms of intermodal transportation, including truck–rail, truck–air, and truck–water, although other combinations are also used. Some carriers have multimodal capabilities, allowing them to utilize the most efficient and economical combinations of intermodal transportation for their customers. The carrier typically determines the mode or modal combinations to use. Customers are not concerned about the combination of modes used as long as the shipment arrives on time!

A recurring issue in the intermodal transportation market is congestion. Equipment shortages, transfer facility bottlenecks, and labor issues create delivery delays and supply chain disruptions. While ocean carriers can add or reduce capacity to meet demand levels, transfer points are not as flexible. During peak activity periods, seaports can struggle to maintain consistent flows in and out of their facilities. Network delays are also problematic for the rail industry. Investments in port automation, network capacity expansion, and equipment are needed to keep improve intermodal freight service.

Figure 11.2	Widely Used Intermodal Transportation Combinations

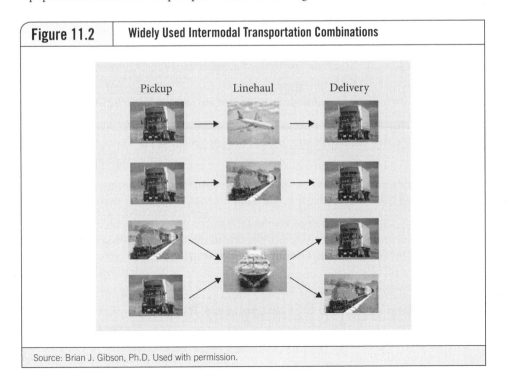

Source: Brian J. Gibson, Ph.D. Used with permission.

On the Line   *The Sixth Mode of*
Transportation

Traditional modes of transportation play a critical role in the movement of physical goods. In contrast, when products like movies, books, software, and music are converted to digital formats, the goods become data that no longer require physical transportation. They can be "transported" via the Internet for direct sale to consumers and the volume is growing. Sales of downloaded music were $6.85 billion in 2014 versus sales of CDs and vinyl albums at $6.82 billion. Sales of digital books reached $5.69 billion in 2014 and are projected to reach $8.69 billion in 2018. And the Netflix streaming subscriber base reached 69 million in the third quarter of 2015.

Given the volume of books, CDs, DVDs, and packaged software that is shifting away from truck and air cargo to electronic formats, there are suggestions that the Internet should be considered the sixth mode of transportation. Robert Walton argues that delivery via the Internet fits the definition of a mode of transportation (the ability to move products from one location to another), provides time and place utility, and eliminates the cost of delivery. Additionally, this "mode" does not use fossil fuels, emit noise, or contribute to roadway congestion. Hence, it is a sustainable mode that does not have negative environmental or social impacts.

In terms of modal capabilities, the Internet offers key strengths. As long as a consumer has a high speed Internet connection, global accessibility to digital products is unlimited. Near instantaneous product availability at low to no cost are also desirable features of the Internet. The primary drawbacks of this mode include a very narrow array of products that can be delivered via the Internet and bandwidth issues that may limit product transferability to due file size.

These challenges notwithstanding, the Internet's operating characteristics compare favorably to the traditional modes of transportation. Walton and others indicate that the Internet is the fastest mode of delivery, provides the greatest service dependability, and offers the best frequency of service as product can move instantaneously, 24 hours a day, 7 days a week. The only downside is its limited capability in the type of "freight" that can be moved.

Based on these capabilities and cost advantages, both product sellers and consumers are wise to leverage this sixth mode of transportation for digital goods commerce.

Sources: James Vincent, "Digital Music Revenue Overtakes CD Sales for the First Time Globally," *The Verge* (April 15, 2015). Retrieved October 22, 2015 from http://www.theverge.com/2015/4/15/8419567/digital-physical-music-sales-overtake-globally; Robert O. Walton, "The 6th Mode of Transportation," *Journal of Transportation Management* (Spring/Summer 2014): 55–61; KnowThis.com, *Modes of Transportation Comparison.* Retrieved October 22, 2015 from http://www.knowthis.com/managing-product-movement/modes-of-transportation-comparison; and, Statistica, *Revenue from e-book Sales in the United States from 2008 to 2018.* Retrieved October 22, 2015 from http://www.statista.com/statistics/190800/ebook-sales-revenue-forecast-for-the-us-market/.

What will be the next modal innovation? Drones and driverless trucks have captured media attention and may be future options. However, there is an alternative delivery method that is already in use. The Internet is a virtual mode of transportation for electronic products. The *On the Line* feature investigates this concept.

11-4 Transportation Planning and Strategy

Understanding the modal options is an important aspect of transportation management. However, before the freight moves, other vital issues must also be addressed. Supply chain professionals must make a series of interrelated transportation decisions and design processes that properly align with the organization's supply chain strategies. These planning issues, highlighted in Figure 11.3, are discussed next.

11-4-1 Functional Control of Transportation

The initial decision for any organization is straightforward but important—determining which department(s) will be responsible for each part of the transportation process. Whenever you buy goods, sell goods, or do both, somebody must make key decisions and manage the process. Even in a simple purchase over the Internet, you have to select a carrier (UPS, FedEx, U.S. Postal Service, etc.), service level (next-day, second-day, etc.), insurance coverage, and a related price. A failure on your part to take responsibility can result in the seller making decisions that do not fit your budget or service needs.

In most organizations, responsibility for transportation decisions falls to one or more of the following departments: logistics, procurement, and marketing. Control can be split into inbound transportation of goods purchased and outbound transportation of goods sold. Typically, the purchasing department controls inbound transportation decisions, while marketing or logistics has responsibility for outbound transportation control. Often, this decision-making structure sacrifices opportunities to generate transportation efficiencies and service improvements. At worst, the split control method relegates decision making to suppliers and customers who prioritize their own needs.

The alternative strategy is to assign transportation decision-making responsibility to the department with supply chain expertise. This logistics or transportation department will coordinate inbound and outbound transportation flows, develop common goals, leverage purchasing power, and procure quality service in support of supply chain excellence. Positive results include access to capacity, improved freight visibility and control, enhanced customer service, and greater control over transportation spending.

11-4-2 Terms of Sale

Terms of sale clarify the delivery and payment terms agreed upon by a seller and buyer. Wise selection of these terms is critical as the decision determines where the buyer's responsibilities begin and where the seller's responsibilities end. They cover issues related to

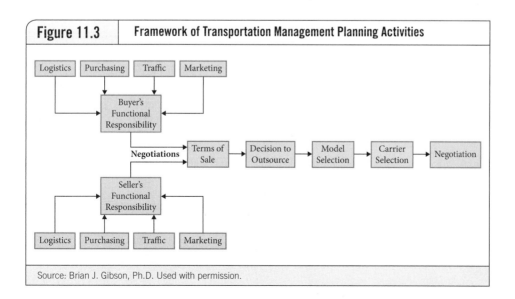

| Figure 11.3 | Framework of Transportation Management Planning Activities |

Source: Brian J. Gibson, Ph.D. Used with permission.

mode and carrier selection, transportation rate negotiation, in-transit freight responsibility, and other key decisions.

Free on board (FOB) terms are used for domestic transactions while International Commercial Terms (Incoterms) are used for international transactions.

11-4-2-1 FOB Terms

Domestic freight control is a straightforward issue. Title and responsibility change hands at the origin or the destination. If the terms are FOB origin, title (ownership) to the goods changes hands at the origin—usually the shipping point or seller's distribution center loading dock. From that point on, the goods belong to the buyer, and any loss or damage is the responsibility of the buyer. If the terms are FOB destination, the title transfers at the destination—typically the buyer's unloading dock. The seller has total responsibility for the goods until they are delivered to the buyer.

A related issue is the responsibility for carrier payment. In general, the seller pays the carrier for the transportation service cost under FOB destination terms, while the buyer pays the carrier under FOB origin terms. However, there are six total options as highlighted in Table 11.4. The option for Freight Prepaid or Freight Collect should be specified with the FOB terms. In cases where the seller has more clout with carriers, it is wise to have the seller negotiate transportation rates under the Freight Prepaid option. Freight Collect is typically used when the buyer has more power with carriers.

11-4-2-2 Incoterms

International transactions often present greater challenges, and parties to the transaction must understand how these terms of sale influence transportation decision making. Even a relatively straightforward international transaction involves long distances, multiple

Table 11.4	**Freight Control and Payment Terms**				
FOB TERM AND FREIGHT PAYMENT RESPONSIBILITY	**WHO OWNS GOODS IN TRANSIT?**	**WHO HANDLES FREIGHT CLAIMS?**	**WHO SELECTS AND PAYS CARRIER?**	**WHO ULTIMATELY BEARS FREIGHT COSTS?**	**BEST USED WHEN _____ HAS GREATER INFLUENCE WITH CARRIER**
FOB Origin, Freight Collect	Buyer	Buyer	Buyer	Buyer	Buyer
FOB Origin, Freight Prepaid	Buyer	Buyer	Seller	Seller	Seller
FOB Origin, Freight Prepaid & Charged Back	Buyer	Buyer	Seller	Buyer. The seller adds freight costs to goods invoice.	Seller
FOB Destination, Freight Prepaid	Seller	Seller	Seller	Seller	Seller
FOB Destination, Freight Collect	Seller	Seller	Buyer	Buyer	Buyer
FOB Destination, Freight Collect & Allowed	Seller	Seller	Buyer	Seller. The buyer deducts freight cost from goods payment.	Buyer

Source: Adapted from Bruce J. Riggs, "The Traffic Manager in Physical Distribution Management," *Transportation and Distribution Management*, June 1968, p. 45.

modes and logistics intermediaries, duties, government inspections, and significant opportunity for damage or delay. Thus, transportation managers must be extremely careful about when and where the title to the goods will change hands.

Incoterms facilitate efficient freight flows between countries. As described by the International Chamber of Commerce, Incoterms are international rules that are accepted by governments, legal authorities, and practitioners worldwide for the interpretation of the most commonly used terms in international trade. They address matters relating to the rights and obligations of the parties to the contract of sale with respect to the delivery of goods sold.[29]

These terms of sale decisions help to clarify the following questions:

- Who will be responsible for control and care of the goods while in transit?
- Who will be responsible for carrier selection, transfers, and related product "flow" issues?
- Who will bear various costs—freight, insurance, taxes, duties, and forwarding fees?
- Who will handle documentation, problem resolution, and other related issues?

Since 1936, Incoterms have been revised and refined seven times. The most recent update, Incoterms 2010, simplified these trade terms. The number of Incoterms options has been reduced from 13 to 11, seven of which apply to all modes of transportation and four of which apply only to water transportation. Among other changes, Incoterms 2010 have been clarified so that they can apply to both international and domestic freight.

The options range from the buyer taking all transportation responsibilities at the seller's location to the seller taking responsibility all the way through delivery to the buyer's location (and numerous locations in between). There are four primary groups of Incoterms—E terms where the buyer takes full responsibility from point of departure, F terms in which the main carriage is not paid by the seller, C terms in which the main carrier is paid by the seller, and D terms where the seller takes full responsibility to an arrival point. Figure 11.4 highlights the respective roles of the seller and buyer under each of the 11 Incoterms.

Taking control of freight through FOB terms or Incoterms can be very beneficial for organizations with the expertise and time to manage the process. Having this control allows you to leverage your purchasing power with specific carriers to achieve lower rates, coordinate inbound and outbound flows, and consolidate freight to achieve greater efficiencies. Other potential benefits include the ability to manage risk, achieve greater freight visibility, and ensure available equipment capacity. Hence, terms of sale can be a strategic opportunity to improve transportation and supply chain performance.

11-4-3 Decision to Outsource Transportation

The organization with FOB freight control and procurement responsibility must analyze the transportation "make or buy" decision. Firms must choose between transporting goods using a private fleet (the "make" option) and using external service providers to move freight (the "buy" option). The decision involves multiple considerations and can be difficult. The primary options are discussed next.

Private fleets account for nearly half of all U.S. freight transportation spending and more than half the miles traveled. Companies like PepsiCo, Walmart, and DuPont move freight on company-owned or company-operated equipment for a variety of economic, customer service, and marketing reasons. A well-run private fleet can operate at costs competitive

Figure 11.4 Incoterms 2010

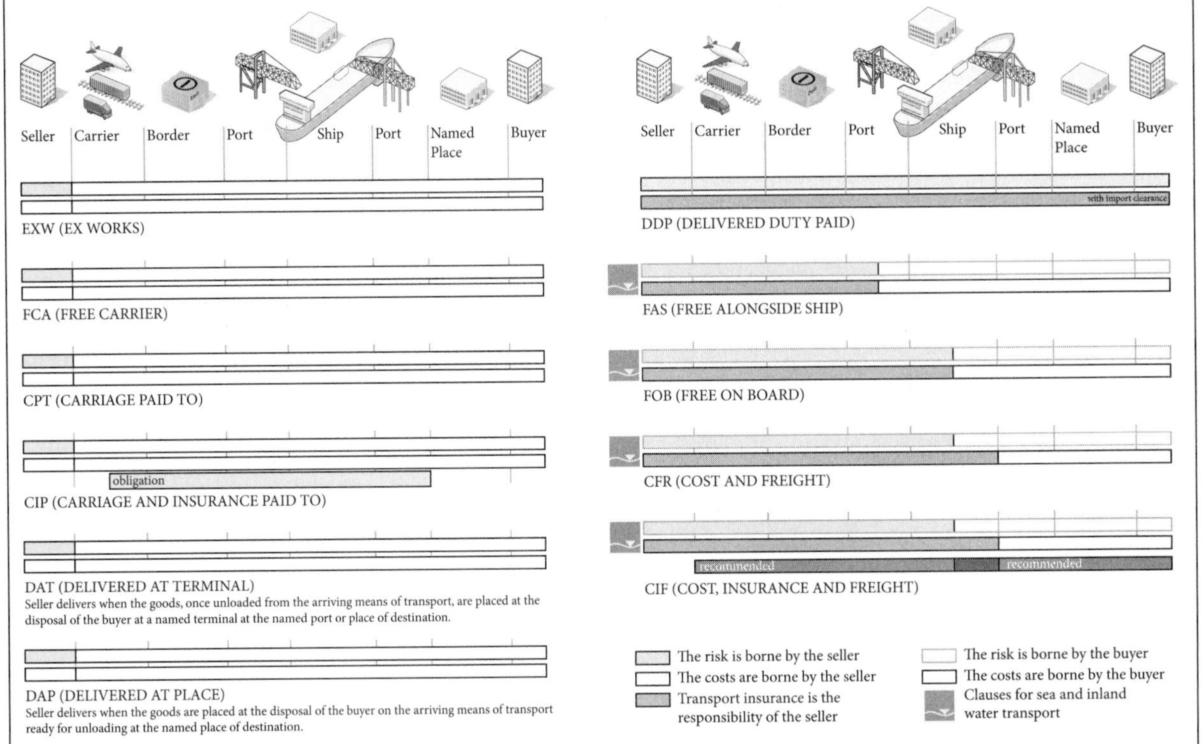

Seller
Carrier
Border
Port
Ship
Port
Named Place
Buyer
EXW (EX WORKS)
FCA (FREE CARRIER)
CPT (CARRIAGE PAID TO)
obligation
CIP (CARRIAGE AND INSURANCE PAID TO)
DAT (DELIVERED AT TERMINAL)
Seller delivers when the goods, once unloaded from the arriving means of transport, are placed at the disposal of the buyer at a named terminal at the named port or place of destination.
DAP (DELIVERED AT PLACE)
Seller delivers when the goods are placed at the disposal of the buyer on the arriving means of transport ready for unloading at the named place of destination.
with import clearance
DDP (DELIVERED DUTY PAID)
FAS (FREE ALONGSIDE SHIP)
FOB (FREE ON BOARD)
CFR (COST AND FREIGHT)
recommended
recommended
CIF (COST, INSURANCE AND FREIGHT)
The risk is borne by the seller
The costs are borne by the seller
Transport insurance is the responsibility of the seller
The risk is borne by the buyer
The costs are borne by the buyer
Clauses for sea and inland water transport

Source: Incoterms® 2010, International Chamber of Commerce.

with for-hire carriers while providing greater scheduling flexibility and control over transit time. Intangible benefits such as the promotional impact and prestige of having highly visible company trucks on the road can also be gained. Many organizations have turned their trailers into 48- to 53-foot rolling billboards.

On the other hand, some organizations decide to use external experts for freight movement and transportation management. Top carriers in all modes offer the capacity, experience, and flexibility to serve a wide variety of customers. These for-hire carriers also offer a variable-cost, simplified alternative to private transportation.

By using for-hire carriers, the customers do not have to incur the large capital cost of starting a private fleet, invest the time needed to build transportation expertise, or take on the challenges (accident liability, regulatory compliance, labor issues, etc.) inherent in operating a private fleet. As a result, more than $867 billion is spent on for-hire freight transportation each year in the United States.

Another alternative to a private fleet is third-party logistics (3PL) which is discussed extensively in Chapter 12. Third-party firms provide a wide array of transportation services. Dedicated contract carriage is one such service of 3PLs (e.g., DHL Supply Chain and Transfreight) and truckload carriers (e.g., Werner Enterprises and J. B. Hunt). Under this arrangement, the 3PL serves as the organization's private fleet and devotes a management team, drivers, and equipment to the relationship.

Another service is traffic management where the 3PL provides transportation planning and tactical decision making, handles administrative functions like freight bill auditing, and coordinates supply chain activities.

Finally, specialized 3PLs provide assistance with the challenges of moving freight internationally. Three types of international 3PLs provide valuable services for organizations that do not have internal global transportation expertise or the freight volume to warrant a full-time staff:

- **International Freight Forwarders** (IFF) help importers and exporters move their goods. Many IFFs consolidate freight in particular service areas, modes of transport, or markets. IFFs are often seen as the travel agents of international freight transportation. These service providers identify and book the best routes, modes of transport, and specific carriers based on customer requirements at competitive rates.

- **Non Vessel-owning Common Carriers** (NVOCC) help organizations move freight in less than container load (LCL) quantities. Unlike IFFs, who usually act as the organization's agent, NVOCCs are common carriers. They book container berths on ships on a regular basis, allowing them to gain advantageous rates from the ocean carriers. They resell the space to customers in smaller increments.

- **Customs Brokers** are individuals or firms licensed by the CBP to act as agents for importers. Brokers are experts at the entry process and, for a fee, help importers avoid Customs clearance pitfalls that delay shipments and increase costs. Brokers prepare and file the necessary Customs entry documents, arrange for the payment of duties, and speed the release of the goods in CBP custody.

11-4-4 Modal Selection

Modal selection is a critical decision that affects how quickly and efficiently products will flow across portions of the supply chain. If an organization with freight control decides to use external service providers, then it must determine which mode(s) of transportation to use. Choosing among the modal options is a function of three factors—modal capabilities, product characteristics, and modal freight pricing.

All modes provide the same basic service of moving freight from point to point in the supply chain. However, Table 11.1 indicated that the modes serve different customer requirements and goods in terms of value, tonnage, and ton-miles. This is because each mode has unique attributes and capabilities that affect its ability to fulfill customer requirements. Table 11.5 summarizes these modal attributes.

Numerous studies have been conducted over the years to identify the most important performance capabilities in modal selection. These studies commonly identify accessibility, transit time, reliability, and product safety as the key determinants in choosing a mode. Cost is another essential consideration in modal selection.

11-4-4-1 Accessibility

Accessibility determines whether a particular mode is able to reach origin and destination points, as well as provide service over the specified route in question. The geographic limitations of a mode's infrastructure or network and the operating scope that governmental regulatory agencies authorize also affect accessibility. Accessibility problems often eliminate a mode from consideration during the selection process.

Table 11.5	Comparison of Modal Capabilities				
MODE	**STRENGTHS**	**LIMITATIONS**	**PRIMARY ROLE**	**PRIMARY PRODUCT CHARACTERISTICS**	**EXAMPLE PRODUCTS**
Truck	• Accessible • Fast and versatile • Customer service	• Limited capacity • High cost	• Move smaller shipments in local, regional, and national markets	• High value • Finished goods • Low volume	• Food • Clothing • Electronics • Furniture
Rail	• High capacity • Low cost	• Accessibility • Inconsistent service • Damage rates	• Move large shipments of domestic freight long distances	• Low value • Raw materials • High volume	• Coal/coke • Lumber/paper • Grain • Chemicals
Air	• Speed • Freight protection • Flexibility	• Accessibility • High cost • Low capacity	• Move urgent shipments of domestic freight and smaller shipments of international freight	• High value • Finished goods • Low volume • Time sensitive	• Computers • Periodicals • Pharmaceuticals • E-commerce deliveries
Water	• High capacity • Low cost • International capabilities	• Slow • Accessibility	• Move large domestic shipments via rivers and canals • Move large shipments of international freight via oceans	• Low value • Raw materials • Bulk commodities • Containerized finished goods	• Crude oil • Ores/minerals • Farm products • Clothing • Electronics • Toys
Pipeline	• In-transit storage • Efficiency • Low cost	• Slow • Limited network	• Move large volumes of domestic freight long distances	• Low value • Liquid commodities • Not time sensitive	• Crude oil • Petroleum • Gasoline • Natural gas

Source: Brian J. Gibson, Ph.D. Used with permission.

- **Accessibility advantage:** Motor carriage, because of its inherent ability to provide service to virtually any location. Given the road networks in most countries, motor carriage is more accessible to sellers and buyers than any other mode for domestic transportation.

- **Accessibility disadvantage:** Air, rail, and water carriers face accessibility limitations due to infrastructure issues. Poor customer adjacency to airports, rail lines, and waterways limit use of these modes unless intermodal service is used. In these cases, air, water, and rail carriers provide long distance linehaul services while trucks provide origin pickup and destination delivery services.

11-4-4-2 Transit Time

Transit time is critical in supply chain management because of its impact on inventory availability, stockout costs, and customer satisfaction. Transit time is the total elapsed time that it takes to move goods from origin to destination. This includes the time required for pickup activities, terminal handling, linehaul movement, and customer delivery. Transit time is impacted by the speed of the mode and the ability of the mode to handle pickup and delivery responsibilities.

- **Transit time advantage:** Air transportation is very fast for the linehaul move but loses some velocity as pickup and delivery activities must be handled by truck.

Motor carriage is also relatively fast because it can provide more direct movement from origin to destination far more often than any other mode.

- **Transit time disadvantage:** Rail, water, and pipeline are extremely slow with
  average transit speeds of 22 miles per hour, 5 to 9 miles per hour, and 3 to 4
  miles per hour, respectively.

11-4-4-3 Reliability

Reliability refers to the consistency of the transit time provided by a transportation
mode. It is easier to forecast inventory needs, schedule production, and determine safety
stock levels if it is known with some certainty when goods will arrive. Reliability is measured by the statistical variation in transit time.

Modal reliability is affected by a variety of factors including equipment and labor availability, weather, traffic congestion, number of required stops, and other factors. Internationally, reliability is impacted by distance, port congestion, security requirements, and
border crossings delays, especially when the two countries do not have a proactive trade
agreement.

- **Reliability advantage:** Motor carriers and air carriers, as they are the most reliable (variability relevant to average transit time). Numerous carriers in both
  modes achieve on-time delivery performance in the 98 percent or greater level.
- **Reliability disadvantage:** Water carriers and rail carriers. Historically, they have
  been slow and consistent, but with the capacity and congestion challenges, they
  have become less consistent. As a result, some customers have reduced their use
  of these modes when possible.

11-4-4-4 Product Safety

Safety is critical to the achievement of customer service, cost control, and supply chain
effectiveness. From a safety standpoint, goods must arrive at the destination in the same
condition they were in when tendered for shipment at the origin. Proper precautions must
be taken to protect freight from loss due to external theft, internal pilferage, and misplace-
ment, as well as damage due to poor freight-handling techniques, poor ride quality, and
accidents. Safety is often pursued through substantial protective packing.

- **Safety advantage:** Air transportation and motor carriage have the best reputa-
  tions for product safety. Their equipment provides excellent ride quality and
  protection from the elements. Faster transit times also reduce the opportunity
  for theft and other mishaps.
- **Safety disadvantage:** Rail and water lag in the product protection area. Goods
  moving via rail encounter a great deal of vibration created by steel wheels on
  steel track, swaying, and jarring from freight cars being coupled at speeds of up
  to 10 miles per hour. Water transportation often exposes goods to the elements
  (corrosive salt water, heat, etc.), excessive movement (sway, pitch, roll, etc.), and
  rough handling during the loading and unloading processes.

11-4-4-5 Cost

The cost of transportation affects modal selection, especially when a low-value commodity needs to be moved. Transportation costs include the rate for moving freight from origin
to destination plus any accessorial and terminal fees for additional services provided. A
number of factors are taken into consideration when freight rates are developed, including weight of the shipment, distance from origin to destination, nature and value of the

product, and the speed required. A detailed discussion of freight ratemaking is provided in Appendix 10B.

- **Cost advantage:** The cost of transportation service varies greatly between and within the modes. In general, pipeline, water, and rail service are low-cost transportation methods. They move large quantities of product over extremely long distances at very reasonable rates, creating a very low cost per ton-mile for their customers. The tradeoff, of course, is slow speed.

- **Cost disadvantage:** Motor carriage and air transportation are high-cost modes. On average, motor carriage is about 10 times more expensive than rail, and air service is more than twice the cost of motor carriage. Despite the premium paid for these modes, the faster speed can result in lower inventory investment and holding costs leading to a net lower landed cost.

Given the pros and cons of each option, modal selection can be difficult. Table 11.6 provides a comparative ranking of modal capabilities. These factors must be considered in conjunction with freight costs, service availability, and ability to fulfill supply chain requirements.

Not every product can be moved by every mode. The nature of a product may eliminate some modes from consideration as they cannot physically, legally, or safely handle the goods. Product size factors—weight, cube, density, and shape—greatly impact modal selection. Lightweight small electronics and apparel are more suitable to air and motor transportation, while heavier, larger, longer products (e.g., lumber) gravitate toward rail and water transportation.

Durability also influences modal selection. Fragile products must be shipped via modes with the best ride quality. Temperature-sensitive goods must move via modes with cooling or warming capabilities. Perishable goods require modes with the fastest transit times. Typically, the superior speed and freight protection capabilities of air and motor carriage serve these low durability, high time-sensitivity products well.

Product value is a critical factor in modal selection. If a company spends too much on transportation relative to the value of a product, then it will not be able to sell the product at a competitive price. Hence, low value bulk commodities tend to move via water, rail, and

Table 11.6	Performance Ranking of Modes				
	MODE OF TRANSPORTATION				
CRITERIA	**TRUCK**	**AIR**	**RAIL**	**WATER**	**PIPELINE**
Accessibility*	1	3	2	4	5
Transit time*	2	1	3	4	5
Reliability*	2	3	4	5	1
Security*	3	2	4	5	1
Cost**	4	5	3	2	1

*1 = Best to 5 = Worst
**1 = Lowest cost to 5 = Highest cost

Source: Edward J. Bardi, Ph.D. Used with permission.

pipelines while higher value finished goods typically move via truck and air. Of course, transportation cost must be considered in light of customer service requirements and cost tradeoffs with other supply chain processes. The cheapest mode may not always be the best choice.

Shipment characteristics cannot be ignored in modal selection. Modal capacities must be matched to the total weight and dimensions of shipments. Origin points, destination points, and specified routes affect modal accessibility and must be factored into selection decisions. Finally, the service requirements of a shipment must be matched to the modal capabilities discussed earlier.

Ultimately, these product, cost, and shipment factors tend to limit modal selection to two or three realistic options. Then, the transportation buyer must determine which mode or combination of modes will create the best balance between modal capabilities, product characteristics, supply chain requirements for speed and service, and freight transportation cost. Short of major price, infrastructure, service quality, or technological changes in the modes, the mode selection decision is not revisited frequently.

11-4-5 Carrier Selection

Carrier selection is a specialized purchasing decision that typically will be made by a supply chain professional that has expertise and experience in the purchase of transportation services. Like the modal decision, carrier selection is based on a variety of shipment criteria and carrier capabilities: transit time average and reliability, equipment availability and capacity, geographic coverage, product protection, and freight rates.

A major difference between modal and carrier selection is the number of options. Modal selection involves six primary options, but the number of carriers varies greatly. In the case of rail transportation, many markets are only served by a single carrier. The choice is limited—either use that railroad or find another mode. At the other extreme is truckload transportation where dozens of carriers serve a particular market. Time and effort must be expended in evaluating potential carrier capability, service quality, and price.

Another difference is the frequency of the decision. Carrier selection requires more active and frequent engagement of the transportation buyer than does modal selection. This engagement does not focus on choosing a new carrier for each freight move; it focuses more on the transportation buyer remaining vigilant and managing the performance of chosen carriers. It is critical to monitor each carrier's service level and freight rates. Should performance deteriorate, it may be necessary to hire a different carrier.

The type of service provided within a mode affects carrier selection. Direct service providers provide point-to-point flows of goods, generating the advantages of speed and safety because freight is handled less and moves without detour to the destination. Indirect service requires interim stops or transfers between equipment. This reduces transit speed and subjects the freight to additional handling but offers lower cost because carriers can consolidate the freight for more efficient transportation.

Because the cost structures are essentially the same for carriers in a given mode, their rates tend to be aligned for a given movement. Thus, service performance is often the key determinant in carrier selection. Carrier selection research suggests that reliability of on-time delivery and on-time pickup, technical capabilities, carrier response to emergencies, information sharing, freight damage experience, carrier financial stability, and total transit time are among the most important criteria to transportation service buyers.[30]

Carrier selection strategy commonly focuses on concentrating the transportation buy with a limited number of quality carriers. Using these core carriers helps the organization leverage its purchasing dollars for lower overall rates and allows the company to focus its attention on other supply chain issues. It also promotes strong relationships with the carriers that produce mutual understanding of requirements, coordination of processes, and service improvement. Being a carrier friendly customer can also give a company priority access to the carriers' limited capacity. The goal is to become a shipper of choice, as highlighted in the On the Line feature.

On the Line   *Courting the Carrier Community*

Freight customers of the trucking industry and the intermodal rail industry are challenged to gain access to needed delivery capabilities. The worsening truck driver shortage, increasing regulation, equipment shortages, and congestion challenges have converged to create a constrained capacity situation. This has shifted the power in shipper–carrier negotiations. Carriers have more business than they can handle which allows them to be selective. They can choose to walk away from customers who are difficult to work with and whose freight is less profitable than other options. In short, the carriers no longer have a great deal of empty equipment to fill at any price.

Given this new normal, what can freight customers do to ensure that they secure the capacity needed to keep their supply chains operating smoothly? The buzz-phrases of the day are being a "shipper of choice" and offering "driver friendly freight" to the carrier community. Simply stated, it means that your operations run smoothly, your freight is handled without challenge, and that you are a customer that carriers trust and want to do business with on an ongoing basis. This is operationalized through the following tactics:

- Collaborate with carriers on capacity requirements. Providing accurate forecasts of equipment and labor needs will help them establish more predictable and profitable routes, driver schedules, and equipment plans.

- Minimize the number of exceptions in the forms of load cancellations and last minute delivery requests. This keeps carriers out of the reactive scramble to find drivers and equipment.

- Simplify financial transactions. Automate processes with freight payment tools, employ attractive payment terms, and pay freight bills in a timely fashion.

- Minimize driver dwell time. Offer flexible pickup and delivery hours, palletize freight for rapid loading and unloading, and loads ready to be dispatched upon driver arrival. In short, keep drivers on the road.

- Provide a pleasant environment for drivers. Streamline gate check-in processes, improve flow patterns, and create a driver lounge for them to rest, do paperwork, and grab a cup of coffee while they wait for dispatch.

Adopting these straightforward practices may be the difference between consistently securing needed capacity from quality carriers and having freight languish while you scramble to find any carrier to accept the load.

Sources: "6 More Ways to Become a Shipper of Choice during a Capacity Crunch," *LDL Voice* (October 2, 2015); Retrieved October 26, 2015 from https://www.loaddelivered.com/articles/6-more-ways-to-become-a-shipper-of-choice-during-a-capacity-crunch/; Rick Erickson, "Choosing to be a Shipper of Choice," *Inbound Logistics*, (April 2015): 58; and, "How to Become Your Carrier's Shipper of Choice," *SupplyChainBrain*, (October 9, 2014). Retrieved October 26, 2015 from http://www.supplychainbrain.com/content/latest-content/single-article/article/how-to-become-your-carriers-shipper-of-choice-2/

11-4-6 Rate Negotiations

After identifying appropriate carriers, service agreements must be established. Some transportation buyers take an adversarial approach and seek to minimize transportation cost. They hold out for the largest possible discount off the published rate regardless of the impact on carrier financial performance or long-term viability. This short-term perspective can lead to service quality degradation or loss of capacity when the carrier finds a more lucrative customer. The buyer will then need to find new service providers.

The alternative is to engage in collaborative negotiations with compatible carriers. These negotiations focus on developing contracts with carriers for a tailored set of transportation services at rates that fairly compensate the carriers. Key negotiation issues for the buyer include equipment availability, freight rates, and service levels. Carriers focus on volume commitments, shipment frequencies, origin–destination combinations, freight characteristics, and related cost issues that influence their ability to profitably serve buyers.

When the parties successfully complete the negotiation, a contract for transportation services is developed and signed. The buyer received tailored services, gains a commitment for scarce capacity, and locks into competitive rates. The carrier receives a relatively stable volume of business across a set of geographic lanes which allows it to improve labor and equipment utilization and reduce the cost of operations. Based on these benefits, it is easy to understand why more than 80 percent of commercial freight moves under contractual rates.

11-5 Transportation Execution and Control

When a shipment needs to be moved across the supply chain, transportation execution processes take center stage. Decisions must be made regarding shipment size, route, and delivery method; freight documents must be prepared; in-transit problems must be resolved; and service quality must be monitored.

11-5-1 Shipment Preparation

The delivery process is set in motion by a customer request, replenishment signal, or prescheduled order. Prior efforts to identify the appropriate mode and carrier, secure capacity, and control transportation spending culminates in shipment preparation and handoff to a carrier for delivery. This carrier assignment is based on the size, service requirements, and destination of the shipment. Transportation cost control and freight protection are also important decision factors.

To ensure maximum effectiveness in the shipment–carrier matching process, many organizations maintain a transportation routing guide. These documents specify the carriers to be used for inbound and outbound deliveries that the organization controls. Routing guides often provide instructions for carton and shipment labeling, insurance and billing requirements, advanced shipping notification, and other pertinent information.

Some routing guides are simple one- or two-page online documents that plainly state shipment requirements. For example, Hallmark's routing guide is easy to read and leaves no room for misinterpretation. It instructs vendors to use FedEx ground and limit parcel shipments to 200 pounds, 20 cartons, and cubic size of 130 inches per carton.[31] 3M and other companies create more detailed routing guides with specific sections for inbound, outbound, and returns freight; regional routing information; origin–destination tables and matrices; and related shipping requirements.

The strategy behind routing guides is to promote supply chain excellence through transportation. Routing guides also help organizations maintain centralized control over the number of carriers used and avoid off-contract or "maverick" buying of transportation services. Another goal is to ensure that contractual volume commitments to specific carriers are achieved, as a failure to meet these commitments can result in higher transportation rates or penalty fees.

In preparing freight for delivery, transportation managers can make cost-saving decisions. Efforts should be made to coordinate inbound and outbound deliveries, specify best routes, and fully utilize container capacity. Multiple orders destined for a single location can be consolidated into a single shipment. The key to reducing cost is having advance knowledge of freight volume, destinations, and service requirements, as well as the lead time, to develop efficient delivery decisions.

The transportation operation is the last line of defense in protecting product integrity and value. It is imperative to use carriers with an effective track record of damage- and shortage-free delivery service. Even when using trusted carriers, a freight shipper must validate that the invoice and shipping documents match the shipment, use protective packaging to avoid damaged en route, and examine the freight container should be examined for cleanliness, leakage issues, and security. The loading process should be monitored for proper freight stacking and stabilization to avoid vibration, product shifting, and other ride quality issues.

11-5-3 Freight Documentation[32]

Freight must be accompanied by documents that spell out the shipment details—the product, destination, ownership, and more. The type and variety of documents required depend on the origin and destination points, characteristics of the freight, mode(s) being used, and carrier handling the freight. Simply stated, the more complex the transportation requirements, the more documents are needed to facilitate the uninterrupted flow of goods through the supply chain. A private fleet delivery of dry groceries from a Kroger distribution center to a Kroger store in the same state will require only a basic bill of lading. In contrast, an intermodal shipment of fireworks moving from China to Texas, will require extensive paperwork.

The most prevalent documents include the bill of lading, freight bill, and claims form.

The **bill of lading** (BOL) is the most important transportation document. It is created by the shipper of the goods to originate the shipment. The BOL provides all the information the carrier needs to accomplish the move, stipulates the transportation contract terms including the scope of the carrier's liability for loss and damage, acts as a receipt for the goods the shipper tenders to the carrier, and in some cases shows certificate of title to the goods. Figure 11.5 shows a typical BOL with the essential types of shipment information contained in the document.

The required BOL type required—inland, ocean, air waybill, multimodal, through, etc.— depends on the mode, trade terms, and shipment details. Also, the BOL is either negotiable or nonnegotiable. A straight BOL is nonnegotiable. The carrier must deliver the goods to the specific receiving organization and destination in return for freight payment. An order BOL is negotiable and serves as a title to the goods. The owner of the goods may transfer title to the goods to another party and reroute the shipment to a location different from the bill of lading information.

Figure 11.5 | **Sample Bill of Lading**

❶ Carrier information

❷ Shipping party/from information

❸ Receiving party/to information

❹ Billing information

❺ Service type

❻ Description of shipment items

❼ Weight of shipment items

❽ COD payment terms

❾ Bill of lading provisions

Note: There are numerous bill of lading types. Key content and location of information may vary by type and the company who has created the bill of lading.

Source: Brian J. Gibson, Ph.D. Used with permission.

The **freight bill** is the carrier's invoice for the fees charged to move the shipment. The freight bill lists the shipment, origin and destination, consignee, items, total weight, and total charges. The freight bill differs from the bill of lading in that the freight bill sets forth the charges applicable to the shipment while the bill of lading sets forth the terms of the shipment and is a document of title.

The total charges specified in the freight bill are based on the rate negotiated by the freight buyer and carrier, the size of the shipment, and supplementary fees for accessorial services. Freight bills are submitted by the carrier when the freight is picked up by carrier (prepaid basis) or when the freight is delivered (collect basis). In most contracts, the freight buyer has a specified number of days to pay the bill after carrier submission and may receive a discount for early payment.

A **freight claims form** is a document that the transportation buyer files with the carrier to recoup monetary losses resulting from the carrier's failure to properly protect the freight. The shipper must file the claim in writing with the carrier before the deadline specified in the contract. Freight claims can be filed for visible damage or shortages that are detected when the product is received and inspected, for concealed losses that are not discovered until packages are opened, or for financial losses due to unreasonable delays. Claims should be supported by photographs of the damage, notations of problems on the delivery receipt, and proof of the damaged goods' monetary value.

Freight claims seek to compensate the transportation buyer an amount equal to the value of the goods had the carrier safely delivered them. Carrier liability is limited if the shipper elected to send the goods under a released value (i.e., valuing the freight at less than its full worth) in exchange for lower freight rates. Carriers are not liable for freight claims if the damage is attributable to some uncontrollable factor such as the following:

- Natural disaster or some other "act of God"
- Military attack or similar "act of public enemy"
- Government seizure of freight or "act of public authority"
- Failure to adequately package the freight or other negligent "act of the shipper"
- Extreme fragility, perishability, or problematic "inherent nature of the goods"

A number of other documents may also be required to move freight efficiently through the supply chain. These include critical transaction documents like the commercial invoice that provides a record or evidence of a transaction between an exporter and importer or the certificate of origin that authenticates the country of origin for the goods being shipped. Both are used for commodity control and duty valuation by the country of import. In addition to the transportation documents described earlier, valuable and sometimes necessary paperwork includes a shipper's letter of instructions, dock receipts, shipment manifests, dangerous goods declaration forms, and insurance certificates.

Documentation-based freight delays and disruptions can be minimized with accuracy, timeliness, and attention to detail. Carriers and governmental authorities may halt the flow of goods if documents appear to be inaccurate, incomplete, or fraudulent. Availability of documents prior to the tendering of goods to carriers is also critical. Most carriers will not accept freight without the necessary paperwork. For international freight, the U.S. Customs 24-Hour Advance Vessel Manifest Rule requires carriers to submit cargo information a full day before it is loaded onto a vessel at a foreign port. If the buyer fails to submit documentation by this deadline, then the carrier will not load the freight which results in a missed voyage and potential supply chain disruptions.

11-5-4 Maintain In-Transit Visibility

Management of the transportation process does not end when the freight and related documents are tendered to the carrier. It is important to control the freight and manage key events as product moves across the supply chain. Visibility of in-transit freight is a key facilitator of this control as it prevents freight from temporarily "falling off the radar screen." The goal of visibility is to provide the location and status of the shipments regardless of the position in the supply chain, enabling transportation buyers to make adjustments as needed to meet customer needs. Accurate and up-to-the-minute shipment data make it possible for organizations to respond to problems as they emerge.

Technology facilitates the ability to monitor product flows. Time-definite carriers and truckload carriers use satellite tracking to maintain equipment visibility. Equipment operators have smartphones, onboard computers with satellite uplinks, and tablet computers to promote frequent and timely contact. Leading integrated carriers like FedEx and UPS offer online tracking capabilities to transportation buyers. Such tools support proactive management of transportation issues before they disrupt the supply chain. These supply chain event management capabilities are detailed in Chapter 14.

11-5-5 Transportation Metrics

The quality of transportation services is tangible—most service requirements are observable and quantifiable. This allows organizations to monitor activities through transportation metrics or key performance indicators (KPIs). Transportation KPIs are objective measures of carrier or private fleet performance that are linked to supply chain success. Data compiled from multiple sources—shipment date and cost from the freight bill, arrival date from the delivery receipt, and shipment damage information from the receiving party—provides the inputs for KPI analysis. These KPIs can be used to benchmark performance against goals and industry leaders.

Customers focus on KPIs targeting transportation service quality. This targets doing things right the first time according to customer-defined requirements. Three of the "Seven Rs" align with quantifiable transportation service quality KPIs—"at the right time" targets transit time, "in the right condition" concentrates on freight protection, and "at the right cost" pertains to rates and billing accuracy. The most common service quality metrics are presented in Table 11.7. Customers must also consider qualitative aspects of service quality such as responsiveness, professionalism, and flexibility.

The focus on lean supply chains and just-in-time operations makes consistent, on-time delivery a critical requirement. Multiple studies suggest that on-time delivery is the most important KPI used by transportation buyers to evaluate their carriers. Timely service facilitates inventory rationalization through lower safety stock levels, provides consistent replenishment to reduce out-of-stock problems, and reduces supply chain uncertainty and the resulting bullwhip effect.

Freight protection is another service quality factor. Shipments must arrive safely and completely. Supply chains supporting just-in-time manufacturing operations and retailers with lean inventories are especially vulnerable to delivery shortages or damage, as they keep little to no safety stock on hand to replace the unavailable goods.

Since transportation rates and service requirements are tailored to a specific customer's requirements, it is imperative that carriers accurately bill customers using the correct shipment data, rate structures, and charges for each load. Incorrect data entry or misapplication of contract provisions can lead to overstatement of rates and accessorial service charges, misrouted freight, incorrect payment due dates.

The ultimate service quality KPI is the execution of perfect deliveries, the ratio of defect-free deliveries to the total number of deliveries made. Transportation buyers should seek out high-quality carriers that consistently provide flawless service that is on time, damage free, accurate, responsive, and cost effective. Defect-free transportation eliminates the need for rework, reduces administrative work, and tempers the use of premium service, as well as promoting customer satisfaction, inventory reduction, and supply chain stability.

Table 11.7	Common Transportation Metrics	
METRIC	**FORMULA**	**TYPICAL TARGET**
On-time Delivery	Total on-time deliveries / Total deliveries	> 95%
Transit Time Average	Sum of transit times / Total deliveries	Low variation around goal
Damage Rate	Total units damaged / Total units shipped	< 1%
Shortage Rate	Total units lost or stolen / Total units shipped	< 1%
Billing accuracy	Total accurate freight bills / Total freight bills	> 99%
Perfect Delivery Index	On-Time % × Damage-Free % × Billing Accuracy %	> 95%
Source: Brian J. Gibson, Ph.D. Used with permission.		

While service quality is critically important for customer satisfaction, transportation service efficiency cannot be ignored. Transportation is the single largest logistics expense, and it is imperative that organizations get the greatest value for their spend. Service requirements must be balanced with the expenses related to moving freight. Keeping transportation costs low in proportion to the value of the goods will create at competitive landed cost. Transportation efficiency KPIs promote these goals.

Aggregate efficiency measures focus on the total transportation spending versus goal, budget, or sales. Item-level KPIs focus on the transportation expense per unit of measure (e.g., pound, case, selling unit). Understanding what is spent to move each unit highlights transportation's impact on the overall cost of goods. This KPI also provides a baseline from which improvement efforts can be made.

Asset utilization is a critical aspect of transportation cost control. The higher the utilization of the equipment, the lower the transportation cost per pound, cubic foot or selling unit. Empty equipment miles must be minimized and cube utilization must be maximized to keep costs under control, reduce resource use, and avoid carbon emissions.

Efficiency measures can also be used to evaluate and improve carrier and private fleet performance. Labor productivity KPIs ensure that equipment operators, freight handlers, and other personnel are performing at acceptable levels. Rapid loading and unloading time improves carrier employee and equipment turnaround time, keeping both in productive use. Efficiency improvements lead to lower transportation operations costs.

Consistent measurement and review of a manageable number of transportation KPIs generates substantial benefits. KPIs help organizations take a proactive, knowledge-based approach to monitoring transportation activities and resolving issues before they negatively affect the supply chain. KPIs also help organizations pinpoint inefficiencies and develop strategies for supply chain cost reduction. Finally, KPI data can be used to analyze cost–service level tradeoffs for future mode and carrier selection decisions.

11-5-6 Monitor Service Quality

Individual transportation KPIs provide valuable nuggets of information but do not give a detailed perspective of a carrier's service quality. Transportation managers must holistically analyze the outcome of their transportation strategy, planning, and decision-making efforts. This is accomplished through a coordinated, ongoing carrier performance monitoring initiative. The focal point of this initiative should be results achieved relative to the carrier's contractual commitments.

One strategy for developing an objective, holistic view of carrier service quality is to develop scorecards with a weighted point plan. The transportation team assigns weight factors to the performance criteria, measures carrier performance, and compares the results to predetermined goals. This produces a performance score which is then multiplied by the weight factor to determine the category score. An overall carrier score is obtained by summing the category scores.

Table 10.5 provides an example scorecard in which the company earned 405 points of a possible 500 points for the evaluation period. This score would be ranked versus other carriers and the carrier would receive feedback from the process. The commentary would include a discussion of positive outcomes and opportunities for improvement. The freight buyer may also use the scorecarding results and carrier rankings as an input to future purchase decisions.[33]

Table 11.8	Transportation Performance Scorecard			
PERFORMANCE CRITERIA	**WEIGHT FACTOR**	**CARRIER PERFORMANCE**	**PERFORMANCE SCORE**	**CATEGORY SCORE**
On-time delivery	35	96.7%	>98% = 5 96.01–98% = 4 94.01–96% = 3 92.01–94% = 2 >92% = 0	140
Loss and damage rate	30	0.6%	<0.5% = 5 0.5–1% = 4 1–1.5% = 3 1.5–2% = 2 >2% = 0	120
Billing accuracy	15	98.1	>99% = 5 97–99% = 3 95–96% = 1 <95% = 0	45
Equipment condition	5	Acceptable	Safe & clean = 5 Poor condition = 0	25
Customer service	15	Outstanding feedback on customer service surveys	Superior = 5 Good = 4 Average = 3 Fair = 2 Unacceptable = 0	75
			Total Score	405

Source: Brian J. Gibson, Ph.D. Used with permission.

11-6 Transportation Technology

The dynamic nature of transportation combined with the wide array of delivery requirements and options create a complex environment for transportation buyers and managers. Multiple factors must be considered when developing strategies and making operational decisions if appropriate and economical decisions are to be made. Fortunately, software and information technology tools have been developed to support transportation planning, execution, and performance evaluation.

The carrier community relies on technology to coordinate the flow of customer freight. Routing and load planning tools promotes optimization of pickup, linehaul, and delivery operations. Dispatching software facilitates the management of drivers, in-transit visibility, and regulatory compliance. Brokerage solutions help to match loads with available capacity and manage the financial aspects of these transactions. Additional tools support the complex to the routine activities, from pricing strategy to documentation preparation. Collectively, this wide array of tools provides carriers with the critical functionality and mobile access needed to manage dynamic transportation networks.

Transportation buyers also require technology to maintain visibility and control of their freight as it flows between origin and destination points. As the old saying goes "knowledge is power" and transportation managers need to know where their freight is, what condition it is in, and when it will arrive. Technology provides this operational knowledge, as well as the ability to plan transportation processes and evaluate results. Carriers are supporting visibility by purchasing technology enhanced freight equipment and communication tools as highlighted in the On the Line Feature.

Transportation buyers and managers leverage a variety of tools and technologies to support supply chain success. Individual applications provide point solutions for activities like load planning optimization, freight rating, and load tendering. Integrated supply chain tools like global trade management software includes transportation management tools for contract and rate management, carrier selection and booking, documentation preparation, and freight audit. The most comprehensive tools are **transportation management systems (TMS)** which support the planning and execution of transportation operations.

On the Line   *Freight Visibility Solutions*

One of the most important requirements of freight customers is knowing where their shipments are located in the network. Visibility solutions help companies monitor the location and current status of their in-transit inventory. Some of these solutions are well-tested while others are relatively new.

One option is to rely on carrier capabilities (as discussed previously in this chapter). They use global positioning satellite tracking, on-board computers, and mobile communication devices to generate shipment status information. One critique of these traditional tools is that they tend to rely on human inputs like keyboard updates to a portal, or phone calls to communicate exceptions. Accuracy and timeliness can be concerns.

A second alternative is to implement control tower software that helps a company to monitor and manage its carriers, logistics service providers, and suppliers. An alternative to ownership is to work with a third party logistics provider that has vast experience with control tower systems already in place. The expected outcomes are transportation savings of 5 to 10 percent, process discipline improvement, and risk reduction.

An emerging option is to embed visibility solutions directly into transportation equipment. Hyundai Heavy Industries and Accenture are integrating digital technology into new ship designs. Using sensors built into the ships, operators will be able to monitor ship location, environmental conditions, and equipment status. By applying real-time analytics to the ship's data, it will be possible to make data-driven decisions that support more efficient operations.

Whatever the method, greater visibility of in-transit freight is a necessity to effectively manage a supply chain. Without visibility, managers are left blind to the activities happening outside their immediate view and are forced to make decisions based on incomplete intelligence.

Sources: Joseph O'Reilly, "Big Data and Big Blue Converge," *Inbound Logistics* (August 2015): 16; Roberto Michel, Logistics Technology: TMS Gets More Warehouse Aware," *Logistics Management* (September 2014): 48–52; and, James A. Cooke, "Control Towers Made Easy," *DC Velocity* (May 2014): 48–49.

11-6-1 Transportation Management Systems

Gartner defines TMS as software used to plan freight movements, do freight rating and shopping across all modes, select the appropriate route and carrier, and manage freight bills and payments.[34] This captures the essence of TMS, presenting it as a melting pot of tools that assist managers in nearly every aspect of transportation from basic load configuration to complex transportation network optimization.

The planning capabilities of TMS support pre-shipment decision making. Buyers are faced with a dizzying number of lane/mode/carrier/service/price combinations in their supply chains. TMS tools allow them to consider a vast array of transportation options in a matter of minutes versus hours or days of manual activity. In addition, the TMS can be linked to order management systems, warehouse management systems, and supply chain planning tools. These links support tradeoffs that optimize overall supply chain performance. Critical TMS planning applications include the following:

- **Routing and scheduling**—Proper planning of delivery routes has a major impact on customer satisfaction, supply chain performance, and organizational success. TMS software uses mathematical methods and optimization routines to identify feasible routes that meet service constraints. Typical TMS output includes a detailed schedule of the routes, cost analysis, and route maps.

- **Load planning**—Effective preparation of safe, efficient deliveries can be accomplished via TMS load optimization programs. Based on product dimensions, loading requirements, and equipment capacity, the TMS software optimizes how shipments should be arranged in the container or on a pallet. The result is reduced damage risk and improved cargo space utilization.

TMS execution tools help transportation managers streamline shipment activities. By automating documentation creation and other repetitive tasks, labor is reduced and inaccuracies are avoided. Other tools post shipment information to a shared network or a Web site to promote shipment visibility and provide greater freight control. Three of the key execution tools include the following:

- **Load tendering**—For a given origin-destination pair and shipment size, multiple carriers may be available, though at slightly different rates. The TMS database identifies eligible carriers and then tenders the freight to the best carrier based on routing guide requirements, cost, transit time, and required service capabilities. This improves contract compliance, service, and freight spending.

- **Status tracking**—Maintaining shipment visibility across the network is a time-consuming task. When linked to satellite tracking, the TMS monitors in-transit shipment location and status. If the shipment is behind schedule, stopped, or off-route, notifications are made so that corrective action can be taken. The On the Line feature discusses visibility tools for in-transit control of freight.

- **Appointment scheduling**—To avoid facility congestion, equipment delays, and operator inefficiency, organizations use TMS capabilities to automate the scheduling function. Many systems support Internet-based access to the scheduling system where carriers can schedule pickup and delivery times at specific dock locations.

TMS analytical tools provide organizations with the ability to evaluate carrier performance, customer service, and transportation spending. TMS software help to assemble and make sense of widely dispersed data that is needed to measure KPIs and assess performance. Useful analytical applications include:

- **Performance monitoring**—TMS tools can automate the measurement of KPIs and dissemination of periodic reports. These dashboards and reports can provide information on overall performance as well as the results in specific segments of the transportation operation. Transportation managers receive timely, objective information upon which decisions can be based.

- **Freight bill auditing**—Payments made to carriers must reflect the contractual rates and the services promised. To ensure that they are neither being overcharged nor undercharged for freight services, many organizations are turning to TMS software to reconcile invoices with their contracts. These tools automate a manual process that did not always catch discrepancies in a timely, accurate manner.

Collectively, these capabilities are driving TMS investment. One industry analyst projects the global TMS market to grow by 7 percent annually through 2019.[35] The anticipated growth is based on the promise of affordable cloud-based solutions with easy installation and rapid return on investment, 10 to 15 percent freight cost reductions, and the ability to use TMS across all modes of service.[36]

The challenge of technology is the constant pace of change. While the software capabilities discussed in this section are today's tools of choice today for managing supply chain flows, they may become yesterday's news. Thus, the most important idea to take away from this section is the importance of information technology in transportation. Simply stated, technology helps us manage the vast volume of data and options in transportation in order to make better decisions regarding modal and carrier selection, routing, packaging, loading, and many other activities. These decisions contribute to greater customer service, tighter cost control, and competitive advantage in the supply chain.

SUMMARY

- Transportation is a dynamic activity and a critical supply chain process. It is the largest logistics cost in most supply chains, and it also directly impacts fulfillment speed and service quality. By providing the physical links between key participants across domestic and global supply chains, transportation facilitates the creation of time and place utilities.

- Managing the transportation process for maximum supply chain impact requires considerable knowledge of transportation options, planning, decision making, analytical skills, and information sharing capabilities.

- Transportation is a key supply chain process and must be included in supply chain strategy development, network design, and total cost management.

- Numerous obstacles—global expansion of supply chains, rising costs, limited capacity, and government regulation—must be overcome to synchronize transportation with other supply chain processes.

- Fulfillment of supply chain demand can be accomplished through five modal options or the intermodal use of truck, rail, air, water, and pipeline transportation.

- Multiple planning activities occur prior to carrier and mode selection. Responsibility for managing the transportation function and freight control decisions must be made with a strategic supply chain focus.

- Mode selection is based on the relative strengths of each modal or intermodal option in terms of accessibility, transit time, reliability, safety and security, transportation cost, and the nature of the product being transported.

- Carrier selection focuses on the type of service required (direct or indirect), geographic coverage, service levels, and carrier willingness to negotiate reasonable rates.

- Most commercial freight moves under contractual rates that are negotiated directly between freight buyers and transportation companies for specific volumes of tailored services at mutually agreed-upon prices.

- Shipment routing guides help organizations ensure internal compliance with service contracts and maintain centralized control over freight tendering decisions.

- Freight documentation provides the details of each shipment, sharing critical information that promotes uninterrupted flows of goods through the supply chain.

- Organizations must continue to manage freight after it has been tendered to carriers by maintaining in-transit visibility of shipments and monitoring carrier performance.

- Numerous metrics are available to evaluate transportation service quality in terms of carrier timeliness, freight protection, accuracy, and perfect deliveries. Service efficiency measures focus on spending proficiency, asset utilization, and labor productivity.

- Transportation management systems and related tools are widely used information technologies that support the effective planning, execution, and analysis of transportation processes.

STUDY QUESTIONS

1. Discuss the role of transportation in the supply chain. Provide examples of how transportation can positively and negatively impact supply chain performance.

2. Describe the major challenges faced by transportation managers in the current environment.

3. What are the primary capabilities, advantages, and disadvantages of each of the basic modes?

4. Using financial Web sites, company Web sites, and search engines, develop a basic overview report (primary service offerings, annual sales, current stock price, and recent news) for one domestic or international transportation company from each Standard Industrial Classification (SIC) system code:
   a. SIC 4011—Railroads, Linehaul Operating
   b. SIC 4213—Trucking, Except Local
   c. SIC 4513—Air Courier Services
   d. SIC 4412—Deep Sea Foreign Transportation of Freight

5. Discuss the primary considerations and issues that must be factored into modal and carrier selection.

6. Should the Internet be considered the sixth mode of transportation? Why or why not?

7. Identify and discuss appropriate modes of transportation for the following items:
   a. Apple iPhones
   b. Under Armour running shoes
   c. Organic fruits and vegetables
   d. Pressure treated lumber

8. Using company Web sites, compare the service offerings for the following transportation companies:
   a. J. B. Hunt (http://www.jbhunt.com) and Old Dominion Freight Line (http://www.odfl.com)
   b. FedEx (http://www.fedex.com/us/ship/) and DHL Aviation (https://aviationcargo.dhl.com)
   c. Maersk Line (http://www.maerskline.com) and Wallenius Wilhelmsen Logistics (http://www.2wglobal.com)
   d. Canadian National Railway Company (http://www.cn.ca) and Florida East Coast Railway (http://www.fecrwy.com)

9. Describe the purpose and value of freight documentation. Discuss the function of the following documents: bill of lading, freight bill, and freight claim.

10. How would a transportation manager monitor the quality of service provided by the carriers used? What types of metrics would be used?

11. What role does information technology play in the management of transportation planning, execution, and analysis?

NOTES

1. Rosalyn Wilson, *26th Annual State of Logistics Report* (Oak Brook, IL: Council of Supply Chain Management Professionals, 2015).

2. David Leonard, "It's Amazon's World. The USPS Just Delivers in It," *Bloomberg Business,* (July 30, 2015). Retrieved October 10, 2015 from http://www.bloomberg.com/news/articles/2015-07-30/it-s-amazon-s-world-the-usps-just-delivers-in-it

3. U.S. Department of Transportation, *About CSA: What Is It?* Retrieved October 11, 2015 from https://csa.fmcsa.dot.gov/about/

4. U.S. Federal Motor Carrier Safety Administration, *Summary of Hours of Service Regulations.* Retrieved October 11, 2015 from http://www.fmcsa.dot.gov/regulations/hours-service/summary-hours-service-regulations

5. U.S. Environmental Protection Agency, *SmartWay.* Retrieved October 11, 2015 from http://www3.epa.gov/smartway/index.htm

6. U.S. Department of Transportation Bureau of Transportation Statistics, *2015 Pocket Guide to Transportation.* Retrieved October 11, 2015 from http://www.rita.dot.gov/bts/sites/rita.dot.gov.bts/files/Pocket%20Guide%202015.pdf

7. Rosalyn Wilson, *26th Annual State of Logistics Report* (Oak Brook, IL: Council of Supply Chain Management Professionals, 2015).

8. U.S. Federal Motor Carrier Safety Administration, 2*015 Pocket Guide to Large Truck and Bus Statistics* (2015). Retrieved October 11, 2015 from http://ntl.bts.gov/lib/54000/54800/54841/2015_Pocket_Guide_-_March_30_2015__For_Web_Publishing_-508c.pdf

9. UPS, *UPS Fact Sheet* (May 27, 2015). Retrieved October 11, 2015 from https://www.pressroom.ups.com/pressroom/ContentDetailsViewer.page?ConceptType=FactSheets&id=1426321563187-193

10. U.S. Federal Motor Carrier Safety Administration, *2015 Pocket Guide to Large Truck and Bus Statistics* (2015). Retrieved October 11, 2015 from http://ntl.bts.gov/lib/54000/54800/54841/2015_Pocket_Guide_-_March_30_2015__For_Web_Publishing_-508c.pdf

11. U.S. Department of Transportation and U.S. Department of Commerce, *2012 Commodity Flow Survey* (February 2015). Retrieved October 11, 2015 from http://www.rita.dot.gov/bts/sites/rita.dot.gov.bts/files/publications/commodity_flow_survey/2012/united_states/table1a

12. Jeff Berman, "ATA Report Drives Home the Dire Situation the Driver Shortage Remains In," Logistics Management (October 6, 2015). Retrieved October 11, 2015 from http://www.logisticsmgmt.com/article/ata_report_drives_home_the_dire_situation_the_driver_shortage_remains_in

13. U.S. Department of Transportation and U.S. Department of Commerce, 2012 Commodity Flow Survey (February 2015). Retrieved October 11, 2015 from http://www.rita.dot.gov/bts/sites/rita.dot.gov.bts/files/publications/commodity_flow_survey/2012/united_states/table1a

14. Association of American Railroads, *Class I Railroad Statistics* (May 26, 2015). Retrieved October 12, 2015 from https://www.aar.org/Documents/Railroad-Statistics.pdf

15. Mark Solomon and Toby Gooley, "State of Logistics Report: U.S. Business Logistics Costs Hit $1.45 Trillion in 2014," *DC Velocity* (July 2015): 15–17.

16. Jeff Berman, "Still on Track, But Not Immune to Challenges," *Logistics Management* (July 2015): 32.

17. Rosalyn Wilson, *26th Annual State of Logistics Report* (Oak Brook, IL: Council of Supply Chain Management Professionals, 2015).

18. Bruce Barnard, "IATA: Global Cargo Revenue Will Rise in 2015 But Rates Will Fall," JOC.com (December 11, 2014). Retrieved October 21, 2015 from http://www.joc.com/air-cargo/international-air-freight/iata-global-cargo-revenue-will-rise-2015-rates-will-fall_20141211.html

19. Graham Newton "Delivered in Style: Cargo Supply Chain Change," *Airlines International* (February 19, 2015). Retrieved October 21, 2015 from http://airlines.iata.org/analysis/delivered-in-style-cargo-supply-chain-change

20. U.S. Department of Transportation and U.S. Department of Commerce, *2012 Commodity Flow Survey* (February 2015). Retrieved October 21, 2015 from http://www.rita.dot.gov/bts/sites/rita.dot.gov.bts/files/publications/commodity_flow_survey/2012/united_states/table1a

21. Rosalyn Wilson, *26th Annual State of Logistics Report* (Oak Brook, IL: Council of Supply Chain Management Professionals, 2015).

22. Institute for Water Resources, *Waterborne Transportation Lines of the United States* (Alexandria, VA: U.S. Army Corps of Engineers, 2014): 3. Retrieved October 21, 2015 from http://www.navigationdatacenter.us/veslchar/pdf/wtlusvl1_13.pdf

23. Statistics, *Number of Ships in the World Merchant Fleet as of January 1, 2014, by Type* (2015). Retrieved October 21, 2015 from http://www.statista.com/statistics/264024/number-of-merchant-ships-worldwide-by-type/

24. *Alphaliner – Top 100.* Retrieved October 21, 2015 from http://www.alphaliner.com/top100/

25. Patrick Burnson, "Ocean Cargo Still Faces Stiff Headwinds," *Logistics Management* (July 2015): 34–35.

26. American Petroleum Institute and the Association of Oil Pipe Lines, *How Many Pipelines Are There?* Retrieved October 22, 2015 from http://www.pipeline101.com

27. American Association of Port Authorities, *Port Industry Statistics: NAFTA Region Container Traffic 1995 – 2014.* Retrieved October 22, 2015 from http://aapa.files.cms-plus.com/Statistics/NAFTA%20REGION%20CONTAINER%20TRAFFIC%20 1995-2014.pdf

28. Association of American Railroads, *Rail Intermodal Keeps America Moving* (May 2015). Retrieved October 22, 2015 from https://www.aar.org/BackgroundPapers/Rail%20Intermodal.pdf

29. International Chamber of Commerce, *Incoterms 2010.* Retrieved October 22, 2015 from http://www.iccwbo.org/incoterms/

30. Shane R. Premeaux, "Motor Carrier Selection Criteria: Perceptual Differences between Shippers and Motor Carriers," *Transportation Journal* (Winter 2002).

31. Hallmark, *Shipping Instructions & Routing Guide.* Retrieved October 23, 2015 from http://corporate.hallmark.com/Vendors/Transportation-Overview.

32. For an extensive discussion of freight documentation, see: John J. Coyle, Robert A. Novack, and Brian J. Gibson, *Transportation: A Supply Chain Perspective*, 8th ed. (Mason, Ohio: South-Western Cengage Learning, 2016): Chapter 10.

33. Brian J. Gibson and Jerry W. Wilson, "Carrier Scorecarding: Purposes, Processes, and Benefits," *Journal of Transportation Management*, Vol. *15*, No. 1 (2004).

34. Gartner, *IT Glossary – TMS (Transportation Management System).* Retrieved October 24, 2015 from http://www.gartner.com/it-glossary/tms-transportation-management-system

35. Technavio, *Global Transportation Management Systems (TMS) Market 2015–2019* (July 2015). Retrieved October 24, 2015 from http://www.fastmr.com/prod/1023941_global_transportation.aspx?dt=p

36. Steve Defillippis, "Nine Tangible Benefits of a Transportation Management System," *Integrated Shipping Solutions Blob* (February 2, 2015). Retrieved October 24, 2015 from http://integratedshipping.com/blog/nine-tangible-benefits-of-a-transportation-management-system-

CASE 11.1

Vibrant Video

Vibrant Video (V²) is a manufacturer of home theater projection systems. The company assembles Ultra HD projectors in Portland, Oregon and sells them online and through specialty electronics stores. The most popular model retails for $4,995 and V² bundles the projector with high fidelity audio components that are purchased from external suppliers.

Due to ongoing delivery challenges with their Pacific Rim suppliers and carriers, V² has decided to buy from suppliers in closer proximity to Portland. The speakers will be supplied by an electronics company with operations in Tijuana, Mexico and the receivers will be purchased from an audio lab in Manchester, New Hampshire.

The purchase contracts have been negotiated in principle. The speaker supplier has given V² two shipping choices under FOB Destination, Freight Collect. The receiver supplier only sells its products FOB Origin, Freight Collect. The remaining issue for the V² transportation director is to evaluate the delivery options that her analyst recommended for each product and make a decision.

Relevant information is provided in the following table:

	SPEAKERS	RECEIVER
Manufactured in	Tijuana, Mexico	Manchester, New Hampshire
V² purchase price	$175 per set	$225 per unit
Weight	28 pounds	5 pounds
Dimensions	30" (L) × 18" (W) × 18" (H)	18" (L) × 8" (W) × 4" (H)
Characteristics	Sturdy, bulky, not easily damaged	Compact, vibration sensitive, theft risk
Freight Terms	FOB Destination, Freight Collect and Allowed	FOB Origin, Freight Collect
Option 1	Weekly LTL delivery 200 units $2,485 Cost per delivery	Weekly Ground delivery 200 units $2,169 Cost per delivery
Option 2	Twice per month TL delivery 400 units $2,946 Cost per delivery	Twice per week airfreight delivery 100 units $2,411 Cost per delivery

CASE QUESTIONS

1. What responsibilities, control, and costs does V2 bear under each of the FOB terms offered?
2. What is the delivery cost and landed cost per unit for each speaker delivery option?
3. Which delivery option do you recommend for the speakers?
4. What is the delivery cost and landed cost per unit for each speaker delivery option?
5. Which delivery option do you recommend for the speakers?
6. What other supply chain issues and costs must SSE take into consideration when making these transportation decisions?

Source: Brian J. Gibson, Ph.D. Used with permission.

CASE 11.2

Bob's Custom BBQs

Bob's Custom BBQs, a manufacturer of outdoor grills, uses three primary carriers to move grills from its Texas factory to home improvement retailers in the United States and Canada. The owner, Bob Flambeau, wants to evaluate the performance of the three carriers and collected data for the following metrics over a three-month period.

PERFORMANCE CRITERIA	ALLIED TRANSPORT	BESTWAY FREIGHT	CERTAINT CARRIERS
On-time delivery	99.5%	98.7%	98.2%
Loads with damage claims	0.9%	1.6%	0.4%
Customer satisfaction ratings	4.6	4.2	3.9
Billing accuracy	99.3%	99.6%	98.2%
Loads rejected	1.3%	2.1%	0.9%

Bob asked his transportation manager to develop a scorecard to help compare the carriers on these five metrics. The manager came up with the following chart:

PERFORMANCE CRITERIA	WEIGHT FACTOR	PERFORMANCE EVALUATION	POTENTIAL SCORE	ACTUAL SCORE
On-time delivery	30	>98.5% = 5 96.01–98.5% = 4 93–96% = 2 <93% = 0	150	
Loads with damage claims	30	<0.5% = 5 0.5–1% = 4 1.01–2% = 2 >2% = 0	150	
Customer satis-faction ratings	20	>4.5 = 5 4.01–4.5 = 4 3–4 = 2 <3 = 0	100	
Billing accuracy	10	>99% = 5 97.01–99% = 4 95–97% = 2 <95% = 0	50	
Loads rejected	10	<1% = 5 1%–2% = 4 2.01–3% = 2 >3% = 0	50	
		Total Score	**500**	

CASE QUESTIONS

1. Calculate the performance score for each of the three carriers.
2. Which carrier would you recommend that Bob consider for elimination? Why?
3. If Bob decides to keep all three carriers, what should each of them work to improve?

Source: Brian J. Gibson, Ph.D. Used with permission.

APPENDIX 11A

Federal Regulation of the Transportation Industry[1]

Federal regulation of transportation has been with us since the Act to Regulate Commerce passed in 1887. The years immediately preceding the enactment of this law were full of turmoil for both shippers and carriers. Inland transportation was basically by railroad, and the carriers charged high rates when possible and discriminated against small shippers. Control over the transportation industry was important to U.S. economic growth, and a stable transportation service supply that would be compatible with the needs of an expanding society was essential.

Regulatory initiatives initially focused on economic issues to ensure competition and fair pricing for freight customers. In the twenty-first century, efforts to regulate the transportation industry have concentrated more on national security, safety of the traveling public, and protection of the environment. Table 11A.1 highlights the major legislative efforts to regulate (and sometimes deregulate) various aspects of the transportation industry.

Table 11A.1	Chronology of Major Transportation Regulation	
DATE	**ACT**	**NATURE OF REGULATION**
Initiation Era		
1887	Act to Regulate Commerce	Regulated railroads and established Interstate Commerce Commission (ICC); rates must be reasonable; discrimination prohibited
1903	Elkins Act	Prohibited rebates and created filed rate doctrine
1906	Hepburn Act	Established maximum and joint rate controls
1910	Mann-Elkins Act	Shipper given right to route shipments
1912	Panama Canal Act	Prohibited railroads from owning water carriers
Positive Era		
1920	Transportation Act of 1920	Established rule of ratemaking; pooling and joint use of terminals allowed; began recapture clause
1933	Emergency Transportation Act	Financial assistance to railroads
Intermodal Era		
1935	Motor Carrier Act	Federal regulation of trucking similar to railroads
1938	Civil Aeronautics Act	Federal regulation of air carriers; established Civil Aeronautics Board (CAB)
1940	Transportation Act	Provided for federal regulation of water carriers; declaration of national transportation policy
1942	Freight Forwarder Act	Federal regulation of surface freight forwarders

Table 11A.1	Continued	
1948	Reed-Bulwinkle Act	Antitrust immunity for joint ratemaking
1958	Transportation Act	Eliminated umbrella (protective) ratemaking; provided financial aid to railroads
1966	Department of Transportation Act	Established U.S. Department of Transportation
1970	Rail Passenger Service Act	Established Amtrak
1973	Regional Rail Reorganization Act	Established Consolidated Rail Corporation
Deregulation Era		
1976	Railroad Revitalization and Regulatory Reform Act	Rate freedom; ICC could exempt railroad operations; abandonment and merger controls began
1977	Airline Deregulation Act	Deregulated air transportation; sunset CAB
1980	Motor Carrier Act	Eased entry restrictions; permitted rate negotiation
1980	Staggers Rail Act	Permitted railroads to negotiate contracts; allowed rate flexibility; defined maximum rates
1984	Ocean Shipping Reform Act	Permitted greater tariff and contracting flexibility for ocean carriers and conferences
1993	Negotiated Rates Act	Provided for settlement options for motor carrier undercharges
1994	Trucking Industry Regulatory Reform Act	Eliminated motor carrier filing of individual tariffs; ICC empowered to deregulate categories of traffic
1994	FAA Reauthorization Act	Prohibited states from regulating interstate trucking
1995	ICC Termination Act	Abolished ICC; established Surface Transportation Board (STB); eliminated most economic regulation of trucking
1996	Maritime Security Act	Authorized a program to assist an active, privately owned U.S.-flagged and U.S.-crewed merchant shipping fleet
1998	Ocean Shipping Reform Act	Eliminated authority of shipping conferences over contracts; modified contract filing requirements
1998	Transportation Equity Act for the 21st Century	Allocated over $216 billion for the maintenance and safety of surface transportation
2001	Aviation and Transportation Security Act	Established the Transportation Security Administration
2002	Homeland Security Act	Moved Coast Guard and TSA into Department of Homeland Security
2010	Compliance, Safety, and Accountability Act	Created scoring system for motor carriers and drivers to promote safer operations
2012	Hours of Service Regulations	Limits truck drivers to 11-hour daily driving limit and 14-hour workday; specifies mandatory off-duty time

Source: John J. Coyle, Robert A. Novack, and Brian J. Gibson, *Transportation: A Supply Chain Perspective*, 8th ed. (Mason, Ohio: South-Western Cengage Learning, 2016), Chapter 3. Reproduced by permission.

Economic Regulation

The need for federal economic regulation of transportation is rooted in the significance of transportation to the overall U.S. economy. Transportation enables business to accomplish the very foundation of economic activity—the exchange of commodities from areas of oversupply to areas of undersupply. The transportation activity benefits all citizens; thus, it can be argued that the government should provide transportation just as it provides public interest functions such as the court system and national defense.

Traditionally, however, private enterprise has provided freight transportation. Fueled by the dollars that shippers spend, transportation companies commit to various transportation services; such resource allocation is more efficient than what a political allocation could produce. Since the free enterprise marketplace has imperfections that may allow monopolies to develop, government control of transportation attempts to allocate resources in the public's interest by maintaining and enforcing the competitive market structure.

Despite arguments for economic regulation of the transportation industry, the regulatory cycle has come full circle to the point where most of the regulation adopted between 1887 and 1973 has been eliminated or reduced. Current federal economic regulation of transportation is very minimal, and marketplace forces are the major controls used to enforce a competitive market structure. Periodically, calls for governmental re-regulation of some transportation activities occur. For example, captive rail shippers with only one service option have called for increased government control over rates that are perceived as punitive. Thus far, legislative efforts to do so have failed.

The lessening of federal economic regulatory controls over transportation began with the passage of the **Airline Deregulation Act** in 1978. This act effectively returned the airline industry to a free marketplace by eliminating most economic regulation. The **Staggers Rail Act of 1980** and the **Motor Carrier Act of 1980** soon followed. These two acts eliminated most of the economic regulation for the railroad and trucking industries. The **Shipping Act of 1984** granted antitrust immunity to ocean shipping conferences in U.S. foreign commerce. These conferences were allowed to set prices and control the capacity available for the transportation.

Further reduction of federal power over the transportation industry occurred in the 1990s. The enactment of the **ICC Termination Act of 1995** eliminated the Interstate Commerce Commission, reduced or eliminated most economic regulation over motor and water carriers, and established the Surface Transportation Board to administer the remaining railroad regulations. The **Ocean Shipping Reform Act** of 1998 modernized and deregulated international ocean shipping.

The current status of federal regulation of the transportation modes is as follows:

- **Motor carriers**—All rate and tariff-filing regulations are eliminated except for household goods and noncontiguous trade (continental United States and Alaska, for example). The common carrier concept is eliminated, but the carriers are held liable for damage. All carriers may contract with shippers. Antitrust immunity is granted to carriers for collective ratemaking (e.g., joint publishing of a freight classification), and the carriers must provide tariffs (containing rates and rules) to shippers upon request. In essence, little federal economic control is exercised over these modes.

- **Railroads**—In theory, rail economic regulation still exists. The STB has jurisdiction over rail rates and rules as well as routes, services, facilities, and mergers. The railroads are subject to the common carrier obligations to provide service to all shippers; to not discriminate against persons, places, or commodities; to charge reasonable rates; and to be liable for damage to the goods. The filing of rail tariffs and contracts is not required. The railroad industry remains the most highly regulated transportation mode, but complete rate deregulation exists over certain types of rail traffic—inter modal freight, for example.

- **Air transportation**—In 1977, economic regulation of air transportation was eliminated; the marketplace determines rates and services. Safety regulation, however, remains a major thrust of federal controls over air carriers. Such safety regulations as the controls over the number of landings and takeoffs permitted at an airport indirectly determine the level of service provided by an air carrier and whether an air carrier can provide service to a particular airport (availability of landing slots).

- **Ocean transportation**—The Shipping Act of 1984 initiated the economic deregulation of the ocean shipping industry, removing the requirement for Federal Maritime Commission (FMC) approval of rates and conference agreements (ocean conferences are groups of carriers that band together to set common prices). The Ocean Shipping Reform Act of 1998 transformed the industry from a common carriage focus with required rate filings to a contract-based system in which pricing is kept confidential. It also greatly diminished the power of ocean conferences.

- **Freight forwarders and brokers**—Both forms of transportation are required to register with the STB, and the broker must post a $10,000 surety bond to ensure the carrier used will receive payment from the broker. However, there are no federal economic controls over the rates or services provided by these two intermediaries. A freight forwarder is considered a carrier and is held liable for freight damage, whereas the broker is not considered a carrier and is not liable for freight damage.

Safety Regulation

Noneconomic regulation primarily focuses on transportation safety, sustainability, promotion, and research issues. Established in 1966, the U.S. Department of Transportation (DOT) mission is to ensure a fast, safe, efficient, accessible and convenient transportation system that meets our vital national interests and enhances the quality of life of the American people, today and into the future.[2] DOT is now partitioned into 11 agencies reporting to the Office of the Secretary.[3] The primary DOT agency for each major mode of transportation is identified in the following paragraphs along with its key safety responsibilities.

The Federal Highway Administration (FHWA) addresses motor carrier industry issues. FHWA provides stewardship over the construction, maintenance and preservation of the Nation's highways, bridges and tunnels. FHWA also conducts research and provides technical assistance to state and local agencies in an effort to improve safety, mobility, and livability, and to encourage innovation.[4]

The mission of the Federal Motor Carrier Safety Administration (FMCSA) is to prevent commercial motor vehicle-related fatalities and injuries. Activities of the Administration contribute to ensuring safety in motor carrier operations through strong enforcement of safety regulations; targeting high-risk carriers and commercial motor vehicle drivers; improving safety information systems and commercial motor vehicle technologies; strengthening commercial motor vehicle equipment and operating standards; and increasing safety awareness.[5]

Two FMCSA safety initiatives that have created challenges for the transportation industry include modification of longstanding hours of service regulation that altered the amount of time that truck drivers can work each day. Confusion about and challenges to the rules, particularly rest period and restart provisions, continue. The **Compliance, Safety, Accountability (CSA)** initiative seeks to improve large truck and bus safety and ultimately reduce commercial motor vehicle crashes, fatalities, and injuries. Concerns regarding the scoring system used to target unsafe carriers have been raised. Data inconsistency, unfairness to small carriers, and a lack of correlation between safety scores and crash occurrences are frequent topics of discussion. In response, the CSA methods are being revised.[6]

The Federal Aviation Administration (FAA) seeks to provide the safest, most efficient aerospace system in the world.[7] Major responsibilities of the FAA include regulation of air safety, promotion of air commerce, and monitoring of air space. In its safety role, FAA issues and enforces regulations and minimum standards covering manufacturing, operating, and maintaining aircraft, operates the airspace, air navigation facilities, and manages air traffic, and conducts safety research and development activities.

The Federal Railroad Administration's (FRA) mission is to enable the safe, reliable, and efficient movement of people and goods for a strong America, now and in the future. This mission is accomplished through issuance, implementation, and enforcement of safety regulations, selective investment in rail corridors across the country, and research and technology development.[8]

The Maritime Administration (MARAD) is responsible for promoting the development and maintenance of an adequate, well-balanced United States merchant marine, sufficient to carry the Nation's domestic waterborne commerce and a substantial portion of its waterborne foreign commerce, and capable of service as a naval and military auxiliary in time of war or national emergency. The Maritime Administration also seeks to ensure that the United States maintains adequate shipbuilding and repair services, efficient ports, effective inter-modal water and land transportation systems, and reserve shipping capacity for use in time of national emergency.[9]

Other safety-focused agencies include the Pipeline and Hazardous Materials Safety Administration, the Federal Transit Administration, and the National Transportation Safety Board. The Environmental Protection Agency plays a key role in setting sustainability standards for the transportation industry.

SUMMARY

Regulation is a dynamic component of the transportation process that is always subject to change. While we are currently in a time of limited economic regulation, governments actively develop transportation policies and regulations to address safety, security, and environmental challenges; meet societal requirements; and adapt to technological change. The intention of such regulation is positive but can have a major impact on the cost, time, and ease with which product flows across the supply chain. Thus, transportation managers must remain vigilant and factor current and pending legislation into their planning processes.

NOTES

1. For an extensive discussion of economic regulation, see John J. Coyle, Robert A. Novack, and Brian J. Gibson, *Transportation: A Global Supply Chain Perspective*, 8th ed. (Mason, Ohio: South-Western Cengage Learning, 2016), Chapter 3.

2. U.S. Department of Transportation, *About Us* (September 28, 2015). Retrieved October 25, 2015 from http://www.transportation.gov/mission/about-us

3. For more information regarding these U.S. DOT agencies and links to their websites, see http://www.transportation.gov/administrations

4. Federal Highway Administration, About (September 17, 2012). Retrieved October 25, 2015 from http://www.fhwa.dot.gov/about/

5. Federal Motor Carrier Safety Administration, *Our Mission* (January 14, 2014). Retrieved October 25, 2015 from https://cms.fmcsa.dot.gov/mission/about-us

6. Federal Motor Carrier Safety Administration, *How Does CSA Work?* Retrieved October 25, 2015 from https://csa.fmcsa.dot.gov/about/csa_how.aspx

7. Federal Aviation Administration, *Mission* (April 23, 2010). Retrieved October 25, 2015 from http://www.faa.gov/about/mission/

8. Federal Rail Administration. *About FRA.* Retrieved October 25, 2015 from https://www.fra.dot.gov/Page/P0002

9. United States Maritime Administration, *What Does the Maritime Administration Do?* Retrieved October 25, 2015 from: http://www.marad.dot.gov/about-us/frequently-asked-questions/#q2

APPENDIX 11B

Basis of Transportation Rates

Transportation ratemaking would be a simple process if carriers sold all transportation services on a ton-mile basis, charging customers X dollars to move each ton of a product each mile. However, carriers do not operate in such a simplistic manner. Multiple factors are considered by carriers and their customers when determining the cost of moving a product from origin to destination. With 33,000 major shipping points in the United States alone, a countless array of commodities with unique characteristics, varying shipment sizes, and specific service requirements, ratemaking is very challenging.

Ratemaking is a sophisticated activity with tremendous efforts being made to optimize the negotiated price of transportation services. Customers recognize the need for carriers to charge rates that earn a reasonable profit margin, or the carrier will not be in business over the long run. This section discusses primary factors that drive the transportation rate development process. To ensure that transportation rates are fair and reasonable for both parties, the following issues must be considered: (1) the cost and value of service, which affect the different rates the carrier establishes for different commodities; (2) the distance between origin and destination; (3) the weight of the shipment; (4) the characteristics of the commodity being transported; and (5) the level of service required.

Cost of Service

Basing rates on the **cost of service** considers the supply side of pricing. The cost of supplying the service establishes the floor for a rate; that is, the supply cost permits the carrier's viability by providing the rate's lower limit (see Figure 11B.1).

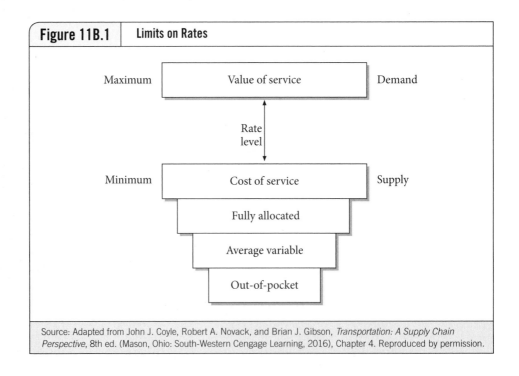

Figure 11B.1	Limits on Rates

Maximum — Value of service — Demand

Rate level

Minimum — Cost of service — Supply

Fully allocated

Average variable

Out-of-pocket

Source: Adapted from John J. Coyle, Robert A. Novack, and Brian J. Gibson, *Transportation: A Supply Chain Perspective*, 8th ed. (Mason, Ohio: South-Western Cengage Learning, 2016), Chapter 4. Reproduced by permission.

The question is: which cost basis should be used? Carriers have used fully allocated (average total) costs as well as average variable costs and out-of-pocket (marginal) costs. In essence, this sets up subfloors to the lower rate limit: the carrier will base the higher limit on fully allocated costs and the lower limit on out-of-pocket costs.

Common and **joint costs** also increase problems with using service cost as a basis for rates. The carrier incurs common costs when moving multiple loads but cannot directly allocate such costs to a particular shipment or customer. A joint cost is a particular type of common cost in which the costs a carrier incurs in producing one unit unavoidably produce another product. For example, moving a commodity from A to B unavoidably produces the movement capacity and cost from B to A—the backhaul. The procedure the carrier uses to assign these common and joint costs determines the cost basis, permitting latitude for cost variations and, consequently, for rate variations.

Value of Service

Value of service pricing considers the demand side of pricing. We may define value of service pricing as "charging what the traffic will bear." This basis considers the product's ability to withstand transportation costs. For example, in Figure 11B.2, the highest rate a carrier can charge to move producer A's product to point B is $0.50 per unit. If the carrier assesses a higher rate, producer A's product will not be competitive in the B market area. Thus, value of service pricing places the upper limit on the rate.

Generally, rates vary by transported product. The cost difference associated with various commodity movements may explain this, but this difference also contains the value of service pricing concept. For higher-value commodities, transportation charges are a small portion of the total selling price. From Table 11B.1, we can see that the transportation rate for diamonds, for a given distance and weight, is 100 times greater than that for coal; but transportation charges amount to only 0.01 percent of the selling price for diamonds, as opposed to 25 percent for coal. Thus, high-value commodities can sustain higher transportation charges, and carriers price the transport services accordingly—a specific application of demand pricing.

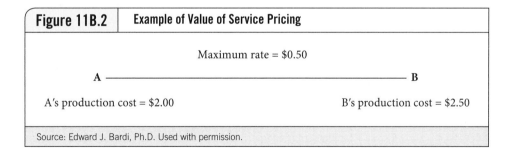

Figure 11B.2	Example of Value of Service Pricing

Maximum rate = $0.50

A ————————————————————————————— B

A's production cost = $2.00   B's production cost = $2.50

Source: Edward J. Bardi, Ph.D. Used with permission.

Table 11B.1	Transportation Rates and Commodity Value		
		COAL	DIAMONDS
Production value per ton*		$30.00	$10,000,000.00
Transportation charge per ton*		<u>10.00</u>	<u>1,000.00</u>
Total selling price		$40.00	$10,001,000.00
Transportation cost as a percentage of selling price		25%	0.01%
*Assumed. Source: Edward J. Bardi, Ph.D. Used with permission.			

Distance

Rates usually vary with respect to **distance**. Typically, the greater the distance the commodity moves, the greater the cost to the carrier and the greater the transportation rate. However, certain rates do not relate to exact point-to-point distance. An example is a **blanket rate** or **zone rate**.

A blanket rate does not increase as distance increases; the rate remains the same for all points in the blanket area the carrier designates. The postage stamp rate is an extreme example of a blanket rate. No matter what distance you ship a first-class letter domestically, your cost as the shipper (sender) is the same. In freight transportation, carriers develop zones that contain a particular area such as a city's commercial zone, a given state, a region, or a number of states, for example. In each case, the transportation rate is the same regardless

Figure 11B.3	Example of the Tapering Rate Principle

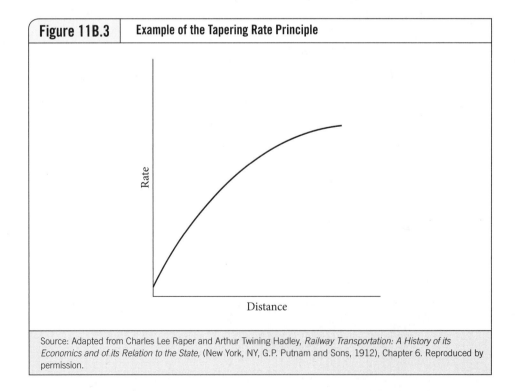

Source: Adapted from Charles Lee Raper and Arthur Twining Hadley, *Railway Transportation: A History of its Economics and of its Relation to the State*, (New York, NY, G.P. Putnam and Sons, 1912), Chapter 6. Reproduced by permission.

of the particular freight pickup or delivery location within the zone. FedEx, UPS, and other small package carriers use zone pricing to simplify the ratemaking process rather than treat every origin and destination point as a unique location for pricing purposes.

While transportation rates increase as distance increases, the increase is not directly proportional to distance. This relationship of rates to distance is known as the **tapering rate principle**. As Figure 11B.3 shows, the rate increases as distance increases, but not linearly. The rate structure tapers because carriers spread terminal costs (cargo handling, clerical, and billing) over a greater mileage base. These terminal costs do not vary with distance; as the shipment's movement distance increases, the terminal cost per mile decreases. The intercept point in Figure 10B.3 corresponds to the terminal costs.

Weight of Shipment

Carriers quote freight rates in cents per hundredweight (actual weight in pounds divided by 100 = hundredweight, or cwt) and determine the total transportation charge by the total weight of the shipment in cwt and the appropriate rate per cwt. The rate per cwt relates to the shipped volume: Carriers charge a lower rate for volume shipments and a higher rate for lower volume quantities. In essence, carriers offer a quantity discount for shipping large volumes. This is partly due to the fact that some of the basic shipment costs like document preparation, shipment pickup, and shipment delivery are spread over a larger amount of freight.

Railroads term these quantity discounts **carload (CL)** and **less-than-carload (LCL)**; motor carriers call them **truckload (TL)** and **less-than-truckload (LTL)**. The CL and TL rates represent the lower, volume rates; and the LCL and LTL rates denote the higher, less-than-volume rates.

One noteworthy exception to the rate–volume relationship is the **any-quantity (AQ) rate**, which bears no relationship to volume shipped. The rate per cwt remains constant regardless of the volume a firm tenders to the carrier for shipment; that is, no quantity discount is available.

Commodity Characteristics

Another ratemaking consideration is the type of product being moved. If carriers must make a special effort to protect freight, devote excess capacity to lightweight freight, or use specialized equipment to handle certain commodities, the cost of providing transportation service increases. The freight price must reflect the increased cost of the additional service to maintain profitability. Hence, carriers consider commodity density, storability, ease or difficulty of handling, and liability issues when developing freight rates.

Freight density reflects the weight *and* volume of freight. If a carrier developed rates on weight alone, bulky and lightweight products (e.g., potato chips) would move very inexpensively versus compact and heavy products (e.g., canned soups) even though the potato chips would take up far more space in the container.

To adjust for density, carriers charge higher rates per cwt for low-density products than they do for higher-density products. For example, air carriers and U.S. small package carriers compare the true weight of the freight and the dimensional weight of the freight (package length × width × height/166), using the higher of the two weights in the calculation of freight rates. This prevents low-density freight from commandeering critical capacity at unreasonably low rates.

Stowability refers to how the product being shipped will affect the space utilization in the container. Certain products ship well and waste little space (e.g., a computer monitor in a narrow box), while other products stow poorly and force a carrier to haul air (e.g., a fully assembled motorcycle). Products resulting in wasted space are typically charged a higher price per unit.

Ease of handling is another ratemaking consideration. The more that goods must be handled, the greater the cost to the carrier. Handling requirements may include repacking goods, cross-docking of LTL shipments, the use of specially trained labor, and the need for special handling equipment. Logically, products with unique handling requirements are charged higher rates by carriers to offset the costs involved in providing the services.

Carriers must also assess their potential liabilities when developing rates. The more susceptible a shipment is to loss, damage, or theft, the greater the carrier's risk. Fragile or easily damaged freight results in more liability claims from shippers. Hence, carriers develop higher rates for valuable products (e.g., appliances) and delicate products (e.g., light bulbs) to offset the financial risk of moving such products. Lower rates are afforded to sturdy products (e.g., wood flooring) that aren't likely to be stolen or damaged.

Efforts have been made to simplify these product characteristic issues. Rather than evaluating every commodity independently, classification systems have been developed to group together products with similar transportation characteristics for the purpose of ratemaking. For example, the trucking industry has long relied on the National Motor Freight Classification (NMFC) as a pricing tool that provides a comparison of commodities moving in interstate, intrastate, and foreign commerce. The NMFC groups commodities into one of 18 classes based on an evaluation of the four transportation characteristics discussed earlier. Together, these characteristics establish a commodity's "transportability."[1]

While the NMFC strives to simplify pricing, there is still a great deal of complexity to manage. Much of this is due to widespread class rate discounting strategies of carriers. To reduce the complexity, some industry experts advocate a product density–based pricing system similar to those used in Europe. Other experts suggest that the use of freight all kinds (FAK) rates that consolidate freight under one class is a time saving device and won't go away with revisions to the NMFC or shifts to density pricing.[2]

Level of Service

Another critical factor in transportation ratemaking is the customer's service requirements. The demand for faster and time-definite service is increasing in all modes of transportation. When a customer requires faster-than-normal service or guaranteed delivery times, carriers often need to break from their standard processes to accommodate the requirement. This could involve dispatching trailers before they are full, putting an additional operator and piece of equipment into service, deviating from normal routes, or a number of other exceptions. Any of these steps will likely reduce the efficiency of the carrier's operations and cause it to incur additional expenses. Thus, customers are charged premium rates to offset the additional costs created by their more demanding service requirements.

FedEx (and many other carriers) offers numerous service-level options and charges accordingly. The current non-discounted rates obtained from the FedEx Web site for moving a single large box weighing 15 pounds from Atlanta to Washington, DC are as follows:

- $157.00 for "FedEx First Overnight" service with delivery by 8:00 AM
- $125.89 for "FedEx Priority Overnight" service with delivery by 10:30 AM
- $121.78 for "FedEx Standard Overnight" service with delivery by 3:00 PM
- $52.32 for "FedEx 2Day AM" service by 10:30 a.m. on the second business day
- $46.01 for "FedEx 2Day" by end of business on the second day
- $39.34 for "FedEx Express Saver" by the end on the third day

As this example reveals, the rates vary even for a few hours time difference. Freight buyers must objectively evaluate their need for extremely fast service because they will pay a major premium for it.

SUMMARY

This appendix provides a primer on transportation ratemaking. It addresses the key factors that should be included in all rate development initiatives—cost and value of service, shipment distance and size, commodity characteristics, and service characteristics. While no ratemaking initiative can ignore these considerations, other factors may be added to the analysis, depending on the situation. An extensive discussion of freight negotiations, mode specific rate issues, and rate types (e.g., released value rates, deferred rates, and incentive rates) can be found in freight transportation textbooks.

NOTES

1. For more information on freight classification, visit http://www.nmfta.org/pages/nmfc.

2. "Density's Destiny," *SMC*[3] *Review* (July 2015): 8–9.

Part IV

The first three parts of this book have focused attention on the foundations and fundamentals of supply chain management, and the key elements of cross-chain logistics processes such as inventory, distribution, and transportation. Hopefully, by this time you have a useful appreciation for the role and importance of supply chain management and an awareness of the many factors, forces, and realities that significantly impact the ability of SCM to accomplish its goals and objectives. Also, an understanding of key elements of overall supply chain processes such as sourcing, operations, demand management, and order management and customer services, have added measurably to your appreciation of the supply chain concept.

Part IV refocuses attention on several key challenges that are of critical importance to the successful functioning of any supply chain in today's business environment. While these challenges have been of significant historical significance, they are quickly changing and are of great contemporary interest as well.

Chapter 12 addresses some of the key types of relationships in supply chain management and reinforces the importance of alignment of people, processes, and technologies to ensure that these relationships are successful. Included is a process model that provides a step-by-step approach to help develop and sustain sound relationships. The overall context of this chapter includes the need for alignment internal to an organization, and with suppliers and customers. Last, information is provided on the topic of using outsourced logistics services, and some guidance for effectively using asset-based providers of logistics services as well as 3PLs and 4PLs to help achieve supply chain objectives.

Chapter 13 provides an understanding of supply chain performance and financial analysis, and various methods to effectively accomplish objectives related to each of these. Discussions include the characteristics of good performance measures, and the various methods used to measure supply chain costs, service, profit and revenue. Income statements and balance sheets can also be very helpful, and use of the strategic profit model provides additional, valuable perspectives on the financial aspects of supply chains. These types of analysis also help to understand and quantify the likely impacts of supply chain service failures. The concluding topic is the utilization of spreadsheet software capabilities to analyze the financial implications of supply chain decisions.

Chapter 14 focuses on two of today's most important areas of supply chain management, that is, managing information flows and the use of technology. Considering the explosion of new technologies and analytical approaches that are now available, it is essential to develop a strategic plan for the use of available technologies to support the development, functioning, and evaluation of supply chains. While significant attention has been focused historically on the role of supply chains in moving physical products from point A to point B, it is now apparent that appropriate technologies are needed to support the best possible planning and execution for such moves. The chapter concludes with a commentary on critical issues impacting technology selection and implementation, and a discussion of innovations in technology that are increasingly impacting supply chains.

Chapter 15 identifies several critical challenges and areas of change for supply chains. The chapter begins with revisiting several key principles of supply chain management that have retained their relevance over time. The content updates our understanding of the critical role played by these principles in today's supply chains, and provides examples of how business organizations are currently using these principles to enrich their supply chains. Among the key areas of discussion for this chapter are: supply chain analytics; omni-channel; sustainability; reverse flows; 3-D printing; and talent management in the supply chain. This chapter, and the text itself concludes with a number of high-level "takeaways" that hopefully will serve as reminders of the importance of SCM and the increasing need to identify and implement new and effective ways to plan, manage, and evaluate supply chains.

Chapter 12

ALIGNING SUPPLY CHAINS

Learning Objectives

After reading this chapter, you should be able to do the following:

- Understand the concept of alignment and its importance to supply chain management.

- Understand the types of supply chain relationships and their importance.

- Introduce a process model that will facilitate the development and implementation of successful supply chain relationships to help achieve alignment.

- Recognize the importance of collaboration and collaborative supply chain relationships.

- Appreciate the potential importance of outsourced logistics services to supply chain management, and the types of value that may be created through the use of third-party logistics (3PL) providers and 4PL™ providers.[1]

- Examine the extent to which various outsourced supply chain services are used by client/customer firms and the types of benefits that are experienced.

- Discuss the role and relevance of information technology-based services to 3PLs and their clients/customers.

- Know the extent to which customers are satisfied with 3PL services and identify where improvement may be needed.

- Understand some of the likely future directions for outsourced logistics services.

Supply Chain Profile   *Why is Strategic Alignment So Hard?*

In today's fast-paced and customer-oriented business environment, superior supply chain performance is a prerequisite to getting and staying competitive. More intense competition among global organizations and global value chains are leading to substantial shifts in what is expected of the supply chain function. Currently, business leaders are demanding more from their supply chains, particularly competitive advantage.

These shifts in expectation force supply chain managers to focus on the entire value chain. It also has led to supply chains becoming a regular topic of conversation at the CEO and board level, with supply chain managers expected to deliver on a much wider set of metrics beyond the traditional cost and working capital. Gone are the days when the popular grails of supply chain management meant simply managing logistics and warehousing. The ability to put in place best-in-class planning processes compounded with the ability to respond quickly to changes on the execution front is becoming more and more critical.

It seems simple, but aligning process, functional, and individual goals with the company's overall direction has always been critical to the success of a supply chain. In the best circumstances, supply chains that have developed a competitive advantage actually work to create their company's vision and direction, not just respond to it.

For example, Amazon continually redefines the retail industry and shapes consumer expectations. Starting with its disruptions to the book industry and electronics retailers, Amazon continues to expand and remain pro-consumer. And with the proliferation of the Amazon effect, consumers now expect free shipping, next day delivery, best prices and large selections from both online and in-store channels. In fact, if we are seriously talking about transformation driving competitive advantage, we must acknowledge that Amazon owes much of its competitive success not only to its enhancements to the online shopping experience, but of at least equal importance, its innovation on supply chain and fulfillment capabilities.

If companies with supply chain operations tightly aligned with business strategy are more successful, why do so few actually try to implement this holistic alignment? One reason is that supply chain professionals may not be intimately familiar with the company's strategic directions, and also may be often too busy with day-to-day demands to worry about big picture issues such as strategy alignment. To begin making progress on this topic, it is essential to first identify what are the challenges and business benefits that can be gained through improved alignment of the supply chain with overall corporate goals, objectives, and strategies. For example, if an organization is focused on "Customer" as a strategic priority and is having challenges in providing the right level of customer service, customer order orchestration processes could be a great starting point to begin the transformation journey.

It is essential to consider that successful strategic alignment will involve capable resources in terms of people, processes, and technologies. A main focus needs to be on having the talent to implement, understand, customize, and extract competitive advantage. We also need to rely on data-driven approaches to decision making, which in turn can help drive transformation and competitive advantage for the organization.

Source: Adapted from Kavitha Krishnarao, *BPO Thought Process*, Capgemini LLC, July 4, 2014.
The original title of this article is "Aligning Supply Chain Strategy to Drive Transformation and Gain True Competitive Advantage."

12-1 Introduction

A distinguishing characteristic of successful supply chains is the ability to achieve "alignment" between people, processes, and technologies that are essential to the planning and operational aspects of supply chains. Essentially, alignment refers to a commonality of functionality and purpose that reinforces accomplishment of supply chain goals and objectives. Three example types of alignment are highly relevant to supply chain management.

- **Supply chain and organizational strategies.** Organizational success requires that the strategies, plans, and functioning of the supply chain are aligned with those of the overall organization. Sometimes referred to as "being on the same page," accomplishment of this objective will help to make sure that the supply chain reinforces what the overall organization is trying to accomplish.

- **Supply and demand.** Principally within an individual organization, alignment between supply and demand will help to maximize the extent to which products and services are available to customers when and where they are needed, and to minimize waste and inefficiency of resources throughout the supply chain.

- **Supply chain and trading partners.** Going beyond the boundaries of an individual organization, there are significant benefits to making sure that the organization, its suppliers, and customers are aligned. To the extent that this is achieved, there is a greater likelihood that improved efficiency and effectiveness of supply chain operations will be experienced.

As indicated throughout this book, many organizations have directed significant attention toward working more closely with supply chain partners, including not only customers and suppliers but also various types of logistics suppliers. Considering that one of the fundamental objectives of effective supply chain management is to achieve coordination and integration among participating organizations, the development of more meaningful "relationships" throughout the supply chain has become a high priority. Also, "collaboration" is viewed as a principal strategy to achieve alignment, and is closely related to the pursuit of effective relationships.

In the interest of examining the topic of supply chain alignment, the structure of this chapter first focuses on the types of supply chain relationships, and how to develop and implement successful supply chain relationships. Second, an in-depth look at the topic of collaboration will highlight how this process can become a valuable element of successful relationships. Last, we will study the importance of the 3PL industry in general and how firms in this industry create value for their commercial clients. The 3PL industry has grown significantly over recent years and is recognized as a valuable type of supplier of logistics services. So, it is essential that the functioning of 3PLs be aligned with the goal and objectives of the customer organization.

As suggested by the late Robert V. Delaney in his *Eleventh Annual State of Logistics Report,* relationships are what will carry the logistics industry into the future.[2] In commenting on the current rise of interest in e-commerce and the development of electronic markets and exchanges, he states, "We recognize and appreciate the power of the new technology and the power it will deliver, but, in the frantic search for space, it is still about relationships." This message not only captures the importance of developing logistics relationships but also suggests that the ability to form relationships is a prerequisite to future success. Also, the essence of this priority is captured in a quote from noted management guru Rosabeth Moss Kanter who stated that "being a good partner has become a key corporate asset; in the global economy, a well-developed ability to create and sustain fruitful collaborations gives companies a significant leg up."[3]

12-1-1 Intensity of Involvement

As suggested by Figure 12.1, the range of relationship types extends from that of a vendor to that a strategic alliance. In the context of the more traditional "vertical" context, a vendor is represented simply by a seller or provider of a product or service, such that there is little or no integration or collaboration with the buyer or purchaser. In essence, the relationship with a vendor is "transactional," and parties to this type of relationship are said to be at "arm's length" (i.e., at a significant distance). The analogy of such a relationship to that experienced by one who uses a vending machine is not inappropriate. While this form of relationship suggests a relatively low or nonexistent level of involvement between the parties, there are certain types of transactions for which this option may be desirable. One-time or even multiple purchases of standard products and/or services, for example, may suggest that an "arm's length" relationship would be appropriate.

Alternatively, the relationship suggested by a strategic alliance is one in which two or more business organizations cooperate and willingly modify their business objectives and practices to help achieve long-term goals and objectives. This type of relationship is more strategic in nature and is highly relational in terms of the firms involved. Also, benefits to the participating organizations include reducing uncertainty, improving communications, increasing loyalty, establishing a common vision, and helping to enhance global performance. Alternatively, strategic alliances can require heavy resource commitments by participating organizations, significant opportunity costs, and high switching costs.

Leaning more toward the strategic alliance end of the scale, a partnership represents a customized business relationship that produces results for all parties that are more acceptable than would be achieved individually. Partnerships are frequently described as being "collaborative," a concept that is discussed further at a later point in this chapter.

Note that the range of alternatives suggested in Figure 12.1 is limited to those that do not represent the ownership of one firm by another (i.e., vertical integration) or the formation

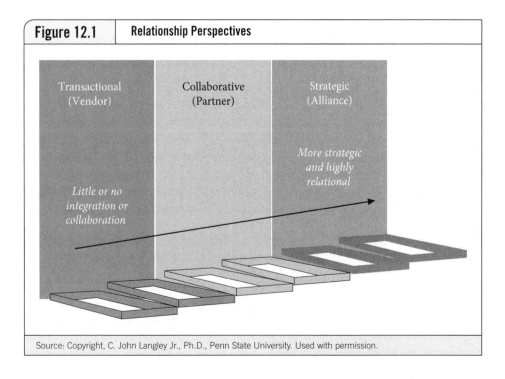

| **Figure 12.1** | **Relationship Perspectives** |

Transactional (Vendor)

Collaborative (Partner)

Strategic (Alliance)

More strategic and highly relational

Little or no integration or collaboration

Source: Copyright, C. John Langley Jr., Ph.D., Penn State University. Used with permission.

of a joint venture, which is a unique legal entity to reflect the combined operations of two or more parties. The concept of vertical integration typically implies significantly greater involvement than the partnership or strategic alliance. Considering that they represent alternative legal forms of ownership, however, they are not discussed in detail at this time.

Regardless of form, relationships may differ in numerous ways. A partial list of these differences follows:

- Duration
- Obligations
- Expectations
- Interaction/communication
- Cooperation
- Planning
- Goals
- Performance analysis
- Benefits and burdens

Generally, most companies feel that there is significant room for improvement in terms of the relationships they have developed with their supply chain partners. The content of this chapter should help to provide understanding of some key ways in which firms may improve and enhance the quality of relationships they experience with other members of their supply chains.

12-1-2 Model for Developing and Implementing Successful Supply Chain Relationships

Figure 12.2 outlines the steps in a process model for forming and sustaining supply chain relationships. For purposes of illustration, let us assume that the model is being applied from the perspective of a manufacturing firm, as it considers the possibility of forming a relationship with a supplier of logistics services (e.g., transport firm, warehouseman, etc.).

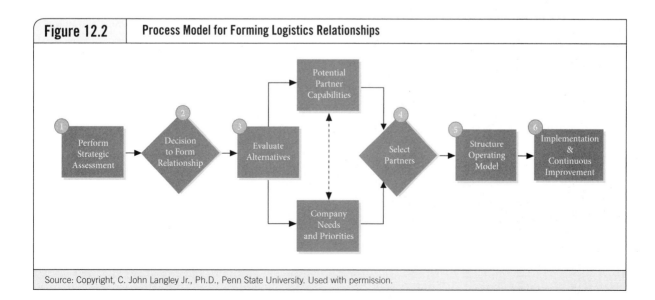

| Figure 12.2 | Process Model for Forming Logistics Relationships |

Source: Copyright, C. John Langley Jr., Ph.D., Penn State University. Used with permission.

12-1-2-1 Step 1: Perform Strategic Assessment

This first stage involves the process by which the manufacturer becomes fully aware of its logistics and supply chain needs and the overall strategies that will guide its operations. Essentially, this is what is involved in the conduct of a logistics audit, which provides a perspective on the firm's logistics and supply chain activities, as well as developing a wide range of useful information that will be helpful as the opportunity to form a supply chain relationship is contemplated. The types of information that may become available as a result of the audit include the following:

- Overall business goals and objectives, including those from a corporate, divisional, or logistics perspective
- Needs assessment to include requirements of customers, suppliers, and key logistics providers
- Identification and analysis of strategic environmental factors and industry trends
- Profile of current logistics network and the firm's positioning in respective supply chains
- Benchmark, or target, values for logistics costs and key performance measurements
- Identification of "gaps" between current and desired measures of logistics performance (qualitative and quantitative)

Given the significance of most logistics and supply chain relationship decisions, and the potential complexity of the overall process, any time taken at the outset to gain an understanding of one's needs is well spent.

12-1-2-2 Step 2: Decision to Form Relationship

Depending on the type of relationship being considered by the manufacturing firm under consideration, this step may take on a slightly different decision context. When the decision relates to using an external provider of logistics services (e.g., motor carrier, railroad, airline, ocean shipping, express logistics provider, 3PL provider), the first question is whether or not the provider's services will be needed. A suggested approach to making this decision is to make a careful assessment of the areas in which the manufacturing firm appears to have core competency. As indicated in Figure 12.3, for a firm to have core competency in any given

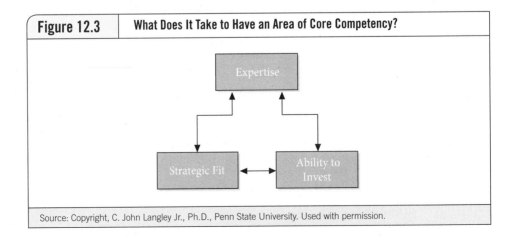

| Figure 12.3 | What Does It Take to Have an Area of Core Competency? |

Source: Copyright, C. John Langley Jr., Ph.D., Penn State University. Used with permission.

area, it is necessary to have expertise, strategic fit, and ability to invest. The absence of any one or more of these may suggest that the services of an external provider are appropriate.

In the relationship decision involves a channel partner such as a supplier or customer; the focus is not so much on whether or not to have a relationship, but on what type of relationship will work best. In either case, the question as to what type of relationship is most appropriate is one that is very important to answer.

Lambert, Emmelhainz, and Gardner have conducted significant research into the topic of how to determine whether a partnership is warranted and, if so, what kind of partnership should be considered.[4] Their partnership model incorporates the identification of "drivers" and "facilitators" of a relationship; it indicates that for a relationship to have a high likelihood of success, the right drivers and facilitators should be present.

Drivers are defined as "compelling reasons to partner." For a relationship to be successful, the theory of the model is that all parties "must believe that they will receive significant benefits in one or more areas and that these benefits would not be possible without a partnership." Drivers are strategic factors that may result in a competitive advantage and may help to determine the appropriate type of business relationship. Although other factors may certainly be considered, the primary drivers include asset/cost efficiency; customer service; marketing advantage; and profit stability/growth.

Facilitators are defined as "supportive corporate environmental factors that enhance partnership growth and development." As such, they are the factors that, if present, can help to ensure the success of the relationship. Included among the main types of facilitators are corporate compatibility; management philosophy and techniques; mutuality of commitment to relationship formation; and symmetry on key factors such as relative size, financial strength, etc.

In addition, a number of additional factors have been identified as keys to successful relationships. Included are factors such as exclusivity, shared competitors, physical proximity, prior history of working with a partner or the partner, and a shared high-value end user.

12-1-2-3 Step 3: Evaluate Alternatives

Although the details are not included here, Lambert and his colleagues suggest a method for measuring and weighting the drivers and facilitators that we have discussed.[5] Then they discuss a methodology by which the apparent levels of drivers and facilitators may suggest the most appropriate type of relationship to consider. If neither the drivers nor the facilitators seem to be present, then the recommendation would be for the relationship to be more transactional, or "arm's length" in nature. Alternatively, when all parties to the relationship share common drivers, and when the facilitating factors seem to be present, a more structured, formal relationship may be justified.

In addition to utilization of the partnership formation process, it is important to conduct a thorough assessment of the manufacturing company's needs and priorities in comparison with the capabilities of each potential partner. This task should be supported with not only the availability of critical measurements and so on, but also the results of personal interviews and discussions with the most likely potential partners.

Although logistics executives and managers usually have significant involvement in the decision to form logistics and supply chain relationships, it is frequently advantageous to involve other corporate managers in the overall selection process. Representatives of marketing, finance, manufacturing, human resources, and information systems, for example, frequently have valuable perspectives to contribute to the discussion and analysis. Thus, it is important to ensure a broad representation and involvement of people throughout the company in the partnership formation and partner selection decisions.

12-1-2-4 Step 4: Select Partner(s)

While this stage is of critical concern to the customer, the selection of a logistics or supply chain partner should be made only following very close consideration of the credentials of the most likely candidates. Also, it is highly advisable to interact with and get to know the final candidates on a professionally intimate basis.

As was indicated in the discussion of Step 3, a number of executives will likely play key roles in the relationship formation process. It is important to achieve consensus on the final selection decision to create a significant degree of "buy-in" and agreement among those involved. Due to the strategic significance of the decision to form a logistics or supply chain relationship, it is essential to ensure that everyone has a consistent understanding of the decision that has been made and a consistent expectation of what to expect from the firm that has been selected.

12-1-2-5 Step 5: Structure Operating Model

The structure of the relationship refers to the activities, processes, and priorities that will be used to build and sustain the relationship. As suggested by Lambert and his colleagues, components "make the relationship operational and help managers create the benefits of partnering."[6] Components of the operating model may include the following:[7]

- Planning
- Joint operating controls
- Communication
- Risk/reward sharing
- Trust and commitment
- Contract style
- Scope of the relationship
- Financial investment

12-1-2-6 Step 6: Implementation and Continuous Improvement

Once the decision to form a relationship has been made and the structural elements of the relationship identified, it is important to recognize that the most challenging step in the relationship process has just begun. Depending on the complexity of the new relationship, the overall implementation process may be relatively short, or it may be extended over a longer period of time. If the situation involves significant change to and restructuring of the manufacturing firm's logistics or supply chain network, for example, full implementation may take longer to accomplish. In a situation where the degree of change is more modest, the time needed for successful implementation may be abbreviated.

Finally, the future success of the relationship will be a direct function of the ability of the involved organizations to achieve both continuous and breakthrough improvement. As indicated in Figure 12.4, a number of steps should be considered in the continuous improvement process. In addition, efforts should be directed to creating the breakthrough, or "paradigm-shifting," type of improvement that is essential to enhance the functioning of the relationship and the market positioning of the organizations involved.

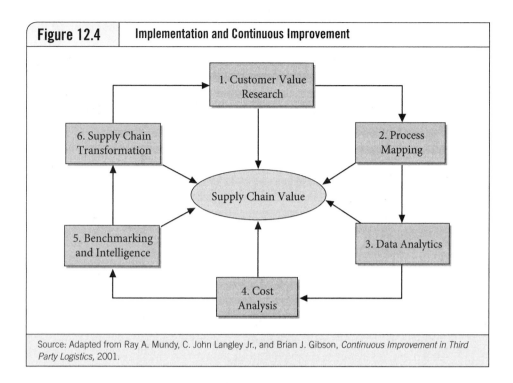

| Figure 12.4 | Implementation and Continuous Improvement |

Source: Adapted from Ray A. Mundy, C. John Langley Jr., and Brian J. Gibson, *Continuous Improvement in Third Party Logistics,* 2001.

12-1-3 Imperative for Collaborative Relationships[8]

Today's supply chain relationships are most effective when collaboration occurs among the participants who are involved. Collaboration may be thought of as a "business practice that encourages individual organizations to share information and resources for the benefit of all."[9] According to Dr. Michael Hammer, collaboration allows companies to "leverage each other on an operational basis so that together they perform better than they did separately."[10] He continues by suggesting that collaboration becomes a reality when the power of the Internet facilitates the ability of supply chain participants to readily transact with each other and to access each other's information. Although when we think of collaboration we often think of people working together, the concept extends to people, process, and technology.

While this approach creates a synergistic business environment in which the sum of the parts is hopefully greater than the whole, it is not one that comes naturally to most organizations, particularly those offering similar or competing products or services. In terms of a logistics example, consider that there was a time when consumer products manufacturers sometimes would go to great lengths to make sure that their products were not transported from manufacturing plants to customers' distribution centers with products of competing firms. While there may have been an underlying logic to this preference, it overlooked the benefits that could occur if the involved parties were more willing to collaborate and share resources in the interest of creating significant logistical efficiencies. It also makes sense, considering that retailers routinely commingle competing products as they are transported from distribution centers to retail stores. When organizations are unwilling to collaborate, real losses may easily outweigh perceived gains.

Most simply, collaboration occurs when companies work together for mutual benefit. Since it is difficult to imagine many logistics or supply chain improvements that involve only one firm, the need for effective relationships should be obvious. Collaboration goes well beyond vague expressions of partnership and aligned interests. It should mean that companies leverage each other on an operational basis so that together they perform better than they did separately. It creates a synergistic business environment in which the sum of the parts is greater than the whole. The following list includes several examples of elements of successful collaboration:

- Well-understood goals and objectives of the participating organizations and the collaboration
- Trust and commitment
- Organizational compatibility and communication
- Equitable sharing of gains and losses
- Benefits greater than going it alone
- Dedication to continuous improvement
- Strategic plan to provide direction to the collaboration

Figure 12.5 illustrates three important types of collaboration: vertical, horizontal, and full. Descriptions of these are as follows:

- **Vertical collaboration** (see Figure 12.5a) refers to collaboration typically among buyers and sellers in the supply chain. This refers to the traditional linkages between firms in the supply chain such as retailers, distributors, manufacturers, and parts and materials suppliers. Transactions between buyers and sellers can be automated, and efficiencies can be significantly improved. Companies can share plans and provide mutual visibility that causes them to change behavior. Examples of vertical collaboration include collaborative planning, forecasting, and replenishment (CPFR), sales and order processing (S&OP), and integrated business planning (IBP). Each of these approaches may help buyers and sellers to better align supply and demand by directly sharing critical information such as sales forecasts, point-of-sale information, etc.

    To be discussed in the next section of this chapter, providers of outsourced logistics services are also key participants in the supply chain. Typically, these organizations facilitate relationships between other organizations in the supply chain, and so they are very relevant to the concept of vertical collaboration.

- **Horizontal collaboration** (see Figure 12.5b) refers to relationships that may be buyer to buyer and/or seller to seller, and in some cases even between competitors (including providers of logistics services). Essentially, this type of collaboration refers to business arrangements between firms that have *parallel* or cooperating positions in the logistics or supply chain process. A horizontal relationship may be thought of as a service agreement between two or more provider firms based on trust, cooperation, shared risk and investments, and following mutually agreeable goals. Each firm is expected to contribute to the specific logistics services in which it specializes, and each works to integrate its services with those of the other providers of supply chain services. An industry example of this would be two or more suppliers that collaborate to help achieve greater efficiency and effectiveness of their supply chain operations. Other examples would include a transportation firm that collaborates with a contract warehousing firm to satisfy the needs of the same customer, and cooperation between a 3PL provider and a firm in the software or information technology business. Thus, these parties have parallel or equal relationships in the logistics process and likely need to work together in appropriate and useful ways to see that the customer's supply chain objectives are met.

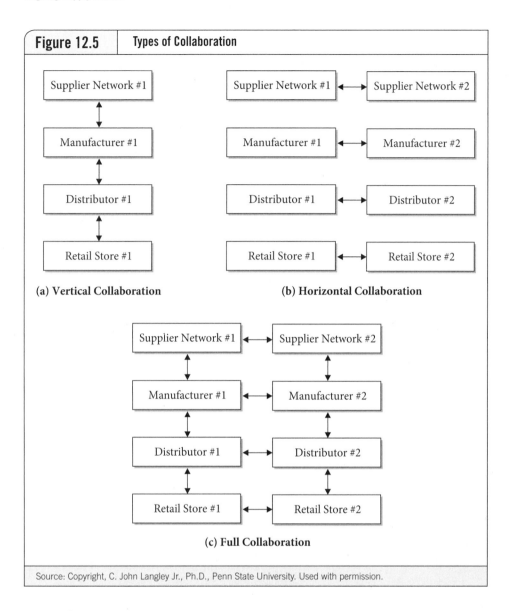

Figure 12.5 | **Types of Collaboration**

(a) Vertical Collaboration

(b) Horizontal Collaboration

(c) Full Collaboration

- **Full collaboration** (see Figure 12.5c) is the dynamic combination of both vertical and horizontal collaboration. Only with full collaboration do dramatic efficiency gains begin to occur. With full collaboration, it is intended that benefits accrue to all members of the collaboration. The development of agreed-upon methods for sharing gains and losses is essential to the success of the collaboration.

In practice, successful collaboration requires overcoming a number of barriers. Typical among these are resistance to change; conflicting business objectives; inconsistent goals and key performance indicators; lack of trust; unwillingness to share information; lack of managerial support; and turf protection. Alternatively, example benefits of successful collaboration may include focus on core competencies of supply chain organizations; increased sharing of information and knowledge; greater responsiveness to customers' needs; creation of competitive advantage over competing supply chains; and more productive and satisfying relationships.

One way of extending the logistics organization beyond the boundaries of the company is through the use of a supplier of third-party or contract logistics services. The following section provides some background information on how best to define this type of logistics provider and what services might be included.

12-2 Third-Party Logistics—Industry Overview

Although there are important distinctions in terminology, the term "third party logistics," or "3PL," generally refers to a broad range of instances where commercial organizations provide and/or manage logistics services on behalf of clients and customers. Over the past 20-30 years or so, the use of external, commercial providers of logistics services has become a routine way for organizations to avail themselves of needed logistics services. As a result, the 3PL industry has become well-developed, and the range of services available has become very comprehensive and responsive to the needs of supply chain users. While organizations still have the discretion to manage and provide these services on an internal, proprietary basis, the global markets for outsourced logistics services represent a significant resource available today.

As this evolution has been underway, firms have directed considerable attention toward working more effectively with their providers and managers of logistics services, in efforts to better serve their customers and work with suppliers, and to enhance the efficiency and effectiveness of their logistics and supply chain activities.

On the Line   *Collaborative Distribution to Achieve Strategic Goals*

In the April, 2015 issue of *Inbound Logistics*, author Lisa Terry provided a very excellent discussion of the topic of "Collaborative Distribution," which helps to maximize asset utilization, reduce transportation costs, and enhance customer satisfaction. Also, by creating operating efficiencies in the transportation area, collaborative distribution plays a key role in helping to alleviate the consequences of the driver shortages that are being faced. Among the various interesting examples highlighted in the article, the following provide useful insights into how supply chain improvements may be experienced through collaborative distribution.

- Well-known beverage company **Ocean Spray** used to ship product more than 1,000 miles from its Bordentown, New Jersey distribution center (DC) to another DC in Lakeland, Florida. Meanwhile, competitor **Tropicana** was sending refrigerated rail boxcars via the nearby CSX terminal to New Jersey. Wheels Clipper, a 3PL provider in Woodridge, Illinois saw the synergies, and proposed an intermodal lane from New Jersey to Florida using Tropicana's empty orange juice boxcars for Ocean Spray's southbound shipments.

- Frisco, Texas-based 3PL **Transplace** matched up two disparate customers with opposite problems but similar routes across the U.S.-Mexico border. Ceramic tile and natural stone provider **Dal-Tile's** heavy loads would weight out, while appliance maker **Whirlpool's** trucks cubed out. Each company used only 20 percent of capacity. Dal-Tile and its co-load partners—which now also include **Convermex**, a maker of plastic cups, plates, and utensils, and **Werner Ladder** with its aluminum and fiberglass ladders—have seen a consistent 20- to 30-percent net reduction in process and resource costs.

- Competing confectioners **The Hershey Company** and **The Ferrero Group** share joint warehousing, transportation, and distribution facilities, creating one North American supply chain. The goal is to improve supply chain efficiency, enhance competitiveness, and reduce carbon dioxide emissions and energy consumption, with fewer vehicles needed to move products to customers.

- **Tupperware** and **Procter & Gamble's** (P&G) European operations both manufacture in Belgium and were shipping significant volumes to Greece—Tupperware via trailers and P&G via intermodal. Tupperware was cubing out, while P&G would weigh out, according to a presentation by Europe's Collaborative Concepts for Co-Modality Project. By consolidating shipments via intermodal, the two companies improved container and weight fill from 55 percent to 85 percent, saved 150,000 truck kilometers, and realized a 17-percent savings in total lane costs.

As demonstrated by these examples, partners in a collaborative distribution project are sometimes in different industries, but more likely occupy different product spaces and share customers. CPG or auto parts suppliers make good collaboration partners because they are more likely to share consignees. Sometimes, different divisions of the same parent company come together to collaborate. In a few cases, collaborating partners are direct competitors.

Source: Lisa Terry, "Collaborative Distribution—Taking Off the Training Wheels," *Inbound Logistics*, April, 2015, pp. 72–77.

12-2-1 Definition of Third-Party Logistics

Essentially, a 3PL firm may be defined as an external supplier that performs or manages the performance of all or part of a company's logistics functions. This definition is purposely broad and is intended to encompass suppliers of services such as transportation, warehousing, distribution, financial services, and so on. 3PLs also may offer additional services such as managing multiple types of logistics services, seeing that these multiple services are "integrated" or managed collectively, and providing "solutions" to logistics/supply chain problems.

Depending on the firm and its positioning in the industry, the terms *contract logistics* and *outsourcing* are sometimes used in place of *3PL*. While some industry executives take care to distinguish among terms such as these, each of these refers broadly to the use of external suppliers of logistics services. Except for the suggestion that the term *contract logistics* generally includes some form of contract, or formal agreement, this text does not suggest any unique definitional differences between these terms. Although most customers who use 3PL's choose to have some formal contract to define the terms of the agreement, it is interesting to note that there also are a number of companies that choose not to have formal contracts with their suppliers of logistics services.

Although the term 3PL is in everyday use, there are a number of participants who are involved in the buying and selling of outsourced logistics services. As indicated below, these may range from 1PL's to 5PL's.

- **1PL** – Shippers or receivers of product moved through supply chain.
- **2PL** – Asset-based logistics providers that physically move product through the supply chain (e.g., motor carriers; railroads; airlines and air cargo; ocean vessels; pipelines; etc.). Many of these alternatives were discussed in detail in Chapter 11 on the topic of Transportation.

- **3PL** – Firms that manage and/or provide logistics services on behalf of their clients and customers.
- **4PL** – Firms that provide broader scope of services to help manage elements of the supply chain.
- **5PL** – Companies that aggregate demands of 3PLs into bulk volumes to negotiate better rates with logistics service providers.

Figure 12.6 illustrates the range of alternatives available to shippers and receivers of product moved through the supply chain. The alternatives begin with the possibility of "insourcing," where the needed logistics services may be provided on a proprietary basis by the shippers and/or receivers in need of these services. Then, in order of increasing strategic involvement, are alternatives relating to 3PLs, 4PLs, and "spinning off" or selling elements of the supply chain. A few more details on each of these may be helpful:

- **3PL** – Defined to include commercial providers or managers of logistics/ supply chain services, 3PLs typically provide services relating to transportation, warehousing and distribution center management, customs brokerage and clearance, contract logistics, freight forwarding, etc. Most of these organizations

Figure 12.6	Evolution of Outsourcing

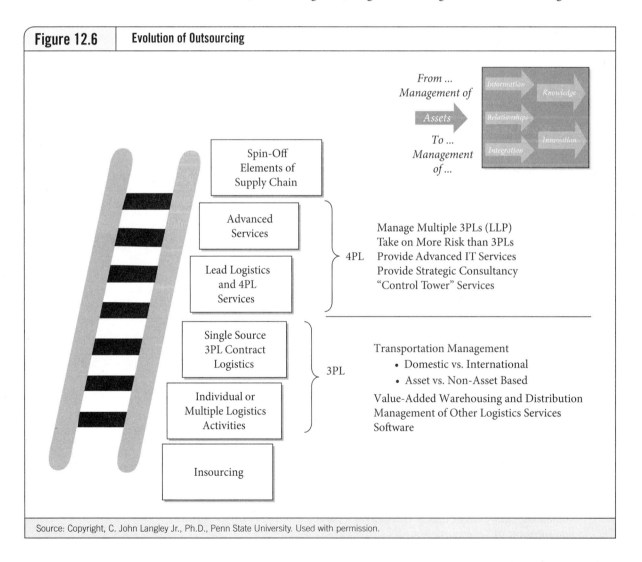

are non-asset based, meaning that the services they manage for customers are actually provided by asset-based suppliers such as trucking companies, warehouse operators, etc. 3PL providers typically manage one or more types of logistics/supply chain services, or perhaps are engaged as single-source providers of logistics services (which refers to managing all logistics services needed by their clients and customers).

- **4PL** – These providers not only provide a broader scope of services to their clients and customers, but typically may be more strategically involved than 3PLs would be. Essentially a supply chain integrator, a 4PL may be thought of as a firm that "assembles and manages the resources, capabilities, and technology of its own organization with those of complementary service providers to deliver a comprehensive supply chain solution.[11] As indicated in Figure 12.6, some of the value-adding services offered by 4PLs include managing multiple providers of 3PL services (i.e., LLP or lead logistics provider); taking on more risk than 3PLs (e.g., taking an equity involvement in inventory ownership); providing advanced IT services; strategic consulting; and "control tower" services that provide comprehensive visibility throughout the supply chain.

- **"Spin-Off" Elements of Supply Chain** – This is a more recent innovation that would occur when a firm divests itself of, or "sells" elements of its supply chain to another organization for reasons typically relating to core competency. Examples of this would include Tommy Hilfiger, Inc., and Liz Claiborne, Inc. selling the supply side of their businesses to Hong Kong based Li & Fung, Inc. The latter is a global expert in sourcing and manufacturing, and there are an increasing number of organizations who are making change of ownership arrangements with Li & Fung to enhance overall organizational and supply chain performance.

12-2-2 Example Services of 3PL Providers

Although there is no shortage of "niche" providers of specific types of 3PL services, a more general trend has been for 3PLs to provide a more comprehensive range of logistics and supply chain services. Among these are transportation, contract logistics, freight forwarding, financial, and information-related services. In recent editions of this text, we have provided a detailed historical perspective on the growth and development of individual types of 3PLs, but this has become less relevant today as many of the current 3PL organizations have grown well beyond the scope of their predecessor organizations. To provide a little background, however, the following notes try to capture the essence of how some of today's 3PLs came into being:

- **Transportation** – Included among the 3PL providers who were founded as a subsidiary or major division of a large transportation firm are companies such as FedEx Supply Chain Services, UPS Supply Chain Solutions, DHL, Ryder Supply Chain Solutions, Schneider logistics, and Penske Logistics. Although it has grown into a highly-diversified supply chain services organization, XPO Logistics, Inc. also would be an example of this type of provider.

- **Contract Logistics** – Generally referring to services relating to warehousing and distribution, examples of organizations that now provide a broad range of supply chain solutions include CEVA Logistics, DSC Logistics, Exel/DHL, Geodis, Penske Logistics, Saddle Creek Corporation, etc. Experience has indicated that these facility-based operators have found the transition to integrated logistics services to be less complex than have the transportation providers.

- **Freight Forwarding** – This logistics activity is essential to the daily flow of global commerce, and involves a wide range of organizations that purchase shipping capacity from asset-based providers and then re-sell to supply chain customers. Examples include C.H. Robinson, DHL, DSV, Expeditors, Hub Group, and Kuehne & Nagel.

- **Financial** – Included are firms providing services such as freight payment and auditing, cost accounting and control, tools for managing shipment visibility, information, and tracking, and consulting and advisory services. Some of the providers in this category include Tranzact Technologies, CTSI, and Cass Information Systems.

- **Information-Related** – In recent years, growth and development of Internet-based, business-to-business, electronic markets for transportation and logistics services have been significant. Since these resources effectively represent alternative sources for those in need of purchasing transportation and logistics services, they may be thought of as a newer, innovative type of third-party provider. As an example, Transplace, Inc. focuses on applying advanced 3PL efficiencies through the use of customized solutions and technologies that scale to the business needs of its customers.

- **Corporate Subsidiaries** – Principal examples of 3PL organizations that initially were divisions or subsidiaries of manufacturing or distributor organizations include Neovia, Inc. (formerly Caterpillar Logistics), IBM Global Business Services, and Odyssey Logistics (founded through merger of Rely Software, Inc. and the former logistics department of Union Carbide Corporation). While the idea that a 3PL firm may emerge from a corporate logistics organization is an interesting one, not all of these conversions have been as successful commercially as the ones listed here.

12-2-3 Global 3PL Market Size and Scope

Global markets and global trade needs continue to evolve, and this translates directly into demand for logistics and supply chain services. Table 12.1 provides global 3PL revenues by region for 2013 and 2014 from Armstrong & Associates, plus a summary of percentage changes in these revenues reported for 2013 to 2014 and the two previous years, and compounded annual growth rates (CAGR) by region for 2006 to 2014.[12] While the CAGR figures for Asia-Pacific and South America are around or near 10 percent, results for North America are 4.3 percent, and those for Europe are slightly in the positive. Looking at the percentage changes in global 3PL revenues by region from 2013 to 2014, and particularly in comparison with the percentages changes reported in the two previous years, positive growth rates were evidenced in North America, Europe and Asia-Pacific, whereas a decline of 6.7 percent was reported for South America. With the exception of the most recent results in South America, the growth rates in the other regions are consistent with modest improvement in other global economies.

Figure 12.7 provides a nearly 20-year look at annual gross revenue/turnover data for the U.S. 3PL market. As indicated, gross revenues were US$56.6 billions in 2000 and increased about three-fold to US$157.2 billions in 2014. Estimates at that time were for this figure to increase to estimated US$195.8 billions in 2018. Interestingly, there has been a steady increase in annual gross revenues over this time frame, with the only exception being the lower revenue figure for 2009 during which the United States was dealing with a recessionary economic environment.

Table 12.1	Global 3PL Revenues Exhibit Modest Growth for 2013–2014					
REGION	**2013 GLOBAL 3PL REVENUES (US$BILLIONS)**	**2014 GLOBAL 3PL REVENUES (US$BILLIONS)**	**PERCENT CHANGE 2013 TO 2014**	**PERCENT CHANGE 2012 TO 2013**[a]	**PERCENT CHANGE 2011 TO 2012**[b]	**CAGR 2006–2014**
North America	$ 177.3	$ 187.6	+ 5.8%	+ 2.9%	+ 6.7%	+ 4.3%
Europe	158.1	174.4	+ 10.3%	+ .01%	– 2.6%	+ 0.7%
Asia-Pacific	255.6	269.6	+ 5.5%	+ 5.3%	+ 23.6%	+ 10.2%
South America	44.9	41.9	– 6.7%	+ 3.0%	+ 12.4%	+ 8.1%
Other Regions	69.0	77.2	+ 11.9%	– .01%	+ 6.4%	
Total	**$ 704.9**	**$ 750.7**	**+ 6.5%**	**+ 2.7%**	**+ 9.9%**	

[a] Source: 2015 19th Annual 3PL Study and © 2014 Armstrong & Associates, Inc.

[b] Source: 2014 18th Annual 3PL Study and © 2013 Armstrong & Associates, Inc.

Copyright © 2015 Armstrong & Associates, Inc., Used with Permission.

Figure 12.7	U.S. 3PL Market 2000–2018E (US$ Billions)

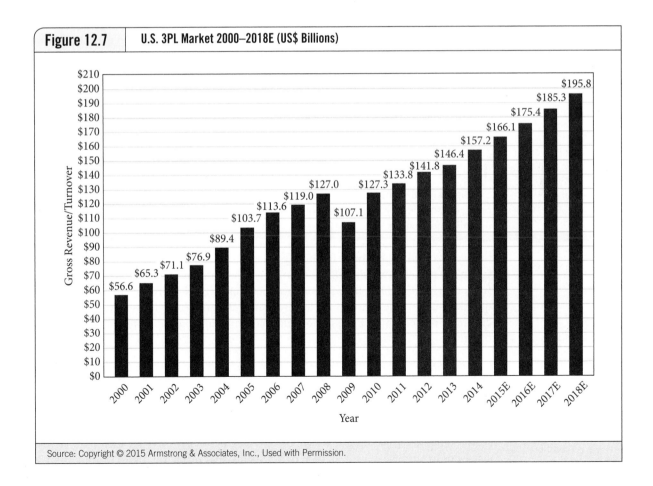

Source: Copyright © 2015 Armstrong & Associates, Inc., Used with Permission.

12-3 Third-Party Logistics Research Study—Industry Details

One significant, ongoing research study, *Third-Party Logistics: The State of Logistics Outsourcing*, is conducted annually by Dr. C. John Langley Jr. of Penn State University and Capgemini Consulting. The *2016 Twentieth Annual Third-Party Logistics Study* provides a comprehensive look at the 3PL industry from the perspectives of users and providers of 3PL services on a global basis.[13] The annual studies provide a continuing source of information on the state of the 3PL industry, and they also address timely, special topics that are relevant to both users and providers of 3PL services.

The principal vehicles for gathering perspectives for use in the annual 3PL studies include the following:

- A survey of global users and providers of 3PL services, administered through the Internet. The intended recipients of the surveys are those involved in the management and leadership of logistics/supply chain activities at customer firms, and executive-level contact at 3PL organizations. The customer surveys include a wide variety of prominent industries.

- Focus interviews with experts who are involved in the purchase, use, or provision of 3PL services, and other experts from industry, consulting, and academia who have valuable knowledge and perspective on the topics of interest. These focus interviews are conducted both in-person and by telephone, and they have proved to be a very valuable source of information.

- Workshops with users of 3PLs in selected cities such as New York, Boston, Chicago, San Francisco, Singapore, Shanghai, Sydney, Amsterdam, Paris, Berlin, and Utrecht (Netherlands). Some of these events were conducted at Accelerated Solutions Environment (ASE) facilities operated by Capgemini in prominent global locations.[14]

12-3-1 Profile of Logistics Outsourcing Activities

Figure 12.8 summarizes the use of specific logistics services that were reported as being outsourced by respondents on a global basis in the *2016 Annual 3PL Study*. Based on this information, the logistics services most frequently outsourced are those that are more operational, transactional, and repetitive in nature. Looking at the results over all of the regions studied, the most frequently outsourced services include domestic transportation (80 percent), warehousing (66 percent), international transportation (60 percent), freight forwarding (48 percent), and customs brokerage (45 percent). Responses to this question support the idea that the less frequently outsourced logistics services tend to be customer-related, involve the use of information technology, and are more strategic in nature.

A strategic issue is how customers feel that 3PLs should position themselves in terms of depth and breadth of service offerings. Based on findings reported over recent years of the study, users of 3PL services indicate significant agreement with the statement that "third-party suppliers should provide a broad, comprehensive set of service offerings" and disagreement with the statement that "third-party suppliers should focus on a limited range of service offerings." This suggests the continued relevance of customer preferences in certain situations for a single-source solution or a "lead logistics manager" role to the provision of integrated logistics services.

| Figure 12.8 | Customers Outsource a Wide Range of Logistics Services |

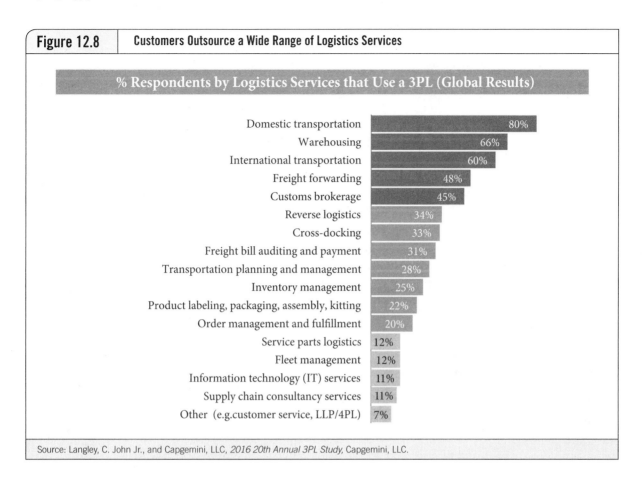

Source: Langley, C. John Jr., and Capgemini, LLC, *2016 20th Annual 3PL Study*, Capgemini, LLC.

12-3-1-1 3PL User Spending Patterns on Logistics and 3PL Services

According to findings from the *2016 20th Annual 3PL Study*, 3PL users reported an average of 50 percent of their total logistics expenditures are related to outsourcing. This compares with an average of 36 percent reported in the previous year, and 44 percent in the year before.[15] Total logistics expenditures include transportation, distribution, warehousing, and value-added services.

12-3-1-2 Benefits of Using 3PLs[16]

The *2016 3PL Study* showed that 70 percent of those who use logistics services (shippers) and 85 percent of 3PL providers said the use of 3PL services has contributed to overall logistics cost reductions, and 83 percent of shippers and 94 percent of 3PL providers said the use of 3PLs has contributed to improved customer service. Moreover, the majority of both groups—75 percent of 3PL users and 88 percent of 3PL providers—said 3PLs offer new and innovative ways to improve logistics effectiveness.

One of the relevant concepts relating to 3PL-shipper relationships is that of alignment, in that 3PLs and customers need to be in agreement on the ways they view their goals and objectives, roles and responsibilities, and a wide range of strategic and operational matters. Among the key takeaways from recent years' global workshops was reinforcement of the importance of openness, transparency, and effective communication between 3PLs and customers; and the ability of both parties to be sufficiently agile and flexible to accommodate current and future business needs and challenges.

Also, the use of "gainsharing" and "collaboration" are still thought of highly by 3PLs and shippers as being useful activities in many relationships. Survey results from the *2016 Annual 3PL Study* suggest that 46 percent of 3PL users and 81 percent of 3PL providers agree that collaborating with other companies, even competitors, can achieve logistics cost and service improvements.

12-3-2 Strategic Role of Information Technology

Each year in the annual 3PL study, 3PL users and providers are asked "which information technologies, systems or tools a 3PL must have to successfully serve a customer in your industry classification." This question always produces interesting and insightful findings, and this year is no different.

Overall, the most-frequently cited technologies as being needed by 3PLs are those that have more execution and transactional-based capabilities. Examples include warehouse/distribution center management (WMS), transportation management planning and scheduling (TMS), visibility, EDI, and the use of web portals for updates and relevant shipment information. Essentially, these types of technologies tend to parallel the types of logistics services that were profiled in the preceding section of this chapter. Table 12.2 summarizes some of these more highly-rated IT capabilities.

Table 12.2	3PL IT Capabilities Viewed as Most Important	
SHIPPERS		**PROVIDERS**
1. Transportation management (execution)		1. EDI
2. EDI		2. Transportation management (execution)
3. Transportation management (planning)		3. Customer order management
4. Warehouse/DC management		4. Transportation management (planning)
5. Visibility (order, shipment, inventory, etc.)		5. Visibility (order, shipment, inventory, etc.)
6. Web portals for booking, order tracking, inventory, etc.		6. Web portals for booking, order tracking, inventory, etc.

Source: Langley, C. John Jr., and Capgemini, LLC, *2016 20th Annual 3PL Study,* Capgemini, LLC.

On the Line

Collaboration Technologies Facilitate 3PL-Customer Relationships

An article in the *Harvard Business Review* in 1996 suggested that "balanced scorecards" could be of significant value in aligning individual, team, and departmental goals. While this approach was met with success, today's supply chains are exponentially more complex…and alignment is even more elusive. As a result, there has been increased collaboration among supply chain participants such as shippers, carriers, and warehouse operators. To further help with these efforts, a new wave of cloud-based collaboration technologies has become available.

"Success lies in understanding and constantly improving your internal processes, especially those that impact customers," explained Elijah Ray, Executive Vice President of Client Solutions at Sunland Logistics, a South Carolina based provider of logistics services that does close to half of its business in the retail sector. "As W. Edwards Deming explained, you can't manage what you can't measure."

Ray is one to know, with his accomplishments including a Six Sigma Master Black Belt and extensive ASQ Certified Quality Manager training. "Sunland makes a point to align its processes with its customer commitments, so the customer is 'always first' in every workflow, scorecard and process," Ray added.

As explained by Bill Fisher, board member at Gap, Inc., diptyque and Lanetix, "with the costs of deploying cloud-based collaboration solutions lower than ever, shippers can work more closely with their logistics service partners to bring their common goals, plans and teams into even greater alignment."

Indeed, many supply chain innovators such as Sunland Logistics rely on cloud-based scorecards that include individual and team KPI's modeled after customers' service level agreements (SLA's). They publish operational dashboards on devices ranging from desktops to smart-phones, which map tasks to individuals based on their expertise. According to Elijah Ray, "our own 'internal LinkedIn' helps us identify the best person to work with our customers. This helps to assure the most relevant expertise is called upon to resolve a particular customer issue."

Bill Fisher applauds the early work of supply chain innovators. "The most successful retailers and manufacturers will be those that align their supply chains—from logistics service providers to carriers—in a unified plan, supported by agile, cloud-based collaboration apps."

Source: Adapted from C. John Langley Jr. and Capgemini LLC, *2016 20th Annual 3PL Study*, Capgemini, LLC, September, 2015.

Figure 12.9 focuses attention on the "IT gap," which is the difference measured each year between the percentage of 3PL users indicating that "IT capabilities are a necessary element of 3PL expertise," and the percentage reporting that they are "satisfied with 3PL IT capabilities." Although the IT gap has narrowed significantly over the time frame indicated, findings from recent years suggest modest decreases in the size of the gap, but it is

| Figure 12.9 | "IT Gap" – Where Do We Go from Here? |

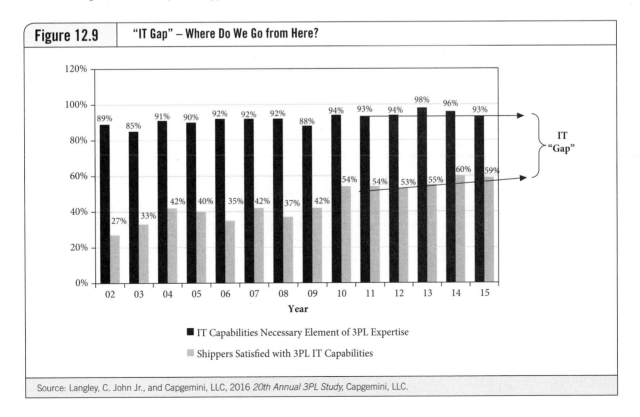

Source: Langley, C. John Jr., and Capgemini, LLC, 2016 *20th Annual 3PL Study,* Capgemini, LLC.

apparent that most shippers do not come close to using the full range of IT capabilities that may be obtained through their relationships with 3PLs. In attempting to analyze the causes of this IT gap, one factor that is significant is the complexity of IT-needs of the shipper organizations, and the extent to which their IT capabilities themselves need to be improved. Also of potential relevance is the relationship internal to the customer organization between the supply chain and IT process areas. The dynamics of this relationship can easily impact and influence dealings between 3PLs and customers regarding the topic of IT capabilities.

12-3-3 Management and Relationship Issues

The need for competency as it relates to the formation and continuation of successful relationships has become critical in today's 3PL industry. Although both providers and users of 3PL services have been improving in their ability to create more productive, effective, and satisfying business relationships, the media is replete with examples of failed relationships. The important question thus becomes "what can we do to improve in this area?"

An interesting finding from one of the earlier year's studies[17] was that the chief executive in the logistics area is the person who clearly is most aware of the need for 3PL services. While available evidence supported the fact that the president or CEO and the finance executive are many times involved with the identification of the need for such services, executives from other areas such as manufacturing, human resources, marketing, and information systems are also aware of such needs but to a lesser degree. If we look specifically at the task of implementing a 3PL relationship, however, it becomes apparent that information systems executives are becoming increasingly involved. This is not surprising, considering the key role of IT in many of today's logistics and supply chain processes.

An insightful topic is that of the "selection" factors that are important to customers as they choose 3PLs with which they want to work. Results of recent Annual 3PL Studies indicate that the most prevalent selection factors are price of 3PL services and quality of tactical, operational logistics services. Looking beyond these two selection criterial others of notable importance include geographic presence in required regions, expected capability to improve service levels, range of available value-added logistics services, and capable information technologies.

In addition, successful 3PL relationships establish appropriate roles and responsibilities for both 3PLs and client firms. While sometimes the use of a 3PL is interpreted simply as "turning over all logistics activities" to an outsourced provider, respondents to recent years' studies suggested that a "hybrid" management structure represents a highly effective way to manage 3PL relationships. Essentially, this reflects a desire on the part of the client firm to have sufficient power over operations for a track record of performance or "trust" factor to be built up. Although most client firms (appropriately) retain control over strategy formulation and direction setting for the logistics areas of responsibility, this hybrid approach to the management of operations is an innovative response to the challenge of successfully managing 3PL–client relationships. Table 12.3 provides a useful summary of some of the expectations that 3PLs and their customers have of each other.

A final issue relates to how customers think of their 3PLs. Approximately two-thirds of customers think of their 3PLs as providers of tactical or operational services, while approximately one-third think of them as strategic or integrative. While it may be tempting to think that the strategic or integrative relationships are superior to or more advanced

Table 12.3	Expectations Setting Relative to 3PL Relationship Management	
CUSTOMERS' EXPECTATIONS OF 3PL PROVIDERS	**3PL PROVIDERS' EXPECTATIONS OF CUSTOMERS**
Superior service and execution (proven results and performance)	Mutually beneficial, long term relationship with company
Trust, openness, and information sharing	Trust, openness, and information sharing
Solution innovation and relationship reinvention	Dedicating the right resources at the right levels, including executives
Capable information technologies to support the relationship	Access to useful data to design solutions and provide desired services to customers
Ongoing executive level support	Clearly defined service level agreements
Service offering aligned with customer strategy and deep industry knowledge	Fiduciary responsibility and overall fairness relative to pricing

Source: Copyright, C. John Langley Jr., Ph.D., Penn State University. Used with permission.

than the tactical, the fact is that the best relationships are those that come closest to meeting the logistics and supply chain needs of the customer as well as the provider. While there are some excellent relationships that are strategic or integrative in nature, there also are some excellent examples that are tactical or operational and that conform closely to the stated needs and requirements of the customer.

12-3-4 Customer Value Framework

Generally, 3PL users across the global regions studied characterized their outsourcing efforts as having been successful. In fact, the percentages of users rating their relationships with 3PLs as being either "extremely" or "somewhat" successful typically falls in the range of mid-high 80 percent to low-mid 90 percent figures.

Based on views from 3PL users, however, there are a number of areas in which they encourage 3PLs to pursue opportunities for improvement. Several of these are as follows:

- Meeting service-level commitments
- Realizing cost reductions
- Avoiding "cost-creep" and price increases once the relationship has commenced
- Effective "onboarding" by 3PLs of new customer relationships
- Ability to form meaningful and trusting relationships
- Information technology capabilities
- Global capabilities
- Strategic management capabilities and consultative/knowledge-based skills

Overall, these opportunities suggests a need to meet service-level and cost objectives and to avoid unnecessary increases in price to the customer once the relationship has commenced. Also, it appears that some 3PLs need to improve in the areas of strategic management, technology, and knowledge-based skills. These suggest expectations by the customers that currently are not being met.

Table 12.4	Future 3PL Industry Trends
• Continued expansion, acquisition and consolidation of 3PL industry	• IT capabilities to become an even greater differentiator
• Expansion of global markets and needed services	• Increased efforts to update, enhance, and improve 3PL provider-user relationships
• Continued broadening of service offerings across supply chain, and broad-based business process outsourcing	• Increased adoption of shared service networks and sometimes collaborative initiatives with traditional competitors
• Two-tiered relationship models (strategic and tactical)	• Emphasis on relationship reinvention, mechanisms for continual improvement, and solution innovation
• Growing range of "strategic" services offered by 3PLs and 4PLs	

Source: Copyright, C. John Langley Jr., Ph.D., Penn State University. Used with permission.

12-3-5 A Strategic View of Logistics and the Role of 3PLs

One major accomplishment of the past 10 to 15 years has been establishing the validity of the logistics outsourcing model and specifically of the 3PL provider. As we look to the future, we already see increasing acceptance of the 4PL model, likely growth in expenditures by current users of 3PL services, and a growing sophistication in the outsourced business approaches that respond to a dynamic set of customer logistics and supply chain needs.

To conclude the discussion of outsourced logistics services as a key element of supply chain relationships, Table 12.4 identifies a number of trends that seem to characterize the future direction of the 3PL sector. Regardless of how quickly these trends become apparent, the topic of logistics outsourcing is likely to be central and critical to the future successes of logistics and supply chain management.

SUMMARY

- There are various types of alignment that are relevant and critical to the success of supply chain management.

- In terms of intensity of involvement, inter-firm relationships may span from transactional to relational and may take the form of vendor, partner, and strategic alliances.

- There are six steps in the development and implementation of successful relationships. These steps are critical to the formation and success of supply chain relationships.

- Collaborative relationships, both vertical and horizontal, have been identified as highly useful to the achievement of long-term supply chain objectives. An example of a vertical relationship is one between buyers and sellers, whereas an example of a horizontal relationship may be between individual suppliers of complementary products to a common customer.

- 3PL providers may be thought of as an "external suppliers that perform all or part of a company's logistics functions." It is desirable that these suppliers provide multiple services and that these services are integrated in the way they are managed and delivered.

- There is a growing need for 4PL relationships that provide a wide range of integrative supply chain services.

- Categorically, 3PLs may be thought of as transportation-based, warehouse/distribution-based, forwarder-based, financial-based, and information-based.

- User experience suggests a broad range of 3PL services utilized; the most prevalent are transportation, warehousing, customs clearance and brokerage, and forwarding.

- While nonusers of 3PL services have their reasons to justify their decision, these same reasons are sometimes cited by users as justification for using a 3PL.

- Customers have significant IT-based requirements of their 3PL providers, and they feel that the 3PLs are attaching a priority to respond to these requirements.

- Although most customers indicate satisfaction with existing 3PL services, there is no shortage of suggestions for improvement.

- Customers generally have high aspirations for their strategic use of 3PLs and consider their 3PLs as keys to their supply chain success.

STUDY QUESTIONS

1. How would you distinguish between the following terms: alignment; relationships; and collaboration?

2. What are the basic types of supply chain relationships and how do they differ?

3. How would you distinguish between a vendor, a partner, and a strategic alliance? What conditions would favor the use of each?

4. What does it take to have an area of "core competency"? Provide an example.

5. Describe the steps in the process model for forming and implementing successful supply chain relationships. What step(s) do you feel is (are) most critical?

6. What are some of the more common "drivers" and "facilitators" of successful supply chain relationships?

7. What is meant by "collaboration" between supply chain organizations? What are the different types of collaboration?

8. What are the basic types of 3PL firms, and which are in most prevalent use?

9. What are some example types of services that may be available from a 4PL provider?

10. What are some of the more frequently outsourced logistics activities? Less frequently outsourced?

11. Why do some firms choose not to use the services of 3PL firms?

12. In what ways are clients/customers counting on 3PLs for involvement with information technology-based services?

13. To what extent are clients/customers satisfied with 3PL services? What is the relative importance of cost, performance, and value creation as determining factors for evaluating and selecting 3PLs?

14. To what extent do clients/customers think of their 3PL providers in a strategic sense? What evidence suggests that this may change in the future, and what kind of change may be expected?

NOTES

1. 4PL and fourth-party logistics are registered trademarks of Accenture, Inc.

2. Robert V. Delaney, *11th Annual State of Logistics Report* (St. Louis, MO: Cass Information Systems, June 5, 2000).

3. Rosabeth Moss Kanter, "Collaborative Advantage: The Art of Alliances," *Harvard Business Review* (July-August 1994).

4. Douglas M. Lambert, Margaret A. Emmelhainz, and John T. Gardner, "Developing and Implementing Supply Chain Partnerships," *The International Journal of Logistics Management!* No 2(1996): 1–17. The content of this section relating to drivers and facilitators has been quoted from this excellent research article.

5. Ibid, 4-10.

6. Ibid, 10.

7. Ibid, 10-13.

8. For an overview of collaborative logistics, see C. John Langley Jr., Ph.D., "Seven Immutable Laws of Collaborative Logistics," 2000 (white paper published by Nistevo, Inc., now a part of Sterling Commerce, an IBM Company).

9. Ibid, 4.

10. Ibid, 2.

11. Accenture, Inc.

12. Armstrong & Associates, 2015. Note that this data was the most recent available at the time of publication of this edition.

13. Ibid.

14. Additional information concerning the Accelerated Solutions Environment (ASE) operated by Capgemini may be found at www.capgemini.com.

15. C. John Langley Jr., Ph.D., and Capgemini, *2016 Twentieth Annual Third-Party Logistics Study.*

16. Ibid.

17. C. John Langley Jr., Brian F. Newton, and Gary R. Allen, *Third-Party Logistics Services: Views from the Customers* (Knoxville, TN: University of Tennessee, 2000).

CASE 12.1

Quik Chips, Inc.

Founded in 2012, Quik Chips (QC) is a joint venture of five competing manufacturers of semiconductor chips used primarily in the production of smartphone and tablet technologies. Essentially, QC provides a full-range of e-Commerce and fulfillment services that help to meet customer demands for increasingly faster turnaround times for these very expensive chips. Although the concept of collaborating with competitors is relatively unique to manufacturers of semiconductor chips, it is not unusual for QC to provide supply chain services to common customers of its members.

Changes and Evolution of Mobile Technologies. Recent years have seen exceptional growth in the demand for smartphone and tablet technologies, and for apps that require an increasing range of chip types and capabilities that support functions of mobile devices such as user interface, texting, gaming, GPS, and other highly-interactive capabilities. This has resulted in a robust group of highly-competitive companies that produce these devices in a few principal geographic regions of the world, including Asia, South America, and Eastern Europe. Considering the need for more expensive, sophisticated chip technologies, these manufacturers have begun to place more emphasis on faster delivery times from their suppliers than on stockpiling inventories of chips to buffer against volatility in demand.

Concept and Capabilities of Quik Chips. Three structural components comprise QC's range of value-added services for its member manufacturers: (1) web-site hosting; (2) supply chain; and (3) logistical fulfillment. QC is a different kind of company in that it does not own, plan, release, or insure any inventory, and does not sell directly to the manufacturers of mobile devices—only its member-manufacturers do. These members provide QC instructions as to what to move and when, and then QC provides a turnkey fulfillment service to see that customers receive the needed chips when and where they are needed. Although the executive offices of QC are located in Singapore, distribution centers with foreign trade zone status are located in Shenzhen, China, Sao Paulo, Brazil, and Prague, Czech Republic.

QC also provides its member-manufacturers with e-Commerce capabilities through its web-hosting service that passes transaction data from customers to the chip manufacturers, using a standardized data format. This "common gateway" for the transfer of information facilitates the operations of the member-manufacturers and also for the customer firms that manufacture the mobile technologies.

Organization and Membership. QC is a not-for-profit organization that provides the types of services described earlier. Membership in the joint-venture is open to other chip manufacturers who must undergo a formal application process, pay a membership fee, and agree to use the services of QC for their shipments to customers. All members have full-access to the capabilities available at QC, and are assessed fees on a pro-rata basis to cover all the costs of the QC operation.

CASE QUESTIONS

1. Describe the elements of the value proposition for the member-manufacturers of Quik Chips. What would be the elements of the value proposition for the mobile technology manufacturers that are served directly by QC?
2. Identify some of the major sources of savings for member-manufacturers of Quik Chips?
3. To facilitate the success of this joint-venture, what are some of the way in which the mobile technology manufacturers should collaborate with QC and its members?

Source: C. John Langley Jr., Ph.D., Penn State University. Used with permission.

CASE 12.2

HQ Depot

June, July, and August are unusually challenging months for HQ Depot, when this Chicago-based retailer experiences significant demand for its products in response to the annual opening of schools and universities in the months of August and September. HQ depot is an omni-channel retailer of a broad range of office supplies and back-to-school items such as computers, printers, and accessories, in addition to more traditional items such as notebooks, filing folders, writing implements, etc. Most of the SKU's available at HQ Depot are imported from a number of emerging and developed markets, such as China, India, Vietnam, Philippines, and Mexico.

Given the very price-competitive market in which HQ depot operates, most of these imported products are shipped by containerships to U.S. west coast ports, and then transported to distribution centers in Chicago, IL, Henderson, NV, and Greenville, SC via intermodal and over-the-road truckload carriers. Most frequently, shipments from these DC's to individual stores, and to home and business addresses for e-Commerce customers, were fulfilled through a combination of truckload, LTL, and express services (particularly for time-sensitive deliveries).

HQ Depot was managing its transportation operations internally, but the company decided it wanted to focus on its core competency, which, according to its SVP Supply Chain, was "maintaining our leadership in the office and school supply industry." The company also wanted to centralize its transportation operations. Looking carefully at the issue of overall performance in the logistics and transportation areas, a significant amount of variability was found in the transit times and service reliability of its store and customer deliveries. Thus the idea of centralizing its logistics operations was consistent in the pursuit of uniformity and control in its fulfillment operations.

Additionally, HQ Depot had set an objective of improving service to some of its outlying stores and customer markets, which clearly would require expansion of its logistics network. According to HQ Depot's VP Logistics, an analysis had begun to study how long it would take and what it would cost to build up the company's transportation capabilities to be able to support such a network. As a key element of this process, a recommendation was being considered to using a 3PL provider to design and operate a system to better manage the transportation of products from DC's to locations of company stores and e-Commerce customers.

In addition, HQ Depot wanted to be able to reach markets for which it did not already have access, which would require expansion of its logistics network. According to the director of logistics, an analysis was undertaken to study how long it would take and what it would cost to build up HQ Depot's transportation capabilities to be able to support such a network. As a result, a recommendation was made to seriously investigate the use of a 3PL provider.

CASE QUESTIONS

1. What rationale is offered by HQ Depot in support of the idea of using a 3PL? Do you agree with the reasons cited for the interest in a 3PL?
2. Based on your understanding of HQ Depot and its business needs, what type of 3PL firm do you feel might be of greatest potential value in terms of a relationship?
3. What steps would you suggest be considered by HQ Depot as it begins to analyze the feasibility of forming a relationship with individual 3PL providers?
4. Once the selection process is complete, what kind of relationship do you feel would be most appropriate: vendor, partner, strategic alliance, or some other option?

Chapter 13

SUPPLY CHAIN PERFORMANCE MEASUREMENT AND FINANCIAL ANALYSIS

Learning Objectives

After reading this chapter, you should be able to do the following:

- Understand the scope and importance of supply chain performance measurement.

- Explain the characteristics of good performance measures.

- Discuss the various methods used to measure supply chain costs, service, profit, and revenue.

- Understand the basics of an income statement and a balance sheet.

- Demonstrate the impacts of supply chain strategies on the income statement, balance sheet, profitability, and return on investment.

- Understand the use of the strategic profit model.

- Analyze the financial impacts of supply chain service failures.

- Utilize spreadsheet computer software to analyze the financial implications of supply chain decisions.

Supply Chain Profile   *CLGN Book Distributors.com*

CLGN Book Distributors.com (CLGN) is an Internet company that began operation in 2001 for the sale and distribution of college textbooks and instructional materials. During the first few years, CLGN struggled with the normal technical glitches associated with an Internet-based company, but the concept of online purchasing of college textbooks proved immensely popular with college students. After obtaining information on the textbook(s) required for a course, the students would use their computers to place their orders, avoiding the dreaded long lines at the campus bookstore.

CLGN's original mission was to be a seller of low-priced college textbooks and instructional materials in the United States. The typical textbook price at CLGN averaged 15 percent below that of the local bookstore, and supplies averaged 20 percent lower. When the cost of shipping was included, the landed cost of the textbook was about 10 percent lower and materials 15 percent lower than purchases at the local bookstore. This lower cost and the convenience of online purchasing resulted in double-digit sales increases every year.

Beginning in 2002, CLGN made a profit and has done so every year since then. In 2015, CLGN had sales of $150 million with a net income of $10.5 million. This net profit margin of 7 percent was above average for business-to-consumer (B2C) Internet companies. However, net income as a percent of sales, or net profit margin, was lower than in the previous years. In 2013 net profit margin was 10.3 percent, and in 2014 it was 9.1 percent. This decreasing profit margin trend was causing considerable concern with top management and CLGN's stockholders.

Following release of the 2015 financial data, Ed Bardi, the CEO of CLGN, held a meeting with the executive committee consisting of the vice presidents of marketing, finance, information systems, and supply chain management. After reviewing the 2015 financial results and discussing the underlying causes for the lower net profit margin, each vice president was given the assignment of examining his/her respective area for process changes that would remove costs while maintaining the same level of service customers expected.

Particular attention was given to the supply chain area because supply chain cost increases exceeded those in other areas of the company. Dr. Bardi also pointed out that during the past year he had been receiving complaints from irate customers regarding late deliveries of orders and receipt of improperly filled orders (wrong items or not all items ordered). Lauren Fishbay, vice president of supply chain management, said she was aware of these problems and was working on solutions for order fulfillment problems as well as the escalating shipping costs. She said her area was developing plans to transition from measuring orders shipped on time and orders shipped complete to measuring the perfect order (orders received on time, orders received complete, and accurate documentation).

Following the executive committee meeting, Ms. Fishbay gathered her operating managers to review the situation and explore alternatives. She asked Tracie Shannon, supply chain analyst, to prepare financial data measuring the supply chain process. Sharon Cox, warehouse manager, was asked to examine the nature and cause of the order fulfillment problems and to suggest solutions. Finally, Sue Purdum, transportation manager, was charged with examining the rising transportation costs and longer, and less reliable, delivery times.

Prior to the supply chain operating managers' meeting, Ms. Fishbay received the following 2015 financial information from Tracie Shannon:

CLGN Book Distributors.com	
INCOME STATEMENT 2015	
Sales		$150,000,000
Cost of goods sold		80,000,000
Gross margin		$ 70,000,000
Transportation	$ 6,000,000	
Warehousing	1,500,000	
Inventory carrying	3,000,000	
Other operating cost	30,000,000	
Total operating cost		40,500,000
Earnings before interest and taxes		$ 29,500,000
Interest		12,000,000
Taxes		7,000,000
Net income		$ 10,500,000

CLGN Book Distributors.com	
BALANCE SHEET 2015	
Assets	
Cash	$ 15,000,000
Accounts receivable	30,000,000
Inventory	10,000,000
Total current assets	$ 55,000,000
Net fixed assets	90,000,000
Total assets	$145,000,000
Liabilities	
Current liabilities	$ 65,000,000
Long-term debt	35,000,000
Total liabilities	$100,000,000
Stockholders' equity	45,000,000
Total liabilities and equity	$145,000,000

Ms. Shannon determined that the inventory carrying cost rate was 30 percent of the value of the average inventory held per year. The corporate tax rate was 40 percent. Total orders in 2015 amounted to 1.5 million ($150 million in sales at an average sale per order of $100). She estimated the lost sales rate to be 10 percent of the service failures caused by late transportation delivery and 20 percent of the service failures caused by improper order fulfillment. The cost of a lost sale per order is the gross profit per order, or $46.67 ($70 million gross margin divided by 1.5 million orders).

Sharon Cox concluded that the cost of a service failure, whether caused by order fulfillment or delivery problems, resulted in an invoice reduction of $10 per order (to appease the customer) and a rehandling cost of $20 per order (to reship the order). Currently CLGN's order fill rate is 97 percent. The causes of the improper order fulfillment could be attributed to the lack of warehouse personnel training. In the current economic environment, it is very difficult to obtain experienced warehouse workers. Other problems could be traced to a lack of discipline regarding order-picking procedures and the computer-generated pick slip. At least $100,000 was required annually for ongoing training.

Sue Purdum traced the escalating transportation costs to the 35 percent increase in residential delivery rates charged by CLGN's ground delivery carrier for standard service (three to five days transit time). The residential delivery rates charged by other ground express carriers were comparable or higher. An alternative to reducing transportation costs was to switch to the U.S. Postal Service, but delivery times would increase and become less reliable. However, CLGN's current on-time delivery performance is only 95 percent because of the longer order processing times at the warehouse and longer transit times via the ground package carrier to residential delivery locations. By using the carrier's expedited ground service, CLGN could improve service and on-time delivery to 96 percent and increase transportation costs by 10 percent.

Given this information, Lauren Fishbay was pondering what actions she should explore with the operating managers in preparation for the next executive committee meeting. She knew whatever course of action she proposed had to be financially sound and provide the greatest benefit to CLGN's stockholders.

Source: Edward J. Bardi, Ph.D. Used with permission.

13-1 Introduction

The CLGN Book Distributors.com case highlights the need for all organizations to be able to measure supply chain performance and link that performance to its impacts on financial performance. Many organizations today have realized that performance metrics are critical to managing the business and achieving desired results. Many organizations want to do the "right things" (effectiveness) and do them "right" (efficiency). However, simply stating those two objectives is not adequate unless there are specific, measurable metrics that enable the organization to gauge whether or not these objectives are achieved.

The purpose of this chapter is to (1) introduce the dimensions of supply chain performance metrics, (2) discuss how supply chain metrics are developed, (3) offer some methods for classifying supply chain metrics, and (4) develop quantitative tools to show how these metrics can be linked to the financial performance of the organization.

13-2 Dimensions of Supply Chain Performance Metrics

Before beginning a discussion of the dimensions of supply chain metrics, it is important to answer two questions. First, what are the differences among a measure, a metric, and an index? Traditionally, the term *measure* was used to denote any quantitative output of an activity or process. Today, the term *metric* is being used more often in place of the term *measure*. What is the difference? A **measure** is easily defined with no calculations and with simple dimensions. Logistics examples would include units of inventory and back-order dollars. A **metric** is more complex to define and usually involves a calculation or a combination of measurements, often in the form of a ratio. Logistics examples would include inventory future days of supply, inventory turns, and sales dollars per stock-keeping unit. An **index** combines two or more metrics into a single indicator. Usually an index is used to track trends in the output of a process. A logistics example of an index is the perfect order.[1]

Second, what are the characteristics of a good metric? Figure 13.1 is an excellent framework that can be used to determine the characteristic of a good metric. Several questions need to be asked to determine if a metric is appropriate for its intended use. A short discussion of the 10 characteristics in Figure 13.1 is necessary here to lay the foundation for the remainder of this chapter.

The first question to be asked about a metric is, "Is it quantitative?" While not all metrics are quantitative, this is usually a requirement when measuring the outputs of processes or functions. Qualitative performance metrics are better suited for measuring perceptions or assigning products or people to categories (e.g., excellent, good, poor). Qualitative metrics are backed up with quantitative data. For example, a transportation carrier might be rated "excellent" if it has only one late delivery for every 100 attempts.

The second question to be asked about a metric is, "Is it easy to understand?" This question is directly related to the fifth question, "Is it defined and mutually understood?" Experience has shown that individuals will understand a metric if they are involved in its definition and calculation.[2] For example, one of the most commonly used metrics in logistics is on-time delivery. This is also one of the most commonly misunderstood

Figure 13.1	**Characteristics of Good Measures**
A GOOD MEASURE	**DESCRIPTION**
• Is quantitative	• The measure can be expressed as an objective value.
• Is easy to understand	• The measure conveys at a glance what it is measuring and how it is derived.
• Encourages appropriate behavior	• The measure is balanced to reward productive behavior and discourage "game playing."
• Is visible	• The effects of the measure are readily apparent to all involved in the process being measured.
• Is defined and mutually understood	• The measure has been defined by and/or agreed to by all key process participants (internally and externally).
• Encompasses both outputs and inputs	• The measure integrates factors from all aspects of the process measured.
• Measures only what is important	• The measure focuses on a key performance indicator that is of real value to managing the process.
• Is multidimensional	• The measure is properly balanced between utilization, productivity, and performance and shows the tradeoffs.
• Uses economies of effort	• The benefits of the measure outweigh the costs of collection and analysis.
• Facilitates trust	• The measure validates the participation among the various parties.

Source: J. S. Keebler, D. A. Durtsche, K. B. Manrodt, and D. M. Ledyard, *Keeping Score: Measuring the Business Value of Logistics in the Supply Chain* (University of Tennessee, Council of Logistics Management, 1999), p. 8. Reproduced by permission from Council of Supply Chain Management Professionals.

metrics in logistics. Disagreements can occur between shippers and customers or between marketing and transportation. Research has shown that if all parties affected by the metric are involved in its definition and calculation, it will be easy to understand.[3]

The third question to be asked about a metric is, "Does it encourage appropriate behavior?" A basic principle of management is that metrics will drive behavior. A well-intentioned metric could very well drive inappropriate behavior. For example, if a warehouse manager is measured by cubic space utilization, he will try to keep the warehouse filled, which could lower inventory turns, drive up inventory costs, and result in product obsolescence.

The fourth question to be asked is, "Is the metric visible?" Good metrics should be readily available to those who use them. A distinction can be made here between a *reactive* metric and a *proactive* metric. Some firms state that metrics are available in the system for employees to see and use. However, this means that they must attempt to find them. These are *reactive* metrics. Leading firms, however, "push" metrics to metrics owners so they can react immediately. These are called *proactive* metrics. In both cases, metrics are visible. However, proactive metrics will be acted upon more quickly because employees need little or no effort to see them.[4]

The fifth question to be asked is, "Does the metric encompass both outputs and inputs?" Process metrics, such as on-time delivery, need to incorporate causes and effects into their calculation and evaluation. For example, a decreasing on-time delivery rate might be caused by late pickups, shipments not being ready on time, or even by production shutdowns. So, the outputs must be somehow related to the inputs.

The sixth question to be asked is, "Does it measure only what is important?" The logistics operation generates huge volumes of transactional data on a daily basis. Many times, firms will measure those activities or processes for which large amounts of data are available. Just because data are available to calculate a metric does not mean the metric is important. In some cases, data are hard to generate for important metrics. For example, data for on-time delivery must be generated by either the carrier or receiving location. Matching arrival data in a timely and accurate manner with bills of lading can be a cumbersome process. So, it is important to decide what is important and then gather the data rather than identifying what data are available and then generating metrics.

The seventh question to be asked about a good metric is, "Is it multidimensional?" Although a single metric will not be multidimensional, a firm's metric program will be. This is where the terms **scorecard** and **key performance indicators (KPIs)** will apply. Many organizations will have a few strategic metrics to manage their logistics operations. These metrics will represent productivity, utilization, and performance in a balanced approach to managing their logistics processes.[5]

The eighth question to be asked is, "Does the process use economies of effort?" Another way to ask this question is, "Do we get more benefits from the metric than we incur costs to generate it?" In many cases, much time and effort are devoted to collecting data to generate a specific metric, while the resulting actions from the metric are minimal. Some firms find this to be the case when they first develop a metric. However, the longer a firm has a metric in place, the more likely there are to be economies of effort.[6]

The last question to be asked about a good metric is probably the most important: "Does it facilitate trust?" If it does not, complying with the other nine characteristics makes little or no difference for the effectiveness of the metric. However, if the first nine characteristics are present for a logistics metric, trust should be an expected conclusion.

Evaluating current or potential logistics metrics is critical to a sound metrics program. Also important to note is that metrics need to change over time; not only the performance standard—for example, 85 percent—but also the individual metric—for example, percentage of orders shipped on time. With regard to the first example, the standard might change to 90 percent as new processes and/or technologies are introduced that enable the organization to consistently exceed the old standard. Advocates of the Six Sigma concept have stressed the focus on continuous improvement, which should result in increasing performance expectations over time.

The second example, indicated previously, regarding changing metrics is also very important. Orders shipped on time and orders shipped complete were frequently used as performance metrics in logistics. These could be considered internal metrics because they focus on the performance of the shipping firm. However, as customer service receives more attention in industry, the metrics have changed to "orders delivered on time" and "orders delivered complete." These are more external metrics because they measure the experience of the customer. Both internal and external metrics are essential components to a balanced approach to logistics performance measurement. Figure 13.2 shows the results of the 2015 Distribution Center Metrics report conducted by the Warehouse Education and Research Council (WERC) asking shippers what performance metrics they use to manage their distribution centers. As can be seen from the results, on-time shipment to customer is the most often used metric to measure distribution center performance for the previous two years.

Figure 13.3 explains how the dimensions and importance of performance measurement have expanded. This figure clearly indicates that expectations have increased since the 1960s and 1970s and that in each of the decades identified there have been important drivers for better performance. Each new decade, however, built upon the improvements in the previous decades.

Figure 13.2	Top 12 Most Popular Measures Used - 2015		
METRICS		**2014 RANK**	**2015 RANK**
1. On-time Shipments – **Customer**		1	1
2. Internal Order Cycle Time, in Hours – **Customer**		2	2
3. Dock to Stock Cycle Time, in Hours – **Inbound Operations**		4	4
4. Total Order Cycle Time, in Hours – **Customer**		3	3
5. Order Picking Accuracy (Percent by Order) – **Quality**		5	5
6. Average Warehouse Capacity Used – **Capacity**		8	9
7. Peak Warehouse Capacity Used - **Capacity**		9	12
8. Backorders as a Percent of Total Orders - **Customer**		11	-
9. Backorders as a Percent of Total Lines - **Customer**		-	-
10. Percent of Supplier Orders Received Damage Free - **Inbound Operations**		7	8
11. Lines Picked and Shipped per Person Hour - **Outbound Operations**		6	6
12. Lines Received and Put Away per Hour - **Inbound Operations**		10	11

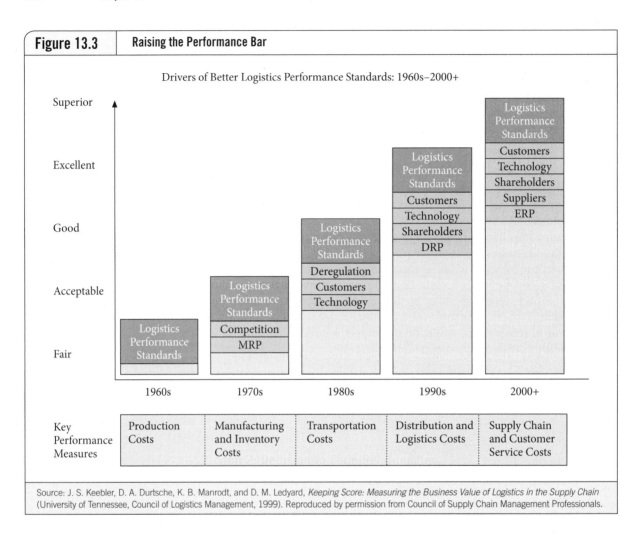

Figure 13.3   **Raising the Performance Bar**

Drivers of Better Logistics Performance Standards: 1960s–2000+

Key Performance Measures	Production Costs	Manufacturing and Inventory Costs	Transportation Costs	Distribution and Logistics Costs	Supply Chain and Customer Service Costs

Source: J. S. Keebler, D. A. Durtsche, K. B. Manrodt, and D. M. Ledyard, *Keeping Score: Measuring the Business Value of Logistics in the Supply Chain* (University of Tennessee, Council of Logistics Management, 1999). Reproduced by permission from Council of Supply Chain Management Professionals.

A question might be raised as to whether or not the focus on performance measurement is a recent event in industry. The answer to that question is a definite "no." Recall from Chapter 2 that the development of the physical distribution and logistics concepts was based upon systems theory with the specific application focused upon least total cost analysis. Total cost is a measure of efficiency and was the rationale supporting physical distribution management. Least total cost was later used to support the logistics management approach.

The focus upon a least total cost system required measuring the tradeoff costs when a suggested change was made in one of the components or elements of the system. For example, this could include switching from rail to motor transportation or adding a distribution center to the distribution network. Cost has long been recognized as an important metric for determining efficiency. This is still true today. However, we have evolved from measuring functional cost to total logistics cost. This means the relevant point of measurement has changed from totally internal to a firm to the collective costs of many firms involved in the supply chain.

The important point to remember is that successful logistics performance measurement relies on appropriate metrics that capture the entire essence of the logistics process. Logistics metrics must also be reviewed to ensure that they are relevant and focus on what is important. A sound, comprehensive set of supply chain performance metrics is critical for an organization to manage its business and identify opportunities to increase profit and market share.

13-3 Developing Supply Chain Performance Metrics[7]

The implementation of new technologies—for example, enterprise resource planning (ERP) systems—and the changing business environment have prompted many firms to reexamine their supply chain metrics programs. Another driving influence for this reexamination has been the desire of organizations to change their supply chain focus from a "cost" center to an "investment" center. In other words, how can organizations justify investments in supply chain processes? This will be discussed in a later section in this chapter. In the meantime, here are some suggestions concerning the successful development of a supply chain metrics program.

First, develop a metrics program that is the result of a team effort. Successful metrics implementations involve development teams comprised of individuals representing functional areas within the firm that will be impacted by the metrics. Because this phase of development requires metric identification and definition, it is critical that all impacted areas agree on the appropriate metrics and their definitions. This agreement will lead to a more successful implementation and use of the metrics to manage the business.

Second, involve customers and suppliers, where appropriate, in the metrics development process. Because customers feel the impact of metrics and suppliers are actively involved in the execution of the metrics, their involvement is also critical to successful implementation.

Third, develop a tiered structure for the metrics. Many organizations develop a small number (usually less than five) of KPIs or "executive dashboard" metrics that are reviewed at the executive level for strategic decision making. Tied to each strategic KPI are tactical and operational metrics. In this hierarchy, operating unit metrics are tied directly to corporate strategic metrics.

Fourth, identify metric "owners" and tie metric goal achievement to an individual's or division's performance evaluation. This provides the motivation to achieve metric goals and use metrics to manage the business.

Fifth, establish a procedure to mitigate conflicts arising from metric development and implementation. A true process metric might require a functional area within an organization to sub-optimize its performance to benefit the organization as a whole. This might result in conflict from the sub-optimized function. For example, achieving the desired on-time delivery metric might require transportation to increase its expenditures, resulting in an unfavorable freight expense. A resolution process must be established to allow the transportation manager to realize the desired on-time delivery goal without being penalized for excess freight expense.

Sixth, establish supply chain metrics that are consistent with corporate strategy. If the overall corporate strategy is based upon effectiveness in serving customers, a supply chain metrics program that emphasizes low cost or efficiency may be in conflict with expected corporate outcomes.

Finally, establish top management support for the development of a supply chain metrics program. Successful metrics programs cost more than expected, take longer to implement than desirable, and impact many areas inside and outside the organization. Top management support is necessary to see the development and implementation of the metrics program to its successful conclusion.

On the Line　　　　　　*Establishing Ocean-Alliance KPIs*

The Global Shippers Forum (GSF) has called for a manageable, but rigorous set of monitoring KPIs that can provide the required level of confidence to customers that ocean shipping alliances can deliver tangible benefits in terms of reduced costs, competitive ocean rates, and improved services for shippers. Chris Welsh, the GSF secretary general, recently outlined the need for shipping alliances to reach out to customers and start showing demonstrable improvements in service quality and innovative solutions for shippers. "Shipping alliances need to take responsibility for monitoring, measuring, and benchmarking their performance on key trade routes to demonstrate enhanced alliance performance and make that information transparent to regulators and their customers as evidence of their commitment to showing the pro-competition benefits of improved alliance services," declared Welsh.

Source: Logistics Management, May 2015, p. 1. Reprinted with permission of Peerless Media, LLC.

13.4 Performance Categories

A number of approaches can be used to classify supply chain performance metrics. Figure 13.4 is one method to use for this type of classification. This figure identifies four major categories with examples that provide a useful way for examining logistics and supply chain performance: (1) time, (2) quality, (3) cost, and (4) supporting metrics.

Time has traditionally been given attention as an important indicator of logistics performance, especially with regard to measuring effectiveness. Figure 13.4 lists five widely used metrics for time. The metrics capture two elements of time: the elapsed time for the activity and the reliability (variability) for the activity. For example, order cycle time might be 10 days, plus or minus 4 days, or 10 days, plus or minus 2 days. Both cycle times have the same absolute length but have different variability. The difference in variability will have an impact on safety stocks in the supply chain (this will be covered further in Chapter 9, which discusses managing inventory in the supply chain). The important point is that metrics should measure both absolute time and its variability.

The second category indicated in Figure 13.4 is cost, which is the measurement for efficiency. Most organizations focus on cost since it is critical to their ability to compete in the market and make adequate profit and returns on assets and/or investments. A number of cost metrics related to logistics and supply chain management are important to organizations.

Some of the cost metrics shown in Figure 13.4 are obvious and easy to understand. For example, total delivered cost or landed cost will have an impact on the prices that will have to be charged in the market. Total delivered cost is multidimensional and includes the cost of goods, transportation, inventory carrying costs, import/export costs, and warehousing. Inventory turns and days sales outstanding are not as obvious. Inventory turns reflect how long an organization holds inventory and its resulting impact on inventory carrying cost (this will be discussed further in Chapter 9). Days sales outstanding impacts service levels to customers and can affect the rate of order fill. The cash-to-cash cycle is receiving increased attention in organizations because it measures cash flow. Organizations are interested in getting their money back as quickly as possible in order to enhance their financial viability.

Quality is the third category of metrics identified in Figure 13.4. Several dimensions in the quality category are important to logistics and supply chain management. The perfect

Figure 13.4	Process Measure Categories

Time

On-time delivery/receipt

Order cycle time

Order cycle time variability

Response time

Forecasting/Planning cycle time

Quality

Overall customer satisfaction

Processing accuracy

Perfect order fulfillment

- On-time delivery
- Complete order
- Accurate product selection
- Damage free
- Accurate invoice

Forecast accuracy

Planning accuracy

- Budgets and operating plans

Schedule adherence

Cost

Finished goods inventory turns

Days sales outstanding

Cost to serve

Cash-to-cash cycle time

Total delivered cost

- Cost of goods
- Transportation costs
- Inventory carrying costs
- Material handling costs

All other costs

- Information systems
- Administrative

Cost of excess capacity

Cost of capacity shortfall

Other/Supporting

Approval exceptions to standard

- Minimum order quantity
- Change order timing

Availability of information

Source: J. S. Keebler, D. A. Durtsche, K. B. Manrodt, and D. M. Ledyard, *Keeping Score: Measuring the Business Value of Logistics in the Supply Chain* (University of Tennessee, Council of Logistics Management, 1999). Reproduced by permission from Council of Supply Chain Management.

order concept is a good example of the increased emphasis being placed upon customer service because it simultaneously measures multiple metrics that must be achieved to get a positive metric.[8] The fourth category indicated in Figure 13.4 offers some supporting metrics such as approval of exceptions to standards.

Another metric classification scheme that has been receiving increased attention is that developed by the Supply Chain Council and contained in the Supply Chain Operations and Reference (SCOR) model. Figure 13.5 is an example of the Level 1 metrics categories. This figure identifies five major categories of metrics that need to be used to measure the performance at Level 1: (1) **reliability**—the performance of the supply chain in delivering the correct product, to the correct place, at the correct time, in the correct condition and packaging, in the correct quantity, with the correct documentation, to the correct customer; (2) **responsiveness**—the speed at which the supply chain provides products to customers; (3) **flexibility**—the flexibility of the supply chain in responding to marketplace changes to gain or maintain competitive advantage; (4) **costs**—the expenditures associated with operating the supply chain; and (5) **asset management**—the effectiveness of an organization in managing assets to support demand satisfaction and including the management of all

Figure 13.5	SCOR Metrics	
ATTRIBUTE	**PERFORMANCE ATTRIBUTE DEFINITION**	**LEVEL 1 METRIC**
Supply Chain Reliability	The performance of the supply chain in delivering: the correct product, to the correct place and customer, at the correct time, in the correct condition and packaging, and with the correct quantity and documentation	Delivery Performance Fill Rates Product Order Fulfillment
Supply Chain Responsiveness	The velocity at which a supply chain provides products to the customer	Order Fulfillment Lead Times
Supply Chain Flexibility	The agility of a supply chain in responding to marketplace changes to gain or maintain competitive advantage.	Supply Chain Response Time Production Flexibility
Supply Chain Costs	The costs associated with operating the supply chain.	Cost of Goods Sold Total Supply Chain Management Costs Value-Added Productivity Warranty / Returns Processing Costs
Supply Chain Asset Management Efficiency	The effectiveness of an organization in managing assets to support demand satisfaction. This includes the management of all assets: fixed and working capital.	Cash-to-Cash Cycle Time Inventory Days of Supply Asset Turn

Source: Adapted from Supply Chain Council (2015). Reproduced by permission.

assets (fixed and working capital).[9] Figure 13.6 identifies metrics in the same categories for Process D.1: Deliver Stocked Product. Figure 13.7 illustrates another perspective in the form of a logistics quantification pyramid, which suggests that performance metrics for logistics and supply chain management should include logistics operations costs, logistics service metrics, transaction cost and revenue.

Transportation is a good example of logistics operations costs. By calculating the trade-offs between using less expensive (slower and less reliable) and more expensive (faster and more reliable) transportation service, an organization can quantify the total cost impact on transportation and inventory costs. Using faster and more reliable transportation will result in higher transportation costs but lower inventory costs, which usually generates in an increase in cash flow for the organization.

Logistics service can fall into any one of the five categories shown in Figure 13.8. Product availability is a logistics metric that is used frequently because it is a good indicator of supply chain performance and its influence on customer inventory requirements, order fill rates, and seller revenue.

Order cycle time (OCT) is another very important logistics service metric. OCT influences product availability, customer inventories, and the seller's cash flow and profit. Once an expected OCT is established for customers, service failures can be measured. One such measure is the number of late deliveries per 100 shipments. From a revenue or cash flow perspective, an organization can calculate the impact of a late delivery on revenue, profit, and cash flow. (This will be discussed further in Chapter 8 that discusses order management and customer service.)

Figure 13.6	SCOR Model: Process D1 Metrics

PROCESS CATEGORY: DELIVER STOCKED PRODUCT	PROCESS NUMBER: D1

Process Category Definition

The process of delivering product that is sourced or made based on aggregated consumer orders/demand and inventory re-ordering parameters. The intention of Deliver Stocked Product is to have the product available when a customer order arrives (to prevent the customer from looking elsewhere). For service industries, these are services that are pre-defined and off-the-shelf (e.g. standard training). Products or services that are "configurable" cannot be delivered through the Deliver Stocked Product process, as configurable products require customer reference or customer order details.

Performance Attributes	Metric
Supply Chain Reliability	Perfect Order Fulfillment
Supply Chain Responsiveness	Order Fulfillment Cycle Time
Supply Chain Agility	Upside Supply Chain Flexibility
	Upside Supply Chain Adaptability
	Downside Supply Chain Adaptability
	Overall Value at Risk
Supply Chain Costs	Total Cost to Serve
Supply Chain Asset Management	Cash-to-Cash Cycle Time
	Return on Supply Chain Fixed Assets
	Return on Working Capital

Source: Adapted from Supply Chain Council (2015). Reproduced by permission.

Figure 13.7	Logistics Quantification Pyramid

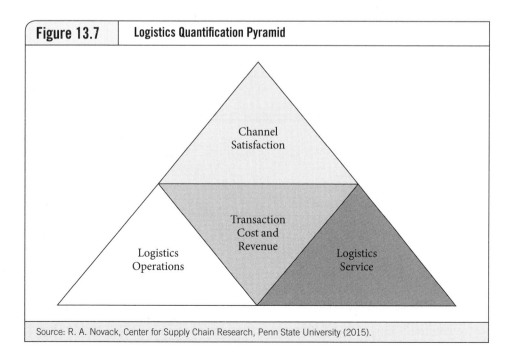

Source: R. A. Novack, Center for Supply Chain Research, Penn State University (2015).

Figure 13.8	Logistics Outputs That Influence Customer Service
	• Product availability • Order cycle time • Logistics operations responsiveness • Logistics system information • Post-sale logistics support

Source: R. A. Novack, Center for Supply Chain Research, Penn State University (2015).

All of the logistics outputs listed in Figure 13.8 can be utilized in some form to develop metrics for service performance. As indicated previously, the service output metrics reflect the quality of service being provided to customers, which is important to sustain and, hopefully, increase revenue and cash flow.

Transaction cost and revenue relates to the value added by logistics. In other words, what is the service and price relationship, and what specifically is the customer's perception of service quality? To add logistics value from the seller's perspective, there are three basic alternatives to consider:

- Increased service with a constant price to the customer
- Constant service with a reduced price
- Increased service with a reduced price

All of these alternatives result in the customers receiving more service per dollar for the price they are paying for the service.

Another perspective on transaction cost and revenue focuses on how a seller's cost influences a customer's profit and on how a seller's service impacts a customer's revenue. If the cost of a seller's logistics service allows a customer to make more profit from the seller's product, the customer should be willing to buy more products from the seller. For example, a manufacturer is able to deliver its product to the buyer's retail store for $0.25 less per case than the competitor can deliver its product to the same store. By keeping the price constant at the shelf, the buyer can realize an additional $0.25 per case profit. Similarly, a manufacturer's logistics service level will have an impact on the retailer's revenues. For example, the same manufacturer in the previous example has an in-stock rate at the buyer's store of 98 percent, compared to 90 percent for the competition. This higher in-stock service level allows the buyer to realize higher revenues from the higher product availability. So, transaction cost and revenue highlight the need to emphasize the impacts of logistics cost and service on supply chain profits and revenues.

Let's look again at the final category shown in Figure 13.7—channel satisfaction, which essentially looks at how logistics cost and service are perceived by channel members. The research in this area is limited. Most of the focus on measurement has been on the perceptions of supply chain members of how well suppliers are performing on logistics cost and service. Leading-edge organizations are beginning to identify the impact of customer satisfaction on revenues and market share.

Overall, much progress has been made during the last few years toward developing appropriate metrics and using them proactively to measure performance in terms of their impact upon the financial results of the organization and its customers. However, as this discussion has highlighted, there is much more to be accomplished. The next section will introduce the supply chain–finance connection, a topic that will reappear throughout the remainder of this book.

13-5 The Supply Chain–Finance Connection

As noted in the supply chain profile at the beginning of this chapter, CLGN Book Distributors.com is focusing its attention on the supply chain process as a means to improve its financial performance. CLGN recognizes the impact supply chain performance has on customer satisfaction and future sales. In addition, the effectiveness of the supply chain process impacts the cost of fulfilling customer orders and transporting these orders to the customer, both of which impact the overall landed cost of the product.

More specifically, the supply chain process influences the flow of products from the supplier to the final point of consumption. The resources utilized to accomplish this flow process determine, in part, the cost of making the product available to the consumer at the consumer's location. This landed cost, then, affects the buyer's decision to purchase a seller's product.

The cost of providing logistics service not only affects the marketability of the product (via the landed cost, or price), but also impacts its profitability. For a given price, level of sales, and level of service, the higher the logistics cost the lower the organization's profit. Conversely, the lower the logistics costs, the higher the profits.

The decision to alter the supply chain process is essentially an optimization issue. Management must view the supply chain alternatives as to their ability to optimize the corporate goal of profit maximization. Some alternatives might minimize costs but reduce revenue, and possibly, profits. By implementing supply chain alternatives that optimize profits, the decision maker is taking the systems approach and trading off revenue and costs for optimum profit.

Supply chain management involves the control of raw material, in-process, and finished goods inventories. The financing implication of inventory management is the amount of capital required to fund the inventory. In many organizations, capital is in short supply but is required to fund critical projects, such as new plants or new warehouses. The higher the inventory level, the more capital is constrained and the less capital is available for other investments.

The recent focus on inventory minimization is a direct response to the competing needs for capital and the difficulty some organizations have in raising additional capital. Logistics techniques such as just-in-time and vendor-managed inventories are directed toward reducing an organization's inventory levels and making more capital available for other projects.

As indicated previously, the level of logistics service provided has a direct impact on customer satisfaction. Providing consistent and short lead times helps manage supply chain inventories and can build customer satisfaction and loyalty. However, the cost of providing this service must also be examined for its impact on a firm's profit and revenue.

Finally, **efficiency** of the supply chain impacts the time required to process a customer's order. Order processing time has a direct bearing on an organization's **order-to-cash cycle**— all of the activities that occur from the time an order is received by a seller until the seller receives payment for the shipment. Typically, the invoice is sent to the customer after the order is shipped. If the terms of sale are net 30 days, the seller will receive payment in 30 days plus the time needed to process the order. The longer the order-to-cash cycle, the longer it takes for the seller to get its payment. The longer the order-to-cash cycle, the higher the accounts receivable and the higher the investment in "sold" finished goods. So the length of the order-to-cash cycle directly relates to the amount of capital tied up and not available for other investments.

13-6 The Revenue–Cost Savings Connection

Throughout this text, attention is given to supply chain efficiency and cost reduction. While process efficiency and cost savings are worthy goals, top management generally refers to corporate improvements in terms of increases in revenue and profit. The apparent conflict between the goals of top management and supply chain management can be readily resolved by converting cost savings into equivalent revenue increases. To improve communications effectiveness with top management, it behooves the supply chain manager to relate efficiencies and cost savings in a language that top management uses—that is, revenue and profit. Appendix 13A contains definitions for some commonly used financial terms.

Logistics and supply chain managers find it advantageous to transform cost reductions into equivalent revenue increases to explain to top management the effects of improved supply chain cost performance. To accomplish this, the following equations can be used:

$$\text{Profit} = \text{Revenue} - \text{Costs}$$

where

$$\text{Cost} = (X\%)(\text{Revenue})$$

then

$$\text{Profit} = \text{Revenue} - (X\%)(\text{Revenue}) = \text{Revenue}(1 - X\%)$$

where

$$(1 - X\%) = \text{Profit margin}$$

$$\text{Sales} = \text{Profit/Profit Margin}$$

Assuming that everything else remains unchanged, a logistics cost saving will directly increase pretax profits by the amount of the cost saving. If a logistics cost saving increases profit by the same amount, the revenue equivalent of this cost saving is found by dividing the cost saving by the profit margin, as shown in the preceding equations. For example, if cost is 90 percent of revenue and the profit margin is 10 percent of revenue, a $100 cost saving is equivalent to additional revenue of $1,000:

$$\text{Revenue} = \text{Cost Saving (or Profit)/Profit Margin}$$

$$\text{Revenue} = \$100/0.10$$

$$\text{Revenue} = \$1,000$$

Table 13.1 provides examples of equivalent revenue for different logistics cost savings using the data found in the supply chain profile for CLGN at the beginning of this chapter. As shown in the table, CLGN has a profit margin of 7 percent. Given this profit margin, a $200,000 logistics cost saving has the same effect as increasing revenue by $2,857,143, a 1.9 percent increase in revenue. Likewise, a $500,000 and $1 million logistics cost savings have equivalent revenue equal to $7,142,857 (4.76 percent revenue increase) and $14,285,714 (9.52 percent revenue increase), respectively.

Table 13.1	Sales Equivalent of Supply Chain Cost Savings				
	CLGN 2015		SALES EQUIVALENT FOR COST SAVINGS OF		
	(000)	PERCENTAGE	$200,000	$500,000	$1,000,000
Sales	$150,000	100.0	$2,857,143[*]	$7,142,857[**]	$14,285,714[†]
Total cost	139,500	93.0	2,657,143	6,642,857	13,285,714
Net profit	10,500	7.0	200,000	500,000	1,000,000

[*]$200,000 cost saving ÷ 0.07 profit margin
[**]$500,000 cost saving ÷ 0.07 profit margin
[†]$1,000,000 cost saving ÷ 0.07 profit margin

Source: Edward J. Bardi, Ph.D. Used with permission.

Table 13.2	Equivalent Sales with Varying Profit Margins			
	PROFIT MARGINS			
	20%	10%	5%	1%
Sales	$50,000	$100,000	$200,000	$1,000,000
Total cost	40,000	90,000	190,000	990,000
Cost saving/profit	10,000	10,000	10,000	10,000

Source: Edward J. Bardi, Ph.D. Used with permission.

The lower the profit margin, the higher the revenue equivalent for a given logistics cost because it takes a greater revenue volume to produce a given profit. Table 13.2 shows the equivalent revenue of a given logistics cost saving with varying profit margins. For a $10,000 logistics cost saving, the equivalent revenue equals $1 million for an organization with a 1 percent profit margin but only $50,000 for an organization with a 20 percent profit margin. Logistics cost savings have a much greater revenue impact for organizations with low profit margins.

In the following section, the financial implications of supply chain strategies are discussed. Following that section, statements contained in the supply chain profile for CLGN Book Distributors.com are analyzed.

13-7 The Supply Chain Financial Impact

A major financial objective for any organization is to produce a satisfactory return for stockholders. This requires the generation of sufficient profit in relation to the size of the stockholders' investment to ensure that inventors will maintain confidence in the organization's ability to manage its investments. Low returns over time will see investors seek alternative uses for their capital. High returns over time, however, will buoy investor confidence to maintain their investments with the organization.

The absolute size of the profit must be considered in relation to the stockholders' net investment, or net worth. For example, if Company A makes a profit of $1 million and Company B makes a profit of $100 million, it would appear that Company B would be a better investment. However, if A has a net worth of $10 million and B $10 billion, the **return on net worth** for a stockholder in Company A is 10 percent ($1 million/$10 million) and for Company B it is 1 percent ($100 million/$10 billion).

An organization's financial performance is also judged by the profit it generates in relationship to the assets utilized, or **return on assets (ROA)**. An organization's ROA is a financial performance metric that is used as a benchmark to compare management and organization performance to that of other organizations in the same industry or similar industries. As with return on net worth, ROA is dependent on the level of profits for the organization.

The supply chain plays a critical role in determining the level of profitability in an organization. The more efficient and productive the supply chain, the greater the profit potential of the organization. Conversely, the less efficient and less productive, the higher the supply chain costs and the lower the profitability.

Figure 13.9 shows the financial relationship between supply chain management and ROA. The effectiveness of supply chain service impacts the level of revenue, and the efficiency affects the organization's total costs. As noted earlier, revenue minus cost equals profit, a major component in determining ROA.

The level of inventory owned by an organization in its supply chain determines the assets, or capital, devoted to inventory. The order-to-cash cycle affects the time required to receive payment from a sale, thereby impacting the accounts receivable and cash assets.

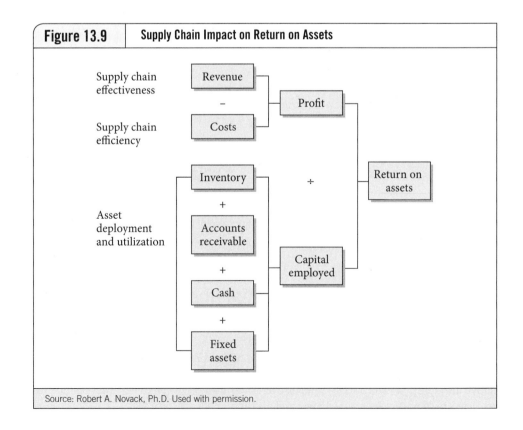

Figure 13.9 | **Supply Chain Impact on Return on Assets**

Source: Robert A. Novack, Ph.D. Used with permission.

Finally, the supply chain decisions regarding the type and number of warehouses utilized impacts fixed assets.

Lastly, Figure 13.9 shows that the calculation of ROA is the division of the profit realized by the capital (assets) employed (profit/capital employed). As noted earlier, the higher the profits for a given level of assets (capital) utilized, the higher the ROA.

Another way to examine the impact of supply chain services and costs can be seen in Figure 13.10. As shown in this figure, cash and receivables for an organization are influenced by supply chain time (OCT/order-to-cash), supply chain reliability (order completion rate and on-time delivery), and information accuracy (invoice accuracy). All of these supply chain services will determine when the customer begins processing the shipment delivery for payment. Inventory investment for an organization is influenced by required service levels and stockout rates for the organization. Property, plant, and equipment investment is impacted by decisions regarding private warehouses and transportation fleets. Decisions regarding the outsourcing activities such as warehousing and transportation will influence current liability levels (accounts payable). Finally, decisions regarding financing for inventories and infrastructure will determine debt and equity levels.

Figure 13.11 summarizes the supply chain strategic areas affecting ROA. The decisions made by the supply chain manager with regard to channel structure, inventory management, order management, and transportation management all have an effect on the level of assets employed or the level of profitability the organization will realize.

Channel structure management includes decisions regarding the use of outsourcing, channel inventories, information systems, and channel structure. By outsourcing supply chain activities, the organization might realize lower supply chain costs (outsourcing firms possess greater functional expertise and efficiencies), a reduction in assets (use of an outsourcing firm's facilities), and increased revenue (from improved supply chain service). Decisions that lower supply chain assets and/or improve revenue through supply chain service improvements result in a higher ROA.

Minimization of channel inventories results in a direct reduction in an organization's assets. The use of improved information systems enables the organization to better monitor inventory levels, production schedules, and demand forecasts to meet current levels

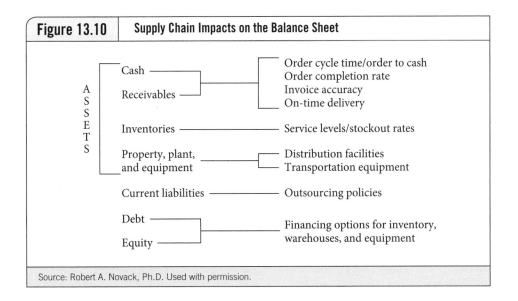

Figure 13.10	Supply Chain Impacts on the Balance Sheet

A
S
S
E
T
S

Cash ———— Order cycle time/order to cash
Order completion rate
Receivables ———— Invoice accuracy
On-time delivery

Inventories ———————— Service levels/stockout rates

Property, plant, ———— Distribution facilities
and equipment ———— Transportation equipment

Current liabilities ———————— Outsourcing policies

Debt ———— Financing options for inventory,
warehouses, and equipment
Equity ————

Source: Robert A. Novack, Ph.D. Used with permission.

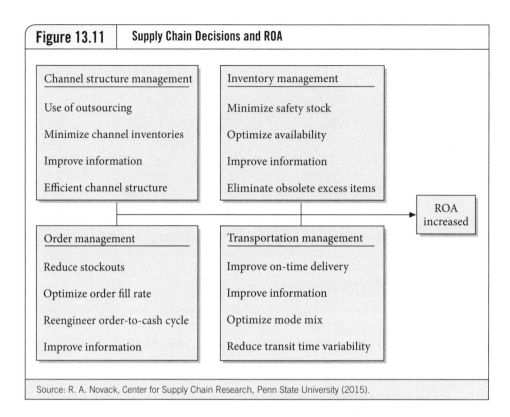

Figure 13.11   Supply Chain Decisions and ROA

Channel structure management

Use of outsourcing

Minimize channel inventories

Improve information

Efficient channel structure

Inventory management

Minimize safety stock

Optimize availability

Improve information

Eliminate obsolete excess items

Order management

Reduce stockouts

Optimize order fill rate

Reengineer order-to-cash cycle

Improve information

Transportation management

Improve on-time delivery

Improve information

Optimize mode mix

Reduce transit time variability

ROA increased

Source: R. A. Novack, Center for Supply Chain Research, Penn State University (2015).

of demand. Streamlining the channel structure through the elimination of unnecessary channel intermediaries—for example, dealing directly with the retailer and bypassing the wholesaler—might eliminate inventory from the channel, as well as reduce the channel cost of transportation and warehousing. The reduction in inventory results in a direct increase in ROA.

Inventory management decisions that reduce inventory (safety stock, obsolete and/or excess stock) and optimize inventory location (in relation to sales or use patterns) reduce the investment in inventory. These decisions require analysis of sales data and inventory levels by channel location, which is readily available with current information systems.

Effective order management not only reduces supply chain costs but also supports increased revenue, the combined effect resulting in a higher ROA. Reducing stockouts implies that sufficient inventories are available to meet demand. Optimizing the order fill rate implies a reduction in the order-to-cash cycle, which reduces the accounts receivable collection time. Reductions in the order processing times, coupled with a reduction in the length of the credit period extended to customers, reduce accounts payable and the cost of capital required to fund accounts payable. All of these reductions in time improve the ROA.

Finally, reducing transportation transit time and the variability of transit time will have a positive impact on revenues as well as on inventory levels. By providing short, consistent transit time, a seller can differentiate its product in the market by lowering the buyer's inventories and stockout costs. This product differentiation should produce increased revenues and a potential for increased profits. Modal optimization affords the opportunity to lower transportation cost by utilizing a lower-cost method of transportation that does not increase other costs above the transportation cost savings. Transportation management decisions, then, offer the opportunity to increase revenues and lower inventories and costs, resulting in a higher ROA.

On the Line — What's the ROI on a Managed Transportation Services Relationship?

Steve Banker, director of supply chain solutions at ARC Advisory Group, feels that measuring the return on a managed transportation service (MTS) relationship will become increasingly important to shippers.

In an MTS arrangement, a shipper contracts with a third party to plan and execute their moves for them. "In other words, instead of having internal partners orchestrate and execute moves, those planners are in the employ of the MTS provider, but work on behalf of the shipper," says Banker.

While there's much fine research on logistics service providers (LSP) and their overall relationships with their clients, there is a scarcity of research focused on specific LSP service lines such as warehousing, freight forwarding, and MTS. A recent survey done in conjunction with Peerless Research Group (PRG), the research division affiliated with *Logistics Management*, was recently conducted to correct this.

"Our goal was to determine the ROI of MTS arrangements, to develop criteria that would sort respondents into a top and bottom performers category, and then to look at what top performers were doing differently from other respondents," says Banker. "This allows shippers engaged in MTS relationships to benchmark their performance."

Banker has plenty of company in the 3PL analyst community when it comes to measuring the wants and needs of shippers. "It's really quite simple," he concludes. "All shippers want is sterling service. In the end, it doesn't matter how few or how many players are involved."

Shippers with managed transportation services (MTS) relationship

Freight savings among those that achieved savings

Savings, but not sure how much — 8%
MTS decreases costs < 2% — 4%
MTS decreases costs 3–5% — 16%
MTS decreases costs 6–8% — 12%
MTS decreases costs 9–11% — 18%
MTS decreases costs > 12% — 9%

Freight costs if not working with MTS provider

Costs would go down 11%
Stay the same 22%
Costs would rise 67%

Source: Adapted from *Logistics Management*, June 2014, p. 56S. Reprinted with permission of Peerless Media, LLC.

13-8 Financial Statements

Let's now turn our attention to two very important financial statements: the income statement and the balance sheet. The data contained in the supply chain profile for CLGN Book Distributors.com will be used in this section. Figure 13.12 presents the CLGN income statement, and Figure 13.13 shows the balance sheet for CLGN. Both financial statements have been prepared using a spreadsheet software program, and the symbol column indicates the symbol and/or equation used for each of the entries.

CLGN's **income statement** shows a net income (NI) of $10.5 million on sales (S) of $150 million, a profit margin of 7 percent. Gross margin (GM) is found by subtracting cost of

Figure 13.12	CLGN Book Distributors.com Income Statement: 2015		
	SYMBOL	(000)	(000)
Sales	S		$150,000
Cost of goods sold	CGS		80,000
Gross margin	$GM = S - CGS$		$ 70,000
Transportation	TC	$6,000	
Warehousing	WC	1,500	
Inventory carrying	$IC = IN \times W$	3,000	
Other operating cost	OOC	30,000	
Total operating cost	$TOC = TC + WC + IC + OOC$		40,500
Earnings before interest and taxes	$EBIT = GM - TOC$		$ 29,500
Interest	INT		12,000
Taxes	$TX = (EBIT - INT) \times 0.4$		7,000
Net income	NI		$ 10,500

Source: Edward J. Bardi, Ph.D. Used with permission.

goods sold (CGS) from sales (S). Earnings before interest and taxes (EBIT) are gross margin minus total operating cost (TOC). Net income (NI) is EBIT minus interest cost (INT) and taxes (TX). The supply chain costs include transportation (TC), warehousing (WC), and inventory carrying cost (IC). Inventory carrying cost is equal to average inventory (IN) times the inventory carrying cost rate (W).

The **balance sheet** in Figure 13.13 indicates CLGN utilized total assets (TA) of $145 million to generate $150 million in sales. Total assets (TA) consist of $15 million of cash (CA), $30 million of accounts receivable (AR), $10 million of inventory (IN), and $90 million of net fixed assets (FA). These assets were financed by debt (liabilities) and stockholders' equity; that is, the $100 million of total debt (TD), consisting of $65 million of current liabilities (CL) and $35 million of long-term debt (LTD), plus $45 million of stockholders' equity (SE), paid for these assets.

13-9 Financial Impact of Supply Chain Decisions

Based on the financial data given in Figures 13.12 and 13.13, an analysis can be undertaken to determine the impacts of alternative supply chain actions available to Lauren Fishbay to improve CLGN's profitability. The basic supply chain alternatives are reductions in the areas of transportation, warehousing, and inventory costs. To determine the supply chain area that affords the largest financial impact and then the focus of initial profit improvement efforts, an analysis is undertaken of the effect of a 10 percent reduction in transportation and warehousing costs and a 10 percent reduction in inventory.

Figure 13.13	**CLGN Book Distributors.com Balance Sheet: December 31, 2015**	
	SYMBOL	**(000)**
Assets		
Cash	CA	$ 15,000
Accounts receivable	AR	30,000
Inventory	IN	10,000
Total current assets	TCA = CA + AR + IN	$ 55,000
Net fixed assets	FA	90,000
Total assets	TA = FA + TCA	$145,000
Liabilities		
Current liabilities	CL	$ 65,000
Long-term debt	LTD	35,000
Total liabilities	TD = CL + LTD	$100,000
Stockholders' equity	SE	45,000
Total liabilities and equity	TLE = TD + SE	$145,000

Source: Edward J. Bardi, Ph.D. Used with permission.

Figure 13.14 shows the financial impact of a 10 percent reduction in transportation costs. First, for 2010, CLGN had a net income of $10.5 million on sales of $150 million, or a profit margin of 7.0 percent. CLGN utilized $145 million in assets to produce this profit, thereby generating a ROA of 7.24 percent. The inventory turn rate for 2015 was 8.0, transportation costs were 4.0 percent of sales, warehousing costs were 1.0 percent of sales, and inventory carrying costs were 2.0 percent of sales.

If CLGN can reduce transportation costs by 10 percent, net income will increase from $360,000 to $10,860,000, and the profit margin will increase to 7.24 percent. ROA will increase from 7.24 percent to 7.49 percent. Transportation costs as a percent of sales will decrease from 4.0 percent to 3.6 percent. Warehousing and inventory carrying costs as a percent of sales will not change (assuming the transportation changes do not result in longer or undependable transit times that would cause inventory levels to increase).

Figures 13.15 and 13.16 show the results of a similar analysis of a 10 percent reduction in warehousing costs and a 10 percent reduction in inventory. In each case, the comparison is made to the 2015 CLGN performance; that is, transportation cost and inventory are computed at the 2015 level when the 10 percent warehouse cost reduction is analyzed. As would be expected, the reduction in warehousing cost and inventory results in increases in profits, profit margin, and ROA.

The analyses contained in Figures 13.14 to 13.16 provide the input data necessary to answer the question regarding which of the basic supply chain alternatives will provide

Figure 13.14	Financial Impact of a 10 Percent Reduction in Transportation Cost		

	SYMBOL	CLGN, 2015 $(000)	TRANSPORTATION COST REDUCED 10 PERCENT
Sales	S	$150,000	$150,000
Cost of goods sold	CGS	80,000	80,000
Gross margin	GM = S − CGS	$ 70,000	$ 70,000
Transportation	TC	$ 6,000	$ 5,400
Warehousing	WC	1,500	1,500
Inventory carrying	IC = IN × W	3,000	3,000
Other operating cost	OOC	30,000	30,000
Total operating cost	TOC	$ 40,500	$ 39,900
Earnings before interest and taxes	EBIT	$ 29,500	$ 30,100
Interest	INT	$ 12,000	$ 12,000
Taxes	TX	7,000	7,240
Net income	NI	$ 10,500	$ 10,860
Asset Deployment			
Inventory	IN	$ 10,000	$ 10,000
Accounts receivable	AR	30,000	30,000
Cash	CA	15,000	15,000
Fixed assets	FA	90,000	90,000
Total assets	TA	$145,000	$145,000
Ratio Analysis			
Profit margin	NI/S	7.00%	7.24%
Return on assets	NI/TA	7.24%	7.49%
Inventory turns/year	CGS/IN	8.00	8.00
Transportation as percentage of sales	TC/S	4.00%	3.60%
Warehousing as percentage of sales	WC/S	1.00%	1.00%
Inventory carrying as percentage of sales	IC/S	2.00%	2.00%

Source: Edward J. Bardi, Ph.D. Used with permission.

the greatest potential for increased profitability. Figure 13.17 contains a comparison of the financial results of the alternative supply chain strategies just examined.

From Figure 13.17, it is evident that CLGN's profit margin will be increased the greatest amount by utilizing a supply chain alternative that reduces transportation costs. This is to be expected, because transportation cost is a larger percentage of sales than the other two supply chain functional areas: 4.00 percent of sales versus 1.0 percent and 2.0 percent for warehousing and inventory, respectively. If the cost to CLGN to realize a 10 percent reduction in these functional areas is the same, it is prudent for Lauren Fishbay to dedicate her resources and efforts to realizing a reduction in transportation costs.

Figure 13.15	Financial Impact of a 10 Percent Reduction in Warehousing Costs		
	SYMBOL	CLGN, 2015 $(000)	WAREHOUSING COST REDUCED 10 PERCENT
Sales	S	$150,000	$150,000
Cost of goods sold	CGS	80,000	80,000
Gross margin	GM = S − CGS	$ 70,000	$ 70,000
Transportation	TC	$ 6,000	$ 6,000
Warehousing	WC	1,500	1,350
Inventory carrying	IC = IN × W	3,000	3,000
Other operating cost	OOC	30,000	30,000
Total operating cost	TOC	$ 40,500	$ 40,350
Earnings before interest and taxes	EBIT	$ 29,500	$ 29,650
Interest	INT	$ 12,000	$ 12,000
Taxes	TX	7,000	7,060
Net income	NI	$ 10,500	$ 10,590
Asset Deployment			
Inventory	IN	$ 10,000	$ 10,000
Accounts receivable	AR	30,000	30,000
Cash	CA	15,000	15,000
Fixed assets	FA	90,000	90,000
Total assets	TA	$145,000	$145,000
Ratio Analysis			
Profit margin	NI/S	7.00%	7.06%
Return on assets	NI/TA	7.24%	7.30%
Inventory turns/year	CGS/IN	8.00	8.00
Transportation as percentage of sales	TC/S	4.00%	4.00%
Warehousing as percentage of sales	WC/S	1.00%	0.90%
Inventory carrying as percentage of sales	IC/S	2.00%	2.00%

Source: Edward J. Bardi, Ph.D. Used with permission.

The largest increase in ROA was generated by the transportation alternative. However, the inventory reduction alternative increased ROA by almost the same amount: 7.49 percent versus 7.42 percent. The financial benefit of an inventory reduction is two-fold: (1) a reduction in the inventory carrying cost and (2) a reduction in assets. Annual inventory turns are increased with the inventory reduction strategy, requiring CLGN to utilize less capital for inventory and making more capital available for other uses in the organization. Thus, an inventory reduction strategy has a double effect on ROA by increasing profits and reducing assets deployed.

Another methodology that can perform the same financial analysis is the **strategic profit model (SPM)**, which makes the same calculations that were made in the spreadsheet

| Figure 13.16 | Financial Impact of a 10 Percent Reduction in Inventory |

	SYMBOL	CLGN, 2015 $(000)	AVERAGE INVENTORY REDUCED BY 10 PERCENT
Sales	S	$150,000	$150,000
Cost of goods sold	CGS	80,000	80,000
Gross margin	GM = S − CGS	$ 70,000	$ 70,000
Transportation	TC	$ 6,000	$ 6,000
Warehousing	WC	1,500	1,500
Inventory carrying	IC = IN × W	3,000	2,700
Other operating cost	OOC	30,000	30,000
Total operating cost	TOC	$ 40,500	$ 40,200
Earnings before interest and taxes	EBIT	$ 29,500	$ 29,800
Interest	INT	$ 12,000	$ 12,000
Taxes	TX	7,000	7,120
Net income	NI	$ 10,500	$ 10,680
Asset Deployment			
Inventory	IN	$ 10,000	$ 9,000
Accounts receivable	AR	30,000	30,000
Cash	CA	15,000	15,000
Fixed assets	FA	90,000	90,000
Total assets	TA	$145,000	$144,000
Ratio Analysis			
Profit margin	NI/S	7.00%	7.12%
Return on assets	NI/TA	7.24%	7.42%
Inventory turns/year	CGS/IN	8.00	8.89
Transportation as percentage of sales	TC/S	4.00%	4.00%
Warehousing as percentage of sales	WC/S	1.00%	1.00%
Inventory carrying as percentage of sales	IC/S	2.00%	1.80%

Source: Edward J. Bardi, Ph.D. Used with permission.

analysis. Figure 13.18 contains the SPM for CLGN for 2015 operations and the 10 percent transportation cost reduction.

The SPM shows the same results as those calculated in Figure 13.14. Two ratios were added to the SPM (1) **asset turnover**, which is the ratio of sales to total assets and indicates how the organization is utilizing its assets in relation to sales, and (2) **return on equity**, which indicates the return the stockholders are realizing on their equity in the organization. Asset turnover was 103 percent for both scenarios, but return on equity increased from

Figure 13.17	Comparison of Supply Chain Alternatives			
RATIO ANALYSIS	CLGN, 2015 $(000)	TRANSPORTATION COST REDUCED 10 PERCENT	WAREHOUSING COST REDUCED 10 PERCENT	INVENTORY REDUCED 10 PERCENT
Profit margin	7.00%	7.24%	7.06%	7.12%
Return on assets	7.24%	7.49%	7.30%	7.42%
Inventory turns/year	8.00	8.00	8.00	8.89
Transportation as percentage of sales	4.00%	3.60%	4.00%	4.00%
Warehousing as percentage of sales	1.00%	1.00%	0.90%	1.00%
Inventory carrying as percentage of sales	2.00%	2.00%	2.00%	1.80%

Source: Edward J. Bardi, Ph.D. Used with permission.

23.33 percent ($10,500/$45,000) for the CLGN 2015 scenario to 24.13 percent ($10,860/$45,000) with the reduced transportation cost scenario.

The preceding analysis and its conclusion examine only the returns from the alternative actions. The risks associated with each must also be considered. The conclusions that *cannot* be made from the preceding analysis are those regarding the risks associated with the added cost necessary to realize the functional cost reductions, the additional capital required to achieve the reduction, and the service implications accompanying the changes. For example, to accomplish the transportation cost reduction, CLGN might have to revert to a mode of transportation that is slower. This could have a negative impact on customer satisfaction and result in lower sales. Or, the warehouse cost reduction might require the expenditure of $500,000 for automated materials handling equipment that increases the assets deployed and reduces the ROA.

The issues above can be added to the financial analysis presented. For example, the added cost associated with reengineering the warehouse or any additional investment in fixed warehouse assets such as facilities or equipment can be added to the financial analysis along with the resulting warehouse cost savings.

Given the financial analysis and the preceding caveats, CLGN has a better insight into the supply chain areas that will result in the greatest improvement in profitability and the accompanying risks (costs). The next section addresses the financial implications of CLGN's supply chain service failures.

13-10 Supply Chain Service Financial Implications

As noted in the supply chain profile, CLGN Book Distributors.com has experienced service failures in the areas of **on-time deliveries** and **order fill rates**. The 95 percent on-time delivery rate means that only 95 percent of CLGN orders are delivered when promised (on-time delivery). Also, only 97 percent of the orders are filled correctly. The alternative view of this service is that 5 percent of the orders are delivered after the promised delivery date and 3 percent of the orders are filled incorrectly.

Figure 13.18   Strategic Profit Model for CLGN 2015 and Reduced Transportation Costs

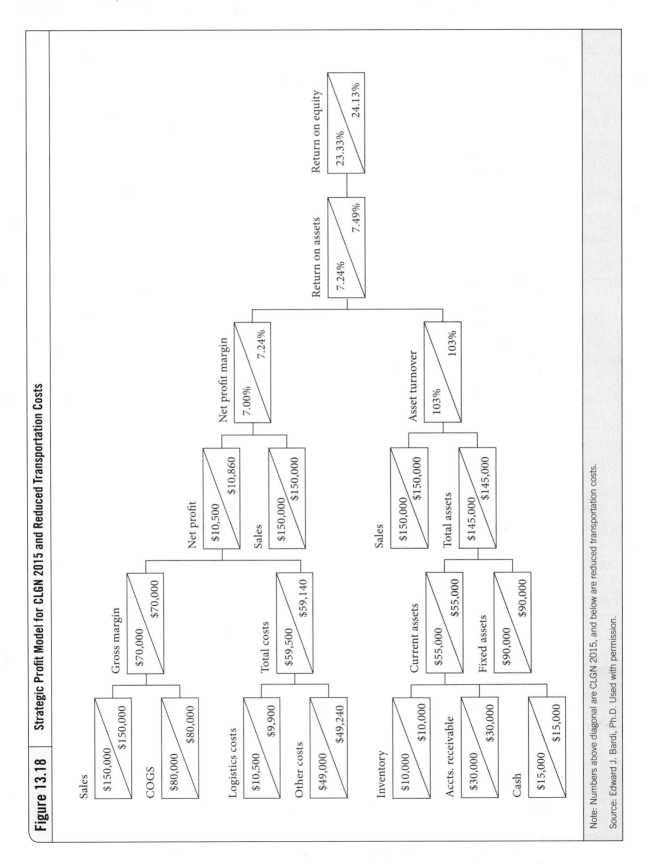

Note: Numbers above diagonal are CLGN 2015, and below are reduced transportation costs.

Source: Edward J. Bardi, Ph.D. Used with permission.

The results of these supply chain service failures are added to the cost to correct the problem and lost sales. Figure 13.19 shows the methodology for determining the cost of service failures. When supply chain service failures occur, a portion of the customers experiencing the service failure will request that the orders be corrected and the others will refuse the orders. The refused orders represent lost sales revenue (refused orders times revenue per order) that must be deducted from total sales. For the rectified orders, the customers might request an invoice deduction to compensate them for any inconvenience or added costs. Finally, the seller incurs a rehandling cost associated with correcting the order such as reshipping the correct items and returning the incorrect and refused items (rectified orders plus refused orders times rehandling cost per order).

Referring to the data provided in the supply chain profile for CLGN's on-time delivery and order fill rates, you will see that the financial impact of improving these two supply chain service metrics is given in Figures 13.20 and 13.21. Assume that there are 1.5 million orders for the year, the average revenue per order is $100, and the cost of goods per order is $53.33. Also, the lost sales rate for on-time delivery failure is 10 percent; for order fill failures, it is 20 percent. The rehandling charge is $20 per rectified and refused order, and the invoice deduction is $10 per rectified order. The costs and assets are those provided in the supply chain profile and used in the previous section. This pertinent information is contained within the boxed area of the spreadsheets in Figures 13.20 and 13.21.

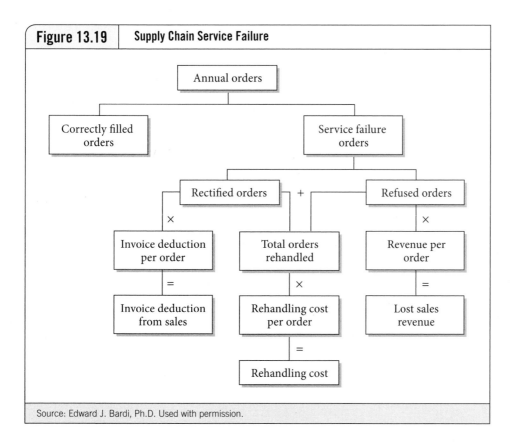

Figure 13.19 | **Supply Chain Service Failure**

Source: Edward J. Bardi, Ph.D. Used with permission.

Figure 13.20 | Financial Impact of Improving On-Time Delivery

	SYMBOL	ON-TIME RATE 55%	ON-TIME RATE 96%	INPUT DATA	95%	96%
Annual orders	AO	1,500,000	1,500,000	%CF	95%	96%
Orders filled correctly	$OFC = AO \times \%CF$	1,425,000	1,440,000	Annual orders	1,500,000	1,500,000
Service failure orders	$SF = AO - OFC$	75,000	60,000	SP = Revenue/order	$100	$100
Lost sales orders	$LS = SF \times LSR$	7,500	6,000	CG = Cost of goods/order	$53.33	$53.33
Rectified orders	$RO = SF - LS$	67,500	54,000	Lost sales rate	10%	10%
Net orders sold	$NOS = AO - LS$	1,492,500	1,494,000	RCO = Rehandling cost/order	$20	$20
Sales	$S = SP \times AO$	$150,000,000	$150,000,000	IDR = Invoice deduction rate	$10	$10
Less: Invoice deduction	$ID = IDR \times RO$	$675,000	$540,000	Transportation cost	$6,000,000	$6,600,000
Lost sales revenue	$LSR = LS \times SP$	$750,000	$600,000	Warehousing cost	$1,500,000	$1,500,000
Net sales	$NS = S - ID - LSR$	$148,575,000	$148,860,000	Interest cost	$3,000,000	$3,000,000
Cost of goods sold	$CGS = CG \times (NOS)$	$79,595,025	$79,675,020	Other operating cost	$30,000,000	$30,000,000
Gross margin (GM)	$GM = NS - CGS$	$68,979,975	$69,184,980	Inventory	$10,000,000	$10,000,000
Rehandling cost	$RC = RCO \times SF$	$1,500,000	$1,200,000	Cash	$15,000,000	$15,000,000
Transportation	TC	$6,000,000	$6,600,000	Accounts receivable	$30,000,000	$30,000,000
Warehousing	WC	$1,500,000	$1,500,000	Fixed assets	$90,000,000	$90,000,000
Inventory carrying	$IC = IN \times W$	$3,000,000	$3,000,000	W = Inventory carrying rate	30%	30%
Other operating cost	OOC	$30,000,000	$30,000,000			
Total operating cost	TOC	$42,000,000	$42,300			
Earnings before interest and taxes	$EBIT = GM - TOC$	$26,979,975	$26,884,980			
Interest	INT	$3,000,000	$3,000,000			
Tax (40% × (EBIT − INT))	TX	$9,591,990	$9,553,992			
Net income	$NI = EBIT - INT - TX$	$14,387,985	$14,330,988			
Profit increase of 1% improvement			($56,997)			

Source: Edward J. Bardi, Ph.D. Used with permission.

Figure 13.21 — Financial Impact of Improving Order Fill Rate

	SYMBOL	ORDER FILL RATE 97%	ORDER FILL RATE 98%	INPUT DATA	97%	98%
Annual orders	AO	1,500,000	1,500,000	%CF	97%	98%
Orders filled correctly	$OFC = AO \times \%CF$	1,455,000	1,470,000	Annual orders	1,500,000	1,500,000
Service failure orders	$SF = AO - OFC$	45,000	30,000	SP = Revenue/order	$ 100	$ 100
Lost sales orders	$LS = SF \times LSR$	9,000	6,000	CG = Cost of goods/order	$ 53.33	$ 53.33
Rectified orders	$RO = SF - LS$	36,000	24,000	Lost sales rate	20%	20%
Net orders sold	$NOS = AO - LS$	1,491,000	1,494,000	RCO = Rehandling cost/order	$ 20	$ 20
Sales	$S = SP \times AO$	$150,000,000	$150,000,000	IDR = Invoice deduction rate	$ 10	$ 10
Less: Invoice deduction	$ID = IDR \times RO$	$360,000	$ 240,000	Transportation cost	$ 6,000,000	$ 6,000,000
Lost sales revenue	$LSR = LS \times SP$	$900,000	$ 600,000	Warehousing cost	$ 1,500,000	$ 1,600,000
Net sales	$NS = S - ID - LSR$	$148,740,000	$149,160,000	Interest cost	$ 3,000,000	$ 3,000,000
Cost of goods sold	$CGS = CG \times (NOS)$	$ 79,515,030	$ 79,675,020	Other operating cost	$30,000,000	$30,000,000
Gross margin (GM)	$GM = NS - CGS$	$69,224,970	$ 69,484,980	Inventory	$10,000,000	$10,000,000
Rehandling cost	$RC = RCO \times SF$	$900,000	$ 600,000	Cash	$15,000,000	$15,000,000
Transportation	TC	$6,000,000	$ 6,000,000	Accounts receivable	$30,000,000	$30,000,000
Warehousing	WC	$1,500,000	$ 1,600,000	Fixed assets	$90,000,000	$90,000,000
Inventory carrying	$IC = IN \times W$	$3,000,000	$ 3,000,000	W = Inventory carrying rate	30%	30%
Other operating cost	OOC	$30,000,000	$ 30,000,000			
Total operating cost	TOC	$41,400,000	$ 41,200,000			
Earnings before interest and taxes	$EBIT = GM - TOC$	$27,824,970	$ 28,284,980			
Interest	INT	$3,000,000	$ 3,000,000			
Tax (40% × (EBIT − INT))	TX	$9,929,988	$ 10,113,992			
Net income	$NI = EBIT - INT - TX$	$14,894,982	$ 15,170,988			
Profit increase of 1% improvement			$ 276,006			

Source: Edward J. Bardi, Ph.D. Used with permission.

Note that the upper portion of the spreadsheet analysis in Figure 13.20 determines the number of service failure orders, lost sales orders, rectified orders, and net orders sold. (The symbols provided in the second column will assist you in creating the spreadsheet analysis.) At the 95 percent on-time delivery rate, 1,425,000 are delivered on time (0.95 × 1,500,000 total orders) and 75,000 orders are delivered late (service failures). Of the 75,000 late orders, the customers will decline 7,500 (10%) and CLGN will lose sales on these orders, or $750,000 ($100 revenue per order × 7,500 lost orders). The rehandling cost is $1,500,000 ($20 per order × 75,000 orders [rectified plus refused]), and invoice deduction is $675,000 ($10 per order × 67,500 orders).

In this example, the 1 percent improvement in on-time delivery (from 95% to 96%) results in net income falling by $56,997. The improved on-time delivery reduces invoice deductions by $135,000 and rehandling cost by $300,000, or a total cost saving of $535,000. However, to realize this cost saving of $535,000, a transportation cost increase of 10 percent or $600,000 is necessary. Since the net income is reduced by $56,997 with the proposed strategy to switch to second-day ground delivery service, CLGN will probably not consider this on-time delivery improvement option.

Figure 13.21 shows that the $100,000 cost to provide training to the warehouse personnel will improve the order fill rate from 97 percent to 98 percent and result in an increase in net income of $276,006. The combined savings of $420,000 (rehandling cost saving of $300,000 and invoice deductions saving of $120,000) are greater than the additional training cost of $100,000.

Given the two options—improve on-time delivery or order fill rate—CLGN would be advised to implement the order fill improvement strategy.

The SPM for these two alternatives is given in Figures 13.22 and 13.23. The profit margin, ROA, and return on stockholders' equity are greater with the order fill rate improvement strategy than with the on-time delivery improvement strategy. For the order fill rate improvement from 97 percent to 98 percent, the ROE increases to 33.71 percent from 33.10 percent, the profit margin increases to 10.17 percent from 10.01 percent, and the ROA increases to 10.46 percent from 10.27 percent.

The financial goal for supply chain management is to increase return to stockholders. Examining alternative courses of action in light of the bottom-line impact (net income) and resultant ROE accomplishes this goal.

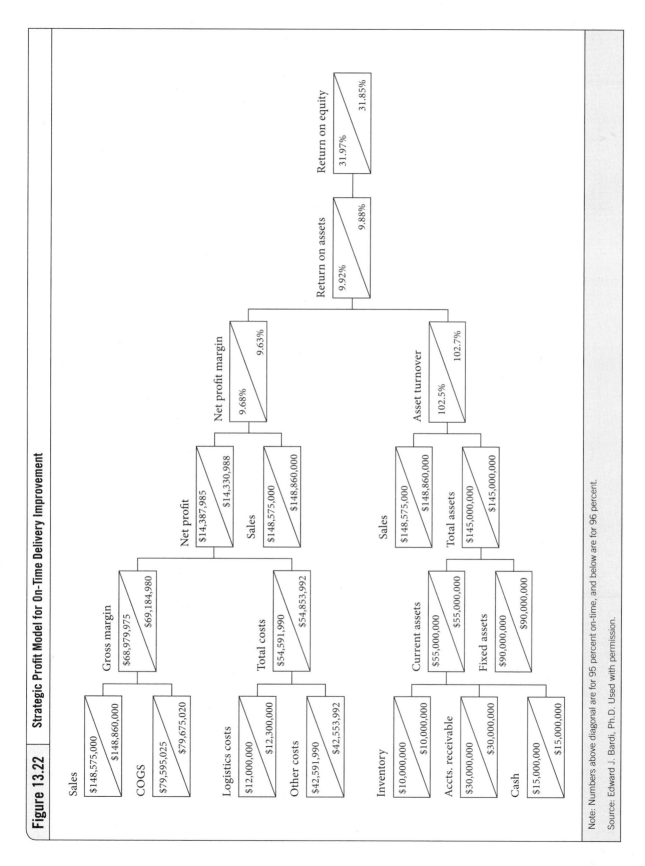

Figure 13.22 Strategic Profit Model for On-Time Delivery Improvement

Note: Numbers above diagonal are for 95 percent on-time, and below are for 96 percent.

Source: Edward J. Bardi, Ph.D. Used with permission.

Figure 13.23 | Strategic Profit Model for Order Fill Rate Improvement

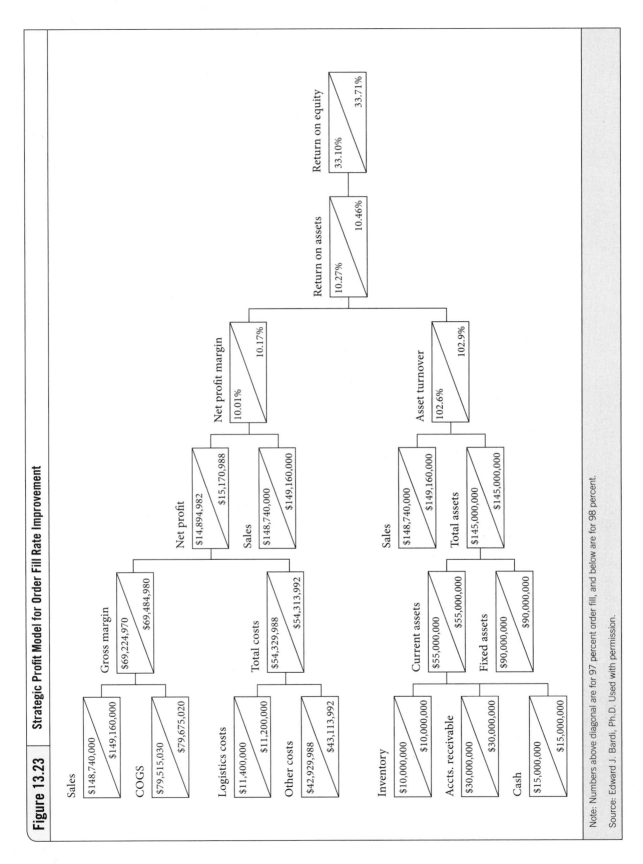

Note: Numbers above diagonal are for 97 percent order fill, and below are for 98 percent.

Source: Edward J. Bardi, Ph.D. Used with permission.

SUMMARY

- Performance measurement for logistics systems and, especially, for supply chains is necessary but challenging because of their complexity and scope.

- Certain objectives should be incorporated into good metrics—be quantitative, be easy to understand, involve employee input, and have economies of effort.

- Important guidelines for metric development for logistics and supply chains include consistency with corporate strategy, focus on customer needs, careful selection and prioritization of metrics, focus on processes, use of a balanced approach, and use of technology to improve measurement effectiveness.

- There are four principal categories for performance metrics: time, quality, cost, and miscellaneous or support. Another classification for logistics and supply chains suggests the following categories for metrics: operations cost, service, revenue or value, and channel satisfaction.

- The equivalent sales increase for supply chain cost saving is found by dividing the cost saving by the organization's profit margin.

- Supply chain management impacts ROA via decisions regarding channel structure management, inventory management, order management, and transportation management.

- Alternative supply chain decisions should be made in light of the financial implications to net income, ROA, and ROE.

- The SPM shows the relationship of sales, costs, assets, and equity; it can trace the financial impact of a change in any one of these financial elements.

- Supply chain service failures result in lost sales and rehandling costs. The financial impact of modifications to supply chain service can be analyzed using the SPM.

STUDY QUESTIONS

1. "Performance measurement for logistics managers is relatively recent. Their focus was previously directed toward other managerial activities." Do you agree or disagree with these statements? Explain your position.

2. What role should employees, in general, play in the development of performance metrics? Why is this role important?

3. "Metrics must focus upon customer needs and expectations." Explain the meaning of this statement. Why have customers become more important for performance measurement? What role, if any, should customers play in developing supply chain metrics?

4. It is generally recognized that organizations go through several phases on the path to developing appropriate supply chain metrics. Discuss the stages of supply development for supply chain metrics. Choose which of the stages of evolution you think would be most challenging for an organization. Explain your choice.

5. Using a spreadsheet computer software program, construct a supply chain finance model and calculate the profit margin; ROA; inventory turns; and transportation, warehousing, and inventory costs as a percentage of revenue for the following:

    Sales = $200,000,000

    Transportation cost = $12,000,000

    Warehousing cost = $3,000,000

Inventory carrying cost = 30%

Cost of goods sold = $90,000,000

Other operating costs = $50,000,000

Average inventory = $10,000,000

Accounts receivable = $30,000,000

Cash = $15,000,000

Net fixed assets = $90,000,000

Interest = $10,000,000

Taxes = 40% of (EBIT-Interest)

Current liabilities = $65,000,000

Long-term liabilities = $35,000,000

Stockholders' equity = $45,000,000

6. Using the supply chain finance model developed for Study Question 5, calculate the impact on profit margin; ROA; inventory turns; and transportation, warehousing, and inventory costs as a percentage of revenue for the following scenarios:

Scenario A

Transportation costs increase = 20%

Warehousing costs decrease = 5%

Average inventory decrease = 10%

Scenario B

Warehousing is outsourced with the following:

Net fixed assets reduced = 20%

Inventory reduced = 15%

Warehousing costs = $0

Transportation costs reduced = 5%

Outsourcing provider costs = $2,500,000

7. Develop a strategic model to depict the scenarios given in Questions 5 and 6.

8. Construct a financial model to determine the redelivery/rehandling cost, lost sales, invoice deduction cost, and net income for the following:
   a. On-time delivery increases from 90 percent to 95 percent, with a 5 percent increase in transportation cost.
   b. Order fill rate decreases from 96 percent to 92 percent with inventory reduced by 5 percent.

Selling price/order = $150/order

Gross margin/order = $35/order

Lost sales rate is as follows:

On-time delivery failure = 15%

Order fill failure = 20%

Annual orders = 200,000

Rehandling cost = $125/order

Invoice deduction/service failure = $150/order

Transportation cost = $1,000,000

Average inventory = $1,000,000

Interest cost = $1,500,000

Inventory carrying cost rate = 25%/$/yr.

Warehousing cost = $750,000

Other operating cost = $500,000

Cash = $3,000,000

Accounts receivable = $4,000,000

Fixed assets = $30,000,000

Tax rate = 40%

NOTES

1. Thomas S. Davis, Center for Supply Chain Research, Penn State University (2010).

2. Robert A. Novack and Thomas S. Davis, "Developing a Supply Chain Performance Metrics Program" (unpublished manuscript, Center for Supply Chain Research, Penn State University, 2007).

3. Ibid.

4. Ibid.

5. Ibid.

6. Ibid.

7. Ibid.

8. Robert A. Novack and Douglas J. Thomas, "The Challenges of Implementing the Perfect Order Concept," *Transportation Journal, Vol. 43*, No. 1 (Winter 2004): 5–16.

9. Supply Chain Council, SCOR Model Version 9.0 2008): 1.2.6.

CASE 13.1

Wash & Dry, Inc.

Wash & Dry (WD) is a small manufacturing company with annual revenues for 2015 reaching $10 million. Located in Bellefonte, PA, WD produces various types of laundry and personal soaps as well as an array of paper products, such as paper towels and napkins. The unique nature of WDs products have allowed it to grow from a start-up in 2010 with revenues of $1 million to where it is today. WDs products are totally sustainable and command a higher price than competitors in the markets they serve. Their products are sold through both mass merchandisers as well as specialty retailers.

WD manufactures it products in two plants in Bellefonte: one dedicated to the soap line and one to paper products. From these two plants, finished products are transported to their distribution center located in Harrisburg, PA. From there, mixed shipments of soap and paper are sent to the retailer distribution centers where they are sorted and mixed with other products going to retail stores.

As a relatively small company, WD had a very unsophisticated set of key performance indicators (KPIs). At the plant, the KPI was "did we make what we were scheduled to make today." At the DC, the KPI was "did we ship what we were supposed to ship today." Although these two KPIs seemed to work in the past, WDs growth and pressure from its retail customers for better service made it necessary for WD to consider developing a more comprehensive set of KPIs.

CASE QUESTIONS

1. If you were hired as a consultant to develop these KPIs for WD, how would you assess what KPIs they should be measuring? In general, what areas of service and cost would these KPIs address? Be sure to include both internal and customer KPIs.

2. What KPIs would you recommend for the manufacturing facility? Why?

3. What KPIs should be used at the distribution center? Why?

4. How would you measure the revenue and profit impacts of these new KPIs?

CASE 13.2

Paper2Go.com

Colleen Starky never thought she would be able to sell paper products to consumers on the Internet. However, after five years in business Paper2Go.com has reached $75 million in revenue. Paper2Go specializes in shipping paper-related products to consumers, including diapers, paper towels, and facial tissue from numerous suppliers. Because these items have a low margin, Colleen knows she needs to control costs and at the same time have high service levels.

Paper2Go receives 500,000 orders annually with an average revenue per order of $150 and an average profit per order of $90. Paper2Go's current order fill rate is 92 percent. Colleen estimates that of the orders not filled correctly or completely, 15 percent of the customers cancel their orders and 85 percent will accept a reshipment of the correct/unfilled items. This rehandling costs Paper2Go $15 per order and is only applicable on the reshipped orders. In an effort to retain customers, Paper2Go reduces the invoice value of rehandled orders by $30.

Paper2Go pays $2,500,000 for transportation, both inbound to and outbound from its warehouses. Its warehousing costs are $1,950,000 annually. Paper2Go has $40 million of debt at an annual interest rate of 12 percent. Other operating costs are $1 million per year and Paper2Go maintains $100,000 in cash at all times.

Paper2Go has an average inventory of $6.7 million. This level of inventory is necessary to help fill consumer orders correctly the first time. The inventory carrying cost rate is 30 percent of the average inventory value per year. Its accounts receivable averages $350,000 per year. Paper2Go owns three warehouses that are valued in total at $85.7 million. The net worth of Paper2Go is $45 million.

Colleen has decided that a 92 percent order fill rate is not acceptable in the market and lost customers and rehandled orders are negatively affecting profits. She has decided to invest $1 million in a new stock locater system for the warehouses, increase inventories by 10 percent, and increase the on-time delivery of inbound shipments by contracting with a new carrier. This carrier upgrade will increase total transportation costs by 10 percent. Colleen hopes these changes will increase the order fill rate to 98 percent. Paper2Go faces a current tax rate of 35%.

CASE QUESTIONS

1. You are the logistics analyst at Paper2Go.com and have been asked to do the following:
   a. Calculate the financial impact of increasing order fill rates to 98 percent from 92 percent.
   b. Develop a strategic profit model of both the old system and the modified system that reflects the suggested adjustments.

Source: Robert A. Novack, Ph.D. Used with permission.

APPENDIX 13A

Financial Terms

Account receivable A current asset showing the amount of sales currently owed by a customer.

Balance sheet A snapshot of everything the company owes and owns at the end of the financial year in question.

Cash cycle The time between payment of inventory and collection of cash from receivables.

Cash flow statement A summary showing the cash receipts and payments from all company financial activities; earnings before interest, taxes, depreciation, and amortization (EBITDA).

Cost of goods sold The total cost of the goods sold to customers during the period.

Cost of lost sales The short-run forgone profit associated with a stockout.

Current assets Cash and other assets that will be converted into cash during one operating cycle.

Current liabilities An obligation that must be paid during the normal operating cycle, usually one year.

Current ratio Current assets divided by current liabilities; measures company's ability to pay short-term debt with assets easily converted to cash.

Debt-to-equity ratio Long-term debt divided by shareholders' equity.

Earnings before interest and taxes (EBIT) Sales minus cost of goods sold and operating costs.

Earnings per share Net earnings divided by average number of shares outstanding.

Gross margin Sales minus cost of goods sold.

Income statement A summary of revenues and expenses, reporting the net income or loss for a specific accounting period.

Inventory carrying cost The annual cost of holding inventory; the value of the average inventory times the inventory carrying cost rate (W).

Inventory carrying cost rate (W) The cost of holding $1 of inventory for one year, usually expressed as a percentage; includes cost of capital, risk, item servicing, and storage space.

Inventory turns Cost of goods sold divided by average inventory.

Liquidity ratio Cash flow from operations divided by current liabilities; measures short-term cash available to pay current liabilities.

Net income (or loss) Final result of all revenue and expense items for a period; sales minus cost of goods sold, operating costs, interest, and taxes.

Operating expense All expenses other than cost of goods sold, depreciation, interest, and income tax.

Operating ratio Percentage of revenues used for operations; operating expenses divided by operating income.

Order-to-cash cycle The time between receiving customer orders and the collection of receivables.

Profit margin Net income divided by sales.

Return on assets Net income divided by total assets.

Return on equity Net income divided by average stockholders' equity.

Shareholders' equity The difference between the value of all the things owned by the company and the value of all the things owed by the company; the investment made by the stockholders at the time the stock was originally issued plus all past earnings that have not been paid out in dividends; sum total of shareholders' investment in a company since it was formed, minus its liabilities.

Working capital Current assets minus current liabilities; working capital finances the business by converting goods and services to cash.

Chapter 14

SUPPLY CHAIN TECHNOLOGY—MANAGING INFORMATION FLOWS

Learning Objectives

After reading this chapter, you should be able to do the following:

- Appreciate the importance of information to supply chain management.
- Explain information requirements in the supply chain.
- Understand the capabilities of an integrated supply chain information system.
- Describe and differentiate between the primary types of supply chain solutions.
- Discuss the critical issues in technology selection and implementation.
- Recognize the technological innovations that are influencing supply chain management.

Supply Chain Profile

Omni-channel Retailing Runs on Information

The rapid evolution of omni-channel retailing has created a colossal service challenge. Retailers must give customers what they want, when they want it, where they want it and at the price they want it. And if the retailer doesn't have the product in-store, then they better get it to the customer's house tomorrow, or Amazon will—with free shipping.

This seamless retail environment requires a highly agile and technology driven supply chain. It must support the customer's ability to buy products in person or remotely using a smartphone, tablet, computer, or kiosk. The retailer must also have the ability to fill the customer's order from multiple facilities in its network —a store, a vending machine, a distribution center (DC), a third-party fulfillment center, or the manufacturer's warehouse.

In this buy from anywhere, fulfill from anywhere world of omni-channel retailing, rapid and accurate data flows are essential. Retailers must be capable of providing customers with online access to inventory levels and locations, shipping options, order cycle times, total order cost, and tracking capabilities. In short, retailers and their supply chain partners must have tightly integrated information systems to support customer engagement, increase sales, boost retention, and drive profits.

What is needed to thrive in this seamless retail environment? A recent survey by Capgemini Group and GS1 US highlights four critical components of success:

Inventory visibility – Information systems must support inventory identification, tracking and control. Automatic product identification tools such as radio frequency identification (RFID) tags can boost inventory accuracy, allowing the retailer to rapidly locate and retrieve inventory for order fulfillment from stores and DCs.

Product information – Key product information and images must be standardized, accurate, and readily retrievable across the supply chain. This supports cross-chain collaboration and brings products to the online marketplace faster.

Customer analytics – Leading retailers are using predictive analytics to gain deeper insight into customer behavior. In turn, the retailers are able to create an individual shopping experience based on rich information sources.

Fulfillment strategy – Retailers must offer flexible, robust order execution using their fulfillment centers, stores, and suppliers. Distributed order management (DOM) software allows the retailers to capture orders and determine the optimal fulfillment location based on inventory availability, cost, transit time, and customer requirements.

The challenge for retailers and their supply chain partners will be to weave these components together in a robust supply chain information system (SCIS). Key elements include DOM, warehouse management systems (WMS) to coordinate inventory management and fulfillment execution, and transportation management systems (TMS) to provide centralized control and visibility of end-to-end omni-channel fulfillment processes. Investment will be necessary and many retailers are pursuing cloud-based technology tools to speed the process at a manageable cost.

Sources: Evan Puzey, "Technology's Role in Improving the Supply Chain," *Supply Chain 24/7* (August 29, 2015). Retrieved September 1, 2015 from http://www.supplychain247.com/article/technologys_role_in_improving_the_supply_chain/Omni-Channel; GT Nexus, "The Omnichannel Retail Supply Chain," (May 6, 2015). Retrieved September 1, 2015 from http://www.supplychain247.com/paper/the_omnichannel_retail_supply_chain/Omni-Channel; and, Patrick Burnson, "Omni-channel Retailing Creates New Challenges for Supply Chain Managers," *Logistics Management* (June 10, 2014). Retrieved September 1, 2015 from http://www.logisticsmgmt.com/article/omni_channel_retailing_creates_new_challenges_for_supply_chain_managers

14-1 Introduction

Knowledge is essential for supply chain success. Information, along with materials and money, must readily flow across the supply chain to enable the planning, execution, and evaluation of key functions. For example, timely, accurate information regarding consumer demand for GoPro cameras is needed by Best Buy to manage its inventory and order additional products. In turn, the Best Buy order information can be used by GoPro to acquire needed components from suppliers to support production. If each organization in the supply chain had to operate without this demand information, it would be very difficult to maintain a proper flow of the right quantities of the right components and models. This could lead to a shortage of hot sellers and an overage of unwanted cameras.

Fortunately, supply chain information technologies can mitigate these problems. Correctly applied, these tools facilitate timely, cost-efficient information sharing between manufacturers, retailers, and logistics services providers, effective execution of the supply chain processes discussed throughout the book, and satisfaction of customer requirements. As the Supply Chain Profile indicates, these technology capabilities are especially important in the high stakes world of omni-channel retailing.

Recognizing the potential of technology, organizations have invested vast sums of money to effectively collect, analyze, and deploy supply chain information. Gartner estimates that sales of supply chain management (SCM) and procurement software applications totaled U.S. $9.9 billion in 2014. That represents a 10.8 percent annual growth rate, led by double-digit gains from SAP and Manhattan Associates.[1]

As supply chains become more global, complex, and data-driven, information technologies must rapidly evolve. Companies need modern tools to help them capture, analyze, and use real-time information. In their quest to create value through technology, CEOs of transportation and logistics company are especially focused on mobile capabilities, data analytics, and cyber security. The executives realize that digital technology investments must be well-planned and be accompanied by measurements of success to drive competitive advantage.[2]

This chapter focuses on the role of information and technology in the supply chain. It is intended to highlight the key information issues and tools that drive supply chain success. We have divided the chapter into five sections that address the following topics: (1) information requirements, (2) systems capabilities, (3) software solutions, (4) technology selection, and (5) innovative information tools. As you will learn, effective technology for the management of information flows is vital for creating responsive supply chains with synchronized processes to meet customer requirements.

14-2 Information Requirements

It has been said that information is the lifeblood of business, driving appropriate decisions and actions. Across the supply chain, store inventory replenishment decisions are based on point-of-sale data, carrier selection is driven by delivery service goals, and production schedules are derived from forecasts. Essentially, information connects the extended supply chain, providing managers with insights about activities taking place at distant supplier and customer locations. These cross-chain insights regarding demand, customer orders, delivery status, inventory stock levels, and production schedules gives managers the ability to properly assess situations and develop appropriate responses.

Figure 14.1 highlights three principle supply chain information requirements that support effective decision making. First, the information in a system must meet quality standards to support fact-based decision making. Second, the information must readily flow within and between organizations. Third, the information must support multiple types of supply chain decisions.

Without these three requirements met, managers will lose their virtual line of sight to inventory, demand, and activities taking place at supplier and customer locations. Blind spots result and opportunities for collaboration will be lost, leaving decisions to be based on educated guesses and internal signals rather than chain-wide knowledge.

14-2-1 Meet Quality Standards

Information quality is a critical characteristic of the vast amounts of data flowing across the supply chain. Value trumps volume and managers must be sure that they are basing decisions on information that is correct. In fact, the seven rights definition of logistics can logically be adapted to information—getting the right *information* to the right *partners*, in the right *quantity*, in the right *format*, at the right *place*, at the right *time*, and at the right *cost*. Change any "right" to "wrong" and the value of the information to supply chain managers will decline.

To ensure that actionable knowledge readily flows across the supply chain, information must display a variety of key characteristics. Chief among these attributes are accuracy, accessibility, relevancy, timeliness, and transferability. Also important are issues of usability, reliability, and value.

Figure 14.1	**Supply Chain Information Principles**

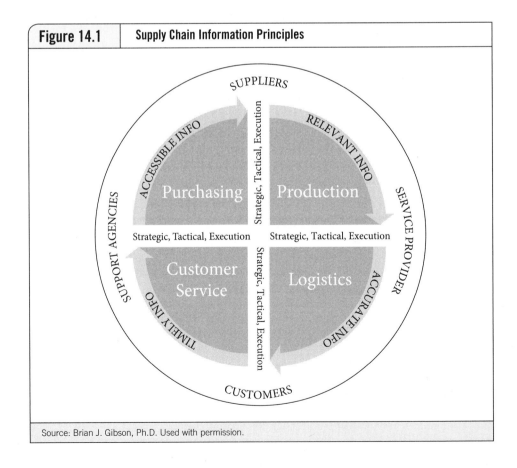

Source: Brian J. Gibson, Ph.D. Used with permission.

14-2-1-1 Accuracy

Supply chain information must depict reality. A true picture of the supply chain that is free of errors facilitates logical decision making. In contrast, decisions based on inaccurate information can lead to inventory shortages, transportation delays, government fines, and unhappy customers. For example, retailers rely upon accurate checkout scans to drive replenishment. If a clerk scans one bottle of soda four times when a customer actually purchases four different flavors, the store-level inventory information becomes inaccurate and the wrong products will be replenished.

14-2-1-2 Accessibility

Accurate information must be available to supply chain managers who have a legitimate need for it, regardless of their location or employer. For example, Kenco supply chain managers need ready access to demand information from Whirlpool to schedule delivery and installation of appliances. Obtaining access to needed information can be difficult because supply chain data often are dispersed among multiple locations on different information systems that are owned by external organizations. Technical issues must be addressed and trust built between the organizations sharing information.

14-2-1-3 Relevancy

Supply chain managers must have access to pertinent information for analysis and decision making. Extraneous data and unnecessary details must be avoided as they shroud important details, waste time, and distract decision makers. When a Honda expeditor logs on to the FedEx Web site to track a critical delivery, he doesn't need to know about every Honda shipment handled by FedEx that day. He wants quick access to the status of the one shipment in question, allowing him to respond accordingly.

14-2-1-4 Timeliness

To be relevant, supply chain information must be up-to-date and available in a reasonable time frame. Timely data flows from a highly synchronized SCIS allow managers to monitor supply chain conditions and respond quickly with corrective actions to avoid problem escalation. For example, rapid discovery of quality problems with a specific model of cable modems would allow a communications company to restock their service trucks with a different brand or model. The defective model would not be installed in customers' homes, reducing frustration and service calls.

14-2-1-5 Transferability

Information also needs to be transferred quickly between locations and system in the supply chain to facilitate accessibility and timeliness. A paper-based supply chain cannot support these requirements. Hence, information must reside in electronic formats that can be readily transmitted and converted. Fortunately the Internet and cloud computing platforms make information transfers relatively easy, inexpensive, and safe, though organizations must take precautions to ensure the security of sensitive data.

14-2-1-6 Usability

Information is useful only if it can drive effective decision making. Up-front efforts must be made to define information requirements and capture appropriate data. This will avoid the time and costs of capturing extraneous data that will not be used by supply chain decision makers. Also, information is only usable if it can be seamlessly shared and translated from one format to another with no discernible loss of data.

14-2-1-7 Reliability

The information contained in reports and transaction data sets must come from reliable and authoritative sources within the organization and from trusted supply chain partners. The data provided must be accurate, unaltered, and reasonably complete to support the intended uses. When incomplete or estimated data is provided, a clear explanation of the missing values and assumptions is needed so that a supply chain manager's analysis can be adjusted accordingly.

14-2-1-8 Value

Achieving these seven quality standards is neither an easy nor a cost-free proposition. The hardware and software needed to capture and disseminate quality supply chain data are quite expensive. A recent study indicates that the average supply chain software spend for licensing, integration, and training is more than a half million dollars.[3] Supply chain executives must ensure that proposed information technology investments truly enhance knowledge and produce tangible performance benefits.

14-2-2 Support Multidirectional Flows

The engagement of multiple stakeholders in supply chain planning and decision making drives a need for multidirectional information flows in a supply chain. Internal information sharing supports cross-functional collaboration and organization-wide performance optimization. For example, a sales and operations planning (S&OP) process will only be successful if marketing, operations, finance, and logistics professionals contribute relevant insights. A failure to do so will prolong the problems of functional silos, myopic planning, and sub-optimal performance.

Information must also flow seamlessly between a company and its supply chain partners. A free flow of information will promote integrated decision making and process synchronization. For example, a steady stream of timely and accurate customer demand data is needed to drive effective upstream production and purchasing decisions by manufacturers and suppliers. Shared insights regarding supplier capacity, production schedules, and inventory availability will facilitate alignment and efficient execution of downstream processes.

Logistics service providers must also be kept in the information loop regarding upstream and downstream customer requirements. This knowledge allows the service providers to marshal the people and equipment resources needed to support inventory requirements and delivery schedules. A failure to communicate with these partners can lead to fulfillment delays and customer dissatisfaction.

Additionally, support agencies must also receive and distribute critical information. Financial institutions participate in the movement of relevant information regarding payments and transactions. Government agencies require ongoing communication regarding trade data and regulatory compliance. Financial consequences can result from a failure to properly establish information flows with these organizations.

14-2-3 Provide Decision Support

With SCM taking on a more important and visible role in most organizations, the need for information greatly expands. Managers at every level of the supply chain require different types of information to excel in their roles. This intelligence is needed for strategic decision making, tactical planning, routing decisions, and execution and transaction processing.[4]

Strategic decision making focuses on the creation of long-range supply chain plans that are aligned with the organization's mission and strategies. The required information is often unstructured and may differ from one project to the next. For example, supply, demand, and operational cost data must be captured from a variety of sources to conduct a strategic network design project. In contrast, a new product development decision requires design, capacity, and supplier capability information. This data is used to evaluate strategic alternatives and conduct what-if analysis using decision support tools.

Tactical planning focuses on cross-organization linkages and supply chain activity coordination. The information must be readily available, support planning processes, and be in a flexible format that can be modified by the supply chain participants for use in their systems. For example, S&OP requires information sharing about demand patterns, promotional plans, supply capacity, inventory, and related data to create a unified operating plan.

Routine decision making leverages operational level information for rules-based decision making. The input data needs to be standardized so that the information system can generate appropriate solutions. For example, an automated transportation routing guide uses a shipment's origin, destination, product characteristics, weight and dimensions, and service level requirements data to recommend an appropriate mode and carrier. Decision makers retain the ability to review and adjust the recommended solution as needed.

Execution and transaction processing uses fundamental information from supply chain databases, customer profiles, inventory records, and related sources to complete fulfillment activities. As discussed earlier in this section, the information must be accurate, readily retrievable, and usable so that it can be processed automatically in a timely fashion. For example, an omni-channel order should be captured, the inventory reserved, and the fulfillment process initiated without human intervention. This will support efficient and rapid order fulfillment.

Ultimately, the information residing in a supply chain must meet all three requirements to drive efficient and effective managerial decision making. Quality information must readily flow to essential stakeholders across the supply chain so that they can take appropriate short-, mid-, and long-range actions in support of supply chain excellence.

14-3 Systems Capabilities

The importance of supply chain information technology is well recognized by leading organizations. Apple, Amazon, Procter & Gamble, and other members of the Gartner Supply Chain Top 25 for 2015 are pursuing greater visibility of end-user demand patterns, digital synchronization of manufacturing with upstream suppliers, and the use of logistics control towers with sensors to reduce risk. Such capabilities are essential for both containing supply chain costs and driving organizational top-line growth.[5]

To compete at this level, a company must succeed on three fronts. First, the system must facilitate excellent performance across the plan, buy, make, move, and return processes of a supply chain. Next, a cohesive network of integrated technologies, skilled people, and robust processes must be established. Finally, common risks must be identified and mitigated to maximize the return on technology investments.

14-3-1 Enable Process Excellence

As supply chains grow increasingly complex, organizations need technology to help them thrive. Managing global relationships, collaborating with logistics service providers, and serving omni-channel consumers requires advanced information systems functionality.

That is, information systems must support cross-chain visibility, agility, velocity, synchronization, adaptability, segmentation, and optimization. When properly deployed, these supply chain process enablers help organizations achieve significantly higher levels of performance on both revenue growth and earnings measures when compared to their industry peers.[6]

14-3-1-1 Cross-chain Visibility

Managers need to control key supply chain activities. Having the most current data about the supply chain is a prerequisite for effective decision making and rapid problem response by managers. Visibility tools provide quick access to global supply chain information, generate supply chain alerts, support management by exception, and facilitate trading partner collaboration. Ultimately, greater visibility supports process variability reduction, performance optimization, and supply chain cost control.[7]

14-3-1-2 Agility

In rapidly changing market conditions, supply chain managers must quickly recalibrate plans and respond to supply and demand volatility. Agile supply chains have the capability, capacity, and flexibility to deliver consistent or comparable cost, quality, and customer service under changing conditions. Appropriately designed systems have strong decision support analytics that model various scenarios. This helps supply chain managers to better understand volatility and respond appropriately.[8]

14-3-1-3 Velocity

The speed of product flows across the supply chain must be aligned with customer expectations. These velocity requirements are situation dependent–emergency replenishment and new product introductions require greater velocity than a normal replenishment of existing products. The ability to adjust speeds accordingly is essential. Capable systems capture order cycle time requirements, sequence orders, and identify the best delivery methods to ensure that fulfillment velocity meets customer deadlines.

14-3-1-4 Synchronization

The goal of a multi-organization supply chain is to function as a single entity that produces and distributes the inventory needed to meet customer requirements. By synchronizing data, resources, and processes, the supply chain partners can coordinate supply and demand over time. Technology facilitates the real-time information sharing between partners that drives consistent insights and collaborative decisions. Inventory optimization software, workforce management applications, and advanced demand management tools have been shown to improve the alignment of supply and demand.[9]

14-3-1-5 Adaptability

Organizations must strategically adapt the design and capabilities of a supply chain to evolving conditions. They can capitalize on demographic trends, political shifts, emerging economies, and other new opportunities through alteration of their supply chain operating model. This requires a flexible, geographically dispersed network supported by strong technology to analyze options and properly allocate network capacity. By linking supply chain technologies to sales and marketing systems, companies can sense and respond to real-time market needs and shape demand when capacity is limited.[10]

14-3-1-6 Segmentation

Organizations must dynamically align their demand and supply response capabilities to optimize net profitability across each customer segment. Offering differentiated service levels to each segment, the organization can increase sales and reduce costs. They avoid the "one size fits all" strategy that under-serves important customers and creates unnecessary costs. Technology can help an organization define logical segments, understand the cost to serve them, and prioritize service execution so that key groups receive appropriate attention.[11]

14-3-1-7 Optimization

To achieve peak supply chain performance, an organization must consider numerous trade-offs, effectively deploy its resources, and make the best possible decision. Supply chain optimization technologies use mathematical modeling tools to quickly run through the options to find the solution that facilitates success for all supply chain stakeholders. These tools can be used to study network design options, determine appropriate inventory levels, develop routing decisions, and more. The goal is to maximize service for the minimal possible operating costs.

These seven supply chain process enablers are by no means comprehensive or static. First, information systems must support initiatives related to supply chain innovation, performance analysis and improvement, risk management, and profitability. Second, these enabling technologies must evolve over time to meet new competitive challenges and changing customer requirements. Supply chain managers would be wise to regularly review these enablers and modify them as needed.

14-3-2 Link Network Elements

Putting the seven process enablers into practice and generating their value is not a simple task. A company cannot purchase software for a single process and expect to fundamentally improve its supply chain. Instead, an investment is required in a SCIS that provides critical knowledge links and automated information flows between internal processes and with external partners. SCIS enable firms to streamline their supply chain processes and provide management with more accurate information about what to produce, store, and move.[12]

It is important to note that immediate success is not guaranteed. Many SCIS implementations have produced less than stellar initial results. The $5.4 billion write-down that Target incurred after its failed expansion into Canada was partly attributed to SCIS issues. One industry expert noted that Target's faulty computer-assisted ordering system left store shelves empty while warehouses were bursting with inventory.[13]

A SCIS initiative will go much smoother and add greater value when time is taken to properly link the technology to people and processes in an intentional and integrated fashion. The technology must be connected across the supply chain. People need to adapt to the full capabilities of the SCIS. And, processes need to be updated to make use of the information that is generated through the SCIS. Figure 14.2 denotes these important people-process-technology linkages.

Properly connected technology generates access to data for informed supply chain decision making. Compared to a manual or partially integrated system, the data in a well-crafted and properly linked network supports data collection and synchronization through automated capture tools. Linking the SCIS across facilities and companies using an Internet or electronic data interchange (EDI) platform allows information to be quickly shared among collaborating companies at low cost.

With a capable, connected SCIS and data that are accurate, standardized, and readily available, focus must turn to the people element of the network. The people tasked with implementing and integrating the technology need the requisite skills, as well as adequate staff and financial resources to complete the work. Also, the day-to-day SCIS users must be

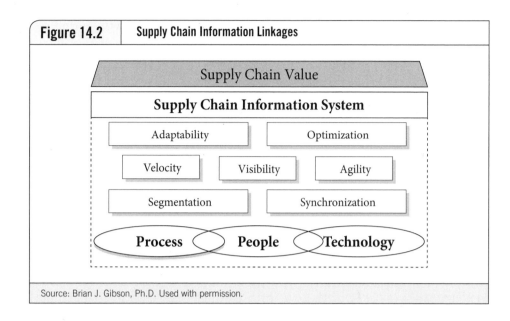

Figure 14.2   Supply Chain Information Linkages

Source: Brian J. Gibson, Ph.D. Used with permission.

properly trained in the appropriate use of the tools. Acclimating users to the SCIS and helping them understand why the tools were adopted will facilitate acceptance and positively impact supply chain performance.

After the technology foundation has been established and users understand the SCIS capabilities, the existing supply chain processes must be reviewed. The risk of not doing this is that inefficient, outdated, or unnecessary processes will be automated, providing little return on the SCIS investment. As needed, operating procedures must be updated and new goals for supply chain productivity, accuracy, timeliness, and cost should be established. Doing so will help supply chain managers fully leverage the process-enhancing capabilities of the SCIS.

The linkage of strong technology, properly trained users, and improved processes, creates a robust operating environment. Using the right SCIS, managers will be properly positioned to effectively plan and execute supply chain processes, make informed decisions, and respond quickly to potential problems. A comprehensive SCIS will also generate scorecards and dashboards that managers can use to continuously monitor, analyze, and improve performance.

14-3-3 Mitigate Known Risks

While information technology holds great promise for enhancing supply chain performance and organizational competitiveness, success is not guaranteed. Supply chain managers must carefully evaluate their technology options and steer clear of the pitfalls associated with systems adoption or upgrades.

A fundamental risk is highlighted by the term "solution." It is unrealistic to assume that supply chain technologies will readily solve or fix flawed supply chains. Technology alone cannot make ill-conceived processes highly productive or make effective use of poor quality data. Managers must avoid buying into the "solution" hype, resolve their process challenges prior to technology adoption, and remember the true role of technology–process enablement.

Weak technology–process alignment is another barrier to success. Software may be chosen by executives and technology specialists that do not understand supply chain processes or requirements. This can lead to ill-fitting solutions that fail to achieve their promise. To mitigate this risk, supply chain managers must be engaged in the technology selection process. It is their responsibility to ensure that the tools fit the need, support collaboration, and provide visibility into all key aspects of the supply chain.[14]

Technology gaps can be a significant problem for organizations. Often, "point solutions" fix an individual supply chain problem but don't address related issues or processes. Also, software may be purchased and deployed in piecemeal fashion, leading to a patchwork quilt of technologies rather than a seamless information network. To reduce these gaps, organizations should create stable enterprise-wide platforms and adopt an integrated supply chain software suite. This will improve data flows between supply chain processes and participants for accurate analysis and informed decision making.

Cross-chain systems integration with suppliers, service providers, and customers is a stumbling block for some organizations. Chief information officers at logistics service providers view integration with customers' information technologies as their single biggest challenge.[15] On the customer side, supply chain network complexity and creating visibility across the supply chain are top challenges.[16] To overcome these integration woes, trading partners need to link their computer systems and transform the supply chain into a network of beneficial relationships.[17]

Poor planning and preparation for technology implementation is also problematic. Some organizations do not create a change management plan. This increases the risk of implementation delays, lost connectivity, and supply chain disruptions. Others fail to address the all-important topics of cultural change, user acceptance, and training. These people issues were cited among the primary reasons why supply chain technology purchases fail to achieve the desired return on investment (ROI).[18] The appropriate action is to follow a staged, logical approach to adopting new technologies and to establish adequate budgets for technology installation, integration, and training.

As these mitigation strategies suggest, systems risks can be overcome. Many organizations successfully deploy SCIS to promote cost control, visibility, and service improvement. The key for supply chain leaders is to view technology implementation as a business improvement project. And, they must actively engage in the planning, purchase, and implementation of new tools. They cannot delegate responsibility and control to the IT team, consultants, or software suppliers.[19]

Realize that developing the systems capabilities of a Gartner Supply Chain Top 25 company is a long-term proposition. Fostering process excellence, linking multiple networks of people, processes, and technology, and mitigating technology risks are huge challenges, even with an established, best-in-class SCIS. Extensive time, financial resources, and top management commitment are required to select, implement, and maintain a quality system that supports supply chain excellence.

14-4 SCM Software

An essential element of a capable SCIS is the software applications that help managers arrange, analyze, and act upon relevant data. The supply chain software market includes technologies that address virtually every activity that occurs in the supply chain. Whether a company needs to develop a sales and operations plan, analyze facility relocation options, or maintain visibility of inventory, relevant software is available.

Supply chain software applications harness the computational power and communication abilities of an SCIS to help managers make timely, appropriate decisions. The primary

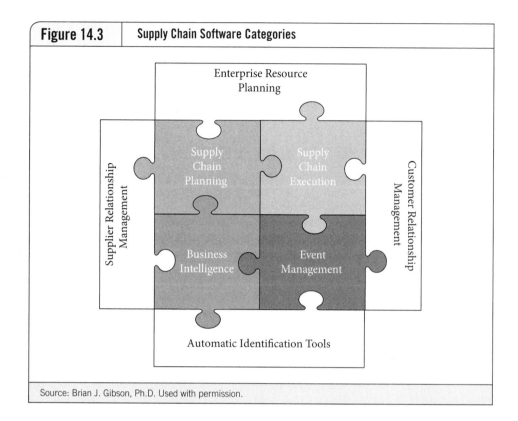

Figure 14.3 | **Supply Chain Software Categories**

Source: Brian J. Gibson, Ph.D. Used with permission.

SCM software categories include planning, execution, event management, and business intelligence (BI). Figure 14.3 displays the categories in a puzzle format to denote the importance of information sharing and cross-solution linkages.

Realize that a coordinated approach to software selection and implementation from the four categories is necessary. An integrated approach to SCM software use will support operational efficiency, customer value, and company profitability.

14-4-1 Planning

Supply chain planning applications help organizations evaluate requirements for materials, capacity, and services so that effective fulfillment plans and schedules can be developed. The tools help managers gain accurate, detailed insight into issues that affect the development of supply chain processes. The solutions use complex algorithms, optimization techniques, and heuristics to achieve supply chain objectives within the stated planning horizon.[20]

SCM planning applications help organizations shift from autonomous planning activities to synchronized planning processes that use real-time data for collaboration across departments, suppliers, and customers. This allows more accurate planning across a range of time horizons (weeks, months, or years) and important issues such as strategic network design, demand forecasting, and the other applications highlighted in Table 14.1. These wide-ranging capabilities are critical as supply chain planning can be quite complex.

Today, supply chain managers need to understand omni-channel demand, forecast at a granular level, and manage resources across multiple supply chains. These needs would be well-served by a robust supply chain planning suite. This integrated collection of software sits on top of a transactional system to provide planning and what-if scenario analysis capabilities.[21]

Table 14.1	Supply Chain Planning Applications
Available/capable to promise	Inventory planning
Sales and operations planning/integrated business planning	Production/factory planning and scheduling
	Vendor-managed inventory/direct point of sale
Collaborative planning, forecasting, and replenishment	Distribution planning
Event planning (promotion, life cycle)	Strategic network design
Demand planning	Inventory strategy optimization
Supply planning	
Production/multiplant capacity planning	

Source: Adapted from Gartner IT Glossary. Retrieved from http://www.gartner.com/it-glossary/scp-supply-chain-planning/

When the applications listed in Table 14.1 are used in an integrated fashion, supply chain managers can view, analyze, simulate, and segment essential data. They get a clearer picture of the available options that support better decisions and drive success. One planning software success story is featured in the On the Line box feature.

On the Line   *Planning Software Drives Forecast Accuracy*

When a company sells bulky, low cost goods like paper products, it is imperative to balance product availability with inventory expense across the supply chain. Shortages lead to lost sales while surpluses generate excess inventory carrying costs. Such was the problem faced by Kimberly-Clark Corp., the maker of Kleenex, Cottonelle toilet paper, and Huggies diapers.

To improve its inventory availability in the right locations, Kimberly-Clark deployed a demand analytics and planning system to improve forecast accuracy. Previously, historical sales forecasts were used to determine store shipments but this proved to be ineffective. The company needed to integrate point-of-sale data into its planning to generate accurate demand-driven forecasts.

To address the situation, Kimberly-Clark adopted a demand-sensing solution from Terra Technology to improve forecasting. Each day, sales information from three major retailers is loaded into the Terra Technology solution, which then recalibrates the shipment forecast for each retailer. The software also evaluates additional information from the retailers such as promotion plans, along with open orders and the legacy demand-planning forecast to generate a new shipment forecast. Kimberly-Clark uses the forecasts to guide internal deployment decisions and tactical planning.

The implementation has been a great success. Kimberly-Clark has improved its forecasts by 15 to 25 percent. This reduces the need for safety stock to protect against forecast errors. As a result, the company has removed $10 million of inventory from its U.S. network without a degradation of customer service.

Sources: James A. Cooke, "Kimberly-Clark Connects its Supply Chain to the Store Shelf," *CSCMP's Supply Chain Quarterly* (Quarter 1, 2013), pp. 42–44; and, Steve Rosenbush, "Kimberly-Clark Sees Data-Drive 'Step Change' in Retail Forecasts," *The Wall Street Journal* (April 16, 2013). Retrieved September 8, 2015 from https://www.terratechnology.com/assets/Uploads/20130416-wsj.pdf

14-4-2 Execution

The recommendations and decisions generated by supply chain planning systems are carried out by supply chain execution applications. The software facilitates desired performance of day-to-day operating tasks required to support customer demand.

Use of execution tools is extensive due to their rapid ROI and positive impact on supply chain performance. Supply chain execution tools purchases reached $3.66 billion dollars in 2014. Investment is expected to grow as companies replace outdated legacy systems in the pursuit of cross-chain collaboration, omni-channel fulfillment capabilities, and transportation efficiencies.[22]

Companies deploy a variety of execution software to implement their strategies and manage supply chain flows of product, information, and money. Effective integration of these tools supports data sharing and cross-chain visibility. The most widely used execution software includes the WMS and TMS discussed in previous chapters. However, the category has greatly expanded as companies seek integrated fulfillment capabilities. Table 14.2 presents the broad array of supply chain capabilities provided by execution tools.

Execution systems are especially important in complex supply chains. TriMas Industries, a global leader in engineered products in six industry verticals, operates a supply chain that spans 60 facilities in 19 countries. By using a TMS to help centralize freight spending and control, TriMas has been able to leverage its volume for lower rates and improve on-time performance. The company has reduced freight costs from 7.2 percent of sales to 4.8 percent of sales.[23]

Table 14.2	Functionality of Supply Chain Execution Applications
Warehouse Management Systems	Transportation Management Systems
Inventory management	Mode and carrier selection
Labor management	Route planning and optimization
Order processing	Dispatching and scheduling
Yard/dock management	Freight audit and payment
Returns management	Performance analysis
Order Management Systems	Global Trade Management
Sales order entry	Trade compliance
Pricing and credit checks	International logistics
Inventory allocation	Global order management
Invoice generation	Global trade financial management
Distributed Order Management	Manufacturing Execution Systems
Order assignment	Work-in-process management

Source: Adapted from Gartner IT Glossary. Retrieved from http://www.gartner.com/it-glossary/sce-supply-chain-execution/

14-4-3 Event Management

Supply chain event management tools collect data in real time from multiple sources across the network and convert them into information that gives managers a clear picture of how their supply chain is performing. The software allows companies to automate the monitoring of supply chain events as they occur on a day-to-day basis. When a problem or exception occurs, managers receive real-time notifications so that corrective action can be taken. Problems such as parts shortages, truck breakdowns, and network disruptions can be avoided or mitigated, saving time and money.

As the geographic scope and number of companies involved in a supply chain grow, the ability to monitor activities exceeds manual capabilities. Hence, supply chain event management tools provide the cross-chain visibility needed to detect, evaluate, and adapt to changing conditions before they snowball into major problems. Work flow rules can be built into an event management system to initiate automated responses that are either preemptive or reactive. [24]

Although they were once stand-alone applications, event management solutions are being integrated into other applications. Monitoring capabilities can now be found in global trade management, warehouse management, transportation management, and manufacturing execution systems. This will help to close the loop between planning and execution to support synchronization of end-to-end activities. For example, large organizations have vastly improved their global connectivity and event monitoring. They are now three times as likely as smaller organizations to have container and unit level visibility of ocean shipments. [25]

14-4-4 Business Intelligence

While execution software offers data extraction and report generation functionality, managers must still interpret the reports and identify areas for improvement. In contrast, BI tools automate the analytical work and present the results in visual formats that are easier to understand. [26] Relevant information becomes readily available to supply chain managers for informed planning and decision making.

In addition to the data collection and analysis capabilities, BI software supports self-service reporting, performance scorecarding versus goals, development of graphical dashboards, and activity monitoring in support of event management. These BI tools also provide access to data residing on multiple SCIS without the need for technology department involvement. Hence, cross-chain collaboration is supported.

Emerging BI go well beyond descriptive information on past performance. These "big data" capabilities are more dynamic, allowing managers to deploy diagnostic, predictive, and prescriptive analytics for greater value. Advanced analytics is the fastest-growing segment of the BI and analytics software market and surpassed $1 billion in 2013, according to Gartner. [27] These BI tools support superior decision making capabilities.

The increased user-friendliness of BI software and the potential payoffs are driving adoption of the tools. When done right, BI helps the organization use root-cause analysis to understand problems. In turn, stronger decision making can drive competitive advantage. BI opportunity areas include generating valuable insights about complex global operations, providing more granular visibility of spending, improving S&OP and demand forecasting, and resolving logistics bottlenecks.[28]

Tangible benefits are derived from strong BI initiatives. According to an Aberdeen Group study, leading BI software users have decreased their landed cost per unit by 0.5 percent, reduced their out-of-stock levels by 7.5 percent, and increased their on-time, in-full orders delivered to customers to 95.4 percent.[29]

14-4-5 Facilitating Tools

Supply chain planning, execution, event management, and BI tools are tremendous advances over the Excel spreadsheets historically used to capture and manage supply chain data. Still, the latest tools cannot truly stand alone as they require data from other sources and managers must align their supply chain decisions with organizational goals and processes. Briefly discussed here are systems and applications that provide critical links between supply chain processes, the organization, and external stakeholders. Collectively, they create a holistic view of the supply chain.

14-4-5-1   Enterprise Resource Planning

Enterprise resource planning (ERP) systems incorporate internal and external systems into a single unified solution that spans the enterprise. ERP systems includes the software that supports business functions and processes, computing hardware for hosting and executing software applications, and back-end network architecture for data communication across and within information systems.[30] A centralized and shared database system links the business processes, allowing information to be entered once and made available to all users.

Though they can be quite expensive and challenging to implement, ERP systems are widely used. A primary appeal lies in the ability of ERP systems to update and share accurate information across business processes. ERP-linked processes typically include accounting and finance, planning, engineering, human resources, purchasing, production, inventory/ materials management, order processing, and more. Primary benefits include process automation, technology cost savings, improved visibility of sales, inventory, and receivables, standardization of processes, and regulatory compliance.[31]

Over time, the traditional separation of supply chain technologies from ERP systems has faded. First, the boundaries are blurring as supply chain tools need to share the information stored in an ERP system. Second, the major ERP systems vendors offer supply chain software that can be readily linked to the ERP system. Though these ERP vendor versions of WMS, TMS, and other tools may not be quite as robust as best-of-breed supply chain software, they do have the advantage of being a one-stop solution and offer common structure that reduces the installation time and effort.[32]

14-4-5-2 Supplier Relationship Management

Supplier relationship management (SRM) is a controlled and systematic approach to managing an organization's sourcing activities for goods and services. SRM seeks to improve communication with suppliers by establishing a common frame of reference for the organizations. SRM software supports the effort by facilitating design collaboration, sourcing decisions, negotiations, and buying processes.[33] SRM software also helps organizations evaluate supplier risk, performance, and compliance throughout the lifecycle of a contract.

The goal of SRM and related software is to consolidate processes, streamline transactions, and improve information flows so that costs can be reduced and the end product for the consumer can be improved. Effective alignment of capable SRM software with strong procurement processes will yield the ability to consistently acquire needed inventory at the best available prices. Interactions will be conducted and managed in a systematic, integrated fashion across the lifecycle of supplier relationships, across business units, and across functions. And, supplier assets, expertise, and capabilities will be leveraged for maximum competitive advantage.[34]

14-4-5-3 Customer Relationship Management

Customer relationship management (CRM) focuses on the practices, strategies, and technologies that companies use to manage and analyze customer interactions and data throughout the relationship lifecycle.[35] CRM software consolidates customer information in a database so business users can more easily access and manage it. The system serves as a vital nerve center to manage the many connections between sellers and buyers in a supply chain. It facilitates information sharing and accessibility.

The goals of CRM software are to improve business relationships with customers, promote retention, and drive sales growth. Each goal requires the organization to learn more about customer needs, behaviors, and demand patterns in order to develop stronger bonds. Though CRM appears to be a marketing tool, the information can also be used by supply chain managers. Better customer insights can promote demand visibility, clarify inventory needs, and drive service improvements.[36]

14-4-5-4 Automatic Identification

By itself, the supply chain software discussed in this chapter provides little value for managers. The software must receive a constant stream of quality data (timely, accurate, relevant, etc.) to maximize ROI. The data capture also needs to be automated to support timely decision making.

Fortunately, supply chain managers can deploy a variety of automatic identification (auto-ID) and data capture technologies to assemble accurate data for analysis, planning, and execution of key processes. These technologies include barcode labels, radio-frequency identification (RFID) tags, optical character recognition tags, and related hardware and software. They work together to recognize objects, collect relevant information, and feed the data directly into the SCIS.

While barcodes are widely used in retail stores for inventory tracking and point of sale activities, RFID is gaining traction in retail distribution and fulfillment processes.[37] RFID makes use of tags and readers. The tag has a microchip that stores and processes information and an antenna that receives and transmits signals. The reader emits a signal to the tags which responds with appropriate information. The reader then sends the results to the SCIS.

Auto-ID tools enhance the visibility and control of products as they move across a supply chain. Automated data collection also improves capture speed, accuracy, and cost efficiency. This facilitates shipment tracking and product traceability, supply chain event management, and inventory replenishment. Auto-ID also provides valuable support for omni-channel fulfillment as highlighted in the On the Line feature.

On the Line   *RFID Supports Omni-channel Success*

As retailers increase customer options for ordering and taking possession of products, the importance of inventory accuracy rises. This is particularly true for the buy online, pick up in store option. When the retailer's Web site indicates that the inventory is available at a particular store and the customer places the order, the product must be in stock and easy to find. Otherwise, the customer will arrive for pick up and find that the order hasn't been or can't be filled. That leads to dissatisfaction and lost sales.

To avoid these embarrassing situations, retailers are turning to RFID technology. This auto-ID tool provides greater than 95 percent inventory accuracy which is a vast improvement over traditional inventory management techniques. It also helps the retail associate quickly locate the inventory within the store or stockroom. Misplaced or hidden inventory no longer create phantom stockouts. Item availability is improved 2 to 20 percent.

Major retailers, including Walmart, Target, Metro Stores, and Macy's, are increasing their item-level tagging of inventory. As a result, spending on RFID technology rose from $541 million in 2013 to $738 million in 2014. The spending trend will continue as more retailers use RFID to boost inventory visibility, accuracy, and in-stock availability.

Sources: "GS1 US Survey Shows Manufacturers and Retailers Embrace RFID to Enhance Inventory Visibility," *PR Newswire* (March 19, 2015). Retrieved September 10, 2015 from http://www.prnewswire.com/news-releases/gs1-us-survey-shows-manufacturers-and-retailers-embrace-rfid-to-enhance-inventory-visibility-300052870.html; MH&L Staff, "RFID Demand Up with Rise of Omni-Channel Retailing," *Material Handling & Logistics* (June 1, 2015). Retrieved September 10, 2015 from http://mhlnews.com/technology-automation/rfid-demand-rise-omni-channel-retailing

14-5 SCM Technology Implementation

As the preceding section indicates, a wide array of software tools support supply chain planning, execution, and control. Companies spend billions of dollars on technology with the goal of making their supply chains more productive. However, the initial purchase does not ensure quick success. Systems integration complexities and training requirements translate into implementation times that can exceed six months at costs that may be twice the software price. Thus, gaining a rapid ROI on technology is challenging.

The key to harnessing the capabilities of supply chain technology within a reasonable time frame is informed decision making. Supply chain managers take the time to develop a clear vision regarding how technology spending will facilitate supply chain strategy and satisfy specific requirements. It is possible to achieve a 12 to 18 month ROI if the managers properly assess their needs, understand their software application and delivery options, and addresses the technical issues before making a purchase decision.

14-5-1 Needs Assessment

The most important step in software selection and implementation is to understand the supply chain that the technology is intended to support. Too often, technology buyers don't understand the processes involved or apply software to outdated processes. This leads to deployments that are poorly matched to needs; unable to link stakeholders; and/or too narrowly focused to support cross-network visibility.

Knowledgeable managers must properly diagnose the situation. Their needs assessment must address the links between effective business processes, appropriate technology, and supply chain performance. They should benchmark their supply chain process capabilities against the needs of their partners. If the current capabilities are deemed inadequate, improvements must be made prior to technology evaluation.

Companies from Amazon to Zara have generated a competitive advantage in their respective industries because they support innovative supply chain practices with technology. They properly view supply chain software as an enabler of process improvement rather than a "quick fix" solution. This ultimately leads to realistic expectations, effective implementation, and greater ROI for SCIS purchases.

14-5-2 Software Selection

Software selection is a multifaceted decision. First, supply chain managers must determine which type of software—planning, execution, event management, or BI—is needed. Additionally, supply chain managers must compare the advantages of commercial software to in-house solutions, choose between single vendor suites and applications from multiple vendors, and consider licensing versus on-demand purchases, among other issues.

14-5-2-1 Development Alternatives

Software can be developed in-house by an organization or it can be purchased from an external vendor. Walmart and Amazon.com have information technology departments to build some internal supply chain applications. Some logistics service providers create in-house solutions as well. While this requires significant resources and development time, the resulting tools are tailored to the company's supply chain requirements. Internal developers can achieve a level of customization that is not possible with off-the-shelf software.

Most organizations do not undertake development due to cost, capability, and priority challenges. They rely on external software vendors to develop and implement supply chain technology. These tools effectively support supply chains that are not overly unique or complex. Because they can be implemented faster than what could be accomplished in-house, are built with interoperability as a key focus, and have some ability to be tailored, vendor-developed tools are the proper choice for most organizations.

14-5-2-2 Solutions Packages

If an organization chooses to purchase software, it has to determine what types of applications are needed and how they should be purchased. One option is to purchase individual applications from leading providers in each software category, commonly called "best-of-breed" solutions. Another option is to buy an integrated software suite from a single vendor as highlighted by Figure 14.4. The middle ground option is to purchase the main applications from a single supply chain software suite vendor and selectively add best-of-breed solutions.

Each strategy has its merits. Single vendor suites require less implementation time and cost versus a variety of tools from different vendors since there are fewer compatibility and connectivity issues. Also, there is only one vendor involved. This reduces complexity and coordination effort. Single vendor suites also require less training time as users only need to learn one package. However, some suites do not contain the advanced functionality or industry-specific capabilities found in best-of-breed applications. They can also be tailored to an individual company's supply chain issues.

The challenge for the technology buyer is to understand the implementation issues; their organization's need for tailored, advanced capabilities; and the constantly changing vendor landscape.

| **Figure 14.4** | **Supply Chain Software Suite** |

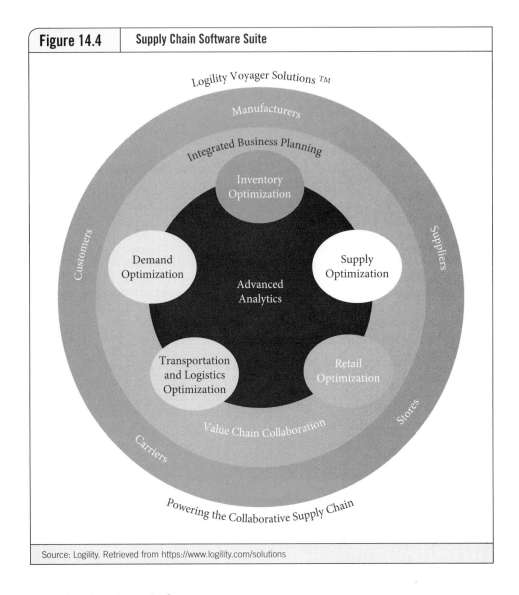

14-5-2-3 Purchase Options

Historically, supply chain software buyers had one option—license software from vendors and install it on the buyer's client-server systems. This is a logical method for supply chain processes with intense computational activity requirements. The downside of licensing is the capital investment and complex deployment. Buyers have to pay for the software up front; address implementation issues; and manage software upgrades, fixes, and maintenance costs.

The Internet and cloud computing have changed the purchase landscape. Buyers can use applications that are not permanently installed on the company's network. In the software as a service (SaaS) distribution model, applications are hosted by a vendor or service provider and made available to customers over a network. One SaaS option is hosted application management in which a technology provider hosts commercially available software for customers and delivers it over the Web. The other SaaS option is software on demand. In this model the provider gives customers network-based access to a single copy of an application created specifically for SaaS distribution.[38]

SaaS is gaining in popularity as more supply chain tools are offered via this method. Fast implementation, low capital requirements, scalability, easy Web-based access, and simplified software upgrades are reasons for deploying this model. However, potential adopters must also review the potential problems of SaaS. Security of sensitive company data must be evaluated. Service outages at the host site, regulatory compliance, and application performance management also warrant attention.[39]

14-5-3 Implementation Issues

Supply chain managers tend to focus on functionality when considering software, but they also must consider the implementation and operational issue. Potentially useful software will become "shelfware" if it is difficult to install, poorly linked to other tools, or too cumbersome to use. Hence, up-front effort must be expended to assess the implementation challenges before making software purchase decisions. The need for training, cultural change, systems interoperability, and data synchronization has already been mentioned. Two additional SCIS implementation issues are discussed as follows.

14-5-3-1 Data Standardization

Given the variety of software vendors, proprietary tools, and legacy systems, coordinating and sharing information across the supply chain can be a significant challenge. Just as different languages, dialects, and alphabets hamper human communication, the variety of systems and programming languages used in SCIS make it difficult to bring data together in an efficient, useful manner.

Though the inconsistent data could be translated, an alternative is to use a standardized format to enhance cross-chain communication. Just as English is the common language of global business, EDI and extensible markup language (XML) enable efficient and accurate computer-to-computer exchange of business data.

EDI provides inter-organizational, computer-to-computer exchange of structured information in a highly standardized, machine-processable format. EDI allows the rapid exchange of large amounts of information, reduces errors, and lowers costs, allowing supply chain partners to work more efficiently and effectively. Nevertheless, EDI does have its drawbacks. Implementation can be complex and transaction fees are incurred when EDI transactions travel across value-added networks.

XML is a robust, logically verifiable text format based on international standards that is simultaneously human-readable and machine-readable. XML provides a flexible way to create structured, common information formats and share both the format and the data via the Internet, intranets, and other networks. XML can be used to define complex documents and data structures such as invoices, inventory descriptions, shipment records, and other supply chain information.

Purchasing software with data standardization capabilities will ensure that information is quickly transferrable in a format that is usable across the SCIS. This will help buyers avoid costly, time-consuming translation efforts and improve SCIS interoperability. Enhanced communication and visibility will also be achieved.

14-5-3-2 Application Integration

Another important issue is seamless integration of software applications. This can be readily accomplished within a self-contained supply chain software suite, but supply chain partners often rely on different vendors, applications, or software versions. The greater the variety of applications, the more challenging the connectivity and information-sharing issues become.

Extensive efforts have been made to improve application integration and foster supply chain information synchronization. Application programming interfaces (APIs) are sets of requirements that govern how one application can talk to another. By sharing some of a program's internal functions, it becomes possible to build compatible applications and readily share data. Service-oriented architecture (SOA) also promotes software integration. SOA defines how two computing entities interact in such a way as to enable one entity to perform a unit of work on behalf of another entity.

Supply chain technology buyers need to understand the challenges of application integration while pursuing improved SCIS connectivity. They must assess and compare integration methods, and then choose those that best fit current needs while providing the flexibility to meet future functionality requirements.

Ultimately, these standardization and integration issues may be the least likely issue to derail a technology implementation initiative. Often, problems occur when obvious issues are overlooked. Thus, supply chain managers must diligently guide the process and plan for possible disruptions. They would do well to follow these 10 golden rules for success:

1. Secure the commitment of senior management.
2. Remember that it is not just an information technology project.
3. Align the project with business goals.
4. Understand the software capabilities.
5. Select partners carefully.
6. Follow a proven implementation methodology.
7. Take a step-by-step approach for incremental value gains.
8. Be prepared to change business processes.
9. Keep end users informed and involved.
10. Measure success with key performance indicators (KPIs).[40]

14-6 Supply Chain Technology Innovations

If there is one constant in SCM, then it has to be ongoing change. That may seem like an oxymoron, but the discipline is continuously evolving to support omni-channel innovation, global network realignment, and customer service enhancement. To achieve success, supply chain managers must effectively leverage current and emerging technologies. Given this environment, it should be no surprise that spending on supply chain software is projected to reach $16.3 billion by 2019.[41]

While most of this spending will occur for existing technologies, some novel applications are gaining traction in SCM. Industry observers point to three technology innovations that hold significant promise for SCM advancement. Each is briefly discussed to conclude the chapter.

14-6-1 Internet of Things

We live in a highly connected world of smartphones and mobile computers. However, there is another level of connectivity that most people don't notice. Connected devices—with sensors, on/off switches, and Internet linkages—already outnumber the world's population and the gap is accelerating. This Internet of Things (IoT) includes Apple watches, Fitbit trackers, and other wearables, home automation systems, electronic toll passes, and other devices used daily by people.

A broad range of IoT business equipment, devices, and mechanisms are already in use. Gartner conservatively estimates that by 2020 there will be more than 26 billion connected devices. Gartner indicates that the IoT trend will influence how supply chains operate.[42] Hence, it is an innovative or "disruptive" technology that warrants attention.

The technology will allow supply chain managers to intelligently connect people, processes, data, and things using IoT devices and sensors. This deeper intelligence will be used to align, synchronize, and automate supply chain activities. Examples of how IoT can enhance supply chain performance include:

- Right-sizing inventory levels – Use sensors to monitor inventory levels in fuel tanks. Trigger a replenishment request when inventory is nearly depleted.

- Modifying storage conditions – Monitor container and facility climate. Adjust temperature and humidity levels to avoid spoilage of food and pharmaceuticals.

- Enhancing in-transit visibility – Track status of shipments as they move across the network. Send new routes to drivers to avoid congested roadways.

- Calibrating factory machinery – Capture equipment performance data. Remotely adjust machine settings or dispatch a maintenance worker for repairs.

Future IoT innovations may radically alter the way supply chains serve end users. It is entirely possible that sensors connected to your refrigerator or your computer printer will be able to track your product usage and trigger automatic replenishment of milk, eggs, and ink cartridges. You will never experience a stockout and the retailer will operate in a true demand-responsive fashion.

A number of security issues must be resolved to bring IoT to its full potential. Increased digitization of information and transfer via the Internet creates data theft risks. Remote tampering with physical infrastructure is possible, and, consumer privacy must be protected against data breaches. To avoid such problems, IoT users must identify their risks and take meaningful steps to mitigate them. This includes reducing the amount of data collected by IoT devices, deploying layered security systems including firewalls, intrusion detection systems, and antivirus tools, segmenting networks, and allowing people to opt-out of IoT initiatives as desired.[43]

Although these issues present real risks, organizations are not shying away from IoT. According to a recent survey, nearly 65 percent of the participants have already deployed or are implementing IoT.[44] SCM applications of IoT technology should lead to compelling improvements in effectiveness and efficiency, further distinguishing forward thinking organizations from their competitors.

14-6-2 Mobile Connectivity

Mobile technology is not a new topic in SCM. In fact, it has been used for nearly four decades since Qualcomm's OmniTracs ushered in mobile two-way satellite-based information services for fleet management. Subsequent introductions and advancements in GPS technology, auto-ID, wireless connectivity, tablets, and smartphones have altered supply chain processes for the better. Improved visibility, asset control, and agility are three benefits of a connected supply chain.

Although mobile connectivity is growing, it has not reached the saturation point in the marketplace. Opportunities for wider adoption are vast as mobile technology problems have faded away. Price points for hardware and communications have fallen, the reliability of mobile technologies has greatly improved, and logical solutions with real ROI are being developed.

Mobile connectivity is critical in the transportation area as freight companies must grapple with the competing objectives of maximizing service and minimizing costs. They need a continuous link with their geographically dispersed drivers, equipment, and cargo. Enhanced geographic information systems data along with real-time and predictive traffic data are needed to effectively plan routes, determine dispatch times, and re-route in-transit freight. These capabilities will help the freight companies to accurately predict arrival times, reduce delivery costs, and decrease energy consumption.[45]

Warehouse operations have long relied on RFID-enabled terminals on forklifts and hand held devices to direct employee activities. Yet, traditional labor management systems are PC-based and tie managers to the office. They need to spend more time on the warehouse floor to gain operational oversight and coach employees, according to a recent survey. Mobile tools and solutions will provide managers with access to critical productivity, work-load management, and exception data regardless of their location. Such capabilities will allow managers to break away from the office and spend much needed time directly engaging with their employees and improving throughput.[46]

Mobility is also a technology priority for manufacturing operations, according to a PwC global chief executive officer survey. Forward thinking manufacturers are integrating mobile capabilities into their quality systems. This allows real-time monitoring of supplier traceability, quality, and non-conformance and corrective actions. Mobile integration of configure, price and quote systems to pricing and inventory systems makes it possible for salespeople to rapidly give customer pricing and delivery dates. And, accessible dashboards on mobile devices will allow managers to monitor production workflow performance. The goals of these initiatives are to make manufacturers more responsive to customers and make manufacturing intelligence the new normal in production operations.[47]

14-6-3 Functional Automation

Automation has long been a part of the manufacturing plant with conveyors moving products between workstations and robots handling welding, painting, and other precision tasks. Warehouse automation has also gained tremendous traction as companies are opening large scale DCs that deploy automated storage, handling, and distribution technologies rather than manual labor. Fulfillment speed and accuracy—two essential elements of omni-channel retailing—are greatly enhanced and there is never an absenteeism issue.

In contrast, the transportation function continues to be a labor-intensive activity, particularly the trucking industry. Connective technologies needed to support driverless vehicles are under rapid development. That may sound farfetched in comparison to IoT appliances and mobile connectivity to software but companies like Daimler AG, Google, and Komatsu are spending significant resources to develop autonomous vehicles.

Daimler's Future Truck 2025 navigates using its Highway Pilot system, enabled by a collection of cameras and radar sensors, while continuously transmitting its position to other drivers and traffic control centers. The pilot program puts a driver in the vehicle to handle driving on city streets. However, it relies heavily on the operational system for highway driving much like an auto-pilot system for an airplane during normal flight operations.[48]

The promises of driverless vehicles are many. First, the prospect of safer truck operation is strong due to the multitude of sensors being used and the elimination of driver fatigue as a crash factor. Second, the driving system is designed to operate at maximum fuel efficiency and reduce emissions. Finally, the technology may be able to address the chronic shortage of truck drivers that hampers industry capacity.[49] This is a long-range prospect as much

Table 14.3	Sources of Additional Information: Supply Chain Technology
SOURCE	**WEB SITE**
Aberdeen	www.aberdeen.com
DC Velocity	www.dcvelocity.com/channels/technology/
Eye For Transport	www.eft.com/technology
Gartner	www.gartner.com
Logistics Viewpoints	logisticsviewpoints.com
Supply Chain 24/7	www.supplychain247.com/topic/category/technology
Supply Chain Digest	www.scdigest.com

Source: Brian J. Gibson, Ph.D. Used with permission.

more testing and proof of concept will be needed to gain regulatory and public acceptance of truly driverless vehicles.

Without question, the innovations described earlier have the potential to drive SCM to new levels of performance. The same is true for future solutions that are in the concept phase today. The only way to keep up with the ever-changing technology landscape is to continuously monitor industry developments. Table 14.3 provides a list of Web sites that will help you stay current on supply chain technology innovations and issues.

SUMMARY

Information is critical to the success of a supply chain and must flow freely between partners. Without accurate, timely information, it is extremely difficult for managers to make effective decisions regarding the purchase, production, and distribution of materials. To facilitate the knowledge links and foster supply chain visibility, most organizations rely upon computer hardware, SCIS, and supportive Internet-based technologies. They realize that real-time information and the ability to dynamically respond to changing conditions in the supply chain are critical to organizational success. Industry leaders are using SCIS to create real-time knowledge, adaptive capabilities, and substantial competitive advantages in their respective markets.

Harnessing information technology in support of supply chain excellence is an ongoing need as SCIS capabilities continue to evolve. Supply chain managers must recognize the critical role of information, understand the software options, choose solutions wisely, and overcome key implementation challenges to generate maximum benefit from information technology. Key concepts from the chapter include:

- To produce actionable knowledge, supply chain information must be high quality, readily flow between organizations, and support a variety of decision types.
- Leading organizations leverage supply chain technology for greater visibility, agility, velocity, synchronization, optimization, and related capabilities.
- A well-designed SCIS links people, processes, and technology in a manner that provides actionable information and enhances decision making.
- Savvy supply chain managers understand the risks involved in SCIS adoption and take an active role in the planning, purchase, and implementation of new tools.

- Supply chain software falls into four general categories: (1) planning tools for forecasting and related activities, (2) execution systems for management of day-to-day processes, (3) event management tools to monitor supply chain flows, and (4) BI applications used to analyze performance.
- ERP, SRM, and CRM systems provide valuable data and platforms that link supply chain processes to the organization and external stakeholders.
- To maximize SCIS investment success, managers must effectively assess the SCM requirements, understand software options, and address the technical issues.
- The technology landscape is ever changing and managers must evaluate how innovations like IoT, mobility, and automation will drive supply chain improvement.

STUDY QUESTIONS

1. Discuss the role of information in the supply chain and how it supports supply chain planning and execution.

2. Describe the attributes of information quality and how they impact supply chain decision making.

3. What are the primary capabilities created by supply chain technology? How can they drive supply chain excellence?

4. Describe how a SCIS enables process excellence and links the essential elements.

5. Review the methods used by supply chain managers to mitigate SCIS implementation risks.

6. Identify the four primary categories of supply chain software and discuss their primary functions.

7. Using company Web sites, develop a profile (types of supply chain software offered, annual sales, and recent news) of the following organizations:
   a. SAP (http://www.sap.com)
   b. Manhattan Associates (http://www.manh.com)
   c. Logility (http://www.logility.com)

8. What is the role of ERP systems in SCM?

9. Discuss the relative advantages of best-of-breed software versus supply chain suites.

10. Why would companies choose to use on-demand software versus licensed software?

11. When preparing to purchase and implement SCIS components, what issues and questions must managers address?

12. How will IoT innovations, mobile connectivity and automation drive change in a supply chain?

NOTES

1. "Gartner Says Worldwide Supply Chain Management and Procurement Software Market Grew 10.8 Percent in 2014," *Gartner Newsroom* (May 12, 2015). Retrieved August 28, 2015 from http://www.gartner.com/newsroom/id/3050617

2. "Global CEO Survey: Transportation & Logistics CEOs Capitalizing On New Technologies," *Supply Chain 24/7* (June 3, 2015). Retrieved August 28, 2015 from http://www.supplychain247.com/article/transportation_logistics_ceos_capitalizing_on_new_technologies/one_network_enterprises

3. Bridget McCrea, "2012 Supply Chain Software Users Survey: Spending Stabilizes," *Logistics Management* (May 2012): 38–40.

4. Cecil B. Bozarth and Robert B. Handfield, *Introduction to Operations and Supply Chain Management,* 4th ed. (Upper Saddle River, NJ: Pearson Education Inc., 2015).

5. Gartner, "Gartner Announces Ranking of Its 2015 Supply Chain Top 25," *Gartner Newsroom* (May 14, 2015). Retrieved September 3, 2015 from http://www.gartner.com/newsroom/id/3053118

6. Jessica Heine, "Deloitte Study: Advanced Supply Chain Capabilities are a Crucial Catalyst for Strong Financial Performance," *Deloitte* (April 14, 2014). Retrieved September 3, 2015 from http://www2.deloitte.com/us/en/pages/about-deloitte/articles/press-releases/deloitte-study-advance-supply-chain.html

7. Stephanie Miles, "Why Supply Chain Visibility Tools are a Good Investment," *Supply Chain Digest* (July 30, 2015). Retrieved September 3, 2015 from http://www.scdigest.com/experts/Amberroad_15-07-30.php?cid=9571

8. Laura Cecere, "Preparing to Run the Race: Supply Chain 2020," *Supply Chain Shaman* (April 25, 2012). Retrieved September 3, 2015 from http://www.supplychainshaman.com/uncategorized/preparing-to-run-the-race-supply-chain-2020/

9. Chris Cunnane, "Supply Chain Synchronization: Matching Supply and ACTUAL Demand," *Logistics Viewpoints* (March 18, 2015). Retrieved September 3, 2015 from http://logisticsviewpoints.com/2015/03/18/supply-chain-synchronization-matching-supply-and-actual-demand/

10. Gregory C. Cudahy, Mark O. George, Gary R. Godfrey, and Mary J. Rollman, "Preparing for the Unpredictable," *Outlook: The Journal of High-Performance Business* (2012). Retrieved September 3, 2015 from http://www.cas-us.com/SiteCollection Documents/PDF/Accenture-Outlook-Preparing-for-the-unpredictable-Supply-Chain-SCM.pdf

11. Mary Holcomb, Tom Nightingale, Tony Ross, and Karl B. Manrodt, *20th Annual Trends and Issues in Logistic and Transportation Study: Operating in the New Normal* (2011). Retrieved September 4, 2015 from http://manrodt.com/pdf/Normal_2011.pdf

12. Kenneth C. Laudon, Jane P. Laudon, and Ahmed Elragal, *"Management Information Systems: Managing the Digital Firm* (Essex, England: Pearson Education Ltd., 2013), p. 319.

13. 24/7 Staff, "Supply Chain Miseries Doom Target in Canada," *Supply Chain 24/7* (January 17, 2015). Retrieved September 6, 2015 from http://www.supplychain247.com/article/supply_chain_miseries_doom_target_in_canada

14. Joe Brady, "The Five Main Supply Chain Challenges Companies Face Today," *Supply Chain Edge* (April 4, 2013). Retrieved September 3, 2015 from http://www.supplychainedge.com/the-edge-blog/the-five-main-supply-chain-challenges-companies-face-today/

15. S. Reynolds and T. Khan, *2012–2013 Transport & Logistics CIO Report.* Retrieved September 3, 2015 from http://www.eft.com/content/it-strategy-logistics-cios-0

16. Sara Pearson Specter, "Trends Transforming Supply Chain Infrastructure,"*MHI Press Release* (February 20, 2013). Retrieved September 3, 2015 from http://www.mhi.org/media/news/12232

17. David Sims, "Integrated Supply Chains Maximize Efficiencies and Savings," *Thomas Register Industry Market Trends* (July 23, 2013). Retrieved September 3, 2015 from http://news.thomasnet.com/imt/2013/07/23/integrated-supply-chains-maximize-efficiencies-and-savings

18. Frank Quinn, "Maximizing Your Return on Investment from Investment in Supply Chain Technology," *Supply Chain 24/7* (June, 2013). Retrieved September 3, 2015 from http://www.supplychain247.com/article/maximizing_your_return_on_investment_from_supply_chain_technology/D4

19. Brian J. Gibson, Joe B. Hanna, C. Clifford Defee, and Haozhe Chen, *The Definitive Guide to Integrated Supply Chain Management.* (Oak Brook, IL: Council of Supply Chain Management Professionals, 2014).

20. ARC Advisory Group, "Supply Chain Sophistication Drives Supply Chain Planning Growth," *Supply Chain Planning* (February 4, 2012). Retrieved September 7, 2015 from http://www.arcweb.com/market-studies/pages/supply-chain-planning.aspx

21. Gartner, "SCP (supply chain planning)," IT Glossary. Retrieved September 7, 2015 from http://www.gartner.com/it-glossary/scp-supply-chain-planning/

22. Josh Bond, "Top 20 Supply Chain Management Software Suppliers," *Modern Materials Handling* (July 2015). Retrieved September 7, 2015 from http://www.mmh.com/article/top_20_supply_chain_management_software_suppliers_2015

23. John D. Schultz, "TriMas Centralizes Freight, Boosts Bottom Line," *Logistics Management* (October 2014), pp. 26–29.

24. Dave Turbide, "Supply Chain Event Management (SCEM)," I.B.I.S. Insights Blog (September 23, 2014). Retrieved September 8, 2015 from http://ibisinc.com/blog/supply-chain-event-management-scem/

25. Bob Heaney, *Supply Chain Visibility: A Critical Strategy to Optimize Cost and Service*, (Cambridge, MA: Aberdeen Group, 2013), pp. 2, 8.

26. Amy Roach Partridge, "Business Intelligence in the Supply Chain," *Inbound Logistics,* (April 2013), pp. 39–46.

27. "Gartner Says Advanced Analytics is a Top Business Priority," *Gartner Newsroom* (October 21, 2014). Retrieved September 8, 2015 from http://www.gartner.com/newsroom/id/2881218

28. "Integrated Business Intelligence Solutions," *Genpact Analytics & Research* (2013). Retrieved September 8, 2015 from http://www.genpact.com/docs/resource-/integrated-business-intelligence-solutions-for-chief-financial-officers

29. Bob Heaney, *Supply Chain Intelligence: Descriptive, Prescriptive, and Predictive Optimization*, (Cambridge, MA: Aberdeen Group, 2015), p. 5.

30. "Enterprise Resource Planning System (ERP System)," *Techopedia Dictionary.* Retrieved September 9, 2015 from https://www.techopedia.com/definition/28432/enterprise-resource-planning-system-erp-system

31. "ERP Creating the Foundation for an Efficient Organization," ITC Infotech. Retrieved September 9, 2015 from http://www.itcinfotech.com/erp/erp-benefits.aspx

32. Bridget McCrea, "ERP vs. Best-of-Breed," *Logistics Management,* (July 2013), pp. 44–47.

33. Cecil C. Bozarth and Robert B. Handfield, *Introduction to Operations and Supply Chain Management,* 4th ed. (Upper Saddle River, NJ: Pearson Education Inc., 2015).

34. Jonathan Hughes, Jessica Wadd, "Getting the Most out of SRM," *Supply Chain Management Review*, (January 2012), pp. 22–29.

35. Margaret Rouse, "Customer Relationship Management Definition," *TechTarget SearchCRM*. Retrieved September 9, 2015 from http://searchcrm.techtarget.com/definition/CRM

36. Rob O'Byrne, "CRM and the Supply Chain," *Logistics Bureau* (July 10, 2013). Retrieved September 9, 2015 from http://www.logisticsbureau.com/crm-and-the-supply-chain/

37. J. Gibson, C. Clifford Defee, and Rafay Ishfaq, *State of the Retail Supply Chain: Essential Findings of the Fifth Annual Report*, (Auburn, AL: Auburn University, March 2015), p. 27.

38. Margaret Rouse, "Software as a Service (SaaS) Definition," *TechTarget SearchCloudComputing.* Retrieved September 10, 2015 from http://searchcloudcomputing.techtarget.com/definition/Software-as-a-Service

39. Charles McLellan, "SaaS: Pros, Cons, and Leading Vendors, *ZDNet*, (March 4, 2013). Retrieved September 10, 2015 from http://www.zdnet.com/article/saas-pros-cons-and-leading-vendors/

40. Jose Favilla and Andrew Fearne, "Supply Chain Software Implementations: Getting it Right," *Supply Chain Management* (October 2005): 241–243.

41. Bond, op. cit.

42. C. John Langley, Jr., "The Internet of What? (of Things, of Course)," *NASSTRAC Newslink*, (November 2015).

43. Jay Vijayan, "5 Ways to Prepare for IoT Security Risks," *InformationWeek DarkReading* (February 24, 2015). Retrieved September 10, 2015 from http://www.darkreading.com/endpoint/5-ways-to-prepare-for-iot-security-risks/d/d-id/1319215

44. Maha Muzumdar and Margie Steele, "The Internet of Things (IoT): Opportunities for Smarter Supply Chains," *Industry Week* (June 3, 2015). Retrieved September 10, 2015 from http://www.industryweek.com/supply-chain/internet-things-iot-opportunities-smarter-supply-chains

45. Mike Mulqueen, "Mobile Technology and Freight Transportation," *Supply Chain 24/7* (March 13, 2014). Retrieved September 11, 2015 from http://www.supplychain247.com/article/mobile_technology_and_freight_transportation/sctusa

46. Peter Schnorbach, "Survey Says? Warehouse Managers Must Get Mobile," *Logistics Viewpoints* (June 11, 2015). Retrieved September 11, 2015 from http://logisticsviewpoints.com/2015/06/11/survey-says-warehouse-managers-must-get-mobile/

47. Louis Columbus, "10 Ways Mobility is Revolutionizing Manufacturing," *Forbes* (April 20, 2015). Retrieved September 11, 2015 from http://www.forbes.com/sites/louiscolumbus/2015/04/20/10-ways-mobility-is-revolutionizing-manufacturing/

48. Fergal Gallagher, "Daimler's Driverless Trucks Could Save Lives and Benefit the Environment," *Tech Times* (June 22, 2015). Retrieved September 11, 2015 from http://www.techtimes.com/articles/62625/20150622/daimler-s-driverless-trucks-save-lives-environment.htm

49. Greg Harman, "Driverless Big Rigs: New Technologies Aim to Make Trucking Greener and Safer," *The Guardian* (February 24, 2015). Retrieved September 11, 2015 from http://www.techtimes.com/articles/62625/20150622/daimler-s-driverless-trucks-save-lives-environment.htm

CASE 14.1

Inflate-a-Dome Innovations

Three years ago, two college roommates—Pat Kelly and Jeff Speer—returned to their tailgating site after a football game only to find a troubling situation. A brief thunderstorm occurred during the game and it turned their tailgating tent into a twisted, unfixable mess. They had pooled some cash together only a few weeks prior to buy the tent. Now that investment was gone.

Frustrated, Pat created a tent that eliminated the metal frame which always seemed to be the fail point of the product. His prototype tent was supported by air-filled tubes that could quickly be inflated with a small battery-operated pump. Jeff created a marketing plan and the two entered a campus competition for new product innovations.

The team won $50,000 and rolled it into a venture called Inflate-a-Dome Innovations (IDI). They hired a friend to build a website, purchased the materials needed to build 50 inflatable tents, and were in business. Using social media and online advertising, IDI began to generate sales and soon had a sustainable business. A few catalog retailers offered to feature Inflate-a-Dome tents in their publications and sales grew.

Needing to manage the operations better, Pat and Jeff hired a friend who was a recent supply chain management grad. Vic Catella quickly assessed the situation and decided that to grow, IDI needed to better control its inventory, production, and transportation. So Vic found some Excel-based freeware and IDI soon had a somewhat better handled on its supply chain. The catalog retailers could transfer orders online, via email, or by phone and IDI was able to create basic production schedules, plan materials needs, and support fulfillment. An online link to the small package carrier made it easy to schedule pickups and track in-transit freight. Life was getting simpler at IDI.

The company was growing at a manageable pace and then life changed overnight. Unknown to the IDI owners, a Hollywood star used ten Inflate-a-Dome tents at her intimate wedding reception. Bad weather quickly rolled in but the tents performed well, saving the day. The story was picked up by the media and soon Pat and Jeff were being interviewed on national morning shows.

Soon thereafter, inquiries began arrive from sporting goods retailers, the NCAA licensing group, and Amazon.com. The IDI owners were elated that volume was about to explode.

In contrast, Vic was greatly worried that inventory variety was about to greatly expand with tents in new colors and emblazoned with college logos. Also, order size and shipment would no longer be one to four units but 50 to 500. He sensed that the simple SCIS that he had built for spare change would no longer suffice. It was time for a real SCIS that could support major clients. It was time for a strategic planning meeting about technology with Pat and Jeff.

CASE QUESTIONS

1. As its customer base grows and becomes more diversified, how will the information requirements of the IDI supply chain change?
2. Given its anticipated volume growth and inventory variety expansion, what supply chain capabilities will IDI need?
3. In preparation for the strategic planning meeting, what technology risks must Vic think about?
4. With limited funds available, what SCM software should Vic recommend? Why?

CASE 14.2

Grand Reproductions Inc.

Grand Reproductions Inc. (GRI) is an authorized manufacturer of products based on popular video games and characters. The Seattle-based company produces collectibles, toys, and other novelty items in its factory outside Chengdu, China. The majority of sales are made to small retailers in the United States and Latin America.

Interest in GRI products has grown thanks to some timely product placements on popular television shows. Danny Gadget, the company's CEO, just received a call from Giga-Mart about carrying the GRI product line for the upcoming holiday season. The call went very well until the Giga-Mart executive asked about GRI's supply chain technology platform and order fulfillment system. Danny had little idea what the person was talking about and provided a somewhat ambiguous response.

The truth of the matter is that GRI has no formal SCIS. The company has talked about using the Internet but order management is largely paper based. From forecasting and inventory control to order fulfillment and customer invoicing, everything has been done by hand on preprinted forms, with the information later entered into Excel spreadsheets.

The Mega-Mart executive sensed the lack of technological sophistication and closed the call by saying: "We really want to carry your products this year but we do have specific standards for digital transfers of orders, point of sale data, and invoices. If you can't effectively interact with our SCIS, then we won't be able to do business with Grand Reproductions."

CASE QUESTIONS

1. To obtain the necessary technological capabilities should GRI license software or purchase access via the Software as a Service model? Explain.
2. What types of software does GRI need to support the Mega-Mart business? What features and capabilities are needed?
3. What roles can the Internet play in GRI's move from manual methods to technology-based information management?
4. What types of technology implementation challenges might GRI face?

Source: Brian J. Gibson, Ph.D. Used with permission.

Chapter 15

STRATEGIC CHALLENGES AND CHANGE FOR SUPPLY CHAINS

Learning Objectives

After reading this chapter, you should be able to do the following:

- Understand current and future strategic challenges and opportunities for supply chains.

- Identify several key principles for supply chain success that have retained their relevance over time.

- Develop a fundamental understanding of supply chain analytics and how they can improve planning, decision-making, and execution in the supply chain.

- Consider the richness of information and insight that can result from the application of supply chain analytics to big data.

- Understand the critical success strategies for retailers operating in an omni-channel environment.

- Appreciate the need for sustainability as it relates to organizations and their supply chains, and to develop effective priorities and approaches to achieve sustainability.

- Assess the roles and importance of reverse flows in the supply chain, and to distinguish between a value stream and waste stream.

- Become familiar with the concept and capabilities of 3-D printing. Also known as additive manufacturing, this emerging technology will have significant impacts on supply chain management.

- Understand the changing roles of supply chain professionals and the process for developing related skills.

- Have a broad and insightful perspective on the concept of supply chain management, and to understand how it can be a key element of success for organizations and their trading partners.

Supply chain practitioners are adept at identifying and adapting to changes in the real world, both in the long and short term. Two examples: One company is preparing its supply chain process for an anticipated explosion of products that don't exist yet, and many logistics and supply chain practitioners are dealing with satisfying consumer demand for instant delivery gratification because of the new "shipment impatience" phenomenon.

Long-term example: *Inbound Logistics* recently met with IBC Advanced Alloys, a Vancouver, British Columbia-based rare metals manufacturer and distributor. The company specializes in beryllium and copper alloys, producing products the aerospace and defense industry needs to build all that futuristic sci-fi stuff that will be reality before we know it.

Given IBC's position upstream in the supply chain, it's an indicator of where change driven by the Internet of Things is taking us. Notably, electronics and circuit board manufacturers are locking up rare metal suppliers now, and streamlining supply chain operations for change that won't be a reality for years. Why? Because the expectation is that the Internet of Things will cause an explosion in demand for circuit boards that bring sci-fi reality to life. Machines talking to machines require sophisticated chipsets that sap rare metal reserves, which calls for global speed in delivery.

IBC realizes the world is changing, and is taking steps *now* to fold that change into its supply chain operations. The velocity of change should impact supply chain planning for the future... right now.

The short-term real-world example of a supply chain adapting to change is the fairly recent behavioral phenomenon of consumer shipment impatience. As a consumer, how many times have you made an online buy based on how fast a vendor could deliver, even if the transportation cost was higher? Ever been left dissatisfied when an e-tailer missed your delivery expectations? Today, many businesses exhibit the same consumerish behavior, and don't seem to care that much about geographical limitations on immediate delivery either. Sourcing from the East? I don't care, I need it now. Selling to China? They don't care, they want it now.

That consumer expectation for speed bleeds over into commercial dealings and impacts supply chain operations. Practitioners have been adept at adjusting to this change by using near-sourcing, omni-channel, and expedited solutions.

There's no stopping innovation, nor new customer demands based on change in the world. As a supply chain practitioner, take the time to look into the future, visualize where change might take your operations, and plan accordingly. The future will be here before you know it. Velocity of supply chain change, meet velocity of change.

Source: Biondo, Keith, "Adapting Your Supply Chain for the Future...Now," *Inbound Logistics*, November 2014.

15-1 Introduction

The primary purpose of this concluding chapter is to provide a capstone or integration of the content of this book. Hopefully, this will provide readers with an opportunity to reflect on past and current advances and accomplishments in supply chain management, and to think about key factors and issues that will help to shape and direct the future of this field of study. To help achieve this purpose, this chapter focuses on two primary objectives:

- To examine seven key principles of supply chain management, ones that have been proven to have a lasting value. The focus will be on updating our understanding of these principles to align with today's supply chain issues and challenges, and also to provide some useful examples of these principles in action.

- To discuss several areas that will be of great significance to the future growth, development, and transformation of supply chains. Included among these areas are: (1) supply chain analytics and big data; (2) omni-channel; (3) sustainability; (4) 3-D manufacturing; and (5) talent.

15-2 Principles of Supply Chain Management[1]

Looking at how disciplines or areas of study evolve over time, it is not unusual to identify a very select number of papers and articles that may be regarded as "classic" or "seminal" articles. In the supply chain discipline, one of these timeless articles is "The Seven Principles of Supply Chain Management," written by David L. Anderson, Frank E. Britt, and Donavon J. Favre, that appeared in the very first issue of *Supply Chain Management Review*. According to Frank Quinn, editor of the SCMR, this was the most requested article in the 10-year history of the publication; it provided a clear and compelling case for excellence in supply chain management.[2] Further, Mr. Quinn added that the insights provided in the article remained remarkably fresh 10 years later.

The purpose of this section is to again recognize these seven principles of supply chain management, provide an interpretation/definition of each, and to suggest some examples from the area of supply chain management that reinforce the extent to which these principles will continue to be relevant, well into the future.

Figure 15.1 lists the seven principles of supply chain management that were discussed in an article that appeared in the very first issue of *Supply Chain Management Review* (SCMR). In addition, Figure 15.1 provides a perspective on each of the seven principles and the extent to which each may be expected to contribute to the objectives of revenue growth, asset utilization, and cost reduction.

15-2-1 Principle 1: Segment Customers Based on Service Needs

This principle suggests a departure from traditional approaches to customer segmentation based on industry, product, or trade channel to an approach that segments customers based on logistics and supply chain needs. Examples would include service requirements, fulfillment priorities, frequency of service, needed support in terms of capable information technologies, etc. Also of importance is to make sure that supply chain services are aligned with the needs of customers, and also are consistent with the financial objectives of the supplier organization.

According to the authors, one successful food manufacturer aggressively marketed vendor-managed inventory (VMI) to *all* customer segments and boosted sales as a result. Regrettably, subsequent activity-based cost analysis found that one segment actually lost nine cents a case on an operating margin basis.

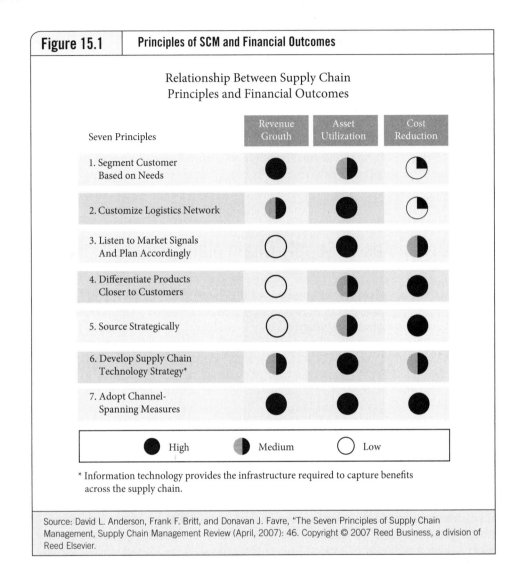

Figure 15.1   Principles of SCM and Financial Outcomes

Relationship Between Supply Chain
Principles and Financial Outcomes

In earlier days, the development by Dell of its direct-to-consumer business model represented a significant change in the computer industry and in the field of supply chain management. More recently, however, the company has transformed its supply chain into a multichannel, segmented model, with different policies for serving consumers, corporate customers, distributors, and retailers.[3] This transformation has resulted in savings by Dell of $1.5 billion in operational costs,[4] and helped to move Dell to the number two spot on Gartner's list of "Top 25 Supply Chains."

15-2-2 Principle 2: Customize the Logistics Network

Historically, many organizations have designed logistics and supply chain capabilities to meet the average service requirements of all customers, or maybe to satisfy the toughest requirements of an individual customer segment. This principle stresses the need for supply chains to be sufficiently adaptable to be responsive to the needs of individual customer segments. These approaches will involve greater complexity and flexibility in the design of supply chains, and will rely on the utilization of real-time decision support tools to meet these needs.

A contemporary example of this principle is that of developing and executing "omni-channel" supply chain strategies. In addition to the need for strategic approaches to managing supply chain capabilities in relation to storefront vs. internet sales, for example, it is also essential to manage a range of supply chain capabilities (e.g., delivery time, pick-up or delivery location, etc.) that may be offered to customers. In the interest of synchronizing some of the supply chain elements needed to respond to sales in these two types of channels, the solution is likely to involve customization of the logistics and supply chain networks. Greater detail regarding omni-channel distribution strategies is included in a later section of this chapter.

15-2-3 Principle 3: Listen to Signals of Market Demand and Plan Accordingly

Although traditional approaches to forecasting continue to have great relevance to planning and developing supply chain capabilities, useful demand planning processes are dependent also on market signals such as point-of-sale information. By seeing that demand planning involves customers and suppliers, this collaborative approach helps to maintain the objective of seeing that supply chain activities and processes are directly responsive to what is currently happening in the marketplace.

This principle is a critical component of contemporary processes such as S&OP (sales and operations planning), IBP (integrated business planning), and IBM (integrated business management). The latter two of these approaches extend the principles of S&OP throughout the supply chain, product and customer needs, and customer demand and strategic planning. The result is a single, seamless management process that develops plans that are based on the signals of market demand.

15-2-4 Principle 4: Differentiate Products Closer to the Customer

When successfully implemented, this principle helps to improve customer service via fewer stockouts and also takes significant inventory carrying cost out of the supply chain. By postponing product differentiation to the latest possible moment and by gaining greater understanding and control of cycle times, supply chain efficiency and effectiveness will be positively impacted.

A traditional example that illustrates this principle is that of canned vegetables being stored "in bright," meaning that the labels on the cans are affixed only when there is certainty as to the specific retailers to which the cans will be shipped. Since companies that produce canned vegetables typically serve a range of customers, the "postponement" of adding the label basically allows the producer to differentiate these products closer to the customer. Benefits from this practice may include reduced inventories and reduced inventory carrying cost, greater responsiveness to the needs of individual customers, and reduced working capital requirements.

A more current example is that of "custom" designed athletic shoes, or "sneakers," that may be ordered by consumers. Essentially, this positions the customer as another "designer" in the product development and purchasing process. So, a key competency of successful shoe retailers (or internet retailers) is to offer customers the ability to customize their footwear to meet their individual needs and preferences. In a broader sense, this example illustrates the value in the marketplace of being able to produce and deliver the customized products that have been ordered. This places significant emphasis on the ability of the supply chain to support this overall process, and to create competitive advantage from being able to differentiate products closer to the customer.

15-2-5 Principle 5: Source Strategically

Over time, customers should expect that the prices they are asked to pay will to some extent reflect the levels of cost that are incurred by their suppliers. This suggests that as a good business practice, customers should have fact-based knowledge of the cost of purchased products and services. The value in having this knowledge is that customers will be better prepared to deal with suppliers that are attempting to recoup their cost increases by way of increasing their prices to customers. Given that excellence in supply chain management suggests that customers and suppliers need to work together in creative, positive ways to meet overall supply chain objectives, useful strategies may include short-term competitive bids, entering into long-term contracts and strategic supplier relationships, outsourcing, and even vertical integration.

More generally, the current interest in "strategic sourcing" is based on the need for a process that is of greater strategic value to the overall supply chain than the traditional functions of purchasing and procurement. As discussed in detail in Chapter 5, the strategic sourcing process can be a great facilitator of improved functioning of supply chains.

An excellent example of a company that became involved in strategic sourcing to find products at the best price from capable suppliers is that of Walmart.[5] As a continuing practice, Walmart establishes strategic partnerships with most of their suppliers, providing them with the potential for long-term and high-volume purchases ... in exchange for the lowest possible prices. Also, Walmart constructed communications and relationship networks with suppliers to improve material flow with lower inventories. Also, this helped significantly to simplify overall supply chain management practices. One major result was that the network of global suppliers, warehouses, and retail stores was described as behaving almost like a single firm.

Another contemporary example is that of Hong Kong based Li & Fung Limited,[6] a global supply chain manager for various consumer goods brands, retailers, hypermarkets, specialty stores, catalog sales, and e-commerce sites. Li & Fung engages in product design and development, sourcing, and logistics on behalf of its many customers, examples of which include Tommy Hilfiger, DKNY Jeans, Hudson's Bay, Calvin Klein, Target, and Walmart.[7]

15-2-6 Principle 6: Develop a Supply Chain-Wide Technology Strategy

The objective here is to utilize enterprise-wide systems to replace inflexible, poorly integrated transactional systems. This approach will help to translate available data into actionable intelligence that can enhance real-world operations. The result will be far superior to traditional approaches that capture large quantities of data that are difficult to assimilate and utilize.

An interesting example of this principle is the RDC (rapid deployment center) strategy that was a central feature of The Home Depot's "direct-to-store" distribution model.[8] Instead of suppliers and vendors shipping directly to Home Depot stores, product is delivered first to one of the 18 RDC's in the company's network. Essentially, each RDC functions as a high-volume, cross-dock facility in The Home Depot's supply chain. To facilitate this overall strategy, The Home Depot centralized all of its warehouse management and yard management technologies on a single-supplier. This is consistent with the objectives of developing a capable supply chain-wide technology strategy.

A major challenge relating to this principle becomes evident when developing strategies for managing global supply chains. Supply chains at The Home Depot are truly global, as they are for numerous organizations in a wide range of industry verticals. The ability to develop and utilize supply chain-wide technologies will be a key element of the overall success of these global supply chains.

15-2-7 Principle 7: Adopt Channel-Spanning Performance Measures

When individual companies in a supply chain are asked a general question about how well their supply chains are doing, the response should be in the context of the extended supply chain that includes the roles played by both customers and suppliers. While it is important for individual organizations to meet their corporate objectives, the realization of supply chain objectives will be essential to the long-term success of the individual participants. Thus, it is essential for these companies to work toward the same goals by understanding what each brings to the supply chain and showing how to leverage complementary assets and skills to the greatest advantage of the supply chain.

The rising popularity of the 4PL concept reinforces the need for channel-spanning (i.e., supply chain spanning) performance measures. Although there are a number of competencies that may be expected from 4PLs, the provision of "control-tower" capabilities applies directly to the principle of adopting supply chain-wide performance measures. In this context, 4PLs focus on providing supply chain transparency and visibility from suppliers, downstream to customers and consumers. Clearly, this makes it possible to create the availability of analytics that may help to determine whether supply chain spanning performance measures are being met.

Clearly, advances in the development and use of mobile and cloud technologies have been significant contributors to better understanding what is going on in the supply chain between "the earliest suppliers and ultimate customers and consumers."

15-2-8 An Update on the Seven Principles of SCM

In response to the comment that "the insights (from this article) remained remarkably fresh 10 years later," lead author Dr. David L. Anderson wrote that he went back and reread the article to see if he agreed. His assessment is captured in the following points:[9]

1. **The seven principles basically survive the test of time.** Although I might include some thoughts around global supply chain risks, add a section on insourcing/outsourcing strategies, update the case studies, and tighten up the procurement strategy discussion, I still believe companies cannot go wrong by adopting these principles as the basis of their supply chain strategies.
2. **We still have a long way to go on supply chain strategy implementation.** The fact that the principles are still relatively fresh implies that many companies have not done the best job implementing strategies that underlie the principles.
3. **Technology and data will be the major game changer going forward.** UPC, RFID, and GPS-related data were not around when we wrote the article. The growing availability of "real-time" supply chain data as well as the tools to enable us to use the data in planning and executing supply chains will be the key factor that separates the winners and losers in supply chain management over the coming decade.

Now that we are nearly another 10 years past the original publication of this timeless article, it is clear that these seven principles continue to be highly relevant to the contemporary challenges related to managing effective supply chains.

15-3 Supply Chain Analytics and Big Data

Chapter 14 provided valuable perspectives on the topics of supply chain technology and managing information flows. Among the key takeaways should be an understanding of information requirements in the supply chain and the capabilities of supply chain information systems. Also included should be an appreciation of some of the specific

---

On the Line   *The Changing Geography of Supply Chains*

In recent years, a number of predictions suggested that more manufacturing would leave Asia and come back to the United States. These are based on factors such as rising wages in China and various emerging markets, as well as the high cost of transporting goods across long distances. So, a logical question relates to what kinds of products are most likely to migrate back to U.S. shores? Part of the answer is in the results of a recent study that concluded capital-intensive industries such as computers and electronics, machinery, fabricated metals, electrical equipment, and plastics and rubber, are likely to lead the way. Another finding is that labor-intensive industries like apparel most likely will stay offshore.

But there are other factors behind the U.S. reshoring trend that have not received as much attention as labor and capital costs. The first is the increasing use of robots. When manufacturers rely on robots rather than on human workers to do repetitive tasks, a plant's location becomes less important. It essentially costs as much to run a robot in Asia as it does in the United States. A robot, moreover, works 24 hours a day, seven days a week without coffee breaks, and doesn't require various types of employee benefits. It's worth noting that the giant contract electronics manufacturer Foxconn reportedly is starting to replace some of its workers with robots in its Chinese factories.

The emergence of additive or 3-D manufacturing is another factor that will promote reshoring. In additive manufacturing, a special printer follows a computer design, applying plastic or metal in layers to make a three-dimensional product. This technology makes it possible for manufacturers to produce high-value, one-of-a-kind items on demand to consumers' specifications, and therefore it is ideally suited for domestic production. Low-value, commodity-type products, such as clothing or garden hoses, will continue to be made offshore.

The return of some manufacturing to the United States will not spell an end to global supply chains, but supply chains in the future may not be as extensive and far-flung as they have been for the past few decades. That's because multinational companies are expected to increasingly embrace the regional theatre concept. One reason is that the rapid growth in consumer spending in developing economies is fueling demand for products. This will encourage manufacturers to maintain plants either in or adjacent to nations like China, India, and emerging markets to serve that demand.

In the not-too-distant future, we could see the development of three major supply chain theaters: one for Europe, one for Asia, and one for the Americas. While more manufacturing undoubtedly will return to the United States and other developed economies where offshoring has been the norm, supply chains will continue to forge global links for some time to come.

Source: Adapted from James A. Cooke, "The Changing Geography of Supply Chains," *CSCMP's Supply Chain Quarterly*, Quarter 4, 2012, p. 9. Used with permission. (James A. Cooke is a principal analyst with Nucleus Research. He previously was Editor of *CSCMP's Supply Chain Quarterly*.)

types of technology that facilitate processes relating to supply chain planning, execution, and control. As highlighted in Figure 14.3 of the previous chapter, the major categories of supply chain software included: enterprise resource planning; customer relationship management; supplier relationship management; and automatic identification tools.

One major topic of great contemporary interest is that of supply chain analytics, and how this resource can contribute significantly to our ability to understand and solve supply chain problems and issues. Central to an understanding of supply chain analytics is to recognize that one of the highest priorities at many organizations today is to take a giant leap from data to information, and then from information to understanding. The brief definitions below are intended to provide an initial awareness of what is meant by these three terms.

- **Data** – unorganized facts that need to be processed (e.g., levels of inventory at ends of financial periods)
- **Information** – data that has been gathered, processed, organized, and structured in a given context (e.g., average levels of inventory and/or levels of inventory by SKU)
- **Understanding** – information that has been examined and studied in the context of specific business situations (e.g., inventory levels in relation to overall economic conditions, weather patterns, etc.)

Essentially, supply chain analytics builds on these concepts and is viewed by INFORMS as "the scientific process of transforming data into insight for making better decisions."[10] Another perspective is from Gartner that states "analytics leverage data in a particular functional process to enable context-specific insight that is actionable."[11] As might be expected, the availability of simple data and facts, coupled with complex data analysis, contributes greatly to the objectives of supply chain decision-making. As indicated by research conducted by Accenture, however, other factors of great relevance to this objective include intuition, personal experience, and consultation with others.[12] So, this helps to underscore the need to appreciate "the art and science of supply chain decision-making."

15-3-1 Supply Chain Analytics Maturity Model

While there are numerous ways to depict a maturity model for supply chain analytics, perhaps the illustration in Figure 15.2 helps to show the various stages and levels of sophistication and robustness that are associated with supply chain analytics.

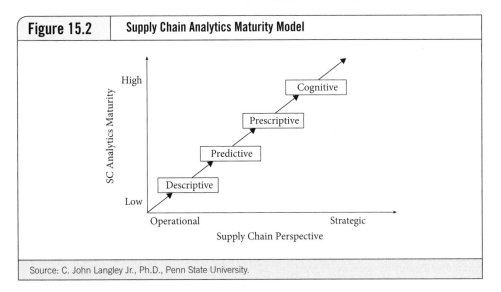

| Figure 15.2 | Supply Chain Analytics Maturity Model |

Source: C. John Langley Jr., Ph.D., Penn State University.

Descriptive. This level incorporates available data to answer questions such as what, where, and when certain supply chain activities, processes, or events are happening? This may take the form of routine data gathering, such as inventory levels, or perhaps ad hoc exercises to address a specific problem. More generally, availability of descriptive data is the foundation of more robust processes relating to competitive intelligence, etc.

The conduct of logistics and supply chain activities and processes can generate exceptionally large amounts of descriptive data. Example sources of this data are listed below:

- Mobile devices
- Telematics – wireless
- Electronic onboard recorders (EOBRs), also referred to as electronic logging devices (ELDs)
- Forecasts and point of sale information
- ERP systems
- RFID tags and bar codes
- Smart sensors
- Other sources

Essentially, descriptive analytics help to provide fundamental information about the functioning of an activity or process, and represent a capable starting point for more advanced and robust types of analytics.

Predictive. The level of inquiry takes a significant step forward in that the predictive stage focuses on questions such as what is likely to happen, what are the likely trends, and what are the results if certain events occur? Answering questions such as these involves formal analyses of available and relevant data, much of which may have been gathered initially for descriptive purposes. In addition, however, it is likely that additional data gathering and analysis may be needed to assure the usefulness and validity of predictions that may be made.

Prescriptive. As the questions shift to the topic of what should be done, this indicates a need for the utilization of prescriptive analytics. When facing the challenge of determining how to configure a large-scale supply chain network, for example, it is essential to use capable tools and processes that can prescribe what needs to be done. As discussed in Chapter 4 of this text, this may indicate the need to apply optimization technologies in an effort to identify a best solution to the current statement of the problem.

One part of the challenge here is to figure out how to convert predictive findings from the previous level to the somewhat elevated aspirations for the prescriptive level. This challenge becomes even more complex when it becomes necessary to address factors, events, and circumstances that are likely to exhibit significant variability in the planning horizon that lies ahead.

Cognitive. Suggesting a helpful definition of this level is considerably more challenging than for the previous three levels. This is because the cognitive level typically introduces social context and meaning into the analytical processes, as well as very high-level mathematical and statistical capabilities. As such, sometimes the results from cognitive analytics include "blinding" insights that may otherwise be difficult to discern.

Characteristically, cognitive approaches address problems that may be ambiguous and uncertain, and where data may change frequently and often is conflicting. Four requirements for cognitive systems include the following:[13]

- Adaptive – ability of systems to learn as information changes
- Interactive – ease of use for those who are doing the analyses; likely will involve cloud capabilities
- Iterative and stateful – identify additional data needs and relevant questions that can enhance the analysis
- Contextual – involve a wide variety of inputs and sources of information

15-3-2 Analytical Resources

Table 15.1 identifies example analytical resources that may be applied to various levels of sophistication to supply chain analytics. While the types and brands of software and technologies that can address supply chain issues are literally too numerous to mention, some of the more widely-used of these include IBM-SPSS,[14] SAS,[15] and Microsoft-Revolution Analytics (R).[16]

Additionally, IBM Watson Analytics is a cognitive system that can help to understand data, learn from it, and reason through it. IBM's Watson has learning capabilities, and for example, can identify patterns in both traditional and unstructured data sets.[17] What this means is that while most analytics technologies help to answer questions and solve problems that are pre-determined, cognitive capabilities can help to outthink the limits of what is already known.

15-3-3 Big Data and the Supply Chain

One of the most exciting and talked-about trends in supply chain management is big data and its potential to gain further insight into supply chain problems and solutions. Big

Table 15.1	Example Analytical Resources
LEVEL OF ANALYTICS	**ANALYTICAL RESOURCES**
Descriptive	Standard and ad hoc reporting
	Data from supply chain partners
	Alerts and notifications
	Query/drill down
Predictive	Forecasting
	Heuristic analysis
	Simulation
	Statistical analysis
	Predictive modeling
Prescriptive	Stochastic optimization
	Scenario planning
Cognitive	IBM Watson Analytics

Source: C. John Langley Jr., Ph.D., Penn State University. Used with permission.

data may be thought of as the process of accumulating, organizing and analyzing very large sets of data to identify patterns, trends and other information of interest. A primary goal of big data is to help organizations better understand the information that resides within the data, and to focus attention on those factors that are most relevant to making well-informed supply chain decisions. While some researchers associate big data with the use of unstructured or semi-structured data, others also include transactions and other structured types of data to be included in big data applications.

Typically, big data may be analyzed using the example technologies and approaches discussed previously in the discussion of supply chain analytics. So, the applications of analytics to big data can help to meet the objectives of descriptive, predictive, prescriptive, and cognitive types of analysis.

Functional vs. Strategic Use of Big Data. Supply chain functional activities such as visibility, transportation management, and warehouse and distribution center management generate significant volumes of data. As a result, it is not surprising that shippers see great potential for improvement through the use of big data and appropriate systems and tools for data analysis. Additionally, shippers see more strategic and IT-based processes such as supply chain planning and network modeling and optimization, as great areas of opportunity to leverage big data. Together, these represent a broad range of potential ways to enhance and improve the functioning and planning of the supply chain.

Supply Chain Examples. The examples below illustrate how the use of big data and capable analytics can help to improve supply chain practices.

- FedEx uses active sensors in high-value merchandise that send out telemetry data, tracking the package's traveling speed and conditions. Applying analytics to this data has the potential to largely reduce supply chain reaction times to avoid delays in shipments.[18] This creates an ability to provide real-time information on the status of shipments and to reroute shipments as may be necessary from time to time. Interestingly, FedEx founder Fred Smith is famous for saying, "The information about the package is as important as the package itself."[19]

- FedEx also uses analytics to actively monitor social networks and video feeds, identifying customer service issues in a more proactive way. Collaboration spaces have been set up through which customers can share information provided by FedEx with customers, partners and suppliers.[20]

- Nike created a database with details on every link of its supply chain from sourcing to vendors across manufacturing and retail. Analytics helps identify the weak links within its supply chains – weak production, unfair labor practices and poor business decisions.[21] As a result, Nike is able to have significant visibility throughout its supply chain, and thus become aware of current and potential situations that may need attention.

- The Boston Consulting Group provides insight regarding the use of big data during the premerger planning for the combination of two large consumer-products companies. To better model the merger of the companies' distribution networks, the use of geoanalytics involved the layering of geographic location data onto delivery data in a way that made it possible to visualize order density and identify pockets of overlap. Vehicle-routing software also enabled rapid scenario testing of dozens of route iterations and the development of individual routes for each truck. Results of this analysis uncovered as much as three hours of unused delivery capacity on typical routes after drivers had covered their assigned miles. Significant savings were projected from a nationwide combination and rationalization of the two networks. Also, the geoanalysis provided insight that would help to create alignment between the two organizations prior to the often difficult postmerger-integration phase.[22]

15-4 Omni-Channel

Looking back in time, the holiday shopping season of 1999 was highlighted by the emergence of a new shopping experience for consumers – the internet. New "e-tailers," such as Amazon, and established retailers, such as Toys R' Us, had established web sites to allow consumers the option of buying gifts on-line or in the store. Expectations for success were high for this new shopping experience as analysts and investors estimated that internet shopping would generate significant revenues for these web sites. While there were some success stories, there were also failures. Many e-tailers had no inventories and relied on wholesalers and/or manufacturers for product availability and had no established delivery network. This strained their ability to promise and deliver the products ordered on-time. Many retailers operated their stores and internet sites as two separate distribution networks with dedicated facilities and unique inventories. This prevented them from being able to share store and internet inventories to make deliveries as promised. While these retailers operated in more than one channel, the concept of omni-channel, as defined today, did not exist in 1999.

Today, the omni-channel concept can be defined as "anytime, anywhere, anyhow, and any device." The idea here is that consumers have the options of where to buy, when to buy, and how to buy from a retailer. Whether a consumer visits a store to purchase goods or uses a smartphone to place an order on a web site, an omni-channel retailer will be able to accept, fulfill, and deliver the order based on the consumer's preference. While technically not an omni-channel retailer, Amazon has had a great impact on the development of the omni-channel concept. Even though consumers cannot buy products at an Amazon store, they can place an order with Amazon for groceries (Amazon Fresh) or non-perishables and get delivery the same day (Amazon Flex) – even within a two-hour time window. This type of fulfillment and delivery network has pushed traditional retailers into using their store and distribution networks to offer the same type of service as Amazon. The ability to handle a consumer order from anywhere, at any time, from any device has a significant impact on the ability for a retailer to offer exceptional customer service.

15-4-1 Strategies for Success

Chapter 4 presented some of the physical distribution/fulfillment networks that are being used in both retail and omni-channel operations. Chapter 8 identified how order management has an impact on product availability, order cycle time, logistics operations responsiveness, logistics system information, and post-sale logistics support. Physical networks and the basics of customer service are a requirement to maintain a presence in an omni-channel environment. This section will briefly discuss five strategies that retailers need to implement to gain a competitive advantage in omni-channel retailing.

One view of the customer. Regardless of whether it is a store or internet purchase, retailers need to realize that they have one consumer who has two channels from which to purchase an item. Previously, many retailers would identify a consumer based on where they purchased their item. This resulted in separate consumer profiles and different product offerings. In today's omni-channel environment, successful retailers focus on the consumer and what is purchased rather than where it is purchased. This allows the retailer to personalize product offerings for consumers with suggestions on what might be added to the shopping cart while they are browsing the web site or to offer consumers discounts on items they buy in the stores. This provides the retailer the opportunity to make better decisions on product allocations to stores and to the web site and to "drive" consumers' purchases to the channel where the inventory is located. This strategy not only increases product availability to the consumer but also increased revenue and decreased inventories for the retailer.

Short-Term Forecasts. Having an accurate forecast of demand in an omni-channel environment is critical to retail success. The ever-increasing array of products offered, coupled with the changing consumer demand by geography and season has made short-term forecasting a necessity to assure product availability at the store or on the web site. One retailer in particular generates 2-3 day short-term demand forecasts by geographic area to determine if short-term demand can be met by existing inventory at its fulfillment centers. If not, inventory is repositioned between fulfillment centers so that orders can be filled. Whereas long-term forecasts (one year) can help plan capacity and inventory decisions for the retailer, short-term forecasts allow retailers to meet current demand. Generating these short-term forecasts requires that the retailer have "one view of the customer" and understand what the consumer buys, where they buy it from, and when they buy it.

Seamless Order Entry and Order Management. Successful retailers understand that their environment is "one consumer/one order" regardless of whether it is a store or internet purchase. They also understand that an order can be generated through a purchase at a store, through a personal computer, through a Smart Phone, or any other type of personal device. This requires that the retailer must have systems that can accommodate orders from various sources (order entry) and channel them through a single order management portal to determine product availability, fulfillment center order picking schedules, and delivery commitments. Allowing consumers multiple order entry points provides them with the convenience to order when and how they desire which will help retailers generate increased "share of wallet" and decreased operating costs.

One View of Inventory. For an omni-channel retailer, the critical issue is not where inventory is positioned within the network but whether it is available to fill an order, regardless of its origin. Traditionally, retailers with web sites maintained two sets of inventories – one to fill store orders and one to fill internet orders. If an order came through their web site for an item not currently available in internet inventory but available in store inventory, the order went unfilled because the inventory pools were considered to be separate. Today, orders are filled with inventory that is the closest to the point of order and which creates the most efficiency for the retailer while meeting the service requirements for the order. If a store needs inventory that is not currently available at the fulfillment center, it could be transferred from another store. If an internet order requires inventory not currently at the fulfillment center for delivery to a consumer, the order can be sourced from a store closest to the demand point. This strategy requires that the retailer have real-time inventory status availability at all of its stocking points—fulfillments centers and stores. While this real-time status is usually not an issue at fulfillment centers, it can pose some challenges at store locations. This will be discussed at the end of this section. This strategy also requires that accounting procedures need to change to accommodate revenue and cost allocations across fulfillment centers and stores. If an internet order is filled from store inventory and shipped, the store loses the revenue from that sale. Some retailers are now crediting the store with a percentage of the revenue from the sale in these instances. However, the one view of inventory strategy is necessary to provide the customer with availability, consistency, convenience, and speed.

Flexible Fulfillment Network. Chapter 4 introduced the various forms of fulfillment networks used in retail today. In an omni-channel environment, these networks must be flexible – which has multiple dimensions. First, flexibility means allowing the customer to determine delivery options which could vary from several days to two hours to store pick-up, and they must be consistent. This means the retailer needs to be able to source from local stores as well as fulfillment centers to fill consumer orders. Second, flexibility means being able to "ramp up" and "ramp down" to meet seasonal patterns. Sears has developed its Cheetah Network which allows it to add or delete stores from its order fulfillment network based on the volume and location of demand. It will source internet orders from its fulfillment centers during peak demand periods until they can no longer handle the volumes or cannot meet requested delivery times. When these scenarios occur, Sears will source order fulfillment to its store network. When demand recedes, Sears will then take stores offline for internet orders.[23] Finally, flexibility means the ability to handle returns through either the fulfillment center network or store network, regardless of where the purchase occurred. This requires systems integration on the part of the retailer but adds a high level of convenience for the consumer.

Changing Store Operations. Store operations in an omni-channel environment are radically different than in the traditional retail model. Inventory visibility at the store level is critical to making delivery commitments. This requires a new level of discipline at the store to scan all items being received in the back room. It also requires the ability to integrate point of sale data at the store to inventory availability in the back room and on the shelf to guarantee product availability. Store design must also adapt to the need for order picking and packing operations as well as for holding items for pick-up by the customer or by a delivery service. Store operations in today's environment must replicate many of the operations traditionally performed at the fulfillment center while maintaining the focus of being a retail store with the proper product assortment and merchandising strategies to facilitate ease of shopping for the consumer.

15-4-2 The Future of Omni-Channel

Retailing has progressed significantly since the holiday shopping season of 1999 in terms of focus and operations. Much of this progress has been accomplished through the use of technology at both the points of order entry and order fulfillment. Personal devices, Smart Phones, and RFID tag technologies have revolutionized how the consumer and retailers interact. Retailers using "Big Data" and data warehouses have allowed them to personalize the shopping experience. What will the omni-channel retail industry look like in ten years? This is anybody's guess, but it will transform based on how technology improvements will facilitate this development. Amazon's drone network would revolutionize home delivery if the technology becomes commercially feasible. Adaptive, or "3-D" printing could allow consumers the convenience of "printing" merchandize at home. The technology is not yet sufficiently developed to allow this. Regardless of the technology influence on omni-channel retailing, the future will certainly continue the strategy of the past that brings products to the consumer (home delivery) rather than having the consumer coming to the products (store shopping). Successful omni-channel retailers need to focus on convenience, consistency of speed, assortment, and information to meet the increasing product and service requirements of the consumer. One end result will be the continued development of new technologies to help manage omni-channel supply chains.

15-5 Sustainability

Sustainability continues to be a topic of interest and concern among various groups with vested interests in the United States and globally. The two previous editions of this text noted the growing awareness and increased attention focused upon sustainability issues as well as the challenges that various organizations and institutions face in resolving these challenges. While there may be some level of general agreement that sustainable practices should be implemented to resolve the plethora of related problems, there are usually advantages and disadvantages associated with the necessary changes. In other words, *some can win while others lose. Consider the case of fossil fuels, especially coal. If we restrict the mining of coal for the production of power, it is likely to reduce pollution levels, but it may increase electricity cost with subsequent price increases as well as raising unemployment levels in states that produce coal. These tradeoffs need to be addressed in developing appropriate government policy.*

As indicated above the goal of sustainability is challenging and it is worth noting at this juncture that the best approach may be to consider sustainability as a journey that will take time and effort to improve. It is also worth pointing out that there has been much progress made over the course of the last several decades. There was a time when sustainable actions and practices were considered by some organizations to represent increased cost that would have to be absorbed with subsequent lower profit or passed off to customers with higher prices or some combinations of the two. Also, it was assumed by some to mean a loss of efficiency placing organizations at a competitive disadvantage, particularly on a global basis.

15-5-1 Benefits and Challenges

In the current economic environment, growing number organizations have conceded that there can be revenue opportunities to offset the costs, especially when sustainability practices are not viewed narrowly as simply recycling and disposal. For example, some organizations have recognized that their consumer packaging practices were not conducive to their objective of achieving sustainability, and made changes which were environmentally friendly and improved efficiency in the supply chain. A well-known example was a change made with the mutual consent of P&G and Wal-Mart to reduce the size of the plastic containers used in the sale of liquid detergents by reducing the water content of the product and making it more concentrated. The consumer had to be convinced that the smaller size bottle would give them the equivalent number of washer loads. Once that was accomplished, the resulting cost reductions in packaging and transportation and the increased efficiency in utilizing space in warehouses and store shelves were notable. It represented a win-win in terms of costs and sustainability. The reduction in unnecessary packaging has become a growing practice among a variety of retail organizations and manufacturers to the benefit of overall environmental sustainability. There are other examples of changes in supply chain practices such as vehicle routing, increased load size, vendor purchasing practices, etc., which have lowered cost and reduced environmental pollution also.

One of the challenges facing organizations is that sustainability has many dimensions. At the most basic level, sustainability requires companies to consider and manage the impact that their supply chain has on both the natural and social environment in which they operate. The latter implies a commitment to social responsibility and may be overlooked since it is usually the most challenging aspect for organizations. For example, the "sweat shop" labor used by suppliers in underdeveloped countries may be difficult to ascertain. Also, the argument is sometime made by indigenous owners and managers, that overall it is beneficial to the employees even if it could be classified as a sweatshop because they have no alternative employment opportunities. The "best-in-class" companies do attempt to manage and control both the natural and social and environmental issues on an integrated basis, but it is challenging especially for human rights issues and product life impacts. It is here that collaborative efforts can play a major role as long as everyone is consistent and in agreement as to what the best practices entail. This is particularly true if the approach, suggested above, to sustainability recognizes that it is a journey with a path of continuous effort. The improvement aspect requires the right balance of people, process and technology. With increase in complexity in supply chains, there is a growing need for improved technology to drive innovation, cost reduction and customer service.

The commitment to improve sustainability can follow many different paths including reduced packaging, alternate modes of transportation (rail versus truck), minimizing transport miles, maximizing shipment size, etc., all of which can also lead to increased profits through lower costs. Other sustainability practices such as distributing and using only fair trade products or insuring humane working conditions at supplier factories can encounter organizational resistance because of increased costs. As some individuals note, cost often drives behavior. However, when companies can get customer buy-in (collaboration), can gain a competitive advantage in the market place for such effort. However, it should be noted that skepticism still remains in some quarters as to the financial viability of such efforts.

15-5-2 Social and Environmental Responsibility

One of the companies frequently noted for their efforts to make sustainability a successful marketing platform is H&M Clothing which has been active in the area of social responsibility for over a decade. They have put forth effort to eliminate toxic chemicals used in raw materials, production washing of materials, dyeing and finishing. The have also been aggressive in reducing water consumption, use of sustainable cotton materials, recycled materials, eliminating abusive and unfair labor practices and reduced energy consumption. Their efforts represent a daunting undertaking because of the large number of small suppliers in their supply chain. However, even H&M as a leader in these areas will express frustration with their efforts to raise awareness and promote efficiency with sustainability in their supply chains.

Another important area for sustainability is the recognition of climatic risk in supply chains. For example, emissions reduction is a goal for many organizations but the results are a "mixed bag." Some blame regulatory bodies for lack of decisive action, and the scientific evidence is not always clear cut for directing efforts of organizations to make improvements. Organizational investment in these efforts brings negativity to the overall drive for sustainable practices. While there is growing evidence of success, there is still a lack of effort and even resistance in some organizations.

One successful approach to overcome organizational resistance is to effectuate collaboration in the supply chain. The power of "partnerships" to establish a joint effort throughout the supply chain among suppliers, producers, customers, logistics service providers, etc. can help make positive changes for mutual benefit of all and the collective approach can often produce more innovation and provide pressure for increased cooperation. The opportunity that today's consumers have for obtaining product information is also becoming an important driver of change and improvement through the social media. Consumers share evaluations and information among each other on a real time basis which is a powerful weapon for many changes including sustainability practices. The information and transparency into organizational practices is a dynamic that cannot be underestimated whether it is about sustainability or racism in organizations.

15-5-3 Reducing Risk

One important dimension of supply chain sustainability that cannot be overlooked is the impact that such efforts can have upon reducing risk. There is a strong feeling among some supply chain experts that the mitigation of risk is the best driver of sustainability initiatives. One of the biggest risks for efficient and effective supply chains is the climate change associated with the pollution of the environment. The growing number disasters associated with weather related events from draught and wildfires to hurricanes and floods have captured the attention of businesses, government agencies and the general public. The human carnage, suffering, and destruction associated with such events is well documented. Supply chains in such countries as Brazil, China and India are potentially more vulnerable because of sustainability issues in those countries. As noted previously, these same countries are important to a growing number of supply chains which should be a concern to all of their collaborators.

15-5-4 "R's" of Sustainability

In this general discussion, mention should also be made of reverse logistics systems and closed-loop logistics or supply chain systems. Both reverse and closed-loop systems are important strategies that impact sustainability in a positive manner. At this point, consideration needs to be given to the so-called R's of sustainability: reuse, remanufacturing, refurbishing, and recycling. Table 15.2 provides a brief description of each of the R's.

It is important to note that sustainability strategies are being designed today also from a business-related or economic perspective as opposed to a public relations approach, as was frequently done in the past. The global, competitive environment requires a broad-based

Table 15.2	Sustainability Approaches
SUSTAINABILITY APPROACHES	**DESCRIPTION**
Reuse	Reuse often requires disassembly, which is a systematic method of separating a product into constituent parts, components, subassemblies, or other component parts. The parts or components may be reassembled for reuse after cleaning, checking, and repair, or the individual components may be reused.
Remanufacturing	Remanufacturing essentially means that a product or part is returned to the market as "good as new." Auto parts, tires, and electronics are frequently remanufactured.
Reconditioning	Reconditioning usually means returning used products to working order but not "good as new."
Recycling	Recycling generally refers to the secondary use of materials. It usually includes glass bottles, cans, newspapers, corrugated material, tires, etc. The recycling is usually performed for individual households by municipal government agencies

Source: Center for Supply Chain Research, Penn State University.

collaborative effort among organizations in a supply chain along with governmental support. Sustainability is a complex issue that will continue to be challenging.

The recycling of consumer and industrial waste has become very widespread, and materials are being reused in a variety of creative forms. Often recycling results in the creation of an entirely new product, for instance, automobile tires into door mats and flooring material. At this point, reverse logistics systems will be discussed in detail since they have become such an important part of the sustainability efforts of business and government organizations.

15-5-5 Reverse Flows

A basic or simple supply chain was illustrated in Chapter 1. The description of this supply chain indicated that there were four important flows to manage: materials, information, financials, and demand. Furthermore, the figure demonstrated that three of the flows could be two-directional. Materials typically flow "downstream" in a supply chain from raw materials sources to the ultimate consumer with value being added to the product along the way. **Reverse flows** can move back through the supply chain for a variety of reasons. Consequently, a number of terms including *reverse logistics systems, product recovery systems, product return networks, enterprise returns management*, and others have been used to indicate the growth in the volume and importance of returns and the need for their efficient and effective management.

Several observations are important at the outset of this section about reverse flows. The forward flow in the supply chain typically has received the most attention since it is so important in terms of customer service, revenue, and cash flow. The reverse direction has often been regarded as a necessary evil or at best a cost center that needs continual scrutiny to control and reduce.

Traditionally, reverse flows were not viewed as adding value for customers or revenue for the manufacturer or producer. In other words, product returns were viewed as a "waste stream," not as a potential value stream. One of the objectives of this chapter is to examine reverse product flows as a potential value stream for a company or an organization. It should be noted that Internet sales have contributed significantly to the increase in reverse flows. Why?

Information and financials (cash) are also important dimensions of reverse logistics and closed-loop supply chains. It was stated in Chapter 1 and other chapters that information is power. Good information contributes to efficiency and effectiveness because it facilitates the flow through the supply chain and reduces uncertainty. Unfortunately, the power of information systems and technology has not received enough emphasis in return flows. Cash or value from returns also needs to be a focus for organizations if they are to receive all the benefits that can come from managing reverse flows. This requires more proactive management to obtain such benefits for companies.

Another observation is that global supply chains present challenges and opportunities for reverse flows. Some European countries have been very proactive in passing so-called **green laws**, primarily for environmental reasons, which means that companies doing business in these countries must be cognizant of these regulations and policies. The green laws usually require reverse flows, for example returning packaging materials. Some underdeveloped countries are very lenient in these areas, which may raise ethical issues for companies doing business in these countries. The differences among countries and the complexity of global supply chains mandate a critical evaluation and analysis of the issues associated with global reverse flows.

Some individuals consider reverse flows for logistics and supply chains as a relatively new phenomenon. In actuality, reverse flows have been a part of logistics and supply chains for many years. Consumer goods companies and transportation companies have always dealt with damaged products that often required returns at some level. For example, many warehouses had a section set aside to repackage cases where only part of the case was damaged. Transportation companies dealt with customers who would not accept damaged products, and they accepted liability for the value of the damaged products. To offset their lost revenue, the transportation companies would usually attempt to sell such products to salvage operators for eventual resale. Historically, beverage bottlers refilled empty bottles for which a deposit may have been paid at the customer level. The empty bottles were returned from the retail level to the beverage bottler. Engines have been repaired and recycled for airlines and other large equipment operations. These repairs required a reverse flow to a centralized location where maintenance would be performed.

According to some experts, a large percentage of what is sold may be returned. No one has an exact measure, and the percentage will vary among industries, but it is estimated that returns can range from a low of about 3 percent to a staggering 50 percent in some sectors. AMR Research estimates that U.S. retailers lose 3 to 5 percent of their gross sales to returns and that this accounts for about 4.5 percent of the cost of logistics. In the consumer electronics industry, the average return rate is estimated at 8.5 percent and in the apparel industry at 19.4 percent. Some additional sector data on returns indicate the following: catalog retailing, 30 percent; durable goods (TVs, refrigerators, etc.), about 4 percent; book industry, 10 to 20 percent; and music and entertainment, 10 to 20 percent.

At the retail level (where most returns originate), Internet returns are about double the counter sale returns. It seems safe to conclude that as Internet sales increase relative to traditional sales, the volume of returns will increase. Another reason for the increase is the customer service policies of some of the large retailers, which make the acceptance of returns ridiculously easy (e.g., "no questions asked," "no receipts necessary," "no time limits," etc.). The problem is then shifted back to the product manufacturer, which has to accept the return and usually deduct the original price from the invoice. As indicated previously, consumer recycling programs have increased in many cities and towns to protect landfills. Also, the high obsolescence rate in technological products has contributed to the growth in reverse flows.

Given the reasons listed earlier for reverse flows, it is not difficult to understand why reverse flows in supply chains have increased, along with present challenges and opportunities for sustainable actions. Other examples or types of reverse flows could be listed, but the above-listed examples should suffice to validate their importance and magnitude. This growth and importance of reverse flows in supply chains deserves additional attention as does closed loop systems. Both topics will be discussed in the appendix for this chapter.

15-6 3-D Printing[24]

For any contemporary book written on innovations in supply chain management, the invention and use of 3-D printing technologies would certainly qualify as a major chapter. Also referred to as "additive manufacturing" (i.e., the process of joining materials such as plastic, ceramics, or metal powders to make objects from 3-D model data, usually layer upon layer until a three dimensional product is created), 3-D printing has exceptional potential not only to facilitate processes and activities in the supply chain, but also to become a "game-changing" innovation in the supply chain. Thus, this represents a truly disruptive technology that can have vast strategic impacts on supply chain management.

Initially used most widely in product prototyping, 3-D printing technology is increasingly being adopted for a number of finished products. The technology is being recognized for its numerous advantages: quick turnaround from design to production; cost-effective production of small lots with special-purpose tooling; design flexibility for complex product structures; and ability to enable product customization. Hence, 3-D printing is a particularly advantageous alternative to conventional manufacturing technologies for products that are high in labor cost, increase their value with customization, require complex tooling for new products, and/or are produced in small quantities.

15-6-1 An Inside Look at 3-D Printing

Despite the advantages and promising growth of these technologies, the high costs of 3-D printing machines, maintenance, and material are to some extent inhibiting wider adoption. Machines for 3-D printing and their maintenance costs can range from less than US $1,000 to many millions of dollars, depending on the process employed. Costs of materials for 3-D printing are also high. Executives at one of the meetings of the Penn State Supply Chain Leaders Forum gave examples of 3-D polymers that can cost 53 to 104 times more than the injection-molding equivalents, and 3-D metal that can be 7 to 15 times more expensive than conventional materials. The price difference is partially due to higher standards of material purity and composition, and to the extra step beyond traditional material processing that is required for 3-D printing. Presently, and while overall demand for 3-D printing materials remains relatively low, many potentially useful materials are not standardized and are available from multiple competing suppliers. Contributing further to the high material prices is the 3-D printer manufacturers' practice of controlling which materials are "certified" for use with their equipment, preventing customers from sourcing materials from the supplier(s) of their choice and creating barriers to entry for third-party material suppliers.

In the near-term, participants at the Penn State Supply Chain Leaders Forum view 3-D printing as being advantageous for fit-to-scale prototypes, low-demand parts with long lead times, and inventory management (because digital inventories can be printed on-demand locally). They speculate that we will see wider adoption of 3-D printing as the associated technologies improve, machine and material costs decline, and companies better understand where those technologies fit into their supply chain processes.

Longer-term, executives believe that 3-D printing technologies may play a key role in "open-source collaboration." Until recently, open-source product design has lagged behind open-source software development projects. The latter possess mature, widely used open-sourced design tools and minimal costs for duplication and distribution of the software code. With advances in 3-D printing technologies, more companies are actively exploring open-source collaboration in the physical-product world. In this environment, the digital design or blueprint files for a physical product can be shared within the growing number of "open-source community" companies and individuals. Prototypes can then be rapidly developed using 3-D printers, and any subsequent improvements made to the design can be redistributed.

15-6-2 Illustrative Examples of 3-D Printing

For example, additive methods may be used to combine parts and generate far more interior detailing. An example is GE Aviation that has switched from traditional manufacturing of fuel nozzles for certain jet engines to the 3-D printing of these parts. Given the expectation of GE Aviation that more than 45,000 of the same design will be needed each year, one might assume that more traditional manufacturing methods would be utilized.

However, the 3-D printing approach was chosen since this technology allows fuel nozzles to be assembled from 20 separately cast parts to be fabricated in one piece. Expectations at GE were that the costs of manufacturing would be reduced by 75%.[25]

Supply chains facilitating the service parts industry are likely to be significantly impacted by the availability of 3-D printing. With efficiently-sized 3-D printing devices located in convenient locations, someone in need of a replacement part would need to download an electronic design from a commercial source and then print the part as desired. In the case of obsolete parts, they could be scanned in 3-D for use when and where they may be needed. Clearly, this type of capability would lead to significant changes to how we manage inventory.

Looking into the future, and once the cost of 3-D printing has become more affordable, it is possible that some household products actually could be manufactured in the homes of consumers. Examples of such products might include plumbing supplies, brackets and fixtures for home improvement, and consumer items such as smartphone cases. This would have significant implications for the logistics industry, as the relevant flows of product would shift from the consumer items themselves to the 3-D printing technologies and the raw materials that are used in their manufacturing processes.

On the Line   *Maersk Uses 3-D Printing for Spare Parts on Ships*

In April of 2014, the United States Navy revealed that they had installed a 3-D printer aboard one of their ships, the USS Essex. This news was somewhat expected as 3-D printing is a technology that has been of continuing interest to the Navy, as well as to other branches of the U.S. military. Although, at the time, the Navy was only testing the machine out, and providing a training mechanism for sailors while the ship was at port, such technology is sure to eventually be used on board ships during actual military operations.

The Navy is not the only group using 3-D printers on board ships. In fact, one of the world's largest container shipping companies, Maersk, headquartered in Copenhagen, Denmark, is using 3-D printers as a way to fabricate spare parts for container ships. The company which currently has a fleet of over 500 containerships, has been transporting goods around the globe for the last 110 years. As of this writing, Maersk revealed that they had installed 3-D printers on board their ships. Although the printers currently are capable of printing with ABS thermoplastics, the company is investigating the possible future utilization of powder based metal laser sintering machines.

When a part breaks on a container ship in the middle of the Ocean, it's certainly not an easy or cheap task to provide a replacement part to that vessel, in a speedy manner. Time equals money when you are shipping millions of products across an ocean, thus 3-D printing seemed to be the perfect solution. Essentially, Maersk engineers in Copenhagen get a call from a ship halfway around the world, send a simple .STL file (blueprint) to a computer on board that ship, and within a few hours a replacement part can be printed out and installed on the vessel.

Certainly the fact that thermoplastics are the only material able to be printed at this time on Maersk's vessels, limits the type of parts able to be fabricated. However, within a few years' time it is likely that more sophisticated laser, metal sintering printers will make their way on board ships from all of the major container shipping companies out there. As prices drop and technology advances, it will be hard to ignore the utility that such machines possess.

Source: Adapted from Brian Krassenstein, "Denmark Shipping Company, Maersk, Using 3-D Printing to Fabricate Spare Parts on Ships," http://3-Dprint.com/9021/maersk-ships-3-D-printers/, July 12, 2014.

15-6-3 3-D Printing Strategic Impacts on Supply Chains and Logistics

Although 3-D printing is in the early stages of development, it is clear that this emerging technology ultimately may have massive impacts on supply chain management. The list below identifies a number of key supply chain concepts, and provides some thoughts as to how they may be changed or enhanced through the use of 3-D printing capabilities. This list is not intended to be comprehensive, but illustrative of some of the game-changing impacts of 3-D printing.

- **Demand-Driven.** Products may be printed when and where they are needed. This results in greater timeliness and responsiveness to demand.
- **Customization/Segmentation.** Depending on cost and demand for products, some may be manufactured traditionally and some through use of 3-D printing.
- **Adaptability and Flexibility.** Significant enhancement by simply modifying electronically-available details for 3-D printing.
- **Range of Product Types.** Easier to print variations of products (e.g., size, color, etc.).
- **Inventory.** Will change inventory management as we know it. Will significantly reduce the need to hold finished goods, parts, and raw materials inventories at strategic locations in the supply chain.
- **Transportation.** Focus will shift to availability of materials used in 3-D printing processes, and then "last-mile" movement of 3-D printed products to customer or consumer locations. Will dramatically change the cost of and need for transportation as we know it.
- **Service and Replacement Parts.** Many will be available via downloading a part design from an online 3-D printing library, then 3-D printing the part as may be needed
- **Globalization.** Significant impacts on global sourcing, manufacturing, and distribution. Will significantly modify our thinking about off-shoring, near-shoring, etc.
- **Decentralized Supply Chains.** 3-D printing closer to markets and customers, without excessive safety stock costs.
- **Small Batch Capabilities.** Will significantly modify the way production economies of scale are relevant to manufacturing and supply chain decision-making. Build-to-order 3-D production will have significant impacts on traditional manufacturer-wholesaler-retailer relationships.
- **Sustainability.** Less waste and need for reverse logistics; lower carbon footprint.
- **Workflows, Value Chains, and Processes.** Overall, these will need to re-thought to take advantage of far-reaching capabilities of 3-D printing. Significant modifications to and streamlining of supply chain networks.
- **Total Landed Cost.** With changes to traditional types of supply chain costs (e.g., transportation, warehousing, inventory, manufacturing, stockouts, etc.), procedures for and calculations of total landed cost will change dramatically.

15-7 The Growing Need for SCM Talent Management[26]

Predictions regarding future developments in SCM tend to focus on technological advancement and process innovation. Additionally, organizations need the right people with the proper skills to staff supply chain leadership roles. These roles are expanding and will continue to do so as C-level executives recognize the value of strong, integrated SCM capabilities for driving business success. These executives are beginning to elevate supply chain leaders to strategic roles and are investing in SCM capabilities to create competitive advantage.

Though the outlook is bright for supply chain professionals, organizations face a future talent supply–demand gap. Numerous studies have highlighted the shortage of promotable SCM talent as a potential roadblock to success. Qualified candidates with the appropriate mix of supply chain skills, general management aptitude, and relevant industry knowledge are in short supply. This problem will continue into the future unless organizations take steps to actively manage and enhance their talent supply chain.

Supply chain talent management is a multi-faceted, dynamic, and challenging activity. There are no quick fixes or easy solutions. Organizations need to adopt a long-term talent management strategy that involves significant planning and a commitment to investment. Effective execution of talent acquisition, development, and advancement strategies will maximize the future capabilities of a company's supply chain team, improve retention, and prepare high potential individuals for leadership roles.

Acquiring new staff to supplement the internal talent pool is the crucial first step in building a high quality SCM team. Hiring properly skilled and culturally aligned talent not only takes care of current staffing needs, it also sets the stage for future retention and growth. These skills are not limited to supply chain expertise. Broader general management skills will also be essential as SCM becomes more ingrained in corporate strategy and the footprint of SCM responsibilities expands. Future supply chain leaders will need to be critical thinkers and problem solvers with abilities to see the big picture, develop integrative solutions, establish contingency plans, and communicate the vision.

To find these broadly skilled supply chain professionals, organizations will need to deploy active recruiting techniques. Simply posting opportunities online and waiting for top candidates to emerge is ineffective in an increasingly competitive recruiting environment. Instead, leading organizations will actively engage SCM candidates through highly effective personal contact methods. They will build recruiting relationships with leading universities, leverage employee referrals, and create online communities via LinkedIn and other sites to facilitate candidate interaction.

Developing talent is the critical second step of building a high quality SCM team. Talented individuals must be quickly acclimated, continuously trained, and properly deployed to meet the supply chain requirements of the organization. Additionally, a proactive professional development program combined with challenging assignments will help reduce the risk of talent turnover. Hence, supply chain leaders will need to immerse future hires in the organization's culture and provide current team members with opportunities to expand their capabilities.

To support the growing need for supply chain talent, organizations will need to build stronger, more thorough development programs that include effective onboarding, ongoing training, and individual guidance. A formal mentoring program will help the transition of newly hired professionals through the learning curves of an unfamiliar role, work environment, and organizational policies. A strong culture of development will encourage active pursuit of skills improvement and professional growth. And, supply chain—human resources collaboration on the SCM talent pipeline will identify high-potential individuals and create customized roadmaps for their development.

Fostering the advancement of top supply chain talent is the third team building step. The last thing an organization wants to do is invest heavily in talent only to have high turnover. A proactive combination of career guidance and challenging assignments will stretch the capabilities and foster the retention of supply chain professionals. This is essential for creating the bench strength and institutional supply chain knowledge that underpin future success.

To avoid talent flight, organizations must provide compelling SCM advancement opportunities via logical career paths, retention strategies, and succession planning. Because relatively few organizations offer clear SCM career paths, there is an imminent need to help individuals plan and manage their advancement. Proactive retention strategies focused on role clarity, financial incentives, and performance feedback from senior executives create a positive culture and contentment. And, adopting a succession planning framework will help organizations to systematically pinpoint high potential SCM talent and groom these individuals for future roles.

Without question, an organization's future success will depend upon its ability to side-step the SCM talent shortage. The solution is to adopt a three-step talent management process that integrates acquisition, development, and advancement. Doing so will establish the broadly skilled talent pool that is ready to lead next generation supply chains.

Figure 15.3 highlights a broader context in which the talent management imperative may be considered. In addition to recruiting the right people, sustaining a high level of business performance requires organizations to continuously adapt and change to deal with today's volatile, complex, and ambiguous market dynamics. When organizations are able to link their people strategies to their business strategies, they gain the ultimate competitive advantage.[27]

Figure 15.3	Effective Talent Management Links People Strategy to Business Strategy

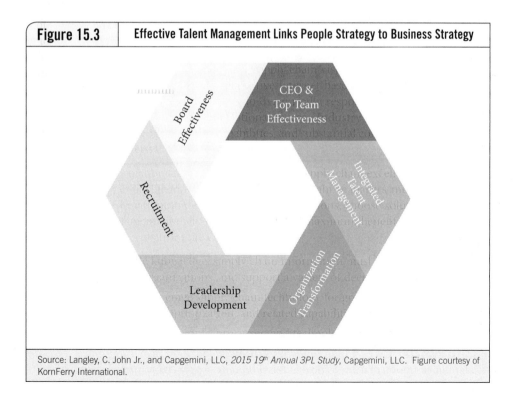

Source: Langley, C. John Jr., and Capgemini, LLC, *2015 19th Annual 3PL Study*, Capgemini, LLC. Figure courtesy of KornFerry International.

On the Line   *Employer Branding in Action*

At The Home Depot, the need to attract supply chain talent is increasing. Not only is the company competing for talent in a market with a low inventory of labor, The Home Depot has narrowed down the number of 3PL partners it is using, moving many of its supply chain responsibilities in house.

To attract and retain employees, The Home Depot is focusing on its massive employer brand, recruiting on college campuses and emphasizing training, said Eric Schelling, head of global talent acquisition for the company. The Home Depot sees every customer as a potential employee, and the company has an employer branding team, which is responsible for shaping the company's employer identity and creating advertising that will reach non-employees. The brand is carried over into all outreach the company does.

Attracting employees can be a challenge, particularly in rural areas where many of The Home Depot's warehouses are located. "The talent pools in those areas are smaller as it is. When you have turnover in those markets it is harder to recruit and train," Schelling said. A critical part of its branding strategy is to treat employees well, pay a competitive wage and ensure employees "have the greatest life possible," Schelling said. For new hires, The Home Depot engages in campus recruiting, and Schelling said the company sees growing interest in positions within the supply chain, which can often attract lines of 50 to 60 students.

Part of The Home Depot employer brand is its internal focus on developing an agile workforce and has an in-depth talent management program that focuses on training and retaining leaders, preparing them for their next role. "We try anything we can for any of our offerings to make sure we develop and engage people and don't lose the talent we have," Schelling said. "Within our retail and supply chain leadership, 90% of all jobs are filled internally."

Source: For more information, refer to "Home Depot on Social Media for Recruitment and Employment Branding," Direct Employers Association, http://www.directemployers.org/2013/10/09/home-depot-on-social-media-for-recruitment-and-employment-branding/

15-8 Closing Thoughts

Hopefully, this book has provided you with a firm understanding of supply chain management from the perspective of logistics functions and processes.

- **Part I – Supply Chain Foundations** – overview of supply chain management, its global dimensions and the role of logistics in the supply chain. Also, emphasis on how to design supply chains is a more traditional sense as well as in the more complex context of omni-channel.

- **Part II – Supply Chain Fundamentals** – beginning with coverage of details relating to strategic sourcing and services, coverage then transitioned to an emphasis on operations, demand management, and order management and customer service. The sequence of these topics related to the structure of the overall process of moving materials to production or value-adding processes, and then to customers and consumers.

- **Part III – Cross-Chain Logistics Processes** – focus here on three types of processes that are critical to the success of supply chain management. Coverage includes managing inventory in the supply chain, distribution, and transportation.

- **Part IV – Supply Chain Challenges and Future Directions** – maybe this closing section of this book falls into the category of being "last but definitely not least." The focus here is on strategic issues that help significantly with the "management" part of supply chain management. Included are aligning supply chains (both internal to organizations and external to their supply chain partners), performance measurement and financial analysis, and supply chain technology. The content relating to strategic challenges and change for supply chains is intended not only to provide a smooth ending for the book, but also to focus on some provocative and innovative aspects of the supply chain. This should be helpful to the readers as they continue to pursue a knowledge and understanding of supply chain management beyond the content of this book.

In closing, there are a number of high-level "takeaways" that the authors would like to highlight. In general, they all support the critical importance of supply chain management to organizations of all types. Thanks for being so attentive and involved for the past 15 chapters, and we wish you the very best in your future endeavors, and particularly as they relate to supply chain management.

- Excellence in supply chain management can be useful pathway to managing an organization's bottom line and top line … and hope to help differentiate the organization in the market place from its competitors.

- To fulfill their responsibilities, people involved in the supply chain typically spend more time interacting with others in their organization than they interact with each other (i.e., meeting and exceeding supply chain objectives requires regular and effective coordination with other process areas on the supply and customer sides of the business.

- Supply chains are impacted by a very wide variety of external and internal factors. The impact of current and future economic, social/political, and environmental trends tends to have a "magnifying" impact on the planning and functioning of supply chains.

- The importance of technology to the future of supply chain management cannot be overstated. While there are many activities and processes in the supply chain that involve the movement of physical products with the use of physical assets, the effective use of technology to manage flows of information and be a critical characteristic of successful supply chains.

- While supply chain management is commonly defined in terms of its mission, goals, and processes, in a much broader sense it actually represents an innovative and very robust way of looking at organizations and how they work with their suppliers and serve their customers.

- The integrating principles of supply chain management also may be viewed as a refreshing context for the management and leadership of the overall organization and its business partners.

- Although we commonly think of various organizations as competing with each other, none of these organizations can meet its goals and objectives without working effectively with its network of suppliers and customers. Thus, the context of supply chains competing with each other is not only an interesting idea, but in fact one that holds true every day in the competitive arena.

- Among the key attributes necessary for long-term success, supply chains must have the ability to change and reinvent, sometimes on a regular basis. Ideally, and instead of being simply responsive to current and future trends, supply chain transformations should be in anticipation of future environments that will affect organizations and their supply chains.

SUMMARY

- "The Seven Principles of Supply Chain Management," published in the *Supply Chain Management Review* is a timeless article that provides useful perspectives on key supply chain issues and priorities that will be relevant well into the future.

- Supply chains generate a wealth of data that can be transformed into information and insight through the use of supply chain analytics. The application of these analytics to big data provide perspectives on supply chains that otherwise would be difficult to discern.

- Traditional retailers that want to compete in the omni-channel environment must change and adopt new strategies to be successful. These strategies start with a new view of the customer and end with how order entry and order fulfillment/delivery are executed.

- Sustainability has become an increasingly important objective for private-sector, for-profit organizations in the twenty-first century. Initially organizations focused upon sustainability because of political and public pressure and their recognition of the importance of their social responsibility.

- Sustainability is a challenging and complex issue because of the diversity of views on the topic, but some supply chain professionals have found it useful to consider sustainability on a broad functional basis—inbound functions, production and operation functions, and outbound or distribution functions.

- An analysis of the benefits of a reverse or return flows program is dependent upon the development of the true costs associated with such a program and comparing them to a realistic measure of the benefits.

- The science of 3-D printing is quickly advancing, and the implications for supply chain management are very significant. Also known as additive manufacturing, this emerging technology will have lasting impacts on the design, configuration, and functioning of supply chains, and on the overall value propositions created by various supply chains.

- The role of supply chain professionals has greatly expanded, creating a shortage of qualified talent. This challenge is expected to continue into the future for organizations that fail to manage their talent supply chain.

- Organizations need to adopt a proactive SCM talent management process to acquire, develop, and retain key individuals for advancement into leadership roles.

- Overall, this book has focused on the foundations, fundamentals, processes, challenges and future directions for supply chain management. Hopefully, this will provide a sound base for more in-depth study and examination of the principles of supply chain management.

STUDY QUESTIONS

1. To what extent have the seven principles of supply chain management remained current? What are some of the major changes that have occurred since they were first developed?

2. Which of the seven principles of SCM do you feel will be most critical to the success of supply chains in the future?

3. Provide an example supply chain issue or problem that you feel may be addressed by each of the key stages in the supply chain maturity model (i.e., descriptive; predictive; prescriptive; and cognitive).

4. Using the internet, identify 2 to 3 traditional retailers that have adopted one or many of the five keys strategies necessary for success in an omni-channel environment. How did they implement this strategy and what were the results?

5. Why is sustainability such a complex and challenging issue for organizations? How can they simplify these challenges from a supply chain perspective?

6. Distinguish between a value stream and a waste stream for reverse flows. Give examples of each.

7. What special challenges and opportunities are presented for reverse flows by globalization? What do you think is the biggest challenge and the greatest opportunity? Why?

8. Aside from the 3-D printing impacts on supply chains that are discussed in this chapter, what do you think are 2 to 3 additional example impacts that could have been mentioned?

9. How is the role of supply chain professionals evolving? What skills will managers need in the future to succeed in this profession?

10. What strategies and steps can organizations pursue to combat the SCM talent shortage?

NOTES

1. Comments in this section about each of the seven principles of supply chain management are based on the content of David L. Anderson, Frank F. Britt, and Donavon J. Favre, "The Seven Principles of Supply Chain Management," *Supply Chain Management Review* (April 2007): 41–46. The authors of this text have supplemented these commentaries with contemporary examples that will help to illustrate the lasting value of these seven principles.

2. Ibid., 41.

3. "Supply Chain Segmentation: 10 Steps to Greater Profits," *Supply Chain Quarterly*, October 25, 2015.

4. Gartner, Inc., "Case Study for Supply Chain Leaders: Dell's Transformative Journey Through Supply Chain Segmentation" (November, 2010).

5. Adapted from Lu, Clara, "Incredibly Successful Supply Chain Management: How Does Walmart Do it?, www.tradegecko.com, May 8, 2014.

6. www.lifung.com

7. Ross, Robert J.S., et al., "A Critical Corporate Profile of Li & Fung, (Worcester, MA: Clark University, Clark Digital Commons), September 12, 2014.

8. Bond, Josh, "The Home Depot Depot Builds an Omni-Channel Supply Chain," *Modern Materials Handling*, February 1, 2015.

9. Dr. David L. Anderson, managing director, Supply Chain Ventures, LLC, http://www.supplychainventure.com.

10. www.informs.org

11. www.gartner.com

12. *Analytics in Action: Breakthroughs and Barriers on the Journey to ROI*, Accenture, 2013.

13. Ferrucci, D. et al. (2010) Building Watson: an overview of the DeepQA Project. Association for the Advancement of Artificial Intelligence, Fall 2010, 59–79.

14. www.ibm.com/software/analytics/spss/

15. www.sas.com

16. www.revolutionanalytics.com/

17. http://www.ibm.com/cognitive/outthink/

18. C. John Langley Jr., Ph.D. and Capgemini Consulting, *2014 18th Annual Third Party Logistics Study*, Capgemini Consulting, 2013, p. 18. The original information appeared at www.slashdot.org , October, 2012.

19. Frederick W. Smith. (n.d.). BrainyQuote.com. Retrieved November 8, 2015, from BrainyQuote.com Web site: http://www.brainyquote.com/quotes/quotes/f/frederickw201582.html Read more at http://www.brainyquote.com/citation/quotes/quotes/f/frederickw201582.html#liMfTuPBwOAgoftk.99

20. Michael Visard, "FedEx CIO Sees Analytics Driving a World of Change," http://insights.dice.com/2012/10/04/fedex-cio-sees-analytics-driving-a-world-of-enterprise-change/#comments, November 4, 2012.

21. C. John Langley Jr., Ph.D. and Capgemini Consulting, *2014 18th Annual Third Party Logistics Study*, Capgemini Consulting, 2013, p. 18. The original information appeared at www.smartplanet.org, November, 2012

22. Boston Consulting Group, bcg.perspectives, "Making Big Data Work: Supply Chain Management," www.bcgperspectives.com, January 27, 2015.

23. Patrick Burnson, "Sears Plays it Cool," *Logistics Management,* February 2015, pp. 24–26.

24. Portions of this section have been adapted from John J. Coyle and Kusumal Ruamsook, "T = MIC²: Game-Changing Trends and Supply Chain's New Normal," *CSCMP Supply Chain Quarterly*, Quarter 4, 2014, pp. 51–57).

25. Richard D'Aveni, "The 3-D Printing Revolution," *Harvard Business Review,* May, 2015.

26. This section is based on: Brian Gibson, Robert Cook, Zachary Williams, and Sean Goffnett, "Talent: An Essential Supply Chain Resource," *CSCMP Hot Topics* (March 2014).

27. Further discussion of this topic is available at C. John Langley Jr., Ph.D. and Capgemini Consulting, *2015 19th Annual Third Party Logistics Study*, Capgemini Consulting, 2014, pp. 28–29.

CASE 15.1

Snoopze's P. O. PLUS

In the Beginning....

Snoopze's is a family owned retail chain that has grown rapidly over the last four decades. The original store was opened in 1975 in Old Fort, Pennsylvania by Bob Snoop. Bob had originally had a service station which sold gasoline and did minor auto repairs. Like many similar establishments Bob also sold cigarettes and confectionary items. At the suggestion of one of his customers, Jack Carson, who was a local plumber, Bob added coffee and donuts (baked by Jack's wife) to his offerings. This had a synergistic impact because many customers who stopped on the way to work early in the morning purchased both coffee/donuts and gas which really enhanced his sales revenue. The success of this idea led Bob to stop doing car repairs and focus upon self-service gasoline sales and other "grab and go" food, drink and convenience items. The success of this business model convinced Bob to purchase of several additional service stations located on busy local roads leading to major places of employment and/economic activity. Two of his brothers joined the organization along with several sons and nephews in the first ten years of operation. The success of Snoopze's businesses led to the opening of several "copycat" operations by competitors in contiguous locations. Bob and his brothers, Steve and Joe decided that it was time to change and enhance the business model and also try to understand the "magic sauce" of their initial success.

Full Speed Ahead...

Two of Bob's nephews were MBA students at the large public university located in central Pennsylvania, and they needed summer internships to satisfy part of their degree requirements. The" Snoop Brothers" thought that this was a win-win opportunity, and decided to fund a strategic study utilizing the talent of the nephews along with one of their professors. The faculty member suggested a SWOT (strengths, weaknesses, opportunities and threats) analysis to begin the project. At this point the company had 25 locations scattered throughout Pennsylvania between Philadelphia and Pittsburgh that sold gasoline, confectionary items, cigarettes and a limited offering of take-out food items for breakfast, lunch and snacks. They operated as a traditional retailer buying what they sold from wholesalers and distributors but had sufficient enough volume to receive price discounts for most items that they sold. That margin along with their operational efficiency provided a reasonable profit, but competition was developing from other similar retailers and some of the gasoline companies that owned and operated similar convenience stores. The SWOT analysis clearly indicated their current business model did not provide much opportunity for growth and expansion, but more importantly, they were very vulnerable to competition. They needed to reduce their costs, improve their operational efficiency and change from model based upon gasoline sales and a limited number of other snack and food items.

Their first major step was to buy a fleet of tanker trucks to pick up their gasoline directly from a major producer to eliminate the wholesaler and deliver to their various locations. It was a risky first step because of the equipment investment and the need for effective equipment and driver scheduling. With the help of a local bank and some capable scheduling software, the outcome was very positive in terms of lowering their cost-of-goods sold position. A serendipitous bonus was the advertising impact of their bright red tank trucks driven by well-trained drivers that were well maintained. The second step included leasing a centrally located warehouse facility to lower distribution costs and improve product availability. The third step was to expand their food offerings to include hot and cold foods "to order" on site which they advertised as M-T-O (Made To Order). As a compliment, their newer locations included some inside and outside seating space. They decided that they had to provide more training for their employees who were required to prepare the food on site. A local vocational school set up a special training program for the needed culinary skills and even some managerial classes for employees that demonstrated the aptitude for advancement. Snoopze's provided financial support and expanding employment opportunities for graduates.

Based upon these changes and an expansion of product offerings, Snoopze's expanded to over 300 locations in seven Mid-Atlantic states with annual sales of over $5 billion. At this point in 2015, they again find themselves at a crossroads for future expansion. The firm is still privately owned by the family, but the second generation (i.e., Ben, Lauren, Matt, Emily and Liz) are the current the Executive Council. They need to consider alternatives for growth that capitalize on their existing strengths. Because they sell so many sandwiches they are building and plan to operate their own bakery to meet their in-store needs for MTO items and to sell separately "off the shelf" to customers. They also have plans underway to provide training not only for their own employees but perhaps others in conjunction with the local Vo-Tech school. They envision these steps as being complementary to their current enterprise and want to do something more "out of the box" like the MTO's which dramatically influenced their business model , changing their image from a gasoline based enterprise that sold snacks and pre-prepared food items to a food enterprise that also sold gasoline.

Here We Go Again.....

The current Executive Council has underwritten a study by the same University that helped 15 years ago to think "outside the box" and exploit their skills and talents for future expansion. The current study that they sponsored recommended a look at four macro areas—sustainability, talent development, technology along with social and demographic trends. The Executive Council concluded that that it had put forth considerable effort in the first two areas and would continue to their current efforts with the understanding that more resources would be devoted to educating a solid group of successful store managers for upper middle management positions providing more upward mobility in the organization. Also, they were intrigued with two other possibilities.

An East Coast competitor, 7-Eleven, was exploring an opportunity to help resolve an issue occurring at the interface of two social-economic trends, namely, increased on-line purchases and a growing number of condominium owners and apartment renters. The latter presented a problem for package deliveries by FedEx, UPS, the USPS, and other local parcel delivery services. 7-Eleven has been investigating the possibility of putting lockers in multiple locations for individuals that are not home during normal delivery hours and do not have a "door step" or porch for packages. 7-Eleven feels that this would provide another revenue stream and attract more customers for additional purchases—"one stop shopping."

Another proposal from several of the third generation family members in their teens and twenties was to expand the "MTO" concept with on-line orders that could be picked up at one of their locations or delivered to their residence, similar to an omni-channel approach as well as some additional options.

CASE QUESTIONS

1. Snoopze's has requested that you analyze the three major options discussed above (i.e., education and training for upper mobility; P.O. related service (stamps anyone?); and on-line ordering with options for pick-up and delivery). Provide a critique of these three options.
2. What are your recommendation(s) for future action?

CASE 15.2

Peerless Products, Inc.

Imagine that Peerless Products, Inc., a well-known manufacturer of consumer electronics, decides to expand its manufacturing in China. The CEO assigns the task to the vice president of manufacturing, and within two years, the company has a plant up and running in Guangdong. Unfortunately, however, Peerless has no overall end-to-end supply chain capability to account for the fact that its lead times have increased by four weeks. This, in turn, has an impact on how the company sells its products, takes orders, plans distribution, sizes warehousing, and manages inbound and outbound logistics throughout the global markets being served by the Chinese plant.

In short, although the company has lowered its product costs, it has increased its supply chain risk and possibly raised its total cost of ownership—taking into account the impact on lost sales. According to Accenture, Inc., risk in the context of global operations may be placed into three buckets: uncontrollable (such as geopolitical instability or natural disasters), somewhat controllable (e.g., volatility of fuel prices), and controllable (for instance, forecasting accuracy or the performance of supply chain partners). Based on a study of 300 companies, however, Accenture found that the more controllable factors constitute the greatest sources of disruption. Up to 35 percent of respondents reported being impacted by natural disasters and 20 percent by geopolitical turmoil. But 38 percent indicated they felt the effects of their supply chain partners' poor performance, and 33 percent had been hurt by logistics complexity, for instance. The consequences of failing to manage those risks are costly indeed, as negative impacts may be experienced in metrics such as sales, return on sales, operating income, return on assets, and inventories.

Although few companies have mastered the management of risk in global operations, many are trying. For example, more than 60 percent of the executives who participated in the global operations study conducted by Accenture indicated that their organizations were manufacturing locally and globally and that they are using contingent suppliers and/or logistics providers. Half said they are intentionally establishing a geographically distributed supply base, and more than half cited increases in inventories and safety stock. Furthermore, 49 percent claimed to have a formal supply chain risk management program in place already.

CASE QUESTIONS

1. Assume you are the CEO of Peerless Products and that you are aware of your company's lack of overall end-to-end supply chain capability. What are some of the high-level, adverse impacts on your business that may occur?
2. What steps would you recommend be taken to help avoid the types of adverse impacts identified above?
3. As CEO, what would be your expectations of the company's vice president of supply chain with respect to the potential problems at hand? How would you compare and contrast expectations of the vice president of supply chain with those of the vice president of manufacturing?

Source: Adapted from Jaume Ferrer, Johan Karlbert, and Jamie Hintlian, "Integration: The Key to Global Success," *Supply Chain Management Review* (March 2007): 26–27. Copyright © 2007 Reed Business Information, a division of Reed Elsevier. Reproduced by permission.

APPENDIX 15A

Reverse Logistics Systems versus Closed Loops

As indicated previously, many terms are used in describing the activities associated with managing reverse flows in a supply chain. Two of these terms are used more frequently and for the purposes of this text are defined as follows:

- **Reverse logistics**—The process of moving or transporting goods *from* their final forward destination for the purpose of capturing value or for proper disposal.
- **Closed-loop supply chains**—Designed and managed to explicitly consider both forward and reverse flows activities in a supply chain.

While these two terms are sometimes used interchangeably, they do have differences. Reverse logistics involves the processes for sending new or used products "back up stream" for repair, reuse, refurbishing, resale, recycling, scrap or salvage. The items in a reverse logistics system are usually returned to a central location for processing. The processing typically involves transporting, receiving, testing, inspecting, and sorting for appropriate action (e.g., repair, refurbishing, or resale). The facility and related processes may be provided by a third-party logistics (3PL) company. The reverse flows may be done independently of the original manufacturer, that is, the system was not designed and managed for forward and reverse flows.

The closed-loop supply chain, on the other hand, is explicitly designed and managed for both flows. In the closed-loop supply chain, the manufacturer is proactive in the processes, and the emphasis is on reducing cost and capturing value. The ultimate goal is for everything to be reused or recycled (i.e., nothing wasted). Several examples are offered here to illustrate closed-loop supply chains.

Figure 15A.1 shows a closed-loop supply chain for cartridge returns. This illustration depicts the program that Xerox introduced in 1991 and expanded in 1998. Customers can return the cartridges in prepaid mailers. The cartridges have to be cleaned and inspected

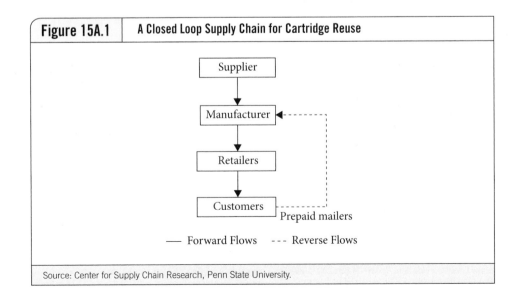

| Figure 15A.1 | A Closed Loop Supply Chain for Cartridge Reuse |

Source: Center for Supply Chain Research, Penn State University.

Figure 15A.2	A Closed Loop Supply Chain for Single-Use Cameras

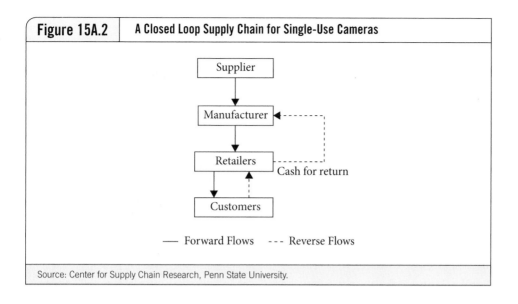

Source: Center for Supply Chain Research, Penn State University.

before refilling. The original system for the rental movies by Netflix was a closed-loop system, as was the system designed by RedBox.

Figure 15A.2 depicts a closed-loop supply chain for single-use cameras. Kodak instituted such a program in the early 1990s to allow the recycling and reuse of parts for its disposable cameras. The process starts with the customer returning the camera to the photo-finisher to develop the film. The photo-finisher batches the cameras to send to a collection center, where they are sorted for shipment to a subcontractor who cleans, disassembles, and inspects them for shipment to a Kodak facility for reloading and resale. The final product containing remanufactured parts and recycled material is indistinguishable to consumers.

The closed-loop supply chain for commercial tire retreading is depicted in Figure 15.3. Frequently, the fleet manager for a trucking fleet, particularly if it is a large fleet, will make arrangements directly with a tire retreader. After receipt of the casings, the retreader will usually retread the same casings and return the retreaded tire to the trucking fleet. This makes the job of balancing supply and demand much easier. For smaller fleet operations, the manager will usually make arrangements with a reseller or tire dealer who will pick up the casings for delivery to the tire retreader and subsequently deliver them back to the fleet. Closed-loop supply chains are also in place for passenger tires. They are more complex because of the need to consolidate casings from retailers, garages, and brokers, which are sold in batches to the retreader. The retreader then has to sell the remanufactured tires, which can present some challenges. Consequently, the balancing of supply and demand is not as easy as it is with commercial tires, and sometimes the retreader has a problem maintaining profitability on passenger tires.

The examples of closed-loop supply chains illustrate the characteristics previously described, namely, that they are explicitly designed and managed for both forward and reverse flows to reduce cost and capture value. While they do not achieve 100 percent return of forward flows, they do recapture a significant percentage. Companies gain an economic and a societal benefit by not having to dispose of the items in landfills. More complex examples of closed-loop supply chains can be found. Xerox, for example, initiated what it called a waste-free system in 1991 for photocopiers that has been very successful. This system involves forward flows, reverse flows, and remanufactured flows. In Europe,

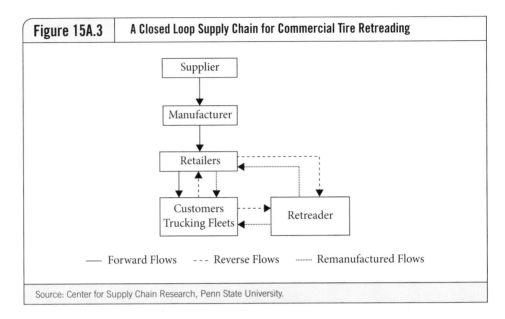

| Figure 15A.3 | A Closed Loop Supply Chain for Commercial Tire Retreading |

Source: Center for Supply Chain Research, Penn State University.

Xerox has a closed-loop supply chain that handles copiers, printers, and office products with a return rate of 65 percent. The reverse flows items may be repaired, be remanufactured, or have parts remanufactured—all with eventual resale. The fourth option in reverse flows is to recycle and dispose where the product has no value.

In contrast to closed-loop supply chains, the reverse logistics process is frequently much more challenging to operate, or it is more difficult to develop a viable value stream. Items may have to be collected from geographically diverse locations, and some items may be considered hazardous materials. The latter could necessitate special handling for collection and disposal. Frequently, the testing, sorting, grading, and inspection are complex and time consuming. Similarly, remanufacturing or reconditioning can be complex and challenging. Resale after remanufacturing may be difficult. In spite of the challenges, companies have come to recognize value stream opportunities if reverse flows are managed carefully and proactively. Major retailers and their suppliers have become proactive in developing more effective reverse flow systems to capture value.

For reverse logistics programs, the three major forces are customer service, environmental issues, and economic benefits. As indicated, the reverse or return processes are substantial in some industries. Understanding the major forces for the reverse flows is important for gaining insight into the challenges and opportunities for efficiency and effectiveness.

Customer Returns

A variety of reasons for customer returns can be given (as indicated previously), including defective or unwanted items, warranty problems, recalls, and misshipments. Given the potential magnitude of such returns, managing the product return process can have a substantial impact on a company's profit and loss statement. The internal channel for return flows will differ depending on the reason for the return. The alternatives include re-inventory for resale, repair or refurbish for return to the customer, or re-inventory for resale or disposal. Industries with high return percentages, such as magazines, books, greeting cards, newspapers, catalog and internal sales, and so forth require internal processes as indicated earlier. Managing these processes efficiently and effectively can have a positive impact on the profit and loss statement. The handling of customer return issues can also have a positive customer service benefit when returns are handled expeditiously with timely cash or credit issuance or product replacement (i.e., it can offer a competitive advantage). The super-retailers (Walmart, Target, Best Buy, etc.) have used this approach as a key element in their customer service policies. It has, however, also contributed to the increase in reverse flows. Companies need to have a balanced approach that accommodates legitimate returns but discourages needless returns. Many retailers have returned to a more conservative approach with product returns to reduce costs.

Environmental Challenges

Recycling and environmental concerns are frequently viewed simultaneously because of their association with regulatory policy at the local, state, and federal level. Social concerns stimulate the development of more environmentally friendly products, new standards, and publicly provided recycling programs. It may be surprising to some individuals, but corporations play an active role in this area as part of their focus on ethics and social responsibility. In fact, the term *triple bottom line* of the three P's—profit, people, and the planet (also known as "the three pillars")—has gained in popularity with corporations, governments, and activist groups in the twenty-first century. The triple bottom line integrates the three P's into the culture, strategy, and operations of companies and thus captures an expanded spectrum of values and criteria for measuring organizational success to include economic, ecological, and social factors.

In addition to the public relations value of such corporate policies, some evidence suggests that when corporations work with their suppliers to reduce waste, reduce pollution, and improve overall "eco-efficiency," they have also been able to improve product quality, cut production times, and increase productivity. The discussion of closed-loop supply chains is an indication of a more proactive approach by companies to be environmentally responsible and use these strategies to enhance their overall financial viability.

Fueled by the growing sense of urgency for environmental action among scientists, consumers, and most governments around the world, the concept of closed-loop supply chain has gained momentum on a global scale. International organizations such as the United Nations and the International Standardization Organization (ISO) initiate frameworks and tools to promote integration of environmental thinking into business practices. For example, the United Nations University/Institute of Advanced Studies launched Zero Emissions Research Initiative (ZERI) in 1994, which was renamed Zero Emissions Forum in 1999. ZERI promoted the concept that all industrial inputs can be completely converted into a final product and that waste products can be converted into value-added inputs for another chain of production. Similarly, ISO first published ISO 14001 in 1996, specifying the operational requirements for an environmental management system that can guide the environmental activities of organizations in most industries.

Economic Value

In reverse logistics systems as well as closed-loop supply chains, economic benefits have become an important emphasis for businesses and even some nonprofit organizations. The potential for viewing reverse flows as a value stream as opposed to a waste stream was identified in a study published over 30 years ago and further amplified in a White Paper published by the Council of Logistics Management (now the Council of Supply Chain Management Professionals). Both studies pointed out that economic benefits can be the primary driver for the establishment of explicit reverse flow processes not otherwise required by customer service (product returns) and governmental requirements. In other words, recycling for reuse and remanufacture has the potential to be a profitable scenario and a value stream.

This has become particularly true in industries that have experienced increasing cost of raw materials, such as the steel industry.

Making reverse flows profitable, however, is a challenge as well as an opportunity. Managing such flows for economic benefit requires careful articulation of the processes and detailed analysis of the costs to determine whether the cost–benefit tradeoffs are positive. The mistake that is commonly made is the assumption that the processes are the same as forward flows and therefore the costs are the same. These assumption will lead to false conclusions.

Achieving a Value Stream for Reverse Flows

The challenge indicated in the previous section of making certain that the proactive management of reverse flows represents an opportunity for enhancing profits through cost reduction or increased revenue is a consideration for both closed-loop supply chains and reverse logistics systems.

From a manufacturing perspective, it may appear to be more costly to remanufacture or refurbish the materials obtained through reverse flows systems than to produce a new product from basic materials or components. Frequently, much of the additional cost is associated with the returns process. Time and distance are often the major cost contributors associated with capturing returns and their residual value. Interestingly, transportation expense is the largest cost component of reverse flows and frequently represents 25 percent or more of the total cost. Using transportation management tools and technology to improve and monitor the transportation network can lower this cost through better scheduling of pickups and deliveries and consolidation of loads to achieve scale economies.

As suggested earlier, one of the major challenges is the estimation of the total cost of the return flow processes. Companies typically have detailed costs associated with forward transportation flow and use historical averages of ton-mile costs to estimate budget costs for the future. In addition, the handling costs associated with returns can be higher because of the sorting, packaging, and random sizes that are typically associated with this activity. As companies gain experience, they can usually reduce handling costs.

Some companies are using activity-based costing (ABC) as a tool to delineate the true costs associated with reverse flows. Quantification of the costs must include all costs associated with the returns processes—labor, transportation, storage and inventory carrying costs, materials handling, packaging, transactional and documentary costs, and appropriate overhead costs. Conversely, accounting for the actual cost savings associated with the materials from reverse flows is important for the tradeoff analysis to determine the economic value added (or the lack thereof).

Once the evaluation for economic value has been completed, it is important to consider the barriers that may impede the implementation of the reverse flows program. These barriers may be internal or external and may include the following:

- Priority relative to other issues and potential projects or programs in the organization
- Inattention or lack of "buy-in" from top-level management in the organization
- Financial resources necessary for operations and asset infrastructure
- Personnel resources required to develop and implement the reverse flows program
- Adequacy of material and information systems to support the returns program
- Local, state, and federal restrictions or regulations

The development and implementation of the articulated and managed reverse flows process requires careful consideration of the preceding list of internal and external barriers. Some organizations may encounter additional barriers. Also, global supply chains may have some additional barriers, but even if they do not, the listed barriers may be more complex on a global basis. Companies that have successfully implemented reverse flows programs give careful consideration to this list of potential barriers prior to attempting to start a program.

The strategic and tactical issues identified earlier for making a reverse flows program a value stream, as opposed to a waste stream, have led some companies to consider a third-party logistics company once the potential program has been rationalized and economically justified. The growth in number and sophistication of 3PLs in the last two decades has made this a very viable option. In fact, some 3PLs specialize in returns and reverse systems. This type of outsourcing may be beneficial for many reasons, but some discussion of the 3PL alternative is appropriate at this point.

As indicated earlier, reverse or closed-loop systems are often very different from forward flow systems. Since managing reverse flows may not be a core competency of an organization, it could be a natural candidate for outsourcing. Obviously, the economic value added of utilizing a 3PL has to be considered. 3PLs can offer some special advantages for global supply chains with information technology that provides visibility of inventory. This is particularly critical when dealing with time-sensitive products such as computers and related peripherals, copy equipment, cell phones, and other personal communication equipment. These products have short life cycles and high obsolescence risk. The value of time for such products is a key consideration in the returns process. Time delays can be very costly in terms of recapturing the value of such product assets.

Total life cycle considerations (TLC) are figuring more prominently into reverse flows management programs and into the 3PL evaluation. It is estimated, for example, that a new printer can lose 20 percent of its value while waiting for disposition. A product's time value function is an important consideration for asset recovery decisions. In fact, just reducing time delays in the reverse flows process can result in significant value being added. The time-sensitive products clearly indicate the importance of logistics processes for reverse flows programs, but even for products with longer life cycles and less risk of obsolescence, logistics processes play a key role in the efficiency of the reverse flows program and the potential for recovering assets that will allow economic value to be added. This is particularly true for retailers and one of the reasons why some of the large mass merchandisers utilize 3PLs so extensively. It was previously pointed out that customer returns at the retail level can reach 50 percent in some instances. Speed and efficient reverse logistics processes are essential in such cases to maximize the value of the returns stream.

Managing Reverse Flows in a Supply Chain

The effective and efficient management of reverse flows in a supply chain requires the careful consideration of a number of key activities or issues. As indicated previously, proactive management of reverse flows can impact the financial position of a company quite positively. On the other hand, the opposite can be true if reverse flows are mismanaged or not carefully managed. The Reverse Logistics Educational Council has recommended careful consideration of the following:

- **Avoidance**—Producing high-quality products and developing processes to minimize or eliminate returns
- **Gatekeeping**—Checking and screening merchandise at the entry point into the reverse flows process to eliminate unnecessary returns or minimize handling

- **Reducing reverse cycle times**—Analyzing processes to enable and facilitate compression of time for returns to enhance value recapture
- **Information systems**—Developing effective information systems to improve product visibility, reduce uncertainty, and maximize economies of scale
- **Returns centers**—Developing optimum locations and facility layouts for returns centers to facilitate network flow
- **Remanufacture or refurbishment**—Preparing and repairing a product for resale as is usually done in closed loop supply chains to maximize value recapture
- **Asset recovery**—Classifying and disposing of returned items, surplus, scrap, and obsolete items to maximize returns and minimize cost
- **Pricing**—Negotiating the best price for products being returned and resold
- **Outsourcing**—Considering a relationship with a third-party organization to handle and manage reverse flows in cases where existing personnel, infrastructure, experience, or capital may not be adequate to implement a successful program
- **Zero returns**—Developing a policy to exclude returns by giving a returns allowance or "destroying" the product in the field
- **Financial management**—Developing guidelines and financial procedures to properly account for charges against sales and related financial issues when items are returned by customers

Subject Index

Note: *Italicized page numbers indicate illustrations or boxes text.*

Name Index

Note: Italicized page numbers indicate illustrations or boxes text.